COMPUTING WITH WORDS

Wiley Series on Intelligent Systems

Editors: James Albus, Alexander Meystel, and Lotfi A. Zadeh

Intelligence through Simulated Evolution: Forty Years of Evolutionary Programming • *Lawrence J. Fogel*

Neuro-Fuzzy Pattern Recognition: Methods in Soft Computing • *Sankar K. Pal and Sushmita Mitra*

Computing with Words • *Paul P. Wang*, Editor

COMPUTING WITH WORDS

Edited by

PAUL P. WANG
Duke University

A Wiley-Interscience Publication
JOHN WILEY & SONS, INC.
New York / Chichester / Weinheim / Brisbane / Singapore / Toronto

This book is printed on acid-free paper. ♾

Published simultaneously in Canada.

For ordering and customer service, call 1-800-CALL-WILEY.

Library of Congress Cataloging-in-Publication Data:

Computing with words / edited by Paul P. Wang.
p. cm. — (Wiley series on intelligent systems)
ISBN 0-471-35374-4 (cloth : alk. paper)
1. Natural language processing (Computer science) I. Title. II. Series.

QA76.9.N38 W37 2001
006.3′5—dc21 2001017597

Printed in the United States of America.

10 9 8 7 6 5 4 3 2 1

CONTENTS

CONTRIBUTORS vii

FOREWORD ix
Lotfi A. Zadeh

PREFACE xi
Paul P. Wang

HOW DO OUR SENSES TALK TO OUR ACTUATORS? 1
James S. Albus and Alexander M. Meystel

1 COMPUTING WITH WORDS: INTRODUCTION, IMPLICATIONS, AND APPLICATIONS 13
Paul P. Wang

2 FROM COMPUTING WITH NUMBERS TO COMPUTING WITH WORDS—FROM MANIPULATION OF MEASUREMENTS TO MANIPULATION OF PERCEPTIONS 35
Lotfi A. Zadeh

3 COMPUTING WITH WORDS: THE PROBLEMS AND SOLUTIONS 69
Alexander M. Meystel and Paul P. Wang

4 GRANULAR RELATIONAL COMPUTING WITH SEMIOTIC DESCRIPTORS USING BK-PRODUCTS OF FUZZY RELATIONS 89
Ladislav J. Kohout, Bobby Granville, and Eunjin Kim

5 COMPUTING GRANULAR WORD MEANINGS: A FUZZY LINGUISTIC APPROACH IN COMPUTATIONAL SEMIOTICS 147
Burghard B. Rieger

6 EXTRACTING INFORMATION FROM TEXT 209
Amit Bagga, Joyce Chai, and Alan Biermann

7 COGNITIVE SCIENCES AND COMPUTING WITH WORDS 235
Benjoe A. Juliano

8 COMBINING LINGUISTIC INFORMATION IN A DISTRIBUTED INTELLIGENT AGENT MODEL FOR INFORMATION GATHERING ON THE INTERNET 251
M. Delgado, F. Herrera, E. Herrera-Viedma, M.J. Martin-Bautista, and M.A. Vila

9 NUMERIC ROBUSTNESS AND LINGUISTIC PERSPICUITY: A HYBRID APPROACH TO KNOWLEDGE ACQUISITION 277
Thomas Whalen and Gwangyong Gim

10 COMPUTING WITH DESCRIPTIVE AND VERISTIC WORDS: KNOWLEDGE REPRESENTATION AND REASONING 297
I.B. Türksen

11 PRINCIPLES OF WORD-BASED KNOWLEDGE REPRESENTATION AND KNOWLEDGE PROCESSING OF CW 329
Alexander M. Meystel

12 FUZZY QUALITATIVE REASONING WITH WORDS 347
Didier Dubois, Allel Hadj-Ali, and Henri Prade

13 BEYOND PROCESS AND ACTION SYMBOLS 367
Tao Yang

SUBJECT INDEX 433

NAME INDEX 447

CONTRIBUTORS

JAMES S. ALBUS, National Institute of Standards and Technology, Gaithersburg, MD 20889

AMIT BAGGA, Avaya Labs Research, Murray Hill, NJ 07974

ALAN BIERMANN, Department of Computer Science, Duke University, Durham, NC 27708

JOYCE CHAI, IBM T.J. Watson Research Center, Hawthorne, NY 10532

M. DELGADO, Department of Computer Science and Artificial Intelligence, University of Granada, 18071 Granada, Spain

DIDIER DUBOIS, IRIT, Université Paul Sabatier, 31062 Toulouse, Cedex 4, France

GWANGYONG GIM, Soong Sil University, Seoul, Korea

BOBBY GRANVILLE, Department of Computer and Information Science, Florida A&M University, Tallahassee, FL 32307

ALLEL HADJ-ALI, Institut d'Informatique, Université Mouloud Mammeri, 15000 Tizi-Ouzou, Algeria

F. HERREA, Department of Computer Science and Artificial Intelligence, University of Granada, 18071 Granada, Spain

E. HERRERA-VIEDMA, Department of Computer Science and Artificial Intelligence, University of Granada, 18071 Granada, Spain

BENJOE A. JULIANO, Department of Computer Science, California State University, Chico, CA 95929

EUNJIN KIM, Department of Computer Science, Florida State University, Tallahassee, FL 32306

LADISLAV J. KOHOUT, Department of Computer Science, Florida State University, Tallahassee, FL 32306

M. J. Martin-Bautista, Department of Computer Science and Artificial Intelligence, University of Granada, 18071 Granada, Spain

Alexander M. Meystel, Department of Electrical and Computer Engineering, Drexel University, Philadelphia, PA 19104

Henri Prade, IRIT, Univesité Paul Sabatier, 31062 Toulouse, Cedex 4, France

Burghard B. Rieger, Department of Computational Linguistics, University of Trier, D-54286 Trier, Germany

I. B. Türkşen, Department of Mechanical and Industrial Engineering, University of Toronto, Toronto, Ontario M5S 3G8, Canada

M. A. Vila, Department of Computer Science and Artificial Intelligence, University of Granada, 18071 Granada, Spain

Paul P. Wang, Department of Electrical and Computer Engineering, Duke University, Durham, NC 27708

Thomas Whalen, Department of Decision Science, Georgia State University, Atlanta, GA 30303

Tao Yang, Department of Electrical Engineering and Computer Sciences, University of California, Berkeley, CA 94720

Lotfi A. Zadeh, Department of Electrical Engineering and Computer Sciences, University of California, Berkeley, CA 94720

FOREWORD

Computing with Words is a compendium of articles authored by experts drawn from a wide variety of fields, ranging from linguistics and cognitive science to databases and control. A unifying aim in these articles is an enlargement of the role of natural languages in scientific theories, especially in information processing, decision, and control. The book is the brainchild of its editor, Professor Paul P. Wang—a person of vision, initiative, and insight.

To see the contents of the book in a proper perspective, a historical observation is in order. It is a deep-seated tradition in science to view the use of natural languages in scientific theories as a manifestation of mathematical immaturity. The rationale for this tradition is that natural languages are lacking in precision. However, what is not recognized to the extend that it should be is that adherence to this tradition carries a steep price. More specifically, a direct and important consequence is that existing theories do not have the capability to operate on perception-based—rather than measurement-based—information. Such information is usually described in natural languages and is intrinsically imprecise, reflecting a fundamental limitation on the cognitive ability of humans to resolve detail and store information. As a consequence, perceptions do not lend themselves to meaning representation through the use of standard methods based on predicate logic. This is the principal reason that existing scientific theories do not have the capability to operate on perception-based information.

In a related way, the restricted expressive power of predicate logic-based languages rules out the possibility of defining in realistic terms many basic concepts, such as causality, similarity, smoothness, and relevance. In this instance, as in many others, the price of precision is overidealization and lack of robustness.

The methodology of computing with words may be viewed as an attempt to harness the highly expressive power of natural languages by developing ways of computing with words or propositions drawn from a natural language. To a limited extent, this has been done in fuzzy logic through use of the concepts of linguistic variable and linguistic if–then rules. Computing with words moves much further in this direction by introducing—as described by me in Chapter 2—the concept of a generalized constraint language (GCL). A key idea that underlies GCL is that the meaning of a proposition drawn from a natural language may be expressed as a generalized constraint in GCL. In this way, reasoning with perceptions described in a natural language may be reduced to propagation of generalized constraints from premises to conclusions.

What is achieved by the use of methods falling under the rubric of computing with words? There are four principal rationales. Briefly stated:

1. The *don't know rationale.* The values of variables and parameters are not known with sufficient precision to justify the use of numbers.
2. The *don't need rationale.* There is no need for numerical values. Linguistic values are sufficient.
3. The *don't want rationale.* Knowledge of detail is counterproductive.
4. The *can't define rationale.* A concept does not lend itself to precise definition. Example: causality.

In addition to these rationales, there is a deeper reason why eventually it will be recognized that computing with words is not an option—it is a necessity. The reason has to do with what may be called *information orthogonality.* More specifically, information orthogonality relates to a condition where the given data provide no information about a sought-after answer to a query. For examples, in probability theory, knowledge of the conditional probabilities of Z given X and Z given Y provides no information about the conditional probability of Z given X and Y. A more down-to-earth example is that the knowledge that one percent of tax returns in the United States are audited tells me nothing about the probability that my tax return will be audited. This may appear to be somewhat counterintuitive, but it is true because the available information is incomplete and worst-case analysis is applied to missing information.

To be able to come up with a nonvacuous answer to a query, it is necessary to draw upon additional information that, as a rule, is perception-based. The methodology of computing with words serves to operate on this information and yield an informative answer to the query.

In the final analysis, what is most important about computing with words is that it serves to import into scientific theories concepts and techniques drawn from linguistics. In this sense, computing with words may be viewed as a "back to natural languages" movement. A move in this direction is dictated by the need to add to existing theories a capability to operate on perception-based information—information that is expressed in a natural language. Such capability would enhance the ability of existing theories to participate in the development of systems that have a much higher MIQ (machine IQ) than those we can design and construct today.

At this juncture, computing with words is still in its initial stages of crystallization. In time, it is likely to become an importnat field in its own right, with wide-ranging impact and many applications. To this end, *Computing with Words* is making an impressive contribution. Professor Wang, the contributors, and the publisher, John Wiley, deserve our thanks and congratulations for producing a volume that is illuminating, informative, authoritative, and reader-friendly.

Berkeley, California
February 27, 2000

LOTFI A. ZADEH

PREFACE

The evolution of artificially constructed languages for digital computers in terms of development, improvement, and fine tuning has reached a maturity that is indeed quite remarkable. Together with other symbolic processing, many researchers would characterize the twentieth century as the *century of syntactics*. On the other hand, even the most advanced high-performance computers are incapable of communicating with humans in natural languages. Current research on Internet and multiple intelligent agents has brought to the forefront the pressing need for natural language processing in digital computers. There is little doubt that the momentum in natural language research in digital computers for human–machine interactions will grow in a dramatic manner. This prospect has triggered some researchers to believe that the twenty-first century will be the century of semantics. Publication of this book on computing with words certainly is a key example of a response to such a need and demand. To say the least, it is certainly timely.

Zadeh's theory of fuzzy set and fuzzy logic has had a very interesting evolution since 1965. Several important and critical turning points can also be identified easily. One significant milestone is the successful application of fuzzy logic as a means of controlling consumer electronic products. Furthermore, the design of sophisticated control systems, cement kilns, unmanned helicopters, steam engines, and trains has also impressed many engineers. All these activities have taken place during 1970s and 1980s, bringing Zadeh's theory to the visible forefront. The credibility of Zadeh's fuzzy set and fuzzy logic hence is thus firmly established. These successful applications have not only been verified by economic value, but also demonstrate the limitations of classical and modern control theory. Systems and control engineers now realize that there is much room to solve complex system problems for which solutions were never before sought. This paradigm shift is marked by the control of set points and trajectories to the control of a task and desirable humanistic goals. This is indeed landmark progress!

The evolution of Zadeh's theory may be summarized in the following chronological order: invention of the fuzzy set, the concept of fuzzy systems, linguistic variables, fuzzy if–then rules and fuzzy graphs, fuzzy sets and information granularity, generalized constraints, and finally, computing with words. This brings up the topic of this project—a book on computing with words. It took us more than two years to assemble the most important leading researchers and the leading topics. Most chapters are the result of the call for papers, of which nearly 60 were received. Some chapters were invited, in order to give our readers a relatively complete picture of the theory and potential applications. Most chapters were written by leading researchers within the fuzzy research community; other chapters are those of natural language researchers. A larger view of computing with words with semiotics and intelligent systems is also visible in this volume.

What is remarkable is that the evolution of Zadeh's theory does not end with computing with words! It was a pleasant surprise to see the publication of Zadeh's computational theory of perceptions in the January 1999 issue of *IEEE Transactions on Circuits and Systems*. The significance of this paper is reflected in the title of the published article: "From Computing with Numbers to Computing with Words—From Manipulation of Measurements to Manipulation of Perceptions." Zadeh's theory has now been generalized and expanded to cover an even wider domain of perception. What is really intriguing is the "back parking a car" example that Zadeh described at Bell Telephone Labs, in 1967, two years after publication of his seminal paper. During that seminar, which only eight researchers attended, his example pointed out quite powerfully the limitations of conventional control methodology. The connection between Zadeh's example and his computational theory of perceptions is quite transparent now with the recent presentation of his consolidated theory.

Both Alex Meystel, the series editor assigned to work with me, and I are grateful to the IEEE and Professor Zadeh for granting permission to republish the article as Chapter 2 in this volume. Chapter 2 is the focus of the commentaries of nearly all other chapters. It is our hope that the content of Chapter 2 will reach a much wider audience than that of electrical engineers. It is also worth mentioning that the Society of Circuits and Systems of the IEEE first realized the importance of mathematical analysis, later to be extended by control, computer, communication, signal analysis, information theory, and cybernetics societies. Zadeh was a true leader in every stage of development in so many different fields.

Although the bulk of this book is about fuzzy expert systems, substantial material on related and larger issues dealing with CW is also included, which increases the fundamental and archival value of Zadeh's theory. Some invited chapters from the natural language processing community, as well as those on current research in the multiple intelligent agent and Internet communities, also contribute considerably to the building of bridges to relevant research communities at large.

We believe that expert systems should make greater use of fuzzy expert system methodology. Through the years, isolated fundings have been devoted to fuzzy expert systems design in governmental, academic, and industrial areas. However, the level of support is small compared to that in the conventional artificial intelligence (AI) community. Research program directors must think seriously about making funds available to launch sincere efforts for major fuzzy expert systems design with the magnitude of, say, the MYCIN project. In fact, this worthy effort is long overdue!

After many years of research effort and a huge transfusion of research fundings, the truth has finally been revealed from nearly all the leading researchers in the established AI community that the central issue in expert systems design relies on successful handling of the linguistics, especially the semantics issues. Zadeh conceived this at a very early stage of his inquiry into the design of expert systems. His centerpiece, of course, is computing with words. This book provides an overview of his theory and implications, with excellent examples.

The significance of Chapter 2 cannot be underemphasized. From computing with numbers to computing with words also means an important paradigm shift from manipulation of measurements to manipulation of perceptions. The remarkable human ability to handle perception is, to say the least, an important model for engineers in learning how to design certain types of desirable and useful engineering systems. Of course, this is a tremendous challenge to be tackled! The latest version of Zadeh's theory, which appears in Chapter 2 of this book, is the generalized theory on which the famous "back parking a car" example is based. This historically significant example has inspired and convinced many researchers by the hundreds and thousands to look at Zadeh's theory seriously. However, many important questions remain unanswered and will probably never be answered unless we know how the human perception, brain, and mind work! However, one thing is certain—that Zadeh has made two very important contributions based on his theory: the invention of a more generalized and novel mathematical methodology of fuzzy sets and fuzzy logic, and the mathematical modeling of natural language and human perceptions.

Considering the research field at large, Zadeh's theory, relatively speaking, is not well known and is often misunderstood. It is our objective to gather all essential background information in one place and build as many bridges as possible to reach as wide an audience as possible. We feel that now is a better time to launch this project because many of Zadeh's theories in the area of fuzzy information manipulation, approximate reasoning, fuzzy inference mechanisms, fuzzy clustering, fuzzy data mining, and so on, are well established. Hence it is more important to us to look to the future rather than looking back at the past.

It is perhaps well established that the human brain is the most complex biological object we know. Kandel and Schwarz estimate about 10^{12} neurons and 10^{15} synatic connections. Daniel Dennett, Tufts University, argues that neurophysiologists, working from the bottom up in an attempt to understand human cognition, and computer scientists, working from the top down, may ultimately both reach their goals. David E. Rumelhart, James L. McClelland, and their colleagues take the middle-of-the-road approach by experimenting with neural networks in order to understand the functioning of the mind. Melanie Mitchell, in reviewing the evolutionary psychology debates, raised the serious question: "Can evolution explain how the mind works?" At Duke University, Max Woodbury, Robert Erickson, and myself have discussed the need for fuzzy set theory and fuzzy logic theory to achieve advancements in brain modeling. It is also well documented that von Neumann believed in the importance of statistics and logic in understanding how the human brain works. Well, fuzzy logic certainly is a generalization of the classical logic that von Neumann was talking about, and there is plenty of evidence that fuzzy sets are crucial in color vision modeling.

Jacob Blum, neural physiologist at Duke University, appears to agree on the real need of new mathematics as an aid to understanding the complexity of perception at the lowest level of the study of perceptions. The phenomena are extraordinarily complex even at the lowest level, not to mention the highest level and those in between. Understanding the neural basis for such higher-level cognitive functions as language and complex problem solving is a very difficult task. CW is aimed at solving difficult semantics problems in natural language. So far, only the handling of adjectives and adverbs has been demonstrated in the course of fuzzy logic control. Much more remains to be accomplished. As far as the theory of perceptions is concerned, we are only at the beginning in figuring out how it works and what the implications would be in terms of producing useful engineering products. And as far as scientific inquiry and the search for truth are concerned, lively debate will never hurt us!

Realization of this project is due to the generous contributions and assistance of many distinguished researchers. First, Professor Zadeh's guidance and inspiration to the contributing authors have been invaluable. We are also grateful to the series editors, Jim Albus and Alex Meystel, for writing an introduction. Editors Andrew J. Smith, Philip Meyler, and G. Telecki of Wiley-Interscience also deserve much credit, especially for their patience in numerous extensions of the publication deadline. For assistance with editing, I express my deep appreciation to my joint conference manager, Anna Menzies, and my son, Samuel W. T. Wang.

In addition, I acknowledge the huge contribution of Alex Meystel, who made this project possible. We chose NIST, nearly at the middle point between Philadelphia and Durham, as our meeting place for working sessions. The patience and support we received from Mrs. Marina Meystel and Mrs. Julia Y. H. Wang cannot be overestimated. Transcription of our conversations by Marina Meystel proved invaluable.

Finally, I would like to show my deep appreciation to Yuan Ze University for offering me a visiting chair professorship, which made possible the long hours I spent writing my chapters.

Duke University
Durham, North Carolina

PAUL P. WANG

The following contributors were present at the Computing with Words Workshop on March 1, 2000 at the Taj Mahal in Atlantic City, New Jersey. First row (from left): Paul P. Wang, Burghard B. Rieger, Lotfi A. Zadeh, and I. B. Türkşen; second row (from left): Alexander M. Meystel, Thomas Whalen, Ladislav J. Kohout, and Benjoe A. Juliano.

HOW DO OUR SENSES TALK TO OUR ACTUATORS?

JAMES S. ALBUS
NIST, Gaithersburg, Maryland

ALEXANDER M. MEYSTEL
Drexel University, Philadelphia, Pennysylvania

In asking this question, we are rephrasing the question asked 40 years ago by J. Y. Lettvin, H. Maturana, W. S. McCulloch, and W. H. Pitts in their classical paper "What the frog's eye tells the frog's brain."[1] First, we are interested in the entire loop from sensors to actuators. Second, in addition to the content in which information is conveyed by sensors, we are interested in the signals, messages, and data structures (i.e., in the *from* in which knowledge of the world is represented. It seems that the entire system is what really matters. And it looks like the system between the sensors and actuator is doing its job by computing with words. Is it? We suggest here that the messages are conveyed in both words and images.

COMPUTING WITH WORDS: A FUNDAMENTAL MECHANISM OR RECENT ADD-ON?

Computing with words is a fascinating new way of looking at a number of problems related to knowledge representation, symbolic reasoning, natural language, and intelligent control. Computing with words uses concepts of fuzzy sets and fuzzy logic to address issues of ambiguity and imprecision in everyday human activities and possibly in information processing of constructed intelligent systems. The concept of *computing with words* provides important insights into problems of

[1] "What the frog's eye tells the frog's brain" was the title of the paper written by J. Y. Lettvin, H. Maturana, W. S. McCulloch, and W. H. Pitts and published in 1959 in *Proc. IRE, 47:*1940–1951.

Computing with Words, Edited by Paul P. Wang.
ISBN 0-471-35374-4

understanding how to design systems that can cope with the complexities of the natural world.

Words are symbols that can be associated with objects, events, groups, classes, situations, concepts, agents, places, regions in space, and periods in time. Words can be used to identify objects and events and to describe states, attributes, values, relationships, and amounts. Names are words that identify things. States and attributes can be represented by words that describe conditions or properties of things. Values can be represented by words that describe what things are worth. Relationships can be represented by words that describe how things are related to each other. Words can be used to describe the world and how it works.

Words provide a vocabulary for language. Using words involves syntax and semantics. Syntax describes how words can be arranged in strings to form grammatical sentences that should carry a meaning. This meaning eventually affects the behavior of an intelligent system. Semantics explicates this meaning: It defines what words and sentences mean. Words have meaning when they represent things, events, situations, and activities in the world. Establishing correspondence words in the language and things in the world is sometimes called *symbolgrounding*. It provides the basis for a concrete meaning in a particular sentence. Note that we are talking about words of human language that serves for communication.

However, words are not what most brains use to represent knowledge about the world. Most creatures in nature have no significant verbal skills. Yet they have the ability to recognize food, preceive danger, identify places, classify other creatures, and remember regions of space that provide safety or have significance in terms of reproductive success.

Many animals make choices and have mechanisms for decision making. Most animals have the ability to visually perceive obstacles and maneuver through the world with great skill and precision at high speed without collisions. Even insects, crustaceans, and fish have highly refined sensory motor skills. Most creatures can distinguish visually between prey and predators. Most can distinguish between potential mates and rivals. Most can recognize and defend territory. Many can manipulate objects with great dexterity. All of these capabilities require the ability to detect and classify objects and events, to track objects over time, and to assign attributes to objects and events. Undoubtedly, the nervous systems of living creatures transmit and store all of this as sets, or packages of signals (one could even all a *sign* or a *symbol* such a package of signals). But none of them require words of natural language that serves the process of communication. It is clear that sensory experience can be transformed into a useful representation of reality without resorting to natural language words, or perhaps, using different "words," not those required for communication.

Representing the world with natural language words requires a very advanced degree of intelligence. Only humans (and perhaps a few of the higher mammals) demonstrate any significant language skills. Computing with words implies the ability to transform sensory signals into verbal descriptions that can be used in logical rules and mathematical formulas. Transforming sensory signals into words requires a great deal of complex computation. Input from the world arrives via sensors embedded in the skin, in the retina, in the cochlea, in the nose and tongue, in the vestibular apparatus, and in the muscles and tendons. All of these different kinds of sensors transform incident energy from the world into signals that are carried to the central nervous system via different afferent neural pathways.

These various signals must be filtered and fused by being processed through many layers of computation before objects and events can be detected and associated with words. For example, arrays of signals from the eyes and skin must first be processed to detect elementary features such as temporal and spatial gradients, edges, and flow vectors. Information from multiple sensors must be processed to detect range, color, and texture. Strings of signals from acoustic arrays must be filtered and processed to detect patterns of frequencies. Elementary features must be grouped into entities. Attributes must be computed and labels assigned. Labeled objects and events must be transformed into a common coordinate frame of reference so that they can be fused into a coherent view of the world with relationships that can be associated with words.

These processes are complicated by the fact that sensory input is almost always ambiguous. It is rare that information about objects or events in the world can be measured directly. For example, photodetectors in a camera or the retina of an eye measure only the intensity of light falling on them. A two-dimensional image on the retina is completely ambiguous with regard to the distance (or range) to points in the image. A signal from a single photodetector is also ambiguous with respect to the shape, size, distance, or class of the object emitting the radiant energy. The visual signal from an entire camera array is ambiguous with respect to the distance, size, and nonvisible characteristics of an object. Perceptual processes must disambiguate the initial signals from sensors by inferring this kind of information, that is by interpreting sensory data in the context of signals from other sensors (such as acoustic, tactile, smell, taste, vestibular, and proprioceptive sensors) and a priori information about the world (such as knowledge of physics, math, logic, and characteristics of the class or classes to which the observed object is recognized as being a member). Range can be inferred from stereo disparity between images in two eyes and vergence between the eyes, or from motion parallax, or from other characteristics of the scene, such as shading, texture, and occlusion boundaries. Size of objects can be inferred from angular size in the image multiplied by the estimated range. Computation of the velocity of perceived objects can be inferred from image flow measurements if the linear and angular motion of the eye or camera is known. Even the most elementary visual feature detection requires inference. When we visually perceive edges between surfaces in the world, these are inferred from gradients in intensity or color images in our visual cortex. We can infer that sounds are coming from a particular direction by computing phase and intensity differences between sound waves in our two ears. In tactile sensing, the shape and surface properties of objects can be inferred from pressure, temperature, vibration, and pain measurements in the skin.

Acoustic signals are also ambiguous. The sound of a footstep may indicate the presence of a loved one or a burglar. In ordinary speech, there are many words that sound the same but mean different things. For example, "attack" and "a tack" are pronounced exactly the same, but have completely different meanings. Yet, the two are rarely confused because of the context in which they are used. Apparently, the brain disambiguates sensory inputs by hypothesizing several possible meanings and choosing the one that best explains the totality of sensory input integrated over an extended window of attention in time and space.

To cope with the ambiguity of sensory input, biological brains have developed sensory processing methods that extract the information needed to construct reliable world models. One of the methods is to hypothesize and test. This process formulates hypotheses to explain the sensory input, and then tests how well each hypothesis predicts experimental observations. Hypotheses that fail to predict observations are discarded. The hypothesis that best predicts observations is accepted. Hypotheses are usually created by grouping prior experiences by similarity.

For example, image features such as edges and surface patches can be grouped into entities such as surfaces and objects. However, there typically are many different ways that features can be grouped into surfaces and objects. Any particular grouping is only one of many possible groupings that might explain the sensory input being observed. Each possible grouping is a hypothesis that must be evaluated and then confirmed or rejected on the basis of its ability to predict future sensory input. Once a grouping is confirmed as an entity, it attributes can be computed and the entity can be classified and named as an object, event, or situation. All of these processes must be completed before computing with words has even a chance to begin.

Because processing information to the level of words is computationally expensive, any brain that uses words must have the ability to focus attention on what is important and ignore what is unimportant. This, of course, requires the ability to distinguish between what is important and what is trivial. Focusing attention, searching, grouping, and classification are carried out at many levels of resolution in multiscale (multigranular, multiresolutional) architectures of top-down and bottom-up processing. Recognition of objects and events as well as decision making requires merging a priori knowledge with current sensory experience.

Thus, the computational power required to perceive the natural world in terms of words is enormous. Only human brains have this capability, attained by virtue of both multiscale representation and using focusing of attention in multiscale processing. But the human brain is a very recent development in evolutionary history. Most brains do not have nearly this level of computing power. This implies that representation of the world in terms of natural language words is a recent development. It suggests that the more simple and fundamental representation of the world in the "prelinguistic" brain is not symbolic but iconic. Natural language words are a recent addition overlaid on the more primitive representation of images and maps.

Of course, the ability to generate symbolic names, attributes, classes, and relationships conveys a tremendous advantage in reasoning about problems and making plans. Precise and complex models of the world often are most efficiently represented in terms of mathematical or linguistic symbols. The advantage of computing with words may be sufficiently large to explain the intellectual differences between humans and other animals. Thus, computing with words is extremely important. But the power of symbolic reasoning in terms of words depends on a vast computational infrastructure supported by more primitive representations. The fundamental representation of the world in the brain is iconic. Representation with words is a thin veneer that has been overlaid on more basic iconic representations only very recently in the evolutionary history of the human species. This should be kept in mind as we contemplate what it means to compute with words.

ESSENCE OF PROBLEMS WITH REPRESENTATION

So, in light of our discussion, what is the essence of this subject: *computing with words*? The essence is in the phenomenon of representation that is related both to perception and to behavior generation. The first subsystem receives signals from sensors, the other outputs the behavior. Communication between these two subsystems should be mediated by a system capable of dealing with words (i.e., transform the way information is represented and learn these representations to use for hypothesizing). Let us call this mediating system a *system of representation* (world representation). Let us address this phenomenon more carefully. The following questions should be answered:

- Why does the representation exist, and what purpose does it serve?
- What are the most likely holders of the representation and the carriers used within the system of representation?
- How are representations processed?

Why "representation," and what is its purposes? The phenomenon of representation can be noted at a very early stage of intelligent systems development. For both natural or artificial goal-oriented systems, the very existence of the phenomenon "system with a goal" is the fact *and* the result of its representation. Indeed, a system is a set of interrelated elements whose parameters and relationships follow a detectable order. If an order is detected, the existence of a purpose can be assumed; otherwise, why keep the order? The order can be considered a partial representation of the purpose (or the goal). Each system is a representation of itself, its goal, and the possible road maps to the goal.

The term *representation* has two meanings:

1. Representation is a *process of mapping* (a) from the reality into a symbolic system, (b) from a symbolic system into another symbolic system, and (c) from a symbolic system into the hardware, or reality (which can formally be considered just another symbolic system).
2. Representation is a *result of the process* of representation described in the preceding paragraph.

The purpose of representation is to provide an internal model of external reality that can be used to analyze the past, predict the future, and plan and control behavior. For artificial or constructed systems, representations are developed and maintained so that the system has information about the state of the world, including objects, events, situations, and relationships. For natural systems, the answer is similar.

Each representation is characterized by its architecture, form, and the embodiment of the representation holder. Representation might be both external and internal (relative to the represented system). Representation can be iconic or symbolic. The purpose of an iconic representation is to represent explicitly, pictorial properties of the world, such as position, orientation, shape, and size. The purpose of a symbolic representation is to capture states, attributes, and relationships of and between objects, events, situations, and classes. All things should be under consideration: words, images, and emotional states including fear, pleasure, pressure, temperature, position, velocity, comfort–fear, pleasure–pain, love–hatred, hunger, thirst, and need for air, among many other nonpictorial meanings.

Thus, representation is a subsystem that interprets messages between the world of perception and the world of behavior generation. At this point we should introduce the concept of *symbol* and a definition that *anything used for representation is considered to be a symbol*. So the system of representation is intrinsically symbolic. The latter definition is important because it provides an opportunity not to make differences among various carriers of representation: by virtue of being used as building blocks or representations *they serve as symbols*.

Symbols are typically considered to be labels for the lumped entities. The question emerges: Can the symbols be continuous? In other words, can the continuum serve as a symbol? The answer is *yes* if the multiresolutional approach is accepted as the protocol for constructing and/or interpreting the system of representation. Then any entity that is a continuum at higher resolution can be grouped into a lumped entity at lower resolution. In the same way, any entity that behaves as a continuum at lower resolution will transform into a multiplicity of lumped entities at higher resolution.

At this point, a discussion of the concept of linguistic variable would seem to be helpful. When in his papers of the 1960s, Lotfi Zadeh talks about *age* (young, average, old) or about *speed* (low, intermediate, high), both are examples of particular linguistic variables (LVs). Each LV has the same mechanism of fuzziness, and everybody uses an intuitively postulated function of membership that determines the convention about the boundaries of the provisional "lump," or a unit of "fuzzy knowledge." So the act of lumping various continua into LVs becomes not an absolute, but a relative issue, and the categorization into a "continuum" or lumped "entity" becomes a provisional issue. Any plausible law (e.g., curve) of membership works well because eventually we supply the system with a feedback, and no matter what low of membership was utilized, the control system works well. This is the bottom line: The apparatus, which was created based on the concept of LV, works in solving realistic problems!

Fuzzy techniques turned out to be an introduction to the multiresolutional and/or multigranular and/or multisclae visions of the world that emerged later. Different zones of fuzziness signified different granularity. Representations are bundled by the value of their granularity. Another term for this was *resolution*. This term focuses not on the property of the world that is being perceived, but upon the property of perception to perceive various things with a different degree of our eyes to be squinted. Although only vision is mentioned, the phenomenon of resolution is undoubtedly also related to other senses. So the level of granularity was not introduced accidentally by our verbalization of the perceived world—it is a property of perception.

CONNECTIONS TO NATURAL LANGUAGE

Words are elements of natural language documents: texts and narratives. Frequently, the term *word* is disconnected from its linkage with natural language because of its computer science meanings: as a set of bits constituting a unit of addressable memory, or as a string of characters from an alphabet. The same disconnection from the natural language and text can happen to the presently emerging body of research related to computing with words. So far, fuzzy set theory was implicitly related to the natural language texts because of the concept of *linguistic variable*. The book *Computing with Words* develops this linkage further; it makes an issue of words that are not are only a part of the dictionary, but rather, a part of the natural language text and its structure.

In this way, many phenomena will be discovered: We will find that the same word has different fuzziness in different contexts, that different words have similar meanings, and that the degree of similarity will affect fuzzy sets. Some people are *older*, and some people are *younger*, and in the context of our conversation the curve of membership can be shifted dynamically as the conversation develops: The meaning and interpretation of words are relative and subjective! But we know that real *words* do not live without text: without expressions and phrases, without sentences and paragraphs, eventually without the context. Words as components of the narrative and/or of natural language documents are richer than LVs: They are not fixed; they are subjected to constant disambiguation. They are parts of fuzzy semantic fields. They are linked with the novel phenomenon of *semantic space*, which is an extension of well-known semantic networks into multidimensional and multiresolutional paradigms (see Chapter 5).

This is how L. Zadeh's intuitions about computing with words (CW) can be interpreted. He wrote: "A key aspect of CW is that it involves a *fusion of natural languages and computation with fuzzy variables*."[1] In other words, the bridge should be constructed and built between natural language processing and knowledge representation based on natural language texts with the methodology of fuzzy system constraints and their propagation so that we could return recommendations as a well-organized natural language text.

It becomes clear that the controversy "computing with numbers versus computing with words" is of minor importance: This was just an additional mapping; it did not change any essence of the process. We still compute with words, even if numbers serve as a technical carrier of representation. We are used to thinking: Computing

[2]See L. Zadeh, Fuzzy logic + computing with words, *IEEE Trans. Fuzzy Syst.* 4(2):103–111, 1996.

with words? Words as opposed to what?" Naturally, as opposed to computing with numbers! You cannot avoid the connection "computing with *words* instead of *numbers*." This connection would not seem controversial if we realize that in a CW domain, we will ascend to *analyzing* with words—this would not counterpose computing with numbers as its antithesis. Everybody uses fuzzy systems—but computes with concrete, nonfuzzy numbers. Fuzzy logic is based on LV, but computers compute with numbers. What else do you need but numbers if the goal is to represent the meaning initially carried within words?

Certainly, *fuzzy logic* is a theoretical emphasis on *computing with words*. But *computing with words* is a much larger issue. *Fuzzy logic* is a subset of *computing with words*. It is one of the tools of computing with words. Fuzzy logic is tremendously useful for systems with *fuzzy variables* but should not necessarily have any traceable direct connection to texts, speech, and natural language as a whole. But *words* are much more powerful because they have all these connections, and we should appreciate this.

We can imagine that somewhere down the road, CW researchers will address such questions as: Perhaps computers should not be encoded in numbers, especially not in binary numbers? Perhaps concepts should be represented in a computer without going through the stage of encoding them with binary numbers that invoke Boolean logic? Perhaps computers *should employ encoding in words*, or at least in multivalued codes that invoke a multivalued logic? However, we do not focus on the imaginary reality of future word-based computers. Perhaps they will be based on a hybrid principle and unify capabilities of both digital and analog computers. We can visualize multivalued logic–based computers as the first step toward truly fuzzy hardware, as might happen in systems using *wetware*. Perhaps this is what a blend of von Neumann and analog computers will be all about? So the code will be in words—and the process of computing will be partially within analog wandering within semantic fields. Perhaps.

CONNECTIONS TO MIND AND PERCEPTION

Let us talk about the area of primary significance for computing with words: the interface between a fuzzy multiresolutional representation and the human mind. The latter is presumed to be a machine for interpreting the meaning of words mainly from speech, natural texts (rooted in speech), and personal perceptions (actually, strongly related to the phenomenon of speech). Shouldn't we focus on the process of going from the speech, the text, the verbal description to a formal model? On the other hand, shouldn't we consider explicitly what kind of symbols are used: words, images, or any another symbolic system?

This problem—mapping the verbal and/or pictorial description into a model—is the foremost problem of the CW area. The central effort is a mapping of words and images into a multiresolutional fuzzy set/logic model. Since a fuzzy controller with "fuzzification/defuzzification" is a tool for moving from one resolution (granularity) to another resolution (granularity), it can be interpreted as a *control with words*. This implies an important statement: *Any fuzzy control is a control with words*. Since *fuzzy* means *multigranular* or *multiresolutional*, our message is: *Any multiresolutional control is a control with words*. Moreover, since any complete controller (that contains both planning and executor) uses two levels or resolution, our statement actually is: *Any control is a control with words*.

We know what fuzzy control is and we know what multiresolutional control is. Are we ready to admit that all controllers are "controllers with words"? Perhaps the phenomenon of a *word* should be broader and deeper than just a "linguistic variable" and should also include at least sensory "images"? Perhaps it should reflect the multiresolutional nature of images and associative links between their components? Clearly, the concept of *fuzzy variable* should exist as an enhancement of the idea of *vairable*. But the concept of controlling with *words* or, rather, controlling with *symbols* would allow us to reach for a totally new vision of the situation.

Further development of this thesis leads to more generalizations. We can call every controller a *controller with words* (or *symbols*) because we can easily explain as follows: This letter (symbol) is "voltage"; this letter (symbol) is "current"; this letter (symbol) is "speed"—so we control the words of a *plant* with words of the *controller*—we control electric motor with words! However, not totally so, because in conventional controllers we submit numbers to the controller, not words such as "low voltage," "middle voltage," the current will be "medium." Actually, nothing prevents us from saying that every controller is a controller with words. Even numbers can be expressed in terms of words. We can define the requirements of a controller in terms of words. Control systems starts with a story, a narrative in a natural language. This story asks, for example, the following:

- How do we want our system to work?
- What might happen (and often happens) to our system that we don't like?
- How are we disturbed by what happens (the losses we encounter)?
- What exactly are the phenomena that we do not like in the functioning of our system?
- Where are the noise and disturbances coming from?
- Under which circumstances does bad accuracy appear?
- What are the advantages that we can gain?

Then, we take this story, and intuitively do the following:

- Abridge the descriptions as much as seems meaningful and reasonable
- Extract the *words of interest* from this story and consider them variables and constraints
- Describe all our knowledge related to the extracted words, with as many details as possible
- Introduce assumptions and simplifications that make the story more balanced and logical
- Neglect a number of seemingly unrelated factors
- Add statements of knowledge that seem to be lacking

All of this is initially expressed in words. Even when we sketch a block diagram and write a set of equations, we do nothing more than encode our verbal descriptions.

This happens at each level of the hierarchy of control, although the story that one has told now belongs to a higher level of this hierarchy (lower resolution). We want to change the situation at each level by introducing planning/executor pairs. We intuitively extract words that are meaningful for us and construct equations around them. When the control system is designed and manufactured, all mathematical equations become important with higher resolution (i.e., with more detail). The descriptions and/or imagery of lower resolution turn out to be extremely important: They guide the high-resolution descriptions.

Yes, we are in the CW business most of our professional lives. This point of view can scarcely be challenged.

PERCEPTION ENTERS THE PICTURE

All these views seems to deserve both detailed consideration and serious analysis. Computing with words emphasizes natural language texts. But words and images exist together and support each other. Neither of them (the texts or the image) can be ignored, because there are elements of the image that affect behavior even if they cannot be verbalized, and there are verbal statements that cannot be translated into the domain of imagery.

The processing of images typically proceeds in a multiresolutional way. Image interpretation typically involves construction of a nested multiscale hierarchy for the partially ambiguous system of labels. Similarly, multiple groups of words, expressions, phrases, sentences, paragraphs, and sections of a document carry respective meanings that form a network of meaning. The collective meaning of groups of documents (corpora) affects the meaning of single words. The fields of meaning for the groups of single words affect the meaning of the units of text that has been mentioned above.

All this brings us to a question: In which form are all these factors represented in the human brain? This is an issue that is usually not addressed in cognitive science and is not reflected in most models of the brain. From the point of view of interpreting the external situation, both images and verbal descriptions are instrumental: They overlap and complement each other. They exist together. When someone tells a story, the listener frequently imagines scenes in which the story takes place. When one sees things happening, one can construct verbal descriptions. These representations coexist and affect the recipient simultaneously. Images emerge while talking, and verbalizations emerge while seeing. We use words in perceptions, but we use more than words. We use images that have not yet been transformed into words. Images support our verbal representations, and vice versa. This may suggest a more generalized approach than just relying on words and images. Computing with words and computing with images may be combined into *computing with thoughts*.[2] This is an interesting idea because

[3]P. Wang communicated to us that this is a point of view expressed by V. Niskanen.

thoughts seem to unify images and words and can be considered as a concept of *multi-symbol fusion* used for representation.

When one thinks about these things within the framework of semiotics, one might find no difference between symbolic representations (in words) and iconic representations (in images). Both are actually symbolic representations; they just utilize different kinds of signs. There is some evidence that in our brain, the descriptive representations (in words) and iconic representations (pictorial images) exist together in joint form. At lower levels the iconic and symbolic representation may be overlaid on each other in the same region of the cortex. At higher levels, language skills tend to be concentrated in the left hemisphere of the brain, and spatial relationships predominate in the right hemisphere. In either case, words and images exist simultaneously and are tightly coupled.

It is often said that one image is worth a thousand words. However, images and words complement each other. The brain achieves its amazing powers through a combination of images and words. This suggests that perhaps we should talk about *computing with words and images*. Perhaps we should consider combining the concepts of computing with words and images into a single concept of *computing with thoughts*. So when we ask a question like "How do our senses talk to our actuators?", the answer should be: "Our sensors are talking in symbols that fuse the modalities of words with modalities of images. In other words, our senses talk to our actuators through the medium of thoughts."

CHAPTER 1

COMPUTING WITH WORDS: INTRODUCTION, IMPLICATIONS, AND APPLICATIONS

PAUL P. WANG
Duke University, Durham, North Carolina

1.1 INTRODUCTION

The goal of this introductory chapter is to explain, comment on, and predict the potential applications of the *computing with words* (CW) theory, developed by Lotfi A. Zadeh. The importance of language and speech to human intelligence has been recognized for many years. For a computer to implement artificial intelligence, it must understand the language and speech of human intelligence as a prerequisite. It is also the firm belief of this writer that Zadeh's theory is unique and innovative. Once research on this theory has been fully developed, CW should be capable of delivering a quality of service beyond human intelligence in at least two very important areas: intelligent information systems and intelligent control systems. Unfortunately, this very significant theory is not as widely known outside the fuzzy research community as it deserves.

In this introductory chapter, the aim is to communicate to a wide audience by relating CW theory to certain important aspects of artificial intelligence with which they are already familiar. Consequently, a great deal of material presented here was taken from the well-known literature to provide immediate reference for readers. Nonetheless, much of the material, especially the commentaries and predicted applications, is original and unique.

1.2 STUDY OF LANGUAGE IN GENERAL

Language is one of the most important human activities in all cultures, regardless of the degree of cultural sophistication [1]. There are many different kinds of natural

Computing with Words, Edited by Paul P. Wang.
ISBN 0-471-35374-4

languages in our world civilization. In written form, language is the most important instrument for recording human activities, thus enabling later generations to know their history and heritage. In spoken form, speech is the primary means of conducting daily communication. Without spoken words, humans must rely on written words or body language.

Historically, language has been studied in several easily distinguishable academic disciplines, each of which defines its own problems, its own method of attacking them, and its accomplishments. This seemingly advantageous position turns out to be more burdensome as we launch CW research. The explosive nature of readily available information as well as the drive to better utilize information creates a challenging research task.

Four distinct schools of language studies may be described briefly as follows [2]:

1. *Linguistics.* Basically, linguists study the structure of language, such as how words form phrases and sentences and what constrains the possible meanings of a sentence. The tools they use include structural analysis, meaning, and mathematical models such as formal language theory and model-theoretic semantics.
2. *Psycholinguistics.* This school studies the processes of human language production and comprehension. Typical questions they ask are: How do people identify the structure of sentences? How are word meanings identified? When does understanding take place? They use experiential methods based on human performance; hence the statistical analysis of observations becomes important.
3. *Philosophy.* At the outset, philosophers worried about how words identify objects in the world—the fundamental issue of how words can mean anything at all. They ask: When does understanding take place? Furthermore, they consider what it means to have beliefs, goals, and intentions. In particular, they ask: How do all these cognitive capabilities relate to language? To achieve their objectives, they employ natural language argumentation using intuition about counterexamples via mathematical logic and model theory.
4. *Computational linguistics.* The goal of the computational linguist is to develop a computational theory of language, taking advantage of the concept of algorithms, data structures, and so on, already known to computer scientists. Furthermore, with the standard artificial intelligence techniques of search and knowledge representation, formal models of knowledge and reasoning become powerful tools to answer such important questions as: How is sentence structure identified? How can knowledge and reasoning be modeled? How can language be used to accomplish specific tasks?

1.3 DEFINITION OF CW

Jean Piaget argued that intelligence is what you use when you don't know what to do. Intelligence is about the process of improvising and polishing on the timescale of thought and action. After all, our language and foresight behaviors are surely aspects of intelligent behavior and they are quite complex [3]. Apart from the philosophical and scientific aspects, language issues hold the key to the success of progress in artificial intelligence. E. Feigenbaum states that most real-world problems in artificial intelligence are linguistic in nature. Our interest and focus in CW has been motivated precisely by the intention to raise the quality of artificial intelligence.

Lotfi A. Zadeh originated the phrase *computing with words.* However, this seemingly perfect choice for a title, surprisingly, has triggered strong disagreements by researchers in various linguistics, artificial intelligence, and natural language processing research communities. They argue that Zadeh's theory is not the only methodology that constitutes computing with words. It can be argued that they are, in fact, computing with words in a strict sense as long as mathematics and digital computers are used. As we mentioned earlier, to accomplish their objectives, linguists use formal mathematical linguistic theory; psycholinguists use statistical analysis; philosophers use mathematical logic; and computational linguists rely heavily on many modern computational tools: algorithms, data structures, search techniques, formal models of knowledge, and so on. However, it is equally true that Zadeh's theory bears his signature definitively and uniquely. As time will prove, his theory is, and will be, very significant both in philosophical argument and in practical applications. In hindsight, the artificial intelligence research community should not have chosen the phrase *artificial intelligence* because it solves only part of the problem. From the fuzzy research community's viewpoint, CW accurately represents Zadeh's 1966 paper, "Fuzzy Logic = Computing with Words" [4].

A formal definition of CW is difficult to cast in stone. However, the following is an attempt to present an outline using simple language. CW provides a mathematical model for the natural language theory. It captures the salient features and characteristics of the semantic aspects of natural language. The theory is especially effective in handling the pragmatic aspects of natural language. The foundation of CW, however, lies in the concept of the fuzzy set and fuzzy logic. Once fully developed, it is possible for a machine to process a set of statements in natural language that contain various uncertainties and draw a conclusion in a single statement that is meaningful and useful to humans.

In natural language, perceptions are handled via descriptions. Zadeh's newest addition to CW is his computational theory of perceptions [5]. To process information presented in the form of perceptions, it is necessary to have a method of representing the meaning of propositions expressed in a natural language in a way that makes meaning amenable to computation. This newly added computational semantics of natural language is a key component of CW. One way to appreciate CW theory is to look at language itself. The progress in natural language theory has, at best, been quite slow during the past half century. CW provides an opportunity for us to do something substantial.

In the next section we explore the mathematical modeling of natural language via CW as well as examine the syntactic and semantic aspects of language theory. Robert Rosen has correctly called twentieth-century science the *age of syntactics.* It has been an age of string processing, word processing, and data processing in which science deals with truth and meaning in language, solely by virtue of form and pattern [6]. So far, CW can accommodate simple form in syntactics—mainly, "if ... then" rules. However, fuzzy constraint network theory can have much more complicated forms of first-order predicate calculus logic and pattern. On the other hand, semantics studies the meaning or significance of the language. Both pattern and meaning enter significantly into the very idea of natural language. But syntax appears objective and scientific, whereas semantics involves conventions and subjectivities that seem to generate hosts of perhaps needless obscurities and ambiguities [6]. It is the semantic aspect of language for which CW is expected to make significant contributions. Fuzzy logic has clearly demonstrated its ability to handle uncertainty, incomplete information, and limitations. CW will do even more.

1.4 MATHEMATICAL MODELING OF NATURAL LANGUAGE USING FUZZY MATHEMATICS

Zadeh is well known as the founding father of fuzzy logic. However, his CW theory is much more fundamental because of its connection to language theory. His concept of the fuzzy set is even more fundamental as a mathematical theory. In this section we examine the fuzzy set from a human cognitive viewpoint, as well as discuss ways in which CW can be used to model natural language. Justification for making use of the fuzzy concept in natural language modeling has deep roots in psychology. Robert Erickson, a researcher with the experimental psychology department at Duke University, has studied natural language extensively from a psycholinguistic point of view. Some time ago, another researcher, Stephen J. Gould, observed in hindsight the need to use fuzzy sets for modeling perceptions [7]:

> The human mind seems to work as a categorizing device.... This deeply (perhaps innately) ingrained habit of thought causes us particular trouble when we need to analyze the many continua that form so conspicuous a part of our surrounding world. Continua are rarely so smooth and gradual in their flux that we cannot specify certain points or episodes as decidedly more interesting or more tumultuous in their rates of change, than the vast majority of moments along the sequence. We therefore falsely choose these crucial episodes as boundaries for fixed categories, and we veil nature's continuity in the wrappings of our mental habits.... We must also remember another insidious aspect of our tendency to divide continua into fixed categories. These divisions are not neutral; they are established for definite purposes by partisans of particular viewpoints.

From this we can see the need for a mathematical definition of a fuzzy set with continuous membership function allowing for a gradual transition during the boundary region. This is not only a natural fit from a mathematical modeling point of view, it is a necessity.

As we try to make practical use of artificial intelligence, we must deal with natural language effectively. The obvious places to begin are the semantics of the words that compose the building blocks of language. To our dismay, we find out that the words, and consequently the language itself, turn out to be the problem. Greg Kimble and William James raised interesting questions about the meaning of words [8]:

> Some of the problems of psychology are the same as those that frustrate public understanding, and for the same reason: The language of psychology is also that of common sense. Language is the agent of cognition, the currency of thinking, the toolbox of communication and the custodian of culture. To be useful, it must map onto the world with some precision. Unfortunately, however, the fact that it does so encourages the faith that the fit is perfect and that truth is in the dictionary. If there is a word for it, there must be a corresponding item of reality. If there are two words, there must be two realities and they must be different.

This quotation points out the fundamental difficulties related to cognitive science, language, and computing with words.

Keeping in mind the goals of technological development and potential commercialization of the CW methodology, we cannot afford to ignore the subtle arguments presented here by important thinkers of the past and present. If we can do something about natural language itself, fine. If not, it is possible that an adaptive approach to CW, as well as the reasoning and inferential power of fuzzy logic, may help. Perhaps the remedy process should begin with a definition of membership functions. At this point, more discussion would certainly be helpful in improving our basic understanding of the situation dealing with the words and the language itself.

James [8] recognized the problem: "Whenever we have made a word . . . to denote a certain group of phenomena, we are prone to suppose a substantive entity existing beyond the phenomena [and] the lack of a word quite often leads to the opposite error. We are then prone to suppose that no entity can be there; and so we overlook phenomena whose existence would be patent to us all, had we only grown up to hear it familiarly recognized in speech." In a similar vein, closer to the technological venture of computing with words, Albert Einstein said [9]: "Science must create its own language, its own concepts, for its own use. Scientific concepts often begin with those used in ordinary language for the affairs of everyday life, but they develop quite differently." Einstein did not let common words shape his science. As it turns out, words and language are problematic as we embark on the task of computing with words.

1.5 RELATIONSHIP BETWEEN CW AND COGNITIVE SCIENCE

Howard Gardner defines *cognitive science* as a contemporary, empirically based effort to answer long-standing epistemological questions, particularly those concerned with the nature of knowledge, its components, its sources, its development, and its deployment [10]. Cognitive scientists harbor the faith that much is to be gained from interdisciplinary studies. At present, most cognitive scientists are drawn from the ranks of specific disciplines: in particular, philosophy, psychology, artificial intelligence, linguistics, anthropology, and neuroscience [10]. Gardner refers to these disciplines together as cognitive science. The hope is that some day the boundaries between these disciplines may become attenuated or perhaps disappear altogether, yielding a single, unified cognitive science.

The unofficial launching of cognitive science took place in the mid-1950s. One might say that cognitive science has a very long past but a relatively short history. Although its roots can be traced to classical times, it has emerged as a recognized pursuit only in the last few decades [10]. In recent years, the limits of the serial digital von Neumann computer become clearer. *Parallel distributed processing* (PDP) provides a different modal view of cognition, a view in which psychological, computational, and neurological considerations are far more intricately linked [11].

Often discussed in cognitive science circles today are the PDP and classical *serial-symbolic* models. Lower-level perceptual processes can be accounted for adequately in terms of PDP models, but higher-level conceptual or linguistic processes (and perhaps even some aspects of perception) will require a more complex, multilevel representational account [10]. Howard Gardner predicts that the pendulum will swing back and forth between PDP and serial symbolic. To date, significant advances have been made in our understanding of visual perception, natural language processing, imaging, categorization, and human rationality. Nevertheless, as Rumelhart and his colleagues note [11], what is difficult to describe in the PDP framework are "the process of thinking, the contents of consciousness, the role of serial processes, the nature of mental models, the reasons for mental simulations, and the important synergistic role of language in thinking and shaping our thought."

Zadeh's proposed theory actually is much broader than simply the applications of fuzzy logic in control engineering. Up to this point I have attempted to explain Zadeh's theory as it relates to cognitive science. This is one of several piecemeal explanations that I will integrate toward the end of the chapter. In a recent article, Zadeh states that there are three basic concepts that underlie human cognition: granulation, organization, and causation [12]. These concepts have been built on the theory of fuzzy set and fuzzy logic.

The issue of causation, in particular, is an important intelligent agent that has been recognized by several prominent researchers, including Marvin Minsky [13]. However, Zadeh's fuzzy version, especially, has been responsible for many outstanding applications of considerable commercial success and economic value. *Granulation* of an object A leads to a collection of granules of A, a *granule* being a clump of points (objects) drawn together by indistinguishability, similarity, proximity, or functionality [12]. In general, granulation is hierarchical in nature. One of Zadeh's familiar examples is the granulation of time into years, months, days, hours, minutes, and so on. The granulation of a two-dimensional space would lead to the familiar notation *resolution* or *sampling frequency* or *size of a pixel*, as occurs in image processing. The impact of the granulation process on image processing is huge from a visual effectiveness viewpoint. From a dynamic control system viewpoint, the granulation hierarchy would lead to a spectrum of multiple versions of mathematical modeling. Contemporary control engineers now consider this necessary for the study of intelligent control systems. To understand better the behavior of dynamic systems, multiple mathematical models of a dynamic system may be needed to finely tune the control. As John Holland has remarked, the desired mathematical model is like a political cartoon—the salient feature should be enhanced. He also noted that the trademark of a good mathematical model is being able to put out more than you put in [13]. However, the issue of granularity is different. For some applications, modeling successfully in several granularities is critical. Spread painting an automobile and planned control of a mobile robot are only two of many actual examples.

Let us now move back one step prior to the completion of a mathematical model in which a decision must be made about the choice of the granule. As Zadeh suggests, a granule is a clump of points (objects) drawn together by indistinguishability, similarity, proximity, or functionality. So far, there is no other known methodology that can do a better job than the fuzzy approach. The definition of the fuzzy set, by its fundamental nature, is a perfect match for the similarity and indistinguishability of conceptual modeling mathematically. The concept of fuzzy relations is nearly ideal, mathematically, for measuring the proximity. Furthermore, the semantic aspect of the label (as a word defined in a language), characterized by linguistic variables, is very rich for language modeling. In addition, the fuzzy set describes ideally information as a utility value. However, this is not the end of the story. These superlative combinations will ultimately be exceeded by many operations and computations of fuzzy mathematics, which, I might note, is extremely different from conventional mathematics. The discussion so far provides a bird's-eye view of the essence of computing with words.

The theory of fuzzy information (represented by fuzzy set) granulation (the multiple resolution concept) has been inspired, according to Zadeh, by the way in which humans granulate information and reason with it [12]. However, the foundation of Zadeh's theory and its methodology are mathematical in nature. The most generalized theory is a combination of fuzzification and granulation. The fuzzification and granular generalization underlies the basic concepts of the linguistic variable—the fuzzy if–then rule—and the fuzzy graph. These concepts have long played a major role in applications of fuzzy logic and differentiate fuzzy logic from other methodologies for dealing with imprecision and uncertainty [12].

Fuzzy logic provides the necessary computations for handling information, while CW provides the semantic interpretations. From a language and speech point of view, CW probably is more important. The impact of fuzzy information granulation theory is likely to be felt most strongly in those fields in which there is a wide gap between theory and reality, according to Zadeh [12]. Natural language processing capabilities would probably revolutionize the way computers are being used. However, the progress of natural language processing, excluding computational method, has been quite slow. This is particularly true for language comprehension and production. With the emergence of cognitive science, of which CW is a part, we may ultimately acquire a deeper understanding of how human language works. To do this we must continue to combine and reconcile the efforts of linguists, psycholinguists, philosophers, and computer scientists. Although still in its infancy, CW offers the potential to play a pivotal role in several research areas. I discuss these further in a later section.

1.6 RELATIONSHIP BETWEEN CW AND ARTIFICIAL INTELLIGENCE

CW is one school of thought in artificial intelligence (AI) research. AI research, which evolved as a means to make better use of the digital computers of the 1950s and 1960s, attempts to develop computers that can complete tasks requiring human intelligence. This goal of putting intelligence in computer hardware, even inventing a complete new architecture for alternative computers—similar to an electronic brain—is a natural challenge for scientists and engineers alike [14]. Zadeh has used CW to address the shortfalls of artificial intelligence, among other things. As mentioned previously, the study of language in artificial intelligence overlaps with psychology, philosophy, and linguistics. These disciplines contribute differently to our understanding behavior and communication.

Artificial intelligence research has led to the development of many diversified expert systems, including those that perform tasks such as medical diagnosis, equipment repairs, computer configuration, financial planning, and hotel yield management [15]. Major AI research topics include:

- Knowledge representation and inference
- Use of search in problem solving
- Expert systems
- Natural language processing
- Vision
- Machine learning and neural networks
- Agents and robots

CW is relevant to each of these topics. However, we focus this discussion on expert systems, natural language processing, and their relation to CW.

In the appendix to his article "Logics of Knowing and Believing," Petr Hájek lists a series of quotations from recognized authorities in the AI field and related domains [14]:

1. "Knowledge processing is vital for A.I."—Lenat and Feigenbaum
2. "Logic is vital for knowledge representation."—Nilsson, Winograd, and Flores
3. "Intelligent systems should be able to reason about their own knowledge."—Winograd and Flores, Hayes-Roth et al., and Halpern
4. "The knowledge of AI systems is typically uncertain and imprecise."—Hayes-Roth et al.
5. "Logics of beliefs as well as probabilistic methods are well established in A.I."—Lotfi A. Zadeh and Peter Hájek

Zadeh's theories on fuzzy sets, fuzzy logic, CW, and the logic of perceptions could lead to improvements in the limitations of AI. However, there has been no significant funding to demonstrate Zadeh's theories even after Michio Sugeno's fuzzy expert system, which was used to control an unmanned helicopter, substantiated Zadeh's research. To cope with the uncertainty and impreciseness noted by Hayes-Roth et al., Hajeck and others maintain that a fuzzy belief logic gives rise naturally to numerical possibility measures [16]. Although the AI community has embraced logics of belief and probabilistic methods for a long time, it has not accepted fuzzy logic with equal enthusiasm. In speaking of the growing use of soft computing, especially fuzzy logic, in the conception and design of intelligent systems, Zadeh stated [17]: "The principal aim of soft computing is to exploit the tolerance for imprecision and uncertainty to achieve tractability, robustness, and low production cost. At this juncture, the principal constituents of soft computing (SC) are fuzzy logic (FL), neural networks (NN), and probabilistic reasoning (PR). . . . In large measure, FL, NN, and PR are complementary rather than competitive."

1.7 NATURAL LANGUAGE PROCESSING

Natural language processing research has always been an important component of artificial intelligence research. CW has the potential to make significant contributions to this research. Natural language processing can be divided into speech and the typed word. A computer is less able to understand spoken language than typed or keyed language because the input is a raw speech signal. Automatic speech recognition becomes the first order of business. A natural language processing system requires considerable knowledge about the structure of language itself. James Allen pointed out the following forms of knowledge necessary for natural language understanding [2]:

1. *Phonetic and phonological knowledge*: how words relate to their sounds.
2. *Morphological knowledge*: how words are constructed from more basic meaning units called *morphemes*. For example, the word *friendly* is derived from the meaning of the noun *friend* and the suffix *ly*, which transforms a noun into an adjective.
3. *Syntactic knowledge*: how words can be put together to form correct sentences. The word sequence is analyzed using knowledge of grammar.
4. *Semantic knowledge*: using information about sentence structure and word meaning to partially understand the entire sentence.
5. *Pragmatic knowledge*: using context to understand the sentence. This might include when, where, by whom, and to whom the sentence was said. In other words, the meaning depends on the situation and use of the sentence. Pragmatic knowledge is one area in which CW can play an important role. Zadeh advocates mathematical modeling of the words and language using fuzzy set theory and interpreting word and sentence meaning via fuzzy logic mathematical operations. For example, the linguistic variable concept enriches the meaning of a word via mathematical modeling. Furthermore, a

meaning is obtained by mathematical quantification. Fuzzy logic theory allows the propagation of elastic constraints of a sentence since the linguistic variable of a word can also be viewed as a constraint.

6. *Discourse knowledge*: how preceding sentences affect the interpretation of the next sentence. This information is especially important in interpreting pronouns and temporal aspects of the information conveyed.
7. *World knowledge*: this includes general knowledge about the world structure that a speaker must possess to maintain a conversation, for example. It also includes what a speaker must know about another speaker's beliefs and goals.

In conclusion, the knowledge required for natural language understanding and processing is very extensive, indeed.

1.8 IDEA OF AUTOMATIC SPEECH RECOGNITION AND UNDERSTANDING ITS DIFFICULTIES

The prospect of communicating with computers using daily speech is extremely attractive [14]. It is fair to say that most of us would like to see an intelligent machine that not only recognizes the spoken word but also understands its meaning. Although the year 2001, which was idealized in the movie *2001—A Space Odyssey*, is already here with us, a computer such as Hal, envisioned by Stanley Kubrick, is nowhere close to being developed. Nor is the robot R2D2 from the George Lucas classic *Star Wars*. Even though dictation machines can possess a 60,000-word vocabulary and provide 95 to 98% accuracy after speaker-dependent training, they still do not *understand* a thing.

According to Lawrence R. Rabiner and Bing-Hwang Juang [18], despite four decades of research, we still are far from developing a machine that can understand spoken discourse on any subject by any speaker in any environment. The primary difficulty in speech recognition is the lack of a simple map from speech signal to word [14]. Speech recognition requires identifying speaker vocabularies, modeling coarticulation (moving one sound to another) and achieving signal robustness, to cite a few examples. The slow progress can be attributed in part to a lack of coordination among the various research communities. As discussed previously, natural language processing requires multidisciplinary research, including linguistics, phonetics, signal processing, AI, pattern recognition, and so on.

1.9 MULTIPLE SPEECH RECOGNITION RESEARCH CONTRIBUTORS AND THEIR INTERDEPENDENCY

A number of midcourse corrections in CW research are needed for better results and improved progress. First, let's look at the various schools of thought. Rabiner and Juang list the following disciplines and their application to one or more speech recognition problems [18]:

1. *Signal processing*: the process of extracting relevant information from speech signals in an efficient and robust manner. Included in signal processing is the form of spectral analysis used to characterize the time-varying properties of the speech signal, as well as various types of signal preprocessing and post-processing to make the speech signal robust to the recording environment (signal enhancement).
2. *Physics (acoustics)*: the science of understanding the relationship between the physical speech signal and the physiological mechanisms (the human vocal apparatus) that produced the speech and through which the speech is perceived (the human hearing mechanisms).
3. *Pattern recognition*: the set of algorithms used to cluster data to create one or more prototypical patterns of a data ensemble and to match (compare) a pair of patterns on the basis of feature measurements of the patterns.
4. *Communication and information theory*: the procedures for estimating parameters of statistical models, the methods for detecting the presence of particular speech patterns, and the set of modern coding and decoding algorithms (including dynamic programming, stack algorithms, and Viterbi decoding) used to search a large but finite grid for a "best" recognized sequence of words.
5. *Linguistics*: the methodology of grammar and language parsing. The relationship between sounds (phonology), words in a language (syntax), meaning of spoken words (semantics), and sense derived from meaning (pragmatics).
6. *Physiology*: understanding the higher-order mechanisms within the human central nervous system that account for speech production and perception. Many modern techniques try to embed this type of knowledge within the framework of artificial neural networks.
7. *Computer science*: the study of efficient algorithms for implementing software or hardware, and the various methods used in a practical speech recognition system. Note that these activities are distinguishable from that of cognitive science discussed previously.
8. *Psychology*: the science of understanding the factors that enable a technology to be used by humans in practical tasks.

It is the area of linguistics in which CW has the most potential to make significant contributions. CW is penetrating, robust, and capable of enhancing the unexplored aspect of natural language potential. We discuss the pragmatics of linguistics in a later section.

The speech and language research community has received a disproportionately low percentage of funds, despite the importance of the field. Attempts to understand the physiology of higher-order mechanisms within the human central nervous system that account for speech production and perception may receive more attention with the recent increase in brain research funding. A case can be made that CW deserves major funding as it connects the fundamental understanding of the speech and technological development of an automatic speech recognition system.

It can also be argued that AI research has a long way to go. Carl Sagan made the following observation [19]: "It by no means follows that computers will in the immediate future exhibit human creativity, subtlety, sensitivity, or wisdom. A classic and probably apocryphal illustration is in the field of machine translation of human languages: a language—say, English—is input and the text is output in another language—say, Chinese."

1.10 ON THE OPTIMISTIC SIDE

The complex issues involved in CW have triggered eight schools of thought and eight major methodologies for solving problems. A review of these bottleneck problems follows.

The same word may be pronounced in many different ways by different speakers, particularly if they have different dialects or are of a different gender [14]. For instance, the Fujian province of China alone has 365 dialects. Even the same speaker will pronounce things slightly differently on different occasions, speaking rapidly or slowly, with varied intonation. There also are words that sound alike, although they have different meanings, such as *there* and *their.*

Speech segmentation is also troublesome, as the temporal gaps between words may be no greater than the gaps within the words themselves in normal speech. It may also be hard to decipher where one word ends and another begins [14]. However, progress has been made and there are automatic methods of segmenting speech into words, phonemes, and so on. If the words are known, their boundaries can be located easily. If words are not known, it is difficult to determine the word sequence and boundaries automatically. Background noise may also complicate analysis. For example, one may have to separate a signal resulting from wind whistling in the trees or a telephone ringing in the background. Although these problems are daunting, they may not be insurmountable.

Speech recognition systems often assume that there is only one speaker; this is known as *speaker independent.* In a single-speaker system, templates used for phoneme matching may come from that speaker. The system may also assume that input consists of one word at a time, with significant pauses between words. Isolated word recognizers deal with such inputs [15]. The third assumption regards a restricted vocabulary, such as "yes" or "no," or the digits zero to nine [14]. Therefore, we can have a restricted system such as a speaker-dependent continuous speech system with a vocabulary of 500 words. State-of-the-art systems might recognize 80 to 90% of the words correctly.

The trend is toward large-vocabulary speaker-independent continuous speech recognition. The design concept is made possible by the availability of faster computers, use of additional training data, better and more refined acoustic modeling, and improved search strategies algorithms. Speech researchers have relied too heavily on linear and linearized models. The speech research community, like so many other research communities, has overutilized the linear and reductionist approach. The approach has been used since Isaac Newton's time, and as the Santa

Fe Research Institute and others have brought to our attention, it must be reexamined critically.

In another vein, let us evaluate natural language processing from the application and economic perspective. Single speech recognition systems are fairly widespread, particularly in telephone applications. One U.S. telephone company uses speech recognition to handle collect calls and other services. Speech recognition systems are also being used for telephone banking services [14]. As discussed earlier, typically, only a small vocabulary is allowed, such as zero to nine digits, "yes," "no," and so on. The dialogue with the user must be focused or prompted to ensure that answers are given in an expected form. Although it is safe to say that a long journey exists for speech recognition research, these examples remind us that progress has been made and that the benefits are well worth the effort.

1.11 PRAGMATICS

The objective of speech is successful communication; that is, the listener should understand the speaker's message [20]. This objective is difficult to achieve; however, it must be accomplished if intelligent systems are to be accepted by users. The most obvious role that CW plays in natural language processing is knowledge of pragmatics. Imagine an intelligent machine successfully using knowledge of word sounds (speech recognition), language structure (syntactic analysis), and individual word meaning (semantics). To understand language, one must know more than the meanings of individual words. One must understand the context of the spoken language. English, particularly, is a context-sensitive language. Furthermore, one must have a basic database and word knowledge base, which are learned in childhood.

Following are four issues central to the study of pragmatics. The discussion of the first two—language as action and handling pronouns—is based on the work of Alison Cawsey [14]. The third area—managing adjectives and adverbs—is an issue widely discussed in the fuzzy research community, while the final issue on dealing with verbs is based on material developed by Tao Yang for this book (Chapter 13).

1. *Language as action.* Language can play the role of communication, such as adding a piece of knowledge. *Loves* (for example, "Paul loves Julia") is a piece of knowledge expressed in an AI language. However, language also plays a much more complex role, as observed by Alison Cawsey [14]. Three typical examples are:

"Where is the tea?"

"Do you have the time?"

"You are late."

These three sentences contain the *speech acts* of informing, requesting, and promising. Behind each speech act, there is a *goal.* If the speaker is denoted by S and the listener by G, the goals are as follows:

1. S wants G to inform her where the tea is.
2. S wants G to tell her the time.
3. S wants G to know that she is annoyed that he is late.

Knowing only the meaning of an utterance is insufficient. One must also understand the goals behind the speech. An analysis of these goals is just one aspect of pragmatics. If language is used to achieve goals, determining what to say is a planning process. Identifying the goals underlying an utterance, in order to respond appropriately, is called a *plan recognition problem* [14]. This is the opposite of planning. In semiotics, a symbol may play an important role in representing a concept. It is an inverse similar to the problem of language in action illustrated by Cawsey. Hopefully, CW will be able to address some of these issues when an intelligent system has to be designed.

2. *Handling pronouns*. Handling pronouns as a pragmatic problem is by no means simple. Sometimes a pronoun may refer to an entity mentioned several sentences earlier [14]. For example, "John buys a new telescope. He sees Mary in the distance. He gets out his telescope. He looks at her through it." To a machine, even an intelligent one, determining the identity of "he," "his," and "her" is no easy task. Furthermore, the problem of identifying the reference point is not restricted to pronouns.

3. *Handling adjectives and adverbs*. Many of Zadeh's CW examples concern the use of adjectives and adverbs. The major difference between CW and conventional artificial intelligence lies in the computational aspect and the role that fuzzy logic plays. Recently, Zadeh pointed out that CW actually equals fuzzy logic [4]. The success of fuzzy logic in solving control problems demonstrates the utility value of CW in managing adjectives and adverbs.

4. *Handling verbs, and the implications*. Tao Yang introduced a computational verb system for developing a new systematic framework of artificial intelligence by embedding the knowledge and experiences of human experts expressed or implied with verbs into machine intelligence (see Chapter 13). He claims that while fuzzy logic provides a computing framework of adjectives and adverbs, it does not cope with verbs. He concludes that fuzzy logic is a quantitative tool for modeling linguistic processes and with static complexities represented by adjectives. We still need another quantitative tool for modeling linguistic processes and for coping with dynamic complexities represented by verbs. Yang's idea is thought provoking and interesting. As a research topic, it could be used to sort out the nontrivial issues for a better understanding and potential applications in natural language processing.

Although we have reviewed only four issues related to pragmatics, it is likely that there are many hidden ones that will surface as more research is conducted. There also are many issues not explored in this chapter: for example, the relationship between fuzzy logic and neural network theory. The nature of word meaning is complicated further by the issue of ambiguity, as many words have multiple meanings. The form in which these various word meanings are represented in the brain has proved elusive [21]. This is as much a question about the structure of memory as it is the representation of word meaning. Neural network has the power to discriminate, and fuzzy logic has the ability to be retrospective. Therefore, the synergy of these two important tools becomes indispensable.

1.12 EVOLUTION OF COMPUTING WITH WORDS

Fundamental papers by Zadeh on the topics of CW include his 1973–1976 papers on linguistic variables, fuzzy if-then rules, and fuzzy graph [22–24]. His paper on computing with words [4] is of particular interest because he points out several directions where fruitful research results can be obtained. His recent work on the theory of fuzzy information granulation, however, provides an even more enhanced foundation for the CW concept. In essence, CW is an integral part of the theory of fuzzy information granulation. In his own words, the point of departure in CW is the observation that in natural language, words play the role of labels of fuzzy granules [12]. In computing with words, a proposition is viewed as an implicit fuzzy constraint on an implicit variable. The meaning of a proposition is the constraint that it represents [20].

From the ultimate application point of view, one may envision the input–system function–output as its mathematical model. In CW, Zadeh specifies the input as the *initial data set* (IDS), which is assumed to consist of a collection of propositions expressed in a natural language. Examples of IDS can be found in Zadeh's memo, "A Theory of Common Sense Knowledge" [20]. Several uncertain and incomplete mathematical structures are embedded in such a collection of propositions. Zadeh identifies the output as the *terminal data set* (TDS), which also is a collection of propositions expressed in natural language. To infer TDS from IDS, the rule of inference in fuzzy logic is used for constraint propagation from premises to conclusion. Although the basic methodology has been around for some time [22–24], many details and implementations are yet to be developed.

According to Zadeh, there are two main rationales for computing with words. First, CW is necessary when the available information is not precise enough to justify the use of numbers [12]. Second, computing with words is advantageous when there is a tolerance for imprecision, uncertainty, and partial truth that can be exploited to achieve tractability, robustness, low-cost solutions, and rapport with reality.

Application potential is quite intriguing. For example, a CW system could allow an accountant to use a microphone to input into a computer income tax data for an entire year.

1.13 FURTHER RESEARCH IN FUZZY LOGIC

Fuzzy logic research is increasing at a rapid pace. There were 3240 papers containing *fuzzy* in the title cited in *Mathematical Reviews* between 1995 and 1998. By comparison, the number of papers cited in 1993 was 521 [25]. Nevertheless, there is a widespread feeling among leading fuzzy logic researchers that more research and more papers on the foundation of fuzzy logic are needed. To have a maximum expressive power for modeling real-world problems, first-order predicate calculus (FOPC) must be used [36]. In CW, the mathematical model for intelligent and complex systems should include FOPC and other mathematical models [26, 36]. The flow of information should be expressed in natural language for the following two reasons:

1. Fuzzy expert systems that capture an expert's experiences use natural language [37].
2. Natural language will be preferred in intelligent control systems whenever and wherever possible. The new concept of completing a *task* in intelligent control calls for the higher command input signal using natural language.

In this regard, the most powerful theory currently is the *fuzzy constraint network* (FCN) [27]. Unfortunately, only a handful of research groups around the world are studying this field. As research is still in its infancy, the theory requires a major investment of time and money. There exists a spectrum of application problems that calls for solutions. In particular, the linguistic variables, fuzzy quantifiers and their interaction and interplays, commonsense knowledge [28], test-score semantics for natural languages and meaning representation [29], and so on, are necessary for a working system. This is only the beginning for research.

The following example demonstrates a specific and fundamental issue concerning FOPC and FCN [28]. We are given the following two propositions:

P: The sun is shining outside.

Q: A lesson is under way in the classroom.

Starting with these two simple propositions, we may construct composite propositions in different ways.

(1) P and Q
(2) Not P
(3) P, though Q
(4) Q, though P
(5) P or Q
(6) Either P or Q
(7) If P, then Q
(8) If Q, then P
(9) Not P, or Q
(10) P, if and only if Q

As one can imagine, there is a huge number of possible composite propositions for FOPC. We can extend this list further, including propositions even more absurd than (8) or (10). In fact, the absurdity of (8)–(10) illustrates the importance of modeling world knowledge. These examples also demonstrate the significance of semantics. The pragmatics of FOPC and FCN for intelligent systems is not only important, it is indispensable, which makes CW research crucial. To increase the expressive power of FOPC for modeling real-world problems, logical function and function of algebraic logic [28] need to be included in the study of complex problem solving. Furthermore, even the operation of forming a composite function of some finite rank should also be investigated.

1.14 GRANULARITY, CW, AND MULTIPLE RESOLUTION DYNAMIC SYSTEMS

For many years it has been widely recognized that mathematical modeling for a dynamic system is not unique and subject to error. The total error can be further aggravated by the source of errors: physics (first principle, heuristic), truncation and round-off errors in computing, approximations in numerical analysis, and so on. As one strives to solve the more difficult problems of intelligent control, it is appealing to use Alex Meystel's multiple resolution mathematical modeling for a complex dynamic system [30,31]. At present, there are several schools of thought on handling this problem. Zadeh proposes using the theory of fuzzy information granularity [12]. Therefore, it is possible that advances in CW research will also enhance research on fuzzy information granularity.

To research the value and need for multiple resolution mathematical modeling, we examine a simple intelligent control problem. The navigation of a mobile intelligent robot can be studied via two mathematical models, one a lower-resolution model and the other a higher-resolution model. The higher-resolution model involves dc servomotors, gears, actuators, and so on, as basic units. Each basic unit can be viewed as a black block that can be quite complicated. All these basic units are driven by different energy sources as far as lower-resolution modeling is concerned. The model does not care about the source of energy as well as the complicated black block. Furthermore, the robot body may be represented by a single-point center of gravity in the lower-resolution model. The mathematical model of lower resolution views the lateral movement (vertical and horizontal axes) and rotational movement (angle movement) as state variables. In this lower-resolution model, one makes a bold assumption that the higher-resolution model always delivers and no fault occurs. This is a critical assumption. To obtain a more complete understanding of the intelligent mobile robot, both versions of the mathematical models are needed.

Semiotics [32] is a new science dealing with a much more generalized control system theory. In semiotics jargon, the formulation of a concept is established from a group of data or measurements. In AI, a proposition is usually represented by a capital English symbol, hence the name *symbolic processing*. There are two reasons for the interaction between CW and the theory of semiotics: (1) In complex control systems, the use of symbols or signs is much more efficient (semiotics view);

and (2) to achieve reasoning, inference, arguments, and so on, of any logical system, the use of symbols is nearly a necessity (AI view).

More important, CW research eventually will enrich and refine the art of information representation, flows, and manipulations. FL and CW provide the attractive properties of adaptability, robustness, and endurance [5]. A visionary paper by James Albus outlines the future of the engineering of mind [32]. Computing with words has been recognized primarily as relating to natural language processing, as discussed in Section 1.7. However, we have projected the utility value of CW to a number of new directions that are of greater significance. This phenomenon is not surprising, as language and speech are fundamentally important to intelligence.

Many questions must be answered if we push research in this direction. One such crucial question regards *grounding*. Grounding is a new concept in semiotics that has not been established clearly with examples. The drive for practicality will produce many examples, however. Suppose that we have the following syllogism:

Premise: x is very high (x measured in feet).

Implication: If x is high, then y should be low (current y measured in amperes).

Conclusion: y should be very low.

All symbols above are fuzzy sets. The conclusion in the syllogism process is also a fuzzy set, which may or may not be inclusive in the dictionary. In this context, the grounding concept in semiotics, denoted by the symbol "very low" with some membership function computed behind the scene, is meant to be the new symbol (words) in the dictionary. Only a finite number of symbols are needed in the dictionary in practical daily use.

1.15 CW AND FUZZY EXPERT SYSTEMS

Fuzzy expert systems will probably dominate future development of expert systems [37]. It is much more agreeable and compatible with daily life. CW provides a means for linking symbolic processing and numeric computations. Symbolic processing is usually accomplished in terms of linguistic variables and is concerned with concepts and qualitative relationships, whereas numeric computations are concerned with precise, detailed algorithmic manipulations of quantitative information [33]. Both aspects of information processing are essential for computer information-processing systems dealing with real-world tasks. The membership function is an important aspect of this linkage.

Pao has constructed the following real-world example that illustrates the need for CW [33]. The personnel manager of a moderate-sized business is informed by the owner that the plant needs a warehouse floor supervisor and that she should hire a suitable person who is "tall" and "not clumsy." Generally, such directions are sufficient in a real-world situation. The personnel manager certainly does not have factual data to back up her idea of what the membership functions should be. But she does have a few data points provided by previous incidents, and she fills in the rest.

Finally, CW will reach some numeric computing involving some intuitive reasoning. A new linguistic variable, "tall $\wedge$ not clumsy," can be computed numerically based on the linguistic variable of "tall" and "clumsy." Extensive fuzzy logic literature will provide the necessary mechanism to do that.

Suppose that the owner had specified instead that the floor supervisor should be "reasonably tall" or "agile," having in mind that agile persons can compensate for lack of height. Therefore, a new linguistic variable, "reasonably tall $\vee$ agile," can be produced from the linguistic variables "reasonably tall" and "agile." Examples of CW in fuzzy expert systems are appealing and show how CW reflects human intelligence.

1.16 CW, LANGUAGE, AND INTELLIGENCE

Since CW involves machine processing of natural language, the essential characteristics of natural language must be understood [21,34]. For this reason we have surveyed many aspects of language theory, with emphasis on two specific items. When we introduce computation to language, we should use the essential and positive features of existing language theory. Also, to fulfill the human expectation of language utilization, we need to consider carefully what kinds of CW research are needed. Birnbaum forcefully asserts that intelligence is a question of learning, of acquiring a memory or knowledge base of sufficient size, and of developing the retrieval mechanisms necessary to use it. Language is intelligence, and we must remember this as we conduct research on computing with words [1].

The view that human language is proof of human intelligence may well be the oldest and most common philosophical cliché [1]. The claim that linguistic behavior shows human superior intelligence can be interpreted in three ways: It may be the things we say; our words give evidence of our thoughts; and the soundness and creativity of our thoughts demonstrate our intelligence [1]. Without linguistic communication, there would be no literature, no science, no law: in a nutshell, no cumulative building of knowledge, theoretical or practical [1]. Language is both enabled and limited by the productive, memorial, perceptual, imaginative, and processing capabilities of human beings [35]. The shape of language and the facts surrounding its employment must be determined in many ways by each of these realities [1]. As one undertakes CW, the limitation appears to be unavoidable; however, enabling appears to be possible as well.

ACKNOWLEDGMENTS

The author wishes to thank Yuan Ze, University of Taiwan, for providing the visiting chair professorship that made it possible for me to write the major portion of this manuscript. Discussions with Drs. Robert Erickson (Experimental Psychology, Duke University), Bryant Pellom (Electrical and Computer Engineering, Duke University), and Robert Lair (Computer Science and Engineering, Yuan Ze University) were very useful.

REFERENCES

1. J. Khalfa, *What Is Intelligence?* Cambridge University Press, New York, 1996.
2. J. Allen, *Natural Language Understanding*, Benjamin-Cummings, Menlo Park, CA, 1987.
3. W. H. Calvin, *How Brains Think: Evolving Intelligence, Then and Now*, Basic Books, New York, 1996, Chap. 1.
4. L. A. Zadeh, Fuzzy logic = computing with words, *IEEE Trans. Fuzzy Syst.*, 4: 103–111, 1996.
5. L. A. Zadeh, From computing with numbers to computing with words—from manipulation of measurements to manipulation of perceptions, *IEEE Trans. Circuits Syst.*, Jan. 1999 (also Chapter 2 of this book).
6. J. Jubak, *In the Image of the Brain: Breaking the Barrier Between the Human Mind and Intelligent Machines*, Little, Brown, Boston, 1992.
7. S. J. Gould, The persistently flat earth, *Nat. Hist.*, Mar. 1994, pp. 12–19.
8. W. James, *Books by James*, Vol. I, 1890, p. 195.
9. A. Einstein and Infeld, *The Evolution of Physics*, 1951.
10. H. Gardner, *The Mind's New Science: A History of the Cognitive Revolution*, Basic Books, New York, 1985.
11. D. E. Rumelhart, J. L. McClelland, and PDP Research Group, *Parallel Distributed Processing: Explorations in the Microstructure of Cognition*, Vol. I, *Foundations*, Vol. II, *Psychological and Biological Models*, Bradford Book/MIT Press, Cambridge, MA, 1986.
12. L. A. Zadeh, Toward a theory of fuzzy information granulation and fuzzy logic, *Fuzzy Sets Syst.*, 90:11–127, 1997.
13. M. Minsky, *The Society of Mind*, Simon & Schuster, New York, 1986.
14. A. Cawsey, *The Essence of Artificial Intelligence.* Prentice-Hall International, Hemel Hempstead, Herts, England, 1998.
15. M. B. Ghalia and P. P. Wang, *Hotel Yield Management*, Tech. Rep. MIFL-4, Machine Intelligence and Fuzzy Logic Research Laboratory, Electrical and Computer Engineering Department, Duke University, Durham, NC, Feb. 1999.
16. V. Ratsch, M. M. Richter, and I. O. Stamatescu (eds.), *Intelligence and Artificial Intelligence: An Interdisciplinary Debate*, Springer-Verlag, Heidelberg, Germany, 1998.
17. L. A. Zadeh, The role of fuzzy logic and soft computing in the conception and design of intelligent systems, in Klement and Slany (eds.), *Fuzzy Logic in AI*, Lecture Notes in AI, Springer-Verlag, Heidelberg, Germany, 1993, p. 1.
18. L. Rabiner and B.-H Juang, *Fundamentals of Speech Recognition*, Prentice Hall, Upper Saddle River, NJ, 1993.
19. C. Sagan, *The Dragons of Eden: Speculations on the Evolution of Human Intelligence*, Random House, New York, 1977.
20. L. A. Zadeh, *A Theory of Common Sense Knowledge*, Memo. UCB/ERL M83/26, 17, Electronics Research Laboratory, University of California–Berkeley, Berkeley, CA, Apr. 1983.
21. T. Halliday (ed.), *The Senses and Communication*, The Open University, Springer-Verlag, Berlin, 1998.

22. L. A. Zadeh, Outline of a new approach to the analysis of complex system and decision processes, *IEEE Trans. Syst. Man Cybern.*, 3:28–44, 1973.

23. L. A. Zadeh, The concept of a linguistic variable and its applications to approximate reasoning, Part I, *Inf. Sci.*, 8:199–249, 1975; Part II, *Inf. Sci.*, 8:301–357, 1975; Part III, *Inf. Sci.*, 9:43–80, 1975.

24. L. A. Zadeh, A fuzzy algorithmic approach to the definition of complex or imprecise concepts, *Int. J. Man–Mach. Stud.*, 8:249–291, 1976.

25. L. A. Zadeh, Growing impact of fuzzy set theory on mathematics, email broadcast to BISC group, June 5, 1998.

26. P. P. Wang, Soft modeling for intelligent and complex systems, Special Issue on Methods and Systems for Interaction, Kasabov and Kozma (eds.), *Inf. Sci. J.*, 123:149–159, 2000.

27. J. Bowen, R. Lai, and D. Bahler, *Fuzzy Semantics and Fuzzy Constraint Networks*, Tech. Rep. TR-91-23, Computer Science Department, North Carolina State University, Raleigh, NC, Sept. 1991; see also R. Lai, Ph.D. dissertation, Computer Science Department, North Carolina State University, Raleigh, NC, 1992.

28. S. G. Gindikin, *Algebraic Logic: Problem Books in Mathematics*, Springer-Verlag, Heidelberg, Germany, 1985.

29. L. A. Zadeh, *Test-Score Semantics for Natural Languages and Meaning Representation via PRUF*, Tech. Note 247, Artificial Intelligence Center, SRI International, Menlo Park, CA, May 1981.

30. J. Albus and A. Meystel, *Intelligent Systems: A Semiotic Perspective*, Vol. 1, National Institute of Standards and Technology, Gaithersburg, MD, 1996.

31. J. Holland, Summary of keynote speeches, in P. P. Wang (ed.), *Proc. 4th Joint Conference on Information Sciences*, Vol. I, Department of Electrical Engineering, Duke University, Durham, NC, Mar. 1997.

32. J. S. Albus, The engineering of mind, banquet speech, in P. P. Wang (ed.), *Proc. 4th Joint Conference on Information Sciences*, Vol. I, Department of Electrical Engineering, Duke University, Durham, NC, Mar. 1997.

33. P. Yoh-Han, *Adaptive Pattern Recognition and Neural Networks*, Addison-Wesley, Reading, MA, 1989.

34. J. L. Casti and A. Karlqvist (eds.), *Real Brain, Artificial Minds*, North-Holland, New York, 1987.

35. T. G. Bever, J. M. Carroll, and L. A. Miller, *Talking Mind*, MIT Press, Cambridge, MA, 1984.

36. C. Y. Tyan, P. P. Wang, S. Rangaswamy, and D. Bahler, A new methodology of fuzzy constraint-based controller design via constraint network processing, *IEEE. Trans. Fuzzy Syst.* 4(2):166–178, 1996.

37. M. B. Ghalia and P. P. Wang, Intelligent system to support judgmental business forecasting: The case of estimating hotel room demand, *IEEE Trans. Fuzzy Syst.* 8(4):380–397, 2000.

CHAPTER 2

FROM COMPUTING WITH NUMBERS TO COMPUTING WITH WORDS—FROM MANIPULATION OF MEASUREMENTS TO MANIPULATION OF PERCEPTIONS

LOTFI A. ZADEH
University of California, Berkeley, California

2.1 INTRODUCTION

In the Fifties, and especially late Fifties, circuit theory was at the height of importance and visibility. It played a pivotal role in the conception and design of electronic circuits and was enriched by basic contributions of Darlington, Bode, McMillan, Guillemin, Carlin, Youla, Kuh, Desoer, Sandberg, and other pioneers.

However, what could be discerned at that time was that circuit theory was evolving into a more general theory—system theory—a theory in which the physical identity of the elements of a system is subordinated to a mathematical characterization of their input/output relations. This evolution was a step in the direction of greater generality and, like most generalizations, it was driven by a quest for models which make it possible to reduce the distance between an object that is modeled—the modelizand—and its model in a specified class of systems.

In a paper published in 1961 entitled "From Circuit Theory to System Theory" [33], I discussed the evolution of circuit theory into system theory and observed that the high effectiveness of system theory in dealing with mechanistic systems stood in sharp contrast to its low effectiveness in the realm of humanistic systems—systems exemplified by economic systems, biological systems, social systems, political systems and, more generally, man-machine systems of various types. In more specific terms, I wrote:

Computing with Words, Edited by Paul P. Wang.
ISBN 0-471-35374-4

> There is a fairly wide gap between what might be regarded as 'animate' system theorists and 'inanimate' system theorists at the present time, and it is not at all certain that this gap will be narrowed, much less closed, in the near future. There are some who feel that this gap reflects the fundamental inadequacy of conventional mathematics—the mathematics of precisely-defined points, functions, sets, probability measures, etc.—for coping with the analysis of biological systems, and that to deal effectively with such systems, which are generally orders of magnitude more complex than man-made systems, we need a radically different kind of mathematics, the mathematics of fuzzy or cloudy quantities which are not describable in terms of probability distributions. Indeed, the need for such mathematics is becoming increasingly apparent even in the realm of inanimate systems, for in most practical cases the *a priori* data as well as the criteria by which the performance of a man-made system are judged are far from being precisely specified or having accurately-known probability distributions.

It was this observation that motivated my development of the theory of fuzzy sets starting with the 1965 paper "Fuzzy Sets" [34], which was published in *Information and Control*.

Subsequently, in a paper published in 1973, "Outline of a New Approach to the Analysis of Complex Systems and Decision Processes" [37], I introduced the concept of a linguistic variable, that is, a variable whose values are words rather than numbers. The concept of a linguistic variable has played and is continuing to play a pivotal role in the development of fuzzy logic and its applications.

The initial reception of the concept of a linguistic variable was far from positive, largely because my advocacy of the use of words in systems and decision analysis clashed with the deep-seated tradition of respect for numbers and disrespect for words. The essence of this tradition was succinctly stated in 1883 by Lord Kelvin:

> In physical science the first essential step in the direction of learning any subject is to find principles of numerical reckoning and practicable methods for measuring some quality connected with it. I often say that when you can measure what you are speaking about and express it in numbers, you know something about it; but when you cannot measure it, when you cannot express it in numbers, your knowledge is of a meagre and unsatisfactory kind: it may be the beginning of knowledge but you have scarcely, in your thoughts, advanced to the state of science, whatever the matter may be.

The depth of scientific tradition of respect for numbers and derision for words was reflected in the intensity of hostile reaction to my ideas by some of the prominent members of the scientific elite. In commenting on my first exposition of the concept of a linguistic variable in 1972, Rudolph Kalman had this to say:

> I would like to comment briefly on Professor Zadeh's presentation. His proposals could be severely, ferociously, even brutally criticized from a technical point of view. This would be out of place here. But a blunt question remains: Is Professor Zadeh presenting important ideas or is he indulging in wishful thinking? No doubt Professor Zadeh's enthusiasm for fuzziness has been reinforced by the prevailing climate in the U.S.—one of unprecendented permissiveness. 'Fuzzification' is a kind of scientific permissiveness; it tends to result in socially appealing slogans unaccompanied by the discipline of hard scientific work and patient observation.

In a similar vein, my esteemed colleague Professor William Kahan—a man with a brilliant mind—offered this assessment in 1975:

> "Fuzzy theory is wrong, wrong, and pernicious." says William Kahan, a professor of computer sciences and mathematics at Cal whose Evans Hall office is a few doors from Zadeh's. "I cannot think of any problem that could not be solved better by ordinary logic." What Zadeh is saying is the same sort of things "Technology got us into this mess and now it can't get us out." Well, technology did not get us into this mess. Greed and weakness and ambivalence got us into this mess. What we need is more logical thinking, not less. The danger of fuzzy theory is that it will encourage the sort of imprecise thinking that has brought us so much trouble."

What Lord Kelvin, Rudolph Kalman, William Kahan, and many other brilliant minds did not appreciate is the fundamental importance of the remarkable human capability to perform a wide variety of physical and mental tasks without any measurements and any computations. Familiar examples of such tasks are parking a car; driving in heavy traffic; playing golf; understanding speech, and summarizing a story.

Underlying this remarkable ability is the brain's crucial ability to manipulate perceptions—perceptions of size, distance, weight, speed, time, direction, smell, color, shape, force, likelihood, truth and intent, among others. A fundamental difference between measurements and perceptions is that, in general, measurements are crisp numbers whereas perceptions are fuzzy numbers or, more generally, fuzzy granules, that is, clumps of objects in which the transition from membership to nonmembership is gradual rather than abrupt.

The fuzziness of perceptions reflects finite ability of sensory organs and the brain to resolve detail and store information. A concomitant of fuzziness of perceptions is the preponderant partiality of human concepts in the sense that the validity of most human concepts is a matter of degree. For example, we have partial knowledge, partial understanding, partial certainty, partial belief and accept partial solutions, partial truth and partial causality. Furthermore, most human concepts have a granular structure and are context-dependent.

In essence, a granule is a clump of physical or mental objects (points) drawn together by indistinguishability, similarity, proximity or functionality (Figure 2.1). A granule may be crisp or fuzzy, depending on whether its boundaries are or are not sharply defined. For example, age may be granulated crisply into years and granulated fuzzily into fuzzy intervals labeled very young, young, middle-aged, old, and very old (Figure 2.2). A partial taxonomy of granulation is shown in Figure 2.3.

In a very broad sense, granulation involves a partitioning of whole into parts. Modes of information granulation (IG) in which granules are crisp play important roles in a wide variety of methods, approaches and techniques. Among them are: interval analysis, quantization, chunking, rough set theory, diakoptics, divide and conquer, Dempster–Shafer theory, machine learning from examples, qualitative process theory, decision trees, semantic networks, analog-to-digital conversion, constraint programming, image segmentation, cluster analysis and many others.

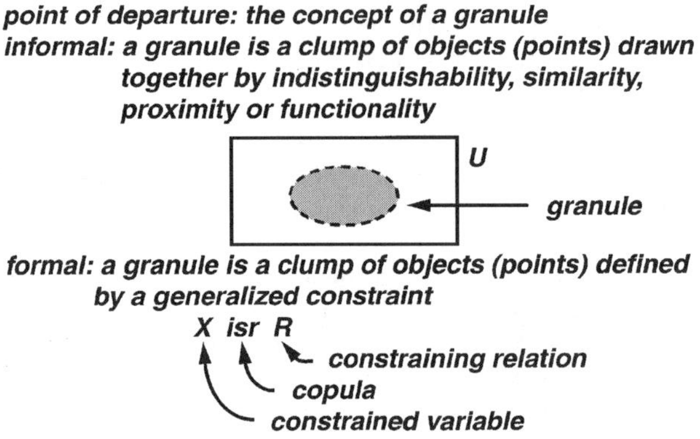

FIGURE 2.1 Informal and formal definitions of a granule.

body → *head + neck + arms + chest + ... + feet*
time → *years* → *months* → *...*
book → *chapters* → *sections* → *paragraphs* → *...*
age → *young + middle-aged + old*
size → *small + medium + large*
distance → *very near + near + not.near and not.far + far + very far*
force → *weak + moderate + strong*

FIGURE 2.2 Examples of crisp and fuzzy granulation.

Important though it is, crisp IG has a major blind spot. More specifically, it fails to reflect the fact that most human perceptions are fuzzy rather than crisp. For example, when we mentally granulate the human body into fuzzy granules labeled head, neck, chest, arms, legs, etc., the length of neck is a fuzzy attribute whose value is a fuzzy number. Fuzziness of granules, their attributes and their values is characteristic of ways in which human concepts are formed, organized and manipulated. In effect, fuzzy information granulation (fuzzy IG) may be viewed as a human way of employing data compression for reasoning and, more particularly, making rational decisions in an environment of imprecision, uncertainty and partial truth.

The tradition of pursuit of crispness and precision in scientific theories can be credited with brilliant successes. We have sent men to the moon; we can build computers that are capable of performing billions of computations per second; we have constructed telescopes that can explore the far reaches of the universe; and we can date the age of rocks that are millions of years old. But alongside the brilliant successes stand conspicuous underachievements and outright failures. We cannot build robots which can move with the agility of animals or humans; we cannot automate driving in heavy traffic; we cannot translate from one language to another at the level of a human interpreter; we cannot create programs which can summarize nontrivial stories; our ability to model the behavior of economic systems leaves much to be desired; and we cannot build machines that can compete with children in the performance of a wide variety of physical and cognitive tasks.

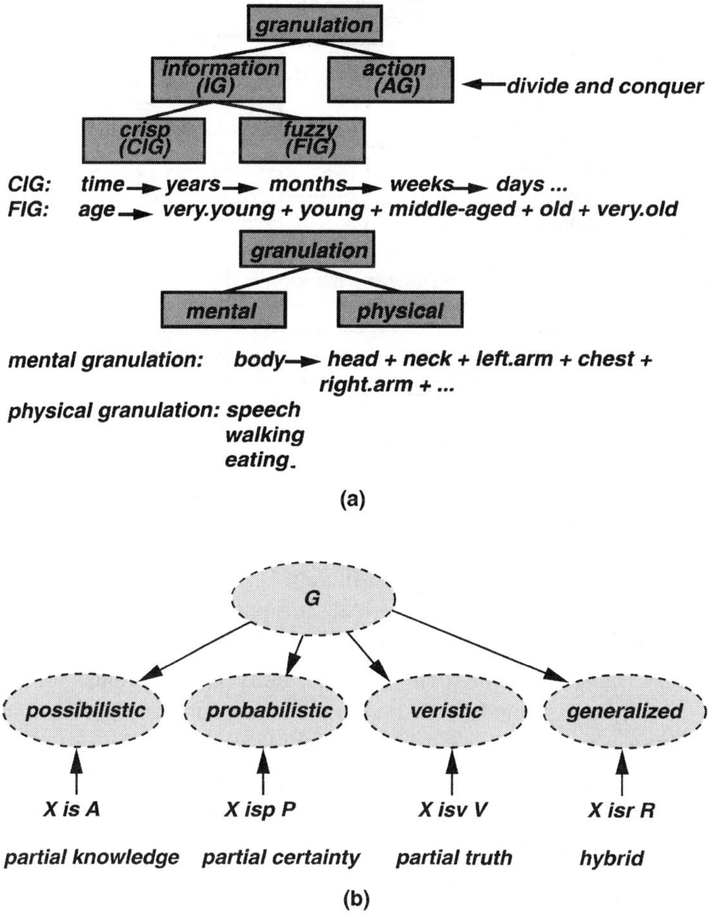

FIGURE 2.3 (*a*) Partial taxonomy of granulation; (*b*) principal types of granules.

What is the explanation for the disparity between the successes and failures? What can be done to advance the frontiers of science and technology beyond where they are today, especially in the realms of machine intelligence and automation of decision processes? In my view, the failures are conspicuous in those areas in which the objects of manipulation are, in the main, perceptions rather than measurements. Thus, what we need are ways of dealing with perceptions, in addition to the many tools which we have for dealing with measurements. In essence, it is this need that motivated the development of the methodology of computing with words (CW)—a methodology in which words play the role of labels of perceptions.

CW provides a methodology for what may be called a *computational theory of perceptions* (CTP) (Figure 2.4). However, the potential impact of the methodology of computing with words is much broader. Basically, there are four principal rationales for the use of CW.

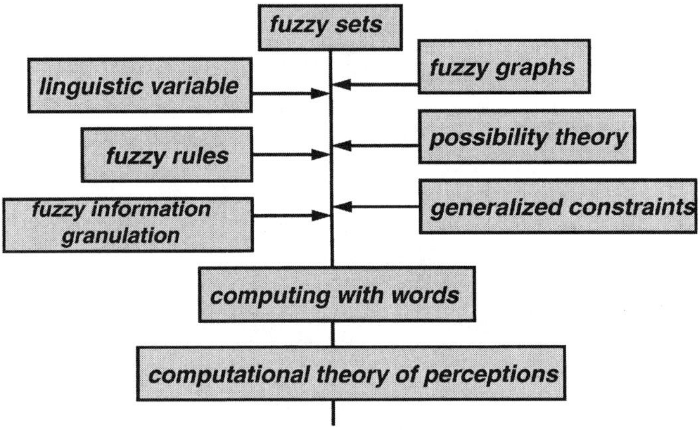

FIGURE 2.4 Conceptual structure of computational theory of perceptions.

1) *The don't know rationale:* In this case, the values of variables and/or parameters are not known with sufficient precision to justify the use of conventional methods of numerical computing. An example is decision-making with poorly defined probabilities and utilities.
2) *The don't need rationale:* In this case, there is a tolerance for imprecision which can be exploited to achieve tractability, robustness, low solution cost, and better rapport with reality. An example is the problem of parking a car.
3) *The can't solve rationale:* In this case, the problem cannot be solved through the use of numerical computing. An example is the problem of automation of driving in city traffic.
4) *The can't define rationale:* In this case, a concept that we wish to define is too complex to admit of definition in terms of a set of numerical criteria. A case in point is the concept of causality. Causality is an instance of what may be called an amorphic concept.

The basic idea underlying the relationship between CW and CTP is conceptually simple. More specifically, in CTP perceptions and queries are expressed as propositions in a natural language. Then, the propositions and queries are processed by CW-based methods to yield answers to queries. Simple examples of linguistic characterization of perceptions drawn from everyday experiences are:

Robert is highly intelligent
Carol is very attractive
Hans loves wine
Overeating causes obesity
Most Swedes are tall
Berkeley is more lively than Palo Alto

perceptions → *Dana is young*
→ *Tandy is a few years older than Dana*

Tandy is (young + few) years old

perceptions → *most students are young*
→ *most young students are single*

---
most^2 *students are single*

perception → *a box contains balls of various sizes, most of which are large*

---
the probability that a ball drawn at random is large is most

(a)

Robert loves women
Mary is a woman

Robert loves Mary

what is rare is expensive
cheap apartments in Paris are rare

---
cheap apartments in Paris are expensive

slimness is attractive
Mary is slim

Mary is attractive

(b)

FIGURE 2.5 (*a*) Examples of reasoning with perceptions; (*b*) examples of incorrect reasoning.

It is likely to rain tomorrow

It is very unlikely that there will be a significant increase in the price of oil in the near future

Examples of correct conclusions drawn from perceptions through the use of CW-based methods are shown in Figure 2.5*a*. Examples of incorrect conclusions are shown in Figure 2.5*b*.

Perceptions have long been an object of study in psychology. However, the idea of linking perceptions to computing with words is in a different spirit. An interesting system-theoretic approach to perceptions is described in a recent work of R. Vallee [31]. A logic of perceptions has been described by H. Rasiowa [26]. These approaches are not related to the approach described in our paper.

An important point that should be noted is that classical logical systems such as propositional logic, predical logic and modal logic, as well as AI-based techniques for natural language processing and knowledge representation, are concerned in a fundamental way with propositions expressed in a natural language. The main difference between such approaches and CW is that the methodology of CW—which is based on fuzzy logic—provides a much more expressive language for knowledge representation and much more versatile machinery for reasoning and computation.

In the final analysis, the role model for computing with words is the human mind and its remarkable ability to manipulate both measurements and perceptions. What should be stressed, however, is that although words are less precise than numbers, the methodology of computing with words rests on a mathematical foundation. An exposition of the basic concepts and techniques of computing with words is presented in the following sections. The linkage of CW and CTP is discussed very briefly because the computational theory of perceptions is still in its early stages of development.

2.2 WHAT IS CW?

In its traditional sense, computing involves for the most part manipulation of numbers and symbols. By contrast, humans employ mostly words in computing and reasoning, arriving at conclusions expressed as words from premises expressed in a natural language or having the form of mental perceptions. As used by humans, words have fuzzy denotations. The same applies to the role played by words in CW.

The concept of CW is rooted in several papers starting with my 1973 paper "Outline of a New Approach to the Analysis of Complex Systems and Decision Processes" [37], in which the concepts of a linguistic variable and granulation were introduced. The concepts of a fuzzy constraint and fuzzy constraint propagation were introduced in "Calculus of Fuzzy Restrictions" [39], and developed more fully in "A Theory of Approximate Reasoning" [45] and "Outline of a Computational Approach to Meaning and Knowledge Representation Based on the Concept of a Generalized Assignment Statement" [49]. Application of fuzzy logic to meaning representation and its role in test-score semantics are discussed in "PRUF—A Meaning Representation Language for Natural Languages" [43] and "Test-Score Semantics for Natural Languages and Meaning Representation via PRUF" [46]. The close relationship between CW and fuzzy information granulation is discussed in "Toward a Theory of Fuzzy Information Granulation and Its Centrality in Human Reasoning and Fuzzy Logic [53]."

Although the foundations of computing with words were laid some time ago, its evolution into a distinct methodology in its own right reflects many advances in our understanding of fuzzy logic and soft computing—advances which took place within the past few years. (See references and related papers.) A key aspect of CW is that it involves a fusion of natural languages and computation with fuzzy variables. It is this fusion that is likely to result in an evolution of CW into a basic methodology in its own right, with wide-ranging ramifications and applications.

We begin our exposition of CW with a few definitions. It should be understood that the definitions are dispositional, that is, admit of exceptions.

As was stated earlier, a concept which plays a pivotal role in CW is that of a granule. Typically, a granule is a fuzzy set of points drawn together by similarity (Figure 2.1). A word may be atomic, as in *young*, or composite, as in *not very young* (Figure 2.6). Unless stated to the contrary, a word will be assumed to be composite. The denotation of a word may be a higher order predicate, as in Montague grammar [12,23].

- ***a word is a label of a fuzzy set***

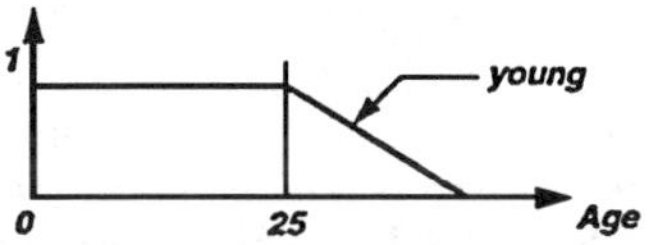

- ***a string of words is a label of a function of fuzzy sets***
  - ***not very young*** $\rightarrow ({}^{2}young)'$
- ***a word is a description of a constraint on a variable***
  - ***Mary is young*** $\rightarrow$ ***Age(Mary) is young***

FIGURE 2.6 Words as labels of fuzzy sets.

In CW, a granule, *g*, which is the denotation of a word, *w*, is viewed as a fuzzy constraint on a variable. A pivotal role in CW is played by fuzzy constraint propagation from premises to conclusions. It should be noted that, as a basic technique, constraint propagation plays important roles in many methodologies, especially in mathematical programming, constraint programming and logic programming. (See references and related papers.)

As a simple illustration, consider the proposition *Mary is young*, which may be a linguistic characterization of a perception. In this case, *young* is the label of a granule young. (Note that for simplicity the same symbol is used both for a word and its denotation.) The fuzzy set *young* plays the role of a fuzzy constraint on the age of Mary (Figure 2.6).

As a further example consider the propositions

$$p_1 = Carol\ lives\ near\ Mary$$

and

$$p_2 = Mary\ lives\ near\ Pat.$$

In this case, the words *lives near* in p_1 and p_2 play the role of fuzzy constraints on the distances between the residences of Carol and Mary, and Mary and Pat, respectively. If the query is: How far is Carol from Pat?, an answer yielded by fuzzy constraint propagation might be expressed as p_3, where

$$p_3 = Carol\ lives\ not\ far\ from\ Pat.$$

More about fuzzy constraint propagation will be said at a later point.

A basic assumption in CW is that information is conveyed by constraining the values of variables. Furthermore, information is assumed to consist of a collection of propositions expressed in natural or synthetic language. Typically, such propositions play the role of linguistic characterization of perceptions.

A basic generic problem in CW is the following.

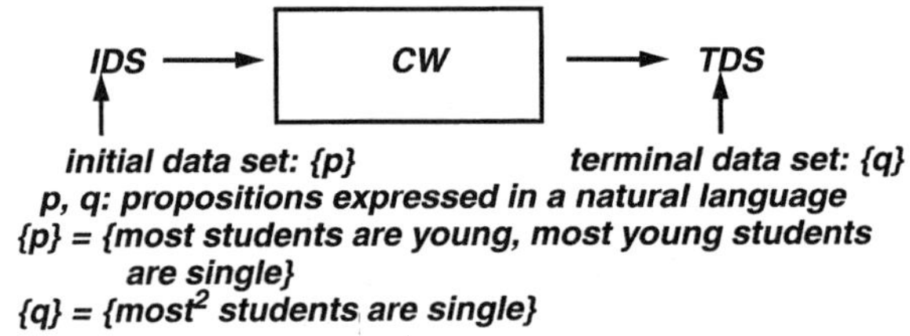

FIGURE 2.7 Computing with words as a transformation of an initial data set (IDS) into a terminal data set (TDS).

We are given a collection of propositions expressed in a natural language which constitute the *initial data set*, or IDS for short.

From the initial data set we wish to infer an answer to a query expressed in a natural language. The answer, also expressed in a natural language, is referred to as the *terminal data set*, or TDS for short. The problem is to derive TDS from IDS (Figure 2.7).

A few problems will serve to illustrate these concepts. At this juncture, the problems will be formulated but not solved.

1) Assume that a function, $f, f : U \to V, X \in U, Y \in V$, is described in words by the fuzzy if–then rules

f: if X is *small* then Y is *small*
if X is *medium* then Y is *large*
if X is *large* then Y is *small*.

What this implies is that f is approximated to by a fuzzy graph f^* (Figure 2.8),

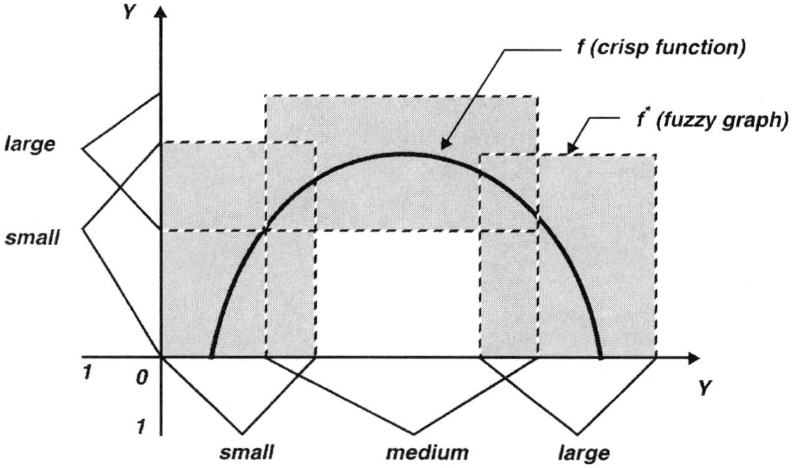

FIGURE 2.8 Fuzzy graph of a function.

where

$$f^* = small \times small + medium \times large + large \times small.$$

In f^*, $+$ and $\times$ denote, respectively, the disjunction and cartesian product. An expression of the form $A \times B$, where A and B are words, will be referred to as a *cartesian granule*. In this sense, a fuzzy graph may be viewed as a disjunction of cartesian granules. In essence, a fuzzy graph serves as an approximation to a function or a relation [38,51]. Equivalently, it may be viewed as a linguistic characterization of a perception of f (Figure 2.9).

In the example under consideration, the IDS consists of the fuzzy rule set f. The query is: What is the maximum value of f (Figure 2.10)? More broadly, the problem is: How can one compute an attribute of a function, f, e.g., its maximum value or its area or its roots if f is described in words as a collection of fuzzy if–then rules? Determination of the maximum value will be discussed in greater detail at a later point.

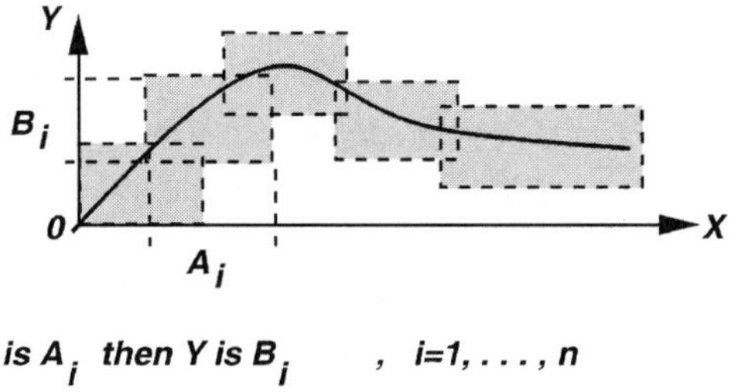

FIGURE 2.9 A fuzzy graph of a function represented by a rule set.

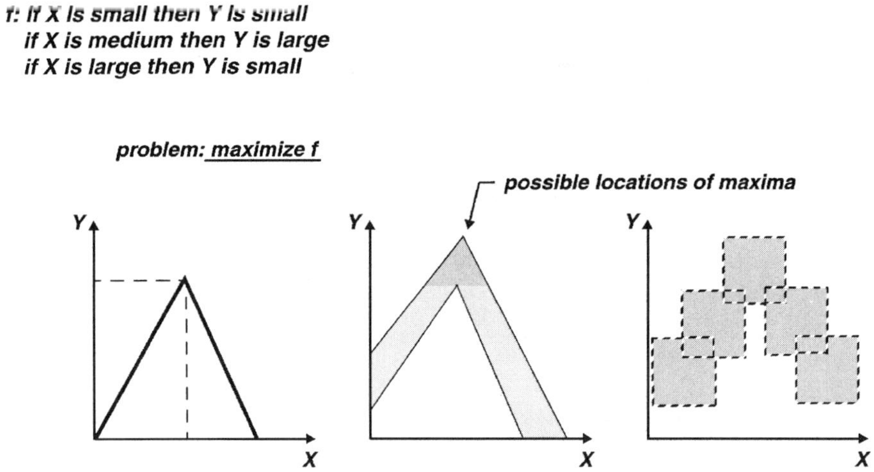

FIGURE 2.10 Fuzzy graph of a function defined by a fuzzy rule set.

2) A box contains ten balls of various sizes of which several are large and a few are small. What is the probability that a ball drawn at random is neither large nor small? In this case, the IDS is a verbal description of the contents of the box; the TDS is the desired probability.

3) A less simple example of computing with words is the following.

Let X and Y be independent random variables taking values in a finite set $V = \{v_1, \ldots, v_n\}$ with probabilities $p_1, \ldots, p_n$ and $q_1, \ldots, q_n$, respectively. For simplicity of notation, the same symbols will be used to denote X and Y and their generic values, with p and q denoting the probabilities of X and Y, respectively.

Assume that the probability distributions of X and Y are described in words through the fuzzy if-then rules (Figure 2.11):

P: if X is *small* then p is *small*
if X is *medium* then p is *large*
if X is *large* then p is *small*.

and

Q: if Y is *small* then q is *large*
if Y is *medium* then q is *small*
if Y is *large* then q is *large*.

where granules *small*, *medium* and *large* are values of linguistic variables X and Y in their respective universes of discourse. In the example under consideration, these rule-sets constitute the IDS. Note that *small* in P need not have the same meaning as *small* in Q, and likewise for *medium* and *large*.

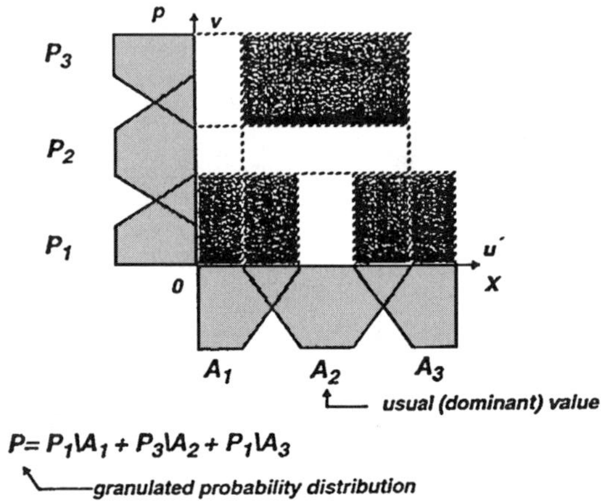

FIGURE 2.11 A fuzzy graph representation of a granulated probability distribution.

The query is: How can we describe in words the joint probability distribution of X and Y? This probability distribution is the TDS.

For convenience, the probability distributions of X and Y may be represented as fuzzy graphs:

$$P: \ small \times small + medium \times large + large \times small$$
$$Q: \ small \times large + medium \times small + large \times large$$

with the understanding that the underlying numerical probabilities must add up to unity.

Since X and Y are independent random variables, their joint probability distribution (P, Q) is the product of P and Q. In words, the product may be expressed as [51]

$$\begin{aligned}(P, Q): \ & small \times small \times (small * large) \\ & + small \times medium \times (small * small) \\ & + small \times large \times (small * large) \\ & + \cdots + large \times large \times (small * large)\end{aligned}$$

where $*$ is the arithmetic product in fuzzy arithmetic [14]. In this example, what we have done, in effect, amounts to a derivation of a linguistic characterization of the joint probability distribution of X and Y starting with linguistic characterizations of the probability distribution of X and the probability distribution of Y.

A few comments are in order. In linguistic characterizations of variables and their dependencies, words serve as values of variables and play the role of fuzzy constraints. In this perspective, the use of words may be viewed as a form of granulation, which in turn may be regarded as a form of fuzzy quantization.

Granulation plays a key role in human cognition. For humans, it serves as a way of achieving data compression. This is one of the pivotal advantages accruing through the use of words in human, machine and man–machine communication.

The point of departure in CW is the premise that the meaning of a proposition, p, in a natural language may be represented as an implicit constraint on an implicit variable. Such a representation is referred to as a *canonical form* of p, denoted as $CF(p)$ (Figure 2.12). Thus, a canonical form serves to make explicit the implicit constraint which resides in p. The concept of a canonical form is described in greater detail in the following section.

As a first step in the derivation of TDS from IDS, propositions in IDS are translated into their canonical forms, which collectively represent *antecedent* constraints.

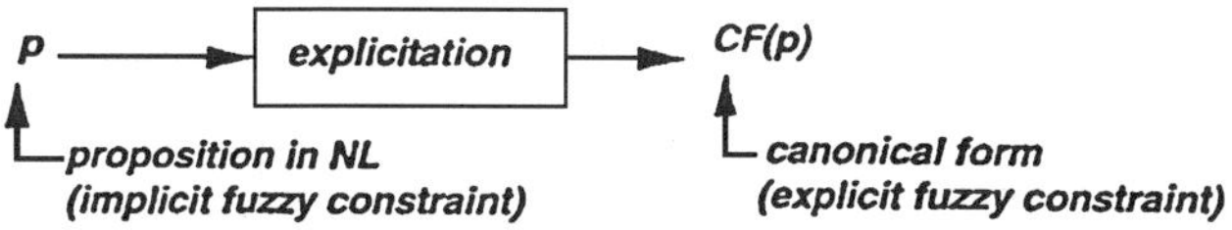

FIGURE 2.12 Canonical form of a proposition.

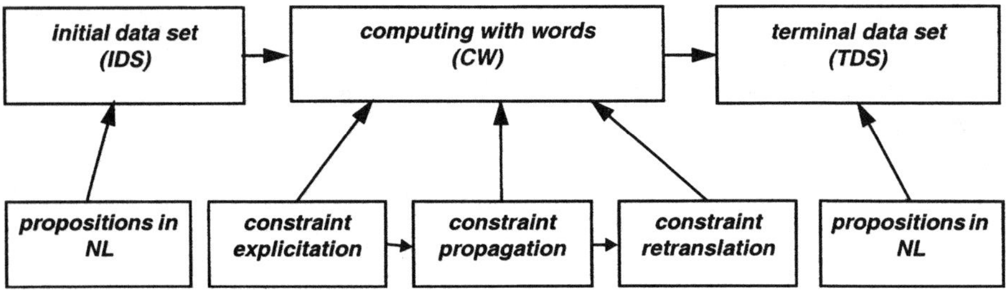

FIGURE 2.13 Conceptual structure of computing with words.

Through the use of rules for constraint propagation, antecedent constraints are transformed into *consequent* constraints. Finally, consequent constraints are translated into a natural language through the use of *linguistic approximation* [10,18], yielding the terminal data set TDS. This process is schematized in Figure 2.13.

In essence, the rationale for computing with words rests on two major imperatives: 1) computing with words is a necessity when the available information is too imprecise to justify the use of numbers; and 2) when there is a tolerance for imprecision which can be exploited to achieve tractability, robustness, low solution cost and better rapport with reality.

In computing with words, there are two core issues that arise. First is the issue of representation of fuzzy constraints. More specifically, the question is: How can the fuzzy constraints which are implicit in propositions expressed in a natural language be made explicit. And second is the issue of fuzzy constraint propagation, that is, the question of how can fuzzy constraints in premises, i.e., antecedent constraints, be propagated to conclusions, i.e., consequent constraints.

These are the issues which are addressed in the following.

2.3 REPRESENTATION OF FUZZY CONSTRAINTS, CANONICAL FORMS, AND GENERALIZED CONSTRAINTS

Our approach to the representation of fuzzy constraints is based on test-score semantics [46,47]. In outline, in this semantics, a proposition, p, in a natural language is viewed as a network of fuzzy (elastic) constraints. Upon aggregation, the constraints which are embodied in p result in an overall fuzzy constraint which can be represented as an expression of the form

$$X \text{ is } R$$

where R is a constraining fuzzy relation and X is the constrained variable. The expression in question is the canonical form of p. Basically, the function of a canonical form is to place in evidence the fuzzy constraint which is implicit in p. This is represented schematically as

$$P \to X \text{ is } R$$

in which the arrow $\rightarrow$ denotes explicitation. The variable X may be vector-valued and/or conditioned.

In this perspective, the meaning of p is defined by two procedures. The first procedure acts on a so-called explanatory database, ED, and returns the constrained variable, X. The second procedure acts on ED and returns the constraining relation, R.

An explanatory database is a collection of relations in terms of which the meaning of p is defined. The relations are empty, that is, they consist of relation names, relations attributes and attribute domains, with no entries in the relations. When there are entries in ED, ED is said to be *instantiated* and is denoted EDI. EDI may be viewed as a description of a possible world in possible world semantics [6], while ED defines a collection of possible worlds, with each possible world in the collection corresponding to a particular instantiation of ED [47].

As a simple illustration, consider the proposition

$$p = \textit{Mary is not young}.$$

Assume that the explantory database is chosen to be

$$\mathrm{ED} = \mathrm{POPULATION}[\mathrm{Name}; \mathrm{Age}] + \mathrm{YOUNG}[\mathrm{Age}; \mu]$$

in which POPULATION is a relation with arguments Name and Age; YOUNG is a relation with arguments Age and μ; and $+$ is disjunction. In this case, the constrained variable is the age of Mary, which in terms of ED may be expressed as

$$X = \mathrm{Age}(\mathrm{Mary}) =_{\mathrm{Age}} \ \mathrm{POPULATION}[\mathrm{Name} = \mathrm{Mary}].$$

This expression specifies the procedure which acts on ED and returns X. More specifically, in this procedure, Name is instantiated to Mary and the resulting relation is projected on Age, yielding the age of Mary.

The constraining relation, R, is given by

$$R = ({}^{2}\mathrm{YOUNG})'$$

which implies that the intensifier *very* is interpreted as a squaring operation, and the negation *not* as the operation of complementation [36].

Equivalently, R may be expressed as

$$R = \mathrm{YOUNG}[\mathrm{Age}; 1 - \mu^2].$$

As a further example, consider the proposition

$$p = \textit{Carol lives in a small city near San Francisco}$$

and assume that the explanatory database is:

$$\begin{aligned}\text{ED} = {} & \text{POPULATION}[\text{Name; Residence}] \\ & + \text{SMALL}[\text{City}; \mu] \\ & + \text{NEAR}[\text{City1}; \text{City2}; \mu]\end{aligned}$$

In this case,

$$\begin{aligned}X &= \text{Residence(Carol)} \\ &=_{\text{Residence}} \text{POPULATION}[\text{Name} = \text{Carol}]\end{aligned}$$

and

$$\begin{aligned}R = {} & SMALL[City; \mu] \\ & \cap_{City1} \; NEAR[City2 = \text{San\_Francisco}]\end{aligned}$$

In R, the first constituent is the fuzzy set of small cities; the second constituent is the fuzzy set of cities which are near San Francisco; and $\cap$ denotes the intersection of these sets.

So far we have confined our attention to constraints of the form

$$X \text{ is } R.$$

In fact, constraints can have a variety of forms. In particular, a constraint—expressed as a canonical form—may be conditional, that is, of the form

$$\text{if } X \text{ is } R \text{ then } Y \text{ is } S$$

which may also be written as

$$Y \text{ is } S \text{ if } X \text{ is } R.$$

The constraints in question will be referred to as *basic*.

For purposes of meaning representation, the richness of natural languages necessitates a wide variety of constraints in relation to which the basic constraints form an important though special class. The so-called generalized constraints [49] contain the basic constraints as a special case and are defined as follows. The need for generalized constraints becomes obvious when one attempts to represent the meaning of simple propositions such as

Robert loves women
John is very honest
checkout time is 11 am
slimness is attractive

in the language of standard logical systems.

A generalized constraint is represented as

$$X \text{ isr } R$$

where isr, pronounced "ezar," is a variable copula which defines the way in which R constrains X. More specifically, the role of R in relation to X is defined by the value of the discrete variable r. The values of r and their interpretations are defined below:

e	equal (abbreviated to $=$);
d	disjunctive (possibilistic) (abbreviated to blank);
ν	veristic;
p	probabilistic;
γ	probability value;
u	usuality;
rs	random set;
rfs	random fuzzy set;
fg	fuzzy graph;
ps	rough set;
.	...

As an illustration, when $r = e$, the constraint is an equality constraint and is abbreviated to $=$. When r takes the value d, the constraint is *disjunctive* (possibilistic) and isd abbreviated to is, leading to the expression

$$X \text{ is } R$$

in which R is a fuzzy relation which constrains X by playing the role of the possibility distribution of X. More specifically, if X takes values in a universe of discourse, $U = \{u\}$, then $Poss\{X = u\} = \mu_R(u)$, where μ_R is the membership function of R, and Π_X is the possibility distribution of X, that is, the fuzzy set of its possible values [42]. In schematic form

$$X \text{ is R} \longrightarrow \begin{cases} \Pi_X = R \\ Poss\{X = u\} = \mu_R(u). \end{cases}$$

Similarly, when r takes the value ν, the constraint is *veristic*. In the case,

$$X \text{ isv } R$$

means that if the grade of membership of u in R is μ, then $X = u$ has truth value μ. For example, a canonical form of the proposition

$$p = \textit{John is proficient in English, French, and German}$$

may be expressed as

$$\text{Proficiency(John)}\\ \quad \text{isv}(1\,|\,\text{English} + 0.7\,|\,\text{French} + 0.6\,|\,\text{German})$$

in which 1.0, 0.7, and 0.6 represent, respectively, the truth values of the propositions *John is proficient in English, John is proficient in French and John is proficient in German.* In a similar vein, the veristic constraint

$$\text{Ethnicity(John)}\\ \quad \text{isv}(0.5\,|\,\text{German} + 0.25\,|\,\text{French} + 0.25\,|\,\text{Italian})$$

represents the meaning of the proposition *John is half German, quarter French and quarter Italian.*

When $r = p$, the constraint is *probabilistic*. In this case,

$$X \text{ isp } R$$

means that R is the probability distribution of X. For example

$$X \text{ isp } N(m, \sigma^2)$$

means that X is normally distributed with mean m and variance σ^2. Similarly,

$$X \text{ isp } (0.2\backslash a + 0.5\backslash b + 0.3\backslash c)$$

means that X is a random variable which takes the values a, b, and c with respective probabilities 0.2, 0.5, and 0.3.

The constraint

$$X \text{ isu } R$$

is an abbreviation for

$$\textit{usually}(X \text{ is } R)$$

which in turn means that

$$\textit{Prob}\{X \text{ is } R\} \text{ is } \textit{usually}.$$

In this expression X is R is a fuzzy event and *usually* is its fuzzy probability, that is, the possibility distribution of its crisp probability.

The constraint

$$X \text{ isrs } P$$

is a random set constraint. This constraint is a combination of probabilistic and possibilistic constraints. More specifically, in a schematic form, it is expressed as

$$\frac{\begin{array}{c} X \text{ isp } P \\ (X, Y) \text{ is } Q \end{array}}{Y \text{ isrs } R}$$

where Q is a joint possibilitistic constraint on X and Y, and R is a random set. It is of interest to note that the Dempster–Shafer theory of evidence [29] is, in essence, a theory of random set constraints.

In computing with words, the starting point is a collection of propositions which play the role of premises. In many cases, canonical forms of these propositions are constraints of the basic, possibilistic type. In a more general setting, the constraints are of the generalized type, implying that explicitation of a proposition, p, may be represented as

$$p \rightarrow X \text{ isr } R$$

where X isr R is the canonical form of p (Figure 2.14).

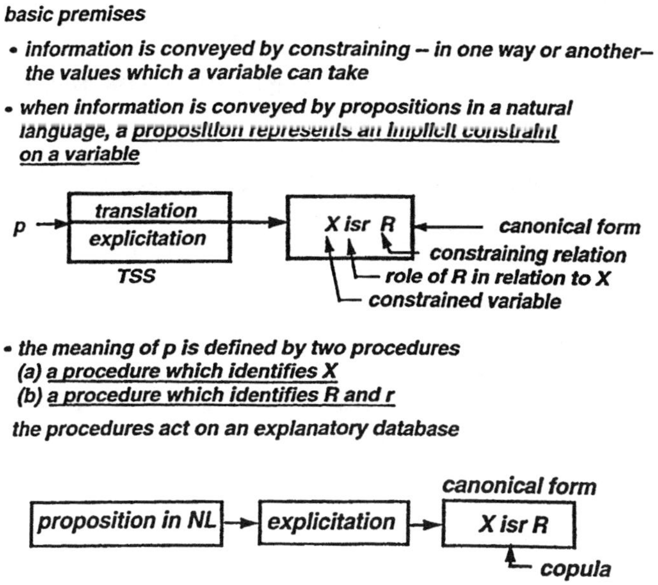

FIGURE 2.14 Representation of meaning in test-score semantics.

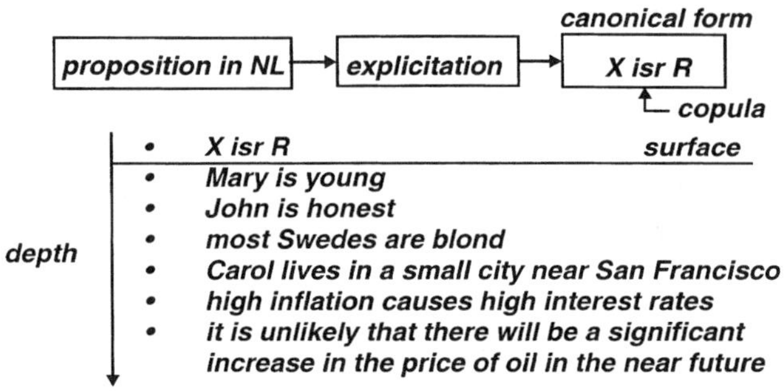

FIGURE 2.15 Depth of explicitation.

As in the case of basic constraints, the canonical form of a proposition may be derived through the use of test-score semantics. In this context, the depth of p is, roughly, a measure of the effort that is needed to explicitate p, that is, to translate p into its canonical form. In this sense, the proposition X isr R is a surface constraint (depth = zero), with the depth of explicitation increasing in the downward direction (Figure 2.15). Thus a proposition such as *Mary is young* is shallow, whereas *it is unlikely that there will be a significant increase in the price of oil in the near future*, is not.

Once the propositions in the initial data set are expressed in their canonical forms, the groundwork is laid for fuzzy constraint propagation. This is a basic part of CW which is discussed in the following section.

2.4 FUZZY CONSTRAINT PROPAGATION AND THE RULES OF INFERENCE IN FUZZY LOGIC

The rules governing fuzzy constraint propagation are, in effect, the rules of inference in fuzzy logic. In addition to these rules, it is helpful to have rules governing fuzzy constraint modification. The latter rules will be discussed at a later point in this section.

In a summarized form, the rules governing fuzzy constraint propagation are the following [51]. (A and B are fuzzy relations. Disjunction and conjunction are defined, respectively, as max and min, with the understanding that, more generally, they could be defined via t-norms and s-norms [15,24]. The antecedent and consequent constraints are separated by a horizontal line.)

Conjunctive Rule 1:

$$\frac{\begin{array}{c} X \text{ is } A \\ X \text{ is } B \end{array}}{X \text{ is } A \cap B}$$

Conjunctive Rule 2: $(X \in U, Y \in B, A \subset U, B \subset V)$

$$\begin{array}{l} X \text{ is } A \\ Y \text{ is } B \\ \hline (X, Y) \text{ is } A \times B \end{array}$$

Disjunctive Rule 1:

$$\begin{array}{ll} & X \text{ is } A \\ \text{or} & \\ & X \text{ is } B \\ \hline & X \text{ is } A \cup B \end{array}$$

Disjunctive Rule 2: $(A \subset U, B \subset V)$

$$\begin{array}{ll} & A \text{ is } A \\ \text{or} & \\ & Y \text{ is } B \\ \hline & (X, Y) \text{ is } A \times V \cup U \times B \end{array}$$

where $A \times V$ and $U \times B$ are cylindrical extensions of A and B, respectively.

Conjunctive Rule for isv:

$$\begin{array}{l} X \text{ isv } A \\ X \text{ isv } B \\ \hline X \text{ isv } A \cup B \end{array}$$

Projective Rule:

$$\begin{array}{c} (X, Y) \text{ is } A \\ \hline Y \text{ is } \text{proj}_V\, A \end{array}$$

where $\text{proj}_V\, A = \sup_u A$

Subjective Rule:

$$\begin{array}{c} X \text{ is } A \\ \hline (X, Y) \text{ is } A \times V \end{array}$$

Derived Rules

Compositional Rule:

$$\begin{array}{l} X \text{ is } A \\ (X, Y) \text{ is } B \\ \hline Y \text{ is } A \circ B \end{array}$$

where $A \circ B$ denotes the composition of A and B.

Extension Principle (Mapping Rule) [34,40]:

$$\frac{X \text{ is } A}{f(X) \text{ is } f(A)}$$

where $f : U \rightarrow V$, and $f(A)$ is defined by

$$\mu_{f(A)}(\nu) = \sup_{u|\nu=f(u)} \mu_A(u)$$

Inverse Mapping Rule:

$$\frac{f(X) \text{ is } A}{X \text{ is } f^{-1}(A)}$$

where $\mu_{f^{-1}(A)}(u) = \mu_A(f(u))$

Generalized modus ponens:

$$\frac{\begin{array}{l} X \text{ is } A \\ \text{if } X \text{ is } B \text{ then } Y \text{ is } C \end{array}}{Y \text{ is } A \circ ((\neg B) \oplus C)}$$

where the bounded sum $\neg B \oplus C$ represents Lukasiewicz's definition of implication.

Generalized Extension Principle:

$$\frac{f(X) \text{ is } A}{q(X) \text{ is } q(f^{-1}(A))}$$

where

$$\mu_q(\nu) = \sup_{u|\nu=q(u)} \mu_A(f(u)).$$

The generalized extension principle plays a pivotal role in fuzzy constraint propagation. However, what is used most frequently in practical applications of fuzzy logic is the *basic interpolative rule*, which is a special case of the compositional rule of inference applied to a function which is defined by a fuzzy graph [38,51]. More specifically, if f is defined by a fuzzy rule set

$$f\text{: if } X \text{ is } A_i \text{ then } X \text{ is } B_i, \;\; i = 1, \ldots, n$$

or equivalently, by a fuzzy graph

$$f \text{ is} \sum_i A_i \times B_i$$

and its argument, X, is defined by the antecedent constraint

$$X \text{ } is \text{ } A$$

then the consequent constraint on Y may be expressed as

$$Y \text{ } is \sum_i m_i \wedge B_i$$

where m_i is a matching coefficient,

$$m_i = \sup(A_i \cap A)$$

which serves as a measure of the degree to which A matches A_i.

Syllogistic Rule [48]:

$$\frac{\begin{array}{l} Q_1 \text{ } A\text{'s are } B\text{'s} \\ Q_2(A \text{ and } B)\text{'s are } C\text{'s} \end{array}}{(Q_1 \otimes Q_2)A\text{'s are } (B \text{ and } C)\text{'s}}$$

where Q_1 and Q_2 are fuzzy quantifiers; A, B, and C are fuzzy relations; and $Q_1 \otimes Q_2$ is the product of Q_1 and Q_2 in fuzzy arithmetic.

Constraint Modification Rules [36,43]:

$$X \text{ is } mA \rightarrow X \text{ is } f(A)$$

where m is a modifier such as *not, very, more, or less*, and $f(A)$ defines the way in which m modifies A. Specifically,

$$\text{if } m = \textit{not} \text{ then } f(A) = A'(\text{complement})$$
$$\text{if } m = \textit{very} \text{ then } f(A) = {}^2A(\text{left square})$$

where $\mu_{2A}(u) = (\mu_A(u))^2$. This rule is a convention and should not be construed as a realistic approximation to the way in which the modifier *very* functions in a natural language.

Probability Qualification Rule [45]:

$$(X \text{ is } A) \text{ is } \Lambda \rightarrow P \text{ is } \Lambda$$

where X is a random variable taking values in U with probability density $p(u)$; Λ is a linguistic probability expressed in words like *likely, not very likely*, etc.; and P is the probability of the fuzzy event X is A, expressed as

$$P = \int_U \mu_A(u) p(u) du.$$

The primary purpose of this summary is to underscore the coincidence of the principal rules governing fuzzy constraint propagation with the principal values of inference in fuzzy logic. Of necessity, the summary is not complete and there are many specialized rules which are not included. Furthermore, most of the rules in the summary apply to constraints which are of the basic, possibilistic type. Further development of the rules governing fuzzy constraint propagation will require an extension of the rules of inference to generalized constraints.

As was alluded to in the summary, the principal rule governing constraint propagation is the generalized extension principle which in a schematic form may be represented as

$$\frac{f(X_1, \ldots, X_n) \text{ is } A}{q(X_1, \ldots, X_n) \text{ is } q(f^{-1}(A))}.$$

In this expression, $X_1, \ldots, X_n$ are database variables; the term above the line represents the constraint induced by the IDS; and the term below the line is the TDS expressed as a constraint on the query $q(X_1, \ldots, X_n)$. In the latter constraint, $f^{-1}(A)$ denotes the preimage of the fuzzy relation A under the mapping $f : U \to V$, where A is a fuzzy subset of V and U is the domain of $f(X_1, \ldots, X_n)$.

Expressed in terms of the membership functions of A and $q(f^{-1}(A))$, the generalized extension principle reduces the derivation of the TDS to the solution of the constrained maximization problem

$$\mu_q(X_1, \ldots, X_n)(\nu) = \sup_{(u_1, \ldots, u_n)} (\mu_A(f(u_1, \ldots, u_n)))$$

in which $u_1, \ldots, u_n$ are constrained by

$$\nu = q(u_1, \ldots, u_n).$$

The generalized extension principle is simpler than it appears. An illustration of its use is provided by the following example.

The IDS is:

most Swedes are tall

The query is: *What is the average height of Swedes?*

The explanatory database consists of a population of N Swedes, $Name_1, \ldots, Name_N$. The database variables are $h_1, \ldots, h_N$, where h_i is the height of $Name_i$, and the grade of membership of $Name_i$ in *tall* is $\mu_{tall}(h_i), i = 1, \ldots, n$.

The proportion of Swedes who are tall is given by the sigma-count [43]

$$\sum Count(tall \cdot Swedes/Swedes) = \frac{1}{N} \sum_i \mu_{tall}(h_i)$$

from which it follows that the constraint on the database variables induced by the IDS is

$$\frac{1}{N}\sum_i \mu_{tall}(h_i) \text{ is } most.$$

In terms of the database variables $h_1, \ldots, h_N$, the average height of Swedes is given by

$$h_{ave} = \frac{1}{N}\sum_i h_i.$$

Since the IDS is a fuzzy proposition, h_{ave} is a fuzzy set whose determination reduces to the constrained maximization problem

$$\mu_{h_{ave}}(\nu) = \sup_{h_1,\ldots,h_N}\left(\mu_{most}\left(\frac{1}{N}\sum_i \mu_{tall}(h_i)\right)\right)$$

subject to the constraint

$$\nu = \frac{1}{N}\sum_i h_i.$$

It is possible that approximate solutions to problems of this type might be obtainable through the use of neurocomputing or evolutionary-computing-based methods.

As a further example, we will return to a problem stated in an earlier section, namely, maximization of a function, f, which is described in words by its fuzzy graph, f^* (Figure 2.10). More specifically, consider the standard problem of maximization of an objective function in decision analysis. Let us assume—as is frequently the case in real-world problems—that the objective function, f, is not well-defined and that what we know about f can be expressed as a fuzzy rule set

$$\begin{aligned} f\text{: } & \text{if } X \text{ is } A_1 \text{ then } Y \text{ is } B_1 \\ & \text{if } X \text{ is } A_2 \text{ then } Y \text{ is } B_2 \\ & \ldots\ldots\ldots\ldots\ldots\ldots\ldots \\ & \text{if } X \text{ is } A_n \text{ then } Y \text{ is } B_n \end{aligned}$$

or, equivalently, as a fuzzy graph

$$f \text{ is } \sum_i A_i \times B_i.$$

The question is: What is the point or, more generally, the maximizing set [54] at which f is maximized, and what is the maximum value of f?

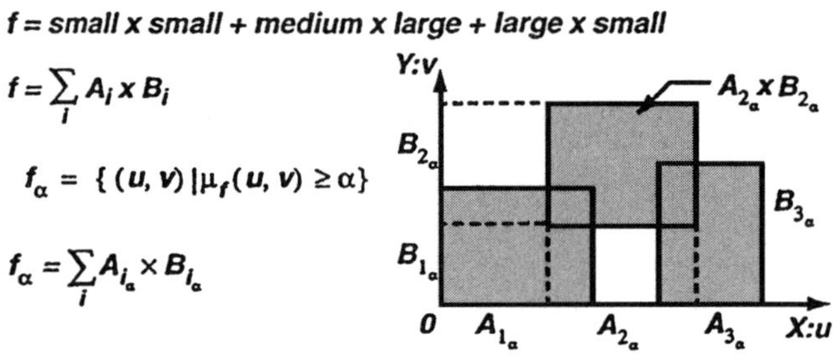

FIGURE 2.16 α-cuts of a function described by a fuzzy graph.

The problem can be solved by employing the technique of *α-cuts* [34,40]. With reference to Figure 2.16, if A_{i_α} and B_{i_α} are α-cuts of A_i and B_i, respectively, then the corresponding α-cut of f^* is given by

$$f_\alpha^* = \sum_i A_{i_\alpha} \times B_{i_\alpha}.$$

From this expression, the maximizing fuzzy set, the maximum fuzzy set and maximum value fuzzy set can readily be derived, as shown in Figures 2.16 and 2.17.

A key point which is brought out by these examples and the preceding discussion is that explicitation and constraint propagation play pivotal roles in CW. This role can be concretized by viewing explicitation and constraint propagation as translation of propositions expressed in a natural language into what might be called the *generalized constraint language* (GCL) and applying rules of constraint propagation to expressions in this language—expressions which are typically canonical forms of propositions expressed in a natural language. This process is schematized in Figure 2.18.

The conceptual framework of GCL is substantively differently from that of conventional logical systems, e.g., predicate logic. But what matters most is that the expressive power of GCL—which is based on fuzzy logic—is much greater than

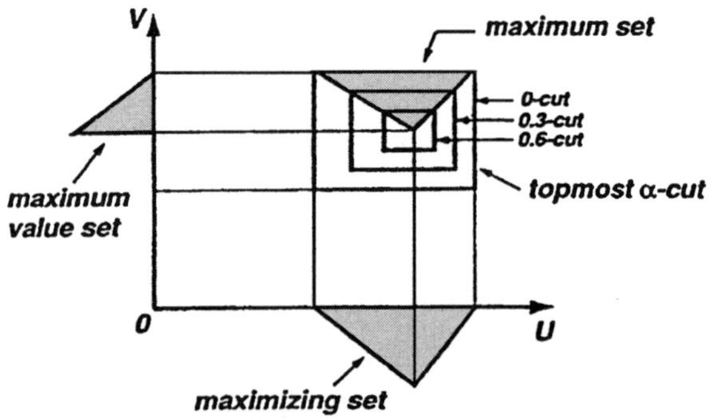

FIGURE 2.17 Computation of maximizing set, maximum set, and maximum value set.

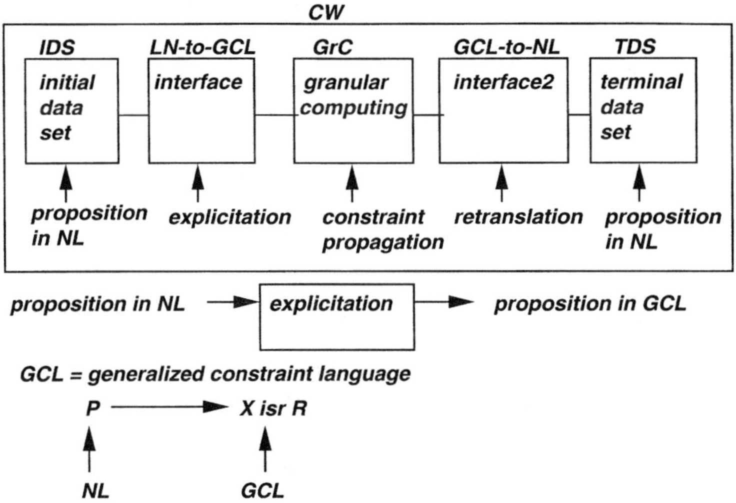

FIGURE 2.18 Conceptual structure of computing with words.

that of standard logical calculi. As an illustration of this point, consider the following problem.

A box contains ten balls of various sizes of which several are large and a few are small. What is the probability that a ball drawn at random is neither large nor small?

To be able to answer this question it is necessary to be able to define the meanings of *large, small, several large balls, few small balls*, and *neither large nor small*. This is a problem in semantics which falls outside of probability theory, neurocomputing and other methodologies.

An important application area for computing with words and manipulation of perceptions is decision analysis since in most realistic settings the underlying probabilities and utilities are not known with sufficient precision to justify the use of numerical valuations. There exists an extensive literature on the use of fuzzy probabilities and fuzzy utilities in decision analysis. In what follows, we shall restrict our discussion to two very simple examples which illustrate the use of perceptions.

First, consider a box which contains black balls and white balls (Figure 2.19). If we could count the number of black balls and white balls, the probability of

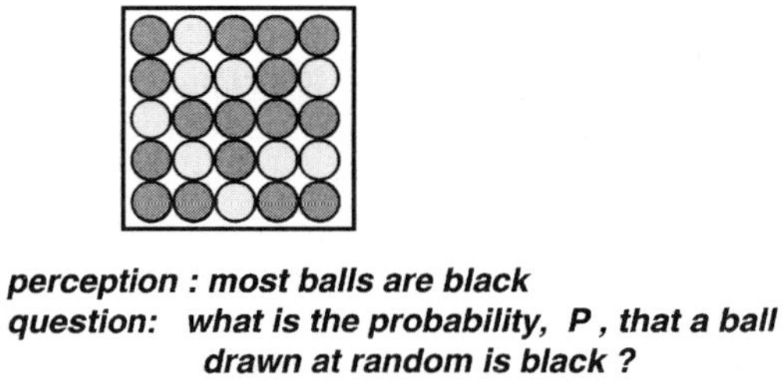

FIGURE 2.19 A box with black and white balls.

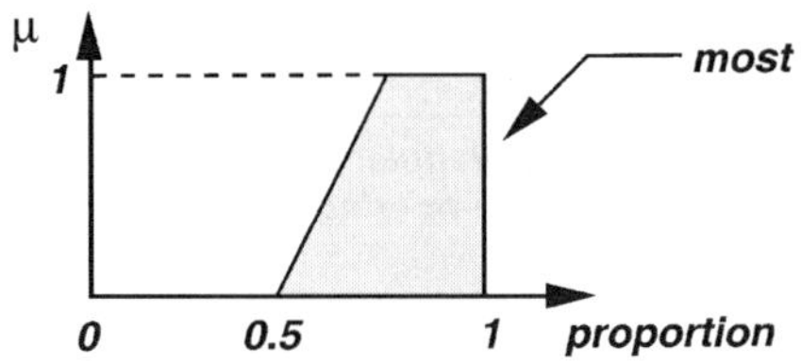

FIGURE 2.20 Membership function of *most*.

picking a black ball at random would be equal to the proportion, r, of black balls in the box.

Now suppose that we cannot count the number of black balls in the box but our perception is that most of the balls are black. What, then, is the probability, p, that a ball drawn at random is black?

Assume that *most* is characterized by its possibility distribution (Figure 2.20). In this case, p is a fuzzy number whose possibility distribution is *most*, that is,

$$p \text{ is } most.$$

Next, assume that there is a reward of a dollars if the ball drawn at random is black and a penalty of b dollars if the ball is white. In this case, if p were known as a number, the expected value of the gain would be

$$e = ap - b(1 - p).$$

Since we know not p but its possibility distribution, the problem is to compute the value of e when p is *most*. For this purpose, we can employ the extension principle [34,40], which implies that the possibility distribution, E, of e is a fuzzy number which may be expressed as

$$E = a\ most - b(1 - most).$$

For simplicity, assume that *most* has a trapezoidal possibility distribution (Figure 2.20). In this case, the trapezoidal possibility distribution of E can be computed as shown in Figure 2.21.

It is of interest to observe that if the support of E is an interval $[\alpha,\beta]$ which straddles O (Figure 2.22), then there is no noncontroversial decision principle which can be employed to answer the question: Would it be advantageous to play a game in which a ball is picked at random from a box in which most balls are black, and a and b are such that the support of E contains O.

Next, consider a box in which the balls $b_1, \ldots, b_n$ have the same color but vary in size, with $b_i, i = 1, \ldots, n$ having the grade of membership μ_i in the fuzzy set of large balls (Figure 2.23). The question is: What is the probability that a ball drawn at random is large, given the perception that most balls are large?

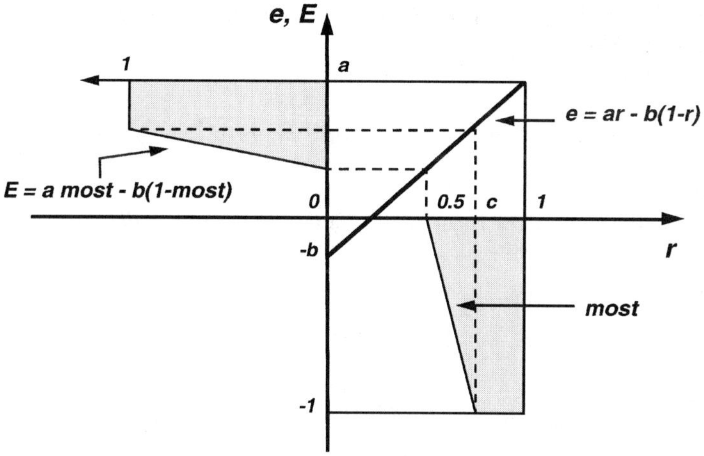

FIGURE 2.21 Computation of expectation through use of the extension principle.

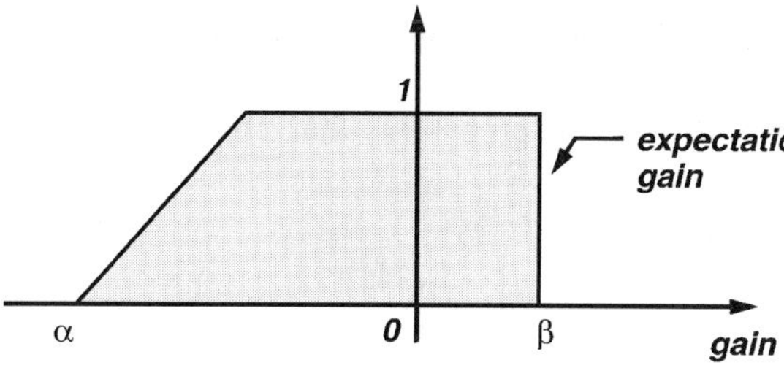

FIGURE 2.22 Expectation of gain.

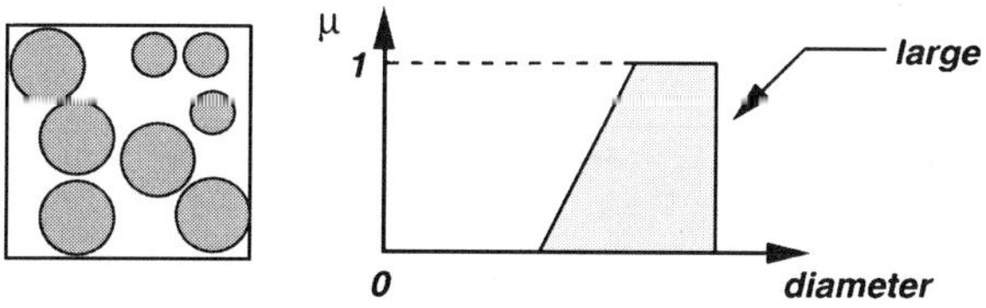

FIGURE 2.23 A box with balls of various sizes and a definition of large ball.

The difference between this example and the preceding one is that the event *the ball drawn at random is large* is a fuzzy event, in contrast to the crisp event *the ball drawn at random is black.*

The probability of drawing b_i is $1/n$. Since the grade of membership of b_i in the fuzzy set of large balls is μ_i, the probability of the fuzzy event *the ball drawn at random is large* is given by [35]

$$P = \frac{1}{n}\sum \mu_i.$$

On the other hand, the proportion of large balls in the box is given by the relative sigma-count [40,43]

$$\sum \mathrm{Count}(large \cdot balls/balls \cdot in \cdot box) = \frac{1}{n}\sum \mu_i.$$

Consequently, the canonical form of the perception *most balls are large* may be expressed as

$$\frac{1}{n}\sum \mu_i \text{ is } most$$

which leads to the conclusion that

$$P \text{ is } most.$$

It is of interest to observe that the possibility distribution of P is the same as in the preceding example.

If the question were: What is the probability that a ball drawn at random is *small*, the answer would be

$$P \text{ is } \frac{1}{n}\sum \nu_i$$

where $\nu_i, i = 1, \cdots, n$, is the grade of membership of b_i in the fuzzy set of small balls, given that

$$\frac{1}{n}\sum \mu_i \text{ is } most.$$

What is involved in this case is constraint propagation from the antecedent constraint on the μ_i to a consequent constraint on the ν_i. This problem reduces to the solution of a nonlinear program.

What this example points to is that in using fuzzy constraint propagation rules, application of the extension principle reduces, in general, to the solution of a nonlinear program. What we need—and do not have at present—are approximate methods of solving such programs which are capable of exploiting the tolerance for imprecision. Without such methods, the cost of solutions may be excessive in relation to the imprecision which is intrinsic in the use of words. In this connection, an intriguing possibility is to use neurocomputing and evolutionary computing techniques to arrive at approximate solutions to constrained maximization problems. The use of such techniques may provide a closer approximation to the ways in which human manipulate perceptions.

2.5 CONCLUDING REMARKS

In our quest for machines which have a high degree of machine intelligence (high MIQ), we are developing a better understanding of the fundamental importance of the remarkable human capacity to perform a wide variety of physical and mental tasks without any measurements and any computations. Underlying this remarkable capability is the brain's crucial ability to manipulate perceptions—perceptions of distance, size, weight, force, color, numbers, likelihood, truth and other characteristics of physical and mental objects. A basic difference between perceptions and measurements is that, in general, measurements are crisp whereas perceptions are fuzzy. In a fundamental way, this is the reason why to deal with perceptions it is necessary to employ a logical system that is fuzzy rather than crisp.

Humans employ words to describe perceptions. It is this obvious observation that is the point of departure for the theory outlined in the preceding sections.

When perceptions are described in words, manipulation of perceptions is reduced to computing with words (CW). In CW, the objects of computation are words or, more generally, propositions drawn from a natural language. A basic premise in CW is that the meaning of a proposition, p, may be expressed as a generalized constraint in which the constrained variable and the constraining relation are, in general, implicit in p.

In coming years, computing with words and perceptions is likely to emerge as an important direction in science and technology. In a reversal of long-standing attitudes, manipulation of perceptions and words which describe them is destined to gain in respectability. This is certain to happen because it is becoming increasingly clear that in dealing with real-world problems there is much to be gained by exploiting the tolerance for imprecision, uncertainty and partial truth. This is the primary motivation for the methodology of computing with words (CW) and the computational theory of perceptions (CTP) which are outlined in this paper.

ACKNOWLEDGMENTS

The author acknowledges Prof. Michio Sugeno, who has contributed so much and in so many ways to the development of fuzzy logic and its applications. This work was supported in part by NASA under Grant NAC2-1177, by the Office of Naval Research under Grant N00014-96-1-0556, by the Army Research Office under Grant DAAH 04-961-0341, and by the BISC Program of University of California at Berkeley. This chapter is an expanded and updated version of a paper entitled "Fuzzy Logic = Computing with Words," which appeared in the *IEEE Transactions on Fuzzy Systems*, vol. 4, 103–111, 1996.

REFERENCES

1. H. R. Berenji, Fuzzy reinforcement learning and dynamic programming, in *Fuzzy Logic in Artificial Intelligence, Proc. IJCAI '93 Workshop*, A. L. Ralescu, Ed. Berlin, Germany: Springer-Verlag, 1994, pp. 1–9.

2. M. Black, Reasoning with loose concepts, *Dialog 2*, pp. 1–12, 1963.
3. P. Bosch, Vagueness, ambiguity and all the rest, in *Sprachstruktur, Individuum und Gesselschaft*, M. Van de Velde and W. Vandeweghe, Eds. Tubingen, Germany: Niemeyer, 1978.
4. J. Bowen, R. Lai, and D. Bahler, Fuzzy semantics and fuzzy constraint networks, in *Proc. 1st IEEE Conf. on Fuzzy Systems*, San Francisco, 1992, pp. 1009–1016.
5. ———, Lexical imprecision in fuzzy constraint networks, in *Proc. Nat. Conf. on Artificial Intelligence*, 1992, pp. 616–620.
6. M. J. Cresswell, *Logic and Languages*. London, U.K.: Methuen, 1973.
7. D. Dubois, H. Fargier, and H. Prade, Propagation and satisfaction of flexible constraints, in *Fuzzy Sets, Neural Networks, and Soft Computing*, R. R. Yager, L. A. Zadeh, Eds. New York: Van Nostrand Reinhold, 1994, pp. 166–187.
8. ———, Possibility theory in constraint satisfaction problems: Handling priority, preference, and uncertainty, *J. Appl. Intell.*, to be published.
9. ———, The calculus of fuzzy restrictions as a basis for flexible constraint satisfaction, in *Proc. 2nd IEEE Int. Conf. on Fuzzy Systems*, San Francisco, CA, 1993, pp. 1131–1136.
10. E. C. Freuder and P. Snow, Improved relaxation and search methods for approximate constraint satisfaction with a maximin criterion, in *Proc. 8th Biennial Conf. on the Canadian Society for Computational Studies of Intelligence*, Ont., Canada, 1990, pp. 227–230.
11. J. A. Goguen, The logic of inexact concepts, *Synthese*, vol. 19, pp. 325–373, 1969.
12. J. R. Hobbs, Making computational sense of Montague's intensional logic, *Artif. Intell.*, vol. 9, pp. 287–306, 1978.
13. O. Katai, S. Matsubara, H. Masuichi, M. Ida, *et al.*, Synergetic computation for constraint satisfaction problems involving continuous and fuzzy variables by using Occam, in *Transputer/Occam, Proc. 4th Transputer/Occam Int. Conf.*, S. Noguchi and H. Umeo, Eds. Amsterdam, The Netherlands: IOS Press, 1992, pp. 146–160.
14. A. Kaufmann and M. M. Gupta, *Introduction to Fuzzy Arithmetic: Theory and Applications*. New York: Van Nostrand, 1985.
15. G. Klir and B. Yuan, *Fuzzy Sets and Fuzzy Logic*. Englewood Cliffs, NJ: Prentice Hall, 1995.
16. K. Lano, A constraint-based fuzzy inference system, in *EPIA 91, 5th Portuguese Conf. on Artificial Intelligence*, P. Barahona, L. M. Pereira, and A. Porto, Eds. Berlin, Germany: Springer-Verlag, 1991, pp. 45–59.
17. W. A. Lodwick, Analysis of structure in fuzzy linear programs, *Fuzzy Sets and Systems*, vol. 38, no. 1, pp. 15–26, 1990.
18. E. H. Mamdani and B. R. Gaines, Eds., *Fuzzy Reasoning and Its Applications*, London, U.K. 1981.
19. M. Mares, *Computation over Fuzzy Quantities*. Boca Raton, FL: CRC, 1994.
20. V. Novak, Fuzzy logic, fuzzy sets, and natural languages, *Int. J. Gen. Syst.*, vol. 20, no. 1, pp. 83–97, 1991.
21. V. Novak, M. Ramik, M. Cerny, and J. Nekola, Eds., *Fuzzy Approach to Reasoning and Decision-Making*. Boston, MA: Kluwer, 1992.
22. M. S. Oshan, O. M. Saad, and A. G. Hassan, On the solution of fuzzy multiobjective integer linear programming problems with a parametric study, *Adv. Modeling Anal, A*, vol. 24, no. 2, pp. 49–64, 1995.

23. B. Partee, *Montague Grammar.* New York: Academic, 1976.

24. W. Pedrycz and F. Gomide, *Introduction to Fuzzy Sets.* Cambridge, MA: MIT Press, 1998.

25. G. Qi and G. Friedrich, Extending constraint satisfaction problem solving in structural design, in *Industrial and Engineering Applications of Artificial Intelligence and Expert Systems, 5th Int. Conf., IEA/AIE-92*, F. Belli and F. J. Radermacher, Eds. Berlin, Germany: Springer-Verlag, 1992, pp. 341–350.

26. H. Rasiowa and M. Marek, On reaching consensus by groups of intelligent agents, in *Methodologies for Intelligent Systems*, Z. W. Ras, Ed. Amsterdam, The Netherlands: North-Holland, 1989, pp. 234–243.

27. A Rosenfeld, R. A. Hummel, and S. W. Zucker, Scene labeling by relaxation operations, *IEEE Trans. Syst., Man, Cybern.*, vol. 6, pp. 420–433, 1976.

28. M. Sakawa, K. Sawada, and M. Inuiguchi, A fuzzy satisficing method for large-scale linear programming problems with block angular structure, *European J. Oper. Res.*, vol. 81, no. 2, pp. 399–409, 1995.

29. G. Shafer, *A Mathematical Theory of Evidence.* Princeton, NJ: Princeton Univ. Press, 1976.

30. S. C. Tong, Interval number and fuzzy number linear programming, *Adv. in Modeling Anal. A*, vol. 20, no. 2, pp. 51–56, 1994.

31. R. Vallee, *Cognition et Systeme.* Paris: l'Interdisciplinaire Systeme(s), 1995.

32. R. R. Yager, Some extensions of constraint propagation of label sets, *Int. J. Approximate Reasoning*, vol. 3, pp. 417–435, 1989.

33. L. A. Zadeh, From circuit theory to system theory, *Proc. IRE*, vol. 50, pp. 856–865, 1961.

34. ———, Fuzzy sets, *Inform. Contr.*, vol. 8, pp. 338–353, 1965.

35. ———, Probability measures of fuzzy events, *J. Math. Anal. Appl.*, vol. 23, pp. 421–427, 1968.

36. ———, A fuzzy-set-theoretic interpretation of linguistic hedges, *J. Cybern.*, vol. 2, pp. 4–34, 1972.

37. ———, Outline of a new approach to the analysis of complex systems and decision processes, *IEEE Trans. Syst., Man, Cybern.*, vol. SMC-3, pp. 28–44, 1973.

38. ———, On the analysis of large scale systems, *Systems Approaches and Environment Problems*, H. Gottinger, Ed. Gottingen, Germany: Vandenhoeck and Ruprecht, 1974, pp. 23–37.

39. ———, Calculus of fuzzy restrictions, in *Fuzzy Sets and Their Applications to Cognitive and Decision Processes*, L. A. Zadeh, K. S. Fu, and M. Shimura, Eds. New York: Academic, 1975, pp. 1–39.

40. ———, The concept of a linguistic variable and its application to approximate reasoning, Part I: *Inf. Sci.*, vol. 8, pp. 199–249; Part II: *Inf. Sci.*, vol. 8, pp. 301–357; Part III: *Inform. Sci.*, vol. 9, pp. 43–80, 1975.

41. ———, A fuzzy-algorithmic approach to the definition of complex or imprecise concepts, *Int. J. Man-Machine Studies*, vol. 8, pp. 249–291, 1976.

42. ———, Fuzzy sets as a basis for a theory of possibility, *Fuzzy Sets Syst.*, vol. 1, pp. 3–28, 1978.

43. ———, PRUF—A meaning representation language for natural languages, *Int. J. Man-Machines Studies*, vol. 10, pp. 395–460, 1978.

44. ———, Fuzzy sets and information granularity, in *Advances in Fuzzy Set Theory and Applications*, M. Gupta, R. Ragade, and R. Yager, Eds. Amsterdam, The Netherlands: North-Holland, 1979, pp. 3–18.

45. ———, A theory of approximate reasoning, *Machine Intelligence*, vol. 9, J. Hayes, D. Michie, and L. I. Mikulich, Eds. New York: Halstead, 1979, pp. 149–194.

46. ———, Test-score semantics for natural languages and meaning representation via PRUF, *Empirical Semantics*, B. Rieger, Ed. Germany: Brockmeyer, pp. 281–349; also, Tech. Rep. Memo. 246, AI Center, SRI International, Menlo Park, CA, 1981.

47. ———, Test-score semantics for natural languages, in *Proc. Ninth Int. Conf. on Computational Linguistics*, Prague, Czech Republic, 1982, pp. 425–430.

48. ———, Syllogistic reasoning in fuzzy logic and its application to reasoning with dispositions, in *Proc. 1984 Int. Symp. on Multiple-Valued Logic*, Winnipeg, Canada, 1984, pp. 148–153.

49. ———, Outline of a computational approach to meaning and knowledge representation based on the concept of a generalized assignment statement, in *Proc. Int. Seminar on Artificial Intelligence and Man-Machine Systems*, M. Thoma and A. Wyner, Eds. Heidelberg, Germany: Springer-Verlag, 1986, pp. 198–211.

50. ———, Fuzzy logic, neural networks, and soft computing, *Commun. ACM*, vol. 37, no. 3, pp. 77–84, 1994.

51. ———, Fuzzy logic and the calculi of fuzzy rules and fuzzy graphs: A precis, *Multiple Valued Logic 1*, Gordon and Breach Science, 1996, pp. 1–38.

52. ———, Fuzzy logic = computing with words, *IEEE Trans. Fuzzy Syst.*, vol. 4, pp. 103–111, 1996.

53. ———, Toward a theory of fuzzy information granulation and its centrality in human reasoning and fuzzy logic, *Fuzzy Sets Syst.*, vol. 90, pp. 111–127, 1997.

54. ———, Maximizing sets and fuzzy Markoff algorithms, *IEEE Trans. Syst., Man, Cybern. C*, vol. 28, pp. 9–15, 1998.

CHAPTER 3

COMPUTING WITH WORDS: THE PROBLEMS AND SOLUTIONS

ALEXANDER M. MEYSTEL
Drexel University, Philadelphia, Pennsylvania

PAUL P. WANG
Duke University, Durham, North Carolina

We are humans not because we have language but because we *are* language.

—Wilhelm von Humboldt

3.1 SEARCHING FOR A NEW GESTALT

This book is an outline for ongoing efforts in the area of computing with words (CW). It was written by a group of 24 authors representing a variety of domains related to CW. Chapter 1 was written by Paul P. Wang, the editor, with the intention of giving an overview of CW in a user-friendly manner. Computing with words is a complex concept and very much an ongoing research issue that touches many disciplines of serious studies. Like any scientific statement, the expression *computing with words* is a metaphor that summarizes, or rather generalizes, a particular situation in science. This metaphor is brought into focus by researchers in an effort to determine an arrangement of existing results related to intelligent systems. Indeed, all subtopics of this area are attached to computer processing of natural language–based information, including knowledge acquisition and organization, linkage between perception and knowledge organization, computer-oriented modeling of self-organized knowledge representation processes within intelligent systems, and planning, control, and self-control of intelligent systems. None of these topics is structurally clear; all are subject to discussion. The intention is to explore the domain in a search for emerging outlines of the nascent scientific discipline.

Computing with Words, Edited by Paul P. Wang.
ISBN 0-471-35374-4

Fifty years ago everything was crystal clear: There was engineering for bridges and turbines, physics for subatomic particles and nuclear energy, and computers for ballistic trajectories now and machine translation in the future. Some discontent was expressed by semioticians and cyberneticists, but the road map for scientific endeavor was clear: Propagate your area, build it up on the skeleton of mathematical equations, and you will make no mistake. Now we are overwhelmed with information that is about to swamp us and consume all productive time, and most of our efforts are oriented toward compressing the information, summarizing the sources, generalizing the description of situations, classifying, categorizing, and clustering the myriads of product descriptions, research results, news articles, technical reports, and requests for proposals. Seemingly, natural language is something that we specialize in continuously from the cradle on, but on which we never focus as we are doing now.

The seeds of the present situation were planted by several major contributions to the scholarly discourse, all of them related not to *what* we analyze, but *how*. This "how" was beyond reach because the phenomenon of thought was beyond scientific endeavor. Said J. Watson [1]: "The behaviorist advances the view that what the psychologists have hitherto called thought is in short nothing but talking to ourselves." After the wall of behaviorist views was torn down in the middle of this century, we saw with surprise that our "talking to ourselves" contains a great deal of natural language, and most of the statements are fuzzy and ambiguous. Thus we embarked on two major activities that are somewhat supplementary: disambiguation and fuzzy calculus.

The need in fuzzy logic and analysis of fuzzy systems is determined by a multiplicity of uncertainties that surround us. Physics is used to fuzziness: The great Heisenberg uncertainty principle declares that there are limits to the accuracy with which we can determine experimentally the values of system coordinates. We are used to talking about the free will of an electron: Its state cannot be described as an exact point in state space; it is a zone, a volume, and somewhere within this volume the phenomenon of the electron is situated (or, at least, we think so). The uncertainty principle is related not only to artifacts of quantum mechanics but works at any scale of world representation. In the same way, we can talk about an uncertainty zone associated with the value of power (and the rate of its change) at the output of a power plant; sure, it will be a "free will of the output power." In the same way, we can talk about the free will of any word, any statement, any definition. There is a zone where the meaning is situated (or, at least, we assume so). However, we won't be able to pin down the meaning more precisely than the zone of uncertainty allows at a particular level of granularity (i.e., scale, resolution).

3.1.1 All That We Do Is Summarizing: The Roots of Fuzzy Representation

At the end of the twentieth century, a silent revolution has happened all over the entire scale of our reality and all existing scientific approaches because of the challenge of complexity. Humanity has survived for a long time without getting involved in this issue—until recently, not even attempting to model it mathematically. Complexity imposes a huge challenge on scientific and engineering methods based on precise models. It is impossible to model a complex system taking every bit of it into account in detail because the system is very complex. Lotfi A. Zadeh recognized this fact quite early. In the history of science, the precise modeling methods were extremely successful. So when fuzzy set theory came into the scientific framework with all its embedded imprecision and vagueness, it encountered many misunderstandings at the beginning.

Thanks to the rapid pace of the Japanese consumer electronics industry, fuzzy control devices based on fuzzy theory have finally gained wide approval and credibility. The fact of the matter is that our brain was (and is) proficient in using the same tools of fuzzy set theory. People just have not yet focused on this issue. It turned out that fuzzy set theory reflects the natural cognitive abilities of human beings. These abilities emerged within our thinking mechanisms and parallel with development of our natural language skills. In CW we get acquainted with these phenomena by learning and using linguistic models for coping with the complexities.

The paradigm of fuzzy sets [2] has emerged as a direct response to multiple, broad needs that became clear, and the terms *membership, containment*, and *fuzzy relations* entered the vocabulary of electrical engineers. Natural language turned out to be the real source of fuzziness as a phenomenon as such terms as *similarly* and *approximately* came under scrutiny [3], and the decision-making process was brought under consideration as a confluence of goals and constraints. Dealing with fuzziness demanded studies of the relation of similarity [4] and thus the concept of linguistic variable [5, 6]. This is when L. Zadeh focused on the fundamental issue of *summarization*, or *generalization* as many call it today.

Logic plays "a basic role in what may well be one of the most important facets of human thinking, namely, the ability to *summarize* information—to extract from the collection of masses of data impinging upon the human brain those and only those subcollections which are relevant to the performance of the task at hand. By its nature, a summary is an approximation to what it summarizes" [6]. Every theory, every statement, even every word in a natural language is a result of a gestalt process [7], which includes summarization or generalization. The following facets of the situation are listed by L. Zadeh in his BISC letter [26]:

1. We do not know how to define what is meant by a summary, nor can we articulate in general terms how to assess the goodness of a summary.
2. A summary is both end-use and length dependent, and, ipso facto, not unique.
3. Summarization cannot be achieved by chunking or, more generally, by divide-and-conquer techniques.
4. Summarization is highly context dependent and requires both local and global understanding.
5. Summarization by omission is not acceptable because it trivializes the problem.

It would be important (for the subsequent presentation) to compare the broadly accepted meanings of two terms: *summarization* and *generalization*. The *American*

Heritage Dictionary (AHD) defines *summary* as "presenting the substance in a condensed form." The *Merriam-Webster Collegiate Dictionary* (MWCD) defines *summary* as "an abstract, abridgment, or compendium ... of a preceding discourse." The term *generalization* in the same sources is defined as follows: "to reduce to a general form, class, or law, to infer from many particulars" (AHD) and "a general statement, law, principle, or proposition" and "the act or process of generalizing," while the verb "generalize" means "to derive or induce (a general conception or principle) from particulars" (MWCD).

It seems that the meaning of *abridgement* as commonly alluded to as regards a summary might be insufficient if significant information is lost in the process of abridgment or if there are structural changes [8]. Generalization presumes that a possible loss of information is avoided by finding a short general equivalent for multiple particularities that can be contained in the discourse. Consider any process of clustering, such as the process of fuzzy rules generation: It always entails loss of information about instantaneous experiences [9]. The same happens during formation of words in a natural language. Zadeh analyzed the processes of fuzziness formation typical for dealing with natural language. Linguistic variables turned out to be a source and the cause of various granularities at which information actually enters the human intelligence [10].

Says Zadeh [6]: "The ability to manipulate fuzzy sets and the consequent summarizing capability constitutes one of the most important assets of the human mind as well as the fundamental characteristic that distinguishes human intelligence from the type of machine intelligence that is embodied in present-day digital computers." After fuzzification, we are solving the problem contemplating solution alternatives formulated in terms of clustered information instead of the elements of the cluster, in terms of the entire set instead of elements of the set, and in terms of assemblies instead of the components of the assembly. Actually, fuzzy set theory was supposed to answer the questions of intelligent systems design starting with representation and ending with decision making and behavior generation. Was it meant to become a regular branch of mathematics? No. It just happened that way. The subject of this book, *Computing with Words*, encompasses a set of issues that are both novel and are opening new, unexplored horizons. This book traces most of the linkages between *fuzzy systems using linguistic variables* and *computing with words*. When Zadeh introduced linguistic variables, it turned out to be the initiation of the great march of fuzzy logic into the domain of computation for decision making.

Yet the need for interlacing generalization with the design of the system and its controller remained. Also, the researchers were driven by an expectation of the guiding role of fuzzy logic in transforming the statements of natural language into statements of the language of intelligent control. In other words, this focus on a generalized, succinct representation remained a hallmark of the intelligence, a feature that earlier had determined fuzzy logic as one of the key tools for *intelligent systems* analysis, which in effect triggered the emergence of multigranular (multiresolutional, multiscale) phenomena and processes typical for *intelligent systems*.

The problem of meaning extraction is one of the difficult problems in the science of logic. Montague [11,12] has demonstrated that the meaning of the text cannot be represented by a syntactic structure related to necessity and possibility because of the fuzziness of words. This issue was addressed by Zadeh in 1978 as a problem of translating from the natural language to a special computer language: a meaning representation language [10].

Zadeh cited the following as examples of fuzzy propositions [13]:

(1) Ronald is *more or less young*.
(2) Miriam was *very rich*.
(3) Harry loves Ann.
(4) X is *much smaller* than Y.
(5) *Most* Swedes are *blond*.
(6) The man in the *dark* suit is *walking slowly toward* the door.
(7) Susanna gave *several expensive* presents to each of her *close friends*.

Zadeh states that statements (5) and (7) contain fuzzy quantifiers and their effect on the meaning can definitely be evaluated [14]; a fuzzy relative clause can be analyzed for proposition (6). The fuzzy set descriptors from (1), (2), (4), and (5) can be the subject of further analysis. However, the meaning of this sentences remains unclear because each of the words used is a summarization, or a generalization for a semantic field. The actual fuzziness of each word depends on the characteristics of such a field. Indeed, even such a simple word as *young* from (1) belongs to a broad enough field:

young **1.** Being in an early period of life, development, or growth. **2.** Of, belonging to, or suggestive of youth or early life. **3.** Vigorous or fresh; youthful. **4.** Lacking experience; immature. **5.** Relating to, or having the characteristics of youth or a young person.

The choice among these five alternatives is a matter of disambiguation that can be performed only in a particular context. Take proposition (2): The fuzziness is determined not only by the fuzzy set descriptor *very* but also by the main word of this phrase; the main word *rich* is a summary of, or a generalization on, many meanings; look at its semantic field:

rich **1.** Having abundant possessions of material wealth. **2.** Having abundant possessions of intellectual or artistic talents. **3.** Having great worth or high value or quality. **4.** Well supplied. **5.** Magnificent; sumptuous. **6. a.** Having an abundant supply. **b.** Abounding, especially in natural resources. **7.** Meaningful and significant. **8.** Very productive and therefore financially profitable. **9. a.** Containing a large number of choice ingredients. **b.** Having or exuding a strong or pungent aroma. **10.** Pleasantly full and mellow.

For a human being, disambiguation of this kind within a context would not be a big problem; however, for automatic *computing with word*, it is. Solutions are proposed based on statistics of particular words typical for definite issues of interest [15, 16]. This process is always linked with prior summarization, or generalization on many sources [17], and after this, an instantiation can be produced. We have to define a path from a summarized or generalized adjective *rich* to its higher-resolution instantiation that dwells on details of fine granularity. All this happens because the source of information remained intimately associated with *natural language*, where various granularities are mixed together in a web of narration. The reality that unfolds under these circumstances is a multigranular reality: No matter what the problem at hand, we must distinguish atomic issues from composite issues [18], or as we would term them today, fine granularity issues from coarse granularity issues; or high-resolution issues from low-resolution issues; or smaller-scale issues from larger-scale issues.

The results of interpretation depend on the totality of the world presented at each resolution (granularity, scale). In the world of a particular granularity, the vocabulary is frequently interpreted in a different way than at other granularities. Much more dangerous for the results of interpretation is the fact that worlds of different granularities are driven by the different axioms and assumptions. This was noted before by J. McCarthy [19]: "Whenever we write an axiom, a critic can say it is true only in a certain context. With a little ingenuity, the critic can usually devise a more general context in which the precise form of the axiom does not hold. Looking at human reasoning as reflected in language emphasizes this point." He calls *nonmonotonicity of reasoning* the process of moving from one level of granularity to another as needed to arrive at an interpretation.

We can deduce that multigranular (multiresolutional, multiscale) representation is presumed. It can be presented in words only—however, it can be presented in multimedia fashion: as a combination of words and images; it will still be organized as a multiresolutional representation [20]. Using multigranular representation is a commonplace, although it is not always done explicitly; sometimes, multiresolutional representations come in disguise (various interpretations of a hierarchical model accepted depend on the school of thought [21]). A system of representation for natural language–connected problems should consist of hierarchically organized levels such that each succeeding level is a result of generalizing (summarizing) the preceding one. This approach is outlined in papers on multiresolutional systems for planning and control [22, 23].

3.1.2 Computing with Words: A New Reality of Intelligent Systems Engineering

Let us be consistent. Now, we know what the systems (intelligent systems) are that we are supposed to focus on. These are systems with thinking, or with elements of functioning that are supposed to approximate thinking. These are systems with the ability to generalize, or summarize, and to reason with available generalizations. These systems are capable of making instantiations: After inference is done within the domain of generalization, we know how to apply the recommendations to any particular case represented by these generalizations. These systems are prone to using constructs of natural language at the input; they are also expected to output natural language statements. We visualize this nascent domain of the study of intelligent systems as a composition of several themes that are organized in a way similar to organization of the parts of this book.

3.2 PROBLEMS AND ISSUES OF COMPUTING WITH WORDS

The *scientific essence* of computing with words requires a symbolic (e.g., semiotical or mathematical) theory. In its stronger meaning, computing with words might be a novel concept of CW-motivated computer architecture, competing with the well-known concept of von Neumann computer architecture and expanding into expected evolving architectures. Von Neumann's computers employ mapping words, images, and symbols into the domain of numbers. The problem solving is being performed in this domain. After this, the solution is mapped back into the domain of world, images, and symbols. A question arises: Is it really necessary to move to the domain of numbers and then return? What if we compute in words directly instead of computing in numbers as everybody does now?

3.2.1 From Computing with Numbers to Computing with Words: Elements of a Theory[1]

Computing with words addresses the issue of the nature of mental computations or the architecture of mind. Concepts of the architecture of mind, contemplated in this book, frequently mimic the block diagrams of the von Neumann computer. The possibility of alternative approaches can be pursued on various conceptual avenues. One of them was unleashed by the idea of a *linguistic variable*, a term coined by Zadeh in 1965. If the idea of linguistic variable is evolved, the concepts of semantic spaces[2] will necessarily follow as the multidimensional spaces of meaning and the operations admissible for these spaces might be explored. The need to analyze the phenomenon of meaning leads us to the medium in which the meaning emerges. This medium is *knowledge representation*.

It is a tradition in science to view the use of natural languages in scientific theories as a manifestation of mathematical immaturity. However, what is not recognized to the extent that it should be is that adherence to this tradition carries a steep price. In particular, a direct consequence is that existing scientific theories do not have the capability to operate on perception-based information. Such important information is usually described in a natural language and is intrinsically imprecise, reflecting a fundamental limitation on the cognitive ability of humans to resolve detail and store information. This is the principal reason why existing scientific theories do not have the capability to operate on perception-based information. Similarly, the restricted expressive power of predicate-logic-based languages denies the possibility of defining many basic concepts, such as causality, resemblance, smoothness, and relevance in realistic terms. The price of mathematical precision is over-idealization and lack of robustness.

[1] Presented by Lotfi A. Zadeh in Chapter 2.
[2] This term was introduced by Burghard B. Rieger in Chapter 5.

In a significant departure from existing methods, the high expressive power of natural languages can be harnessed by constructing what is called a *precisiated natural language* (PNL). This is a subset of a natural language (NL), a subset that is equipped with constraint-centered semantics based natural language (CSNL) and is translatable into what is called the *generalized constraint language* (GCL). A central concept of GCL is that of a generalized constraint expressed as X isr R, where X is the constrained variable, R is the constraining relation, and isr (pronounced *ezar*) is a variable copula in which r is a discrete-valued variable whose value defines the way in which R constrains X.

Among the principal types of constraints are the following: possibilistic constraint, $r =$ blank, with R playing the role of the possibility distribution of X; veristic constraint, $r = v$, in which case R is the verity (truth) distribution of X; probabilistic constraint, $r = p$, in which case X is a random variable and R is its probability distribution; $r = rs$, in which case X is a fuzzy set–valued random variable (fuzzy random set) and R is its fuzzy set–valued probability distribution; and fuzzy graph constraint, $r = fg$, in which case X is a fuzzy set–valued variable and R is its fuzzy set–valued possibility distribution.

With these constraints serving as basic building blocks, which are analogous to terminal symbols in a formal language, more complex (composite) constraints may be constructed through the use of a grammar. Simple examples of composite constraints are: X isr R and X iss S; and if X isr R, then Y iss S, or, equivalently, Y iss S if X isr R. The collection of composite constraints forms the generalized constraint language (GCL). The semantics of GCL is defined by the rules that govern combination and propagation of generalized constraints. These rules coincide with the rules of inference in fuzzy logic (FL).

A key idea in PNL is that the meaning of a proposition, p, in PNL may be represented as a generalized constraint that is an element of GCL. Thus, translation of p into GCL is viewed as an explicitation of X, R, and r. In this sense, translation is equivalent to explicitation. The translate of p in GCL is referred to as its *canonical form* [CF(p)]. These concepts form the core of what is called *constraint-oriented semantics of natural languages* (CSNL).

In what ways does the concept of a precisiated natural language serve to enlarge the role of natural languages in scientific theories? Standing out in importance are the following.

1. By serving as a base for the methodologies of computing with words (CW) and the computational theory of perceptions (CTP). The importance of these methodologies derives from the fact that in real-world settings decision-relevant information is frequently a mixture of measurements and perceptions. Existing methods of decision analysis are measurement based and do not have the capability to operate on perception-based information. The computational theory of perceptions adds this capability to existing theories and thereby enhances their ability to deal with realistic problems.

2. By making it possible to compute with words rather than with numbers when numerical values of decision-relevant variables are not known with sufficient precision to justify the use of numerically based methods.
3. By making it possible to define concepts that are perception based rather than measurement based. Examples of such concepts are the concept of a usual value of a random variable, the concept of smoothness of a function, the concept of optimality in multicriterion optimization, and the concept of relevance in database search. In particular, in the context of decision analysis, it becomes possible and, in many cases, advantageous, to define the goals, constraints, dependencies, probabilities, utilities, and risk aversion in PNL rather than analytically or numerically. These are but a few examples of ways in which PNL-based methods can be used as addenda to existing numerically based methods.

The concept of a precisiated natural language and the associated methodologies of computing with words and the computational theory of perceptions open the door to a wide-ranging generalization and restructuring of existing theories, especially in the realms of information processing, decision, and control. In this perspective, what is very likely is that in coming years a number of basic concepts and techniques drawn from linguistics will be playing a much more important role in scientific theories than they do today.

3.3 THEORETICAL FUNDAMENTALS OF COMPUTING WITH WORDS

We believe that the efforts of numerous philosophers and scientists devoted to meaning extraction and truth representation are the fundamentals and the roots of computing with words. We should not pretend that we unveiled the problem and discovered the direction toward the solution. Nevertheless, we will discuss this area without alluding to the vast and productive results in philosophy of meaning and truth representation. There is a tacit scientific tradition of formulating both the problem and the solution within the domain of science. Thus our focus will be on the science of natural language and computer science, including linguistics and semiotics.

In each particular science, the feeling of an invisible boundary is always present. If one is trying to push the limits and receive the answers about reality from a particular scientific discipline, one always bumps into an invisible impenetrable obstacle no matter what discipline it is: physics, chemistry, astronomy, and so on. This obstacle is the language of this scientific discipline, which almost never allows for a direct and crisp translation into a natural language. And the science of natural language has its obstacle, too: the area of *thinking*, since the latter is carefully avoided by the science of psychology, including cognitive science. In this book we attempt to determine the motivation for CW research in two interlaced topics: *thinking* and *natural language*.

3.3.1 Models and Mechanisms of Thinking: A Multigranular Approach[3]

The goal of the analysis of thinking processes is to demonstrate the significance of the semiotic approach in the area of computing with words and intelligent systems in general. The massive and diverse contribution of scholars from a variety of domains allowed integrating some of the prior results. The intention was to sketch some possible avenues of simulating thinking processes in a contemporary computer. From *computing with numbers* toward *computing with words*, then toward *computing with thoughts*—this is the way that can be foreseen in the area of intelligent systems analysis and simulation.

We have introduced elementary operations of thinking, we evolved them into composite operations, and we ended up with operations of generalization and instantiation. These are the operations that produce concepts, generate metaphors, and summarize complex and long descriptions into simple and short summaries. It turns out that they can be simulated via a more understandable and reproducible set of operations, including focusing of attention, combinatorial search, and grouping. This is the arsenal of artifacts required for dealing with natural language when computing with words.

3.3.2 The Meaning of Words Is Granular: A Fuzzy Computational Semiotics[4]

Computing with words should deal directly with natural language, which is observable and accessible evidence of the processes of human cognition. Both cognitive processes and language structures are characterized by information granulation, organization, and causation. This thesis represents yet another version of bringing out the most useful of computing with words. This version details the intricate relationships among CW, cognitive science, and linguistics.

The theory of computing with words allows us to envision *semiotic cognitive information processing systems* (SCIPs). The heart of a semiotics characterization, of course, is a multilevel representational system. For dynamic cognitive models of natural language understanding, the system's theoretical view suggests that we accept natural language discourse as multiresolutionally structured results of semiotic processes. The body of representation required for applying relevant techniques is introduced in the form of semantic space. These theses are illustrated by a number of procedures whose properties are discussed as being implemented to realize language understanding by machine as a semiotic enactment of meaning constitution.

3.3.3 Extracting Information from Text[5]

So how can we apply the achievements of our information technology to help a person to scan large volumes of text (corpora) efficiently and end up with a discovery of

[3] Presented by Alexander M. Meystel in [27], Chapter 4, and partially in Chapter 11.

[4] Presented by Burghard B. Rieger in Chapter 5.

[5] Presented by Amit Bagga, Joyce Chai, and Alan Biermann in Chapter 6.

significant facts? The traditional approach has been to specialize on a narrow semantic domain and to construct a processor aimed at retrieving information in that domain only. Researchers have generally believed that the information extraction problem is so difficult that each such system must be oriented toward a particular user since there are many peculiarities of the individual domains.

To address the problem of creating such systems economically, some researchers have looked at techniques for automatic or semiautomatic construction of lexicons or sets of extraction rules for the domain. Most of these techniques have applied machine learning approaches to rules based on texts that have been annotated semantically. Either a preannotation of text is done by a human expert, or the rules are postprocessed by a human expert.

A domain-independent information extraction system is outlined that can be built if it can include a self-modifying feature that enables it to adapt to new domains automatically. Admittedly, any user knows the peculiarities involved and is able quickly to train the system to collect specific target facts. This is done by scanning a series of example articles using a special text-processing interface and leading the system through a particular retrieval routine. Then the system acquires the patterns that are to be used in the retrieval and applies them to any large database of text to extract the information of interest.

The creation of such a general-purpose extraction system requires the solution of many problems. For example, the word *bank* refers to a financial institution and not to the edge of a river. Any pattern designed to select financial institutions runs the risk of firing on river banks unless a mechanism is included to distinguish them. This mechanism is called *word sense disambiguation.*

3.3.4 Cognitive Sciences and Computing with Words[6]

Cognitive science explores and models the wide variety of exceptional physical and mental capabilities that human beings seem to possess. Many of them are performed without the need for precise measurements and accurate computations. As far as the cognitive sciences are concerned, computing with words and both of its components—the theory of fuzzy information granulation and the computational theory of perceptions—must be understood as a feasible modeling framework in developing theories of cognition. This is exemplified in a number of tasks that humans perform where "fuzzy information granulation seems to be employed in making rational decisions in an environment of partial knowledge, partial certainty and partial truth" [24]. It is possible to expect that the long-standing tradition of dealing with perceptions by converting them into measurements will slowly get phased out. People are recognizing that "the conversion of perceptions into measurements is infeasible, unrealistic or counter productive" [25].

The exponential growth in computational power available through today's computing devices is making the move from representing measurements to representing

[6] Presented by Benjoe A. Juliano in Chapter 7.

perceptions in a verbal (or otherwise symbolic) form seem to be more feasible. This will lead to an increase in the role of natural languages in scientific and industrial research. This should affect substantially the paradigm in the discipline of cognition. A concerted effort among the cognitive science community and those supporting the computing with words movement should bring about more concrete and interesting results that will take us closer to a unified theory of cognition. We should all recognize this. After all, most of the researchers in the area of intelligent systems, including intelligent control, fuzzy logic, and neural networks, are cognitive scientists, to some degree or other, in our quest to understand more about ourselves, our cognitive capabilities, and all our limitations.

3.4 FROM LINGUISTICS TO FUZZY GRANULARITY: KNOWLEDGE REPRESENTATION

The topic of *knowledge representation* for computing with words is characterized by our intention to demonstrate that natural language is the entrance to the most powerful system of representation adequate to solving a vast multiplicity of problems. Our brain is dealing with knowledge, and a huge part of this knowledge seems to be represented in a way relevant to natural language. The phenomenon of *knowledge* is a key factor in our computing. It does not seem that we compute in *numbers*; rather, we compute in *entities*, or speaking in a more pragmatic manner, in *objects, events*, and *actions*. It seems that our mind tends to compute using all of the available carriers of knowledge, and these carriers emerge as a result of lumping representations in space as well as in time. So what do we arrive at, words? It seems that words are unavoidable. However, visual images should also be found among the ground structures. But why only visual images? All kinds of perceptual inputs should be represented, possibly, with the help of a flexible structure of symbols.

The tendency to lump thoughts in words and other symbols seems to be plausible. The possibility of dealing with continua of meanings without lumping them into symbols is looming, and there is a suspicion that our brain employs this capability, too. Even in this book, there is a temptation to address thinking processes that expand beyond the customary world of words. It would be prudent to anticipate that not only are words the carriers of meaning: It is safe to propose that these carriers are both *words* and any type of perceptual *images*. Still, it leaves us not totally satisfied. Perhaps there are other symbols, too? (What is this: other symbols?) In the beginning of this paragraph an expression to "lump thoughts in words" was used, from which a variety of ideas might percolate[7]: for example, that the phenomenon of thought is a continuous one and that its discretization into words brings the meaning to our consciousness.

[7]Obviously, we are talking about the phenomena of generalization/summarization.

3.4.1 Combining Linguistic Information in a Distributed Intelligent Agent Model for Information Gathering on the Internet[8]

Linguistic variables are variables whose values are not numbers but words or sentences in a natural or artificial language. The management of linguistic information uses operators such as *comparison* or *aggregation*. Delgado et al. propose the concept of a linguistic weighted averaging (LWA) operator as a tool to aggregate linguistic weighted information. This operator is very helpful, as it incorporates more flexibility in the information-gathering and communication process.

The results presented in this chapter are very timely because they are applicable to information handling in a distributed intelligent agent model on the Internet. The authors have worked out an example in sufficient detail to show how promising applications on the Internet can be carried out. The usefulness of the concept of the linguistic variables and CW is fully demonstrated, at least in certain aspects, in an important and timely topic of research. The operators in general are important in the processing of fuzzy information. The significance is enhanced when we have more complicated uncertainty modeling, such as multiple agents on the Internet.

3.5 LEARNING: KNOWLEDGE ACQUISITION IN FUZZY GRANULAR SYSTEMS

3.5.1 Numeric Robustness and Linguistic Perspicuity: A Hybrid Approach to Knowledge Acquisition[9]

Two dimensions of knowledge are introduced. The first dimension is articulate versus inarticulate knowledge (quality versus quantity). The second dimension is declarative versus procedural knowledge (fact versus skill). The hybrid approach to knowledge acquisition uses robust numerical models, perspicuous linguistic models, and human expertise. The first step in generating a hybrid model is to fit a first-order model to a set of training examples containing predictor variables and a criterion variable. The second step is to convert the numerical outputs of the first-order model into a consistent set of ordinal categories based on the quantiles of the numeric model's output. The ordinal category assigned each training case, paired with the case's predictor variable values, makes up the training data for the second-order model generated by the rule induction algorithm.

Automated knowledge acquisition (AKA) refers to a body of techniques that accept a database of examples and generate a formal system that displays expertlike behavior. Each example consists of a set of predictor variables and one or more criterion variables; the resulting formal system takes the predictor variables for new cases as inputs and outputs the predicted value(s) of the criterion variable(s). The concept of AKA is very similar to the concept of machine learning. Three important

[8]Presented by M. Delgado, F. Herrera, E. Herrera-Viedma, M. J. Martin-Bautista, and M. A. Vila in Chapter 8.

[9] Presented by Thomas Whalen and Gwangyong Gim in Chapter 9.

classes of AKA techniques are regressionlike techniques, supervised artificial neural networks, and rule induction.

The rule sets that simple example-based inductive mechanisms create can help knowledge engineers and domain experts during the early stages of knowledge acquisition. A computer-generated expert system, especially in the form of if–then rules, can do a better job of inspiring an expert to make improvements and corrections than a blank page and a request to "tell what you know" can. There is no guarantee that knowledge structures arising from AKA will represent meaningful ontological categories or causal relations. However, they can stimulate a human expert to better conceptualization and communication of his or her expertise.

Traditional epistemology has assumed that we acquire and represent knowledge symbolically by a collection of declarative sentences (or sentencelike expressions) that represent facts about the world. We observe ourselves conversing, writing, and lecturing by means of natural or technical language, and stating conclusions based on making inferences through transmitted sentences. Knowledge that is built up by joining together groups of sentencelike expressions is referred to as *articulate* knowledge, since the word *articulate* means "composed of distinct, meaningful syllables or words."

Some of what we know how to do, we can also explain using natural language, perhaps augmented with a technical vocabulary. However, there are also many things we know how to do without being able to state linguistically how we do them. The former case we refer to as *articulate procedural knowledge*, the latter as *inarticulate procedural knowledge*. Inarticulate knowledge is difficult to express in "meaningful syllables or words" in part because it is a relatively seamless unity of sensation perception, and action—it does not consist of conceptual "sections united by joints." Even some of our declarative knowledge has an inarticulate element; for example, we may be able to name an image without being able to describe it or give rules for recognizing it. Much of the discipline of knowledge engineering has consisted of techniques for turning inarticulate knowledge into articulate knowledge prior to transcribing the knowledge into symbolic computer codes.

3.5.2 Principles of Word-Based Knowledge Representation and Knowledge Processing for CW[10]

Computing with words presumes relying on having problems of knowledge representation resolved prior to starting various CW procedures. The theories of *knowledge representation and organization* for CW are related to the notion of *fuzzy syntax, knowledge organization, and interpretation*—to formation of *fuzzy semantic fields*, and *knowledge generation and utilization*—to *fuzzy pragmatics*. These three areas belong to the body of semiotics and are applicable to knowledge transmitted by any kind of sign system. We focus on the subset of it denoted by a term we have not defined yet: *word-based knowledge* (WBK).

[10]Presented by Alexander M. Meystel in Chapter 11.

Theoretical approaches relevant to CW are extremely diversified, and they are dispersed within sources related to application domains. Their consideration would first require a discussion of general principles of WBK representation for CW. The following principles of dealing with WBK should be discussed as a prerequisite for developing the theory of computing with words: (1) principle of thesaural interpretation of words assignment (labeling), (2) principle of entity-relational WBK representation, (3) principle of multiresolutional representation coarsening/refinement, or principle of nested hierarchical representation, (4) principle of heterogeneity, or principle of multiple WBK representation systems, (5) causality principle, (6) principle of efficiency, (7) principle of incompleteness, (8) feedforward principle, (9) principle of feedback, (10) principle of limited resource, (11) principle of continuity, and (12) principle of creativity. These principles are organized in a manner that allows for consecutive building up the conceptual background with a gradual increase in complexity of the issues involved.

3.6 REASONING WITH WORD-BASED KNOWLEDGE

Next we introduce the issue of *reasoning*, where all the consequences of computing with words come out as advantages, or failures, and the perspectives of our new approach possibly reside. Undeniably, all tools of representation are as good as the result of them can be applied for reasoning. For developing the most advanced actions and behaviors, the phenomenon of *reasoning* is required. The original lumping is performed in our perceptual system (e.g., in vision). Even very underdeveloped creatures can distinguish their prey from the background; thus the mechanisms of reasoning should provide for and deal with *lumping*. Perhaps such lumping and memories of lumping are equivalent to *words*. Nevertheless, the human ability to lump visually is affected by our existing word-based knowledge representation and the way we reason about it. Probably, images generate a pra-vocabulary of representation, and animals compute in something like this "primordial" vocabulary, which relies on the simplest tools of reasoning.

The growth of the volume of computations led to more sophisticated signs and symbols; words emerged. Then other symbols invade our mind together with the mechanisms for reasoning about them. This was stimulated by the need to increase the efficiency of our overburdened system of verbal representation. This is how the abstract numbers emerged instead of having three different words for 10 sheep, 10 apples, and 10 fingers. In any case, this evolution from reasoning with images, to reasoning with words, to more abstract reasoning with signs/symbols is unquestionable.

3.6.1 Computing with Descriptive and Veristic Words: Knowledge Representation and Reasoning[11]

Within a framework of fuzzy system modeling, it is the general practice to initiate reasoning within the domain of linguistic knowledge either acquired from an expert

[11] Presented by I. B. Türkşen in Chapter 10.

via an interview and/or from an algorithm data processing of historical information. It is usually expressed in terms of *descriptive words*. The *veristic words* that assert the truth of the descriptive knowledge is expressed either implicitly or explicitly. When the veristic assessment is expressed explicitly, it is possible to form fuzzy truth tables and to derive FDNF (fuzzy disjunctive normal forms) and FCNF (fuzzy conjunctive normal forms) expressions. Both FDNF and FCNF expressions allow us to construct metalingustic expressions and solve problems of containment and equivalence. Thus the laws of reasoning are developed for two adjacent levels of resolution (granularity and scale), and the processes of generalization and instantiation are supported by theoretical apparatus.

It is quite clear that in computing with words, we need to implement several stages of development in building a rule base for system modeling, analysis, prediction, decision, and control. Based on the classical theory of DNF and CNF, it is possible to generalize many of the new results that provide a bird's-eye view of what needs to be accomplished in CW to set the stage for implementation of a practical working system.

3.6.2 Fuzzy Qualitative Reasoning with Words[12]

Human beings employ mostly words and qualitative descriptions when providing assessments of situations or reasoning about complex physical or human systems. The order-of-magnitude reasoning is investigated in terms of closeness and negligibility relations. It is shown that computation can be handled at the word level. Qualitative reasoning has to be propagated about relative orders of magnitude where fuzzy constraints express closeness or negligibility relations.

Fuzzy relations can indeed provide appropriate semantics for inference rules about relative orders of magnitude. It is emphasized that reasoning with relative orders of magnitude can be seen as a particular type of fuzzy constraint satisfaction problem. Fuzzy qualitative reasoning with words is demonstrated to be a rigorously proven and practically important tool of CW. Qualitative reasoning is a well-established subarea in artificial intelligence. The way this particular type of reasoning is handled in a fuzzy set setting could exemplify a substantial part of computing with words. CW is more than just dealing with linguistic variables. Linguistic variables are at the core of Zadeh's approximate reasoning methodology. It is more than approximate reasoning applied to fuzzy relative orders of magnitude, in the sense that the fuzzy approximate reasoning machinery is fully captured at a purely symbolic level by means of rules from which the formal parametrized labels are inferred at the word level and are interfaced with a semantics expressed in terms of fuzzy sets when needed.

[12]Presented by Didier Dubois, Allel Hadj-Ali, and Henri Prade in Chapter 12.

3.6.3 Granular Relational Computing with Semiotic Descriptors Using BK-Products of Fuzzy Relations[13]

The importance of fuzzy relational representation is demonstrated here within a CW setting. Fuzzy relational BK-products[14] have been demonstrated with all their power and usefulness. Relational representation makes it possible to perform all the computations and decision making in a uniform relational way by means of these special relational compositions (BK-products). This integration is extended further by showing how the relational approach can be used for computing with words.

The basic concepts of CW emphasize the importance of information granularity and construction of representations at various granularities (scales and resolutions). Then the semiotics and relational properties as well as BK-products of relations are a built-in component of the relational operations. A new generic architecture for fuzzy relational computing with words is introduced.

3.7 BEHAVIOR GENERATION IMPLIED FROM WORDS

All thinking processes succeed if they result in successful behavior. Neither concepts nor intellect are goals for an intelligent system as a whole. Its goal is its output behavior. Thus *behavior generation and control* with words are addressed. Several chapters of this book are dedicated to control with words or using verbs in behavior generation. Something is lacking, though: Why not "control with images" or "using nice-looking curvatures in behavior generation"? On the other hand, in the domain of behavior generation, the processes are not intrinsically lumped into corresponding words. In most cases, lumping is practiced by our minds, to make our decision-making processes easier. Errorless movements of animals accurately reaching the goal are performed as a result of joint activities of thousands of elementary muscle tissues without apparent decomposition of the continuous motion into lumped elementary components. When we analyze these movements, we tend to assign labels to them, just as we assign labels to continuous automobile maneuvers: U-turn, backing up, and so on. This creates doubts: Do we really compute with words? Perhaps not just with words; perhaps visual images should be incorporated into the discourse.

3.7.1 Computational Verb Systems: Computing with Perceptions[15]

For a full-scale expert system, verbs and their handling are extremely important. In a sense, verbs are the basic building blocks for transferring and representing human experience. Because of the unique world of verb systems, their significance in linguistics, especially semantics, cannot be overestimated. Mathematical and quantita-

[13] Presented by Ladislav J. Kohout, Bobby Granville, and Eunjin Kim in Chapter 4.
[14] The results obtained by Kohout and Bandler.
[15] Presented by Tao Yang in Chapter 13.

tive treatment within the CW framework will enhance the utility value of CW in a rather large way in the future.

In English grammar, as well as in the grammars of other human natural languages, phrases that use nouns and verbs are two types of elementary elements. According to Yang, nouns represent things that are found or perceived by humans, while verbs are words that are generated and/or acted by humans. The term *computational verb* is introduced by the author. To embed the dynamic experiences coded by verbs into machines, verbs are modeled explicitly and quantitatively by dynamic systems called *computational verbs*. Thus a verb used in symbolic logic, unfortunately, loses its dynamics. The backbone of the computational verb system is the pattern thinking, which is utilized very efficiently by human brains. These views invite many prospective debates to the main issues of CW.

In the discussion of comparative role of noun and verb phrases, the philosophical argument and historical notes are of considerable interest. The important factor of "time arrow" should be taken in consideration in the discussion of the issue.

Yang's physical interpretation in his prologue is also of substantial interest. He says that an electronic digital computer is a simulation running in an analogue computer based on electromagnetic dynamics of silicon. Similarly, a human linguistic system is a symbolic simulation running in an analogue structure called the human brain. The author raises an interesting question: Why can the human species survive complexities painlessly while digital computers (no matter how powerful they may be) can not? The answer is that our brains simulate the complexities in correct ways while the digital computers so far simulate them inappropriately.

REFERENCES

1. J. B. Watson, *Behaviorism*, W. W. Norton, New York, 1930.
2. L. A. Zadeh, Fuzzy sets, *Inf. Control*, 8:338–353, 1965.
3. R. E. Bellman and L. A. Zadeh, Decision-making in a fuzzy environment, *Manage. Sci.*, 17:141–164, 1970.
4. L. A. Zadeh, Similarity relations and fuzzy ordering, *Inf. Sci.*, 3:177–200, 1971.
5. L. A. Zadeh, Fuzzy languages and their relation to human and machine intelligence, in *Proc. International Conference on Man and Computer*, Bordeaux, France, 1972, pp. 130–165.
6. L. A. Zadeh, Outline of a new approach to the analysis of complex systems and decision processes, *IEEE Trans. Syst. Man Cybern.*, 3:28–44, 1973.
7. W. Kohler, *Gestals Psychology*, Liveright, New York, 1970.
8. L. J. Kohout, The dynamics of generalization: from fuzzy linguistic statements to concepts and constructs, in *Intelligent Systems: A Semiotic Perspective, Proc. 1996 International Multidisciplinary Conference*, Vol. I, *Theoretical Semiotics*, Gaithersburg, MD, 1996, pp. 77–82.
9. R. R. Yager and D. P. Filev, Generation of fuzzy rules of mountain clustering, *J. Intell. Fuzzy Syst.*, 2:209–219, 1994.

10. L. A. Zadeh, The concept of a linguistic variable and its application to approximate reasoning, Part I, *Inf. Sci.*, 8:199–249, 1975; Part II, *Inf. Sci.*, 8:301–357, 1975; Part III, *Inf. Sci.*, 9:43–80, 1975.
11. R. Montague, in R. Thomason (ed.), *Formal Philosophy: The Collected Papers of Richard Montague*, Yale University Press, New Haven, CT, 1974.
12. D. Dowty, *Word Meaning and Montague Grammar*, D. Reidel, Dordrecht, The Netherland, 1979.
13. L. A. Zadeh, PRUF: a meaning representation language for natural languages, *Intl. J. Man–Mach. Stud.*, 10:395–460, 1978.
14. L. A. Zadeh, A computational approach to fuzzy quantifiers in natural languages, *Comput. Math.*, 9:149–184, 1983; abridged version in *Proc. 4th Conference of the Canadian Conference for Computational Studies of Intelligence*, Saskatoon, Saskatchewan, Canada, 1982, pp. 116–120.
15. W. Gale, K. Church, and D. Yarowsky, A method for disambiguating word senses in a large corpus, *Comput. Human.*, 5–6:415–439, 1992.
16. T. Pedersen, R. Bruce, and J. Wiebe, Sequential model selection for word sense disambiguation, in *Proc. 1997 Conference on Applied Natural Language Processing (ANLP-97)*, Washington, DC, Apr. 1997.
17. H. T. Ng and H. B. Lee, *Integrating Multiple Knowledge Sources to Disambiguate Word Sense: An Exemplar-Based Approach*, Tech. Rep., Defence Science Organization, Singapore, 1996.
18. L. A. Zadeh, A fuzzy-algorithmic approach to the definition of complex or imprecise concepts, *Int. J. Man–Mach. Stud.*, 8:249–291, 1976.
19. J. McCarthy, Generality in artificial intelligence, *Commun. ACM*, 30(12):1030–1035, 1987.
20. A. Simon, J.-C. Pret, and A. P. Johnson, A fast algorithm for bottom-up document layout analysis, *IEEE Trans. Pattern Anal. Mach. Intelli.*, 19(3):273–277, 1997.
21. P. P. Wang, Soft modeling for intelligent and complex systems, in A. M. Meystel (ed.), *Proc. 1997 International Conference on Intelligent Systems and Semiotics: A Learning Perspective*, Gaithersburg, MD, 1997, pp. 415–421.
22. A. Meystel, Theoretical foundations of planning and navigation for autonomous mobile systems, *Int. J. Intell. Syst.*, 2(2), 1987.
23. J. Albus and A. Meystel, A reference model architecture for design and implementation of intelligent control in large and complex systems, *Int. J. Intell. Control Syst.*, 1(1):15–30, 1996.
24. L. A. Zadeh, Toward a theory of fuzzy information granulation and its centrality in human reasoning in fuzzy logic, *Fuzzy Sets Syst.*, 90(2):111–127, 1997.
25. L. A. Zadeh, From computations with measurements to computations with perceptions, *Abst. BISC Seminar*, Sept. 16, 1999.
26. L. A. Zadeh, An e-mail letter to BISC-group, October 21, 1998.
27. A. Meystel, *Semiotic Modeling and Situation Analysis: An Introduction*, AdRem, Bala Cynwyd, PA, 1995.

CHAPTER 4

GRANULAR RELATIONAL COMPUTING WITH SEMIOTIC DESCRIPTORS USING BK-PRODUCTS OF FUZZY RELATIONS

LADISLAV J. KOHOUT
Florida State University, Tallahassee, Florida

BOBBY GRANVILLE
Florida A&M University, Tallahassee, Florida

EUNJIN KIM
Florida State University, Tallahassee, Florida

4.1 RELATIONAL ARCHITECTURES FOR COMPUTING WITH SEMIOTIC DESCRIPTORS

We have been engaged in the development of fuzzy relational architectures for intelligent systems and robotic systems [46]. The integrating framework is provided by means of fuzzy relational computations. Relational representation makes it possible to perform all the computations and decision making in a uniform relational way by means of special relational compositions, BK-products [60]. The purpose of this chapter is to extend this integration further by showing how the relational approach we have developed can be used for computing with words (CW).

The chapter starts with an overview of basic notions of computing with words, emphasizing particularly the importance of information granularity. The semiotics and some relational properties of granularity are touched upon in Section 4.3. The mathematics of relations and BK-products of relations are reviewed in Section 4.4. Section 4.5 is concerned with the semiotics of relational computations. In the

Computing with Words, Edited by Paul P. Wang.
ISBN 0-471-35374-4

remainder of the chapter a new generic architecture for fuzzy relational computing with words is described.

4.1.1 Scope and Merits of Relational Computations

The conceptual content of computations is often neglected by computer scientists outside the area of artificial intelligence (AI) and knowledge engineering. But this important domain should interact with soft computing methods. In the realm of intelligent systems we need integration of the approaches of soft computing and computing with words. Relational computing platforms may facilitate such integration.

Zadeh singles out three areas of computer applications—numerical analysis, large databases, and knowledge engineering—as highly important in construction of information-intelligent systems. Unfortunately, in computer science these are often treated separately. It is the conceptual analysis within the semiotic framework, *placed into* the formal and computational setting of fuzzy relations, that can provide the essential integration of these three important areas. It can also link these with the new important area of symbolic mathematical computing.

Kohout, Anderson, Bandler, Stabile, and others have shown in a series of papers (e.g., Refs. 38,53,54,67,74,75, and 77) that fuzzy relations present a *unifying framework* for integrating different techniques, such as fuzzy approximate reasoning, interval computations, logic inference using nonassociative compositions of relations, semiotic descriptors, and diffuse computations in neural networks.

We have departed radically from established practice and used fuzzy relational structures not only for inference and knowledge representation, but also for providing *dynamic protection* structures [34,57] in order to increase the trustworthiness of intelligent systems. We also use fuzzy relational methods for retrieval of objects in knowledge and databases [58].

Conceptual computations based on semiotic descriptors are at the heart of our integrative approach to computing with words. The methodology that is used as a working tool in this endeavor is the activity structures methodology [41,43,45]. It uses the general systems constructs that forge integration of essential tools of computer science and engineering within the framework of cross-disciplinary interaction with other disciplines.

Activity structures methodology is designed to deal with concurrent activities and is directly compatible with fuzzy relational methods. It provides a good model of concurrent activities, in which both desirable and undesirable side effects can be captured in fuzzy relations and their dynamic effects computed by fast fuzzy relational algorithms [41,43,45,46,51,55].

The methods of knowledge elicitation, knowledge representations, and fuzzy relational algorithms for analysis need to be integrated into a coherent framework to deal with the problems of building CW systems. There is a lesson to learn from knowledge engineering. Our activity structures [41,45] can provide tools for such integration (see also Ref. 43, in particular Chap. 10). Semiotic aspects are discussed in that book in Section 10.9.

4.2 BASIC NOTIONS OF COMPUTING WITH WORDS

4.2.1 What Is Computing with Words?

According to Zadeh [89], CW should provide a conceptual framework for computing and reasoning with words rather with numbers. The basic idea underlying CW is that, in general, information is conveyed by constraining the values that a linguistic variable can take.

1. The information given is represented as a collection of propositions expressed in a natural language.
2. Each proposition is viewed as an implicit constraint on an implicit variable.
3. For the purposes of computation, it is necessary to make such constraints explicit.
4. This leads to the concept of a *canonical form* which serves to make explicit (both) the variable that is constrained and the constraining relation.
5. Once the implicit constraints in the premise propositions are made explicit through the use of canonical forms, the rules of inference in fuzzy logic can be employed to propagate fuzzy constraints from premises to conclusions.
6. Finally, the constraints induced are translated into a natural language.

Conceptual computations take such interrelationships into consideration. One of the approaches that can capture the semiotics of computing with concepts is the activity structures methodology [43] mentioned briefly above. This methodology is rooted in the interdisciplinary approach of general systems, making it applicable not only in computer science and engineering, but also eminently suitable for interdisciplinary integration of computing with other disciplines. Within the activity structures approach we define semiotic descriptors [45] that are in certain mutual semantic relationships, much as in physics, where the measured quantities are related via conceptual dependencies of dimensional analysis. The only difference is that semiotic descriptors are linguistic entities that provide linguistic constraints, while dimensionless entities of dimensional analysis of physics yield mathematical constraints. Both can be expressed algebraically, however, within an appropriate calculus of relations.

4.2.2 Fuzzy Logics: A Tool for Decision Making

In decision making, extensions of sets and decision logics to the fuzzy domain are highly desirable. From the standpoint of science, a statement is either true or false. Every physician, lawyer, or manager, however, knows that some statements may not be simply true or false, but just irrelevant. Furthermore, certain management decisions may be graded by the degree of their plausibility. This fact is conveniently captured by fuzzy sets.

Klir [37] succinctly explains why scientific, engineering, and management methodologies are enhanced substantially by allowing grades of membership in sets and relations, and degrees of truth in propositions. All four characteristics are extremely important in the context of the computing with words by means of granular structures.

1. Fuzzy sets and logics possess far greater capability to capture irreducible measurement uncertainties than their classical counterparts. This makes a better bridge between mathematical models and the associated physical reality.
2. The capability of fuzzy sets to capture gradual transitions from one set to another considerably enhances their expressive power. Hence, by using these, one can deal effectively with a broader class of problems.
3. An important feature of the theory of fuzzy sets and relations is their capability to capture the vagueness of linguistic terms in statements of natural language, thus providing us with a greater capability to model more realistically human commonsense reasoning, decision making, and other aspects of human cognition.
4. Fuzzy sets and logics are powerful tools for managing complexity and controlling computational costs.

Both fuzzy sets and fuzzy logics can be subsumed in the more universal framework of fuzzy relations. Ordinary non fuzzy sets and relations then become special cases of our more universal framework of fuzzy relations. Fuzzy relations themselves are many-valued logic-based extensions of crisp (i.e., nonfuzzy) mathematical relations. This extendibility property guarantees that any fuzzy computation will default into a standard crisp (i.e., nonfuzzy) computation with crisp (nonfuzzy) data.

4.2.3 Role of Fuzzy Information Granulation in CW

The notion of *granularity* was introduced into fuzzy sets by Zadeh. In his interpretation, granulation involves a decomposition of the whole into the parts, and conversely, *organization* involves an integration of parts into the whole. The notion of granularity is helpful in studies of any system with complex structures. To deal with granularity in intelligent systems, the potential of fuzzy logic to approximate is to be explored. According to Zadeh [89]: "Exploitation of the tolerance for imprecision is an issue of central importance in Computing with Words (CW). In CW, a word is viewed as a label of a granule; that is, a fuzzy set of points drawn together by similarity, with the fuzzy set playing the role of a fuzzy constraint on a variable."

In semiotic terms, a word w is a label of a granule g, and conversely, g is the denotation of w. The denotation may be a higher-order predicate. In this chapter we deal primarily with *relations* in their *predicate form*.[1] Because a granule g is a fuzzy constraint on a variable, the denotation also induces a correspondence between words and fuzzy variables.

[1]It should be realized that the predicate form R_P of a relation R is in general intensional while its satisfaction set R_S is always extensional. For the definition of R_P and R_S, see Section 4.4.1.

Given a query in words that defines a computational task or problem, the appropriate semantic constraints that are contained implicitly in natural language propositions have to be made explicit—that is, the appropriate denotations have to be produced.

From this information new constraints have to be computed according to what is required, in order to reach the conclusion of that computational problem. The computed solution has to be expressed in linguistic form again, pairing the solution–denotation with the appropriate labels.

Put in operational terms, two main issues arise in CW:

1. *Representation of fuzzy constraints.* The constraints are implicit only in the propositions expressed in a natural language. The methods for making these explicit are required.
2. *Fuzzy constraints propagation.* The fuzzy constraints in premises have to be propagated to conclusions. Appropriate calculi of fuzzy constraint propagations are required.

Zadeh [89, p. 110] succinctly expressed the two main challenges of CW that have to be dealt with to be successful. The first is linked to the issue of representation of fuzzy constraints: "Given a collection of premises expressed in a natural language, we can, in principle, express them in their canonical forms and thereby explicate the implicit fuzzy constraints. For this purpose we have to employ test-score semantics. However, in test-score semantics we do not have at present effective algorithms for the derivation of canonical forms without human intervention. This is a problem that remains to be addressed." The second challenge is linked with fuzzy constraint propagation: "In using fuzzy constraint propagation rules in computing with words, applications of the extension principle generally reduce to the solution of a non-linear program. What we need—and do not have at present—are approximate methods of solving such programs which are capable of exploiting the tolerance for imprecision."

At the current state of the art, it is possible to deal with Zadeh's challenge if the problem is restricted to a specific metaframework that provides a sufficiently general set of constraints within which the conversion can be done automatically by a computer with human supervision. This requires having generic canonical forms that can be specialized within a specific knowledge domain according to the topic at hand.

Relations in their predicate form, together with special relational compositions, offer the required *parallelism* between the algebraic form of relational predicates and restricted linguistic statement in a natural language. This parallelism is twofold:

1. *Logical parallelism*: a correspondence of meaning of logical and linguistic operators
2. *Semiotic parallelism*: a denotational correspondence—linguistic forms and relational semiotic descriptors denoting the same granules

Logical parallelism is enforced by the operational and dynamic properties of BK-products of relations. How this works is explained in Section 4.4 when we give the needed elementary mathematical and logic prerequisites concerning relations, their products and generalized morphisms.

Semiotic parallelism requires development of a rich generic semiotic framework, in particular the framework of general systems constructs, semiotic descriptors, and algebra of relational properties that are used for classifying granules employed in computations according to their taxonomical types, which are partly generic and partly dependent on the nature of knowledge of the application domain described by linguistic statements.

We start with the latter and discuss the link of relational properties with relational specification of granules in Section 4.3.1. This will naturally lead us to multiple levels of relational systems where the fuzzy objects are structural configurations of granules. This is illustrated in Section 4.7 by a case study of a granular system taken from the medical domain.

4.3 SEMIOTICS AND MATHEMATICS OF GRANULARITY

4.3.1 Relational Characterization of Types of Granularity

The notion of granulation as an activity leading to producing a granule is described by Zadeh [90] as follows: "Granulation of an object A leads to a collection of granules of A, with a granule being a clump of points (objects) drawn together by indistinguishability, similarity, proximity or functionality. ... When we talk about fuzzy information granulation we are not talking about a single granule; we are talking about a collection of fuzzy granules which result from granulating a crisp or fuzzy object."

We shall be concerned with *similarity* and *functionality* as the organizing principles forming granules. In relational terms, what Zadeh calls similarity is a fuzzy relation that is reflexive, symmetric, and transitive. An entire family of fuzzy similarity relations can be formed by functionalities. Each distinct function may draw together points into a different fuzzy similarity class. Because different functionalities can be related, collections (families) of granules might also be related by functional correspondences or congruences induced by the granules-forming process.

So we are concerned with two kinds of relations with special properties that characterize special kinds of granules structurally:

1. *Similaritylike*: fuzzy tolerances, which are reflexive and symmetric, and fuzzy equivalences, which are transitive tolerance relations
2. *Orderlike*: preorder and (partial) order

The equivalence relation underlies every classification, and it is indeed the case that every well-organized *system* of classification (such as those of zoology and botany) can be subsumed in a single fuzzy equivalence relation. Of the *orderlike* relation there are two subspecies: *order* (the mathematicians' "partial order")—reflexive, transitive, and antisymmetric—and *preorder*—reflexive and transitive with no restriction as to symmetry or antisymmetry. The latter is much more common in empirical cognitive data, especially in its fuzzy version, from economic preferences to implications (by definition or use) among keywords in the realm of information retrieval and among constructs in the realm of cognitive attribution.

The orderlike relational structures are of particular interest because they are also linked to human cognition. Analyzing complex problems requires that people employ multiple levels of abstraction, simultaneously embedding layers of meaning and representation. Relational descriptions clarify how these levels are utilized in reasoning of experts. Hence they are important not only in the design of intelligent systems, but also in computing with words, because of their connections to the issues of granularity.

In 1971, Zadeh extended mathematics concerning reflexivity, symmetry, and transitivity to fuzzy relations in a now classic paper [88]. From the point of view of applicability of relational methods to representation and analysis of structures, this is a very significant extension, as it allows for approximation of the crisp structures by fuzzy ones. Thus one may identify approximate similarities, approximate equivalences and orders, and so on, in relational structures representing knowledge.

4.3.2 Semiotic Relational Models for Capturing Granularity

Granulation is in fact an organizing principle that is related to abstraction. When granules are formed at a particular resolution level, some features are not distinguished because of lack of information, and some features are irrelevant in the given context. Other features are relevant and factor objects into some, often coherent, "fuzzy clouds" called *granules*. To explore the granular structures in computing with words, we need in addition to abstract principles of aggregation, some concrete means for acquisition, representation, and further computational processing of granular structures. Relational semiotic structures are such representation media.

Scheme for Constructing Semiotic Relational Models. To capture the real world in a symbolic representation that adequately reflects the properties and relationships about the entities of this world, some general normative principles that safeguard against distortions of representations have to be obeyed. Only representations so safeguarded ought to be used for information-intelligent systems.[2]

In this chapter we discuss symbolic representations of a relational type to be used for the representation of knowledge in information-intelligent systems exploring the paradigm of computing with words. In our applications we are concerned with multi-environment intelligent systems [53] that combine and interleave the information of various scientific, engineering, and societal domains as required by real-world appli-

[2]The name information-intelligent systems was coined by Zadeh to emphasize the importance of information-processing aspects in those intelligent systems whose primary purpose is to process, analyze, and interpret information [76]. This was done to distinguish these systems from intelligent controllers, systems in which the purpose is to perform primarily control engineering tasks. In many applications of intelligent systems (e.g., manufacturing) it is necessary to combine aspects of intelligent control with intelligent information management [47].

cations [22,73]. In such multienvironment applications, it is essential to deal with the context dependency [71] and locality of meaning [49] and relevance.

Semiotic system models capturing the *relevance of the given situation* can be constructed computationally by applying the following steps [7,45]:

1. Select features judged to be significant; discard the irrelevant ones (proper subset of the original).
2. Reduce details by grouping similar cases together (partition of the data into equivalence classes or blocks).
3. Represent the result of step 2 in a model (isomorphism).

Relational semiotic structures thus obtained may contain intrinsic relational properties that represent some invariants of meaning.

Information about relational properties possessed by semiotic relational structures is important for invariant representation of various semantic features in an appropriate semantic space. This is so because relational properties extract important semantic distinctions between various concepts captured by these structures. For example, knowledge of interactions of various parts of a relational structure is one such important issue.

One may ask: What are the actual mechanisms for selection of relevant features? The answer is that this depends on the nature of the agent or system that performs this selection [49]. Although we are concerned here with artifacts, computing systems, such selection is also performed in natural systems, by perceptual mechanisms in an animal or human brain. We cannot go into detail here; see Ref. 43 for a deeper discussion of these issues.

Approximation of Meaning in Fuzzy Semiotic Models. Because in fuzzy relations, relational properties may hold or be absent either fully or *to a degree*, the extension to *fuzzy relations* gives us important tools for approximation of meaning.

Computing closures and interiors over relations that have some properties partially but not completely provides an additional mechanism that makes it possible to generate approximate meaning invariants in semiotic relational structures. This is supported computationally by fast fuzzy relational algorithms [6,11] for computing fuzzy closures and interiors of relations of required properties.

Combined with the modeling procedure above, fuzzy relations also provide high-level knowledge representation language and computational procedures that can be used for identification and representation of granules contained intrinsically in empirical data. Such data can be obtained, for example, by linguistic questionnaires and repertory grids from which we can computationally extract relational representations of linguistically expressed knowledge.

4.3.3 Locality of Granular Structures and the Problem of Relevance

So far, we have discussed special cases of granular structures: for example, crisp or fuzzy equivalences, similarities, congruences, and hierarchies that exhibit the *global property*: All elements of the granular structures must participate because of the (global) reflexivity. It is, however, well known that fuzzy logics may be local [87, pp. 283–335]. This is necessarily reflected in the systems of granules—these may be local as well. *Locality* means that not all the points will participate in a particular granular structure.

Although standard relational properties (both crisp and fuzzy), such as reflexivity, symmetry, and classes of relations with special properties such as tolerances, equivalences, and partial orders are well understood, their potential has not been used either in connection with issues of granularity or with computing with words. The major reason was the essential drawback of the standard global theories, which postulate that the properties of a relation must be shared by all the elements of a relation. Unfortunately, in the majority of papers on relational calculi, including Zadeh's pioneering paper on fuzzy relations, the relational properties are global, utilizing only the standard notion of (global) reflexivity. This also explains why the potential of the relational methods for knowledge representation and reasoning has not yet been utilized effectively in CW.

The contribution of Bandler and Kohout crucial for multilevel knowledge representation was to provide an adequate definition of *locality* that was new for both crisp (nonfuzzy) and fuzzy relations [6,10,11]: Where R is any fuzzy relation on X, the local equality of R is the relation E_R given by $(E_R)_{ii} = \bigvee_j(\vee(R_{ij}, R_{ji}))$, $(E_R)_{ij} = 0$ *if* $j \neq i$. In 1982, Bandler and Kohout introduced [6,10] local reflexivity and *local composed properties*, such as local tolerance, local preorderness, and local equivalence, in addition to global properties of that kind. This was an extension not only of the fuzzy theory of relations but also of the crisp theory.

Using the definition of local equality above, *local reflexivity* is defined as follows: R is locally reflexive if and only if $E_R \sqsubseteq R$. The definitions of all other compound local properties are obtained by replacing reflexivity by local reflexivity.

The notion of local properties is essential for applications and was embedded into the software tool Trisys, which has been used for testing of local properties and comparing partial relational structures [11,59] in solving problems in engineering, medicine, and business. The capability of correct relational computing with relations possessing local properties is also crucial for the success of the relational methods in CW applications.

It should be clearly understood that semantic space representations are not formed by relations alone but also by operations on relations. Relations together with a plethora of operations form complex structures that can be nested in various ways. Such structures are definitely needed when dealing not only with sentences but also with fragments of texts formed by aggregating the individual sentences.

4.3.4 Role of Fuzzy Relational Products in Computing With Words

In computational science we do not want to talk just about the mechanisms that conceptually describe how CW proceeds. Our ultimate goal is to build computing systems that *can* compute with words. For this we need higher-level computational structures (e.g., fuzzy generalized quantifiers) that operate over the semantic spaces represented inside systems for computing with words. In our approach an important role is played by BK-products (compositions) of relations. We represent semantic spaces by n-ary relational structures in their intensional form. This representation of relations in predicate form is a richer representation than just n-ary Cartesian products of fuzzy sets.[3]

One may ask why we use relational representations. One important reason is that a relational representation of knowledge structures makes it possible to perform all the computations and decision making in a uniform relational way [59], by means of *special relational compositions* called *triangle* and *square products*. The *triangle subproduct* $R \lhd S$, *triangle superproduct* $R \rhd S$, and *square product* $R \square S$ were introduced by Bandler and Kohout in 1977 and are referred to as in the literature *BK-products* [17,19,27]. The *square product*, however, stems from Riguet (1948) [81], needing only to be made explicit [10]. The products were more recently rediscovered and described in 1986 by Doignon, Monjardet, Roubens, and Vincke [20] and Fodor, [23] and in the crisp version by C. A. R. Hoare and others.

The theory and applications of BK-relational products have made substantial progress since 1977. See the survey in Ref. 59, which includes a list of 50 selected references on the mathematical theory and applications of BK-products in various fields of science and engineering. Particular new uses have been found by Kerre and DeBaets [17–19].

BK-products have been applied in various fields of science and engineering, medicine, information retrieval, handwriting recognition, cognitive structures analysis, relational computer architectures, decision making, and generating search strategies for resolution-based theorem proving. An important use of BK-products has been in building fuzzy cognitive mental maps and investigating their changes induced by learning. Examples include capturing and the analysis of mental construct relationships with the help of Trisys software. Some interesting problems addressed were: physiotherapists changing their view as the result of treatment of atypical patients [5], people perceiving architectural environments, acquisition of cognitive maps capturing differences in the way experts and novices use concepts in problem solving [13,33], and others. All these applications required the use of fuzzy semiotic relational structures for relational representation of semantics, and sufficiently powerful relational computational software for processing empirical data. This lead Bandler, Kohout, and their associates to the development of relational computational methods and software for that purpose, and to the development of *fuzzy semiotic representation structures*, discussed in Section 4.5.3. In our opinion, these methods and techniques are also essential for computational handling of granularity in CW.

[3] It should be clearly understood that a Cartesian product of sets is only a satisfaction set representation of relation (i.e., its extension), not the relation itself. For more detailed discussion of these very important issues, see Ref. 48.

4.4 FUZZY RELATIONAL METHODS

In previous sections we have outlined basic principles of computing with words and argued the advantages of combining relational computations with some basic semiotic notions. In this section we present the basics of the calculus of relations, with emphasis on the BK-products of relations. Section 4.5 is devoted to the semiotics of relational computations.

4.4.1 Role of Calculus of Relations in Computing With Words

The mathematical definitions of three families of fuzzy products—*triangle subproduct* $x(R \triangleleft S)z$, *triangle superproduct* $x(R \triangleright S)z$, and *square product* $x(R \square S)z$, which are needed in the sequel—are presented in this section together with some examples of their use.

Mathematical Definitions of BK-Products in Logic Notation: Binary Crisp and Fuzzy Relations. A binary (two-place) relation R between two sets X and Y is a *predicate* with two empty slots. When an element x of X is put into the first slot and an element y of Y into the second, a grammatical statement ensues, which may be either true or false if the relation is crisp. For a fuzzy relation a degree of truth is assigned to that predicate. For any element x_i in X, the *afterset* x_iR is the subset of Y consisting of those elements to which x_i is related via R. Similarly, for any element y_j in Y, the *foreset* Ry_j is the subset of X consisting of those elements related by R to y_j. If R is a crisp relation, these are crisp sets; if R is fuzzy they are fuzzy sets, with membership degrees given by the degrees of the truth of the relation. The symbol R_{ij} denotes the *degree* to which the ordered pair of elements (x_i, y_j) is related by the predicate R. The set of all ordered pairs that are related by a given relational predicate R_p is called the *satisfaction set* R_S of relation R. R_P is in general *intensional*, only if the relations satisfy the axiom of extensionality may it be extensional. On the other hand, R_S is always extensional.

Where R is a relation from X to Y and S a relation from Y to Z, a *product relation* $R{*}S$ is a relation from X to Z determined by R and S. There are several types of product used to produce product relations, each distinctive in its *intention* and *use* [10,59].

The mathematical definitions of *triangle subproduct* $x(R \triangleleft S)z$, *triangle superproduct* $x(R \triangleright S)z$, and *square product* $x(R \square S)z$ are presented below. Each product type performs a *different logical action* on the intermediate sets, as *each logical type* of product enforces a *distinct specific meaning* on the resulting product relation $R{*}S$. We shall see in Section 4.5.1 what impact this distinction of different logical actions enforced by different types of BK-products of relations has on the meaning of semiotic descriptors of composed relations.

In the definitions of BK-products that follow, R_{ij} and S_{jk} represent the fuzzy degrees to which the respective statements x_iRy_j and y_jSz_k are true.

Product Type	Many-Valued Logic Formula
Circle product	$(R \circ S)_{ik} = \bigvee_j (R_{ij} \bigwedge S_{jk})$
Triangle subproduct	$(R \triangleleft S)_{ik} = \bigwedge_j (R_{ij} \rightarrow S_{jk})$
Triangle superproduct	$(R \triangleright S)_{ik} = \bigwedge_j (R_{ij} \leftarrow S_{jk})$
Square product	$(R \square S)_{ik} = \bigwedge_j (R_{ij} \equiv S_{jk})$

The formulas above define the products in logic notation form. This is advantageous computationally, because finite relations can be expressed and manipulated by a computer in the matrix form. For example, relational products can be computed as products of relational matrices.

For crisp nonfuzzy relations, each type of product has only one realization, which is given by the uniqueness of two-valued logic: Each logic connective is a unique, well-known Boolean connective. When the relations are fuzzy, there is a further wide choice of realization for each of the four product kinds, because of the plethora of many-valued logic-based candidates for the role of *implication operator* and other connectives. Despite this multiplicity of versions of each of the many-valued logic connectives $\wedge, \vee, \rightarrow, \leftarrow$, and $\equiv$, the distinct character and difference of each product type are preserved.

The symbols for the logic connectives AND and OR, both *implications* and *equivalence* in the formulas above, represent some many-valued logic connectives, chosen according to the properties of the products required. The best known connective in fuzzy logic are max*(x,y)* and min*(x,y)* for standard fuzzy OR and AND, respectively. The other well-known pair are the *bold connectives* (also called Łukasiewicz *connectives*) $x \vee y = \min(1, x + y)$ and $x \wedge y = \max(0, x + y - 1)$.

In the examples given in the sequel we use the Łukasiewicz implication given by $x \rightarrow_5 y = \min(1, 1 - x + y)$ and Kleene–Dienes implication given by the formula $x \rightarrow_6 y = \max(1 - x, y)$ for computation of BK-products. The details of choice of the appropriate many-valued connectives are discussed in Refs. 5, 8, 9, 59, and 64, where the reader can also find lists of other useful connectives that have been used in many of applications of BK-products but are not mentioned here.

It is important to distinguish what we call *harsh products* (defined above) from a different family, the family of *mean products*. Given the general formula

$$(R@S)_{ik} ::= \#(R_{ij} * S_{jk})$$

a *mean product* is defined by replacing the outer connective # by $\sum$ and normalizing the resulting product appropriately. The mean products are very important in some applications, although their mathematical theory does not take such a neat form as that of the harsh products.

BK-Relational Products in Set Notation. The table of relational products given above contains definitions based on many-valued logic notation, which uses the logic connectives $\bigwedge$, and $\rightarrow$, $\leftarrow$, $\equiv$ for triangle subproduct, superproduct, and square product, respectively.

There exists, however, another form of definition of relational products, based on notation using the concept of set inclusion and equality [3,4]. The link between set-based definitions of BK-products with definitions expressed in logic notation is provided by the theory of fuzzy power sets [3]. These two different forms of relational compositions are algebraically equivalent, producing the same mathematical results. Distinguishing these forms is, however, important for practical reasons. *Logic notation* is useful when constructing fast and efficient computational algorithms. It is also more transparent when dealing with logical aspects of fuzzy relations. *Set-theoretical notation*, given below, is, however, important for conceptual interpretation of the meaning of semiotic descriptors and forming verbal interpretation of relational forms in the context of computing with words.

Products in Set Notation

Circle product	$x(R \circ S)z \Leftrightarrow \delta(xR \text{ intersects } Sz)$
Triangle subproduct	$x(R \triangleleft S)z \Leftrightarrow \delta(xR \subseteq Sz)$
Triangle superproduct	$x(R \triangleright S)z \Leftrightarrow \delta(xR \supseteq Sz)$
Square product	$x(R \square S)z \Leftrightarrow \delta(xR = Sz)$

where $\delta(X) \in [0,1]$ represents the degree to which the statement X holds.

4.5 SEMIOTICS OF RELATIONAL COMPUTATIONS

4.5.1 Semiotic Aspects of Triangle and Square Products of Relations

From Linguistic Labels of Relational Products to Semiotic Descriptors. In representing knowledge structures capturing the meaning of relations in a particular knowledge domain (e.g., in medicine or industrial engineering), not only quantitative but also qualitative notions are involved. Product relations formed by relational products represent new entities composed from the original data. Each relation possesses meaning carried by its linguistic label. The label carries a concrete interpretation within a particular knowledge domain. This interpretation also determines the meaning of the composed relation computed by the relational product. Let us look at an easily understandable example taken from the health care domain. Many examples could be quoted from other fields, but medical examples are most easily understandable without extra technical descriptions.

If R is the relation between *patients* and *individual symptoms*, and S a relation between *symptoms* and *diseases*, $R * S$ will be a relation between *patients* and *diseases*. The diagnostic clinical interpretation of each distinct logical type (e.g., the triangular square product type) of these product relations has a distinct clinical meaning:

$x(R \circ S)z$	Degree to which patient x has at least one symptom of illness z
$x(R \triangleleft S)z$	Degree to which x's symptoms are among those that characterize z
$x(R \triangleright S)z$	Degree to which x's symptoms include all those that characterize z
$x(R \square S)z$	Degree to which x's symptoms are exactly those of illness z

Methods of combining linguistic labels with BK-products provide a natural conceptual framework for knowledge representation and inference from imprecise, incomplete, or not totally reliable knowledge that has successful applications in knowledge engineering [60]. In the context of CW, these methods provide a basis for a structured method that allows us to capture semantic interrelationships of fuzzy granules. This helps us to find reliable and consistent subsets within otherwise ambiguous or incomplete data. It also helps in measuring the degree of inconsistency and incompleteness of the spurious parts relative to some perspective or norm of evaluation. All that is needed when devising adequate methods of approximating meaning.

Comparison of Structures and Investigating Their Properties. BK-relational products can also be used to compare relational structures. Thus if R is any relation (perhaps itself a product of other relations) from X to Y, we call R^T the *transposed relation* (often called *converse*, or sometimes, *inverse*), in which y is related by R^T to x exactly when x is related by R to y. This well-known converse is important in constructing new relational structures from basic (primary) relations that are already given. In particular, $R * R^T$ is a relation from X to X, and $R^T * R$ a relation from Y to Y. Here is an example from the medical field using the specific relations mentioned above:

$x_i(R \lhd R^T)x_k$	Patient x_i's symptoms are among these of x_k.
$x_i(R \square R^T)x_k$	Patient x_i has exactly the same symptoms as x_k.
$y_j(R^T \lhd R)y_l$	Whenever symptom y_j occurs, so does y_l (in this group of patients).
$y_j(S \square S^T)y_l$	Symptom y_j characterizes exactly the same diseases as does y_l.

Relations so constructed might exhibit relational properties that reveal important characteristics and interrelationships of the source of information from which they were generated (see Section 4.3). Hence methods for detecting various relational properties of given relations have important practical applications.

4.5.2 Semiosis, Granularity, and Interpretation

In this section we look at the role of semiotic descriptors in representation of knowledge by relational structures in a more general semiotic framework. We have seen from earlier examples how fuzzy relations can manipulate semantic information that is carried by linguistic labels. We have seen that the logic component of meaning imposed on different types of BK-products was defined strictly mathematically. But the logic semantics does not fully define the meaning of the linguistic labels that carry the conceptual meaning of the relations composed. The information has to be supplemented by the meaning of semiotic descriptors.

It is helpful to put this in more general terms: A *fuzzy semiotic representation structure* (FSRS) consists of a pair of structures, $<$ FRS, SD $>$. FRS is a fuzzy relational structure consisting of a family of fuzzy relations, and SD is a collection of semiotic descriptors [43,45]. The main goal of semiosis is the interpretation of signs and symbols, specifically recognition of their meaning. The meaning interpretation unit is a very complicated one.

The meaning of something can be different depending on the scale that is used for representation. This makes the notion of granularity very important. *Levels of granularity*, also referred to as *levels of resolution*, are closely related to generalization. Interpretation and meaning depend on context. A process considered with all its details cannot be properly understood unless the details irrelevant within a particular context or perspective are cleared away.

4.5.3 Triadic Distinction of Semiotics: Syntax, Semantics, and Pragmatics

One of the classic notions of semiotics is the triadic distinction *syntax–semantics–pragmatics*, coined by Morris in the late 1930s. That is the place where the duality *semiotics–mathematics* comes in. In logic methods of proofs, only the *form*, the syntactic composition, plays a role. In the *logic theory of models*, the primary goal is to interpret syntax in semantic metastructures. But what we need here is the fully fledged duality syntax–semantics and the pragmatics of emergence of either of these. Here fuzzy logic can play an important role: We have a duality of linguistic descriptors and fuzzy structures to which these descriptors apply. In our relational setting, *numerical* will be extended to the many-valued logic valuation of relational structure, and *symbolic* will be represented by semiotic descriptors, which are special instances of linguistic labels.

Now we have to link fuzzy semiotic representation structure with the semiotic triangle. The semiotic triangle has three vertexes: *name, meaning*, and *object* represented. The vertex name maps into a semiotic descriptor (SD), and the vertex meaning is represented by an FRS. The vertex object maps into the object of the real world characterized by the pair <FRS,SD>. See Figure 4.1 for more detail.

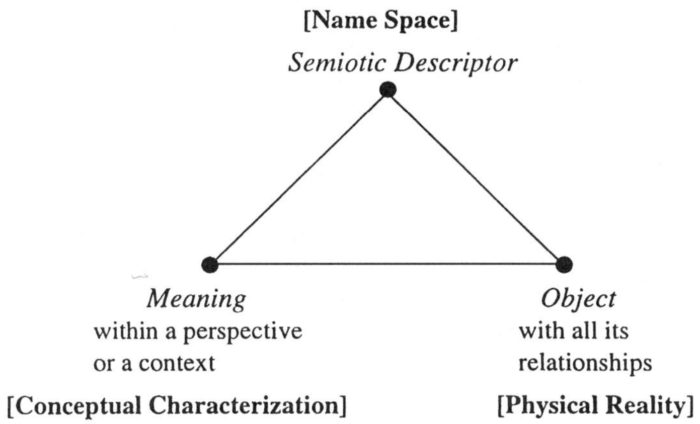

FIGURE 4.1 Semiotic triangle.

In the next section we introduce some general conceptual categories of semiotic descriptors. In Section 4.7 we look at a specific relational model from the domain of medicine. First we give an overview of the global relational structure of the medical relational knowledge-based system Clinaid. This is followed by a more detailed explanation of the meaning and purpose of semiotic descriptors at different levels of granularity employed in Clinaid.

4.5.4 Conceptual Categories of Semiotic Descriptors

Fuzzy semiotic representation structure has to be enriched by the choice of appropriate generic categories of semiotic descriptors. In AI terminology this means selecting the appropriate *ontologies*. The following conceptual categories of semiotic descriptors are used in activity structures methodology [42,43,45]: (1) objects, (2) attributes, (3) values, (4) agents, (5) perspectives, (6) contexts, and (7) views. Each category represents a specific level of granularity. Each level of granularity may possess conceptual refinements that are interlinked with other granular structures. Each conceptual category has specific meaning that can be understood and interpreted by a domain expert.

Objects. In manufacturing applications, objects are, for example, either parts of a manufactured product or products, or whole technologies, depending on the resolution level.

Attributes. Attributes are characterized by *linguistic descriptors*. In manufacturing applications, examples of these are low raw material cost, small processing windows, high temperature, good lubricity, low variance in raw material costs, and so on. But attributes can also be characterized by *measurable* physical or fiscal parameters, such as temperature, lubricity, cost reducing potential, potential investment, cost, and so on. In medical applications, these are signs, symptoms, and syndromes.

Interactions. Interactions are special kinds of relations. For example:

REL_1,5 Low variance in raw material costs $\rightarrow$ low cracking probability
REL_2,3 Good processing control $\rightarrow$ low raw material cost

Values. These are either linguistic variables or numerical variables determining the degree to which an object possesses an attribute.

Agents. In the context of our manufacturing applications [69,70], agents are the observers (e.g., engineers or accountants) assessing the degree to which an attribute is possessed by an object. For example, in Refs. 22, 36, and 69, describing the evaluation of a low-pressure turbine (LPT) cover plate for a jet engine, the observers were engineers evaluating to what degree various attributes can be assigned to the LPT plate.[4]

[4]The work on manufacturing applications has been supported by NSF Grants DMI 9525991 and DMI 9726027 (PI: L. J. Kohout). The industrial partner in these two projects was Pratt & Whitney.

In medical and health care applications these were, for example, clinicians, physiotherapists, or computer systems such as the Dexteron system, used to record the handwriting of neurological patients for neurological investigations.

Perspectives. An object or a family of objects can be evaluated within different perspectives. For example, an LPT cover plate can be evaluated from the perspective of an engineer or from the perspective of a business analyst performing value analysis of the part, or from the perspective of an accountant. Each perspective may employ attributes that are different from the attributes of a different perspective for the same object. Some attributes may, however, be shared by different perspectives. A patient may be evaluated from the perspective of a neurologist or surgeon.

Contexts. Each object or family of objects can appear in several different contexts. For example, an LPT cover plate may appear in the context of an ingot process, forging process, extrusion process, or other process. In medical diagnostics contexts may be different body systems, for example (see Section 4.7.2 for further details).

Views. Even in one particular perspective or context, different experts may assess differently the objects and situations in which objects appear. These different views of different experts can be captured by repertory grids and compared by relational methods using algorithms provided by Trisys [11].

4.5.5 Logic of Questions and Relational Queries

After presenting the notion of afterset and foreset, which provide useful computational mechanism for representing queries, we look at some examples.

Aftersets and Foresets of Relations. For a crisp relation R from X to Y, the *afterset* of an element $x_i \in X$ is a subset of Y, a collection of those y_j which make the statement x_iRy_j true; in symbols,

$$x_iR = \{y_j | x_iRy_j\}.$$

Conversely, the *foreset* of an element y_j is the subset of X given by

$$Ry_j = \{x_i | x_iRy_j\}.$$

Mnemonically and semantically, an afterset consists of all those elements which can correctly be written after a given element, a foreset of those which can correctly be written before it. An afterset or foreset may well be empty.

A relation is known completely if all its foresets or all its aftersets are known. For a fuzzy relation, the degree of truth from the interval [0,1] is associated with each element y_i of an afterset or with each element x_j of a foreset, respectively.

The notions of afterset and foreset of an element can be extended to afterset and foreset of a set in (at least) two distinct but equally important ways:

1. The *inclusive afterset* of $A' \in \mathcal{P}(A)$ and the *inclusive foreset* of $B' \in \mathcal{P}(B)$ are, respectively,

$$A'R = A' \circ R = \{b \in B \mid \exists a \in A' \quad \text{such that} \quad aRb\}$$
$$RB' = R \circ B' = \{a \in A \mid \exists b \in B' \quad \text{such that} \quad aRb\}.$$

2. The *exclusive afterset* of $A' \in \mathcal{P}(A)$ and the *exclusive foreset* of $B' \in \mathcal{P}(B)$ are, respectively,

$$[A']R = A' \rhd R = \{b \in B \mid \forall a \in A', aRb\}$$
$$R[B'] = R \lhd B' = \{a \in A \mid \forall b \in B', aRb\}.$$

Use of Foresets and Aftersets in Resolving Relational Queries. The foreset–afterset formulas can be used with advantage for computing the answers to relational queries (cf. Section 4.8.3). Let us look next at some examples. Let us fix the meaning of the sets and relations used in our examples.

P	Set of patients
S	Set of signs and symptoms
D	Set of diseases
R	Relation from P to S (patient data)
Q	Relation form S to D (diagnostic knowledge)
T	Relation from P to D: the diagnoses computed by $(R \lhd Q)$
$D(p_i)$	Set of all diseases that the patient p_i has
D_k	Abbreviation defined by $D_k = \mu(d_k)$
P_i	Abbreviation defined by $P_i = \mu(p_i)$

Example 4.1. The query "What are the diseases involved in patient p_i?" will be expressed in foreset–afterset notation as p_iT. The answer to this query, the set $D(p_i)$, will be expressed by the formula

$$D(p_i) = p_iT = p_i(R \lhd Q).$$

Let us illustrate the use of logic notation for evaluation of the query. We shall compute the degree $\mu(d_k)$ to which the patient p_i may have a disease d_k that is contained in the set $D(p_i)$ indicated for the patient by the answer to the query. We have

$$\mu(d_k) = \delta[d_k \in D(p_i)] = D_k = P_i \wedge \Big[\bigvee_j (R_{ij} \rightarrow Q_{jk})\Big].$$

Example 4.2. The query "What are the diseases similar with respect to the (simultaneously present) set S' of signs/symptoms?" can be computed by the *symmetric* exclusive afterset of the set S' and relation Q. In symbols, $D(S') = S' \square Q$. Using the logic notation, we obtain

$$D_j = (S' \square Q)_j = \bigwedge_i (S'_i \equiv Q_{ij}).$$

4.6 ARCHITECTURES FOR FUZZY RELATIONAL COMPUTING WITH WORDS

In fuzzy semiotic representation structures (FSRSs), one puts fuzzy sets and relations into correspondence with semiotic descriptors. Let us call this correspondence *internal SD correspondence*. The FSRSs defined in Section 4.5.2, which "twin" fuzzy relational structures (FRS) with semiotic descriptors (SD), give additional power to relational methods. This is explored with advantage in information-intelligent systems as well as in various other uses of relational computations.

Semiotic descriptors (SDs), however, are also in a correspondence with words of natural language and with linguistic statements (LSs) composed of these words. Let us call this correspondence of SD with LS *external linguistic correspondence* of FSRS. This correspondence factors out a *restricted fragment of natural language* (RFNL) that is application-domain dependent. It will be different for different specialties of medicine or for different branches of engineering.

The FRS component of fuzzy semiotic representation structures (FSRSs) is in correspondence with RFNL. Thus when used in applications, the FRS component of FSRSs is also in correspondence with a restricted fragment of natural language (RFNL). Let us call this *external logical correspondence* of FSRS.

This triple of correspondences—FRS–SD, SD–RFNL, and FRS–RFNL—makes it possible to utilize fuzzy relational architectures based on BK-relational products as the inner part of a CW system, forming what we shall call the "core system" of the CW relational architecture.

Figure 4.2 shows the block structure of a fuzzy BK-product architecture for computing with words. It consists of three subsystems:

1. *Front end*: fuzzy CW translator
2. *Core system*: BK-product relational architecture
3. *Back end*: OpenMath communication interface

Front End. The front end is a generic subsystem that can be connected to a variety of different BK-product relational architectures. Its function is to provide translation

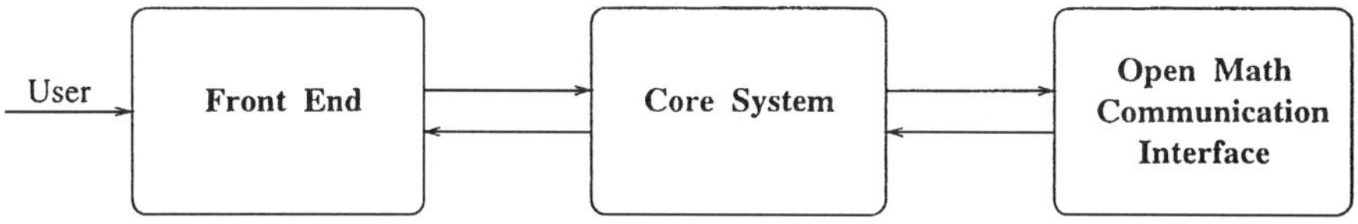

FIGURE 4.2 Fuzzy BK-product architecture.

of the natural language statements in RFNL to the canonic relational form represented in FSRS. These relational forms, in turn, are used by the core system for relational computations. It also performs the reverse translation of the computational results from FSRS to RFNL.

Core System. The core system design utilizes our experience in application of relational methods in various knowledge domains. The triangle relational products together with fast fuzzy relational algorithms [6,11] were applied to various practical problems in a number of scientific fields. For example, in the analysis of medical diagnosis: diagnostic data and patient management processes [5,8,67], medical sign and symptom comparison [16,65], information retrieval [35,58,66,68], handwriting classification [63], industrial engineering [69], business [78], and other areas [55].

Clinaid [34,38,52] and Dexteron [63,65] are designs of relational systems intended for use in clinical medicine. Trisys [11], on the other hand, is a system for general relational analysis. These systems have common generic features. This makes it possible to design the front end to be a generic system compatible with all our BK-product relational architectures.

In all these applications, relational representation linked with the semiotic descriptor structures plays a crucial unifying role. The relational structures provide a computational interpretation and representation of the semiotic categories defined by the semiotic descriptors.

The semiotic descriptors (SDs) capture the denotational meaning of concepts of a specific application domain. The objects denoted by SDs are the concepts and processes that the computer is required to emulate in a relational computational model. The generic categories of semiotic descriptors described in Section 4.5.4 provide a generic semiotic structure for a wide class of relational architectures of information-intelligent systems. In a particular application domain, these have to be enriched by domain-specific types of semiotic descriptors. See Section 4.7.4 for an example.

In this chapter we use as an example the medical knowledge-based system Clinaid to demonstrate the structure of relational architectures. This is necessary for fuller understanding of the relational methods for CW. The ways the semiotic descriptors specific to the medical domain are used in the medical knowledge-based system Clinaid are discussed in Section 4.7.

Back End. The core system may require cooperation with mathematical systems for symbolic computation and/or numeric computation when solving problems in a scientific or engineering domain. Access to such systems (e.g., via the Internet) can be facilitated by the back end. As this is a large topic, also dependent on the future development of the OpenMath international standard [1], we touch only briefly on this topic in the final section of the chapter.

4.7 INFORMATION-INTELLIGENT SYSTEMS USING RELATIONAL COMPUTATIONS AND GRANULARITY

The front end–fuzzy CW translator converts linguistic expressions to relational representations in multidimensional semantic spaces that are manipulated by the relational CW *core system* (see Figure 4.2). The actual computation (fuzzy inference) is performed by fuzzy BK-products (compositions) of relations. The results of these computations are then translated back to linguistic form, communicating some sentences from the front end to the user of the CW system. How the core system works we demonstrate on a specific example, a relational system called Clinaid [38,52,74].

In this section we summarize the main features of the relational architecture of the medical knowledge–based system Clinaid. This is intended as a specific example of the core system that is used as the middle part of a relational architecture for computing with words (cf. Section 4.6). The core system exchanges information with the front end translator, described in Sections 4.8 and 4.9.

4.7.1 Dynamics of the Medical Diagnostic Process and Its Use in the Translation Process

To make it possible to compute with words, there must be a natural correspondence between the linguistic structures used by the user of a CW system to define the problem and its relational representation in a CW system. We shall look now briefly at such a correspondence in the field of medical diagnosis that is introduced by the nature of clinical activities.

The activity structure of relational computation in Clinaid mirrors the clinician's activity [52,56]. At least the following four components applied iteratively characterize the clinicians' activity while treating a patient [56, Fig. 4.1, Sec. 4.1.3]:

1. Observation
2. Conceptual classification and filtration of relevant observational data for decision making
3. Decision
4. Clinical action

These comprise *concurrent evaluation* of competing hypotheses, *context dependence* of inference, and *incompleteness* of approximate clinical data.

All these basic components interact strongly with one another. This interaction of the structures manifests itself in the character of the dynamic process of inference: Not only static logic components but also their dynamic interactions generate important logical properties. One of these properties is *context dependence* of logical inference in a clinical context [38, Sec. 4.2.2, 74]. Context dependence has direct impact not only on the correctness of inference, but necessarily brings about the *multiplicity* of contexts in which the inference process should operate correctly.

Superficially, it would seem that the relation between signs, symptoms, and illnesses suffices for performing an adequate diagnostic inference. However, investigation of the logical structure of medical knowledge shows that this is not the case. This leads to the following problems [51]:

1. *Problem of incompleteness.* Not all signs and symptoms characterizing the disease are always observable or present.

2. *Problem of locality of inference*. Not all signs and symptoms are relevant in a particular given diagnostic context [52, Sec. 4.10.5.2].
3. *Problem of complexity of inference*. The complexity of exhaustive matching of all disease descriptors and indicators (e.g., signs, symptoms, tests) may be forbiddingly high [38, Sec. 4.6.2, p. 17].

In terms of functional activity structures [43], the inferential process focuses its activity into a particular area of locality, according to the context, which is *semantically* controlled by the *syndromes*. Once the inference is focused into one or several body systems, then within each body system, the context is controlled by introducing an appropriate questioning strategy [61] in which syndromes play an essential role.

Exploratory knowledge elicitation based on the concepts discussed in this section [2, 14, 15, 43, 60] provides information required for building fuzzy semiotic relational structures needed for relational computations of Clinaid. It provides the external linguistic correspondence defining the semiotic descriptors SD of the FSRS. See Section 5.7.4 for the resulting families of SDs. More detailed description of these families can be found in Ref. 38 (Chap. 1 and Sec. 4.7).

It also partially determines the external logical correspondence of RFNL with the fuzzy relational structure (FRS) of FSRS that is utilized in the core system architecture. In particular, the information concerning the locality and incompleteness of medical data helps in selecting the appropriate many-valued logic used in the definition of BK-products.

4.7.2 Clinaid Generic Architecture

The Clinaid approach differs significantly from more conventional AI approaches in its potential capabilities. Clinaid chooses to use fuzzy relations to capture a large amount of clinical knowledge in a structured way and to make it easier to deal with the parallelism that is essential for a multicenter approach. There are 11 body systems in the Clinaid specification [38]:

1. Cardiovascular
2. Respiratory
3. Central nervous system
4. Muscular and peripheral nervous system
5. Renal
6. Endocrine
7. Blood and reticuloendothelial
8. Reproductive
9. Skeletal
10. Gastrointestinal
11. Psychological

Each body system is a semantic abstraction that provides a different context for the input information. Each sign or symptom has a different meaning in a different body system. We can say that each body system represents knowledge from the *perspective* of the corresponding medical specialty.

The average size of the knowledge structure of a body system indicates that the problems of efficiency and correctness of inference are not insignificant:

Signs and symptoms per body system	200–400 approximately
Diseases per body system	100–400 approximately
Total number of body systems	11

To deal with the complexity of the entire medical field spanning 11 body systems, Clinaid uses fuzzy relational inference. This allows us to explore fully the advantages of granularity of medical knowledge.

The structural relationships of collections of granules are also reflected in the system architecture of Clinaid. Our approach is grounded on two essential features that are built into the system [50]:

1. Plurality of control and inferential centers
2. Inference via triangular relational products

The plurality of centers requires their *mutual cooperation*. Briefly, the plural centers cooperate as follows:

1. Each center is adapted to dealing with a particular portion of the common task.
2. Each center filters out different aspects of data, according to the context or to what its special competence is.

The power of this way of organizing things comes jointly from the *specialization* of the former and the *simplification* of the latter. How the *common task* is *subdivided* and how the centers are coordinated are of course delicate and crucial questions [39], but assuming that they can be achieved successfully, the advantages of subdivision are evident:

1. Each center deals only with a small portion of systemic knowledge.
2. The centers can operate in parallel.

These provide a major weapon against combinatorial explosion, with the following desirable consequences:

1. Inference and meta-inference are both expressible as relations.
2. Inference is computable in parallel.
3. The relational inferential and knowledge representation structure can be mapped into natural linguistic structures.

4. The horizontal dimension of a computational activity is across the centers and induces parallelism.
5. The vertical dimension of computational activity performs switching of the context between various levels of granularity.

Figure 4.3 displays a partial snapshot of Clinaid's computational activity, which shows how the fuzzy relational inference proceeds. The signs and symptoms presented by a clinician initiate the activity at two levels of granularity: namely: the

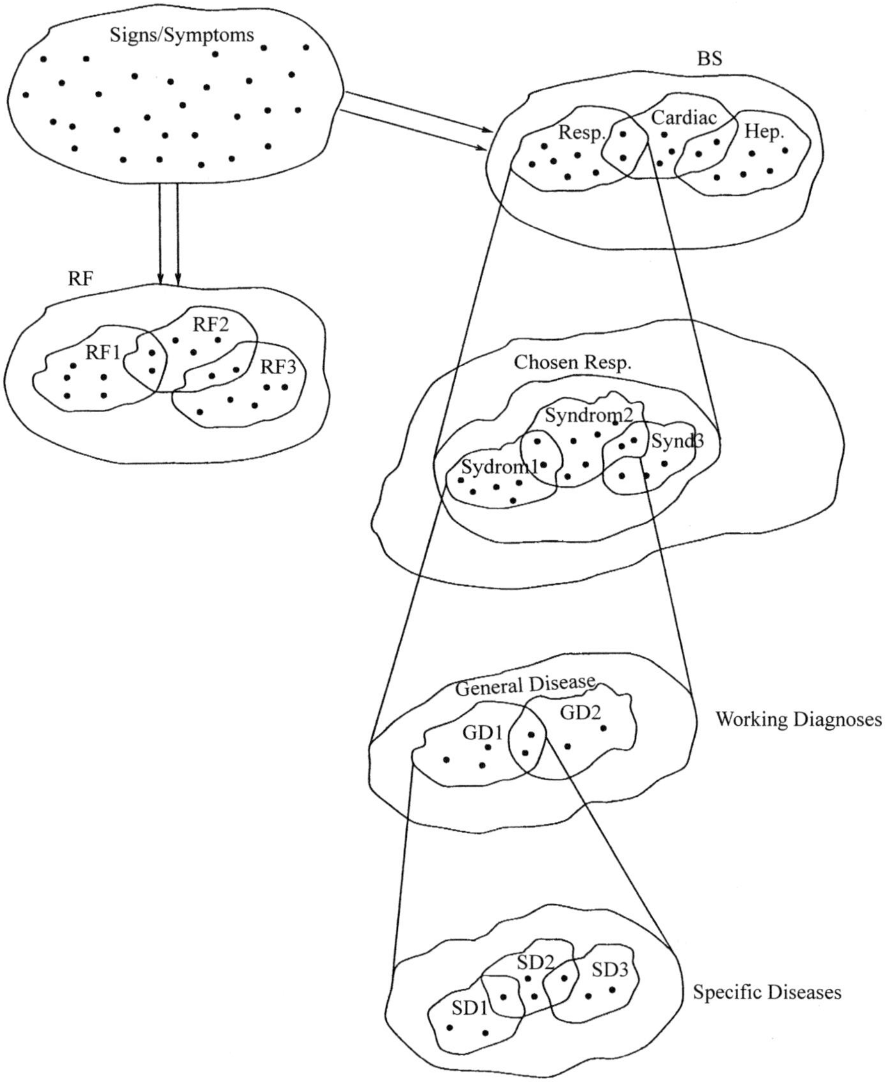

FIGURE 4.3. Granular activities for Clinaid diagnostic unit.

level of risk factors (RFs) and the level of body systems (BSs). At the level of body systems, three out of 11 BS centers become active concurrently in this particular example: respiratory BS, cardiac BS, and hematological BS.

Each center executes a vertical thread of granular activities (VTGA). The VTGA for the respiratory system is depicted in Figure 4.3. When the respiratory BS becomes active, it performs its computations over the *syndrome* granular space (GSP). The refinement of this particular VTGA continues down to the granular space of *general diseases*, ending at the granular space of *specific diseases*. Figure 4.3 shows the family of three *working diagnoses*, SD1, SD2, and SD3, each consisting of several specific diseases.

In the inference we use a plurality of mathematical relational systems, each system being based on a specific many-valued logic. All these systems form together a generic family that has in common generic logical types of relational operations, such as triangle or square relational products. It should be understood that the essential condition placed on the properties of any fuzzy theory is that for nonfuzzy (crisp) data, all the theories must default into the same classical (two-valued) semantic theory of mathematical relations.

4.7.3 Semiotics of the Modes and Strategies of Inference

Any inferential process in Clinaid is characterized by its conceptual *semantics* and *dynamics* [41,43]. The functional activity structure capturing diagnostic activity can be divided (particularized) into two distinct parts:

1. *Semantic component.* The semiotic descriptor structure captures the semantic definitions of all relevant diagnostic concepts.
2. *Pragmatic component.* The dynamic descriptor structure captures the clinician's inferential strategy and logic.

The *dynamic descriptor structures* are driven by the context, which is provided by the patient diagnostic data provided by the clinician. *Semiotic descriptors*, on the other hand, are concerned primarily with determining the meaning of the individual disease descriptors within the body systems, thus determining the medical content of the knowledge base by providing diagnostic definitions of the individual body systems.

The inferential process focuses its activity into a particular area of locality, according to the context, which is *semantically* controlled by the *syndromes*. Once the inference is focused into one or several body systems, then within each body system, the context is controlled by introducing an appropriate questioning strategy [61]. The answers of the clinician to the questions by Clinaid represent the pragmatic component.

Thus the system moves from ignorance to adequate knowledge. In doing so, the system passes dynamically through various intermediate states. In these dynamic states, it has only partial information; hence strategies of inference generate partial conclusions. The dynamics of inference is such that several partial conclusions can be kept under consideration until further diagnostic activity can distinguish between them. As more than one possibility is being considered at once, the system implements a form of concurrent inference [77].

4.7.4 Multicontext Fuzzy Relational Inference of Clinaid

Diagnostic Knowledge Structures: Levels of Organization and Granularity. We have seen that a good method of dealing with complexity reduction is to subdivide the activities. This decreases the size of the problem to be resolved at any particular stage. This hierarchical manner of subdividing the activities reveals the structure of processes that can be executed in parallel and allows the inference to proceed rapidly. Clinaid uses classificatory knowledge to diagnose diseases. Different portions of the taxonomy are used at different resolution levels, yielding different kinds of granularity.

As more information is obtained from the patient and presented by the doctor to the system, groups of unrelated diseases can be eliminated from the diagnostic path. This makes it possible to increase the resolution level and utilize finer granularity as the diagnostic inference progresses. This process continues until the final diagnostic conclusion the working diagnosis, is reached.

Dealing with the Inferential Context by Means of Granular Refinements. The diagnostic unit of Clinaid deals with a *multiplicity* of contexts provided by the various body systems and other factors. Deep knowledge concerning *individual contexts* takes into account cross-contextual similarities and differences. We distinguish (1) the *context of different body systems* and (2) the *context of different diagnostic levels* within the supercontext of a specific body system.

The inferential process is performed in a hierarchical or heterarchical manner, involving the following conceptual levels, each with a different granularity:

1. Symptoms and signs level
2. Risk factors level
3. Body system level
4. Syndrome level
5. General disease level
6. Specific disease level
7. Aetiological level

The activation of levels within the specific body system represented in a center of the diagnostic unit is ordered by the following sequence:

$$\text{(bodysystem)} \Rightarrow \text{syndromes} \Rightarrow \text{general diseases} \Rightarrow \text{working diagnoses}$$

Signs and symptoms of a patient entered into the system are matched with the knowledge structures distributed within the individual levels of a specific center.

The stream of computations passes through the levels of the foregoing sequence, in an iterative manner.

The knowledge represented at each level is captured in a relational structure and the inference is performed by the relational products composing the knowledge items of the levels with the information items entered into the level from its environment.

Complexity of clinical inference within the multiple context is reduced by the diagnostic hierarchy, which uses *syndromes* as the main instrument. Syndromes are essential when dealing with a multiplicity of body systems of general medicine, as they help to focus the inference within a particular context, excluding those combinations of signs and symptoms that are irrelevant within the context that the syndromes define.

A *syndrome* is defined as a cluster of signs and symptoms that appear together and characterize a specific group of diseases. This cluster consists of signs and symptoms that when viewed in probabilistic or statistical terms are mutually dependent.

The knowledge contained in syndromes and similar semantic constraints, in addition to that contained in the relationship of signs and symptoms to diseases, vastly reduces the complexity of the inferential task as well as increasing its reliability. Without the use of such constructs, the inferential process might have difficulty in reaching a conclusion.

Semiotic Descriptors and Fuzzy Relational Knowledge Structures of Individual Diagnostic Levels. In this subsection we present the semiotic descriptors for activity structures concerned with the activities of the diagnostic unit. We concentrate here mostly on the semiotic descriptors, as these present the link between the structures and contexts of individual body systems and their environments. This determines the partitioning of the architecture of the diagnostic unit of Clinaid.

Let us list the medical meaning (semiotic descriptors) of all sets entering into the relations at individual levels:

B	Set of body systems
G	Set of general diseases
D	Set of specific diseases
I	Set of investigations
P	Set of patients
S	Set of symptoms and physical signs
Y	Set of syndromes

Each granule has been factored by a different function or class of functions. The way the granule is manipulated depends on the purpose and the context of its use.

- *Definition of the relation "symptoms and signs to body systems"*

$$SB \in \mathcal{F}(S \rightarrow B)$$

The relation SB relates the set S of symptoms and physical signs to individual body systems B. The aim of this relation is to select the body systems relevant to patient information presented.

- *Definition of the relation "symptoms and signs to syndromes"*

$$SY_i \in \mathcal{F}(S \rightarrow Y)$$

This is a family of fuzzy relations, as there is a different relation SY_i for each body system. The aim of this fuzzy relation is to identify possible syndromes. By identifying the appropriate syndromes, the complexity of search for diseases can be reduced, since a syndrome is a cluster of relevant symptoms and physical signs.

- *Definition of the relation "syndromes to general diseases"*

$$YG_i \in \mathcal{F}(Y \rightarrow G)$$

The fuzzy relation YG_i shows the degree of relevance of syndromes Y to different general diseases G. The aim of this fuzzy relation is to identify the general diseases of the patient. There is a separate relation for each body system.

- *Definition of the relation from "general diseases G to investigations I"*

$$GI \in \mathcal{F}(G \rightarrow I)$$

There are several possible types of investigation I, tests, or examinations that can be performed to explore each general disease. In fact, the fuzzy relation GI shows for each general disease the possible number of investigations, with their degree of relevance. The aim of this fuzzy relation is to identify the possible investigations that can be performed for a particular general disease which ultimately can contribute to the identification of specific disease(s).

- *Definition of the relation from "investigations results J to specific diseases D"*

$$JD \in \mathcal{F}(J \rightarrow D)$$

The results of the investigations, tests, or examinations can lead to the identification of specific diseases. These investigation results can contribute by identifying specific diseases with a varying degree of certainty. The relation JD shows the results of investigations which yield specific diseases with different degrees of relevance (certainty). The aim of this relation, accepting the results of an investigation, is to be able to confirm, reject, or change the priority of the specific disability.

Interval Inference in Clinaid. The relational inference mechanism of Clinaid has been extended to cover fuzzy interval inference. An example of the end result of such inference is depicted in Figure 4.4. Providing the results of relational inference of Clinaid in the form of interval representation offers a useful method of translation from intervals to linguistic statements. To translate from the interval representation

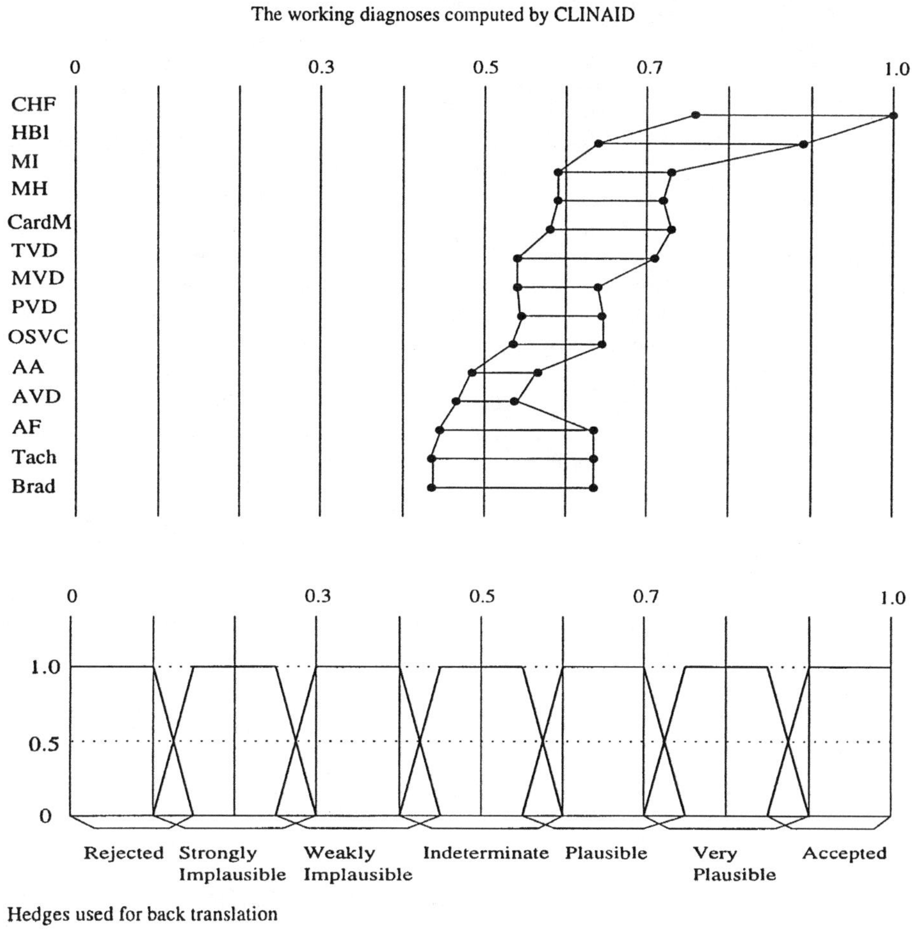

FIGURE 4.4. Interval inference in Clinaid.

of the working diagnosis to an equivalent set of linguistic statements, the normative family of linguistic hedges is required. Such a family is depicted at the bottom of Figure 4.4.

Applying the *principle of the maximal overlap* between the interval set of working diagnoses and the normative set of linguistic hedges, the output set of linguistic statements is produced (see Table 4.1).

The linguistic form is:

> The hypothesis that patient <NAME> has <DISEASE> is <EPISTEMIC VALUE>.
>
> The granular refinement inference passed through <BODY SYSTEM> and <SYNDROME>.

TABLE 4.1. Working Diagnoses

Syndrome	Disease	Fuzzy Interval	Translation
Acute cardiac failure (ACF/[0.72, 0.57])	Congestive heart failure	[1.0, 0.76]	Accepted or very plausible
	Heart block	[0.89, 0.64]	Very plausible or plausible
	Myocardial infarction	[0.73, 0.59]	Plausible
	Malignant hypertension	[0.72, 0.59]	Plausible
	Cardiomyopathy	[0.73, 0.58]	Plausible
Murmurs in structural cardiac and blood vessel lesions (MRM/[0.56, 0.48])	Tricuspid valve disease	[0.73, 0.57]	Plausible
	Mitral valve disease	[0.71, 0.54]	Plausible or indeterminate
	Pulmonary valve disease	[0.64, 0.54]	Plausible or indeterminate
	Occlusion of superior vena cava	[0.64, 0.53]	Plausible or indeterminate
	Aneurysm of aorta	[0.56, 0.48]	Indeterminate
	Aorta valve disease	[0.53, 0.46]	Indeterminate
Dysrythmia (DSR/[0.63, 0.43])	Atrial fibrillation	[0.63, 0.44]	Indeterminate or plausible
	Tachycardia	[0.63, 0.43]	Indeterminate or plausible
	Bradycardia	[0.63, 0.43]	Indeterminate or plausible

For example, the actual disease for the case shown in Table 4.1 would be reported by the phrase:

> The hypothesis that patient *x* has *Congestive Heart Failure* is *Accepted OR Very Plausible.*
>
> The granular refinement inference passed through *Cardiac Body System* and *Acute Cardiac Syndrome.*

4.8 FRONT END SYSTEM FOR RELATIONAL COMPUTING WITH WORDS

As explained in Section 4.6.1, the user presents a sentence to the front end, which converts the sentence to relational representations and communicates it to the core system. The results computed by the core system are then translated back to linguistic form and presented to the user of the CW system by the front end.

The front end is a generic subsystem that can be connected to a variety of different BK-product relational architectures. Its main functions are:

- To translate the natural language statements from a restricted fragment of natural language (RFNL) to the canonic relational forms represented within fuzzy semiotic relational structures
- To communicate these translations to the core system that performs relational computations
- To perform the reverse translation of the computational results from FSRS to RFNL

Our design of the front end explores natural affinities of restricted natural language input representation of knowledge of a particular knowledge domain (using linguistic variables, hedges, and linguistic predicate structures) with the deep knowledge concerning the same domain expressed in the relational form (cf. Section 4.5) that pertains. Translation process is done under the supervision of the user, so that the user can check the correctness of relational interpretation as well as of the retranslation from relational notation to RFNL.

4.8.1 Front End Translator Prototype

The current prototype [26] gives the user a form of practical English query language (EQL) in which to pose questions about the useful fuzzy relational computations and searches [25]. In more concrete terms, the front end subsystem can:

- Translate linguistic predicate information to mathematical relational notation and vice versa
- Create the hierarchical classification of objects and specify any necessary restrictions placed on the objects
- Provide the means for formulation and verification of syntactic and semantic restrictions
  - Syntactic restrictions include such limitations as permitting only the specified forms from a given list of English linguistic predicates, queries, and limited graphical representation forms.
  - Semantic restrictions, on the other hand, refer to the application-specific requirements that maintain the relational dependency of subobjects given by a preorder.[5]

Graphical communication is often as effective as purely linguistic communication, and both these forms fall into the realm of semiotics. For this reason, our aim is to provide three mutually translatable modalities of representation of relational computations: (1) linguistic, (2) mathematical, and (3) graphical. In the remaining part of this chapter we describe the design of the current prototype.

4.8.2 Front End Functional Requirements

In this section we describe our solutions of selected substantial issues that arise in design of the front end of a relational system for computing with words (CW). We address the following topics:

[5]Concrete examples from specific applications are hierarchies and similarities of diseases, signs, and symptoms in the medical domain [38]; subtopics and documents retrieved in fuzzy relational information retrieval [58]; heuristic hierarchies of terms and theorems in resolution theorem provers [72]; and preorders and equivalences of cost parameters in affordability studies for the aeronautical industry [36].

1. English query to metaformula translations
2. Back translation (metaformula to EQL query) support
3. Knowledge specification of user's environment
4. Dynamic protection/security
5. Help facilities
6. Linguistic quantifier translations
7. Support function tools

Query to Metaformula Translations. The metaformula is a canonic relational product that is in a computer-interpretable form. The core activity of the translator is to parse the user-entered English query into subphrases. This is necessary to construct the appropriate metaformula that represents in the relational form the *logical* and *epistemic* meaning of the query presented for computation. Hence this formula contains two semiotic components:

1. A relational logical form that can determine the degree of truth that certain relational properties exist within a specific fuzzy relational structure
2. Associated applied meaning conveyed by the semiotic descriptors attached to the relational form

Back Translation: From a Metaformula to an EQL Query or a Statement. The result of computations have to be translated from the relational form back into the linguistic form. On occasion a user also needs to translate a metaformula into the appropriate EQL syntax. To facilitate these tasks, the front end provides a back translation tool that displays an English query or a statement translated from a given relational metaformula. First, the semiotic descriptors used in the metaformula are expanded to the corresponding representative names. Then the back translator is called to restructure the corresponding query statement. Finally, the newly restructured query is then displayed to the user along with the original metaformula.

Knowledge Specification of Users' Environment. The proposed front end is a generic shell that may be used in different knowledge domains. Therefore, the domain expert has to supply the domain knowledge needed for operating the front end in that domain. This involves:

- Defining the data dictionary with specific primary set categories and the participating elements used in relations
- Deciding on other application parameters needed to install the environment of interest

The Clinaid fuzzy knowledge-based system environment (described in the preceding sections) was chosen as the domain on which a detailed front end prototype study is made.

Multiple Levels of Protection. Various ways of accomplishing protection will be used. The protection mechanism employed serves to regulate security issues and prohibit certain capabilities using static and dynamic techniques [43, Chap 5–8; 57]. This makes it possible to have high-level protection requirements represented relationally.

Help Facilities. We introduce dynamic levels of help that will be invoked according to the expertise and skills of particular users. Some of the help facilities are general; others provide more details of the task at hand. This enables the help descriptions and explanations presented to be domain specific. The variety of choices is dependent on the content of domain-specific knowledge supplied. Also, context-sensitive help traits are maintained through an awareness of the current functional activity performed by the front end at the request of the user. The help function keeps track of the current and recent functions processed. It anticipates the intentions of users by observing the syntax required and informs the users of alternatives needed to refine their query. The final form of the English structured query is displayed for user verification—acceptance or rejection. Interactive help messages are used within the users' query to aid in supplying users with specific assistance in forming their queries.

Translation of Linguistic Qualifiers. Each fuzzy linguistic variable and hedge is associated with a specific value. These values are used to adjust the underlying fuzzy measures involved in the query analysis. This approach allows further qualification of already fuzzy incomplete data. It provides the user with some of the advantages of fuzzy set theory: specifically, the ability to use naturally vague fuzzy modifiers to represent already vague English terms. For example, a user can use such vague expressions as "very high fever," "a little swelling," "an occasional cough," and so on [26].

Support Function Tools. The front end subsystem must furnish the system support functions necessary for realization of the activities discussed above. The following is the acceptable minimum:

- Provide a log function that records the transactions for subsequent review.
- Save and restore application's data dictionary to and from disk.
- Access to file maintenance functions (create, edit, copy, and delete files).
- Allow user control of implication logic, α-cut value, selecting harsh or mean product calculation methods.
- Help via presenting contents of the data dictionary of a specific application environment.
- Help via displaying non-application-specific generic knowledge data.
- Show the relations and the fuzzy assertions used in deriving conclusion.
- Display current values of system parameters.
- Show sample queries upon request.

- Display checklist paradigm that assists in determining fuzzy membership values.
- Display relational preorders as Hasse diagrams, graphs showing equivalence classes and their preordering.
- Allow the user the option to adjust or modify the system in a "what if" mode to change and explore the modified behavior of the system.
- Allow user to vary the choice of the implication operator used in computation of products.

4.8.3 Front End/User Dialogue Scenario

Users should be able to make system requests that are flexibly defined at the initial setup of the shell of the CW system when the knowledge domain of the core subsystem is chosen. The requests can be classified into several categories. The first category are domain-independent purely relational requests, such as:

Which domain elements participate in the product relation $(R \triangleright S)$?

What range elements participate in the product relation $(R \triangleright S)$?

List the different compositional inferences for the derived relation _____.

Back translate (to English query) the relational product formula $(R \triangleright S)$.

Trace the derivations of relational products to original relations. Map an alternative path.

Analyze the completeness of the assigned values or weights for a given relation using property closures and/or property interiors.

Do the reflexive and transitive properties hold for the relation _____?

Display the Hasse diagram of the relation S.

List the afterset (matrix row) attribute objects of the relation __R.

List the foreset (matrix column) attribute objects of the relation S__.

Set α-cut level.

The second category of system requests is domain dependent. Examples of such queries follow.

Give the degree of involvement of each body system for patient z.

What are the diseases involved in patient x?

What are the body systems involved with disease k?

What are the syndromes involved with disease k?

What are the signs/symptoms involved with disease k?

What are the diseases involved with syndrome y?

What are the signs/symptoms related to body system _____?

What are the body systems related to sign/symptom _____?

What are the signs/symptoms contained in syndrome _____?

What are the syndromes related to sign/symptom _____?
What are the signs/symptoms related to disease _____?
What are the diseases related to sign/symptom _____?
What are the diseases related to body system _____?
What are the body-systems affected by disease _____?
What are the diseases related to syndrome _____?
What are the syndromes related to disease _____?
What are the syndromes related to body system _____?
What are the body systems related to syndrome _____?

The third category are requests that involve some modal terms, such as *necessary* or *possible*. Here are some examples:

What are the syndromes necessarily present, given the following simultaneously present signs/symptoms: _____?
What are the syndromes suggested by the following simultaneously present signs/symptoms: _____?
What are the diseases similar with respect to the following simultaneously present group of signs/symptoms: _____?

4.9 DESIGN REQUIREMENTS OF THE FRONT END

A computing system that computes with words is not exempt from the requirements that any trustworthy computer system should satisfy. A CW system should be reliable, with good computer protection against the intruders that may cause malicious damage over the Internet. Hence the front end should function as a shell that also provides the user with the capability to use relational product structures to implement security, protection, and other system control functions. The basic configuration of the front end is shown in Figure 4.5. Various control functions are summarized in Figure 4.6. In the sequel we focus primarily on the EQL translator of Figure 4.5, as it is the most essential part with respect to CW.

4.9.1 Design of the Parser Subsystem

The front end prototype system has to provide the user with a suitable level of natural language interactive communication methods which are driven by interrogative statements. In this, the parser subsystem [6] plays the key role.

[6] In order to interpret a language sentence, this sentence has to be parsed. In human brain, parsing is usually done on a subconscious level, but it is the necessary prerequisite to all attempts to understand the meaning of a sentence. Dyslexia and some other brain malfunctions demonstrate that parsing is necessary. Similarly, in any system that processes the natural language, parsing has to be implemented.

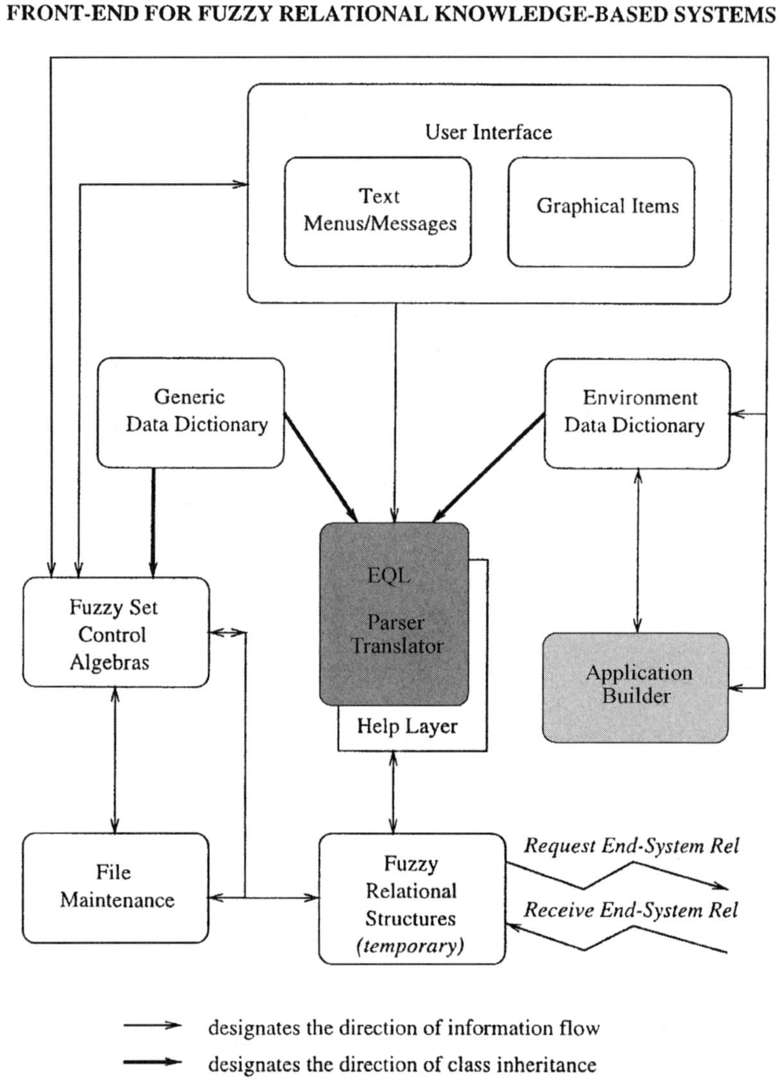

FIGURE 4.5. Basic configuration of the front end (prototype system).

Query Grammar. The set of natural language queries used in a specific expert domain is not an unrestricted set of English questions. It is composed of a finite set of carefully structured queries that meet the user's needs when extracting information from fuzzy relational structures.

Since the number of possible user queries can be rather large, the allowable queries are represented by a rule specification method rather than by individually listing each allowable query. A grammar specified in Backus–Naur form (BNF)

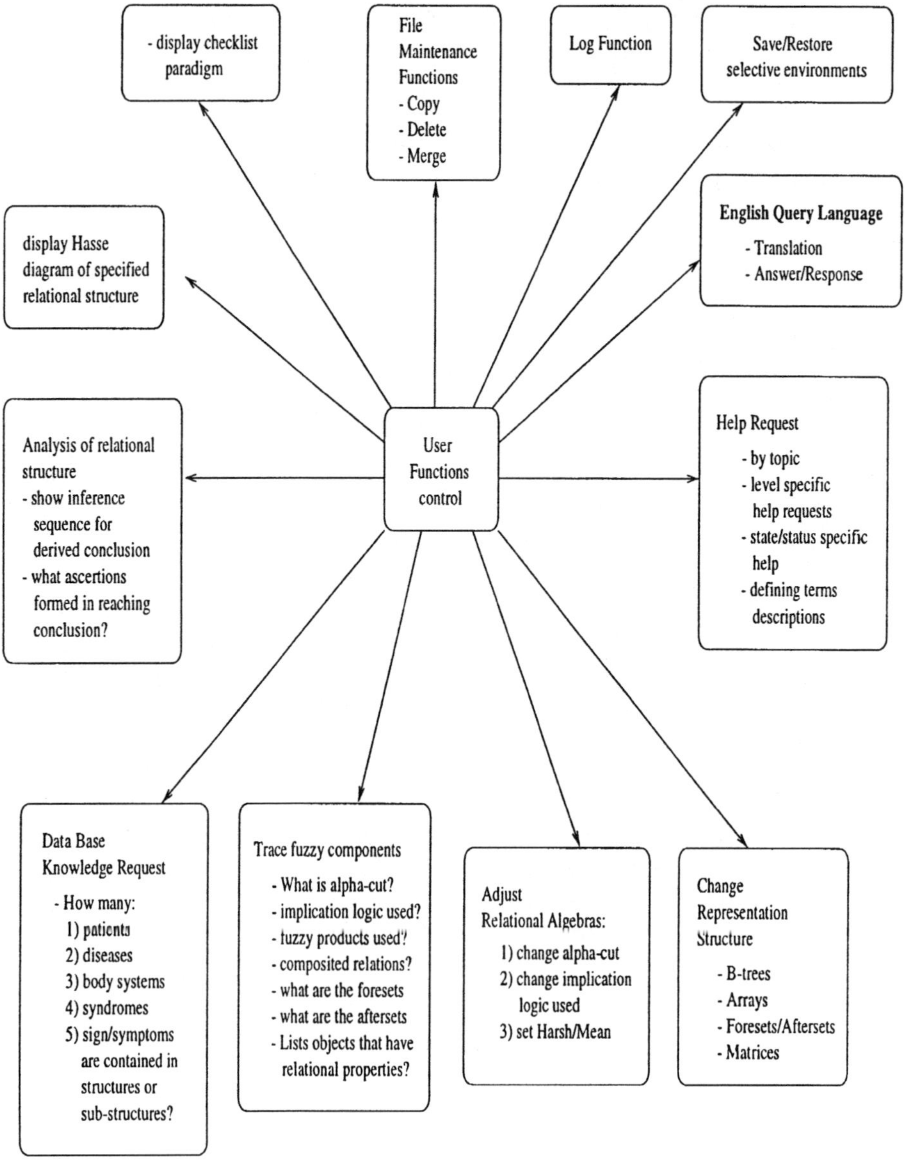

FIGURE 4.6. Front end user control options.

establishes the building blocks used to construct the elements of the query sets, as in diagramming an English sentence.

The grammar rules can generate a complex set of English queries or interrogative statements about the existence of specific relations or subrelations in the fuzzy relational knowledge base. A language grammar includes history, spelling, pronunciation, and rules of meaning (semantic usage). The grammar specifies which syntactic elements can be put together in a particular order to be grammatically correct. The presence or absence of certain items (articles such as *the*, *a* or *an*) does not establish any semantic difference in the query's fuzzy value. The sole purpose of such items is to make the query a grammatically correct English statement.

If the query request is not grammatically correct, the system will prompt the user and switch into an interactive help mode. Several choices can be given to help the user obtain an appropriate query that meets the grammatical properties. User interactive assistance will be offered to guide the user in forming their query correctly. The query's grammar subsystem is constructed to specify the variable forms of the basic input query. A grammar is chosen to allow some flexibility for incorporating adjustments in acceptable query forms.

The grammatical subsystem in the current prototype includes the following information components:

- Data dictionary
- English language query structure
- Knowledge-based (fuzzifications) information

The *data dictionary* consists of all relations, together with the relational elements used in the user's modeled environment. This data structure takes the form of class objects that maintain lists of the category or class names for all entities that may take part in a fuzzy relation. It is a representation of semiotic descriptors, examples of which appeared in Section 4.7.4.

Sorted lists of class semiotic descriptors and class names are used to locate the linked list of member element names directly. The front end maintains these lists of entity names to transcribe the symbolic representations used by the machine. Therefore, the end system is required to store only the coded symbols or abbreviations known to the front end and not the English names of relational objects.
The following lists will be used to store the data dictionary items:

- Primary class set (PS): full-names list
- Primary class set: semiotic character descriptors list
- Primary class set: elements (PEs) list
- Knowledge-based relations/addresses
- Linguistic variables list
- Linguistic hedges list

An exhaustive list of all primary set names that can be used in a query must be contained in the table of primary class sets (PS). Each name should correspond to the actual objects within the application environment on which relations are made. The query, "What is the degree to which the signs/symptoms for body system x are included in the signs/symptoms for disease y?," for instance, will require the category set consisting of: names signs/symptoms, body systems, diseases. This can be found in the table of primary sets names. A PS is structured as a separate object that contains the following lists of associated subobject names that pertain to it:

- List of primary element names
- List of linguistic variables or null (empty)
- List of linguistic hedges or null (empty)

The data dictionary is partitioned into two categories: (1) domain[7]-independent knowledge-based items, and (2) domain-dependent knowledge-based items. Once a relation is needed, a request will be given to the core system knowledge structure for the actual membership values of that relation.

English Query Language Structure. Ideally, the grammar should allow a variety of query structures. The proposed query grammar EQL identifies a basic syntax model from which a number of useful interrogative statements can be constructed to analyze fuzzy relational structures. EQL defines a grammar syntax suitable for either written or oral presentation of the input query. Here the basic form of the EQL syntax will be described clearly with examples. Several user queries can be structured from this basic form.

Each query is partitioned into four phrases with abbreviations as follows:

1. Header phrase (h-phrase)
2. Antecedent relational phrase (a-phrase)
3. Product relational phrase (p-phrase)
4. Subsequent relational phrase (s-phrase)

Each standard query has the ordered sequence of phrases

$$\text{h-phrase} \mid \text{a-phrase} \mid \text{p-phrase} \mid \text{s-phrase}$$

An example of a query is given in Figure 4.7. This figure shows how the linguistic query is partitioned into the separate phrases.

Each correctly structured phrase in the query is parsed individually using a leftmost derivation approach. Parsing of the sample query displayed in Figure 4.7 produces the relational formula that is displayed at the top of the figure. In that formula, the symbol @ denotes generically BK-relational products. The type of the product is determined by the contents of the p-phrase. Let us assume for illustration that @ is a subproduct $\triangleleft$.

The purpose of parsing activity of each phrase of the example query can be summarized as follows:

[7]*Domain* in this context means the *knowledge domain* (e.g., neurology, psychology, electrical engineering, control engineering).

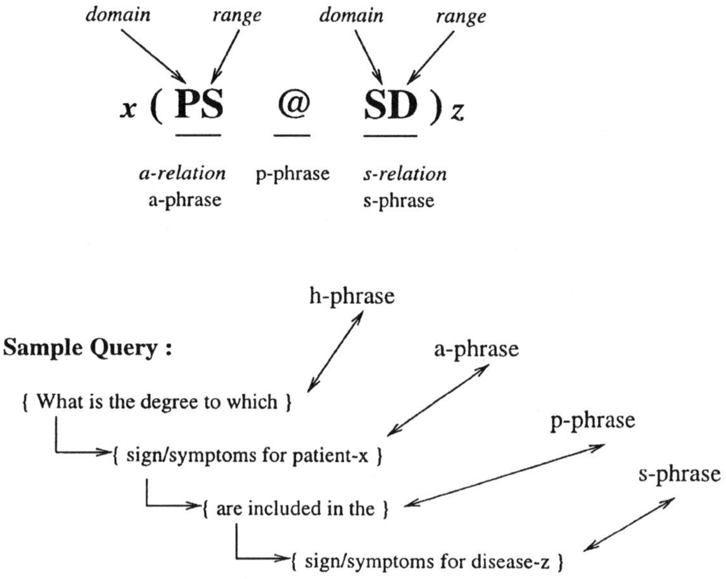

FIGURE 4.7. Fuzzy relation's product formula/English query.

- The h-phrase is used to control certain parameters during execution of the query. Its allowable structure will cause certain pre- and postextraction procedures to be performed (see the next section for details).
- The a-phrase will derive the relation afterset xPS.
- The p-phrase will derive the triangle subproduct $\triangleleft$.
- The s-phrase will derive the relation's foreset SDz.

Finally, the query extraction formula $x(PS \triangleleft SD)y$ will be produced by all the derivations combined.

Header Phrases of a Query. A number of header phrases (h-phrases) can be used to form the head of the query. Each phrase triggers certain optional computations that adjust certain default parameter settings for the application environment of current interest. When necessary, new h-phrases can easily be added to the list. This technique allows for some ease in setting and resetting the optional parameters by incorporating the triggers within the query itself.

Different h-phrases can be structured from the basic BNF descriptions illustrated in Figure 4.8. The phrase "What is the degree to which ..." causes the normal calculation of fuzzy relational measures to be computed for a single class/element in the class of attributes (symptoms of a patient in Figure 4.7). When interval relational computation is required, the term *range* is added to the h-phrase to request the interval result.

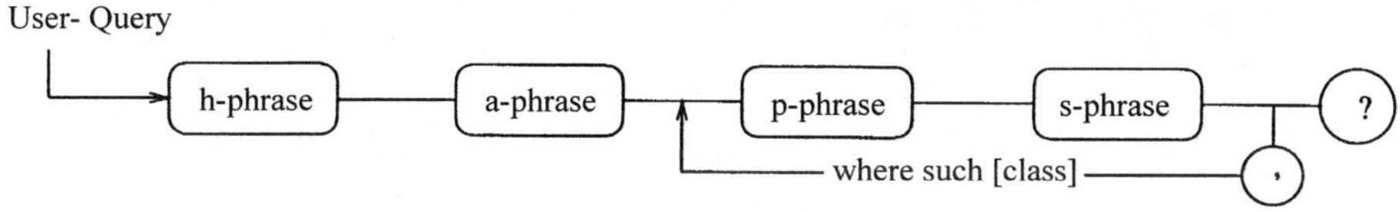

h-phrase := [WHAT IS THE [crisp] DEGREE TO WHICH]
| [WHAT ARE THE [crisp] DEGREES TO WHICH]
| [WHAT IS THE RANGE OF [crisp] DEGREES TO WHICH]
| [WHAT ARE THE RANGES OF [crisp] DEGREES TO WHICH]

FIGURE 4.8. Query h-phrase structured grammar diagram.

Antecedent and Subsequent Phrases of a Query. The h-phrase is followed syntactically by two similar phrases separated by a predicate or product phrase. These two phrases are described as the antecedent phrase (a-phrase), the phrase before the predicate; and the subsequent phrase (s-phrase), the phrase appearing subsequent to the predicate (after). Both phrases have the same structure; each holds different information from the query. The a-phrase and s-phrase have two clauses separated by a preposition. The first clause of the a-phrase is represented by the *range set class* name of the first relation followed by a preposition and then the second clause. A limited number of prepositions are permitted: *of*, *for*, *with*, and *from*. An example is given in Figure 4.9 that shows these individual mappings. The second clause of the a-phrase represents the *domain set class* with element name (class element) from the first relation.

The linguistic variable can be used in the specification of the query's class/element pair. Here, the ordering of the class/element pair is important. The class name must precede the element name. Each class/element component can be found in the predicate part of both the a-phrase and the s-phrase. Structured similarly to the a-phrase, the first clause of the s-phrase has the domain set attribute name of the second relation. This name must be the same name as the one used for the range set of the first relation. After the preposition *of*, *for*, *with*, or *from*, the second clause of the s-phrase is considered the range set class element name for that phrase. Linguistic modifiers such as *high* or *low*, and their modifiers or hedges, such as *very*, *extremely*, or *most*, are permitted in both class element names of a set. This is true provided that the primary element's primary set in question allows linguistic quantifiers. Not all primary set elements are permitted to use linguistic modifiers. This can be controlled from the data dictionary. The primary set *patients*, for instance, does not permit linguistic quantifiers. Figure 4.9 shows the structured diagram of the class/element name.

Product Phrase of a Query. The product phrase corresponds to the standard circle, square, and triangle product symbols found in query extraction formula representation form (Figure 4.10). Direct mapping from the small number of allowable text phrases to the corresponding product symbol can be realized from this figure. The limited number of choices for each symbol type are found to be sufficient for building a variety of users' queries. These metasymbol types can be back-translated into

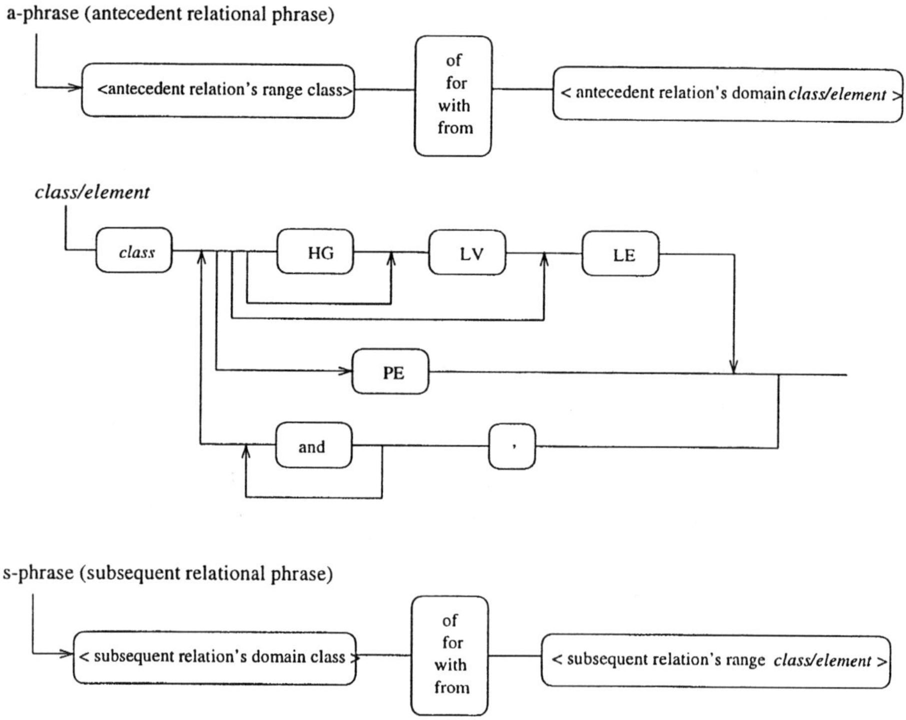

FIGURE 4.9. Query a-phrase/s-phrase structured grammar diagram.

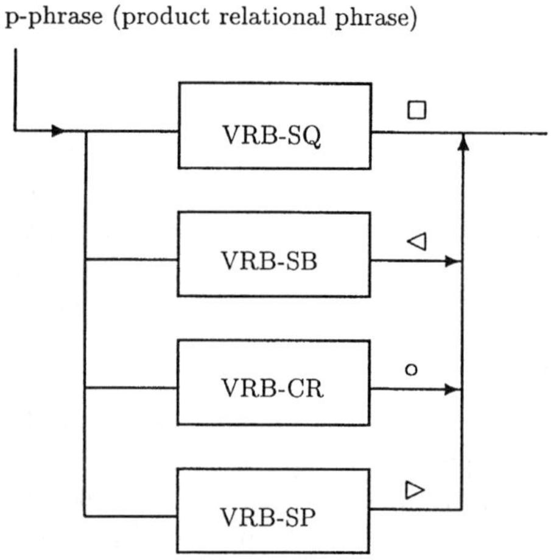

VRB-SQ::= ARE EXACTLY [THE] SAME
| ARE IDENTICAL TO [THE]

VRB-SB::= ARE INCLUDED IN [THE]
| ARE CONTAINED IN [THE]

VRB-CR::= INCLUDED AT LEAST ONE
| HAVE AT LEAST ONE
| CONTAIN AT LEAST ONE

VRB-SP::= INCLUDE ALL [[OF] THE]
| HAVE ALL [[OF] THE]
| CONTAIN ALL [[OF] THE]

FIGURE 4.10. Query p-phrase structured grammar diagram.

linguistic phrases as specified by the BNF expression shown at the right-hand side of Figure 4.10. If a product symbol is given, it will be matched with an appropriate natural language product phrase, and if the phrase is given, the product symbol would be returned.

Knowledge Base of Fuzzy Relational Structures. The front end serves as a shell that contains none of the knowledge base fuzzy relations that are used for relational computations by means of linguistic query interrogations. The fuzzy relations required for this purpose are maintained by those core systems to which the front end is linked.

The front end aids users with context-sensitive help about the underlying data dictionary and the core subsystem base relations. Its overall purpose is to provide the user with interactive means of deriving useful meaning from different product compositions of fuzzy relations. It also provides log-on security and incorporated protection by limiting data access to sensitive data using assigned capability levels.

4.9.2 English Query Language Interpreter

The English query is used as a natural means for posing questions about the existence of certain subrelations within a fuzzy relational KBS. A method is needed for transforming the English query into machine-usable form. Each group of words must be interpreted and then translated into one of the fuzzy product relation formulas. The English query language interpreter (EQL) serves this purpose. These resulting fuzzy product formulas have the theoretic properties that are needed for extracting information from the fuzzy relation knowledge-based structures. Figure 4.7 has shown the basic abstract form of a fuzzy product relation together with a sample English query. The stages of the EQL interpreter are described in the following sections. Transforming the English queries into appropriate metalanguage formulas involves several stages (preprocessing, lexical analysis, parsing, and semantic processing).

First, the entire query is scanned for errors: All possible checks are presented to the user before the error pass is finished. Interactive assistance will be available upon demand to guide the user in forming a query. Additionally, a list of closely matched queries will be displayed upon demand. Then fuzzy semantic analysis is processed on the query until the translation is verified by the user. A diagram of the EQL interpreter is shown in Figure 4.11.

Syntax Analysis of Query. The syntax analysis phase is performed by the lexical analyzer and the parser. The analysis of a query expression is checked item by item (word by word) by the parser. If both the a- and s-relation attributes exist in the data dictionary, its fuzzy relation's matrix form is located. Any linguistic modifiers are also verified and passed to the semantic analysis phase. The syntax analyzer performs checks to see that each item in the query agrees with the BNF descriptions for the grammar and for the application environment.

The translation passes perform the following activities:

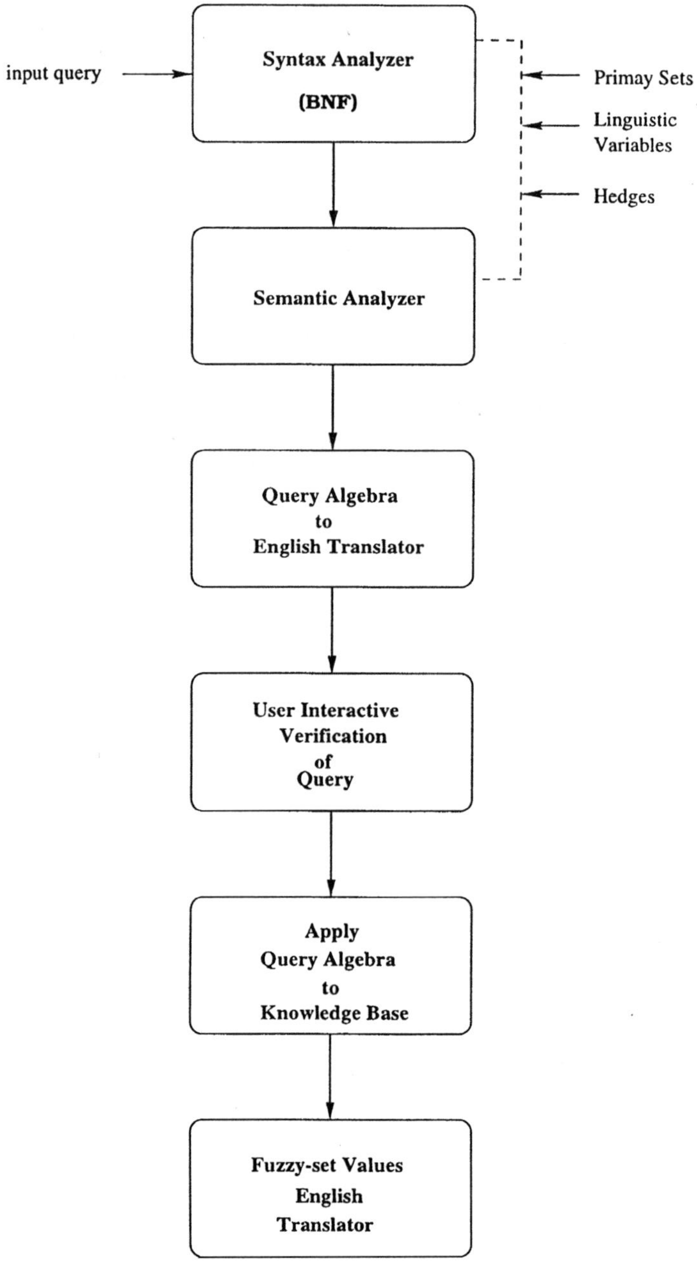

FIGURE 4.11. English query language (EQL) interpreter.

- *Pass 1.* Unnecessary words are stripped from the query (preprocessing), substituting one space for any number of embedded multispaces.
- *Pass 2.* Lexical analyzer, parser, and query generator translate the source query into intermediate forms.

Lexical Analyzer Phase. The scanner or tokenizer translates each query into words, the smallest usable form. A *token* is an indivisible lexical unit (keyword). Each token matches a single lexeme. *Lexemes* are translated (mapped) to tokens. Tokens are represented as enumerated types. Each noun, verb, adverb, article, adjective, conjunction, and preposition will be identified as specified in the knowledge base. Unspecified prepositions are ignored, because in the limited domain the presence of prepositions does not alter the meaning. The lexeme and look-ahead word are used to disambiguate the tokens. We utilize a small number of token types for specifying this grammar. Although in the data dictionary a variety of specific names can be formed as instances of a token type, unnecessary choices should be avoided, as too many token types make the parser large. The parser calls the lexical analyzer when a new token is needed. It returns the token and associated lexeme. Thus one can replace the lexical analyzer without affecting the rest of the translation processes.

Query Parser. An English query is parsed by breaking it up into component parts in order to analyze it grammatically. The parser verifies the agreement of the range class of an *a-relation* with the domain class of an *s-relation*. The translator performs much of this query decomposition in the parsing phase. For example, the following query can be divided into the basic phrases of a general query: "What is the degree to which signs/symptoms for patient x are among signs/symptoms for patient y?"

- The tokens "What is the degree to which" form the h-phrase.
- The tokens "signs/symptoms for patient-x" form the a-relation phrase.
- The tokens "are among" form the p-phrase.
- The tokens "signs/symptoms for patient-y" form the s-relation phrase.

Table 4.2 specifies the syntax-generic abbreviations for the grammar. The *parse tree* structure is very similar to the structure formed by a conventional sentence diagram. The syntax diagram or *syntax tree* shows the syntactic relationships between the parts of the query. Unlike the sentence diagram a tree structure can easily be represented by a computer. The query sentence is the entire computer program as seen by the translator. Again, a pass convets a token stream into a parse tree (structural representation of the query sentence being parsed). Separate linguistic quantifier values may generate value adjustments to be combined later with the fuzzy relational membership values themselves. A final pass creates an intermediate language representation metaformula form from which the product composition relation in question can be generated.

TABLE 4.2. Syntax Generic Abbreviations (Non-Application-Specific)

PS	Primary class sets	(e.g., body systems, signs/symptoms, disease, etc.)
PE	Primary element	(members of a specific primary class set)
LE	Linguistic element (nouns)	(modifiable primary element)
LV	Linguistic variables	(noun modifiers of linguistic elements)
HG	Linguistic variables hedges	(modifiers of linguistic variables)
ME	Member element	(a member element with/without modifiers)
CE	Class/element	(PS name with one or more PE names)

Syntactic Errors with Solutions: Warnings. Once an error is discovered, one of the following error messages is displayed and the necessary assumptions are made to continue checking for additional errors:

a-relation subject is not defined
a-relation object is not defined
p-relation subject is not defined
p-relation object is not defined
a-relation is not specified
p-relation is not specified
unrecognizable term __
problem in product relation phase
a-relation's range class does not match p-relation's domain class

Help will display a list of suggested tokens from the data dictionary in an attempt to match the problem term.

Semantic Analyzer. Semantic analysis involves procedures to derive meaning of the input query using the information provided by the syntax analyzer. The restricted domain is searched for corresponding grammatical substructures used to convey meaning through the use of appropriate numerical values that represent hierarchical and behavioral relationships. Conceptual meaning is, therefore, largely relative to the data of the application domain and knowledge suitable for the environment under study. Interpretation is dependent on the values supplied, along with the settings for the theoretical parameters chosen. Output from the EQL interpreter is a fuzzy BK-product formula which itself causes certain analyses to be computed for the two fuzzy relations specified.

The fuzzy product connector metaformula is structured from the representation forms provided by the parser. The fuzzy values of relations together with the database parameters for α-cut and choice of implication operator will be used to calculate the degree to which the product between the given relations holds.

Semantics of Linguistic Quantifiers. Linguistic modifiers reduce or intensify the degree of measurement for modifiable primary class set elements. The use of fuzzy linguistic variables and hedges in a query permits the underlying membership values of relations to be adjusted temporally. No permanent change to the relation's values is realized. Hence a linguistic query can specify different tolerance levels at which to measure BK-products of fuzzy relations. Linguistic variables are value-terms naturally used to test for a specific level of fuzzy membership. A linguistic hedge can be described as an adverb that modifies a linguistic variable (adjective). Therefore, hedges are permitted in the query only when an associated linguistic variable follows. Lists of allowable hedges and variables are linked to each primary element (noun) that permits linguistic modifiers. All unrecognized adjectives and adverbs found in the query are ignored. Hedges allow for fine tuning of the linguistic variables (primary set elements) as with "more" or "less." Specific hedge modifiers and values are stored in the data dictionary. Together the linguistic variable and hedge strengthen or weaken the intensity of the value measured. Notice that the hedge will strengthen in the direction of the linguistic variable. Since both linguistic properties (linguistic variables and hedges) will allow membership value changes, it is practical to apply all linguistic adjustments at the end, just prior to computing a query's response. Articles such as *the*, *an*, and *a* are ignored in the translation since they have no effect on the semantic weights.

A number of primary classes do not permit linguistic modifiers on their element terms. The element terms of those primary classes that do permit linguistic modifiers are called *linguistic elements* (LEs). These are the nouns used to represent the primary class/sets elements that are modifiable by linguistic constructs.

Back Translation: Semantic Interpreter. The back translator is utilized in order to:

- Restructure an English query statement from a given fuzzy relational metaformula. This restructured query is then displayed and compared by the user for acceptance or rejection. Also, an English explanation of certain analysis criteria of an individual fuzzy relational structure could be provided.
- Translate back to the natural language the result of computation expressed as a relational formula or metaformula.

Because we work with restricted fragment of natural language (RFNL), this back translation can be performed by a modified "reverse run" of the translating mechanisms described earlier.

4.9.3 Implementation of Prototype

The front end prototype FEF_KBS is implemented as a number of distinct objects in order to achieve maximum flexibility and reusability of designed objects. Each object is implemented as a class object in the object-oriented language C++. This language was chosen because of its popularity and ease in porting to different platforms. A number of class functions or methods are defined for each class object. The definition header files for the class objects provides the specifics of the methods used.

The front end will accept a natural language interface query written in the EQL syntax form to cause BK-product computations and analysis on the fuzzy relations defined in the knowledge-based system for Clinaid and other fuzzy relational systems using BK-products. Three main types of knowledge structures are used in the implementation: (1) generic knowledge, (2) application-specific semiotic knowledge, and (3) application-specific fuzzy relational structures.

The *generic knowledge* component includes those default parameters and tables that are contained in the empty front end shell. These are prescribed for a number of application environments, whereas *application-specific semiotic knowledge* applies only to the natural language terms and semiotic descriptors normally used in the environment being modeled. Unlike the fixed form of generic and application-specific knowledge, *fuzzy relational knowledge* can be structured in a variety of forms. Conceptually, the matrix is the simplest, most direct form by which to represent the last type of knowledge structure, fuzzy relations. Computation of BK-products over matrix representation is done by using logic notation-based forms (cf. Section 4.1.1). This allows for easy indexing.

Other computer representations of relations, such as threaded trees combined with foreset–afterset–based data structures, can be used instead [55,62,84]. The later representation, which is based on the foreset–afterset form of relations (cf. Section 4.5.5) uses, on the other hand, the set notation (cf. Section 4.1.2) for computation of BK-products.

4.10 BACK END: COMMUNICATION WITH OTHER COMPUTING SYSTEMS

It is important to make our systems capable of communication with other types of systems. For this, one needs to utilize suitable high-level Internet protocols and standards. One such international standard is developed by the OpenMath international consortium.

The central task of OpenMath is "to provide a means of exchanging semantic information encoded as a character string." Thus an encoded message is communicated by the sender and interpreted ("understood") by the receiver of the message within the context of some application [1].

Because of the variety of levels of understanding, this becomes reminiscent of characteristics of human languages. Indeed, it is argued that "the similarities between human language perception and the extraction of mathematical information from the OpenMath string can be exploited quite fruitfully." The analogy with a model of linguistic understanding composed of several independent language modules working in parallel motivates the semiotic stages of evaluation and interpretation of OpenMath-exchanged messages. We explore the linguistic paradigm for OpenMath proposed several years ago by Andreas Strotmann. When applied to our problem, it yields the following communication structure:

1. *Morphological module*: identifies words (morphemes) and labels them with their possible syntactic properties

2. *Syntax component*: consists of several subcomponents represented by a syntactic tree
3. *Logic component* (formal semantics module)
4. *Semantic component*

Scenaria for communicating mathematical objects between two or more participants would benefit by extending the linguistic paradigm by concepts concerned in viewing languages in a broader framework, as a dynamic communication process within a context. We also employ the distinction that the Prague Linguistic Circle made between *topic* and *focus* [40,44].

4.11 CONCLUSIONS: PRESENT AND FUTURE OF THE RELATIONAL CW APPROACH

The description of a prototype of a CW system presented in Sections 4.6 to 4.9 shows that the actual implementation of even a simple CW system has to use many advanced computer science techniques. We examine next how our prototype implementation relates to some basic computational processes outlined by Zadeh in his pioneering paper on computing with words [89]. In Section 4.2, the conceptual structures for CW as defined by Zadeh were described.

The architectural principles and design details by which the basic CW-computational process is realized in our prototype CW system by means of BK-product relational computing architectures were described in Sections 4.6 to 4.9.

The basic generic problem of CW [89] is solved conceptually by a CW-computational process that consists of the following activities:

1. The initial data set (IDS), a collection of propositions expressed in a natural language (NL) is converted by constraints explication into a canonical form of expression. This makes variables constraints and constraint relations explicit.
2. From the IDS we wish to infer an answer to a query expressed in NL. This is done by constraint propagation.
3. The answer is converted by constraint retranslation to NL and is referred to by Zadeh as the terminal data set (TDS).

Next we demonstrate the correspondence of Zadeh's [89] CW-computational process just described with the components, modules, and activities of our CW prototype. In our prototype, the *initial data set* (IDS; cf. Zadeh [89], p. 104) is confined to natural language (NL)-restricted sentences. Each sentence consists of four subsentence segments of the following form: $\langle$*h-phrase, n-phrase, p-phrase, s-phrase* $\rangle$ (cf. Section 4.9.1, Figures 4.7 to 4.9).

The constraint explication [89, pp. 105–106] we perform by translation of the IDS to relational structures in propositional form [10]. This is done by a query language interpreter consisting of a *lexical analyzer* and a *query parser* (cf. Section 4.9.2).

The *explanatory database* (ED) (Zadeh's term; cf. [89, p. 205]) which is used for constraints explication consists of *two modules* in our prototype, generic data dictionary (GDD) and the environment data dictionary (EDD). The data in both GDD and EDD contain *semiotic descriptors*. Semiotic descriptors in GDD are generic, pertaining to the entire family of knowledge domains. In EDD, on the other hand, the semiotic descriptors belong to a particular relevant knowledge domain, such as medicine, industrial engineering, or business value analysis, depending on the application. Instantiation of the explanatory database (ED) is performed by fuzzy set control algebras, an application builder, and by the information transmitted from the core system to the front end.

The *constraint propagation* is performed by the core system (in our example, Clinaid; cf. Section 4.7). *Constraint retranslation* (cf. [89, Fig. 4.3 and p. 104] is performed in our prototype within the front end by a *back-translation semantic interpreter* (cf. Section 4.9.2).

Our prototype demonstrates practical realizability of CW using fuzzy relational architectures. These architectures employ fuzzy nonassociative BK-products of relations as operations that operate on intensional propositional forms of fuzzy relations. For building of systems that compute with large IDS, TDS, and explore large explanatory databases (EDs), new computer representations of fuzzy relations are required [62]. The current prototype detects errors in incorrectly phrased NL sentences, but corrections have to be provided by the user. Automatic correction of grammatically incorrect sentences will have to be incorporated in the future, using the techniques described in Ref. 80. In this approach, parsing of the query, constraint explication, and constraint propagation are done dynamically, as mutually communicating dynamic concurrent processes exploring an entire family of EDs.

Because most of the literature on relations is about extensional satisfaction sets (e.g., building structures by Cartesian products), one may get a wrong impression that the propositional relational structures in predicate form used in Sections 4.7 and 4.8 can simply be replaced by fuzzification of conventional semantic nets; to assume this is, however, a serious mistake. First, relations in their predicate form are intensional, and only under special circumstances can then be reduced to their extensional (i.e., satisfaction set) form. Second, as in the test score semantics of Zadeh, in BK-products-based relational computations, Frege's principle of compositionality might not always hold. The compositionality principle requires that the meaning of a proposition be composed from the meanings of its *constituents*. In test score semantics of Zadeh [86], the *composants* are implicit rather than explicit. By allowing the meaning to be composed from its composants instead of its constituents, test-score semantics achieves a higher expressive power that is possible under Frege's principle of compositionality.

In general, higher-level representation of relational architectures is done in terms of concurrent parallel centers (cf. Section 4.7), processes, and communication agents [49]. Computationally this leads to partial relational structures [49], generalized morphisms [48], and branching quantifiers [30], where compositionality does not always hold. The relationship of these issues with Hintikka's notions of parallelism, learnability, and invariance [31], and independence friendly logics [30] ought to be investigated further.

Jaakko Hintikka's analysis of the issue of compositionality [29,31,32] in mathematical and philosophical logic yielded the following dependency graph:

$$\text{learnability} \Longrightarrow \left.\begin{array}{l}\text{parallelism}\\ \text{invariance}\\ \text{determinacy}\end{array}\right\} \Longrightarrow \text{compositionality.}$$

These intricate notions of Hintikka that together make the Fregean concept of compositionality are linked to the important distinction between surface information and depth information made by Hintikka [28]. This distinction of Hintikka is also important for understanding where the expressive power of the combination of the semiotic descriptors with the means of logic[8] comes from. According to Hintikka [28, p. 22]: "*Depth information* is the totality of information we can extract from a sentence by all the means that logic puts to our disposal. *Surface information*, on the contrary, is only that part of information which the sentence gives us explicitly."

IDS contains surface information, while the interrelationships of semiotic descriptors expressed by BK-products contribute to deep information. It follows that special relational properties which provide metalogic of granulation (cf. Sections 4.3.1, 4.3.3, and 4.7) characterize the logic component of semantic space that is closely linked to the language structure. The constraints imposed by the scheme of Section 4.3.2, on the other hand, are domain-of-application dependent. A more detailed discussion of the need to distinguish the general logical questions from ontological and epistemological questions (which are logic dependent) can be found in Ref. 42.

The important feature of the NL sentences is that they are not always compositional. From this it follows that structural relationship of sentences in large aggregates of meaning (i.e., texts are of paramount importance in computing with words). It would, however, be a mistake to assume that a given text is the entire source of meaning. *Text interpreters* and their *mutual communication* are equally important. We have given elsewhere an example of a text with two different interpretations in a fuzzy ED (explanatory database) [21].

In the context of computing with words, the semiotic notions of the Prague Linguistic Circle [79,82] are very important. The basic components of the Prague approach (eg., Refs. 24, 44, 83, and 85) are as follows:

- The language is approached as a teleological functional system, where the reference made to the outside world by an utterance is understood to be the function of language.
- Language is approached as a semantic system, where a linguistic sign and *communication* are two fundamental concepts.

[8]For example, relational constraints expressed by BK-products and special properties of relations.

- The basic element of the naming process is the world.
- The basic element of the communicative process is the sentence.
- Communicative process is the process by which the units of meaning are brought into mutual relationship.

In our design of systems for computing with words, we have to take into account the multiplicity of functional relationship [40] of language to the extralinguistic reality, which gives rise to the hierarchies in language organization, and in turn induces a complex relationship between sign and denotation. We have to clearly understand that both the Saussurean dichotomy sign–content (significant–signified) and the conventional semiotic triangle are simplified special cases of this more intricate functional relationship. In the Prague approach each sign may have several functions, and each function can be expressed by several signs. This is, for example, also the case for medical semiotics, as can clearly be seen from our account of Clinaid granular structures presented in Section 4.7.

REFERENCES

1. J. Abbot, A. van Leuwen, and A. Strotmann, OpenMath: communicating mathematical information between cooperating agents in a knowledge network, *J. Intell. Syst.*, 8(3–4):401–426, 19 (Special Issue: Improving the Design of Intelligent Systems: Outstanding Problems and Some Methods for Their Solutions).
2. J. Anderson, A. Behrooz, and L. J. Kohout, Knowledge elicitation: an exercise in identification and verification of medical knowledge, in L. J. Kohout, J. Anderson, and W. Bandler (eds.), *Multi-environmental Knowledge-Based Systems*, Ashgate (Gower), Aldershot, Hants, England, 1992, Chap. 6.
3. W. Bandler and L. J. Kohout, Fuzzy power sets and fuzzy implication operators, *Fuzzy Sets Syst.*, 4:13–30, 1980; reprinted in D. Dubois, H. Prade, and R. Yager (eds.), *Readings in Fuzzy Sets for Intelligent Systems*, Morgan Kaufmann, San Mateo, CA, 1993, pp. 88–96.
4. W. Bandler and L. J. Kohout, Fuzzy relational products as a tool for analysis and synthesis of the behaviour of complex natural and artificial systems, in P. P. Wang and S. K. Chang (eds.), *Fuzzy Sets: Theory and Applications to Policy Analysis and Information Systems*, Plenum Press, New York, 1980, pp. 341–367.
5. W. Bandler and L. J. Kohout, Semantics of implication operators and fuzzy relational products, *Int. J. Man–Mach. Stud.*, 12:89–116, 1980; reprinted in E. H. Mamdani and B. R. Gaines (eds.), *Fuzzy Reasoning and Its Applications*, Academic Press, London, 1981, pp. 219–246.
6. W. Bandler and L. J. Kohout, Fast fuzzy relational algorithms, in A. Ballester, D. Cardús, and E. Trillas (eds.), *Proc. 2nd International Conference on Mathematics at the Service of Man*, Universidad Politechnica de las Palmas, Las Palmas, Canary Islands, Spain, June 28–July 3, 1982, pp. 123–131.
7. W. Bandler and L. J. Kohout, *Modelling for Computer Scientists*, notes, M.Sc. in computer systems course, Department of Computer Science, Brunel University, London, 1983.

8. W. Bandler and L. J. Kohout, A survey of fuzzy relational products in their applicability to medicine and clinical psychology, in L. J. Kohout and W. Bandler (eds.), *Knowledge Representation in Medicine and Clinical Behavioural Science*, an Abacus Book, Gordon and Breach, New York, 1986, pp. 107–118.
9. W. Bandler and L. J. Kohout, Fuzzy implication operators, in M. G. Singh (ed.), *Systems and Control Encyclopedia*, Pergamon Press, Oxford, 1987, pp. 1806–1810.
10. W. Bandler and L. J. Kohout, Relations, mathematical, in M. G. Singh (ed.), *Systems and Control Encyclopedia*, Pergamon Press, Oxford, 1987, pp. 4000–4008.
11. W. Bandler and L. J. Kohout, Special properties, closures and interiors of crisp and fuzzy relations, *Fuzzy Sets Syst.*, 26(3):317–332, June 1988.
12. W. Bandler and L. J. Kohout, Universal construction of fuzzy preorders by means of triangle superproducts of relations, *Int. J. Gen. Syst.*, in press, 1997.
13. W. Bandler, V. Mancini, and L. J. Kohout, Investigating the structures of knowledge and thought, in G. E. Lasker (ed.), *Advances in Computer Science*, International Institute for Advanced Studies in Systems Research and Cybernetics, Ottawa, Ontario, Canada, 1989.
14. A. Behrooz, L. J. Kohout, and J. Anderson, Identifying the expertise of the expert, in *AAMSI Congress Proc.*, American Association for Medical Systems and Informatics, Washington, DC, 1987.
15. A. Behrooz, L. J. Kohout, and J. Anderson, Knowledge elicitation—the first step towards the construction of expert systems: the outline of a method, in L. J. Kohout, J. Anderson, and W. Bandler (eds.), *Multi-environmental Knowledge-Based Systems*, Ashgate (Gower), Aldershot, Harts, England, 1992, Chapt. 7.
16. B. Ben-Ahmeida, L. J. Kohout, and W. Bandler, The use of fuzzy relational products in comparison and verification of correctness of knowledge structures, in L. J. Kohout, J. Anderson, and W. Bandler (eds.), *Knowledge-Based Systems for Multiple Environments*, Ashgate (Gower), Aldershot, Hants, England, 1992, Chapt. 16.
17. B. DeBaets and E. Kerre, Fuzzy relational compositions, *Fuzzy Sets Syst.*, 60(1):109–120, 1993.
18. B. DeBaets and E. Kerre, A revision of Bandler–Kohout composition of relations, *Math. Pannonica*, 4:59–78, 1993.
19. B. DeBaets and E. Kerre, The cutting of compositions, *Fuzzy Sets Syst.*, 62(3):295–310, 1994.
20. J. P. Doignon, M. Monjardet, B. Roubens, and P. Vincke, Biorders families, valued relations and preference modelling, *J. Math. Psychol.*, 30:435–480, 1986.
21. F. Dowlatshahi and L. J. Kohout, Intentional possibilistic approach to dealing with incompleteness, vagueness and uncertainty, *Fuzzy Sets Syst.*, 25:277–295, 1988.
22. B. Dubrosky, L. J. Kohout, R. M. Walker, E. Kim, and H. P. Wang, Use of fuzzy relations for advanced technology cost modeling and affordability decisions, in *Proc. 35th AIAA Aerospace Sciences Meeting and Exhibit*, Reno, NV, Jan. 6–9, 1997, pp. 1–12; AIAA paper 97-0079.
23. J. C. Fodor, Traces of fuzzy binary relations, *Fuzzy Sets Syst.*, 50(3):331–341, 1992.
24. B. R. Gaines and L. J. Kohout, The fuzzy decade: a bibliography of fuzzy systems and closely related topics, *Int. J. Man–Mach. Stud.*, 9:1–68, 1977; reprinted in M. M. Gupta, G. N. Saridis, and B. R. Gaines (eds.), *Fuzzy Automata and Decision Processes*, Elsevier North-Holland, New York, 1988, pp. 403–490 (a critical survey with bibliography).

25. B. Granville and L. J. Kohout, An intelligent front-end for relational decision support architectures based on BK-products of fuzzy relations, in P. P. Wang (ed.), *Proc. 2nd Joint Conference on Information Sciences*, Wrightsville Beach, NC, Sept. 28–Oct. 1, 1995, pp. 605–608.
26. B. C. Granville, An empirical study of a query-language front-end processor using BK-products for fuzzy relational knowledge-based systems, Ph.D. dissertation in preparation, Department of Computer Science, Florida State University, Tallahassce, FL, 1998.
27. P. Hájek, A remark on Bandler–Kohout products of relations, *Int. J. Gen. Syst.*, 25(2): 165–166, 1996.
28. J. Hintikka, *Logic, Language-Games and Information: Kantian Themes in the Philosophy of Logic*, Clarendon Press, Oxford, 1973.
29. J. Hintikka, The prospects of convention *t*, *Dialectica*, 30:61–63, 1976.
30. J. Hintikka, *The Principles of Mathematics Revisited*, Cambridge University Press, Cambridge, 1996.
31. J. Hintikka and J. Kulas, *The Game of Language*, D. Reidel, Dordrecht, The Netherlands, 1983.
32. J. Hintikka and G. Sandu, Tarski's guilty secret: compositionality, in *Proc. 1997 Tarski Colloquium*, Vienna, 1997.
33. B. Juliano and W. Bandler, *Tracing Chains-of-Thought: Fuzzy Methods in Cognitive Diagnosis*, Physica-Verlag, Heidelberg, Germany, 1996.
34. V. Kaliappan, L. J. Kohout, and J. Anderson, Design of a well-protected patient record unit for multi-centre knowledge-based system clinaid, in K.-P. Adlasnik, G. Grabner, S. Bengtsson, and R. Hansen (eds.), *Proc. 10th International Congress (MIE-91)*, Berlin, Aug. 19–22, 1991, European Federation for Medical Informatics, *Lecture Notes in Medical Informatics*, Springer-Verlag, Berlin, pp. 309–313.
35. E. Keravnou and L. J. Kohout, A system for experimental verification of deviance of fuzzy connectives in information retrieval applications, in A. Ballester, D. Cardús, and E. Trillas (eds.), *Proc. 2nd International Conference on Mathematics at the Service of Man*, Universidad Politechnica de las Palmas, (Las Palmas, Canary Islands, Spain, June 28–July 3), 1982, pp. 384–387.
36. E. Kim, L. J. Kohout, B. Dubrosky, and W. Bandler, Use of fuzzy relations for affordability decisions in high technology, in R. A. Adey, G. Rzevski, and A. K. Sunol (eds.), *Applications of Artificial Intelligence in Engineering XI*, Computational Mechanics Publications, Bilerica, MA, 1996.
37. G. J. Klir, Fuzzy logic: its meaning and significance, *IEEE Potential*, 1995.
38. L. J. Kohout, I. Stabile, W. Bandler, and J. Anderson, Clinaid: medical knowledge-based system based on fuzzy relational structures, in M. Cohen and D. Hudson (eds.), *Comparative Approaches in Medical Reasoning*, World Scientific, River Edge, NJ, 1995, pp. 1–25.
39. L. J. Kohout, Control of movement and protection structures, *Int. J. Man–Mach. Stud.*, 14:394–422, 1981.
40. L. J. Kohout, On functional structures of behaviour, in L. J. Kohout and W. Bandler (eds.), *Knowledge Representation in Medicine and Clinical Behavioural Science*, an Abacus Book, Gordon and Breach, New York, 1986, pp. 69–94.
41. L. J. Kohout, Activity structures as a tool for design of technological artifacts, *Syst. Cybern. Int. J.*, 18(1):27–34, 1987.

42. L. J. Kohout, Theories of possibility: meta-axiomatics and semantics, *Fuzzy Sets Syst.*, 25:357–367, 1988.

43. L. J. Kohout, *A Perspective on Intelligent Systems: A Framework for Analysis and Design*, Chapman & Hall and Van Nostrand, London, 1990 (in 1991, received an international prize from the International Institute for Advanced Studies in Systems Research: "The best book of the year in the area of AI Systems").

44. L. J. Kohout, Quo vadis fuzzy systems: a critical evaluation of recent methodological trends, *Int. J. Gen. Syst.*, 19(4):395–424, 1991.

45. L. J. Kohout, Activity structures: a methodology for design of multi-environment and multi-context knowledge-based systems, in L. J. Kohout, J. Anderson, and W. Bandler (eds.), *Knowledge-Based Systems for Multiple Environments*, Ashgate (Gower), Aldershot, Hants, England, 1992, Chap. 5.

46. L. J. Kohout, Distributed architectures for computer aided manufacturing (CAM) and other embedded robotic systems, in L. J. Kohout, J. Anderson, and W. Bandler (eds.), *Multi-environmental Knowledge-Based Systems*, . Ashgate (Gower), Aldershot, Hants, England, 1992, Chap. 13 (the activity structures approach originated by the author is applied to the design of robotic systems).

47. L. J. Kohout, Toward a unified theory of intelligent autonomous control systems, in A. Kandel and G. Langholz (eds.), *Fuzzy Control Systems*, CRC Press, Boca Raton, FL, 1994, pp. 19–54.

48. L. J. Kohout, Boolean and fuzzy relations, in P. M. Pardalos and C. A. Floudas (eds.), *The Encyclopedia of Optimization*, Kluwer, Boston, 1999.

49. L. J. Kohout, Foundations of knowledge engineering for systems with distributed intelligence: a relational approach, in A. Kent and J. G. Williams (eds.), *Encyclopedia of Microcomputers*, Marcel Dekker, New York, 1999, Vol. 24, pp. 127–158.

50. L. J. Kohout, J. Anderson, and W. Bandler, Clinical computer aids based on assymetrical products of relations, in *Progress Report 1*, SERC Research Grant GR/C 172.3, Brunel University and Kings College Medical and Dental Schools, University of London, London, Aug. 1983.

51. L. J. Kohout, J. Anderson, W. Bandler, A. Behrooz, S. Gao, and C. Trayner, Activity structures based architectures for knowledge-based systems, Part I: dynamics of localised fuzzy inference and its interaction with planning, *Fuzzy Sets Syst.*, 44(4):405–420, 1991.

52. L. J. Kohout, J. Anderson, W. Bandler, S. Gao, and C. Trayner, CLINAID: a knowledge-based system for support of decisions in the conditions of risk and uncertainty, in L. J. Kohout, J. Anderson, and W. Bandler (eds.), *Knowledge-Based Systems for Multiple Environments*, Ashgate (Gower), Aldershot, Hants, England, 1992, Chap. 10.

53. L. J. Kohout, J. Anderson, and W. Bandler, *Knowledge-Based Systems for Multiple Environments*, Ashgate (Gower), Aldershot, Hants, England, 1992 (awarded "Outstanding Scholarly Contribution Award" by the Systems Research Foundation in 1993).

54. L. J. Kohout, J. Anderson, S. Gao, and W. Bandler, On a transformation of triangle product inference structure of Clinaid into fuzzy neural network architecture with variable treshold, in P. P. Wang (ed.), *Proc. Joint Conference on Information Sciences: 3rd Annual International Conference on Fuzzy Theory and Technology*, Duke University, Nov. 13–16, 1994, Durham, NC, pp. 304–307.

55. L. J. Kohout and W. Bandler, Relational-product architectures for information processing, *Inf. Sci.*, 37:25–37, 1985.

56. L. J. Kohout and W. Bandler, Knowledge representation, clinical action and expert systems, in L. J. Kohout and W. Bandler (eds.), *Knowledge Representation in Medicine and Clinical Behavioural Science*, an Abacus Book, Gordon and Breach, New York, 1986, pp. 1–8.
57. L. J. Kohout and W. Bandler, Computer security systems: fuzzy logics, in M. G. Singh (ed.), *Systems and Control Encyclopedia*, Pergamon Press, Oxford, 1987.
58. L. J. Kohout and W. Bandler, The use of fuzzy information retrieval techniques in construction of multi-centre knowledge-based systems, in B. Bouchon and R. R. Yager (eds.), *Uncertainty in Knowledge-Based Systems*, Lecture Notes in Computer Science, Vol. 286, Springer-Verlag, Berlin, 1987, pp. 257–264.
59. L. J. Kohout and W. Bandler, Fuzzy relational products in knowledge engineering, in V. Novák et al. (eds.), *Fuzzy Approach to Reasoning and Decision Making*, Academia, Prague, Czech Republic, and Kluwer, Dordrecht, The Netherlands, 1992, pp. 51–66.
60. L. J. Kohout and W. Bandler, Use of fuzzy relations in knowledge representation, acquisition and processing, in L. A. Zadeh and J. Kacprzyk (eds.), *Fuzzy Logic for the Management of Uncertainty*, Wiley, New York, 1992, pp. 415–435.
61. L. J. Kohout, S. Gao, and H. Kalantar, Design of questioning strategies for knowledge-based systems, in L. J. Kohout, J. Anderson, and W. Bandler (eds.), *Knowledge-Based Systems for Multiple Environments*, Ashgate (Gower), Aldershot, Hants, England, 1992, Chap. 11.
62. L. J. Kohout and M. Harris, Computer representation of fuzzy relations by means of threaded trees, *J. Fuzzy Logic Intell. Syst.*, 3(1):41–64, 1993 (ISSN:1225–1127).
63. L. J. Kohout and M. Kallala, Evaluator of neurological patients' dexterity based on relational fuzzy products, in *Proc. 2nd Expert Systems International Conference*, London, Oct. 1986, Learned Information, NJ, 1986, pp. 1–12.
64. L. J. Kohout and M. Kallala, Choice of fuzzy optimal logics for pattern classifiers by means of measure analysis, in *Proc. 7th International Congress on Cybernetics and Systems*, Imperial College, London, Sept. 1987.
65. L. J. Kohout and M. Kallala, The use of fuzzy information retrieval in knowledge-based management of patients' clinical profiles, in B. Bouchon and R. R. Yager (eds.), *Uncertainty in Knowledge-Based Systems*, Lecture Notes in Computer Science, Vol. 286, Springer-Verlag, Berlin, 1987, pp. 275–282.
66. L. J. Kohout, E. Keravnou, and W. Bandler, Automatic documentary information retrieval by means of fuzzy relational products, in B. R. Gaines, L. A. Zadeh, and H.-J. Zimmermann (eds.), *Fuzzy Sets in Decision Analysis*, North-Holland, Amsterdam, 1984, pp. 383–404.
67. L. J. Kohout, E. Keravnou, W. Bandler, C. Trayner, and J. Anderson, Construction of an expert therapy adviser as a special case of a general system protection design, in R. Trappl (ed.), *Cybernetics and Systems Research 2*, North-Holland, Amsterdam, 1984, pp. 97–104.
68. L. J. Kohout, E. Th. Keravnou, and W. Bandler, Design of an information retrieval system using triangle and square products of fuzzy relations for thesaurus construction, in *Proc. IFAC International Symposium on Fuzzy Information, Knowledge Representation and Decision Analysis*, Marseille, France, July 19–21, 1983, Pergamon Press, Oxford, 1983.
69. L. J. Kohout and E. Kim, Global characterization of fuzzy logic systems with para-consistent and grey set features, in P. Wang, (ed.), *Proc. 3rd Joint Conference on*

Information Sciences (JCIS'97): 5th International Conference on Fuzzy Theory and Technology, Research Triangle Park, NC, Mar. 1997, pp. 238–241; in Vol. 1, *Fuzzy Logic, Intelligent Control and Genetic Algorithms*, Duke University, Durham, NC, 1997.

70. L. J. Kohout and E. Kim, The role of semiotic descriptors in relational representation of fuzzy granular structures, in J. Albus (ed.), *Intelligent Systems and Semiotics: A Learning Perspective (ISAS'97)*, pages Gaithersburg, MD, Sept. 22–25, 1997, pp. 31–36; NIST Spec. Publ. 918.

71. L. J. Kohout and E. Kim, Semiotic descriptors in fuzzy relational computations, in J. H. Albus and A. Meystel (eds.), *Proc. IEEE International Symposium on Intelligent Control, IEEE International Symposium on Computational Intelligence in Robotics and Automation and Intelligent Systems and Semiotics: Joint conference on the Science and Technology of Intelligent Systems*, Piscataway, NJ, Sept. 14–17, 1998, pp. 828–833.

72. L. J. Kohout and Yong-Gi Kim, Generating control strategies for resolution-based theorem provers by means of fuzzy relational products and relational closures, in B. Lowen and M. Roubens (eds.), *Fuzzy Logic: State of the Art*, Kluwer Academic, Boston, 1993, pp. 181–192.

73. L. J. Kohout, V. Mancini, W. Bandler, and I. Stabile, Intelligent machine retrieval of satellite-age data for human environmental understanding, in P. P. Wang (ed.), *Proc. Joint Conference on Information Sciences: 3rd Annual International Conference on Fuzzy Theory and Technology*, Duke University, Durham, NC, Nov. 13–16, 1994, pp. 28–31.

74. L. J. Kohout and I. Stabile, Interval-valued inference in medical knowledge-based system Clinaid, *Interval Comput.*, 2(3):88–115, 1993.

75. L. J. Kohout and I. Stabile, Relational computations in medical KBS CLINAID: the means for integrating interval, symbolic logic and neural network techniques, in T. Furuhashi et al. (eds.), *Proc. First On-Line Workshop of Soft Computing*, Society of Fuzzy Theory and Systems (SOFT), Nagoya University, Nagoya, Japan, Aug. 1996, pp. 228–233; *http://www.bioele.nuee.nagoya-u.ac.jp/wsc1*.

76. L. J. Kohout and I. Stabile, Improving the design of intelligent systems: outstanding problems and some solutions, *J. Intell. Syst.*, 8(3–4):225–238, 1998.

77. L. J. Kohout, I. Stabile, H. Kalantar, M. San-Andres, and J. Anderson, Parallel interval-based reasoning in medical knowledge-based system Clinaid, *Reliable Comput. (Special Issue on Parallel Systems)*, 1(2):109–140, 1995.

78. L. J. Kohout and G. Zenz, Activity structures and triangle BK-products of fuzzy relations: a useful modelling and computational tool in value analysis studies, in R. Mesiar et al. (eds.), *Proc. World Congress of International Fuzzy Systems Association (IFSA'97)*, Prague, Czech Republic, June 1997, Vol. IV, pp. 211–216.

79. L. Matejka (ed.), *Sound, Sign and Meaning: Quinquagenary of the Prague Linguistic Circle*, University of Michigan, Ann Arbor, MI, 1978, No. 6.

80. S. Nagarajan and L. J. Kohout, Fuzzy syntactic and semantic analyzer, in R. Lowen and M. Roubens (eds.), *Proc. 4th IFSA World Congress (IFSA'91)*, Brussels, Vol. *Artificial Intelligence*, International Fuzzy Systems Association, 1991, pp. 149–152.

81. J. Riguet, Relations binaires, fermetures, correspondances de Galois, *Bull. Soc. Math. Fr.*, 76:114–155, 1948.

82. P. Steiner and J. Vachek, Semiotics in Bohemia in the 19th and early 20th centuries: major trends and figures, in R. W. Bailey, L. Matějka, and P. Steiner (eds.), *The Sign: Semiotics*

Around the World, University of Michigan, Ann Arbor, MI, 1978, pp. 207–226; book series: Michigan Slavic Contributions, No. 9.

83. B. Trnka, *Selected Papers in Structural Linguistics: Contributions to English and General Linguistics Written in the Years 1928–1978*, Mouton, New York, 1982.
84. D. Tsonis and L. J. Kohout, Data structures for computer representation of fuzzy relations, in P. P. Wang (ed.), *Proc. Joint Conference on Information Sciences: 3rd Annual International Conference on Fuzzy Theory and Technology*, Duke University, Durham, NC, Nov. 13–16, 1994, pp. 32–34.
85. J. Vachek and Dušková (transl. and ed.), *Praguiana: Some Basic and Less Known Aspects of the Prague Linguistic School*, W.A. Benjamin, Menlo Park, CA; co-edition with Academia, Publishing House of the Czechoslovak Academy of Sciences, Prague, Czech Republic, 1983.
86. L. A. Zadeh, in R. Yager et al. (eds.), *Fuzzy Sets: Selected Papers I*, Wiley, New York, 1987.
87. L. A. Zadeh, in G. Klir and B. Yuan (eds.), *Fuzzy Sets: Selected Papers II*, World Scientific, New York, 1996.
88. L. A. Zadeh, Similarity relations and fuzzy orderings, *Inf. Sci.*, 3:177–200, 1971.
89. L. A. Zadeh, Fuzzy logic = computing with words, *IEEE Trans. Fuzzy Syst.*, 4(2):103–111, 1996.
90. L. A. Zadeh, Toward a theory of fuzzy information granulation and its centrality in human reasoning and fuzzy logic, *Fuzzy Sets Syst.*, 90(2):111–127, 1997.

CHAPTER 5

COMPUTING GRANULAR WORD MEANINGS: A FUZZY LINGUISTIC APPROACH IN COMPUTATIONAL SEMIOTICS

BURGHARD B. RIEGER
University of Trier, Trier, Germany

The methods and goals of the scientific enterprise may tell us little about human thought in general, just as the symbolic systems constructed appear to differ radically from natural languages in their formal and semantic properties. If so, the picture that has guided the most important work on these topics in the last century may be seriously misconceived.

—N. Chomsky

5.1 INTRODUCTION

The notion of *computing with words* (CW) hinges crucially on the employment of natural language expressions. These are considered to provide not only the representational structures of what can semantically be meant but also the operational means of what can cognitively be understood by processing these structures. They allow for decomposition of wholes into their constituents or parts (*granulation*), or conversely, for composition and integration of parts into wholes (*organization*), and for the association of causes with effects (*causation*). According to Zadeh's early introduction of the notion of granularity [69] and his recent elaboration of that concept [71] as *theory of fuzzy information granulation* (TFIG), human cognition may be understood to be based on and structured by processes of granulation, organization, and causation. These are meant to specify different types of mind/brain activities that can be characterized as being computational in nature and hence to be modeled mathematically and/or procedurally. Although this characterization suggests different modes of mind/brain activities, to be distinguished sharply both as the enactment of processes and as the results these processes produce—a distinction we will

Computing with Words, Edited by Paul P. Wang.
ISBN 0-471-35374-4

have to draw and obey in what follows—there is the need for yet another discrimination to be made in order to clarify what we will deal with here. It is tied to the first and concerns the way in which mind/brain activities are made accessible in different ways by techniques, models, or disciplines.

Whereas cognitive approaches tend to model mind/brain processes based on the evaluation of (in parts linguistic) data generated in (more or less) sophisticated experiments of human thought and understanding, much more immediate results of cognitively most relevant mind/brain activities—not the experimentally reduced segments of them—are being made accessible in the form and structure of natural language discourse. Other than approaches in cognitive linguistics that model the human language faculty under theoretical premises outlined below, some processes of language understanding require and can be modeled along observable but as yet unexploited traces of meaning constitution which speakers/writers and hearers/readers enact in situations of communicative language use.[1] This enactment is tied to representational or semiotic functions, based on regularities of entity usages[2] which not only generate observable structures but serve in turn to allow these functions being activated to modify these structures simultaneously. Thus the complexities of natural languages themselves may be taken as a salient paradigm for information granulation in both its fuzzy and crisp modes of structural representation and functional processing. It appears that the conception of fuzzy and/or crisp granulation—once the process–result ambiguity and its cognitive–linguistic ambivalence is solved as addressed by a facet of the symbol–matter problem [30]—lends itself easily to a unifying view of how natural language understanding or meaning constitution may be arrived at as a computational process on structural entities adequately identified.

The way that structural linguists used to and still do categorize (segment and classify) observable natural language phenomena as tokens, such as phones, morphs, and utterances, to constitute abstract linguistic entities as types, such as phonemes, morphemes, and phrases, will be shown to be based on these very processes, however imperfectly. What may procedurally be derived either as *soft linguistic categories* or fuzzy *granules* represented by vectors, distributions, or *fuzzy sets* for (numerical) computation has so far been overgeneralized and abstracted to form crisp categories represented by signs (symbols) for (string) manipulation. Certainly, linear aggregation of these symbols serve to understand and control one type of observable natural language phenomena as part of string formation or formal grammar. Its core concepts of well-formedness (*syntax*) and truth function (*semantics*) were made explicit by way of specifying conditions of formal correctness and derivational compositionality. Their symbolic representations in the form of productions or rewrite rules—allowing for recursive application and generative string formation—not only constituted a wealth of symbol aggregation systems (*formal languages*) but were also employed to model comparable properties (in processes) of natural language string formation.

[1]In the sense of employment and act of being used under certain conditions and to a particular communicative purpose.

[2]In the sense of customary practice and manner of using that may establish and modify rules and standards.

However, whereas applying formal rules would allow us to specify generative properties and truth-functional constraints in formal constructs such as sentence and proposition, other properties of natural language expressions, which are communicationally more relevant (e.g., making sense by having specific meaning in situational contexts which are to be understood), tended to be abstracted away. The process of understanding natural language discourse below and above formal sentence reconstruction is, by and large, still in need of principled analysis, formal representation, computational simulation, and procedural realization.

To follow this line of structural, functional, simulative, and enactive modeling, traits of traditional approaches to cognition and natural language processing as forwarded by *linguistics proper* (LP), *computational linguistics* (CL), and language processing in *artificial intelligence* (AI) research will be reviewed to identify points of departure from which to advance our understanding of how natural languages function the way they do. Some presuppositions will have to be revised to understand how communicative employment of languages is based not only on (*use*) but also establishes (*usage*) structural constraints[3] which may be made explicit by assumptions motivated by systems theory and/or by empirically testable hypotheses derived from systems theory. It will be argued that the introspective assessment and judgment of any speaker's own language faculty on linguistic functions and the correctness of singular sentences or phrasal structures as conceived by an ideal speaker's/hearer's *internal language* (IL) is not at all sufficient, let alone superior to modern means of empirical investigation of masses of natural language discourse or *external language* (EL) as produced by real speakers/writers. Instead, some of the inadequacies of models of natural language processing that competence-oriented linguistics have inspired so far will hopefully be revealed to be due to unwarranted abstractions from relevant characteristics (e.g., contextuality, vagueness, variability, adaptivity, and openness, to name only the most salient) of processes of natural language communication. Other than these idealizations, which purportedly allow immediate access to cognitively relevant entities, we shall argue for an empirically controlled understanding of functional sign constitution which does not readily abstract from the emergent structures, which models of a more semiotically cognitive information processing (SCIP) may bring about. It is hoped to collect and produce some evidence that the traces of such processing cannot only be identified, but that these identification procedures may also be employed to systematically (re)construct fuzzy information granulation procedurally.

In *fuzzy linguistic* (FL) models of *computational semiotics* (CS), the situatedness of natural language communication is considered conditional. This requirement is met by corpora of *pragmatically homogeneous texts* (PHTs) which assemble language material which is situationally constrained by a number of variables (e.g., communicative media or domain, register, topic, author) whose values (e.g., newspaper, report, economy) define the PHT profile the texts incorporated will satisfy. There is good reason to assume that such PHT collections realize the organized structure of natural language discourse [i.e., integrating parts into wholes (sign

[3]See footnotes 1 and 2.

formation)] as well as the causative functions [i.e., associating causes with effects (meaning constitution)]. The inherent structuredness of a PHT corpus gives rise to multiresolutional representations of meaning functions which may be explored to model (crisp and fuzzy) SCIP granules. Based on the empirically well founded observation and rigorous mathematical description of universal regularities in natural language discourse, these regularities can be shown to structure and constitute (different levels of) processes and/or their representational results when made to operate on pragmatically homogeneous texts of either performed or intended communicative interaction in actual situations. Only such a performance-oriented semiotic approach will give a chance to formally reconstruct and model procedurally both the significance of entities and the meanings of signs as a function of a first- and second-order semiotic embedding relation of situations (or contexts) and of language games (or cotexts) which corresponds to the two-level actualization of cognitive processes in language understanding [54].

Following this introduction is an exploration of the cognitive background (Section 5.2) with an outline of cognitive modeling (Section 5.2.1), the relation of language and linguistics (Section 5.2.2), and the cognitive linguistic approach (Section 5.2.3) as opposed to the fuzzy linguistic approach (Section 5.2.4). The conception of computational semiotics (Section 5.3) is developed along the line of an information systems view (Section 5.3.1), the notion of semiotic enactment (Section 5.3.2), and the idea of (re)constructive procedures (Section 5.3.3) considered obligatory on combining situation and language game semantics in a procedural frame of semiotics. This is then tied to fuzzy linguistics (Section 5.4) with the formal derivation and structured representation of word space (Section 5.4.1) and semantic hyper space (Section 5.4.2) as computed from natural language data and actual discourse. Under the heading of "(Re)Constructing Reference" (Section 5.5) the semiotic cognitive information processing system devised so far is submitted to an experimental test (Section 5.5.1) placing it into a language environment of particular, restricted situational conditions (Section 5.5.2) whose operational processes and results (Section 5.5.3) are produced to illustrate the SCIP system's performance. After these somewhat preparatory sections in a realization of semiotic computing with words (Section 5.6) we outline, illustrate, and discuss functions (operating on the semantic hyper space data) and structures (resulting and emerging from that processing) as dispositional dependency structures (Section 5.6.1) and as semiotically generalized constraints (Section 5.6.2), and their representational properties (Section 5.6.3) as constituting a realizational model of semiosis. Finally, in the conclusion (Section 5.7) we summarize some of the innovative points that may also hint at envisaged areas of possible extension, both theoretical and applicational.

5.2 COGNITIVE BACKGROUND

For the past decades, the concept of symbolic representation together with the computer metaphor have appeared to offer an adequate framework to deal with cognitive processes scientifically. Formally grounded by logical calculi and implemented as algorithms operating on representational structures, cognition is considered a form of information processing in the cognitive sciences. Thus cognitive theory has long identified the complex of language understanding as a modular system of subsystems of information processing that could be modeled accordingly. The alliance of logics and linguistics, mediated mainly by (language) philosophy in the past and by (discrete) mathematics since the first half of this century, has long been (and partially still is) dominant as to how natural languages and their functioning should be explicated and how their processing could be modeled. In replicating (and in parts also supplementing) semiotically motivated strata of systematic sign description and analysis, different levels of modular aggregation of information—external and/or internal to a processing system—have been distinguished in cognitive models of language understanding. They partially correspond to and cut across the syntactics–semantics–pragmatics distinction in the semiotic relatedness of signs, the utterance–discourse–corpus levels of performative language analysis, and the hierarchy of morphophonological, syntax-sentencial, and lexicosemantic descriptions in structural models of linguistics. It is ironic, however, that the dramatic increase in computational power and symbol manipulation means has changed the fundamentals of many scientific disciplines, even creating new ones, but has allowed linguistically oriented disciplines, even new ones, to adhere to the lore of seemingly well grounded and traditionally dignified concepts (e.g., phrase and sentence, predicate and proposition, grammatical correctness and formal truth) in describing natural language structures and their functions.

In view of our as yet very limited understanding of the processes constituting natural language understanding which cognitive models and implemented systems of computational natural language processing explicatively offer or demonstrate, it may well be suspected that some of the problems encountered by these model constructions are due to the modeling tools and representational formats they employ in depicting and manipulating entities (elements, structures, processes, and procedures) considered to be relevant or even essential to an understanding of the communicative use of natural languages by humans.

5.2.1 Modeling Cognition

An earlier attempt by Varela et al. [66] to classify model constructions as produced in cognitive science had led us to distinguish three types of approaches, based on their characteristics:

1. *Cognitive approach*: presupposes the existence of an external world structured by given objects and properties and the existence of representations of (fragments of) this world internal to the system, so that the cognitive systems' (observable) behavior of action and reaction may be modeled by processes operating on these structures.
2. *Associative approach*: described as dynamic structuring based on the model concept of self-organization, with cognitive systems constantly adapting to changing environmental conditions by modifying their internal representations of them.

3. *Enactive approach*: may be characterized as being based on the notion of structural coupling. Instead of assuming an external world and systems' internal representations of that world, some unity of structural relatedness is considered to be fundamental of, and the (only) condition for, any abstracted or acquired duality in notions of the external and internal, object and subject, and reality and its experience.

Whereas the first two approaches apparently draw on the traditional rationalistic paradigm of mind–matter duality—the former static, the latter dynamic—by assuming the existence of external world structures and internal representations of it, the third type does not. Considering the importance that the notions of formatting and representation (both internal and external to an information-processing system) have gained in tracing processes on the grounds of their observable or resulting structures, it appears to be justified [55] to add a fourth type:

4. *Semiotic approach*: focuses on the notion of semiosis and may also be characterized by the process of enactment, complemented, however, by representational impact. For example, it is considered fundamental to the distinction of cognitive processes from their structural results, which due to the traces these processes leave behind, may emerge in some form of knowledge whose different representational modes comply with a distinction between internal or tacit knowledge (i.e., memory), on the one hand, and of external or declarative knowledge (e.g., language discourse), on the other.

According to these types of cognitive modeling, computational semiotics (CS) can be characterized as aiming at the dynamics of meaning constitution by realizing processes of simulated[4] multiresolutional representation [27] within the frame of an ecological information-processing paradigm [54]. CS does not depend on rule-based or symbolic formats for (linguistic) knowledge representations, nor does it subscribe to the notion of (world) knowledge as static structures that may be abstracted from and represented independently of the way they are processed. Instead, knowledge structures and the processes operating on them are modeled as procedures that can be implemented as algorithms.

In particular, the emergence of sign structures as a self-organizing process may be studied on the basis of combinatorial and selective constraints universal to all natural languages. Both (linguistic) entity and structure formation as well as (semiotic) sign and symbol function may thus be reconstructed as two aspects of one type of process, constituting and at the same time acquiring syntagmatic constraints on linear agglomeration, and paradigmatic constraints on selectional choice of elements in

[4] The necessity to distinguish sharply between simulation and realization [30] in modeling living systems was clarified in desirable detail by Pattee (see below). It may be related to the even more fundamental issue addressed by Casti [9], who compared the internal structural simplicity (or complexity) of model constructions against their external behavioral complexity (or simplicity) by way of their observable and measurable performances. These interdependencies and some of their semiotic aspects will, however, have to be dealt with in a separate paper.

natural language discourse. It is extending traditional linguistic analyses that have long—however coarsely—identified and represented their findings as morphophonemic, lexicosemantic, phraseosyntactic, and situational or pragmasemantic types of structures. Their regularities may now be exploited at a much finer grain and represented in higher and dynamically adapting resolutions by text-analyzing algorithms operating on different levels of structuredness. Ideally, these algorithms accept natural language discourse as input and produce, via intermediate levels of (not necessarily symbolic) representations, interpretable structures of consistent regularities as output. Whereas the intermediate (internal) representations on different levels may be understood as the semiotic system's (hidden) layers of information processing, the system's output structures would represent its state of adaptation to the (external) structures of its environment as signaled and mediated by the natural language discourse processed.

Thus *semiotic cognitive information processing* (SCIP) can be defined as the cognitive processing of information by humans and/or machines whose semioticity consists of the multilevel representational performance of dynamic (working) structures emerging from and at the same time being modified by such processing, which simultaneously constitutes meaning.

5.2.2 Language and Linguistics

Anything we know or believe about the world can—more or less precisely—be communicated verbally. We do so by language means, employing words, forming phrases and clauses, and producing discourse whose meanings are understood to convey, stand for, designate, refer to, or deal with topics and subjects, entities and domains, structures and processes in the real world (past, present, or future), or be altogether fictitious, in an entertaining and/or educating sense of understanding. Natural language discourse in the form of spoken or written texts (still) is the most flexible and, as such, highly efficient means to represent knowledge and to convey learning to others.

What appears to be conditional for this kind of textual understanding is humans' language faculty: the performative ability to identify, recognize, produce, and structure fragments of real-world material stimuli according to internal (although externally conditioned) principles. Traditional approaches in linguistics proper (LP), computational linguistics (CL), and parts of artificial intelligence (AI) claim to be interested in and based on (a subset of) these principles, which they call language competence. Their research endeavors have developed structural and procedural conceptions for (certain aspects of) the process of language understanding. The distinction drawn between linguistic knowledge as represented formally in rule-based formats, and world knowledge, whose structuredness is mediated by symbol representational formats, has allowed us to combine both in a controlled way to model language processing by machine. However, important features characteristic of natural language understanding processes, such as contextuality, vagueness, robustness, adaptivity, distributivity, and dynamism, had to be overlooked or put aside intentionally because of the representational formats chosen and the way this choice determined the (entities of) processing. Consequently, computational processing of natural languages as based on relevant CL and AI research is presently faced by—and partially even undergoing—fundamental scrutiny. It may broadly be characterized by challenges concerning some of the founding assumptions and basal hypotheses implied in their research goals (*Erkenntnisinteresse*), by critical evaluation of their methodological standards in the light of empirical disciplines' quantitative research methods (*Untersuchungsmethoden*), and by redefinition of the (proper) linguistic domain of language research objects in general (*Forschungsgegenstände*).

Ruling Tradition: Linguistic Competence. According to Chomsky [11], the cognitive study of natural language phenomena has to be concerned primarily with the principles underlying language understanding [i.e., the structure and the organization of the human language faculty (*competence*)]. It is believed that it may (theoretically) be analyzed and (formally) be characterized well without empirical exploration of observable language data as produced in situations of communicative interaction by real speakers/hearers (*performance*). In a more recent move [13] the speaker's language knowledge or competence has been reformulated as *internalized* or *I-language* whose set of entities (called a *lexicon*) aggregatable according to a set of rules (called a *computational system*) constitutes the proper domain (called a mental grammar) of linguistic inquiry. Accordingly, the speakers' performative language use, termed *externalized* or *E-language*, became marginal to that domain and was considered cognitively uninteresting. One of the results that the ongoing discussion [60] may produce is the understanding that the grounding of cognitive linguistic research so far might turn out to be based on a too-principled abstraction of language reality [61] as experienced—individually and collectively—in communicative discourse interaction.

Taking account of some language regularities and structures that are empirically traceable but may not be identified within the categorial framework of established linguistic concepts[5] and in view of corresponding tendencies in cognitive linguistics, CL and AI research has come up with some solutions that resulted in increasing complexity and/or narrowing scopes of systems dealing with natural language structures and functions, whereas some empirical studies of performative language phenomena were able to provide valuable insights and explanations because of their domains' objects and methods complementary to those of competence-centered linguistics. Moreover, it appears that empirical approaches based on quantitative-statistical as well as fuzzy-theoretical model constructions may allow for a more semiotic understanding of the functioning of language signs as used by interlocutors in communicative interaction.

[5]Phenomena such as linear short-distance orderings (*Nahordnung*) of performative language entities (e.g., co-occurrences) whose regularities are deprived of rule-based notations but can easily be represented and processed as numerical expressions of correlation values with any precision, are an example in point here. They appear to be the observable results of structuring principles which have been overlooked by competence theoretic investigations only because they do not comply with linear long-distance orderings (*Fernordnung*) that are constitutive of linguistic categories as represented by symbols and processed by familiar grammar formalisms [15,18,20].

Procedural Challenge: Language Performance. As is well known, computational models of natural language analysis and generation are based on correct structural descriptions of input strings and their semantic interpretations. This is made possible by rule-based representations of (syntactic and lexical) knowledge of a language and of the (referential and situative) world knowledge concerned in formats on which grammar formalisms and deductive inferential mechanisms can operate. Notwithstanding the considerable advances in the development and theoretical testing of increasingly more complex systems, this kind of cognitive (or knowledge-based) language processing (based on monotone logics, symbolic representations, rule-based operations, sequential processing, etc.) and the essential statics of their representational structures were challenged—although for differing reasons—by connectionist and empirical approaches. These were particularly successful in simulating dynamic properties of processes of cognitive natural language processing (based on the theory of dynamic systems, subsymbolic or distributed representations, numerically continuous operations, parallel processing, etc.) in *artificial neural network* (ANN) models [8,28,33]. There were new insights gained into the wealth of structural patterns and functional relations observed in *very large language corpora* (VLLC) of communicative natural language performance. These insights have partly been specified by results from models of quantitative and statistical analyses (based on probability and possibility theory, stochastic and fuzzy modeling, numerical mathematics and nonmonotone logics, strict hypothesizing and rigorous testing, etc.) [1,23].

The performance of operational ANN implementations applied successfully to problems of string segmentation and classification, to adaptive learning and acquisition, to linguistic entity recognition and identification tasks without prior knowledge of rule-based entity definitions, and so on, seemed to allow for everything from controversial skepticism to wildly speculative enthusiasm. Focusing on some of the earlier and more serious contributions to this discussion that the controversy of connectionistic versus rule-based approaches to models of natural language processing has fueled [17,59,63,64], one will find—overall and in the majority of cases—that these are brought forward from an undisputed epistemological position characteristic of and common to cognitive linguistics. Proponents from both sides seem to accept that language competence, its principles, components, and their organization, is of primary concern to linguistics proper and hence is the basal objective for computational linguistics, too. Following the discussion so far, there is a predominant interest in the theoretical aspects of what the different, even hybrid model constructions would claim and may justifiably be said to explain [7, 21, 33], not, however, what aspects of new theory constructions or older theoretical constructs' modifications would be necessary to cover and explain hard-core results of empirical and quantitative approaches in language research.

The reasons for this delay are manifold, as the availability of masses of performative language data not only require the methodological mastery of a whole spectrum of tools and methods, new to most linguists, but also tend to imply some compensating shift from language competence toward language performance studies corresponding to a wider domain of research objects for linguistics proper

[16] which many computational linguists would refrain from. However, in view of the formal complexity and applicational limitations that rule-based cognitive models show, on the one hand, and considering the surprisingly efficient practicability of stochastic parsers [14,4] and statistical machine translation systems [5,6], on the other, there are good reasons to expect some revision of assumptions and basal hypotheses defining cognitive linguistics. To name only one of the most prominent is the availability (and globally increasing number) of very large language corpora.[6] These will facilitate investigating types of natural language properties whose categorial vagueness (uncertain, underdetermined, fuzzily delimited, etc.) or dubious observability (sparse data, uncertain information, etc.) had left them inaccessible and too often irrelevant to language research. Meanwhile, the processing of VLLC has given abundant evidence that categorial concepts common in traditional linguistics must be considered highly problematic. When applied tentatively to classify structures that can easily be identified procedurally by quantitative-numerical means, an increasing number of borderline cases, variations, and ambiguities are encountered which cannot be dealt with consistently within the traditional categorial framework. As these problems appear to result from mappings of structurally highly related data sets to inadequate categories only, these ought to be avoided from the very start. Consequently, classical categorial conceptions in linguistics have begun to be scrutinized and may possibly be substituted by soft categories [55] before there is substantial hope to improve chances to understand and to explain knowledge as some form of (world and/or language) structures emerging from information-processing models that can truly be called semiotic.

5.2.3 Cognitive Linguistic Mechanisms: Strata

In a rare venture into discussing systematically how cognitive (i.e., knowledge-based) information-processing mechanisms may be provided together with the knowledge bases on which they are meant to operate, and how these knowledge structures may be related to observable language data, Bierwisch [3] sketches a hierarchy of information-processing mechanisms whose representational format (sets of rewrite rules operating on structured data) allows algorithms to be formulated and implementations found to guarantee their computability. According to this schema (Figure 5.1) and starting with the morphophonological level, an information-processing mechanism M_1 is postulated which accepts utterances as input and produces some associated *structures* as output. In doing so, however, the mechanism's performance will be determined not only by the external input strings but also by some internal knowledge of elements and rules that allow us to agglomerate the structures

[6]The Trier dpa-Corpus comprises the complete textual material from the basic newsreel service of 1990–1993 (720.000 documents), and the author thanks Deutsche Presseagentur (dpa), Hamburg, for providing these data for research purposes. After cleaning of editing commands, the Trier dpa-Corpus consists of approximately 180 million (18×10^7) running words (tokens), for which an automatic tagging and lemmatizing tool is under development. It is this German text corpus which provides the performative data of written language use for current (and planned) fuzzy linguistic and computational semiotic projects in our university department.

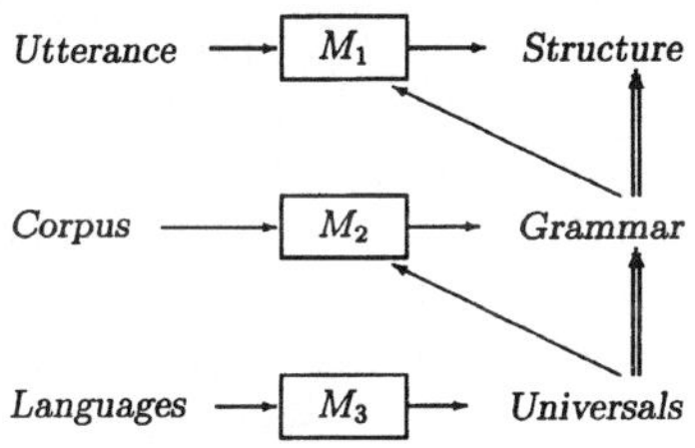

FIGURE 5.1 Schema of the model hierarchy of cognitive linguistic strata determined by mechanisms M_1 to M_3 that constitute structure, grammar, and universals from utterance, corpus, and languages, respectively, identifying and defining the principled constraints universals $\rightarrow M_2$ and grammar $\rightarrow M_1$ on these strata (according to Bierwisch [3]).

identified. The acquisition and representation of this internal knowledge is hypothesized as resulting from a process M_2, which includes a multitude of rudimentary, incomplete, and tentative M_1-type processes. M_2 is assumed to be a complex information-processing mechanism whose inputs are *corpora* of utterances together with environmental information, and whose outputs will be the *grammars* underlying these utterances. Again, this mechanism's results are postulated to be not only and completely determined by the external inputs but also by internal structures believed to control the human language faculty in a fundamental way as *linguistic universals.* These may (or may not) be assumed to be derivable as results of an information-processing mechanism M_3 whose input is as comprehensive (or unspecified) as the word *languages* might allow.

Taking the relation of inclusion for $M_1 \subset M_2$ to hold also for $M_2 \subset M_3$, and considering M_1, M_2, and M_3 computationally specifiable procedures of language-analyzing processes instead of mere metaphors for some (more or less plausible) mechanisms of the human mind, it appears reasonable to consider M_3 a (multilevel and structured) collection of all the processes of methodical analysis, representation, comparison, identification, interpretation, and so on, for sets of utterances from different languages. This includes the processes in M_1 as a device that explicitly specifies an utterance's structure relative to a given grammar, and the processes in M_2 as a system that generates a grammar from a corpus of utterances relative to the given set of universals M_3. The modeling setup allows for the notion *universals* $\Rightarrow$ *grammar* $\Rightarrow$ *structure* to be understood as variables of theoretical constructs hinged on empirical regularities observed in *languages, corpora*, and *utterances*, respectively. Whereas the latter are considered external language realizations, the former are hypothesized to be constraints internal to any natural language or cognitive information-processing system which may be represented externally only under the competence linguistic approach to cognitive modeling. Thus (following the double arrows in Figure 5.1), these will form a hierarchy of linguistic[7] abstractions, not

[7]The term is polysemous in English, as it might similarly be understood as the adjectival form of language and linguistics. To allow for a distinction of these two meanings which other languages have in fact lexicalized (by different words), we confine linguistic to denote properties (theories, models, methods, goals, concepts, etc.) of linguistics as the scientific discipline investigating natural languages, and languagelike to refer to observable or experiential language phenomena.

of language entities which may formally be specified by (other types of) linguistic abstractions and represented by symbols.

The model theoretical and operational problems inherent in this setup concern the (nonuniversal and highly restrictive) representational format which is assumed to enable the denotation of universals, grammar, and structure, and the essentially top-down[8] nonrecursive propagation of externally presented but internally processed results of these mechanisms. Thus completeness of M_3 in identifying universals and representing them externally is crucial for the efficient performance of M_2, which is to employ these universals as internal, procedural constraints in order to identify syntactic regularities successfully. Represented externally in a rule-based format, these rules will constitute possible formal grammars. Grammars, in turn, are meant to provide the internal procedural constraints in M_1 in order to let these mechanisms' identification processes represent their findings successfully as discretely categorized external structures.

Distinguishing between these two types of structuredness, either external or internal to the mechanisms *M* as introduced by Bierwisch, not only anticipates important components of Chomsky's notion of *mental grammar* and his distinction of *E*- and *I*-languages. But the distinction is also indicative of the *endo–exo dichotomy*, whose introduction on this level of modeling may be questioned as an ad hoc abstraction from, not a result of, the procedural unity that a systems theoretical view on information processing allows us to keep up in semiotic modeling. The mechanisms M_1 to M_3, if provided, easily translate to sets of procedures that determine and simulate but hardly realize a living system's ability to process environmental input (external structures) according to procedural constraints known to the system (internal structures) in order to produce not only some results as a material part of the (external) environment but simultaneously also some feedback affecting the system's (internal) structure.

In fact, it appears not at all conclusively compelling to assume that such constraints and their procedural enactment need to be represented in a format of rule-type expressions. Certainly, according to an ecologically motivated systems theoretical perspective, enacting these processes under boundary conditions as determined by the external surroundings or the systems' internal structuredness, or both, will have to be exposed to certain input structures to produce specified output structures. But identifying their status of being simultaneously internal and external to the processing system is tantamount to the methodological dilemma, which can be solved solely on the grounds of revising the representational mode and the formatting constraints that the model construction has to be decided on to allow. Apparently, Chomskyan linguistics has restricted both these modes to consist of abstract principles of language competence whose assumed determinacy subsequently allowed for symbol representations in the form of rewrite rules or productions. These, in turn, gave rise to the foregoing model hierarchy of discrete strata which only lately, under pressure of urgent practical solutions to circumvent difficulties resulting from the dilemma's methodical obstructions, became meshed by unification mechanisms in corresponding grammar formalisms.

[8] Although in Figure 5.1 these strata are given in inverse (bottom-up) order.

In trying to relate these strata to observable performative language data structures in order to mediate observable language regularities with theoretical constructs supposedly representing principles underlying these constructs, the methodological shortcomings of the cognitive linguistic approach are revealed. It suffers from competence theoretically inspired idealizations and theoretical abstractions (e.g., universals, grammars, sentences) whose symbolic notations and formal expressions may only be scrutinized for their syntactic correctness but lack empirically observable and experimentally testable procedures that relate formal expressions—supposedly representing competent speakers' language understanding faculties—to performative language regularities observable in discourse and detectable by realized (symbolic) abstractions, not as a result of it.

5.2.4 Fuzzy Linguistic Procedures: Tiling

It is *structural linguistics* (SL) that has given substantial hints on how abstract linguistic entities (types) may be identified from observable language items (tokens) by segmentation and classification of resemblances of entities' distributional patterns as employed and discovered in communicative discourse. The structuralistic view of natural languages has produced the seminal distinctions of *langue-parole* (de Saussure), on the one hand, and of competence/performance or I-language/E-language (Chomsky), on the other, providing modern linguistics with two different realms of language description and linguistic analysis. It is grounded in the possibility to abstract (formal) linguistic entities from (empirical) language data and in the discovery of principles of combinatorial constraints responsible for string formation in natural languages. Tied to comparative operations, these allow us to segment token strings of language discourse and to categorize segments as classes of types of linguistic entities.[9]

An overview of linguistic approaches to word semantics, from traditional (crisp) models to semiotic structures of (fuzzy) word meaning analysis, representation, and processing, lends itself quite naturally to illustrate the point to be made here. By taking up the lore of terminological distinctions, some of the organizational and granular aspects underlying traditional linguistic categorizing may be revealed: closed classes (*functional words*) as opposed to open classes (*contents words*), the latter consisting of simplicia (lexical) and compounds of (morphologically) either derivational or flexional origin, and the former breaking down in logical constants (e.g., and, or, not, all, if... then) and linguistic functions (e.g., at, by, for, in, on) with characteristic functional equivalences on various levels across different languages. In particular, the open class of contents words display the mechanisms of

[9]From an enactive approach to modeling cognition, the very possibility of distinguishing these segmented token observations from classified type abstractions corresponding to them can be considered evidential for natural language discourse as an instantiation of structure which serves both as a controlling constraint and an emergent result when employed. It is this two fold ontology that renders communicative discourse a structural coupling whose analytical use can be made by any semiotic cognitive information-processing (SCIP) system properly attuned to that natural language environment.

morphologically relevant sign aggregation and entity formation regularities most clearly, which led structural linguists to identify the fundamental constraints (universals) that control the linear combinability and multilevel formation of language structures in distinguishing restrictions on their linear aggregation (syntagmatics) from restrictions on their selective replacement (paradigmatics). This distinction allows within any sufficiently large set of strings of natural language discourse to ascertain syntagmatic regularities of linear element aggregations on level n, whose characteristic distributional patterns can be classified to form paradigms that generally acquire aggregational element status again on level $n+1$, and so on. As such, constraints have been detected in both directions (bottom-up and top-down) and represented for different levels ($n-1$, n, $n+1$) of linguistic entity formation. Some of these entities may indeed be identified with the well-established traditional strata of linguistic analysis and description of language phenomena.

The combinatorial redundancies resulting in observable (language) regularities may not only—if sufficiently overt—be expressed by (linguistic) symbols and their linear aggregations be represented by sets of (deterministic) rules formatted accordingly. But also less overt observable redundancies may quite as well be taken as an efficient (i.e., recursively applicable) principle of complexity reduction by multiresolutional bottom-up representational organization or top-down information granulation. Detecting and identifying regularities, then, allows for at least two kinds of multiresolutional modeling:

1. The categorial type of constraints symbolized by fully deterministic if–then rules will result in a rather coarse three-level hierarchy (Figure 5.1) of symbolic representations of mechanisms or crisp information granules.
2. Identifying regularities as probabilistic or possibilistic constraints will produce a continuous covering or multilevel tiling (Figure 5.2) of dynamic distributional representations realized as procedures or fuzzy information granules.

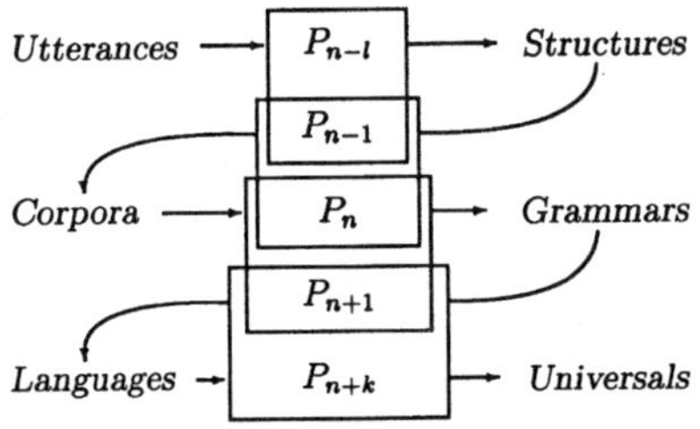

FIGURE 5.2 Schema of model tiling or (overlapping) computational semiotic coverage of procedures P_{n-l} to P_{n+k} for the analysis and representation of (detected) language regularities in utterances, corpora, and languages and of (constituted) fuzzy linguistic or soft categories mediating between structures → corpora and grammars → languages (according to Rieger [54]).

Thus we can distinguish sharply between cognitive crisp categorial, rule-based, symbolically represented linguistic mechanisms[10] and soft categorial, regularity-based, distributedly represented semiotic procedures whose computations transform structured input data according to its immanent regularities to yield new, structural representations emerging from that computation (as hypothesized by fuzzy linguistics and realized in procedural models of computational semiotics).

The elements of these new model structures are value distributions or vectors of input entities that depict properties of their structural relatedness, constituting multidimensional (metric) space structures (semiotic spaces) instead of formally correct string expressions from externally interpreted calculi (formal languages). As a weaker or soft analog to the principles of formal languages, these space-structure elements may, however, be interpreted as systems of subsystems of fuzzy sets allowing set-theoretical operations to be exercised on these representations that do not require categorial (crisp) definitions of concept formations or predefined propositional structuredness.

Other than cognitive linguistic and competence theoretical mechanisms, the proposed [55] cognitive semiotic and language performative procedures redefine the modularity of language understanding as an overlapping covering of computational processes. The classical and coarse three-stage description and modeling of linguistic regularities (Figure 5.1) will be replaced—or rather complemented [38]—by a multistage covering or tiling of semiotic procedures P_{n-l} to P_{n+k} (Figure 5.2). This allows for the definition of more adequate soft categories or intermediate representations to fit regularities of entities on any level. Their essentially cognitive character will not be borrowed from predefined strata (and their purportedly related abstract categories) but can be derived as a result of the algorithms' analyzing and representational performance [i.e., the ability to transform linearly structured entities (strings) of one level to multidimensional structures of entities (vectors) on another]. Their (numerical) specificity and (procedural) definiteness, as well as their subsymbolic, distributional format appear to provide for higher phenomenological compatibility and more cognitive adequacy in modeling processes and results of entity formation than traditional levels of categorial representation whose symbolic mediation and syntactic correctness could formally be scrutinized but not tested empirically or experimentally [38].

How this is achieved by analyzing the linear or syntagmatic and the selective or paradigmatic constraints that natural language structure imposes on the formation of (strings of) language signs on whatever level of entity formation has been derived elsewhere [50] in some detail and is illustrated more concisely below.

[10]Although these mechanisms may also be translated to procedures and—when implemented as algorithms—to operational processes, they do not hereby acquire *semiotic* status. Other than transforming hidden structures into their representations by exploiting n-level inherent constraints of training data to constitute $(n+1)$-level significations of them (i.e., realization), cognitive linguistic systems claiming to be procedural are confined to transforming input structures according to symbolically predefined representational formats external to the structuredness they are meant to model (i.e., simulations).

5.3 COMPUTATIONAL SEMIOTICS

Inspired by information systems theory [54], human beings may be taken as living systems whose knowledge-based processing of represented information makes them cognitive, and whose sign and symbol generation, manipulation, and understanding capabilities render them semiotic. Due to our own daily experience of these systems' performance and ability in representing results of cognitive processes, in organizing these representations, and in modifying them according to changing conditions and states of system–environment adaptedness, it is argued [55] that the semiotic approach to modeling human cognition—constituting *computational semiotics*—will have to be grounded in such complex semiotic cognitive information processing. Consequently, it has to be based on the representational structures resulting from and initiating such processing (i.e., natural language discourse). In the aggregated form of pragmatically homogeneous text (PHT) corpora [35], communicatively performative natural language discourse provides a cognitively revealing and empirically accessible system whose multifaceted structuredness may serve as a guideline for the cognitively motivated, empirically based, and computationally realized research in the semiotics of language.

5.3.1 Information Systems View

The ecological view of information processing arose out of the investigation of animal–environment interaction which formed the basis of Gibson's theory of perception [19] and the school of ecological realism [66] that has been based on it. Following an ecological paradigm of systems theory (providing a concept of pragmatic information [67] relative to system–environment situations) and accepting the cognitive point of view (implying that information processing is knowledge based), human beings appear to be not just natural information-processing systems with higher cognitive abilities. Instead, they have to be considered very particular cognitive systems whose outstanding plasticity and capability to adapt to changing environmental conditions are essentially tied to their use and understanding of natural languages in communicative discourse. It seems that the language faculty expands their learning potential well beyond experimental experience into realms of virtual reality (*Gedankenexperimente*). The basic idea of model construction in terms of such an ecological theory of information systems [54] is that the processing structure of an information system is a correlate of those structures which such a system is able to process in order to survive.

Ecological Information Processing. Life may be understood as the ability to survive by reproduction and adaptation to changing requirements in the real world. In terms of the ecological theory of information systems, faculties such as perception, identification, and interpretation of structures (external or internal to a system) can hence be conceived of as a form of information processing which (natural or artificial) systems—due to their own structuredness—are able to perform. Thus living systems receive or derive information from relevant portions of their surrounding environments, they learn from experience, and they change their behavior accordingly. In contrast to other living systems which transmit experiential results of environmental adaptation only biogenetically[11] to their descendants, human information-processing systems have additional means to convey their knowledge to others. In addition to the vertical transmission of system-specific (intraneous) experience through (biogenetically successive) generations, humankind has complementarily developed horizontal means of mediating specific and foreign (extraneous) experience and knowledge to (biogenetically unrelated) fellow systems within their own or any later generation. This is made possible by a semiotic move that allows us not only to distinguish processes from results of experience but also to convert the latter to knowledge, facilitating it to be reused, modified, and even improved in learning. The vehicle and medium of this move are *representations* [i.e., material systems (abstract languages)] formed of recurrent structures (both elementary and composite) constituting sign functions of arbitrary complexity (textures) that may be realized in communicative processes, called *actualization*.

Modes of Representation. In terms of the theory of information systems, representations (textures)—whether internal or external to the systems—function like virtual environments.[12] Considering the system–environment relation, virtuality may generally be characterized by the fact that it dispenses with the identity of space–time coordinates for system–environment pairs which normally prevails for this relation when qualified to be indexed real. It appears that the dispensation of this identity (i.e., space–time dispensation) is not only conditional for the possible distinction of systems (mutually and relatively independent) from their environments, but also establishes a notion of representation which may be specified as exactly that part of a time-scaled process that can be separated and identified as its outcome or result in being (or becoming) part of another time scale.[13] Accordingly, immediate or space–time-identical system–environments without representational form may well be distinguished from mediate or space–time-dispensed system–environments whose particular representational import (texts) corresponds to their particular bivalent timely status both as longer-term material (composed of language signs having

[11]According to standard theory, there is no direct genetic coding of experiential results but rather, indirect transmission of them by selectional advantages which organisms with certain genetic mutations gain over others without them to survive under changing environmental conditions.

[12]Simon's (1982) remark that "there is a certain arbitrariness in drawing the boundary between inner and outer environments of artificial systems.... Long-term memory operates like a second environment, parallel to the environment sensed through eyes and ears" [62, p. 104] is not a case in point here. Concerned primarily with where to place the boundary, he does not seem to see its placing as a need to be justified or derived as a consequence of some possibly representational processes we call semiotic. As will become clear in what follows, Simon's distinction of inner (memory structure) and outer (world structure) environments is not concerned with the special quality of language signs whose twofold environmental embedding (textual structure) cuts across that distinction, resolving both in becoming representational for each other.

[13]It is tempting to extend the conception of different linear time scales to that of differently scaled time cycles, particularly in view of the resolutional power of representations and their semiotic processing in computational models, which can only be alluded to here.

virtual meaning) and as shorter-term structure [in need of being (re)cognized in order to be understood].[14] This double identity calls for a particular modus of actualization (understanding) that may be characterized as follows: For systems appropriately adapted and tuned to such virtual environments, actualization consists essentially in a twofold embedding to realize:

1. The spatiotemporal identity of pairs of immediate system–environment coordinates which will let the system experience the material properties of texts as signs (i.e., by functions of physical access and mutually homomorphic appearance of structures). These properties apply to the percepts of language structures presented to a system in a particular discourse situation.
2. The representational identity of pairs of mediate system–environment parameters which will let the system experience the semantic properties of texts as meanings (i.e., by functions of identification, granulation, organization, emergence, activation, and modification of structures). These virtual properties apply to the comprehension of language structures recognized by a system to form the situation described.

Hence, according to the theory of information systems, functions such as interpreting signs and understanding meanings translate to processes that extend the fragments of reality accessible to a living (natural and possibly artificial) information-processing system beyond reality's material manifestations.[15] This extension applies to both the immediate and mediate relations a system may establish according to its own evolved adaptedness or dispositions (i.e., innate and acquired structuredness, processing capabilities, and represented knowledge).

5.3.2 Semiotic Enactment

Semiotic systems' ability to actualize environmental representations does not merely add to the amount of experiential results available, but also constitutes a significant change of experiential modus. This change is characterized by the fact that processes of experience may be realized as being different and hence be separable from the results of that experience. Whereas in immediate system–environment situations, processes without traceable representations appear to be indistinguishable from their

[14]In view of natural languages discourse there is yet another distinction to be mentioned, although not enlarged upon here, which is due to systems' theoretical verbal or auditor differences, as opposed to written or optically mediated language environments for interlocuting systems. Whereas the former may be characterized for participating systems as either space–time identical (e.g., face-to-face communication) or space-dispensed (e.g., videophone conversation) environments, the latter or scripture-based interaction will generally dispense with the space–time coordinates' identity of system–environment pairs concerned (e.g., papyri), allowing, however, space identity (e.g., mural inscriptions).

[15]It might be argued that—if anywhere—the problem of modeling consciousness (whether posed as a soft or hard problem [10] or neither [29] could be addressed on these grounds, that is, as an integral quality of system–environment situations whose dynamics as mediated by self-organizing material structures acquire interpretable meanings for SCIP systems properly attuned (with the understanding that the notion of attunement is semiotic, whereas adaptation is functional).

results, mediate system–environments are constituted by this very distinction.[16] Being able to distinguish experiential modi like these is tantamount to the emergence of virtual experiences which have not to be made but can instead just be tried and tested, very much like hypotheses in experimental settings (thought experiments). The results of such tentative experiencing may become part of a system's adaptive knowledge as acquired in immediate system–environments, but may also—other than in immediate, however characteristic of mediate system–environments—be neglected or selected, accepted or dismissed, varied and repeatedly actualized, and reused without any risk for the system's own survival, stability, or adaptedness.

This somewhat experimental quality of textual representations, which increases the potentials of adaptive information processing beyond the system's life span, is constrained simultaneously by dynamic structures corresponding to knowledge. The builtup, employment, and modification of these structural constraints[17] are controlled by procedures whose processes determine cognition and whose results constitute adaptation. Systems properly attuned to textual system–environments have acquired these structural constraints in language learning and can perform certain operations efficiently on them in language understanding. These are prerequisites to (re)cognize mediate (textual) environments, to respond to their needs for—and to enact the systems' own abilities of—actualizing a process whose mutual (and threefold) relatedness Peirce identified to constitute what he called semiosis.[18] Systems capable of and tuned to such knowledge-based processes of actualization will in the sequel be referred to as semiotic cognitive information-processing (SCIP) systems [52, 53].

In modeling SCIP system performances, the concept of representation has to be considered fundamental to the computational semiotic approach to cognition, allowing us to realize—instead of simulating—the experiential distinction of semiotic processes of cognition from their results which emerge—due to the traces these processes leave behind—in some structures (knowledge). Different representational modes of this structure not only comply with the distinction of internal or tacit knowledge (as in modeling memory), on the one hand and of external or declarative knowledge (as in representations of discourse), on the other[19], these modes also

[16] Splitting up experience in experiential processes and experiential results—the latter being representational and in need of procedural actualization by the former—appears to be at the base of all endo–exo distinction of structures being internal, from those being external to an information-processing system which thereby becomes separated from its environment.

[17] What Simon [62] calls memory in accordance with his questioning of the inner–outer distinction of cognitive systems and their environments.

[18] See footnote 22.

[19] Whereas tacit knowledge cannot be represented other than by the immediate system–environments' corresponding states, explicit knowledge is bound to acquire some formal properties in order to become externally presented and thereby part of mediate system–environments. Natural languages obviously provide these formal properties—as partly identified by research in linguistic competence (principled knowledge and acquisition of language)—whose enactment—as investigated in studies on natural language performance (production and understanding of texts)—draws cognitively on both bases of (explicit and tacit) knowledge.

relate to different types of (distributional versus symbolic) formats, (connectionist versus rule-based) modeling, and (stochastic versus deterministic) processing.

It is on this range of correspondences that fuzzy linguistics (FL) is based and tries to exploit to come up with a unifying framework for most of the different approaches followed so far. Soft categorizing appears to be a prerequisite for fuzzy linguistic models, examples of which will illustrate the notion of dynamic structures emerging from corpora of natural language discourse.

5.3.3 (Re)Constructive Procedures

In systems theory it is common to look at systems in two ways: externally by its behavioral characteristics, that is, the way a system performs in processing (some controlled or known) input and producing (observable or measurable) outputs, and internally by the structural characteristics, that is, the number and kind of variables in the system and how these variables are connected to each other.

From the model constructor's position it was pointed out [31] that the matter–symbol, material–sign, or structure–function distinctions are difficult to determine in (primitive) organisms' behavior, quite contrary to the sharp distinction drawn in models of dynamic physical behavior.[20] This is due primarily to the fact that only from the modeler's external view does the organisms' processing of environmental information appear to be based upon principled structures (representations) of processing results, whereas an organism's own (internal) processing may in fact do very well without such representational structures and apparently survives on merely performing some sorting procedures or classification functions, allowing us to identify the relevant (and to ignore the irrelevant) components in its surroundings, possibly (but not necessarily) based on prior experience in similar situations. Therefore, relating structure to function may well be considered but another aspect of how the notion of representation (internal or external to a system) can be realized instead of simulated in a system–environment model of cognitive information processing.

> First, simulations and realizations belong to different categories of modeling. Simulations are metaphorical models that symbolically "stand for" something else. Realizations are literal, material models that implement functions. Therefore, accuracy in a simulation need have no relation to quality of function in a realization. Secondly, the criteria for good simulations and realizations of a system depend on our theory of the system. The criteria for good theories depend on more than mimicry, e.g. Turing Tests. Lastly, our theory of living systems must include evolvability. Evolution requires the distinction between symbolic genotypes [types of language entities], material phenotypes [tokens of language entities], and selective environments [situations of communicative language use]. Each of these categories has characteristic properties that must be represented in artificial life (AL) models [30, p. 63][21]

[20] "As external modelers we need to know the detailed chemical structure of DNA to understand, and perhaps to design, the chemical correlates of its function, but to perform its semantic function in the cell only the cell's classification of the base sequence is relevant to the synthesis of proteins" [31, p. 12].

[21] My additions in brackets.

For cognitive models of natural language processing the system's theoretical view suggests to accept natural language discourse as analyzable and empirically accessible evidence for tracing such processes. Thus natural language discourse might reveal essential parts of the particularly structured, multilayered information representation and processing potential to a system analyzer and model constructor in rather the same way as this potential is accessible to an information-processing system trying to understand these texts. There is an important difference, however, in dealing with the natural language material that is part of an information-processing system and its analyzer, on the one hand, and also part of an information system engaged in processing its discourse environment, on the other. Distinguishing between the object–modeler relation and the system–environment relation is to be active in and part of different information-processing situations of which only the latter can be said to be directly accessible to the modeler via attunement.

It is this lack of being properly attuned to the semiotic principles underlying natural language understanding systems which prompts cognitive linguists to fall back on situations they are attuned to: namely, natural language understanding whose formal abstractions they believe to be provided by principled IL representations of language competence. But whereas in communicative language understanding one can—and even has to—take the semiotics of signs and the constitution of meanings for granted and beyond questioning (i.e., signs and meanings are meant to be understood, no matter whether fully or only partially, whether correctly or even wrongly), the purpose of modeling that very process (i.e., how structures become signs, meaning is constituted, and language understood) must not. Trying to understand (conditions of possible) understanding of signs and meanings cannot rely on the simulative processing of (symbol) structures whose representational status is declared by drawing on a preestablished semantics (known by the modeler, made accessible to the model, but not at all compulsory for the system modeled). Instead, modeling processes of meaning constitution or understanding will have to realize that very function in an implemented and operational information-processing system which is able to render some structure—in a self-organizing way—representational of something else, and also allows to identify what that structure is to stand for. This is, very briefly, what establishes a symbol or sign-meaning relation whose semantics is a way of representing this relation in an overt and intelligible sense to other (natural and/or artificial) SCIP systems. The notions of discourse situation and of language game will serve to mediate the dynamics of semiosis and the procedural approach to model SCIP systems as based on natural language discourse.

Discourse Situations. Situations (comprising system, environment, and processing) are considered cognitive inasmuch as the system's internal (formal and procedural) knowledge has to be applied to identify and recognize structures external to the system (meaning interpretation). These situations become semiotic whenever the internal knowledge applied to identify and interpret environmental structures is derived from former processes of external structure identification and interpretation, and applied as the result of self-organizing feedback through different levels of (inter-)mediate representation and organization. This process (of meaning constitution or structure understanding) is the multiple enactment of the threefold relation which is called—following Peirce—semiosis.[22] The triadic relation allows for different ontological abstractions of language:

1. As a component (sign) in a system's external environment (i.e., material discourse as a physical space–time location)
2. As a constituent of virtuality which systems properly attuned experience as their environment (object) (i.e., structured text as an interpretable potential of meanings)
3. As a process of actualization (interpretant) in a particular system–environment situation (i.e., understanding as the constitution of meaning)

According to Barwise and Perry [2], any language expression is tied to reality in two ways: by the discourse situation, allowing an expression's meaning to be interpreted, and by the situation described allowing its interpretation to be evaluated truth-functionally. Within this relational model of situation semantics, meaning may be considered the derivative of information processing, which (natural or artificial) systems, due to their own structuredness, perform by recognizing similarities or invariants between situations that structure their surrounding realities (or fragments thereof).

By ascertaining these invariants and by mapping them as uniformities across situations, cognitive systems properly attuned to them are able to identify and understand those bits of information that appear to be essential to form these systems' particular views of reality: a flow of types of situations related by uniformities such as individuals, relations, and time–space–locations. These uniformities constrain a system's external world to become its view of reality as a specific fragment of persistent (and remembered) courses of events whose expectability (by their repetitiveness) renders them interpretable or even objective.

In semiotic sign systems such as natural languages, such uniformities also appear to be signaled by sign types, whose employment as sign tokens in texts exhibit a special granular form of structurally conditioned constraints. Taking the entity word as an example from the granular tiling of semiotic sign structures, these words and the way they are used in discourse by the speakers/hearers do allow us not only to convey/understand meanings differently in different discourse situations (efficiency), but at the same time, the discourses' total vocabulary and word usages also provide an empirically accessible basis for the analysis of structural (as opposed to referential) aspects of event types and how these are related by virtue of word uniformities across phrases, sentences, and texts uttered. Thus as a means for the intensional (as opposed to the extensional) description of (abstract, real, and actual) situations, the regularities of word usages may serve as an access to and a representational format for those elastic constraints which underlie and condition any word

[22] "By semiosis I mean [. . .] an action, or influence, which is, or involves, a coöperation of three subjects, such as sign, its object, and its interpretant, this tri-relative influence not being in any way resolvable into actions between pairs" [32, p. 282].

type's meaning, the interpretations it allows within possible contexts of use, and the information its actual word-token employment may convey on a particular occasion.

Under these preliminary abstractions, the distinction between (the format of) the representation and (the properties of) the represented is not so much a prerequisite but rather more of an outcome of semiosis (i.e., the semiotic process of sign constitution and understanding). Consequently, it should not be considered a presupposition or input to, but a result or output of the processes which are to be modeled procedurally and implemented as a computational system justified to be named semiotic.

Language Games. According to Wittgenstein [68], the notion of language game[23] characterizes a very fundamental type of discourse situations "complete in themselves, as complete systems of human communication" and concerned solely with the way signs are used. Operationalizing this notion and analyzing a great number of texts for usage regularities of terms can reveal essential parts of the concepts and hence the meanings conveyed by them. This approach, as conveyed in Ref. 37, has also produced convincing evidence that an analytical procedure chosen appropriately can be identified with a mechanism that simultaneously solves fundamental representational tasks if based on algorithms that simulate the combinatorial constraints operational in syntagmatics and paradigmatics, known to be universal to all natural languages.

This philosophical concept of language game can be combined with the formal notion of situation, allowing for the identification of a cognitive system's (internal) structure as well as the (external) structure of that system's environment. Being tied to the observables of actual language performance enacted by communicative language use also opens up an empirical approach to procedural semantics and computational semiotics. Whatever can formally be analyzed as uniformities in Barwiseian discourse situations may eventually be specified by word-type regularities as determined by co-occurring word tokens in samples of pragmatically homogeneous texts as representations of language games. Going back to the fundamentals of structuralistic descriptions of regularities of syntagmatic linearity and paradigmatic selectivity of language items, the quantitative, two-level analyses of discourse entities' correlational behavior will allow for a multiresolutional word meaning and world knowledge representation whose dynamism is a direct function of elastic constraints established and/or modified in language communication.

As has been outlined in some detail elsewhere [40, 43, 47, 57], the meaning function's range may be computed and simulated as a result of exactly those (semiotic) procedures by way of which (representational) structures emerge and their

[23] "These are ways of using signs simpler than those in which we use the signs in our highly complicated everyday language. Language games are the forms of language with which a child begins to make use of words [. . .] If we want to study the problem of truth and falsehood, of the agreement and disagreement of propositions with reality, of the nature of assertion, assumption, and question, we shall with great advantage look at primitive forms of language in which these forms of thinking appear without the confusing background of highly complicated processes of thought" [68, p. 17] and—we might add—their symbolic and/or formalized representations.

(interpreting) actualization is produced from observing and analyzing the domain's regular constraints as imposed on the linear ordering (syntagmatics) and the selective combination (paradigmatics) of natural language items in communicative language performance. For natural language semantics this is tantamount to (re)presenting a term's meaning potential by a fuzzy distributional pattern of the modeled system's state changes—rather than by a single symbol—whose structural relations are to depict the system's potential interpretations of its environment. Whereas symbolic representations have to exclude, distributional representations will automatically include the (linguistically) structured, pragmatic components which a SCIP system will both embody and employ as its representational and procedural import to identify and interpret its environmental structures by means of its own structuredness.

Semiotic Attunement. In a systems-theoretic approach, attunement replaces the notion of static knowledge structures as realized in cognitive information-processing models so far, by a dynamic conception of structuredness. It defines knowledge as an open, modifiable, and adaptive system whose organization can be conceived as a function of the system's own processing or knowledge acquisition. This can only be achieved, however, by allowing semiotic entities to have their own (perhaps yet unknown) ontology. It might not (or not fully) be accounted for[24] by predicative and propositional representations or rule-based and truth-functional formats, which tacitly make believe that semiotic entities can be characterized and their functions modeled exclusively by crisp categorial structures and associated processing of well-defined rules for symbol manipulation.

It cannot be overstated that system analyzers and model constructors dealing with semiotic processes in natural language understanding should not rely on the granular adequacy of established linguistic categories to represent semiotic entities. Instead, they have to make every provision that their ideas about the modeling of both the representation and the processing are not unduly predefined by longstanding but possibly inadequate formats. Rule-based models of syntactic processing as well as truth-functional models of (sentence) meaning appear to be as inadequate as predicative and propositional formats of semiotic entity representation and processing. Thus the aim of modeling semiotic processes is to find and employ representational formats and algorithmicable procedures which do not prematurely decide and delimit the range of semiotically relevant entities, their representational formats, and the modes of processing.

One of the advantages of computational models of semiotic processes would be that the entities considered relevant need not be defined prior to model construction but will emerge from the very processing that the model realizes or is able to enact. It appears that—if any—this property of models does account for the intrinsic (co- and contextual) constraining of the meaning potentials characteristic of natural lan-

[24]With reference to the intrinsic interdependencies of Peirce's "tri-relative influence," identified within a system–environment processing situation above as "an action, or influence, which is, or involves, a coöperation of three subjects, [sign, object, interpretant . . .] not being in any way resolvable into actions between pairs" [32, p. 282].

guage discourse, which renders them semiotic in a meaning (or function)-constituting sense, which may also be identified to be the core of understanding.

Representing a system's environment (or fragments thereof) such that representations not only take part in a system's direct (immediate) environment (via language texts) but may be understood as virtual in the sense that new (mediate) environments (via textual meanings) can also be processed has been introduced explicitly elsewhere [52, 53, 57]. This view is again dependent on how a system's attunement to these kinds of situated discourse can be tied to the formal concept of situation [2] and the analytical notion of language game [68] phenomenologically (re)interpreted. The combination of both lends itself easily to operational extensions in empirical analyses and procedural simulations of processes that may grasp essential parts of meaning constitution realized as a process of understanding.

5.4 FUZZY LINGUISTICS

Recent research findings give rise to some well-founded assumptions as to whether—and if so, how—semiotic models will help to emulate the way that structures may emerge from orders of some kind and how these orders relate to or evolve from regularities that multitudes of repeatedly observable entities show. Modeling this kind of processes is to define procedures for which algorithms can be found that at the same time detect the regularities concerned and assemble their results to form (intermediate) representations. Properties of these procedures may resemble (or can even be identified with) the observable (or experiential) entities which could indeed be responsible for (if not identical with) the use and emergence of (sign-functional) structures in language understanding systems, both natural and artificial. As more abstract (theoretical) levels of representation for these processes—other than their procedural modeling—are not (yet) available, and as any (formal) means of deriving their possible results—other than by their (operational) enactment—are (still) lacking, it has to be postulated that these processes, independent of all other explanatory paradigms, will not only relate to but will produce different representational levels of entity formation. They do so in a way that Marr [26] characterized as being formally controlled or computable, which can be modeled procedurally or algorithmized and which may empirically be tested or implemented. Procedural models of this kind are understood to denote a class of (re)presentational (i.e., modeled) (re)constructions of entities whose interpretation is not (yet) tied to an underlying theory which would provide the semantics for the entities (or expressions) that these type of models present. Instantiating their defining procedures as implemented algorithms will result in processes that produce some (abstract) structures whose visualizations can then only be compared to those structures originally observed to hold for and be characteristic of the object modeled.

Structural linguistics has contributed substantially to how language items come to be employed in communicative discourse the way they are. The fundamental constraints have been identified that control the multilevel combinability and formation of language entities[25] by distinguishing the restrictions on linear aggregation of elements (*syntagmatics*) from restrictions on their selective replacement (*paradigmatics*). Regularities may be described by computational procedures whose varying degrees of combinatorial determinacy will not only detect different patterns of elements' linear distributions but may also be identified with the constraints being applied to constitute the syntagmata and paradigmata observed. Defining structures of this kind can neither be provided extensionally as sets of elements, nor intensionally as lists of properties with which the elements concerned would have to comply, because both modes would presuppose prior with which knowledge and understanding of what is to be defined. Not so the procedural definition by an algorithmic or computational operation whose enactment will instantiate a process in space–time to select the elements concerned according to their structural (i.e., syntagmatic and paradigmatic) relatedness. Moreover, this mode could provide for the semioticity of entities whose vagueness and reconstructive openness will be accounted for more satisfactorily by the dynamism of distributive as opposed to symbolic representational formats. They allow us to map structured input data according to its immanent regularities to yield new, structural representations emerging from that computation (as hypothesized by performative linguistics and realized in procedural models of computational semiotics). Components of these new structures are distributions or vectors of entity–value pairs that depict self-regulatory properties of input entities' structural relatedness, constituting multidimensional (metric) space structures (semiotic spaces). Their elements may also be interpreted as (labeled) fuzzy sets allowing set-theoretical operations to be exercised on these representations that do not require categorial (crisp) definitions of concept formations. Computation of letter (morphic) vectors in word space, derived from characteristic n-grams of letter or grapheme distributions [38, 39], as well as of word (semic) vectors in semantic space [42, 43], derived from word-type correlations of word token distributions in discourse, will serve to illustrate the operational flexibility and granular variability of these representational formats [51] derived from semiotic functions in language performance which traditional linguistic categories fail to identify.

5.4.1 Word Space

If the basic hypotheses in structural linguistics hold according to which the entity formation in natural language sign systems is governed by the recursively applied principles of syntagmatic and paradigmatic constraints, then these constraints, restricting theoretical combinability of items to form redundancies in order to make new entities emerge, should be found applicable on the morphophonetic and/or the morphographemic level of language to form labeled morphic structures (words)

[25]Reference is made to segmentation and classification of observable strings of entities (on level n), which make it possible to identify and segment entities within characteristic cotextual distributions whose classifications allow for these classes to become new entities on level $(n + 1)$ string formation, which again may be segmented and classified, and so on. Thus, words (on level n)—being (granularly) decomposable into syllables $(n - 1)$, into graphemes/phonemes $(n - 2)$,—will compose to aggregated (organized) strings of phrases (on level $n + 1$), sentences $(n + 2)$, and texts $(n + 3)$, and so on.

as well as on the word level to form labeled semantic structures (meanings). In what follows, the level of written (or morphographemic) sign representation is preferred[26] to that of the sound (or phonomorphic) level to illustrate soft categorizing in German [39] by fuzzy linguistic procedures [55] modeling semiotic functions.

The following notations will be used to outline the computational semiotic approach on the morphic level:

- n-grams are n-elementary strings of entities. For $n \geq 2$ they may be analyzed as ordered pairs of adjacent items (letters, graphs, sign strings, word strings, etc.) which are the basis of
- Abstractions over such items, which may procedurally be determined as soft categorial types (corresponding to characters, graphemes, morphemes, syllables, words, etc.) that have procedurally been defined as
- Fuzzy subsets of multidimensional sign inventories Z^n with $n > 1$:

$$\tilde{X}_n := \{(x, \mu_n(x)) \ : \ x \in Z^n\} \subseteq Z^n \times [0, 1] \tag{5.1}$$

  Their elements' grades of membership are defined by the membership function

$$\mu_n : Z^n \rightarrow [0, 1] \tag{5.2}$$

  whose
- Membership values $\mu_n(x)$ may be computed inductively as the overall tendency of linear chaining of items in language corpora. For an n-elementary string $x \in Z^n$, let $H_n(x)$ be the frequency of x occurring in a corpus. Then for any
- Bigram $x = (y, z) \in Z^n, y \in Z^{n-1}, z \in Z$, the coefficient

$$\mu_n(x) = \frac{H_n(x)}{II_{n-1}(y)} \tag{5.3}$$

  with $Z = \{z_1, \ldots, z_m\}$ will yield for each $y \in Z^{n-1}$ a vector

$$(\mu_n(y, z_1), \ldots, \mu_n(y, z_m))^{\mathrm{T}} \in IR^m \tag{5.4}$$

  The set of all vectors reflect the morphological structure of the corpus analyzed, which is the numerically specified basis for the procedural definition of
- Soft categories, which may procedurally be specified by restricting a system of fuzzy subsets of observed syntagmatic (string) distributions according to their paradigmatic (selective) distributions observed. These may be interpreted to represent elastic constraints operating on the language items' chaining tendencies, which structure the corresponding corpus.

[26]The reason is that VLLCs of written language discourse are more readily available than phonetic discourse transcripts and that the distance between phonemic realization and graphemic representation in German is less than in English or French, where the sound-writing discrepancies are more frequent, causing graphemic analyses of these languages to be noisier.

TABLE 5.1. Grapheme (Letter) Combinatorics with (Theoretically and Factually) Possible and Actually Occurring Types of n-Grams in German According to a Subset of the Trier dpa-Corpus

n-gram	F_n (factual occurrence)	$T_n = \|Z^n\|$ (theoretical possibility)	$100 \cdot \frac{F_n}{T_n}\%$	$A_n = m \cdot \|F_{n-1}\|$ (actual possibility)	$100 \cdot \frac{F_n}{A_n}\%$
1	31	31	100.000	31	100.000
2	817	961	85.015	961	85.015
3	10,175	29,791	34.154	25,327	40.174
4	54,470	923,521	5.898	315,425	17.268
5	164,045	28,629,151	0.572	1,688,570	9.715
6	357,632	887,503,681	0.040	5,085,395	7.032
7	634,767	27,512,614,111	0.002	11,086,592	5.725
Size of test corpus:		3,648,326	(signs)	502,587	(words)

The presentation of the development of soft categories as elastic constraints (operating on different levels) can be simplified by their formal introduction as (n-ary) fuzzy relations and their corresponding numerical formats of transition matrices (of higher orders).

For written German discourse analyzed on a type-setting level with m discernible types of signs (letters) and maximum lengths n of strings, there are quite a number of theoretically possible (Table 5.1, column $T_n = Z^n$) crisp n-ary relations:

$$
\begin{aligned}
Z = T_1 &= \{x_1 && : x_1 \in Z\} \\
T_2 &= \{(x_1, x_2) && : x_1, x_2 \in Z\} \\
T_3 &= \{(x_1, x_2, x_3) && : x_1, x_2, x_3 \in Z\} \\
\vdots \quad & \quad \vdots && \quad \vdots \\
T_{n-1} &= \{(x_1, \ldots, x_{n-1}) && : x_1, \ldots, x_n \in Z\} \\
T_n &= \{(x_1, \ldots, x_n && : x_1, \ldots, x_n \in Z\}
\end{aligned}
$$

Of these, however, those that must be computed are only those that are not only actually possible (column A_n) but have actually been observed to occur: that is, $F_n \subseteq F_{n-1} \times Z$ (Table 5.1, column F_n) :

$$
\begin{aligned}
Z = F_1 &\subseteq \{x_1 && : x_1 \in Z\} \\
F_2 &\subseteq \{(x_1, x_2) && : x_1 \in F_1, x_2 \in Z\} \\
F_3 &\subseteq \{(x_1, x_2, x_3) && : (x_1, x_2) \in F_2, x_3 \in Z\} \\
\vdots \quad & \quad \vdots && \quad \vdots \\
F_{n-1} &\subseteq \{(x_1, \ldots, x_{n-1}) && : (x_1, \ldots, x_{n-2}) \in F_{n-2}, x_{n-1} \in Z\} \\
F_n &\subseteq \{(x_1, \ldots, x_n) && : (x_1, \ldots, x_{n-1} \in F_{n-1}, x_n \in Z\}
\end{aligned}
$$

Fuzzy relational modeling according to (5.3) and (5.2) shows that even for higher n, only bigrams have to be traced and computed, due to the $(n-1)$ary relations computed on the preceding level of representation. It is this principle of procedural self-similarity of n-ary agglomerative steps which allows for the treelike trie[27] representation of entities that are labeled (by soft categorial n-relative letter transitions) and are an outcome of procedural constraints (over n levels of processing) which produce a dynamically structured system of fuzzy relations that depicts the overall transition tendencies of a grapheme sign. For the letter d, this soft grapheme structure is given in Figure 5.3, illustrating subregularities of morphic word formation.

5.4.2 Semantic Hyperspace

Again following the procedural approach in computational semiotics, the reconstruction of linguistic functions or meanings of words is based on the fundamental distinction of natural language items' agglomerative or syntagmatic and selective or paradigmatic relatedness. Consequently, the core of the analytical and/or representational formalism can be characterized as a two-level process of abstraction (called α- and δ-abstraction) on the set of fuzzy subsets of the vocabulary, providing the word types' usage regularities or corpus points, and on the set of fuzzy subsets of these, providing the corresponding meaning points as a function of those word types which are being instantiated by word tokens as employed in pragmatically homogeneous corpora of natural language texts.

Quantitative Linguistic Data. The basically descriptive statistics used to grasp these relations on the level of words in discourse are centered around a correlational measure (5.9) to specify intensities of co-occurring lexical items in texts, and a measure of similarity (or rather, dissimilarity) (5.13) to specify differing distributions of correlation values. Simultaneously, these measures may be interpreted semiotically as providing for set-theoretical constraints or formal mappings α (5.11) and δ (5.15), which model the meanings of words as a function of these words' differences in usage regularities.

As a first mapping function, α allows us to compute the relational interdependence of any two lexical items from their textual frequencies. For any pragmatically homogeneous corpus

$$K = \{k_t\} \qquad t = 1, \ldots, T \tag{5.5}$$

of texts k_t, having an overall length

$$L = \sum_{t=1}^{T} l_t \qquad 1 \leq l_t \leq L \tag{5.6}$$

[27]This neologism, coined by Knuth [22], refers to a graph representation of an organizational structure for efficient storage and retrieval of linearly related entities. But whereas Knuth's trie structures are based on frequencies of entity occurrences, our soft category representations of graphemes are based on relative frequencies of n-agglomerative entity transitions computed separately on each level n for all letters observed.

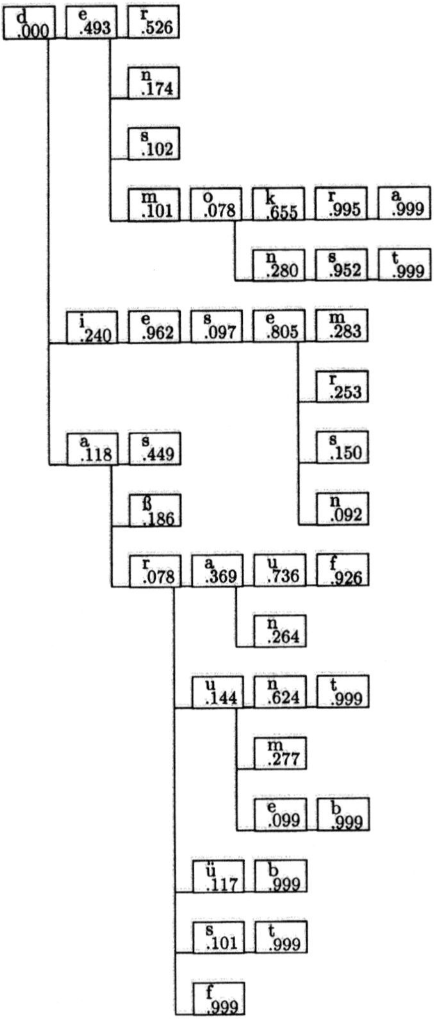

FIGURE 5.3 Tree representation of procedural soft category $\tilde{d}$ depicting (part of) the hierarchy of graded letter agglomeration tendencies according to decreasing transitions (in 7-grams) of word beginnings in a sample of the Trier dpa-corpus of German newspaper texts. Clearly, word formation of gender cases of definite articles (*der, den, des, dem, die, das*) as well as demonstrative pronouns *diesem, dieser, dieses, diesen*) are revealed (among others) as cotextually determined dispositions which signify the grapheme (letter) *d*.

measured by the number l_t of word tokens per text and a vocabulary

$$V = \{x_n\} \qquad n = 1, \ldots, i, j, \ldots, N \tag{5.7}$$

of N word types x_n of different identity i, j whose frequencies are denoted by

$$H_i = \sum_{t=1}^{T} h_{it} \qquad 0 \leq h_{it} \leq H_i \tag{5.8}$$

the modified correlation coefficient $\alpha_{i,j}$ allows us to express pairwise relatedness of word types $(x_i, x_j) \in V \times V$ by numerical values ranging from -1 to $+1$. These are calculated from co-occurring wordtoken frequencies comparing their observed h_{it} against their expected h_{it}^* values for any text t in the following way:

$$\alpha(x_i, x_j) = \frac{\sum_{t=1}^{T}(h_{it} - h_{it}^*)(h_{jt} - h_{jt}^*)}{\left[\sum_{t=1}^{T}(h_{it} - h_{it}^*)^2 \sum_{t=1}^{T}(h_{jt} - h_{jt}^*)^2\right]^{1/2}} \qquad -1 \leq \alpha(x_i, x_j) \leq +1, \tag{5.9}$$

where $h_{it}^* = H_i l_t / L$ and $h_{jt}^* = H_j l_t / L$. Evidently, as normalized by the denominator in this expression, pairs of items (x_i, x_j) that frequently either co-occur in, or are both absent from, a relatively graded majority of texts will be positively correlated, $\alpha(x_i, x_j) \leq +1$, and called *affined*; those pairs of which only one (and not the other) item occurs frequently will be negatively correlated, $\alpha(x_i, x_j) \geq -1$, and hence called *repugnant*.

As a fuzzy binary relation,

$$\tilde{\alpha} : V \times V \rightarrow I \tag{5.10}$$

can be conditioned on $x_n \in V$, which yields a crisp mapping

$$\tilde{\alpha} \,|\, x_n : V \rightarrow C \qquad \{y_n\} =: C, \tag{5.11}$$

where the tuples $\langle (x_{n,1}, \tilde{\alpha}(n, 1)), \ldots, (x_{n,N}, \tilde{\alpha}(n, N)) \rangle$ represent the numerically specified syntagmatic usage regularities that have been observed for each word type x_i against all other $x_n \in V$ and can therefore be abstracted over one of the components in each ordered pair. This α-abstraction (Table 5.2) defines an element $y_i \in C$.

$$x_i(\tilde{\alpha}(i, 1), \ldots, \tilde{\alpha}(i, N)) =: y_i \in C. \tag{5.12}$$

Hence the regularities of usage of any lexical item will be determined by the tuple of its affinity/repugnancy values toward every other item of the vocabulary. As these may be interpreted as coordinate values, the tuples can be represented by points y_n in a vector space C spanned by the number of axes N, each of which corresponds to an entry x_n in the vocabulary V.

Considering C a representational structure of abstract entities y_n constituted by syntagmatic regularities of word-token occurrences in pragmatically homogeneous discourse, the similarities and/or dissimilarities between these abstract entities will capture the corresponding word types' paradigmatic regularities. These can be modeled by the δ-abstraction, which is based on the numerically specified evaluation of differences between any two such points $y_i, y_j \in C$. These point representations will be closer to each other the less the usages (tokens) of their corresponding lexical items $x_i, x_j \in V$ (types) differ. The differences may be calculated by a distance mea-

TABLE 5.2. Formalizing (Syntagmatic/Paradigmatic) Constraints by Consecutive (α and δ) Abstractions over Usage Regularities of Items x_n and Their Differences y_n to Form Meaning Representations z_n, Respectively

$$
\begin{array}{ccccc}
 & \alpha\text{-abstraction} & & \delta\text{-abstraction} & \\
V \times V & \Downarrow & C \times C & \Downarrow & S \times S \\
\begin{array}{cccc}
\tilde{\alpha} & x_1 & \dots & x_N \\
x_1 & \alpha_{11} & \dots & \alpha_{1N} \\
\vdots & \vdots & \ddots & \vdots \\
x_N & \alpha_{N1} & \dots & \alpha_{NN}
\end{array}
& \xrightarrow{\tilde{\alpha}|x_i} &
\begin{array}{cccc}
\tilde{\delta} & y_1 & \dots & y_N \\
y_1 & \delta_{11} & \dots & \delta_{1N} \\
\vdots & \vdots & \ddots & \vdots \\
y_N & \delta_{N1} & \dots & \delta_{NN}
\end{array}
& \xrightarrow{\tilde{\delta}|y_j} &
\begin{array}{cccc}
\zeta & z_1 & \dots & z_N \\
z_1 & \zeta_{11} & \dots & \zeta_{1N} \\
\vdots & \vdots & \ddots & \vdots \\
z_N & \zeta_{N1} & \dots & \zeta_{NN}
\end{array} \\
 & \Uparrow & & \Uparrow & \\
 & \textit{Syntagmatic} & & \textit{Paradigmatic} & \\
 & & \text{Constraints} & &
\end{array}
$$

sure δ of, say, a Euclidian metric:

$$\delta(y_i, y_j) = \left[\sum_{n=1}^{N} (\alpha(x_i, x_n) - \alpha(x_j, x_n))^2 \right]^{1/2} \qquad 0 \leq \delta(y_i, y_j) \leq 2\sqrt{n}. \tag{5.13}$$

Thus δ will serve as a second mapping function to represent any item's differences in usage regularities measured against those of all other items. As a fuzzy binary relation, also,

$$\tilde{\delta} : C \times C \to I \tag{5.14}$$

can be conditioned on $y_n \in C$, which again yields a crisp mapping

$$\tilde{\delta} \,|\, y_n : C \to S \qquad \{z_n\} =: S, \tag{5.15}$$

where the tuples $\langle (y_{n,1}, \tilde{\delta}(n, 1)), \dots, (y_{n,N} \tilde{\delta}(n, N)) \rangle$ represent the numerically specified paradigmatic structure that can be derived for each syntagmatic usage regularity y_j against all other $y_n \in C$. These distance values can therefore be abstracted again analogous to (5.12), this time, however, over the other component in each ordered pair. The δ-abstraction (Table 5.2) defines an element $z_j \in S$ termed the meaning point in S:

$$y_j(\tilde{\delta}(j, 1), \dots, \tilde{\delta}(j, N)) =: z_j \in S \tag{5.16}$$

By identifying $z_n \in S$ with the numerically specified elements of potential paradigms, the set of possible combinations $S \times S$ may be constrained structurally and evaluated without (direct or indirect) recourse to any preexistent external world. Introducing a Euclidian metric

$$\zeta : S \times S \to I \tag{5.17}$$

a hyperstructure $\langle S, \zeta \rangle$ or semantic hyperspace (SHS) is declared, constituting the system of meaning points as an empirically grounded and functionally derived representation of a lexically labeled knowledge structure.

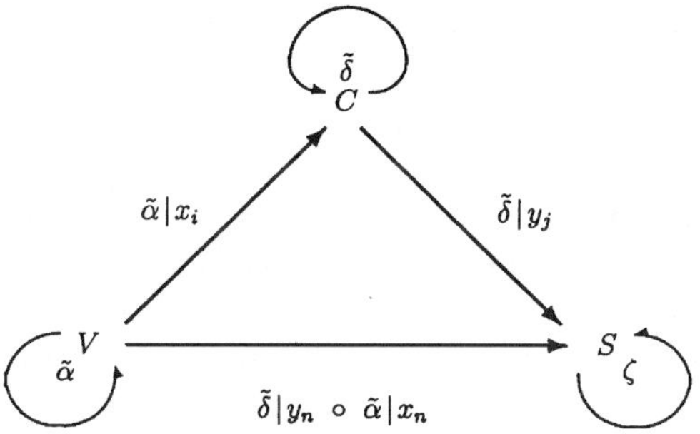

FIGURE 5.4 Fuzzy mapping relations $\tilde{\alpha}$ and $\tilde{\delta}$ between the structured sets of vocabulary items $x_n \in V$, of corpus points $y_n \in C$, and of meaning points $z_n \in S$.

Semiotic Functions. As a result of the two-stage consecutive mappings, any meaning point's position in $\langle S, \zeta \rangle$ is determined by all the differences (δ or distance values) of all regularities of usage (α or correlation values) each lexical item shows against all others in the discourse analyzed. Without recurring to any investigator's or test person's word or world knowledge (semantic competence), but solely on the basis of usage regularities of lexical items in discourse (communicative performance), some global structure is derived procedurally from natural language discourse by computational processes which construct and simultaneously identify topological positions of meaning points $z_i \in \langle S, \zeta \rangle$ as meaning representations of corresponding vocabulary items $x_i \in V$. This consecutive mapping function is called semiotic because it (re)constructs part of the process of natural language understanding as a function of language items' differences of usage regularities as observed and made measurable in discourse whose meaning emerges from that mapping and is depicted and represented in the resultant topological structure of SHS. The semiotic mapping can formally be stated as a category of morphisms [65] or a set-theoretical composition of two restricted (fuzzy) relations $\tilde{\delta} \,|\, y$ and $\tilde{\alpha} \,|\, x$ (Figure 5.4). Thus consecutive application of (5.11) on input texts and (5.15) on output data allows us to model the meanings of words as a fuzzy set-theoretical composition, a category of semiotic morphisms, or computationally, as a two-level function of differences (paradigmatic selection) of usage regularities (syntagmatic aggregation) as schematized in Table 5.2.

5.5 (RE)CONSTRUCTING REFERENCE

Processing natural language texts the way these algorithms do would appear to grasp some relevant portions of the ability to recognize and represent and to employ and modify internally the structural information available and accessible externally to a system that is capable of processing language regularities. A semiotic cognitive information-processing (SCIP) system endowed with these capabilities and performing similarly in building up an internal representation of its processing results would consequently be said to have constituted some—however shallow—text understanding. The problem is whether (and if so, how) the contents of what such a system is said to have understood can be tested (i.e., made accessible) other than by the language texts in question and/or without committing to a particular semantics whose presuppositions would inevitably determine all possible interpretations.

So far, a system of word meanings (lexical knowledge) has been modeled in $\langle S, \zeta \rangle$ as a relational data structure whose linguistically labeled elements (meaning points) and mutual distances (meaning differences) form a system of potential stereotypes. Although on first sight these points appear to be symbolic meaning representations, it is worth mentioning here again that in fact each such point is determined by a fuzzy set or value distribution of pairs of word type and numerical value. Meaning representation via points (or vectors) in semantic hyperspace (SHS) is a matter of the position a point (or the direction a vector) takes among others, and it is this position (or direction) that interprets the lexical label attached to it, not vice versa. Therefore, based on SHS structure as computed from the items' usages in the discourse analyzed, the meaning of a lexical item may be described as a fuzzy subset of the vocabulary, a meaning point's vector, or a meaning point's topological environment delimiting the central point's position indirectly as its stereotype [36, 49].

This variability of representational formats complies with the semiotic notion of understanding and meaning constitution according to which the SHS may be considered the core or base model of a multilevel conceptual knowledge representation system [37]. Essentially, it separates the format of a basic (stereotype) word meaning or concept representation from its latent relational forms of organization for particular cognitive purposes. Whereas the former may be thought of as a comparatively stable (or long-term), although dynamic topologically structured (associative) memory, the latter can be characterized as a collection of structuring procedures that (re)organize the memory data according to cognitive tasks to be solved under situational (or short-term) conditions[28]

As we have separated cognitive processes from their resultant structures above, so may we distinguish here between the short-term process in a situational embedding (employment or activation) and its long-term structure as an addressable representation of knowledge (stereotype or concept) with the semiotic implication that the structures depend on the processes, and vice versa, to let addressable representations emerge and cognitive processes be enacted. Thus the duality of the inner–outer distinction or system–environment opposition may be mediated (or even suspended) by processes operating on some supposedly common, basal representational structures[29] whose efficient (re)organization can be modeled only procedurally. What

[28]This notion not only corroborates but extends ideas expressed in the theories of priming and spreading activation [25], now allowing, for example, for the dynamic and task-oriented generation of paths (along which activation might spread) but no longer being confined to predefined static relations. The situational generation of these paths actually allows us to model priming as a realized cognitive function rather than a simulation of processes related with it in the past.

[29]Representational formats will be called *basal* if they can provide a frame for the formal unification of categorial, concept-hierarchical, truth-functional, propositional, phrasal, or other intermediate representations.

appears disturbing as a consequence of the process–result distinction in the first instance is that the procedural models of cognitive processes, not the processes themselves, produce accessible results in representational structures which, depending on the way they are addressed, will result in the (more or less subjective) internal or endo view the system develops, and in a (more or less objective) external or exo view of the surrounding environment that constitutes the system's reality by virtue of its endo structure.[30] However, on second thought, the computational semiotician finds herself or himself engaged in a constitutive part of the very process of meaning constitution (semiotic function) which she or he was trying to model as a process of knowledge-based information processing (cognitive function). Apparently, realizational models of semiotic aspects of cognition will produce emergent representational results which are open to perspectival (endo–exo) interpretation, whereas simulative models will not.

To find out (and preferably to be able to test) what of the structural information inherent in natural language discourse (defined and structured by the text analytical, computational processes described above) might be involved in mediating or constituting that duality, an experimental setting has been designed. It is based on the assumption that some representational level or core structure, similar to the one modeled by SHS, ought to be postulated to be considered a common base for different notions of meaning or content of natural language expressions developed by theories of referential and situational semantics as well as some structural or stereotype meaning theories.

5.5.1 Experimental Testing

For the purpose of testing semiotic processes of meaning constitution, situational complexities have to be reduced by abstracting away irrelevant components, hopefully without oversimplifying the issue and trivializing the problem. Therefore, the propositional form of natural language predication (undoubtedly the common basis of traditional meaning theories) will not be done away with or neglected. Instead, it will be employed to construct and generate in a controlled way the natural language material that is to be used for training and for testing the system; however, the propositional structure will not determine the way this training material is to be processed in the test. To have semantically well-defined and truth-conditionally-clear language expressions of propositions denoting referentially doubtless facts in a specified situation would appear to be a necessary condition for a test (or *experimentum crucis*) to show whether or not a nonpropositional processing of strings of propositions in pragmatically homogeneous texts can result in a structure either identical or at least similar to the facts described in these texts and/or related in some regular way to the denoted structures referred to by these texts.

To give a general view of the approach first, the experimental setting is imagined to consist of an artificial mobile system in a two-dimensional environment, with

[30]It appears that what Pattee [31] named semantic closure and characterized as a specific relation between the material (performative) and the symbolic (representational) aspects of any organism's behavior is another perspectival view on this phenomenon.

some objects at certain places which are to be identified[31] The system's channels of perception allowing to form its own or endo view of its surroundings are extremely limited, and its ability to act (and react) is heavily restricted compared to that of natural or living information-processing systems. What makes such an abstract system a semiotic one is that whatever it might gather from its environment, it will not be the result of decoding processes, which would necessarily call for that code to be known to the system. Instead, any result will be constituted according to the system's (co- and contextually restricted) susceptibility and processing capabilities to (re)organize the environmental data and to (re)present the results in a dynamic structure that determines the system's knowledge (susceptibility), learning (change), and understanding (representation).

This postulate obviously rules out immediately any traditional approaches to cognitive modeling. They do not see the need of an endo–exo differentiation and are satisfied instead with well-established formalisms (in syntax, semantics, predicate logics) that not only allow us to distinguish, describe, and represent different levels of natural language structures but apparently also determine and control the processing of what these levels are meant to model. Consequently, knowledge-based representations were conceived corresponding to the cognitive processes believed to operate on them, depending on and according to the convictions held about the way natural language expressions are to be analyzed and interpreted, and not as they might be understood by humans. It is still difficult to accept that the syntactic and semantic analysis (parsing and interpretation) of natural language expressions is more of a fault-tracing and fault-correcting machinery than a model of default mechanism underlying natural language understanding.[32] This is one of the reasons why cognitive models in linguistics appear to have persistently narrowed the general (and semiotic) scope of natural language understanding to become identified with structure processing. Accordingly, language processing appeared to be reducible to a problem of inventing symbolic representations for (both world and linguistic) knowledge structures which rules of formal syntax and semantics could be made to operate on (memory). However, identifying textual discourse solely with propositional function, and ascribing to it syntactic structures of sentences whose truth-conditional interpretation is determined by a referential semantics which, in turn, seems to allow for the definition of predicate meanings according to properties believed to be observed, recognized, identified, and named in the world around and external to the cognitive systems, is to favor a very particularized understanding of natural language understanding which is hardly tenable. It also appears scarcely convincing why some (admittedly well understood) formalisms representing certain functional results on different levels of (more or less arbitrary) abstractions should also provide the only levels and modules to study and investigate the (as yet enigmatic) processes related to (or even underlying) these or other cognitive functions in language under-

[31] As will become clear in what follows, so far this identification concerns the places and does not (yet) apply to the objects.

[32] The difference may be seen as an analog of the phenomenological distinction made by existential philosophy between efficient modes of immediate understanding (*Dasein*) and deficient modes in need of object constitutional explication (*Welt*).

standing by humans. It is this governing hypothesis of the structure–function relation—purportedly clear-cut and in no need of representational scrutiny—underlying models of language processing in cognitive linguistics that is questioned.

The experimental setting developed to allow for such a test of language understanding without committing to the semiotically unwarranted presuppositions of sentencial and truth-conditional reconstructions of language processing is still tentative (Figure 5.5). It hinges on the assumption that cognitive information processing will both operate on and produce structures as a condition for and/or a result of such processing. These structures have to have some space–time extension (i.e., are in principle observable apart from and independent of being processed cognitively). The processes operating on and modifying them can also in principle be dealt with independent of their temporal duration by procedures that can be defined as

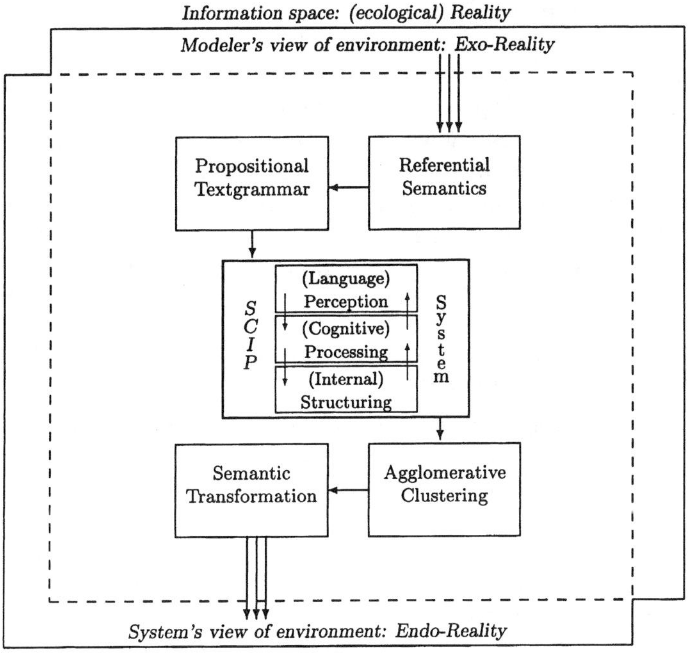

FIGURE 5.5 Situational setting of a SCIP system within an environment which is defined to allow for the system's view of it (endo reality) to differ from what the external observer's view (exo reality) might be. This is achieved by keeping the system's (nonpropositional) faculties of language processing strictly apart from the (propositional) way the language data are generated as a truth-functional correct textual protocol description of system–environment relations serving as their structural coupling. Note that grammar (lexicon, syntax) and semantics are not part of the system's language processing (linguistic knowledge) and that the visualization modules (cluster analysis, semantic transformation) applied to the system's internal representation (knowledge or understanding) are external to the system's semiotic processing. These components are introduced exclusively to formally specify and control the system's environment as its language input and to allow for a semantic interpretation and visualized image of the internal structure of the system's acquired knowledge at a time.

processes abstracted from their temporality. Procedures can be represented formally, their notational format parsed and checked for correctness, their expressions interpreted or compiled for execution, and provided that a suitable automaton is available, become initial for the enactment of processes in time again, not only having a certain duration but also the effect of operating on and modifying structures which in fact (not only in principle) are observable as (input/output-related) changes.

This two-sided independence facilitates procedural cognitive models to relate structured language expressions, which can be analyzed (or observed) without being understood, to language understanding processes, which can be conceived (as procedures) being abstracted from their temporal duration. It appears that by this move, procedures and algorithms found to model some aspects of cognitive information processing for language comprehension can be tested against—not on the grounds of—any accepted, well-defined model of cognitive (language) understanding. Test results would have to be considered positive for all cases in which the contents of the same language expressions is represented or depicted in either identical (or at least similar) results for both models.

Thus to enable intersubjective scrutiny, the (unknown) results of an abstract artificial (SCIP) system's (well-known) processing of natural language discourse is compared to the (well-known) traditional (LP and CL)[33] interpretations of the (unknown) processes of natural language meaning constitution.[34] Therefore, the propositional form of natural language predication will be used here to control both the format and the contents of the natural language training material, not, however, to determine the way it is processed to model understanding.

5.5.2 Situational Conditions

For the purpose of testing semiotic processes, their situational complexity has been said to be in need of an abstractive reduction that does not oversimplify the issue or trivialize the problem. Trying to achieve this, situational parameters have to be determined guaranteeing:

1. That the three main components of the experimental setting, the system, the environment, and the discourse are specified by sets of conditioning properties. These define the SCIP system by way of a set of (partly procedural) parameters such as orientation, mobility, perception, and processing (Table 5.3). The SCIP environment is defined as a set of formal entities such as reference plane, objects, grid, direction, and location (Tables 5.4). The SCIP discourse material coupling system and environment (structural coupling) as language mediation is structured first by a number of whole–part-related (granular) entities such as corpus, text, sentence, and word (Table 5.5), of

[33]That is, linguistics proper (LP) and cognitive/computational linguistics (CL).

[34]The concept of knowledge underlying the employment of adjectival terms here is meant to be understood in the sense that "known" generally refers to having some well-established (however controversial, experiential, scientific, intersubjective) models to deal with, whereas "unknown" refers to the lack of such models.

TABLE 5.3. Collection of SCIP Systems' Formal Properties [a]

SCIP System:	$\{\mathcal{O}, \mathcal{M}, \mathcal{P}, \mathcal{C}, \mathcal{A}\}$
Orientation:	$\mathcal{O} := \{\vec{N} = (0,1), \vec{E} = (1,0), \vec{S} = (0,-1), \vec{W} = (-1,0)\}$
Mobility (pace):	$\mathcal{M} := \{k(0,1), k(1,1), k(1,0), k(1,-1), k(0,-1), k(-1,-1), k(-1,0), k(-1,1) : k = 1\}$
LanPerception:	$\mathcal{P} := \{K := \{k_t\}, L := \sum_{t=1}^{T} l_t, V := \{x_i\}, H_i := \sum_{t=1}^{T} h_{it} : i = 1, \ldots, j, \ldots, N\}$
CogProcessing:	$\mathcal{C} := \{\alpha, \delta, \zeta, \ldots\}; \mathcal{A} := \{\tilde{\alpha}\vert x, \tilde{\delta}\vert y, \ldots\}$
Semantics:	**none**
Syntax:	**none**

[a] Neither syntactical nor semantic knowledge is defined as provided for the system.

TABLE 5.4. Collection of SCIP Environments' Formal Properties

SCIP Environment:	$\{\mathcal{R}_E, \mathcal{R}_O, \mathcal{R}_R, \mathcal{D}, l_{\mathcal{R}}\}$
Reference plane:	$\mathcal{R}_E := \{P_{n,m} : \exists R_{n,m} \in \mathcal{R}_R(n_0, m_0, g), P_{n,m} \in R_{n,m}\}$
Reference objects:	$\mathcal{R}_O := \{\square, \Delta, \ldots\}$
Reference grid:	$\mathcal{R}_R(n_0, m_0, g) := \{R_{n,m} = [(n-1)g, ng] \times [(m-1)g, mg], 1 \leq n \leq n_0, 1 \leq m \leq m_0, g > 0\}$
Directions:	$\mathcal{D} := \{\vec{N} := (0,1), \vec{O} := (1,0), \vec{S} := (0,-1), \vec{W} := (-1,0)\}$
Object location:	$l_{\mathcal{R}} : \mathcal{R}_O \longrightarrow \mathcal{R}_E$

TABLE 5.5. Collection of Conceptual Restrictions That Define Language Material Entities Constituting the Coupling of SCIP System and SCIP Environment Structurally

SCIP Structural Coupling:

Word: the entity (sign) identified as vocabulary element (type) whose occurrences in (linear) sets of entities (tokens) are countable

Sentence: the (nonempty, linear) set of words to form a correct expression of a true proposition denoting a relation of system position (SP) and object location (OL)

Text: the (nonempty, linear) set of sentences with identical pairs of core predicates denoting SP–OL relations resulting from linear movement of the system to positions directly adjacent

Corpus: the (nonempty) set of texts comprising descriptions of (any or all) factually possible SP–OL relations within a specified systemic and environmental setting

which sentence and text require further defining restrictions to become specified by a formal syntax (Table 5.6) and referential semantics (Table 5.7).

2. That the system's environmental data are provided by a corpus of (natural language) texts comprising correct expressions of true propositions denoting how system positions relate to object locations (SP–OL relations for short).

TABLE 5.6. Syntax of Text Grammar for the Generation of Strings of Correct Descriptions of Possible SP–OL (System Position and Object Location) Relations

T(ext):	=	$\{S_i \mid S_i \longrightarrow S_{i+1} : \mathcal{M} \wedge \{KP_1, KP_2\} \in S_i \wedge \{KP_1, KP_2\} \in S_{i+1} \wedge \forall KP_j \in S_i \cup S_{i+1};\ j = 1, 2; i = 1, \ldots, I\}$
$\mathcal{M}$	:=	$\{k(0,1), k(1,1), k(1,0), k(1,-1), k(0,-1), k(-1,-1), k(-1,0), k(-1,1) : k = 1\}$
S_i	$\longrightarrow$	NP VP
NP	$\longrightarrow$	N
VP	$\longrightarrow$	V PP
PP	$\longrightarrow$	HP KP
N	$\longrightarrow$	$a\langle triangle \mid square \rangle$
V	$\longrightarrow$	*lies*
HP	$\longrightarrow$	$\langle extremely \mid very \mid rather \rangle \langle near \mid far \rangle$
KP	$\longrightarrow$	$\langle on\ the\ left \mid on\ the\ right \rangle \mid \langle in\ front \mid behind \rangle$

TABLE 5.7. Semantics to Identify Denotationally True Core and Hedge Predicates (Under Crisp and Fuzzy Interpretation) in Correct Sentences Being Generated for Fixed (Unchanged) Object Locations (OLs) and Mobile (Varying) System Positions (SPs)

Core predicates (KPs) as $>$ and $<$ relations of system positions x, y and object locations n, m (0-coordinates down the left) for all orientations N, E, S, W of the system

North x, y	*in front*	*behind*
on the left	$>m, <n$	$>m, >n$
on the right	$<m, <n$	$>m, <n$

East x, y	in front	behind
on the left	$<m, <n$	$>m, <n$
on the right	$<m, >n$	$>m, >n$

South x, y	*in front*	*behind*
on the left	$<m, >n$	$>m, <n$
on the right	$>m, >n$	$<m, >n$

West x, y	*in front*	*behind*
on the left	$>m, >n$	$<m, >n$
on the right	$>m, <n$	$>m, <n$

Hedge predicates (HPs) as distances of SP-OL (crisp and fuzzy interpretations): by number of grid points ($|x - n|$ and $|y - m|$)

Crisp 1.0	1	2	3	4	5	6	7	8	9	10
extremely near	1	1	0	0	0	0	0	0	0	0
very near	0	0	1	1	0	0	0	0	0	0
rather near	0	0	0	0	1	0	0	0	0	0
rather far	0	0	0	0	0	1	0	0	0	0
very far	0	0	0	0	0	0	1	1	0	0
extremely far	0	0	0	0	0	0	0	0	1	1

Fuzzy 1.1	1	2	3	4	5	6	7	8	9	10
extremely near	1	1	0.7	0.2	0	0	0	0	0	0
very near	0.2	0.7	1	1	0.7	0.2	0	0	0	0
rather nearby	0	0	0.2	0.7	1	0.7	0.2	0	0	0
rather far	0	0	0	0.2	0.7	1	0.7	0.2	0	0
very far	0	0	0	0	0.2	0.7	1	1	0.7	0.2
extremely far	0	0	0	0	0	0	0.2	0.7	1	1

These material world relations are described according to the formally specified syntax and semantics (representing the exo view or described situations).

3. That the system's internal picture of its surroundings (representing the endo view or discourse situations) is to be derived from this language environment

other than by way of propositional reconstruction (i.e., without syntactic parsing and semantic interpretation of sentence and text structures).

Consequently, the exo knowledge allowing designers of the experimental setting to control the propositional encoding and decoding of environmental information in texts which the system—being placed in that environment as specified in such a way—would have to process had to be kept strictly apart from the SCIP system's endo capacities, into which it was definitely not to be included. Thus the system's own nonpropositional processing would have to allow for some results which, as the system's internal representation, would not be interpretable as mere repetitious reproductions or as an application of knowledge structures made available to it externally. Instead, it would have to have in principle a chance to be different from (however comparable to) the exo view of its environment as specified by propositional descriptions. This is tantamount to the quest for a representation whose format allows visualization of endo-computed adjacencies and comparison to exo-defined relations.

5.5.3 Processes and Results

The procedures enabling semiotic processing operate in a situational setting that consists of a two-dimensional environment with the objects of a triangle and a square at certain places (Figure 5.6*a*). A SCIP system will have to identify them on the grounds of sets of natural language expressions it is exposed to which describe SP–OL relations correctly. Although the SCIP system's perception is limited to its

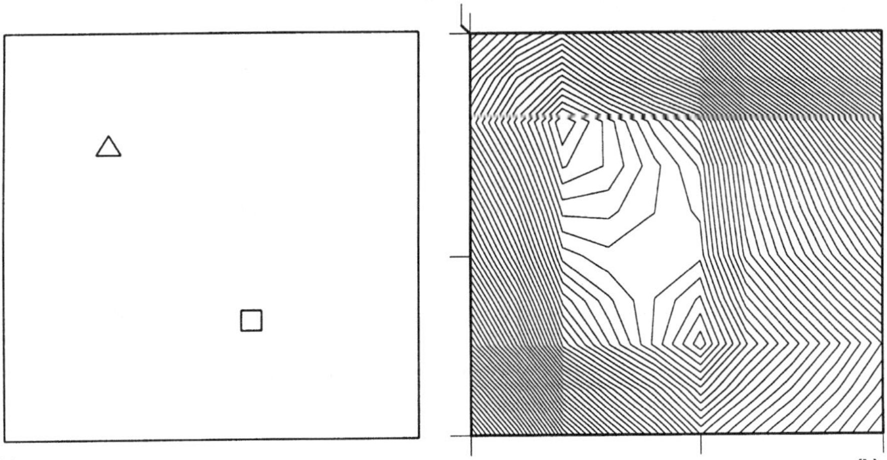

(a) (b)

FIGURE 5.6 (*a*) Reference plane with location of objects (△ and □) propositionally described by texts in the training corpus; (*b*) resulting two-dimensional image (right) of SCIP system's endo view after processing the text corpus, showing regions of potential object locations (iso referentials) as computed under crisp hedge interpretation.

(formal) language-processing capabilities (which do not entail any knowledge of syntax or of semantics), and as its ability to act (and react) is restricted to stepwise linear movement and global processing of discourse information, it will come up with some acquired internally represented structure corresponding vaguely to its external environment (Figure 5.6*b*) when visualized to allow for a comparison.

What makes the processing of such a system semiotic is that it will not apply any (symbolically) coded knowledge (of linguistic structures and their semantics) during that processing, but as such knowledge is not made available to it will instead be confined to its own computing capabilities in (re)organizing the environmental data and (re)presenting its results.

The example layout is illustrated by the object locations in the reference plane (Figure 5.6*a*). It provided the base for the cognitive situations to be described which consisted of all possible system positions (SPs) and orientations $\mathcal{O}$ relative to the two object locations (OLs). The language expressions describing these relations were generated automatically for given OLs and all possible SPs according to the formal syntax (Table 5.6) and semantics (Table 5.7) specified above. The resulting corpus comprises some 12,432 word tokens of 26 word types in 2483 sentences and 684 texts. This training set of generated language material was then exposed to the SCIP system, which perceived it as environmental data to be processed according to its specified faculties (Table 5.3): namely, language perception $\mathcal{P}$ (i.e., identifying and counting string entities of different types), according to (5.5), to (5.8); cognitive processing $\mathcal{C}$ (i.e., computation and organization), according to (5.9) to (5.11) as well as (5.13) to (5.15); and abstracting $\mathcal{A}$ (i.e., formation and representation of new entities), according to (5.12) and (5.16), as introduced above.

In the course of processing, the composite morphisms (Figure 5.4) as summarized in the two-level mapping abstractions (Table 5.2) result in the semantic hyperspace (SHS). Its intrinsic structure reveals some properties that can be made visible in a four-stage process:

1. Applying methods of average linkage cluster analysis allows us to identify (Figure 5.7) structurally adjacent word types (e.g., entity labels of object and predicate candidates) [45, 54] comparable to Kohonen self-organizing semantic maps [24, 58], which yield comparable though internally less structured results.
2. Their numerical hedge interpretation provides the SP–OL distance values whose directional core interpretations determine virtual regions of object locations relative to the system's central position in an intermediate Endo $1_{i,j}$ data structure (Table 5.8). From this intermediate representation the system's processing arrives at its own internal perception of the environment by
3. Computing the transformation according to (6.18) to yield the Endo$2_{m,n}$ data determining the system's endo view of its environment, which is an orientation-independent structure (Table 5.9). It can be visualized in another format as

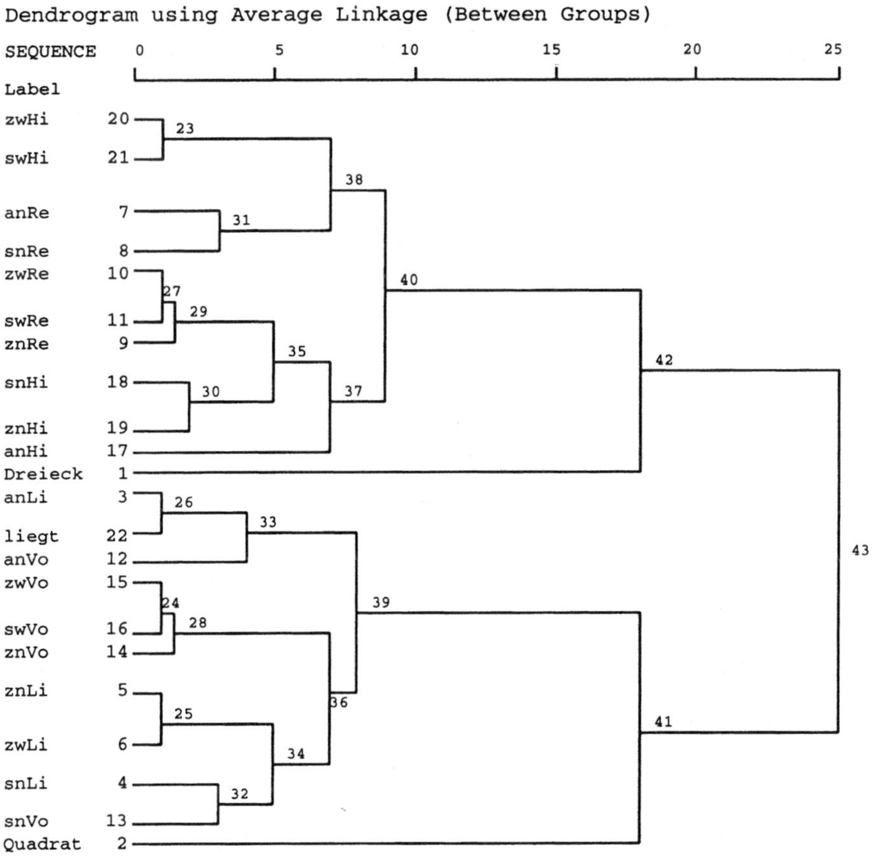

FIGURE 5.7 Dendrogram of internal SHS structure of labels of hedged core predicate adjacencies as analyzed from textual object location descriptions relative to system positions oriented south. a, *Extremely*; s, *very*; z, *rather*; w, *far*; n, *near*; Li, *on the left*; Re, *on the right*; Vo, *in front*; Hi, *behind*; Dreieck, *triangle*; Quadrat, *square*; liegt, *lies*.

4. A holistic representation comparable to the referential plane now structured by a pattern of polygons that connect regions of equivalent denotational likelihood—called isoreferentials—of possible object locations in a two-dimensional format (Figure 5.6*b*) or in a three-dimensional image (Figure 5.8) according to the texts processed.

Transforming the $\text{Endo1}_{i,j}$ data matrix (Table 5.8) to the $\text{Endo2}_{m,n}$ data matrix (Table 5.9) according to the equation

$$Endo2_{m,n} = \sum_{i=m}^{m+10} \sum_{j=n}^{n+10} Endo1_{i,j} \tag{5.18}$$

TABLE 5.8. Endo1$_{i,j}$ Value Distribution of Sums of Grid Point Marks According to (Crisply Interpreted) Hedged Core Predicate Adjacencies as Found in the Cluster Dendrogram Computed from the Semantic Space Data of Texts Which Describe SP–OL Relations for a Mobile System (∇) Oriented South

BEHIND

	0	0	0	0	0	0	0	0	0	0		0	0	0	0	0	0	0	0	0	0	
	0	0	0	0	0	0	0	0	0	0		0	0	0	0	0	0	0	0	0	0	
	0	0	2	2	2	2	4	4	4	4		1	1	1	1	1	1	0	0	0	0	
	0	0	2	2	2	2	4	4	4	4		1	1	1	1	1	1	0	0	0	0	
	0	0	2	2	2	2	4	4	4	4		1	1	1	1	1	1	0	0	0	0	
	0	0	5	5	5	5	2	2	2	2		1	1	1	1	1	1	0	0	0	0	
	0	0	5	5	5	5	2	2	2	2		1	1	1	1	1	1	0	0	0	0	
	0	0	5	5	5	5	2	2	2	2		1	1	1	1	1	1	0	0	0	0	
	0	0	4	4	4	4	2	2	2	2		1	1	1	1	1	1	0	0	0	0	
	0	0	4	4	4	4	2	2	2	2		1	1	1	1	1	1	0	0	0	0	
RIGHT											∇											LEFT
	0	0	1	1	1	1	1	1	1	1		6	6	3	3	3	3	0	0	0	0	
	0	0	1	1	1	1	1	1	1	1		6	6	3	3	3	3	0	0	0	0	
	0	0	1	1	1	1	1	1	1	1		3	3	7	7	5	5	0	0	0	0	
	0	0	1	1	1	1	1	1	1	1		3	3	7	7	5	5	0	0	0	0	
	0	0	1	1	1	1	1	1	1	1		3	3	4	4	4	4	0	0	0	0	
	0	0	1	1	1	1	1	1	1	1		3	3	4	4	4	4	0	0	0	0	
	0	0	1	1	1	1	1	1	1	1		3	3	4	4	4	4	0	0	0	0	
	0	0	1	1	1	1	1	1	1	1		3	3	4	4	4	4	0	0	0	0	
	0	0	0	0	0	0	0	0	0	0		0	0	0	0	0	0	0	0	0	0	
	0	0	0	0	0	0	0	0	0	0		0	0	0	0	0	0	0	0	0	0	

IN FRONT

TABLE 5.9. Endo2$_{m,n}$ Showing Regions of OL (Object Location) Likelihood Computed for Each Grid Point *m,n* by Superimposing Locality Patterns from Endo1$_{i,j}$ Values According to (5.18)

NORTH

	226	240	251	232	213	194	164	141	118	95	
	240	260	274	257	240	223	192	168	144	120	
	251	274	295	284	271	258	226	201	176	151	
WEST	237	262	289	285	277	269	238	216	194	172	EAST
	223	250	280	280	276	272	242	223	204	185	
	209	238	271	275	275	275	246	230	214	198	
	191	222	258	269	276	283	258	243	228	213	
	173	206	245	263	277	291	270	256	242	228	
	144	176	214	236	254	272	256	244	232	220	
	119	150	187	212	233	254	242	232	222	212	

SOUTH

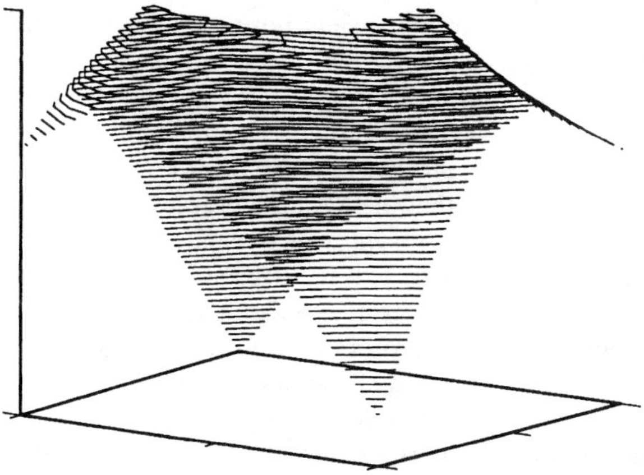

FIGURE 5.8 Three-dimensional profile according to Table 6.9 data of the SCIP system's endo view of its reality, showing highest potentials for object locations (OLs) under crisp hedge interpretation, as computed from the training corpus of texts describing these locations relative to system positions (SPs) in the reference plane.

is a line- and columnwise summation of values which can be viewed as a replica of the system's stepwise movement along grid points in the reference plane which allowed us to generate the SP–OL descriptions. Therefore, the matrix $Endo2_{m,n}$ (Table 5.9) contains the structural information for an external observer's image of the system's endo view as computed globally from the corpus of texts that described SP–OL relations in a predicative and propositional way. The overall picture of (interpolated) points corresponding to degrees of even referential likelihood (iso referentials) produces two object locations (OLs) by way of two- and three-dimensional scattergrams (Figure 5.6*b* and 5.8, respectively) and denotes the potential objects clearly, however fuzzy.

The fuzziness of this image is quite remarkable insofar as it does not concern the object locations themselves but rather the referential space around them, allowing for their differentiation. This sort of holistic and indirect way of specification, as opposed to the direct way by stating two coordinate values to determine a location, is self-including and organized around the entities to be specified. It does not, therefore, need (or rely on) any categorial presuppositions of how points may be defined exterior to the self-organizing process whose emergent results structure space in a way to allow it to become (potentially) referential. It should be noted here, however, that the initial format of visualization chosen to be a two-dimensional plane spanned by orthogonal coordinates is not a situational necessity of the space concept but only the most conventionalized frame for representing definite locations by abstracting from their situational embedding.

What can be concluded from what has been outlined so far? The strict separation of the computational processes from their results on the system's side now corresponds to the sharp distinction between the formal specification to control the propositional generation of descriptive language material and the image of the object locations (OLs) relative to varying system positions (SPs) of which this language material is a referentially true description. As the language material is in both cases the medium of representation for objects located in the reference plane at certain places, it serves well as the postulated structural coupling for testing a SCIP system's performance to collect and represent referential information from discourse. It is worthwhile noting here again that the SCIPS's processing is neither based on, nor does it involve, any knowledge of syntax or semantics on the system's side.

As soon as gradation (or fuzziness) is included as a consequence of a co- and contextual[35] situatedness—that is, according to the SCIP system's basal assumption by way of textual language descriptions of object locations relative to system positions (described situations) and their actualization or understanding by the system concerned (discourse situations)—the representational frame is immediately extended by structural information that more conventional (symbolic) frames of (rule based) representations can cope with only by adding other dimensions ad hoc.

The nonpropositional processing of a set (corpus) of sets (texts) of correct language expressions (sentences) of true meanings (propositions) describing object locations (fixed) relative to system positions (changing) resulted in a topology (dynamic) of labeled meaning points. Being in a vector space format (SHS), its intrinsic structure was made visible by three consecutive stages of representations. These visualizations were based on the $crisp_{1.0}$ interpretations of the hedges. Using instead the $fuzzy_{1.1}$ definitions (Table 5.7) to interpret the adjacencies of hedged core predicate labels as analyzed in the cluster dendrogram (Figure 5.7) has produced comparable images of emerging structuredness that was visualized accordingly in the form of three-dimensional iso referentials (Figure 5.9).

What is surprising, though, is the fact that these exo representations of the system's endo view appear to provide a more immediate image of the referential space structure under $fuzzy_{1.1}$ than under $crisp_{1.0}$ interpretations of hedges. Derivable from the fuzzy semantic data is a more clearly structured image without the transform of intermediate data structures which are needed according to (5.18) in the case of crisp semantic interpretation of the data. A still very tentative explanation may be offered by assuming that the fuzzy interpretation of hedged core predicate adjacencies on this (representational) level appears to enhance the effect that the changing positions of the system produce on the situational level. Described by differing language expressions to denote varying but definite SP–OL relations (of system positions and object locations) under crisp interpretation of hedges, these variations seem to be mimetically enlarged in the $fuzzy_{1.1}$ definitions of hedged predicates. As the SCIP system was conceived as a mobile one, restricted by the defining conditions and properties (Table 5.3), its changing positions were constitutive for the controlled generation of (language) descriptions of (very restricted) referential situations. Therefore, it might not be too startling to find the overall structure emerging from nonpropositional processing of pragmatically homogeneous propositional descriptions of situations no longer in want of a computational transformation. It may be

[35]The cotextual embeddedness of language entities is preserved in our definitions of word, sentence, text, and corpus (Table 5.5), whereas the contextuality is determined by the structural SCIP system–environment coupling (Figure 5.5) procedurally enacted by our model of language sign processing.

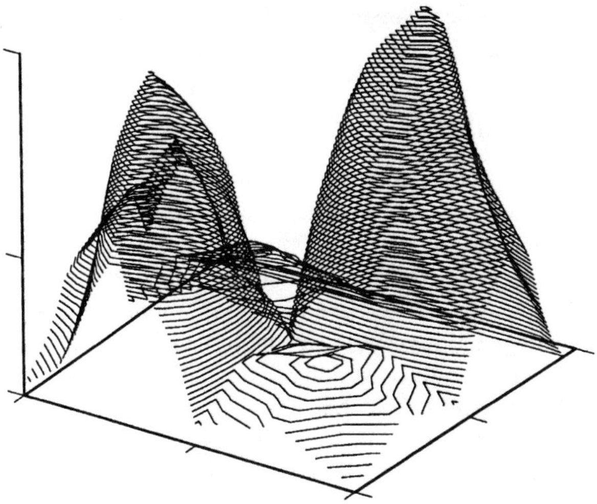

FIGURE 5.9 Three-dimensional image of the SCIP system's endo view of regions showing highest potentials for object locations under $fuzzy_{1.1}$ hedge interpretation, as computed from the training corpus of texts describing these locations relative to system positions in the reference plane.

concluded that its results can apparently be compensated or rather anticipated by the more semiotic substitute or, rather, principle intrinsic to natural language structuring (i.e., by fuzzy instead of crisp definitions and interpretations of hedges).

5.6 SEMIOTIC COMPUTING WITH WORDS

The problem of visualizing results of computational procedures developed to model and realize semiotic processes whose numerical representations by definition do not have an immediate interpretation is apparent. Confining to the level of semantic word meaning constitution, various techniques have been developed and applied in the past [45–49] to analyze, scrutinize, and visualize emergent structures in distributed representations of vectors of labeled meaning components as determined by functions of differences of usage regularities computed from natural language discourse corpora. These approaches were able to demonstrate the definite noncontingency of meaning points $z \in S$ in semantic hyperspace (SHS). Hence its structure may serve as a base for a number of procedures to operate on. Their algorithmic implementations as well as the results produced by these algorithms allow us to demonstrate the semiotic quality of procedural models of nonsymbolic information processing, illustrating their meaning constitutional performance and their ability to represent such meanings in a usable, easily interpreted format of treelike graphs whose hierarchically structured connotative dependencies (CDSs) [41], associative dependencies (ADSs) [44], and dispositional dependencies (DDSs) [56] converge in a particular type of semantic relatedness of co- and contextually sensitive focal perspectivity.[36]

5.6.1 Semantic Dispositional Dependencies

Following the semiotic understanding of meaning more as a constitutional process rather than an entity of invariable constancy or static representation, the SHS presented may be considered part of a word meaning/world knowledge representation system which separates the format of basic (stereotyped) meaning components (meaning points) from their latent (dependency) relational organization as meaning potential (semantic dispositions). Whereas the former is a static, topologically organized multidimensional memory structure, the latter can be characterized as a dynamic and flexible structuring process which (re)organizes and thereby transforms the basic relatedness of the elements it operates on.

This is achieved by a recursively defined procedure that produces a hierarchical ordering of the SHS's meaning points, which can be represented as a tree structure organized under a given aspect (root node) according to and in dependence of its neighbors' co- and contextual relevancy. Taking up ideas from cognitive theories of semantic memory, priming, and spreading activation [25], the DDS algorithm was devised to operate on the semantic space data and to generate a dispositional dependency structure (DDS) in the format of an n-ary tree. Given one meaning point's position, the algorithm will:

1. Take that meaning point's label as a start.
2. Stack labels of all its neighboring points by their decreasing distances.
3. Instantiate the DDS tree, with a head or root node being the starting point's label. The process continues to
4. Take the label from the top of the stack as the next daughter node.
    - 4.1. List the labels of all its neighbors.
    - 4.2. Intersect the list with nodes in the tree.
    - 4.3. Determine from the intersection the least distant one as the mother node in the tree.
5. Link the daughter to the mother node identified, and
6. Repeat step 4 either
    - 6.1. Until step 2 is empty, or
    - 6.2. Other stop condition (preset number of nodes to be processed, maximum distance from starting point, etc.) is reached
7. To end.

[36]These tree structures differ according to their underlying procedures and algorithms which were developed to operationalize different aspects of (connotative, associative, and dispositional) dependencies. Their potentiality is visualized in possible meaning relations which these algorithms assemble and organize under the root node's focus in a hierarchy of dependency graphs which are represented in a perspectively structured form.

Apparently, although the DDS algorithm can simply be characterized as a greedy, encapsulated minimal spanning tree (MST) generating procedure [34] which consumes all meaning points $z_n \in \langle S, \zeta \rangle$, this encapsulation serves a meaning-constituting purpose catching semiotic properties of emergence and representation of structure which are tied to its contextuality. Where the MST is searching for the shortest-possible connection between points qualifying for tree node relatedness, the DDS is looking for the highest meaning similarities, that is, for the shortest-possible distance relations between points which are determined as semiotically derived representations of meaning components as computed from textual structures (discourse). It is this property that allows the algorithm's search space to be reduced and semantically constrained on the starting point's or root node's topological environment (capsule) which renders the tree perspective (i.e., aspect-dependent and structurally context sensitive).

The tree-structured graphs[37] may serve as a visualization of the discriminating relatedness that any labeled meaning point $z_i \in \langle S, \zeta \rangle$ chosen as root node will produce according to this and other points' adjacencies in the SHS data structure (Figure 5.10). Their primal topological relatedness in SHS—being determined by and reconstructed operationally as a function of the differences of usage regularities of word distributions in the texts analyzed—will thus allow for a directed, nonsymmetric relation (dependency) being procedurally declared and induced on the SHS structure of meaning points z_i, depending on the start area (i.e., the meaning point's position chosen as the tree's root node). Such topology-based dependencies guarantee that from all related meaning points the most relevant will also be related in the tree structure generated. The dependencies which may be weighted will vary in degree by the tree level they occur in, and in context according to the semantic aspect (or starting point chosen as root node) under which it is algorithmically generated. This type of tree has been named a *dispositional dependency structure* (DDS) because it may be considered a dynamic structure whose generation and assembly of possible meaning points will vary according to the modifications of the SHS structure from which it is derived.

5.6.2 Semiotically Generalized Constraints

The DDSs can be considered an alternative procedural format of fuzzy information granulation which extends the rule-based frame as introduced by the concept of generalized constraint [70] and exemplified in Ref. 71 as unconditional constraints. According to Zadeh [71], a generalized constraint on values of X is expressed as X *isr* R, where X is a variable that takes values in a universe of discourse U, *isr* is a variable copula with r being a discrete variable whose values define the way in which R constrains X, and R is the constraining relation. For r the different values defined are equality, possibility, verity, probability, probability value, random set, and fuzzy graph and the related (definitional, operational, procedural, computa-

[37]The figures present fragments of trees of a SHS structure that was computed from a sample of texts from the German daily newspaper (Die Welt, 1964, Berlin edition); $\oplus$ marked nodes hide conflated subtrees not expanded here; the numerical values stated are direct ζ-distances from the root node.

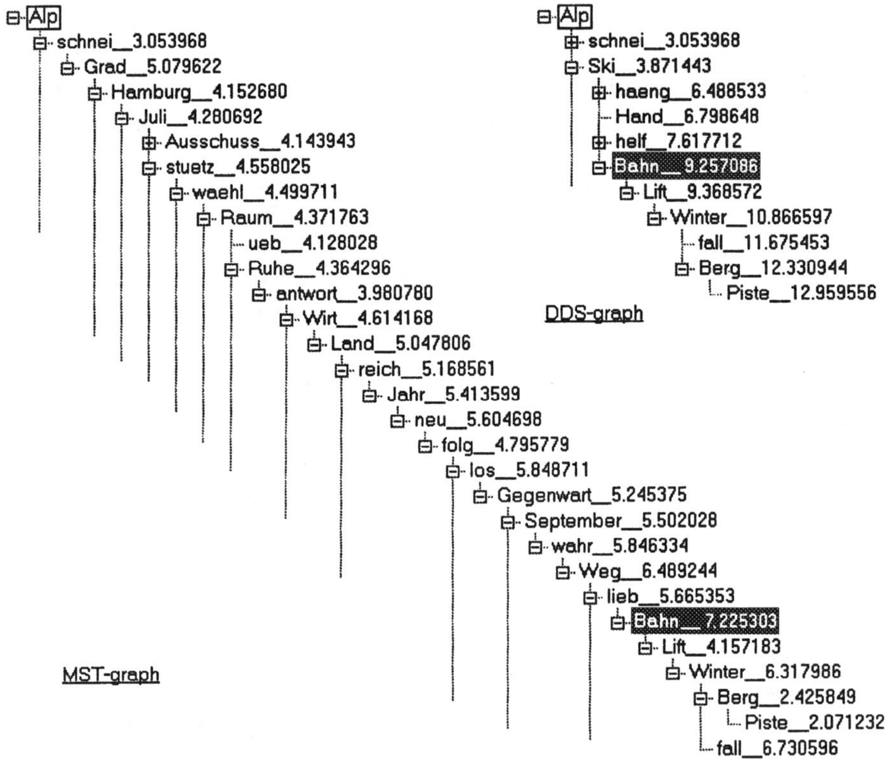

FIGURE 5.10 Fragment of MST graph of Alpen/*Alps* (root) as generated from the semantic space data ($V = 345, H_i \geq 10$) of a German newspaper sample (*Die Welt*, 1964, Berlin edition), contrasted with a fragment of the DDS tree (upper right) as generated for the same root node Alpen/ and from the same SHS data.

tional) interpretations are given. It is important to observe that r relates to R in a predicative sense specifying the interpretation of R (generally being a distribution of grades of membership) as possibilities, truth values, probabilities, or composites thereof. The distinction of functional types of r to control the interpretation of R is necessary for rule-based mechanisms of inferential processing but may become obsolete for algorithmic procedures in CS operating on well-defined value distributions. "In addition to the types of constraints defined above there are many others that are more specialized and less common. A question that arises is: What purpose is served by having a large variety of constraints to choose from? A basic reason is that, in general setting, information may be viewed as a constraint on a variable" [71, p. 117].

However, as has been shown above, constraints cannot only be induced by predicative expressions of truth-functional propositions but may also be induced by word meanings, provided that these are modeled by procedurally determined weighted dependency relations in SHS data derived from natural language discourse analyzed in a fuzzy linguistic manner. Taking the concept of a generalized constraint to hold also for the levels of sentence meanings (proposition) as well as for word meanings (DDS), the TFIG notational format introduced may be translated to $X \simeq \{z_n\}$, where X is a variable that takes values $z_i \in \langle S \rangle$ with $S \subseteq U$. A semiotically generalized constraint on values of X is expressed by $X\ dds_i\ S$, where DDS_i relates z_i to S in a specifying way by restricting SHS procedurally in generating the tree structure from meaning point z_i as its root, and z_n as its discrete variable whose values define different dependency paths which constrain S.

It should be noted here that the notion of dependency path is a structural representation of a dynamic concept of *granular word meaning*, which induces a reflexive, symmetric, and weakly transitive relation between relevant meaning components. It allows for the procedural definition and computational enactment of semantic inferencing on the word level, very much like the rule-based models of inferencing in granular fuzzy information processing based on fuzzy rules, or the syntagmatically defined propositional formats of symbolic processing in (cognitive linguistic) sentence semantics based on crisp logic calculi.

Thus a DDS tree can be said to (re)present meaning points—top down—as granular components whose dependency-related hierarchy determines its—bottom up—organization by way of a structured potential for choice made accessible by restrictions on the SHS $\langle S, \zeta \rangle$. Their actualized access then will be causative for the constitution of the meaning associated with (or rather enacted by) the expression of the root node's z_i language label $x_i \in V$ or vocabulary item employed in discourse.

5.6.3 Representational Properties

There are a number of consequences to be derived from DDS properties, of which the following seem interesting enough to be listed and commented on briefly:

1. To illustrate the contextual sensitivity which distinguishes the DDS algorithm from minimal spanning trees (MST) [34], for example, the latter (Figure 5.10) has been generated from the same data with the same starting node. Note that the subtrees of Bahn (*track, course, trail*), identical in both the MST and DDS trees, are found on extremely different levels (MST 23 compared to DDS 3)[38]
2. The procedural (semiotic) approach replaces the storage of fixed and ready set relations of (semantic) networks in AI by source- or aspect-oriented induction of relations among meaning points by means of the DDS procedure.
3. DDSs' dependencies may be identified with an algorithmically induced relevance relation which is reflexive, nonsymmetric, and (weakly) transitive, as illustrated by the dependency paths' listings of node transitions les/*to read* $\Longrightarrow$ schreib/*to write* and its (partial) inverse schreib $\Longrightarrow$ les (Figures 5.11 and 5.12).

[38] The numerical MST values given are direct ζ-distances between nodes (mother–daughter pairs).

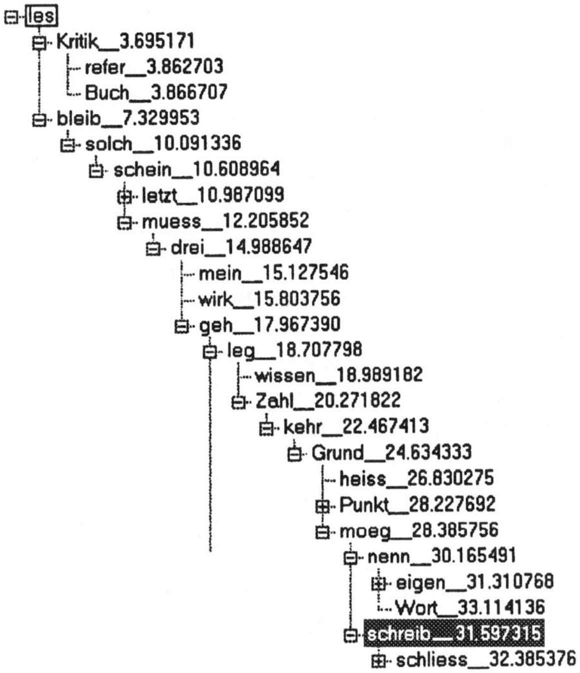

FIGURE 5.11 Dependency path of lesen/*to read* $\Longrightarrow$ schreiben/*to write* as traced in DDS tree of les.

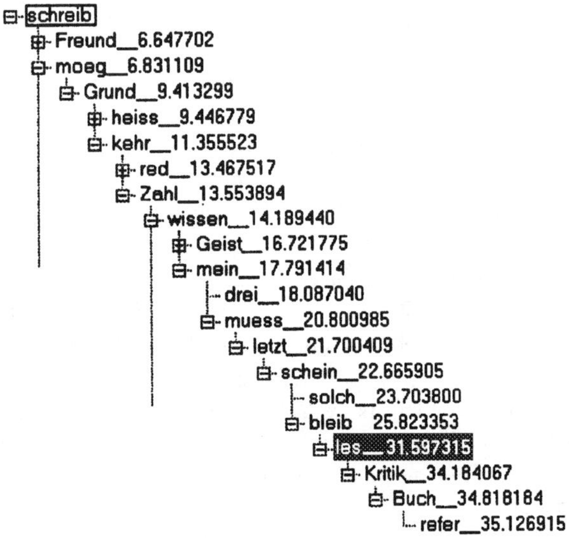

FIGURE 5.12 Dependency path of schreiben/*to write* $\Longrightarrow$ lesen/*to read* as traced in DDS tree of schreib.

4. The relevance relation gives rise to the notion of criteriality, which allows us to estimate to what degree a meaning compound (daughter node) contributes to the meaning potential a root node's DDS is to represent. It will render the DDS a weighted tree and may be specified numerically as a function of any node's level and ζ-distance by

$$Cr_i(d)_{\kappa+1} = Cr_i(m)_{\kappa} e^{-\zeta(d,i)/[\lambda+\zeta(d,m)]} \tag{6.19}$$

with i, m, and d for root, mother, and daughter nodes, respectively, and the counters κ for (left to right) nodes and λ for (top down) levels in the tree.

5. As the criteriality values are decreasing monotonously from 1.0 (root), they may be interpreted as membership values that reflect the relevance related, softly structured collection of components (nodes) in the DDS as a fuzzy meaning potential. Applying the set-theoretical extensions for logical operators (*and, or, non*, etc.) opens new possibilities of generating composite meaning points (Wort/*word* $\vee$ Satz/*sentence*) and (Wort $\wedge$ Satz) in Figure 5.13 and Figure 5.14 without assuming a propositional structure and to get these composites' structural meanings determined by their DDSs as computed from the SHS data.

6. The experiments run for semantic inferencing (SI) based on DDS have turned out to be very promising. SI appears to be feasible without the need to have to state the premises in a predicative or propositional form prior to the concluding process. The DDS algorithm lends itself easily to the modeling of analogical reasoning processes by parallel processing of DDS trees.

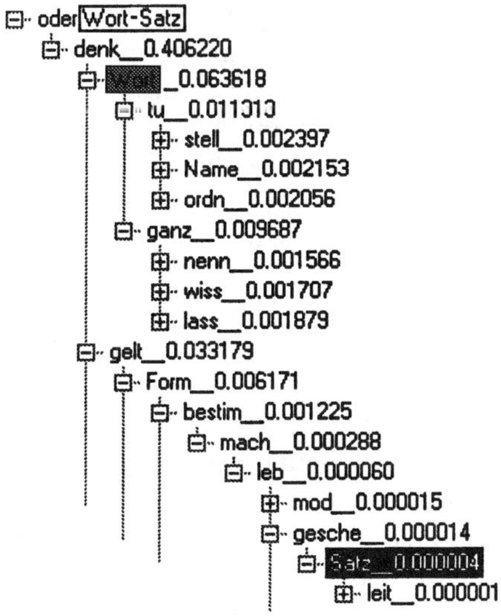

FIGURE 5.13 Fragment of DDS of Wort/*word* $\vee$ Satz/*sentence* as generated from OR-adjunction (max.) of meaning points in semantic space.

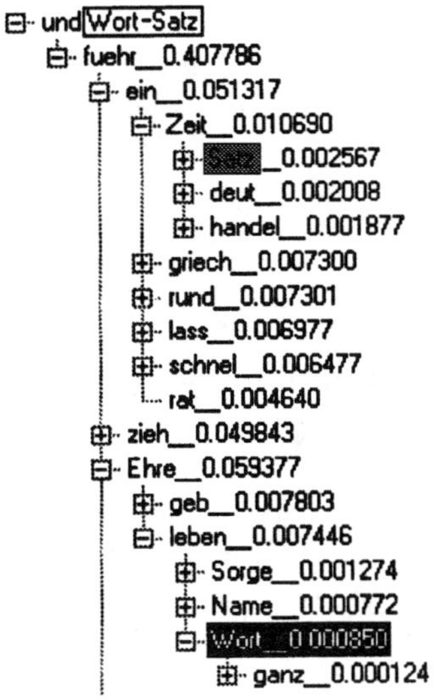

FIGURE 5.14 Fragment of DDS of Wort/*word* ∧ Satz/*sentence* as generated from AND-conjunction (min.) of meaning points in semantic space.

As illustrated in Figure 5.15, the semantic inference process will start from two (or more) root nodes as semantic premises (here three: Alpen/*Alps*, Programm/*program*, and Winter/*winter*), it will then initiate the two (or more) DDS processes concerned, each of which—in selecting its daughter nodes—will tag the respective meaning points in the semantic space. The stop condition for this process, which proceeds (least distance or highest criteriality) breadth first through the respective DDSs, is defined to be the first meaning point found to be tagged already by one (and all) other processes active. This point (here: reis/*travel*) will be considered the (first) candidate inferred or concluded from the premises (with the option to extend the number of candidates under different stop conditions). The dependencies activated (bottom line of Figure 5.15) are three paths: first: *Alps* → *join* → *drive/propel* → *spa* → *travel*; second: *program* → *service* → *support* → *choose* → *exercise* → *space/locality* → *travel*; and third: *winter* → *lift* → *course/track* → *ski* → *danger* → *join* → *drive/propel* → *spa* → *travel*. They translate to the premises' inference paths, resulting in the concluded meaning (reis/*travel*) whose connotative embedding is provided by the subtrees shown according to its semantic relatedness mediated by the text material analyzed.

The semantic inference (SI) procedure may also give some hints on how to exploit central aspects of efficient word usages, which result in what is linguistically perceived as homonymous/polysemous meanings of lexical items when isolated from their cotexts. As connotativity of words in discourse is the functional core of structural meaning, opaque compounds common in German can be resolved on the grounds of DDS graphs used in semantic inferencing. This can well be illustrated by differences in connotations that words not only acquire due to other words they occur with in strings of texts, but which also indicate their new semantic values,

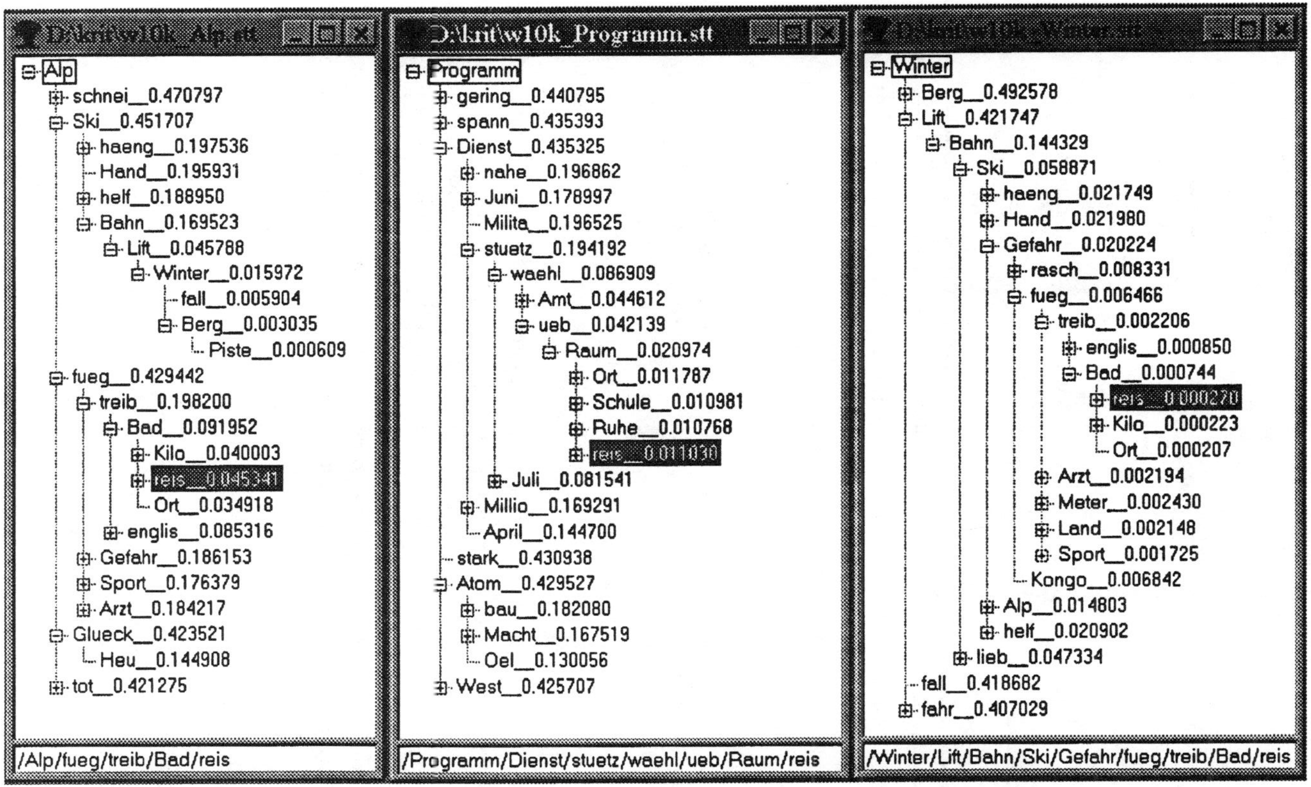

FIGURE 5.15 DDS-based semantic inference (on criteriality values) from Alpen/*Alps*, Programm/*program*, and Winter/*winter* (premises) to reis/*travel* (conclusion) as computed from the semantic space data.

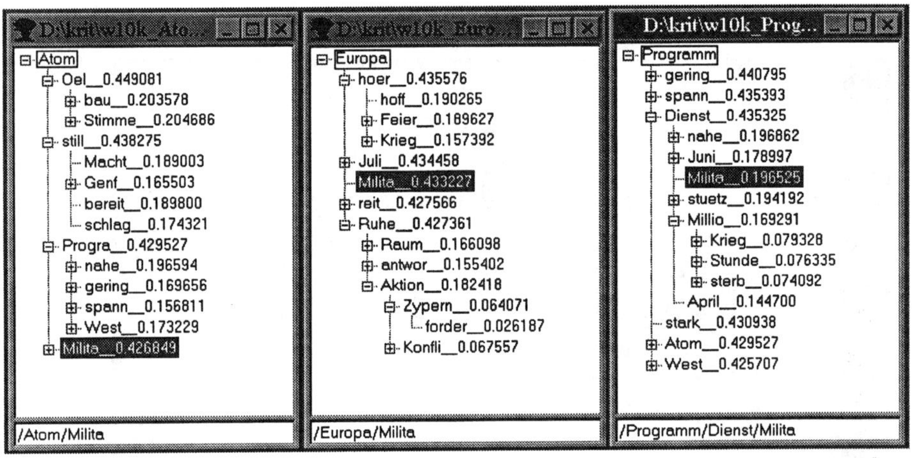

FIGURE 5.16 DDS-based semantic inference (on criteriality values) from Atom/*atom*, Europa/*Europe*, and Programm/*program* (premises) to Militär/*military* (conclusion) as computed from the same semantic space data.

which therefore may serve as a structural means of representation. Depending on other lexical items in their cotextual environments (particularly obvious via compounding as in *Alpenprogramm, Atomprogramm, Europaprogramm*, or *Winterprogramm*), their meanings can well be determined, instead of being defined propositionally, by their granular organization as represented by DDS graphs and their inferential processing.

The two items Atom/*atom* and Europa/*Europe* have been chosen here as alternative premises for the semantic inference (SI) procedure with program, contrasting *Alps*, and *winter* in Figure 5.15 above. This resulted in semantic dependencies as shown in Figure 5.16, depicting and conveying a notion of Militärprogramm/*military program* according to the dependencies listed (*program/service/military*), rather different from Reiseprogramm/*travel plan*, with its divergent dependencies (*program/service/support/chose/exercise/locality/travel*) generated in Figure 5.15.

5.7 CONCLUSIONS

Devising representational structures which result from semiotic processing of natural language discourse as modeled by semiotic cognitive information processing (SCIP) systems is to explore syntagmatic and paradigmatic constraints on different levels of item combinability in pragmatically homogeneous texts. Although still tentative, hopefully SCIP systems do contribute to a deeper understanding of how entities and structures are constituted that may indeed be called semiotic (i.e., not only have an objective (material) extension in space–time), but beyond that, can be understood as having interpretable (semantic) meaning.

For natural as well as artificial SCIP systems, to be able to identify signs and to interpret them as representational of what they stand for, they need to have not only an adaptive structure that is able to perform accordingly, but which is also self-organizing in a semiotic (i.e., meaning constituting) sense of performance. As has often been and still is experienced, most of automatic symbol processing devices available so far do not serve the purposes too well when applied to deal with problems of natural language understanding which we find difficult to describe, analyze, or define at present in a principled way. Procedural modeling and computational realization of living organisms' cognitive behaviors would appear to offer some chances for moderate progress in that respect.

From a cognitive science point of view, mind/brain activity is essentially computational information processing which can be modeled accordingly (i.e., as rule-based symbol processing mechanisms). From a systems-theoretic perspective, the fundamentals of cognition are viewed as a means of structuring an environment as perceived by (artificial or natural) information-processing systems. The semiotic grounding of such structuring (process) adds the means of representing this structure (result) in some—not necessarily symbolic—format in order to preserve or to communicate some of it to other systems. This combination of structuring process and structured result as mediated by representations (memory) gave rise to the theory of semiotic cognitive information processing systems, whose test bed is natural language understanding. It might add coverage of considerable complexities of sign-based cognitive processes. Apparently, soft computing with words has embarked in tackling central issues stemming from these complexities by relaxing the widely deterministic machinery of rule-based symbolic models employed for information processing by machine so far.

The dynamics of semiotic knowledge structures and the processes operating on them essentially consist in their recursively applied mappings of multilevel representations, resulting in a multiresolutional granularity of fuzzy word meanings which emerge from and are modified by such text processing. Test results from experimental settings (in semantically different discourse environments) illustrate the SCIP system's granular language understanding and meaning acquisition capacity without initial explicit morphological, lexical, syntactic, and semantic knowledge.

Due to the centrality of semiosis and its pivotal role in language understanding, SCIP systems are designed to emulate the process of sign and/or meaning constitution by machine without (necessarily) replicating the procedural components and/or representational means as employed and enacted by humans. Following the systems theoretical approach, the modeling basically places an information-processing system into an environment whose structural coupling, as realized by the mediating processes and their representational results, allows for the distinction of both. When we think of natural language structures and their actualization in discourse understanding in these terms of representation and process, the generality of the conception lends itself easily to accommodate hierarchically structured restrictions on modes of processing (granulation, organization, causation) which determines categorial differences of entities to be dealt with. Thus data processing according to predefined rules is distinguished from information processing under given and preestablished interpretations; information processing is called cognitive whenever these interpretations have to be derived from sets of principled structures according to certain mechanisms the processing system is endowed with as its (internal or external) knowledge base. Cognitive information processing will become semiotic to the extent in which this knowledge is acquired, structured, and/or modified according to the system's own processing capabilities and intrinsic structuring principles. They allow not only for the (internal) representation of results of such processing, but also for their (externalized) representation (sign structures), giving access to them by way of mediation. Mediation can be defined as the capacity of sign structures to activate the associated functions in SCIP systems properly attuned. This is roughly what understanding natural language sign structures translates to in a SCIP system–environment situation.

Favoring such a semiotic (re)orientation has practical importance as a possible application. As information proves to be essential to any decision process and vital to optimal ones, the availability, support, and affordance of relevant data, information, and understanding become a prerequisite to correct decisions which, ideally, are to be found in order to act, plan, or decide accordingly. For these processes, some components may be identified whose semiotic (i.e. sign and meaning constitutive relatedness) has by and large been overlooked so far. It can be envisaged, however, that it may be specified operationally and incorporated systematically to replenish and improve the explicative understanding of what language understanding—beyond the anatomy of planned decisions of/for action and its modes of (possible, if not even necessary) realization processes—is going to mean.

REFERENCES

1. S. Armstrong-Warwick (ed.); Using large corpora, I and II, Special issues; *Comput. Linguist.*, 19(1/2); 1993.
2. J. Barwise and J. Perry; *Situations and Attitudes*, MIT Press, Cambridge, MA, 1983.
3. M. Bierwisch, Logische und psychologische Determinanten der Struktur natürlicher Sprachen, in Scharf (ed.), *Naturwissenschaftliche Linguistik*, Nova Acta Leopoldina, NF 54, Nr. 245, Halle (J.A. Barth), 1981, pp. 176–187, 841–851.
4. T. Briscoe and J. Carroll, Generalized probabilstic LR parsing of natural language (corpora) with unification-based grammars, *Comput. Linguist.*, 19(1):25–59, 1993.
5. P. Brown, S. DellaPietra, V. DellaPietra, and R. Mercer, The mathematics of statistical machine translation: parameter estimation, *Comput. Linguist.*, 19(2):263–311, 1993.
6. P. Brown et. al., A statistical approach to language translation in Vargha (ed.)., *COLING-88*, Budapest, John von Neumann Society of Computing Science, ICCL, Budapest, 1988, pp. 71–76.
7. H. Bunke (ed.), *Advances in Structural and Syntactic Pattern Recognition*, World Scientific, Singapore, 1992.
8. G. A. Carpenter and S. Grossberg (eds.), *Pattern Recognition by Self-Organizing Neural Networks*, MIT Press, Cambridge, MA, 1991.

9. J. L. Casti, Simple and complex models in science, in Kornwachs and Jacoby (eds.), *Information: New Questions to a Multidisciplinary Concept*, Akademie, Berlin, 1996, pp. 209–228.
10. D. Chalmers, Facing up to the problem of consciousness, *J Consciousness Stud. Controversies Sci. Human.*, 3(2):200–219, 1995.
11. N. Chomsky, *Language and Problems of Knowledge: The Managua Lectures*, Current Studies in Linguistics, Vol. 16, MIT Press, Cambridge, MA, 1988.
12. N. Chomsky, *Language and Thought*, Anshen Transdisciplinary Lectureship Monographs, Vol. 3 Moyer Bell Wakefield, RI, 1993.
13. N. Chomsky, *The Minimalist Program*, Current Studies in Linguistics, Vol. 28, MIT Press, Cambridge, MA, 1995.
14. K. Church, A stochastic parts program and noun phrase parser for unrestricted text, in *Proc. 2nd Conference on Applied Natural Language Processing*, ACL, Austin, TX, 1988, pp. 136–143.
15. K. W. Church and P. Hanks, Word association norms, mutual information, and lexicography, *Comput. Linguist.*, 16(1):22–29, 1990.
16. K. W. Church and R. L. Mercer, Introduction to the special issue on computational linguistics using large corpora, *Comput. Linguist.*, 19(1):1–24, 1993.
17. J. Fodor and Z. Pylyshyn, Connectionism and cognitive architecture: a critical analysis, *Cognition*, 28(1): 3–71, 1988.
18. W. Fucks, On Nahordnung and Fernordnung in samples of literary texts, *Biometrica*, 1954(2):116–132, 1954.
19. J. Gibson, *The Ecological Approach to Visual Perception*, Houghton Mifflin, Boston, 1979.
20. D. Hindle and M. Rooth, Structural ambiguity and lexical relations, *Comput. Linguist.*, 19(1):103–120, 1993.
21. G. Hinton (ed.), *Connectionist Symbol Processing*, MIT Press, Cambridge, MA, 1992.
22. D. E. Knuth, *The Art of Computer Programming, Vol. 3, Sorting and Searching*, Addison-Wesley Reading, MA, 1973.
23. R. Köhler and B. Rieger (eds.), Contributions to quantitative linguistics, *Proc. First Quantitative Linguistics Conference (QUALICO-91)*, Kluwer Academic Publishers, Dordrecht The Netherlands 1993.
24. T. Kohonen, *Self-Organization and Associative Memory*, 3rd ed., Springer Series in Information Sciences, Springer-Verlag, New York, 1989.
25. R. Lorch, Priming and search processes in semantic memory: a test of three models of spreading activation, *J. Verbal Learn. Verbal Behav.*, 21:468–492, 1982.
26. D. Marr, *Vision*, W.H. Freeman, San Francisco, 1982.
27. A. Meystel, *Semiotic Modeling and Situation Analysis: An Introduction*, AdRem, Bala Cynwyd, PA, 1995.
28. L. Nadel, L. Cooper, P. Culicover, and R. Harnish (eds.), *Neural Connections, Mental Computation*, MIT Press, Cambridge, MA, 1989.
29. K. O'Hara and T. Scott, There is no hard problem of consciousness, *J. Consciousness Stud. Controversies Sci. Human.*, 3(4):290–302, 1996.
30. H. Pattee, Simulations, realizations, and theories of life, in Langton (ed.), *Artificial Life*, Santa Fe Institute Studies in the Science of Complexity, Vol. VI, Addison-Wesley, Reading, MA, 1989, pp. 63–77.

31. H. Pattee, Evolving self-reference: matter, symbol, and semantic closure, *Commun. Cognit. Artif. Intell.*, 12(1/2):9–27, 1995.
32. C. Peirce, Pragmatism in retrospect: a last formulation, in Buchler (ed.), *The Philosophical Writings of Peirce*, Dover New York, 1906, pp. 269–289.
33. R. Pfeiffer, Z. Schreter, F. Fogelman-Soulié, and L. Steels (eds.), *Connectionism in Perspective*, North-Holland, Amsterdam, 1989.
34. R. C. Prim, Shortest connection networks and some generalisations, *Bell Syst. Tech. J.*, 36:1389–1401, 1957.
35. B. Rieger, Bedeutungskonstitution: Einige Bemerkungen zur semiotischen Problematik eines linguistischen Problems, *Z. F. Literaturwiss. Linguist.*, 7(27/28):55–68, 1977.
36. B. Rieger, Semantische Dispositionen: Prozedurale Wissenstrukturen mit stereotypisch repräsentierten Wortbedeutungen, in B. Rieger (ed.), *Dynamik in der Bedeutungskonstitution*, Papers in Textlinguistics, Vol. 46, Buske, Hamburg, 1985, pp. 163–228.
37. B. Rieger, *Unscharfe Semantik: Die empirische Analyse, quantitative Beschreibung, formale Repräsentation und prozedurale Modellierung vager Wortbedeutungen in Texten*, Peter Lang, Frankfurt, 1989.
38. B. Rieger, Vorwort, in *Empfehlungen der GLDV zur Konturierung des Faches Computerlinguistik*, Trier GLDV, Sept. 1989.
39. B. Rieger, Fuzzy Modellierung linguistischer Kategorien, in Feldweg and Hinrichs (eds.), *Lexikon und Text*, Lexicographica Series Maior, Vol. 73, Niemeyer, Tübingen, Germany, 1996, pp. 155–169.
40. B. B. Rieger, Fuzzy word meaning analysis and representation in linguistic semantics: an empirical approach to the reconstruction of lexical meanings in East- and West-German newspaper texts, in Nagao and Fuchi (eds.), *Proc. 8th International Conference on Computational Linguistics (COLING-80)*, International Committee on Computational Linguistics, Tokyo, 1980, pp. 76–84.
41. B. B. Rieger, Connotative dependency structures in semantic space, in B. Rieger (ed.), *Empirical Semantics II: A Collection of New Approaches in the Field*, Quantitative Linguistics, Vol. 13, Brockmeyer, Bochum, Germany, 1981, pp. 622–711.
42. B. B. Rieger, Feasible fuzzy semantics: on some problems of how to handle word meaning empirically, in Eikmeyer and Rieser (eds.), *Words, Worlds, and Contexts: New Approaches in Word Semantics*, Research in Text Theory, Vol. 6, de Gruyter, New York, 1981, pp. 193–209.
43. B. B. Rieger, Fuzzy representation systems in linguistic semantics, in Trappl, Findler, and Horn (eds.), *Progress in Cybernetics and Systems Research*, Vol. XI, McGraw-Hill International, London, 1982, pp. 249–256.
44. B. B. Rieger, Procedural meaning representation: an empirical approach to word semantics and analogical inferencing, in Horecky (ed.), *Proc. 9th International Conference on Computational Linguistics (COLING-82)*, Linguistic Series, Vol. 47, North-Holland, New York, 1982, pp. 319–324.
45. B. B. Rieger, Clusters in semantic space, in Delatte (ed.), *Actes du Congrès International Informatique et Science Humaines*, Laboratoire d'Analyse Statistique des Langues Anciennes, Liège Belgium, 1983, pp. 805–814.
46. B. B. Rieger, Generating dependency structures of fuzzy word meanings in semantic space, in Hattori and Iounu (eds.), *Proc. 13th International Congress of Linguists*, Comité International Permanent des Linguistes, Tokyo, 1983, pp. 543–548.

47. B. B. Rieger, Semantic relevance and aspect dependancy in a given subject domain, in Walker (ed.), *Proc. 10th International Conference on Computational Linguistics (COLING-84)*, International Committee of Computational Linguistics, Stanford, CA, 1984, pp. 298–301.
48. B. B. Rieger, Inducing a relevance relation in a distance-like data structure of fuzzy word meaning representations, in Allen (ed.), *Data Bases in the Humanities and Social Sciences, Proc. 4th International Conference on Data Bases in the Humanities and Social Sciences* (*ICDBHSS-83*), Paradigm Press, Osprey, FL, 1985, pp. 374–386.
49. B. B. Rieger, Lexical relevance and semantic disposition: on stereotype word meaning representation in procedural semantics, in Hoppenbrouwes, Seuren, and Weijters (eds.), *Meaning and the Lexicon*, Foris Publications, Dordrecht, The Netherlands, 1985, pp. 387–400.
50. B. B. Rieger, Distributed semantic representation of word meanings, in: Becker, Eisele, and Mündemann (eds.), *Parallelism, Learning, Evolution: Evolutionary Models and Strategies (WOPPLOT-89)*, Lecture Notes in Artificial Intelligence, Vol. 565, Springer-Verlag, New York, 1991, pp. 243–273.
51. B. B. Rieger, *On Distributed Representation in Word Semantics*, Forschung. TR-91-012, International Computer Science Institute, Berkeley, CA, 1991.
52. B. B. Rieger, Meaning acquisition by SCIPS, in Ayyub (ed.), IEEE *Transactions: Joint International Conference on Uncertainty Modeling and Analysis (ISUMA-NAFIPS-95)*, North American Fuzzy Information Processing Society and IEEE Computer Society Press, Los Alamitos, CA, 1995, pp. 390–395.
53. B. B. Rieger, Situations, language games, and SCIPS: modeling semiotic cognitive information processing systems, in Meystel, and Nerode (eds.), *Architectures for Semiotic Modeling and Situation Analysis in Large Complex Systems, 10th IEEE Symposium on Intelligent Control*, AdRem, 1995, Bala Cynwyd, PA, pp. 130–138.
54. B. B. Rieger, Situation semantics and computational linguistics: towards informational ecology—a semiotic perspective for cognitive information processing systems, in Kornwachs and Jacoby (eds.), *Information: New Questions to a Multidisciplinary Concept*, Akademie, Berlin, 1996, pp. 285–315.
55. B. B. Rieger, Computational semiotics and fuzzy linguistics: on meaning constitution and soft categories, in A. Meystel (ed.), *A Learning Perspective: Proc. 1997 International Conference on Intelligent Systems and Semiotics (ISAS-97)*, National Institute of Standards and Technology, Washington, DC, 1997, pp. 541–551; NIST Spec. Publ. 918.
56. B. B. Rieger, Tree-like dispositional dependency structures for non-propositional semantic inferencing: on a SCIP approach to natural language understanding by machine, in Bouchon-Meunier and Yager (eds.), *Proc. 7th International Conference on Information Processing and Management of Uncertainty in Knowledge-based Systems (IPMU -198)*, Paris (Edition EKD), 1998, pp. 351–358.
57. B. B. Rieger and C. Thiopoulos, Semiotic dynamics: a self-organizing lexical system in hypertext, In Köhler and Rieger (eds.), *Contributions to Quantitative Linguistics, Proc. First Quantitative Linguistics Conference (QUALICO -191)*, The Netherlands, Kluwer Academic Publishers, Dordrecht, 1993, pp. 67–78.
58. H. Ritter and T. Kohonen, Self-organizing semantic maps, *Biol. Cybern.*, 61:241–254, 1999.
59. H. Schnelle, Die Herausforderung des Konnektionismus in der kognitiven Linguistik, in Friemel, Müller-Schönberger, and Schütt (eds.), *Forum-90: Wissenschaft und Technik*, Informatik-Fachberichte, Vol. 259, Springer-Verlag, New York, 1990, pp. 42–58.

60. H. Schnelle, Welcher Sprachwissenschaft auf der Spur? Plädoyer für größere Klarheit und Toleranz, *Z. F. Sprachwissensch.*, 13(1):110–120, 1994.
61. H. Schnelle, Reflections on Chomsky's "Language and Thought," *Theor. Linguist.*, 22 (1/2):105–124, 1996.
62. H. A. Simon, *The Sciences of the Artificial*, 2nd ed., MIT Press, Cambridge, MA, 1982.
63. P. Smolensky, On the proper treatment of connectionism, *Behav. Brain Sci.*, 1988(11): 1–74, 1988.
64. P. Smolensky, Connectionism and constituent structure, in Pfeiffer (ed.), *Connectionism in Perspective*, North-Holland, New York, 1989, pp. 3–24.
65. C. Thiopoulos, Semiosis und Topoi, Ph.D. thesis, Universität Trier, Pfaffenweiler, 1992.
66. F. Varela, E. Thompson, and E. Rosch, *The Embodied Mind: Cognitive Science and Human Experience*, MIT Press, Cambridge, MA, 1991.
67. E. Weizsäcker, Erstmaligkeit und Bestätigung als Komponenten der Pragmatischen Information, in E. Weizsäcker (ed.), *Offene Systeme I: Beiträge zur Zeitstruktur von Information, Entropie und Evolution*, Klett, Stuttgart, 1974, pp. 82–113.
68. L. Wittgenstein, in R. Rhees (ed.), *The Blue and Brown Books*, Blackwell, Oxford, 1958.
69. L. A. Zadeh, Fuzzy sets and information granularity, in Gupta, Ragade, and Yager (eds.), *Advances in Fuzzy Set Theory and Its Application*, North-Holland, Amsterdam, 1979, pp. 3–18.
70. L. A. Zadeh, Outline of a computational approach to meaning and knowledge representation based on a concept of a general assignment statement, in Thoma and Wyner (eds.), *Proc. International Seminar on AI and Man-Machine Systems*, Springer-Verlag, Heidelberg, 1986, pp. 198–211.
71. L. A. Zadeh, Toward a theory of fuzzy information granulation and its centrality in human reasoning and fuzzy logic, *Fuzzy Sets Syst.*, 90(3):111–127, 1997.

CHAPTER 6

EXTRACTING INFORMATION FROM TEXT

AMIT BAGGA, JOYCE CHAI, and ALAN BIERMANN[1]
Duke University, Durham, North Carolina

6.1 INTRODUCTION

The task of an information extraction system [12] is to find and return to the user key facts from a text database related to a given query. Of course, a large fraction of the database may have some relation, weak or otherwise, to the user's request, and the system must select only a limited subset. In fact, the user's request induces the fuzzy set, relatedness, on the database and the system has the task of retrieving those facts with high membership values in this set.

The traditional approach to building such systems has been to specialize on a narrow semantic domain and to construct a processor aimed at retrieving information in that domain only. Researchers have generally believed that the information-extraction problem is so difficult that each such system must be hand constructed because of the many peculiarities of the individual domains. Examples are those featured by the Message Understanding Conferences [13,15]: terrorist attacks, management transitions in industries, and the launching of space vehicles.

To address the problem of creating such systems economically, some researchers have looked at techniques for automatically or semiautomatically constructing lexicons [23,24,26,30] or extraction rules for the domain [7,16,17,20,25,28]. Most of these techniques have applied machine learning approaches to learn rules based on texts that have been annotated semantically. Either preannotation of text is done by a human expert, or the rules are postprocessed by such an expert.

The research reported here proposes that a domain-independent information extraction system can be built if it can include a self-modifying feature that enables

[1]A. Bagga is currently at Avaya Labs Research, Murray Hill, New Jersey; J. Chai is currently at IBM T.J. Watson Research Center, Hawthorne, New York.

Computing with Words, Edited by Paul P. Wang.
ISBN 0-471-35374-4

it to adapt automatically to new domains. The theory is that the user should know the peculiarities involved and be able to train the system quickly to gather the specific target facts. This is done by scanning a series of example articles using a special text-processing interface and allowing the user to lead the system through the retrieval steps desired. Then the system acquires the patterns that are to be used in the retrieval and applies them to any large database of text to extract the information of interest.

As an example, suppose that a person wishes to collect information about programming jobs offered by banks. They might use the following article to demonstrate to the system a desired retrieval.

> Springfield's largest bank, First Savings and Loan, is seeking high-level programmers with five or more years of C++ development experience. This respected institution is offering three-year contracts with competitive salaries and liberal benefits.

Specifically, they can apply the system internal parser to break the text into significant phrases:

Springfield's largest bank
First Savings and Loan
is seeking
high-level programmers
with five or more years of C++ development experience
This respected institution
...
...
etc.

Then they can use the system-provided commands to indicate that the pattern *bank-is seeking-programmers-with experience* is going to be useful for the desired retrievals. Finally, they can invoke an automatic generalization routine to loosen the constraints on the pattern so that it can fire on a variety of specific wordings that may vary greatly from the original. For example, the user might want the system to extract some or all of these:

IBM Corporation has a need for computer scientists...
The city of Boston is hiring computer analysts with Java experience...
Several computer companies in the area need expertise in C++ and Java...
Oracle is advertising for experts for the creation of new database products...
First Federal Savings is looking for programmers to code security systems...

The creation of such a general-purpose extraction system requires the solution of many problems. For example, the word *bank* in the example refers to a financial institution and not to the edge of a river. Any pattern designed to select financial institutions runs the risk of firing on river banks unless a mechanism is included to distinguish them. Called *word sense disambiguation*, this must be done automatically by the information extraction system. Another problem relates to facts that are separated in the discourse across clauses or different sentences. Suppose that the user is interested, in the example above, in the pattern *banks-offering-contracts* which requires that the system discover that the phrases with head nouns *bank* and *institution* refer to the same entity. Called *noun phrase coreference*, this is another problem that must be solved automatically in the information extraction system. In the extreme case, the information needed may be spread across several different articles separated in time and space and the system may be expected to gather it together. Finally, the problem of doing the generalization must be solved. How does one discover that the First Federal Savings is a bank which is an institution that the user might be interested in. How does the system know to fire on such words as *computer scientist*, *analyst*, *expert*, *worker*, or even *people* when it has seen only the token *programmer*? Furthermore, when multiple documents all have facts about "John Smith," how does the system know that it is actually talking about the same person or different persons with the same name? These problems and related ones constitute the core areas of study needed to create the domain-independent system described above. Their solution is the subject of this chapter.

Specifically, we first describe in this chapter a new trainable information extraction (IE) system [8]. With our approach, any user, based on his or her interests, can train the system on different domains. The system learns from the training and outputs the structured target information automatically. The system uses many powerful mechanisms to create useful generalizations from the user's inputs. For example, if the user specifies one example of a desired extraction, our system automatically tries generalizations of the terms and every permutation of the ordering of significant words. The system gives the user the opportunity to judge the level of generalizations being made and to tune them to his or her particular needs. Where modifications of the rules are deemed successful by the user, those rules are incorporated into the extraction set. Following the description of the information extraction system, we will describe a system that resolves both noun phrase coreference and event coreference across documents. Although the two systems are currently independent, we plan to use the output of the cross-document coreference system to improve the performance of the information extraction system. The coreference annotated output can be used to merge entities and events extracted across documents, thereby making easier the task of the IE system by providing multiple documents regarding an entity or event of interest. This methodology adds tremendous power to an extraction system by enabling it to gather facts from disparate sources and bring them together to obtain more completeness to the retrieval.

6.2 INFORMATION EXTRACTION SYSTEM

6.2.1 System Overview

Our *trainable information extraction system* (TIMES) includes four major subprocesses: tokenization, lexical processing, partial parsing, and rule learning, and generalization [1]. The general structure of TIMES is shown in Figure 6.1. The first stage of processing is carried out by the tokenizer, which segments the input text into sentences and words. Next, the lexical process acquires lexical syntactic/semantic information for the words. To achieve this, a preprocessor is used for semantic classification. The preprocessor can identify special semantic categories such as e-mail and Web addresses, file and directory names, dates, times, dollar amounts, telephone numbers, zip codes, cities, states, countries, names of companies, and many others. The syntactic information is retrieved from the CELEX database[2] and the semantic information is from WordNet [22]. Following the lexical processing, a partial parser, which is based on a set of finite-state rules, is applied to produce a sequence of non-overlapping phrases as output. It identifies noun phrases (NGs), verb phrases (VGs), and prepositions (PGs). The parser uses 14 finite-state rules to identify noun phrases, seven rules to identify verb phrases, and one rule to identify prepositions. Verb phrases are further categorized as verb active, verb passive, verb be, verb gerund, and verb infinitive.[3] The last word of each phrase is identified as its *headword*. The phrases, together with their syntactic and semantic

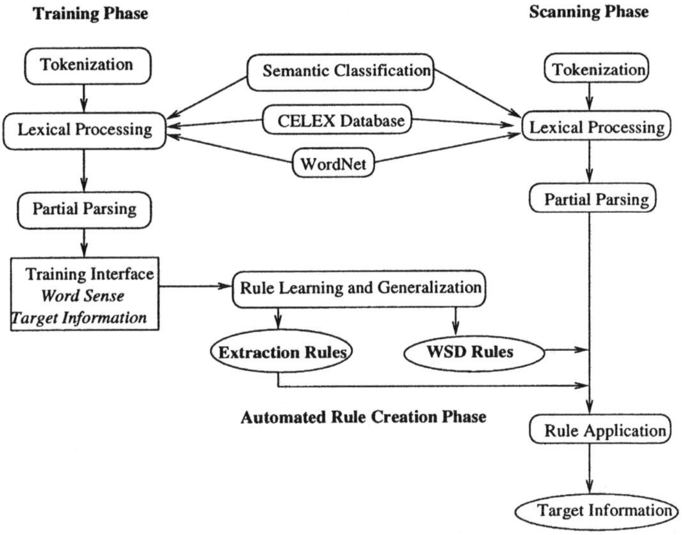

FIGURE 6.1. System overview. (Copyright AAAI.)

[2]Available through Linguistic Data Consortium: http://www.ldc.upenn.edu/.

[3]Thank you to Jerry Hobbs of SRI for providing the finite-state rules for the parser.

information, are used in rule learning and generalization. Based on the training examples, the system automatically acquires and generalizes a set of rules for future use.

The system has three running modes, which implement training, automated rule creation, and scanning, respectively. In the training phase, the user is required to train the system on sample documents based on his or her interests. That is, the user specifically points out the desired information in the text. Because the WordNet hierarchy depends on word senses, in the training phase the system also requires some semantic tagging by the user. This phase tends to use minimum linguistic and domain knowledge so that it can be used by the casual user. The rule creation phase builds a set of useful rules, including both extraction rules for information of interest and word sense disambiguation (WSD) rules for sense identification. The scanning phase applies the learned rules to any new body of text in the domain.

We use precision, recall, and F-measure [29] to give a quantitative evaluation of the system. The recall score measures the ratio of information correctly extracted against all relevant information in the texts. The precision score measures the ratio of correct information extracted against all information extracted. To define precision and recall more precisely, if n is the number of entities identified relevant by the system, m is the number of entities that are relevant from the text, a is the number of entities correctly identified by the system, then recall = a/m, precision = a/n. It is difficult to evaluate the system since the measures of recall and precision are often equally important yet negatively correlated. *F-measure* combines the measure of precision and recall to get a single measure. Recall and precision can have relative weights in the calculation of the F-measure, giving it the flexibility to be used for different applications. The formula for calculating the F-measure is

$$F = \frac{(\beta^2 + 1.0) \times P \times R}{\beta^2 \times P + R}, \tag{6.1}$$

where P is precision, R is recall, and β is the relative importance given to recall over precision. If recall and precision are of equal weight, $\beta = 1.0$. The F-measure reported in the following sections is based on $\beta = 1.0$.

6.2.2 WordNet

In contrast with most IE systems, which heavily rely on handcrafted domain-specific knowledge, TIMES acquires lexical semantic information from WordNet. WordNet is developed at Princeton University's Cognitive Center [22]. It provides a tool to search dictionaries conceptually rather than merely alphabetically. The 1.5 version contains approximately 95,600 different word forms organized into some 70,100 word meanings or sets of synonyms. The most useful feature of WordNet to the natural language processing (NLP) community is its attempt to organize lexical information in terms of word meanings (or concepts) and semantic relations. The meaning (or concept) is represented by a *synset*, which is a set of synonymous words representing a certain meaning. An example of a synset is {*girl, miss, missy, gal, young lady, young woman, fille*}. A semantic relation is a relation between meanings. For instance, for nouns, there are "part of," "is a," "member of," and similar relationships between concepts.

Consider the following example from Ref. 22: The synsets {*board, plank*} and {*board, committee*} each serve as unambiguous designators of two different meanings (or senses) of the noun *board*. Also associated with each synset is a short English description (gloss) of the meaning expressed by the synset. So the synset {*board*} (a person's meals, provided regularly for money), consisting only of the noun *board* itself, can be distinguished from the other senses by the gloss associated with it.

In addition, WordNet attempts to organize different senses of a word based on the frequency of use of the senses. For example, a list of all the synonyms of *board* yields eight different synsets, each designating a different sense of the noun. The most commonly used sense (sense 1) is {*board,plank*}, while the least commonly used sense (sense 8) is {*board*} [a flat portable surface (usually rectangular) designed for board games].

An important relationship present in WordNet that is used extensively in our system is the hyponymy/hypernymy (the subset/superset, or ISA) relationship. A concept represented by the synset $\{x, x_1, \ldots\}$ is said to be a *hyponym* of the concept represented by the synset $\{y, y_1, \ldots\}$ if native speakers of English accept sentences constructed for such frames as *An x is a (kind of) y*. If this holds, we can also say that $\{y, y_1, \ldots\}$ is a *hypernym* of $\{x, x_1, \ldots\}$ [22]. For example, {*maple*} is a hyponym of {*tree*}, and {*tree*} is a hyponym of {*plant*}. Hyponymy is transitive and asymmetrical, and it generates a hierarchical semantic structure in which a hyponym is said to be below its superordinate. Such hierarchical representations are also called *inheritance systems:* A hyponym inherits all the features of the more generic concept and adds at least one feature that distinguishes it from its superordinate and from any other hyponyms of that superordinate. So *maple* inherits features of its superordinate, *tree*, but is distinguished from other trees by the hardness of its wood, the shape of its leaves, and so on.

In TIMES, WordNet is used to provide the sense information during the training. Based on the training, the system automatically generates a set of rules to disambiguate word senses [10]. We found that in most cases, in a specific domain, senses tend to remain the same. Furthermore, the most frequently used senses are applied very often. For example, we trained 24 articles with 1129 headwords from the "triangle.jobs" domain, and found that 91.7% of headwords were used as sense 1 in WordNet.

6.2.3 Training Phase

TIMES provides a convenient training interface for the user. Through this interface, the user identifies the information of interest (i.e., the target information). One issue in training is the trade-off between the user's effort and the system's learning cost. TIMES requires some minimum training from the user, which is to identify the target information for the training articles and assign the correct sense to the words if their senses are not used as sense 1 in WordNet. (Sense 1 is the most frequently used sense in WordNet. The training interface provides sense definitions so that the user would know which sense to choose.) By default, the system will assign sense 1 to the headwords if no other specific sense is given by the user. If the user performs the minimum training (i.e., identifying target information and assigning senses), the system will learn the rules based on every phrase in the training sentences. Since the system will try all kinds of combinations of those phrases, the resulting learning cost will be relatively high. If besides the minimum training, the user decides to select the important phrases from the training examples, the rules can be learned based only on the important phrases. Thus the training effort is increased, and the system learning cost is reduced. Furthermore, if the user has sufficient expertise and decides to create rules for the system (the rules could be generated from the training articles or from the user's own knowledge), more training effort is required and the system learning cost is further reduced. In general, to make the system easily and quickly adapted to a new domain, computational linguists and domain experts can apply their expertise if they prefer; casual users can provide the minimum training and rely on the system learning ability.

For example, suppose that the training sentence is "IBM has a need for Java programmers to work at Raleigh, NC for one month." The user of our system will employ the interface to indicate the key target information in this sentence which is to be extracted. The target information is: companies that have job openings (use *COMPANY* to represent this target), positions available (*POSITION*), and locations of those positions (*LOCATION*). Based on the user's input, the system internally generates a record as shown in Table 6.1. In this table, the first column lists seven important phrases from the sentence; the second column is the target information specified by the user. If a phrase is identified as a type of target information, this phrase is called a *target phrase*. For example, "IBM," "Java programmers," and "Raleigh, NC" are three target phrases. The third column lists the specific semantic types classified by the preprocessor for each important phrase. The fourth column lists the headwords for the important phrases. If a phrase can be identified as a special semantic type, the headword is the name for that semantic type; otherwise, the headword is the last word in the phrase. The fifth column lists the syntactic categories identified by the partial parser. The last column is the sense number for the headwords. From the information in Table 6.1, the system will create an initial template rule as shown in Figure 6.2 for doing extraction. Furthermore, the system applies a supervised learning algorithm to generate useful rules for disambiguating word senses based on different contexts [10].

6.2.4 Specific Rules

In general, rules in the system are pattern-action rules. The pattern, defined by the left-hand side (LHS) of a rule, is a conjunction (expressed by $\wedge$) of *subsumption functions* $S(X, \alpha, target(\alpha))$. X is instantiated by a new phrase when the rule is applied, α is the concept corresponding to the headword of an important phrase in the training sentence, and $target(\alpha)$ is the type of target information identified for α.

TABLE 6.1. Internal Structure for a Training Example

Important Phrase	Target	Semantic Type	Headword	Syntactic Category[a]	Sense
IBM	*COMPANY*	company-type	company	NG	1
has	none	none	has	VG	1
a need	none	none	need	NG	1
for	none	none	for	PG	1
Java programmers	*POSITION*	none	specialist	NG	1
at	none	none	at	PG	1
Raleigh, NC	*LOCATION*	city-type	city	NG	1

[a]NG, noun phrase; VG, verb phrase; PG, preposition.

$$S(X_1, \{company\}, COMPANY) \wedge S(X_2, \{has\}, none)$$
$$\wedge S(X_3, \{need\}, none) \wedge S(X_4, \{for\}, none)$$
$$\wedge S(X_5, \{programmer\}, POSITION) \wedge S(X_6, \{at\}, none)$$
$$\wedge S(X_7, \{city\}, LOCATION) \longrightarrow$$
$$FS(X_1, COMPANY), FS(X_5, POSITION), FS(X_7, LOCATION)$$

FIGURE 6.2. Initial template rule/most specific rule.

The action in the right-hand side (RHS) of a rule, $FS(X, target(\alpha))$, fills a template slot, or in other words, assigns the type of target information $target(\alpha)$ to the phrase X.

The subsumption function $S(X, \alpha, target(\alpha))$ essentially looks for subsumption of concepts. It returns true if the headword of X is subsumed to the concept α. If all subsumption functions return true, the RHS actions will take place to extract X as a type $target(\alpha)$. In the following sections, the subsumption function is referred to as a *rule entity.*

For example, the initial template rule (i.e., the most specific rule) in Figure 6.2 says that if a pattern of phrases $X_1, X_2, \ldots, X_7$ is found in a sentence such that the headword of X_1 is subsumed by (or equal to) *company*, the headword of the second phrase X_2 is subsumed by *has*, and so on, one has found the useful fact that X_1 is a *COMPANY*, X_5 is a *POSITION*, and X_7 is a *LOCATION*. (In the most specific rule, the headwords of important phrases are used directly as α in subsumption functions. They are referred to as *specific concepts*.) Apparently, the initial template rule is very specific and has tremendous limitations. Since the occurrence of exactly the same pattern rarely happens in the unseen data, the initial template rule is not very useful. We need to generalize these specific rules.

6.2.5 Rule Generalization

The rule generalization is a two-dimensional model that combines syntactic (horizontal) and semantic (vertical) generalization [11].

Syntactic Generalization. From our early experiments we noticed that the optimum number of entities required in the rules varied for different types of target

1. $S(X_1, \{company\}, COMPANY) \wedge S(X_2, \{need\}, none)$
$\wedge S(X_3, \{programmer\}, POSITION) \longrightarrow FS(X_1, COMPANY)$
2. $S(X_1, \{company\}, COMPANY) \wedge S(X_2, \{need\}, none)$
$\wedge S(X_3, \{programmer\}, POSITION) \longrightarrow FS(X_3, POSITION)$

FIGURE 6.3. Example of syntactically generalized rules.

information. In the job advertisement domain, when a token is classified as the dollar-amount semantic type, it is the target salary information 95% of the time. A rule with one rule entity suffices. Rules with more entities are too specific and will lower the performance. For example, in Figure 6.2, by removing the second, fourth, sixth, and seventh entities, the most specific rule becomes two rules with three entities in Figure 6.3. Since two target phrases remain and in our convention, each generalized rule corresponds to only one target phrase, two rules are necessary to capture two types of target information. When these two rules are applied for unseen data, the first will extract the target information *COMPANY* and the second will extract *POSITION*. On the other hand, since the number of constraints on the LHS are reduced, more target information will be identified. By this observation, removing entities from specific rules results in syntactically generalized rules.

Furthermore, syntactic generalization is also aimed at tackling paraphrase problems. For example, by reordering entities in the rule generated from the training sentence "Fox head Joe Smith...," it can further process new sentence portions, such as "Joe Smith, the head of Fox,...," "the head of Fox, Joe Smith,...," or "Joe Smith, Fox head...." This type of syntactic generalization is optional in the system. This technique is especially useful when the original specific rules are generated from the user's knowledge.

Therefore, syntactic generalization is designed to learn the appropriate number of entities and the order of entities in a rule. By reordering and removing rule entities, syntactic generalization is achieved. More precisely, syntactic generalization is attained by a combination function and a permutation function. The combination function selects a subset of rule entities in the most specific rule to form new rules. The permutation function reorders rule entities to form new rules.

Combination Function. If a training sentence has n important phrases, there are n corresponding rule entities, $e_1, \ldots, e_n$ (each e_i is a subsumption function). The combination function selects k rule entities and forms the LHS of the rule as $e_{i1} \wedge e_{i2} \ldots \wedge e_{ik}$ (the order of the entities is the same as the order of the corresponding phrases in the training sentences). At least one of k entities corresponds to a target phrase. If $i(1 < i \leq k)$ entities are created from i target phrases, i rules will be generated. These rules have the same LHSs and different RHSs, with each corresponding to one type of target information. Rules created by the combination function are named *combination rules*. For example, in Figure 6.3, $k = 3$ and $i = 2$; therefore, two rules are necessary to identify two different types of target information.

Permutation Function. The permutation function generates new rules by permuting rule entities in the combination rules. This function creates rules for processing

1. $S(X_1, \{need\}, none) \wedge S(X_2, \{programmer\}, POSITION)$
$\wedge S(X_3, \{company\}, COMPANY) \longrightarrow FS(X_3, COMPANY)$
2. $S(X_1, \{need\}, none) \wedge S(X_2, \{programmer\}, POSITION)$
$\wedge S(X_3, \{company\}, COMPANY) \longrightarrow FS(X_2, POSITION)$

FIGURE 6.4. Example of permutation rules.

paraphrases. Rules created by the permutation function are named *permutation rules*. For example, the permutation function can generate rules in Figure 6.4 by reordering rule entities in Figure 6.3. While rules in Figure 6.3 are created based on the sentence "IBM has a need for Java programmers. . .," the permutation rules can process a paraphrased sentence, such as "There is a need for Java programmers at IBM."

Semantic Generalization. Syntactic generalization deals with the number and order of the rule entities. However, each rule entity is still very specific. For a rule entity $S(X,\alpha,target(\alpha))$, semantic generalization is designed to replace α with a more general concept. Thus it will cover more semantically related instances.

A concept is defined in WordNet as a set of synonyms (synset). For a word *w*, the corresponding concept in WordNet is represented by $\{w, w_1, \ldots, w_n\}$, where each w_i is a synonym of *w*. Given a word *w*, its part of speech, and its sense number, the system can locate a unique corresponding concept in the WordNet hierarchy if *w* exists in WordNet. For a word, especially a proper noun, if the preprocessor can identify it as a special semantic type expressed in a concept in WordNet, a virtual link is created to make the concept of this special noun as the hyponym of that semantic type. For example, "IBM" is not in WordNet; however, it is categorized as a kind of $\{company\}$. The system first creates the concept of "IBM" as $\{IBM\}$, then creates a virtual link between $\{IBM\}$ and $\{company\}$. For any other word *w*, if it is not in WordNet, and it is not identified as any semantic type, the concept of *w* is $\{w\}$ and is virtually put into WordNet, with no hierarchical structure. Therefore, every headword of an important phrase should have a corresponding concept in WordNet.

Let α be a concept in WordNet. The hypernym hierarchical structure provides a path for locating the superordinate concept of α, and it eventually leads to the most general concept above α. (WordNet is an acyclic structure, which suggests that a synset might have more than one hypernym. However, this situation doesn't happen often. In case it happens, the system selects the first hypernym path).

Therefore, semantic generalization acquires the generalization for each rule entity by replacing the specific concept with a WordNet concept. For example, rules in Figure 6.3 could be generalized to rules in Figure 6.5. In our early work [9], we have applied a statistical generalization tree model to determine the optimal

1. $S(X_1, \{group, ...\}, COMPANY) \wedge S(X_2, \{need, ...\}, none)$
$\wedge S(X_3, \{professional, ...\}, POSITION) \longrightarrow FS(X_1, COMPANY)$
2. $S(X_1, \{organization, ...\}, COMPANY) \wedge S(X_2, \{need, ...\}, none)$
$\wedge S(X_3, \{engineer, ...\}, POSITION) \longrightarrow FS(X_3, POSITION)$

FIGURE 6.5. Example of semantically generalized rules.

semantic generalization degree automatically based on the user's feedback. This approach made it possible for the system to adapt to user's needs.

Two-Dimensional Generalization. The two-dimensional generalization model is a combination of semantic (vertical) generalization and syntactic (horizontal) generalization. Our method applies a brute force algorithm, which performs semantic generalization on top of syntactically generalized rules generated from the training set and then applies those rules again on the training set. Based on the training examples and a threshold, the system selects useful rules.

The *relevancy_rate* $rel(r_i)$ for rule r_i is a fuzzy measure of relatedness. It is defined as the percentage of the correct information extracted by the r_i. A threshold is predefined to control the process. If $rel(r_i)$ is greater or equal to the threshold, r_i will be put in the rule base for future use.

The procedure for generating generalized rules is the following:

1. Predefine N, the maximum number of entities allowed in the rule.
2. For each target phrase in the training sentence, based on the important phrases in the sentence, generate all combinations rules with number of entities from 1 to N, as well as their permutation rules.
3. For every rule, generate all possible semantically generalized rules by replacing each entity with a more general entity with a different degree of generalization.
4. Apply all rules to the training set. Based on the training examples, compute relevancy-rate for each rule.
5. Select rules with relevancy-rate above the defined threshold. If two rules r_1 and r_2 both have n entities, and if each entity of r_1 corresponds to a more general or the same concept as that of r_2, the system will choose r_1 for future use if $rel(r_1)$ is greater than or equal to the threshold and eliminate r_2.
6. Sort the rules with the same number of entities to avoid rule repetition.

By following this procedure, the system will generate a set of useful rules that are both syntactically and semantically generalized. Those rules will be applied to unseen documents. First, the system applies rules with N number of entities to the unseen sentence. If some matches are found, the system identifies the target information as what is extracted by the most rules and then processes the next sentence. If there is no match, the system applies rules with fewer entities until either there are some matches or all the rules (including those with one entity) have been applied. By doing so, the system will first achieve the highest precision and then gradually increase recall without too much cost in precision.

6.2.6 Experiments

Our experiments were conducted based on the domain of *triangle.jobs* newsgroup. Eight types of target information were extracted:

1. *COMPANY (COM.)*: the name of the company that has job openings
2. *POSITION (POS.)*: the name of the position available
3. *SALARY (SAL.)*: the salary, stipend, or compensation information
4. *LOCATION (LOC.)*: the state and city where the job is located
5. *EXPERIENCE (EXP.)*: years of experience
6. *CONTACT (CON.)*: the phone number or e-mail address for contact
7. *SKILLS (SKI.)*: the specific skills required, such as programming languages, operating systems, and so on
8. *BENEFITS (BEN.)*: the benefits provided by the company, such as health, dental insurance, and so on

There were 24 articles for training and 40 articles for testing. These 64 articles were randomly selected. Training articles were grouped into three training sets. The first training set contained 8 articles; the second contained 16 articles, including ones in the first set; the third training set consisted of all 24 articles. In all of the experiments, the relevancy-rate threshold was set at 0.8 unless otherwise specified.

Syntactic Generalization. The first experiment tested the impact of pure syntactic generalization. The system only generated combination rules and permutation rules without semantic generalization. Figure 6.6 shows that rules with pure syntactic generalization (represented by "*All*") achieve better performance (in terms of F-measure) than rules with a fixed number (one, two, or three) of entities.

In particular, different types of target information require different numbers of entities in the rules. As shown in Figure 6.7, for both *COMPANY* and *EXPERIENCE*, no rule with one entity was learned from the training set. For the target information *SALARY*, the rules with one entity performed much better (in terms of F-measure) than those with two entities or three entities. For the target information *LOCATION*, the rules with two entities performed better than those of one entity and three

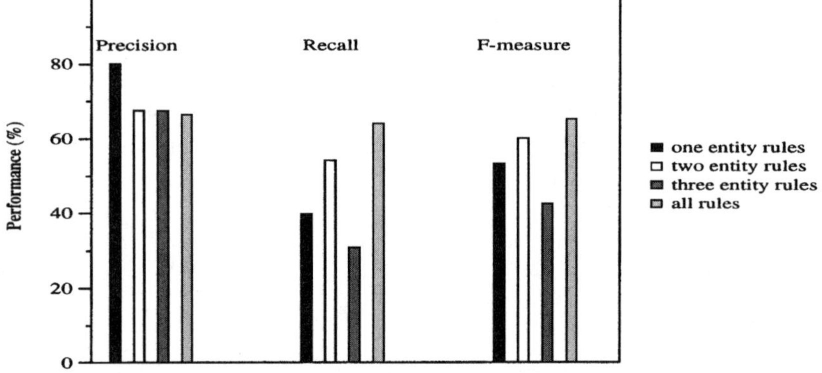

FIGURE 6.6. Effect of rules on overall performance in pure syntactic generalization.

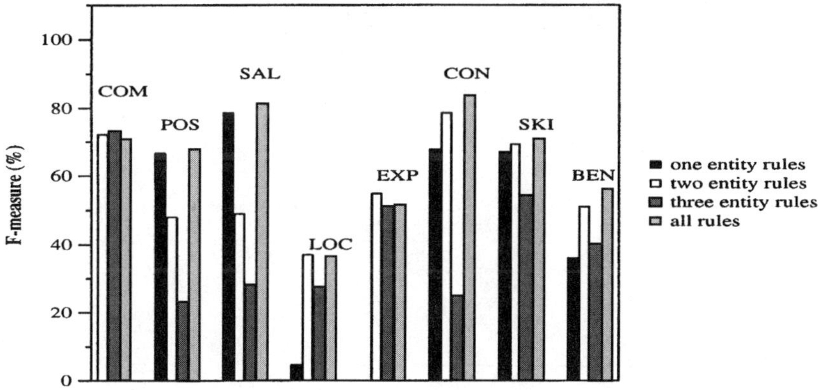

FIGURE 6.7. F-measure on single fact extraction in pure syntactic generalization.

entities. For the target information *COMPANY*, the rules with three entities perform the best. Thus for different types of information, the best extraction requires different numbers of entities in the rules. However, the appropriate number of entities for each type of information is not known in advance. If applying rules with the fixed number of entities, a less than optimal number of entities will cause a significant loss in the performance. By applying our approach, for each type of information, the performance is either better (as in the *SALARY* row), or slightly worse (as in the *COMPANY* row). The overall performance of the application algorithm is better than that achieved by the rules with the fixed number of entities.

Two-Dimensional Generalization. When the semantic generalization is added to the model, the evaluation of the effectiveness of WordNet becomes important. In this experiment, the system generated rules both syntactically and semantically. In those rules, some entities were only generalized to include the synonyms of the specific concept from the training sentence; some were generalized to direct hypernyms (one level above the specific concept in the conceptual hierarchy), and some were generalized to various higher degrees. The question is: Even though the rules have been learned from the training examples, are they reliable? To achieve good performance do we need to put some upper bound on the generalization degree for the entities? To answer that, we used $h_{\max}$ as the limit for the degree of generalization for each entity. We modified the rules only to generalize each entity to the $h_{\max}$ level above the specific concept in WordNet hierarchy. We applied those rules (the threshold was 1.0) with different limitations on semantic generalization to the 24 training documents and 40 testing documents.

As in Figure 6.8, for the training set, with no upper bound on the semantic generalization degree in the rules, the system had an overall 86.6% F-measure, with very high (92.7%) precision. When the various limits on the generalization degree were applied, the performance was still about the same. This indicated that the rules were indeed learned from the training examples, and these rules represented the training examples sufficiently well.

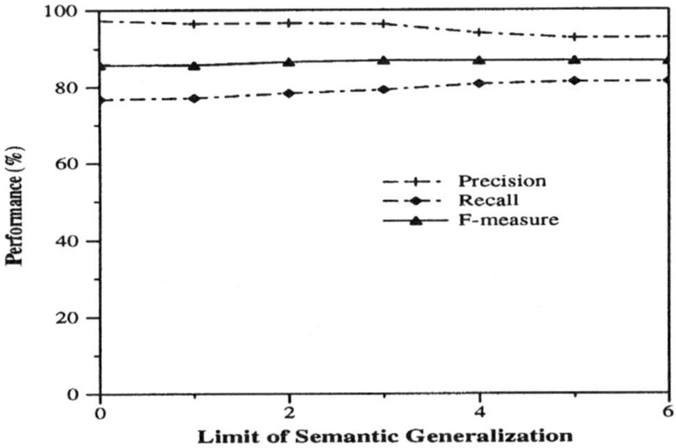

FIGURE 6.8. Effect of limit semantic generalization on training data.

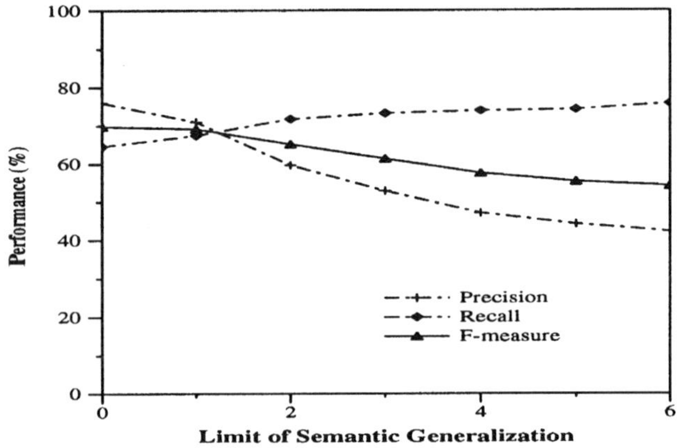

FIGURE 6.9. Effect of limit semantic generalization on testing data.

We then applied the same set of rules on the testing data. As shown in Figure 6.9, without an upper bound on the semantic generalization, the system achieved an F-measure of only 54.2%. However, when the upper bound on the degree of generalization was $h_{max} = 0$, which only generalized the entities to include the synonyms of the specific concepts, the overall performance was about 70%. When $h_{max} = 0$, the overall performance was also about 70%. The results indicated that further restriction on the semantic generalization degree could enhance the performance. WordNet hypernyms are useful in achieving high recall but with a high cost in precision. WordNet synonyms and direct hypernyms are particularly useful in balancing the trade-off between precision and recall and thus improving the overall performance.

We compared the experimental results from rules with pure syntactic generalization and the rules with two-dimensional generalization (with a limit of $h_{max} = 1$ on the semantic generalization). As shown in Figure 6.10, when the training set is small, the semantic generalization can be particularly helpful. The F-measure

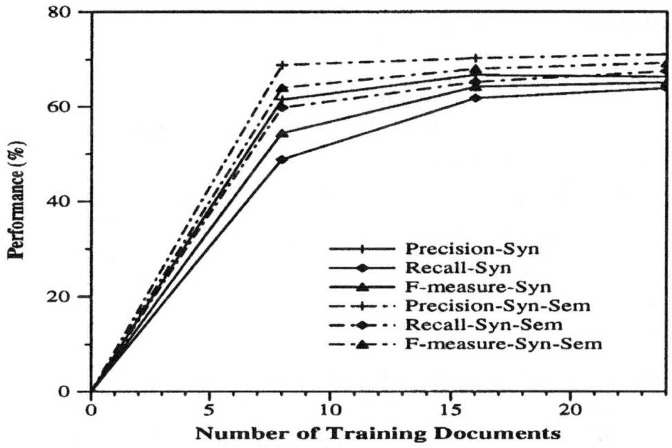

FIGURE 6.10. Performance versus training effort in both syntactic and two-dimensional generalization.

increased about 10% when the training set had only eight articles. The F-measure for training 16 articles is about the same as that from training 24 articles. Thus no more training is necessary. This result implies that for the two-dimensional rule generalization approach, there is a performance upper bound in this domain. If we would like to break this upper bound, generalizing only concepts and orders of the rules may not be enough. We should approach other strategies for generalization.

The semantic generalization can be particularly effective for extracting certain types of information. Comparing Figures 6.7 and 6.11, we can see that the semantic generalization is especially useful for extracting both *LOCATION* and *BENEFITS* facts. The performance was improved about 30% in F-measure for those two facts.

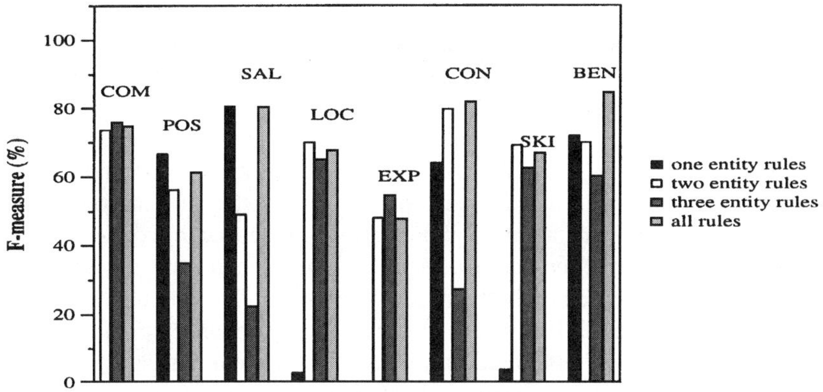

FIGURE 6.11. F-measure on single-fact extraction in two-dimensional generalization.

6.2.7 Discussion

Automated rule learning from examples can also be found in other systems, such as AutoSlog [23], PALKA [21], RAPIER [7], and WHISK [28]. AutoSlog uses heuristics to create rules from the examples and then requires the human expert to accept or reject the rules. PALKA applies a conceptual hierarchy to control the generalization or specification of the target slot. RAPIER uses inductive logic programming to learn the patterns that characterizes slot fillers and their context. WHISK learns the rules by starting with a seed example and then selectively adding to a rule, terms that appear in the seed example.

TIMES differentiates itself in the sense that it learns rules by interleaving syntactic and semantic generalization. It decides automatically the number, the order, and the generalization/specification of constraints. It learns these three aspects in each rule, whereas other systems concentrate on one or two aspects. Furthermore, most of those systems focus on the improvement of performance by refining learning techniques in an environment of large databases of examples. TIMES is designed to provide a paradigm where rule learning makes it possible to build an IE system based on minimum training by a casual user. Indeed, TIMES emphasizes the usability to the casual user. When a large amount of preannotated information is not available and when the user is not experienced enough to tag the information, how does one make an IE system effective based on minimum training? In our experiments we intentionally chose a small training set, since for a casual user, a large amount of training is difficult. The experimental results suggest that the two-dimensional generalization obtains reasonable performance while the effort and time involved in the training is reduced dramatically.

Most information extraction systems are created based on handcrafted domain-specific knowledge. This is because the lexical semantic definitions given by the generic resources sometimes cannot meet the actual needs of the specific domain. No use is made of existing general lexical semantic resources by any of the MUC systems. NYU's MUC-4 system [18] made some attempt at using WordNet for semantic classification. However, they ran into the problem of automated sense disambiguation because the WordNet hierarchy is sense dependent. As a result, they gave up using WordNet. TIMES attempts to integrate WordNet with WSD techniques [10]. The use of WordNet hypernyms in the two-dimensional generalization could raise the recall performance from 65% to 76% (see Figure 6.9), at the cost of precision. However, we found that the WordNet synonyms and the direct hypernyms are particularly useful in balancing the trade-off between precision and recall. The use of WordNet enhanced overall performance by 5%. Despite the typographical errors, incorrect grammars, and rare abbreviations in the free text collection, which make information extraction more difficult, in this domain the two-dimensional generalization model based on both syntactic and semantic generalization achieved about 69% (see Figure 6.10) F-measure in overall performance.

In the remainder of this chapter we discuss a different system: a system that resolves cross-document coreference. We believe that use of such a system will greatly improve the performance of IE systems.

6.3 CROSS-DOCUMENT COREFERENCE

Cross-document coreference occurs when the same person, place, event, or concept is discussed in more than one text source. Computer recognition of this phenomenon is important because it helps break the "document boundary" by allowing a user to examine information about a particular entity or event from multiple text sources at the same time.

Resolving cross-document coreference has been considered to be a difficult problem that requires the output of an information extraction system [19]. However, recent research has shown that cross-document coreferences for both entities and events can be resolved accurately [3,4].

6.3.1 Cross-Document Coreference and Information Extraction

Despite the success of the Message Understanding Conferences, the performance of information extraction systems has hit a barrier commonly referred to as the *60% barrier* on MUC-like data sets. The two main causes for this barrier are:

1. There are too many ways of presenting the same fact (information) in text. The tail of the frequency distribution of a fact is too long to justify the effort used to train the system manually on all possible ways of phrasing a fact.
2. The systems are able to extract information written explicitly in text. The extraction of more implicit information is much harder and currently beyond the state of the art.

We feel that IE systems can break the 60% barrier by using the output of a cross-document coreference system. Using a cross-document coreference system will enable an IE system to work with several articles about an entity or event (as opposed to one, currently). The presence of several such articles will increase the chances that one or more of the articles will contain a pattern on which the IE system has been trained. In addition, it increases the chance that the information contained in one or more of the articles will be present in a more explicit way.

6.3.2 Cross-Document Coreference: The Problem

Cross-document coreference is a distinct technology from named entity recognizers such as IsoQuest's NetOwl and IBM's Textract because it attempts to determine whether name matches are actually the same person (not all John Smiths are the same). Neither NetOwl nor Textract have mechanisms that try to keep same-named persons distinct if they are different people.

Cross-document coreference also differs in substantial ways from within-document coreference. Within a document there is a certain amount of consistency which cannot be expected across documents. In addition, the problems encountered during within-document coreference are compounded when looking for coreferences across documents because the underlying principles of linguistics and discourse context no longer apply across documents. Because the underlying assumptions in cross-document coreference are so distinct, they require novel approaches.

6.3.3 Architecture and Methodology

In this section we describe a cross-document coreference resolution system that resolves coreferences for both entities and events using the vector space model. Figure 6.12 shows the architecture of the system, which is built on the University of Pennsylvania's within-document coreference system, CAMP [5,6] (as described in Section 6.3.4).

Our system takes as input the coreference-processed documents output by CAMP. It then passes these documents through the SentenceExtractor module, which extracts, for each document, all the sentences relevant to a particular entity of interest. The VSM-Disambiguate module then uses a vector space model algorithm to compute similarities between the sentences extracted for each pair of documents.

Details about each of the main steps of the cross-document coreference algorithm are given below.

1. For each article, University of Pennsylvania's CAMP system is run on the article. It produces coreference chains for all the entities mentioned in the article. For example, consider the two extracts in Figures 6.13 and 6.15. The

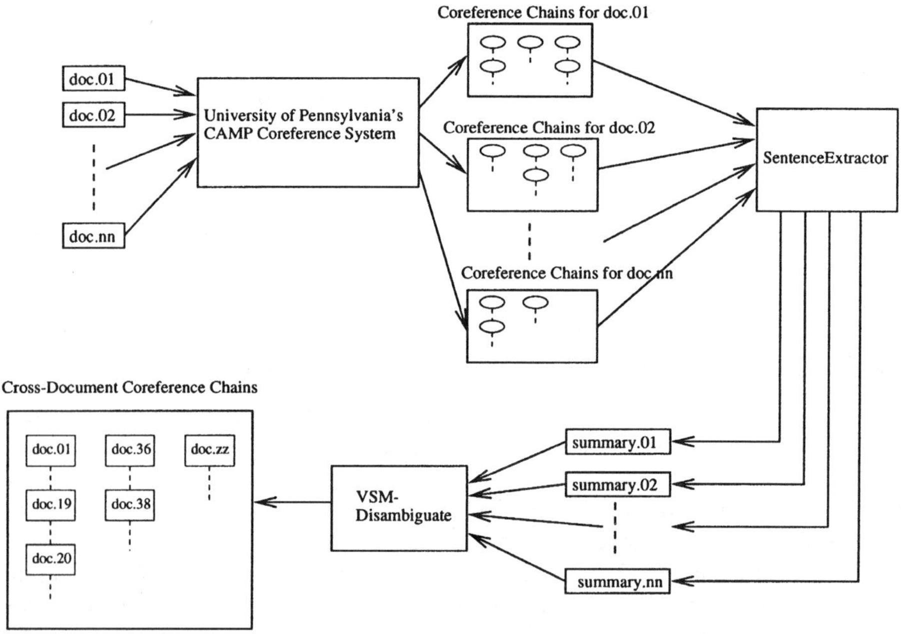

FIGURE 6.12. Architecture of the cross-document coreference system.

John Perry, of Weston Golf Club, announced his resignation yesterday. He was the President of the Massachusetts Golf Association. During his two years in office, Perry guided the MGA into a closer relationship with the Women's Golf Association of Massachusetts.

FIGURE 6.13. Extract from doc.36.

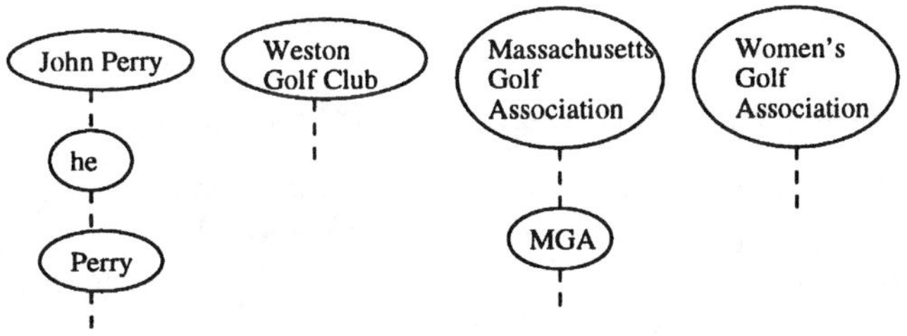

FIGURE 6.14. Coreference chains for doc.36.

Oliver "Biff" Kelly of Weymouth succeeds John Perry as president of the Massachusetts Golf Association. "We will have continued growth in the future," said Kelly, who will serve for two years. "There's been a lot of changes and there will be continued changes as we head into the year 2000."

FIGURE 6.15. Extract from doc.38.

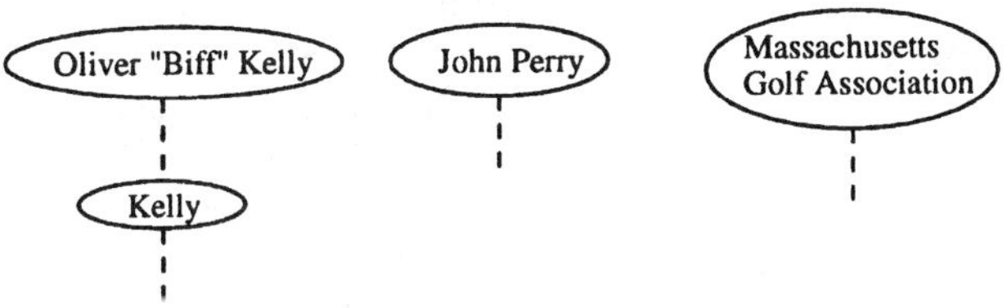

FIGURE 6.16. Coreference chains for doc.38.

coreference chains output by CAMP for the two extracts are shown in Figures 6.14 and 6.16.

2. For the coreference chain of interest within each article (e.g., the coreference chain that contains "John Perry"), the SentenceExtractor module extracts all the sentences that contain the noun phrases that form the coreference chain. In other words, the SentenceExtractor module produces a summary of the article with respect to the entity of interest. Therefore, for doc.36 (Figure 6.13), since at least one of the three noun phrases ("John Perry," "he," and "Perry") in the coreference chain of interest appears in each of the three sentences in the extract, the summary produced by SentenceExtractor is the extract itself. On the other hand, the summary produced by SentenceExtractor for the coreference chain of interest in doc.38 is only the first sentence of the

extract because the only element of the coreference chain appears in this sentence.

3. For each article, the VSM-Disambiguate module uses the summary extracted by the SentenceExtractor and computes its similarity with the summaries extracted from each of the other articles. Summaries having similarity above a certain threshold are considered to be regarding the same entity.

6.3.4 University of Pennsylvania's CAMP System

The coreference chains output by CAMP enable us to gather all the information about the entity of interest in an article. This information about the entity is gathered by the SentenceExtractor module and is used by the VSM-Disambiguate module for disambiguation purposes. Consider the extract for doc.36 shown in Figure 6.13. We are able to include the fact that the John Perry mentioned in this article was the president of the Massachusetts Golf Association only because CAMP recognized that the "he" in the second sentence is coreferent with "John Perry" in the first. It is this fact which actually helps VSM-Disambiguate decide that the two John Perrys in doc.36 and doc.38 are the same person.

6.3.5 Vector Space Model

The vector space model used is the standard vector space model used widely in information retrieval [27]. The model performs a fuzzy comparison between pairs of summaries by estimating the similarity between the summaries in the form of a real number between 0 and 1. In this model, each summary extracted by the Sentence-Extractor module is stored as a vector of terms. The terms in the vector are in their morphological root form and are filtered for *stop words* (words that have no information content, such as *a*, *the*, *of*, *an*, ...). If S_1 and S_2 are the vectors for the two summaries extracted from documents D_1 and D_2, their similarity is computed as

$$\mathrm{Sim}(S_1, S_2) = \sum_{\text{common terms } t_j} w_{1j} \times w_{2j},$$

where t_j is a term present in both S_1 and S_2, w_{1j} the weight of the term t_j in S_1, and w_{2j} the weight of t_j in S_2.
The weight of a term t_j in the vector S_i for a summary is given by

$$w_{ij} = \frac{tf \times \log(N/df)}{\sqrt{s_{i1}^2 + s_{i2}^2 + \cdots + s_{in}^2}},$$

where *tf* is the frequency of the term t_j in the summary, N the total number of documents in the collection being examined, and *df* the number of documents in the collection in which the term t_j occurs. $\sqrt{s_{i1}^2 + s_{i2}^2 + \cdots + s_{in}^2}$, the *cosine normalization factor*, is equal to the Euclidean length of the vector S_i, where s_{in}^2 equals the square of the product $tf \times \log(N/df)$ for the term t_n in vector S_i.

For each summary S_i, the VSM-Disambiguate module, computes the similarity of that summary with each of the other summaries. If the similarity computed is above a predefined threshold, the entities of interest in the two summaries are considered to be coreferent.

6.3.6 Experiments

We tested our cross-document system on two highly ambiguous test sets. The first set contained 197 articles from the 1996 and 1997 editions of the *New York Times*, and the second set contained 219 articles from the 1997 edition of the *New York Times*. The sole criterion for including an article in the two sets was the presence of a string matching the "/John.*?Smith/" and the "/resign/" regular expressions, respectively.

The goal for the first set was to identify cross-document coreference chains about the same *John Smith*, and the goal for the second set was to identify cross-document coreference chains about the same *resign* event. The system did not use any *New York Times* data for training purposes. The answer keys were created manually, but the scoring was completely automated.

Analysis of the Data. There were 35 different *John Smiths* mentioned in the first set of articles. Of these, 24 of them had only one article which mentioned them. The other 173 articles were regarding the 11 remaining *John Smiths*. The background of these *John Smiths*, and the number of articles pertaining to each, varied greatly. Descriptions of a few of the *John Smiths* are: chairman and CEO of General Motors, assistant track coach at UCLA, the legendary explorer, the main character in Disney's *Pocahontas*, and the former president of the Labor Party in Great Britain. In the second set, there were 97 different *resign* events. Of these, 60 were involved in chains of size 1. The articles were regarding resignations of several different people, including Ted Hobart of ABC Corp., Dick Morris, Speaker Jim Wright, and the possible resignation of Newt Gingrich.

6.3.7 Scoring the Output

To score the cross-document coreference chains output by the system, we had to map the cross-document coreference scoring problem to a within-document coreference scoring problem. This was done by creating a metadocument consisting of the file names of each of the documents on which the system was run. Assuming that each of the documents in the two data sets was about a single *John Smith*, or about a single *resign* event, the cross-document coreference chains produced by the system could now be evaluated by scoring the corresponding within-document coreference chains in the metadocument.

B-CUBED Scoring Algorithm. We used the B-CUBED scoring algorithm [2] to score the within-document coreference chains in the metadocument. This algorithm looks at the presence and absence of entities from the chains produced. Therefore, we compute the precision and recall numbers for each entity in the document. The

$$\text{Precision}_\text{i} = \frac{\#\ of\ correct\ elements\ in\ the\ output\ chain\ containing\ entity_i}{\#\ of\ elements\ in\ the\ output\ chain\ containing\ entity_i}$$

$$\text{Recall}_\text{i} = \frac{\#\ of\ correct\ elements\ in\ the\ output\ chain\ containing\ entity_i}{\#\ of\ elements\ in\ the\ truth\ chain\ containing\ entity_i}$$

FIGURE 6.17. Definitions for precision and recall for an entity i.

numbers computed with respect to each entity in the document are then combined to produce final precision and recall numbers for the entire output.

For an entity i, we define the precision and recall with respect to that entity in Figure 6.17. The final precision and recall numbers are computed by the following two formulas:

$$\text{final precision} = \sum_{i=1}^{N} w_i \times \text{precision}_i$$

$$\text{final recall} = \sum_{i=1}^{N} w_i \times \text{recall}_i,$$

where N is the number of entities in the document and w_i is the weight assigned to entity i in the document. For all the examples and the experiments in this chapter we assign equal weights to each entity (i.e., $w_i = 1/N$). But we also plan to look at the possibilities of using other weighting schemes.

6.3.8 Results

Figure 6.18 shows the precision, recall, and F-measure [14] (with equal weights for both precision and recall) using the scoring algorithm for the *John Smith* data set.

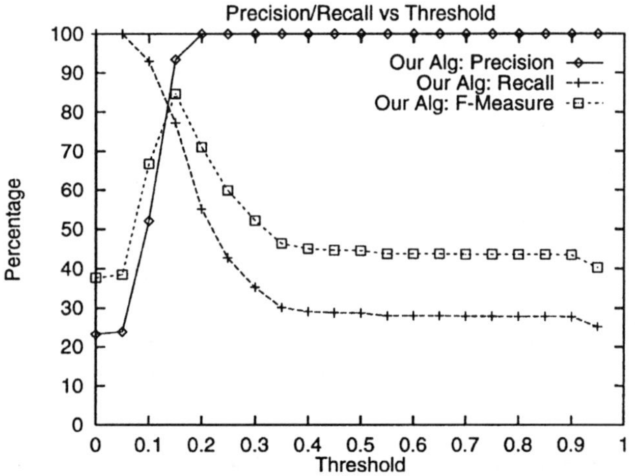

FIGURE 6.18. Precision, recall, and F-measure with training on the summaries for the *John Smith* data set.

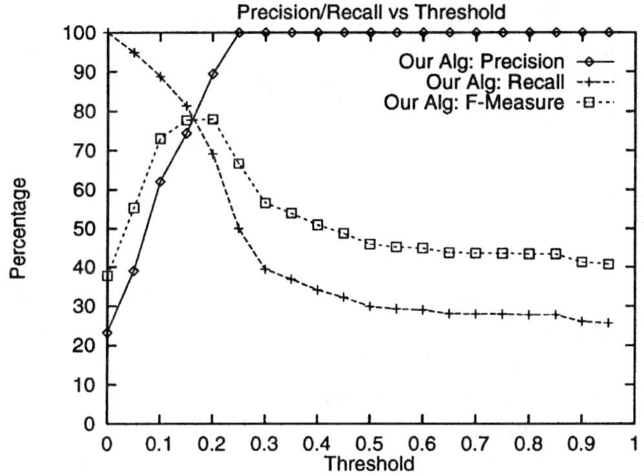

FIGURE 6.19. Precision, recall, and F-measure with training on entire articles for the *John Smith* data set.

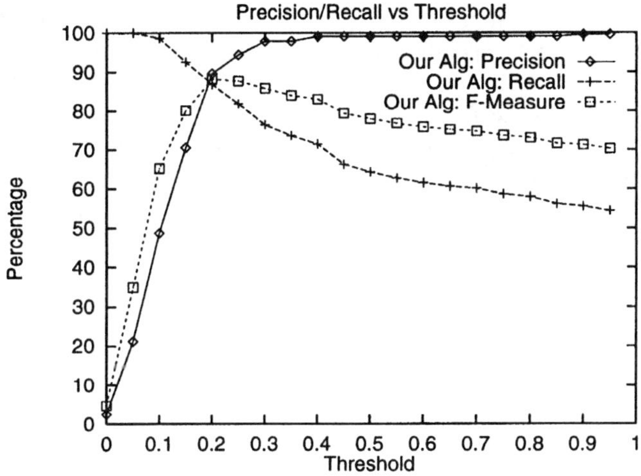

FIGURE 6.20. Precision, recall, and F-measure for the *resign* data set.

The vector space model in this case constructed the space of terms only from the summaries extracted by SentenceExtractor. In comparison, Figure 6.19 shows the results when the vector space model constructed the space of terms from the articles input to the system (it still used the summaries when computing the similarity). The importance of using CAMP to extract summaries is verified by comparing the highest F-measures achieved by the system for the two cases. The highest F-measure for the former case is 84.6%, and the highest F-measure for the latter case is 78.0%. In comparison, for this task, named-entity tools (such as NetOwl) would mark all the *John Smiths* the same. Their performance using the scoring algorithm is 23% precision and 100% recall.

Similarly, Figure 6.20 shows the same three statistics for the *resign* data set. The best precision and recall achieved by the system when using the scoring algorithm was 90% and 87%, respectively. This occurs when the threshold for the vector space model was set to 0.2.

6.4 CONCLUSIONS

The ubiquity of machine-readable free text on almost every topic creates a need for information extraction software that can access it. Simultaneously, users have specific needs that may not be serviced by software products aimed at particular domains or by products that are based on keyword technologies. New approaches are needed which enable a user to style a search specifically to his or her own needs and which use modern information extraction methods to glean detailed facts from a large corpus. The methodologies of this chapter provide a user with a powerful tool for efficiently training a system to do just the search the user wants. It gives the user the ability to scan sample articles and demonstrate exactly the extractions that he or she wants. It gives the user the ability to adjust the generalization level as needed to either broadly gather all items that may have weak resemblance to the training or to filter out only a tightly specified few items that strongly resemble the training samples. That is, it enables the user to adjust the return to include a broad range of membership levels in the fuzzy set relatedness or to restrict the response to high membership levels only. The methodology makes available to the user all the power that comes from utilizing a parser, WordNet, the coreferencing system, and the combination and permutation mechanisms for rule generalization.

Tremendous additional power comes from such a system when it can do cross-document coreference because the resources from disparate sources can be combined to answer questions. A theory of cross-document coreference is also described here that can further enhance the information extraction capabilities of a system.

REFERENCES

1. A. Bagga, J. Chai, and A. Biermann, The role of WordNet in the creation of a trainable message understanding system, in *Proc. 9th Conference on Innovative Applications of Artificial Intelligence (IAAI-97)*, 1997.
2. A. Bagga and B. Baldwin, Algorithms for scoring coreference chains, in *Proc. First International Conference on Language Resources and Evaluation Workshop on Linguistics Coreference*, May 1998.
3. A. Bagga and B. Baldwin, Entity-based cross-document coreferencing using the vector space model, in *Proc. 36th Annual Meeting of the Association for Computational Linguistics and the 17th International Conference on Computational Linguistics*, Aug. 1998, pp. 79–85.
4. A. Bagga and B. Baldwin, Cross-document event coreference: annotations, experiments, and observations, in *Proc. ACL'99 Workshop on Coreference and Its Applications*, June 1999, pp. 1–8.

5. B. Baldwin et al., University of Pennsylvania: description of the University of Pennsylvania system used for MUC-6, in *Proc. 6th Message Understanding Conference (MUC-6)* [14], pp. 177–191.
6. B. Baldwin et al., Description of the University of Pennsylvania's MUC-7 System, in *Proc. 7th Message Understanding Conference (MUC-7)* [15].
7. M. Califf and R. Mooney, Relational learning of pattern-match rules for information extraction, in *Proc. Computational Language Learning'97*, 1997.
8. J. Chai, Learning and generalization in the creation of information extraction systems, Ph.D. thesis, Department of Computer Science, Duke University, Durham, NC, 1998.
9. J. Chai and A. Biermann, Corpus based statistical generalization tree in rule optimization, in *Proc. 5th Workshop on Very Large Corpora (WVLC-5)*, 1997.
10. J. Chai and A. Biermann, The use of word sense disambiguation in an information extraction system, in *Proc. 11th Conference on Innovative Applications of Artificial Intelligence (IAAI-99)*, 1999.
11. J. Chai, A. Biermann, and C. Guinn, Two dimensional generalization in information extraction, in *Proc. 16th National Conference on Artifical Intelligence (AAAI-99)*, 1999.
12. J. Cowie and W. Lehnert, Information extraction, *Commun. ACM*, Jan. 1996.
13. DARPA: TIPSTER text program, *Proc. 4th Message Understanding Conference (MUC-4)*, June 1992.
14. DARPA: TIPSTER text program, *Proc. 6th Message Understanding Conference (MUC-6)*, San Mateo, Nov. 1995, Morgan Kaufmann, San Francisco, 1995.
15. DARPA: TIPSTER text program, *Proc. 7th Message Understanding Conference (MUC-7)*, Apr. 1998.
16. D. Freitag, Toward general-purpose learning for information extraction, in *Proc. 36th Annual Meeting of the Association for Computational Linguistics*, 1998.
17. M. Graven, D. DiPasquo, D. Freitag, A. McCallum, T. Mitchell, K. Nigam, and S. Slattery, Learning to extract symbolic knowledge from the World Wide Web, in *Proc. 15th National Conference on Artificial Intelligence*, 1998.
18. R. Grishman, C. Macleod, and J. Sterling, New York University Proteus System: MUC-4 test results and analysis, in *Proc. 4th Message Understanding Conference*, 1992.
19. R. Grishman, Whither written language evaluation? in *Human Language Technology Workshop*, San Mateo, CA, Mar. 1994, Morgan Kaufmann, San Francisco, 1994, pp. 120–125.
20. S. Huffman, Learning information extraction patterns from examples, in *Connectionist, Statistical, and Symbolic Approaches to Learning for Natural Language Processing*, 1996.
21. J. Kim and D. Moldovan, Acquisition of semantic patterns for information extraction from corpora, in *Proc. 9th IEEE Conference on Artificial Intelligence for Applications*, 1993.
22. G. Miller, WordNet: an on-line lexical database, *Int. J. Lexicog*, 1990.
23. E. Riloff, Automatically constructing a dictionary for information extraction tasks, in *Proc. 11th National Conference on Artificial Intelligence*, 1993.
24. E. Riloff, An empirical study of automated dictionary construction for information extraction in three domains, *AI J.*, Aug. 1996.
25. E. Riloff and R. Jones, Learning dictionaries for information extraction by multi-level bootstrapping, in *Proc. 16th National Conference on Artificial Intelligence*, 1999.

26. B. Roark and E. Charniak, Noun-phrase cooccurrence statistics for semi-automatic semantic lexicon construction, in *Proc. 36th Annual Meeting of the Association for Computational Linguistics*, 1998.
27. G. Salton, *Automatic Text Processing: The Transformation, Analysis, and Retrieval of Information by Computer*, Addison-Wesley, Reading, MA, 1989.
28. S. Soderland, Learning information extraction rules for semi-structured and free text, Special Issues on Natural Language Learning, *Mach. Learn. J.*, 1999.
29. B. Sundheim, Overview of the fourth message understanding evaluation and conference, in *Proc. 4th Message Understanding Conference (MUC-4)*, June 1992.
30. C. Thompson and R. Mooney, Automatic construction of semantic lexicons for learning natural language interfaces, in *Proc. 16th National Conference on Artificial Intelligence*, 1999.

CHAPTER 7

COGNITIVE SCIENCES AND COMPUTING WITH WORDS

BENJOE A. JULIANO
California State University, Chico, California

> The basic concepts of linguistic variable, fuzzy if–then rule, and fuzzy graph have long played a major role in the applications of fuzzy logic. These concepts differentiate fuzzy logic from other methodologies for dealing with imprecision and uncertainty.
>
> —Lotfi A. Zadeh

7.1 INTRODUCTION

Humans have a wide variety of exceptional physical and mental capabilities. Some human tasks are performed without the need for precise measurements and accurate computations. Consider, for example, the task of driving in heavy traffic. Depending on how bad the traffic situation is, humans make their own judgments as to how to handle the circumstances. (Notice that although how "bad" traffic is can be measured by some indication of expected delays, characterizing just how bad the situation is does not really require precise measurements.) A particular driving situation may require passing at least one vehicle in front of you. Such a decision normally arises from some indication that the vehicle immediately in front is "too slow." Before the pass is actually done, we need to see if there are any vehicles approaching from the opposite lane. If there is at least one, we decide how fast they are approaching. We also need to check if there are any vehicles behind us in the passing lane that are getting ready to pass our vehicle. If so, we again make a judgment regarding how fast they are approaching. Additionally, if we are nearing our exit, we need to decide if there is enough time to pass the vehicle(s) in front of us so as not to miss the exit

Computing with Words, Edited by Paul P. Wang.
ISBN 0-471-35374-4

ramp. Regardless of the traffic situation, the act of driving often requires that one maintain control of the vehicle by keeping it more or less "centered" on a particular lane—again, without the need for accurate computations. What is amazing is that we do not realize how much comes into play in making such a decision when driving in heavy traffic, but sometimes it almost appears instinctual how we manage such tasks. (Some may argue that perhaps the smartest thing to do is avoid traffic altogether, be it by finding an alternative route or by waiting until the situation gets "better.") There are numerous other tasks such as this one: playing a game of golf, assessing the quality of a bottle of wine, recognizing distorted speech in a noisy environment, and summarizing a story. Crucial to these intelligent capabilities, as Lotfi Zadeh has put it, is humans' remarkable ability to compute with words. Computing with words (CW) is another important contribution that Lotfi Zadeh has to offer from his highly acclaimed fuzzy set theory [19]. In this chapter we look into the cognitive sciences, their relationship to CW, and their significance in soft computing (see Refs. 23 and 24 for definition).

The chapter begins with an overview of the cognitive sciences as described by Von Eckardt [14]. CW's connection to this overview is then discussed. Next, a brief look at artificial intelligence and how CW relates to some issues in AI is presented. One of the important issues emphasized next is that of knowledge representation. Finally, important points discussed in this chapter are summarized into a paradigm shift that is slowly growing in popularity: numbers versus words! Whenever possible, the author notes other chapters in the book that present ideas that are related to the current discussion.

7.2 THE COGNITIVE SCIENCES

Von Eckardt [14] defines *cognitive science* as "a field that studies cognition by drawing on resources of a number of disciplines, including cognitive psychology, AI, linguistics, philosophy, neuroscience, and cognitive anthropology." As such, Zadeh's CW fits into the arena of research problems probed by these disciplines. For example, Zadeh [22,26] also recognizes granulation (decomposition of whole into parts), organization (integration of parts into whole), and causation (association of causes with effects) as important aspects of cognition and intelligence. Von Eckardt [14] also points out that there really is no single cognitive science field; rather, it is a collection of cognitive sciences. Although this collection does not exhibit a common, agreed-upon research paradigm and there is little consensus on specific goals and metatheoretical assumptions, there is agreement on the subject matter being the study of the human adult's normal, typical cognition (ANTCOG). ANTCOG encompasses aspects of individual differences, group differences, cultural variation, pathology, development, neural realization, and others. Some of the uncertain (and controversial) questions regarding the cognitive sciences include:

1. Whether the cognitive sciences include study of the cognition (or intelligence) of human-made computers

2. Whether the cognitive sciences include study of the cognition (or intelligence) of nonhuman animals
3. Whether the cognitive sciences include study of human mental phenomena other than cognition (such as emotion)

In attempting to describe the cognitive sciences, Von Eckardt [14] also identifies three sets of assumptions that seem to embody the closest description of the cognitive science research framework: the domain-specifying assumptions, substantive assumptions, and methodological assumptions.

7.2.1 Domain-Specifying Assumptions

According to Von Eckardt [14], the three domain-specifying assumptions of the cognitive sciences are:

D1. *Identification assumption.* The domain of ANTCOG consists of the human cognitive capacities.

D2. *Property assumption.* Pretheoretically conceived, the human cognitive capacities have a number of important properties (the basic general properties of cognition):
   (a) Each capacity is intentional (involves states that have content or are "about" something).
   (b) Virtually all of the capacities are pragmatically evaluable (can be exercised with varying degrees of success).
   (c) When exercised successfully, each of the evaluable capacities has a certain coherence or cogency.
   (d) Most of the evaluable capacities are reliable (typically, exercised successfully).
   (e) Most of the capacities are productive (manifest in a practically unlimited number of novel ways).

D3. *Grouping assumption.* The cognitive capacities of the typical normal adult make up a theoretically coherent set of phenomena, or a system (e.g., with sufficient research it will be possible to arrive at a set of answers to basic questions of the research framework that constitute a unified theory and that are empirically and conceptually acceptable).

The *identification assumption*, D1, ascertains a general description of what the study of ANTCOG consists of. Although some of the disciplines within the cognitive sciences investigate areas of human cognitive development, this assumption points out that the main focus would still be the cognitive capacities of adult humans. These cognitive capacities include reasoning, judgment, decision making, summarization, problem solving, and so on.

Some additional specifics regarding the domain of the cognitive sciences are presented as the *property assumption*, D2. For example, each of the cognitive capacities listed in the last sentence of the preceding paragraph is intentional. The primary intention for reasoning is to support or explain how one has arrived at a particular decision, and the intention in making decisions is to resolve an existing situation or set of situations. Similarly, humans naturally exercise reasoning and decision making with varying degrees of success (although an incorrect decision does not necessarily mean that it is a bad one!).

Based on the properties of evaluable human cognitive capacities itemized in D2, the *grouping assumption*, D3, makes the case for coherence among theories. Typically, theories within a field or discipline may clash or contradict one another. One might expect that with multiple fields conducting research in the same general area of ANTCOG, even more dissidence would ensue. The restrictions imposed by D2 will hopefully prevent such disagreement and even facilitate unified theories among the cognitive sciences.

7.2.2 Substantive Assumptions

According to Von Eckardt [14], the two substantive assumptions of the cognitive sciences are:

SA1. *Computational assumption*

- C1. *Linking assumption.* The human cognitive mind/brain is a computational device (computer); hence the human cognitive capacities consist, to a large extent, of a system of computational capacities.
- C2. *System assumption.* A computer is a device capable of automatically inputting, storing, manipulating, and outputting information in virtue of inputting, storing, manipulating, and outputting representations of that information. These information processes occur in accordance with a finite set of rules that are effective and that are, in some sense, in the machine itself.

SA2. *Representational assumption*

- R1. *Linking assumption.* The human cognitive mind/brain is a representational device; hence the human cognitive capacities consist of a system of representational capacities.
- R2. *System assumption.* A representational device is a device that has states or that contains within it entities that are representations. Any representation will have four aspects essential to its being a representation: (1) it will be realized by a *representation bearer*; (2) it will represent one or more *representational objects*; (3) its *representation relations* will be grounded somehow; and (4) it will be interpretable by (i.e., it will function as a representation for) some currently existing *interpreter.* In the mind/brain representational system, the nature of these four aspects is constrained as follows:

R2.1. *Representation bearer.* The representation bearer of a mental representation is a computational structure or process, considered purely formally.

R2.2. *Representational content.* Mental representations have a number of semantic properties.

(1) They are semantically selective.

(2) They are semantically diverse.

(3) They are semantically complex.

(4) They are semantically evaluable.

(5) They have a compositional semantics.

R2.3. *Ground.* The ground of a mental representation is a property or relation that determines the fact that the representation has the object (or content) it has.

(1) This ground is naturalistic (nonsemantic and nonintentional).

(2) This ground may consist of either internal or external factors.

R2.4. *Interpretant.* Mental representations are significant for the person in whose mind they "reside." The interpretant of a mental representation *R* for some subject *S* consists of the set of all possible determinate computational processes contingent upon entertaining *R* in *S*.

SA1 embodies the information-processing system view adopted (or at the least considered) by most, if not all, of the subdisciplines of the cognitive sciences. This assumption facilitates the representation of theories of cognition in computer programs for testing, validation, and evaluation. Another important feature is SA1's *system assumption*, C2, which highlights the relationship between information and representation. SA2 emphasizes the significance of knowledge representation as a cognitive capacity. The four aspects listed in SA2's *system assumption*, R2—the representation bearer, representational objects, representation relation, and interpretant—bear a close resemblance to similar and related theories of intelligent agents and their interaction with their surrounding environment (which may include other intelligent agents). R2 also emphasizes the representational constraints for these four aspects.

7.2.3 Methodological Assumptions

According to Von Eckardt [14], the 11 methodological assumptions of the cognitive sciences are:

M1. Human cognition can be studied successfully by focusing exclusively on the individual cognizer and his or her place in the natural environment.

The influence of society or culture on individual cognition can always be explained by appealing to the fact that this influence is mediated through individual perception and representation.

M2. Human cognitive capacities are sufficiently autonomous from other aspects of mind, such as affect and personality, that to a large extent, they can be studied successfully in isolation.

M3. There exists a partitioning of cognition in general into individual cognitive capacities such that each capacity can, to a large extent, be studied successfully in isolation from each of the others.

M4. Although there is considerable variation in how adult human beings exercise their cognitive capacities, it is meaningful to distinguish, at least roughly, between "normal" and "abnormal" cognition.

M5. Although there is considerable variation in how adult human beings exercise their cognitive capacities, adults are sufficiently alike when they cognize that it is meaningful to talk about a "typical" adult cognizer, and it is possible to arrive at generalizations about cognition that hold (at least approximately) for all normal adults.

M6. The explanatory strategy of cognitive science is sound. In particular, answers to the original basic equations can, to a large extent, be obtained by answering their narrow information-processing counterparts (i.e., the revised basic questions).

M7. In choosing among alternative hypothesized answers to the basic questions of the research framework, one should invoke the usual canons of scientific methodology. That is, ultimately, answers to the basic questions should be justified on empirical grounds.

M8. A complete theory of human cognition will not be possible without a substantial contribution from each of the subdisciplines of the cognitive sciences.

M9. Information-processing answers to the basic questions of cognitive science are constrained by the findings of human neuroscience.

M10. The optimal research strategy for developing an adequate theory of the cognitive mind/brain is to adopt a coevolutionary approach—that is, to develop information-processing answers to the basic questions of cognitive science on the basis of empirical findings from both the nonneural cognitive sciences and the neurosciences.

M11. Information-processing theories of the cognitive mind/brain can explain certain features of cognition that cannot be explained by means of lower-level neuroscientific accounts. Such theories are thus, in principle, explanatorily ineliminable.

Assumption M1, focusing on the individual cognizer and its natural environment, allows observation and self-introspection as an acceptable methodology in the cognitive sciences. M2 and M3 facilitate the consideration of distributed models of cognition by noting that cognitive capacities are autonomous, and to some extent can each be investigated in isolation. Assumption M4 recognizes the importance of discerning "normal" versus "abnormal" cognition in adult human beings. Human diversity is taken into consideration under assumption M5, which also mentions "typicality" and how this can be generalized into theories that apply to all normal adults.

It seems that in methodological assumption M6, Von Eckardt [14] is again relying on generalizations as being applicable to the information-processing system model. As is further supported in M7, theoretical information-processing system-based models must be verified and validated empirically, which in this case, could be achieved through software simulation and/or hardware implementations.

Methodological assumptions M8 through M11 clearly emphasize the inherently multidisciplinary trait of the cognitive sciences. M8 stresses more-or-less equal significance among all subdisciplines of the cognitive sciences. In M9, the importance of research findings from human neuroscience is pointed out. This is crucial in supporting nonneural findings that pertain to any of the human cognitive capacities. M11 comes from the opposite direction: Some features of cognition are best explained by nonneural approaches. Finally, M10 recommends a coevolutionary research strategy where both the nonneural cognitive sciences and the neurosciences cooperate and coordinate their efforts.

7.2.4 Initial Account: Connection to Computing with Words

Von Eckardt's [14] characterization of the cognitive sciences, its primary research thrust (the study of ANTCOG), and its research framework gives us a general view of how the cognitive sciences and CW are related. Zadeh [25,26] points out that underlying some of the more remarkable human cognitive capacities is "the brain's crucial ability to manipulate perceptions—perceptions of distance, size, weight, time, force, color, direction, number, similarity, likelihood, and truth, among others." In this regard, his computing with words (CW) [25], theory of fuzzy information granulation (TFIG) [26], and computational theory of perceptions (CTP) [27] may prove insightful to the cognitive sciences. We explore all these in another section.

7.3 WHAT ABOUT ARTIFICIAL INTELLIGENCE?

Artificial intelligence (AI) [9] is a subdiscipline of the cognitive sciences. Since there is already a separate chapter in this book devoted to AI, we briefly discuss two views from AI in this section. These are Nilsson's [8] three theses that formulate a logical approach to AI, and Lenat's [4,5] three points regarding AI and the threshold of knowledge. At the end of the section we take a look at Lenat's [6] CYC project and the implications for CW. In particular, the role of common sense in intelligent behavior is emphasized.

Wagman [15,16] discussed Nilsson's [8] three theses that formulate a logical approach to AI. This approach includes encoding of declarative knowledge in the language of predicate calculus. Nilsson's three theses are:

1. *Knowledge of the environment.* Intelligent machines will have knowledge of their environment.
2. *Centrality of declarative knowledge.* The most versatile intelligent machines will represent much of their knowledge about their environments declaratively.
3. *Reliance on predicate calculus.* For the most versatile machine, the language in which declarative knowledge is represented must be at least as expressive as first-order predicate calculus.

Notice that Nilsson's [8] three theses are related to Von Eckardt's [14] system assumption R2 under representational assumption SA2. For example, in thesis 1, Nilsson points out that intelligent systems require knowledge of their surrounding environment. Clearly, knowledge representation is the underlying feature in cognizing the surrounding environment. This is where thesis 2 and thesis 3 highlight the significance of declarative knowledge in a logical approach to AI. Since Nilsson believes that intelligent systems will rely heavily on knowledge of their environment, most of their knowledge will be represented declaratively.

Wagman [15,17] also presents what Lenat [5] refers to as the three major findings and hypotheses of AI. These three items emphasize the relationship between AI and the threshold of knowledge:

1. *Knowledge principle.* If a program is to perform a complex task well, it must know a great deal about the world in which it operates; without knowledge, search and reasoning are all that is left, and they are not sufficient.
2. *Breadth hypothesis.* To behave intelligently in unexpected situations, an agent must be capable of falling back on increasingly general knowledge and analogizing to specific but superficially far-flung knowledge.
3. *AI as empirical inquiry.* Premature mathematization, or focusing on toy problems, washes out details from reality that later turn out to be significant; thus ideas must be tested experimentally, falsifiably, on large problems.

Similar to Nilsson's [8] first thesis, Lenat's [5] *knowledge principle* emphasizes the significance of knowledge in intelligent systems. Knowledge includes concepts, facts, representations, methods, models, metaphors, and heuristics about the domain of endeavor. The latter type of knowledge is important because searching can become costly. Lenat's *breadth hypothesis* underscores the significance of commonsense knowledge for intelligent behavior in unexpected situations. This affects both knowledge representation and search techniques since it implies requiring an ontology of the knowledge base, representation of metaknowledge, and metarules to guide and constrain search operations. Wagman [15] warns about differentiating between efficient organization versus "deep, self-heightened comprehension of [a system's] own electronic information." Finally, Lenat's *AI as empirical inquiry* is related to Von Eckardt's [14] methodological assumption M7, which highlights the significance of empirical testing.

Lenat [6] has put his three major findings of AI into practice in his ongoing CYC [5,6,11] electronic encyclopedia project. Although he recognizes the fact that "any intelligent computer would understand that occasional mistakes and inconsistencies are inevitable and can even serve as valuable learning experiences," he had dropped the use of certainty factors, probabilistic weights, to sentences given to CYC. He also states that "as humans we tolerate inconsistency all the time." Perhaps this is why Lenat puts a lot of emphasis on commonsense knowledge. He indicates this by stating that "it takes common sense to understand each other," as well as "it takes common sense to stay focused, and to learn." He points out that today's computers lack the capacity to comprehend most of our speech and text intelligently simply because they lack the common sense, the shared knowledge and experience, that we humans have. To drive the point regarding the significance of commonsense knowledge even further, Lenat [6] gives the following example: "Before we let robotic chauffeurs drive around our streets, I'd want the automated driver to have general common sense about the value of a cat versus a child versus a car bumper, about children chasing balls into streets, about young dogs being more likely to dart in front of cars than old dogs (which, in turn, are more likely to bolt than elm trees are), about death being a very undesirable thing, and so on. That 'and so on' obscures a massive amount of general knowledge of the everyday world without which no human or machine driver should be on the road, at least not near me in any populated area." Perhaps we need to revisit the question about knowledge representation before we get into the details of CW and the cognitive sciences. In the next section we take a brief look at what researchers have done in the area of knowledge representation.

7.4 KNOWLEDGE REPRESENTATION

Markman [7] defines knowledge representation through the following statement: "In the study of mind, cognitive scientists seek explanations of mental life, which consists of perceptions, emotions, social interactions, and cognitive abilities. In many of these explanations, they refer to goals, beliefs, mental images, concepts, and other mental entities. They are also concerned with retrieval, analogy, inferencing, reasoning, categorization, and many other processes that create, combine, and use the information *in our heads*." Hence he identifies the components of a representation as follows:

- A represented world
- A representing world
- A consistent set of relationships between the represented and representing worlds
- Processes that make use of this information in the representing world

This is somewhat similar to Von Eckardt's [14] *system assumption* R2 of *representational assumption* SA2 in the cognitive sciences. In answering the question as to what mental representations are used by humans, we are faced with a question regarding what formats are used for the information that makes up mental life (and how the information is used).

Perhaps one of the most influential knowledge representation schemes is Quillian's [10] semantic network model. This knowledge representation scheme assumes that information is organized into a network of nodes representing concepts and links representing relations between concepts. These links can represent constraints that can be either excitatory or inhibitory in nature. Quillian used semantic networks as a proposal for the structure of long-term memory. In his model, memory is searched by passing activations across links. The model assumes that finding intersections among concepts in a network could be used to determine the meaning of a sentence. This was used as a basis for text comprehension. The initial model did not work as planned simply because finding intersections among concepts was insufficient for sentence meaning. What was needed was language to provide new information about a situation, where sentences are used to construct new knowledge. This is in contrast to just stating relations among known concepts via links between these concepts. In other words, additional processing mechanisms were required to allow semantic networks to model this situation. Some improvements over the original Quillian model include Anderson's [1] ACT, which combines semantic networks with rule-based production systems to carry out complex problem-solving tasks, and Thagard's [13] ECHO, which uses rule-based processes to set up a constraint satisfaction network that models the simultaneous satisfaction of multiple constraints by passing activation through the network.

Markman [7] also points out that structured representations are able to create more complex representations of a situation by embedding relations into other relations (called *higher-order relational structures*). The reason for this is that higher-order structures encode important psychological elements such as causal relations and implication. Another highly influential knowledge representation scheme considers the hypothesis that human concepts consist of either *objects* or *events*. The main difference between these two types of concepts is that objects have prominent *spatial extent*—generally, objects do not change rapidly over time, objects have enduring entity, and objects contain both perceptual and conceptual information. On the other hand, events have prominent *temporal extent*—they are used to track movements and interactions of different objects over some specified time. This is why events are used for planning, prediction, and narrative comprehension. The most influential theory of event representation is Schank and Abelson's [11] scripts. They posited that people represent events with scripts. In their model, a mental script is composed of chains of scenes that determine what a set of actors do in a given situation. The events are temporally ordered and causally connected.

What is the significance of these knowledge representation schemes to cognitive models? Markman [7] gives the following seven proposals for the use of representation in cognitive models:

1. Cognitive models must be based on representations that actually represent.
2. Cognitive models must adopt multiple approaches to representation.
3. Cognitive models must use representations at multiple grain sizes (level of abstraction).
4. Cognitive models must be clear about the specification of processes.
5. Cognitive models must attend to the details of processing as well as to its gross form.
6. Cognitive models must attend to social context.
7. Cognitive models must attend to the relationship between the individual and the world.

Again, note that these proposals are related to the ideas presented in our description of the cognitive sciences and one of its subdisciplines, AI.

7.5 COMPUTING WITH WORDS

Zadeh [26] recognizes that among the basic concepts that underlie human cognition, the three most important are granulation, organization, and causation. He loosely defines *granulation* as involving decomposition of whole into parts, *organization* as integration of parts into whole, and *causation* as the association of causes with effects. In this section we discuss the connection between Zadeh's [25] computing with words (CW) and the cognitive sciences. We do this by looking into two theories that underlie CW: Zadeh's [26] *theory of fuzzy information granulation* (TFIG) and Zadeh's [27] *computational theory of perceptions* (CTP).

7.5.1 Zadeh's Theory of Fuzzy Information Granulation

Since information granulation (IG) involves decomposition of whole into parts [26], fuzzy IG facilitates modeling and consideration of any uncertainty involved in the procedure. The fuzziness stems from the natural fuzzy characteristic of such concepts as distance, time, and speed (see Ref. 21) when used as an integral part of decision making as well as in many other human cognitive capabilities (see Ref. 20). Fuzzy information granulation is "a mode of granulation which underlies the concepts of linguistic variable, fuzzy if–then rule, and fuzzy graph." Zadeh [27] defines a *granule* as a clump of objects or points that are drawn together by a generalized constraint such as indistinguishability, similarity, proximity, or functionality. Typically, a granule is a fuzzy set. *Granulation* of an object A results in a collection of granules of A. A detailed discussion of Zadeh's TFIG is given in Ref. 26.

According to Zadeh [26], the basic structure of fuzzy IG involves granulation, attribution, and valuation. These are related as shown in Figure 7.1. Zadeh also notes that the fuzziness of granules (e.g., objects, events), their attributes (e.g., length, height, weight), and their values (e.g., long, heavy, early) is characteristic of the

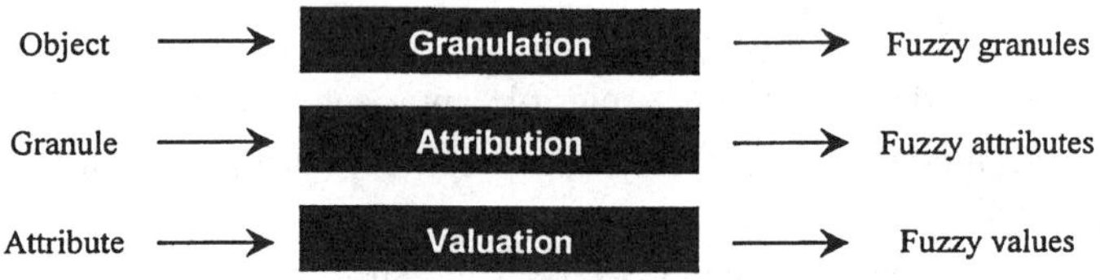

FIGURE 7.1. Structure of fuzzy information granulation.

ways in which human concepts are formed, organized, and manipulated. He emphasizes that TFIG is a basis for CW; in effect, CW is an integral part of TFIG.

Fuzzy IG can be viewed as a mode of generalization that may be applied to any concept, method, or theory. One of a few modes of generalization listed by Zadeh [26] is *f.g.-generalization*, a combination of fuzzification (replacement of a crisp set with a fuzzy set) and granulation. F.g.-generalization's pivotal role in TFIG and in fuzzy logic, in general, becomes apparent with the structure of fuzzy information granulation (see Figure 7.1). The structure exhibits granulation, but it also embodies fuzzification of items concerned (most specifically, the right side of the figure). F.g.-generalization is also known as *f-granulation* or *fuzzy granulation.*

Recall that we had started this chapter by noting how some of the exceptional physical and mental capabilities humans have are performed without the need for precise measurements and accurate computations. Although the TFIG provides a basis for CW as a means of capturing and modeling these intelligent tasks, it seems clear that another tool is required. What is needed is a methodology for reasoning and computing with perceptions rather than measurements. This is provided by Zadeh's [27] computational theory of perceptions (CTP), which is briefly discussed in the next section.

7.5.2 Zadeh's Computational Theory of Perceptions

Zadeh's [27] computational theory of perceptions (CTP) provides a methodology for reasoning and computing with perceptions rather than measurements. Since perceptions tend to be less precise and less accurate than measurements, if follows that the CTP is based on the methodology of CW. According to Zadeh, in the CTP, words play the roles of labels of perceptions, and more generally, perceptions are expressed as propositions in a natural language. In other words, natural languages may be viewed as systems for describing perceptions. Hence computing and reasoning with perceptions is reduced to computing and reasoning with words.

In the computational theory of perceptions, meaning representation is based on what is referred to as constraint-centered semantics of natural languages (CSNL). According to Zadeh [27], a concept which plays a central role in CSNL is that of a generalized constraint. A generalized unconditional constraint is expressed as X *isr* R, where X is the constrained variable; R is the constraining (fuzzy) relation, which is called the generalized value of X; and *isr* (pronounced "ezar") is a variable copula in which the value of the discrete variable r defines the way in which R constrains X. Among the basic types of constraints listed by Zadeh are equality constraints ($r{:}=$), possibilistic constraints (r:*blank*), veristic constraints ($r{:}v$), probabilistic constraints ($r{:}p$), random set constraints ($r{:}rs$), usuality constraints ($r{:}u$), and fuzzy graph constraints ($r{:}fg$). Details of Zadeh's CTP as a theoretical account of reasoning with perceptions are given in Ref. 27.

The significance of CTP may be inferred by referring to the structure of fuzzy IG as given in Figure 7.1. In the arrangement given, objects are perceived. Moreover, granules, their attributes, and their values are, to a large extent, all perceived. Hence the CTP provides a means to develop a model of the human capability to reason with perception-based information. In providing the CTP, Zadeh [27] hopes that incorporation of the machinery of the computational theory of perceptions to existing theories may eventually lead to theories that have a superior capability to deal with real-world problems. He foresees such integration, making it possible to conceive and design systems with a much higher machine IQ (MIQ) than current machines have today.

7.6 CONNECTIONS: A DISCUSSION

In analyzing the ANTCOG framework adopted by the cognitive sciences, it seems natural to consider the human cognitive capacities as the binding framework with which all the cognitive sciences are related to one another. Zadeh's CW should seriously be taken into consideration by the cognitive sciences as a workable model for the higher mental processes of humans and its associated inherent features of uncertainty. Zadeh [27] also points out that although there has been an "exponential improvement in the capability of computers to process extremely large volumes of information at a very high speed, at a considerably low cost and with very high reliability," the aim is not to develop better number-crunching models of cognition. Instead, technology should be viewed as providing a better platform for computing with words instead of numbers!

Computing with words, as well as the TFIG and CTP in particular, seem to provide the necessary framework for modeling such cognitive capabilities, such as concept formation, sentence construction and processing, analogical reasoning, and so on. These naturally complex tasks (although as humans, we seem to perform them with such ease) can be modeled better with consideration of Zadeh's work on CW. According to Zadeh [26], the two main rationales for CW are:

1. CW is a necessity when the information available is not precise enough to justify the use of numbers.
2. CW is advantageous when there is a tolerance for imprecision, uncertainty, and partial truth that can be exploited to achieve tractability, robustness, low solution cost, and better rapport with reality.

Additionally, Von Eckardt's [14] characterization of the cognitive sciences also makes some important points that we need to take into consideration. Foremost is the recognition that the cognitive sciences is a vastly diverse set of disciplines that have a common theme: the investigation and understanding of human cognition. Also, as pointed out in methodological assumption M8, a complete theory of human cognition will not be possible without a substantial contribution from each subdiscipline of the cognitive sciences.

An example of such a cross-disciplinary approach is the work presented in Refs. 2 and 3 by Juliano and Bandler. Their research on the use of fuzzy graph structures and fuzzy relational methods for cognitive diagnosis considers work done in other areas of the cognitive sciences. Juliano and Bandler present the basic framework of their methodology in Ref. 3 with a structure similar to Zadeh's TFIG structure. Then in Ref. 2, Juliano and Bandler expound on the use of fuzzy graph structures called fuzzy cognitive maps (FCMs) to model the use of similarities and discrepancies when humans form conceptual categories as part of our higher mental activities.

Perhaps as part of this call for stronger cross-disciplinary work, Zadeh [26] presents a challenge to the AI community. He posits that for most naturally complex tasks that humans perform with ease, the decision-relevant information is f-granular. Recent successes and failures in AI and in the use of some knowledge representation schemes also seem to indicate the need for a different perspective, as Yager [18] points out. Hence Zadeh states that for an intelligent machine to perform everyday tasks such as parking a car, driving through heavy traffic, estimating a person's age from voice, and so on as effortlessly as humans can, a machine must have the capability to process f-granular information. His conclusion is that fuzzy information granulation is an integral part of human cognition; "without the methodology of fuzzy IG in its armamentarium, AI cannot achieve its goals."

7.7 SUMMARY

We started this chapter by recognizing the wide variety of exceptional physical and mental capabilities that humans seem to possess. Some, if not most, of these tasks are performed without the need for precise measurements and accurate computations. As far as the cognitive sciences are concerned, computing with words and its associated theories—the theory of fuzzy information granulation (TFIG) and the computational theory of perceptions (CTP)—must be taken seriously as a feasible modeling framework in developing theories of cognition. This is exemplified in a number of tasks that humans perform where "fuzzy information granulation seems to be employed in making rational decisions in an environment of partial knowledge, partial certainty and partial truth" [26].

Zadeh [27] recognizes the move from computing with numbers to computing with words as a paradigm shift. He predicts that the long-standing tradition of dealing with perceptions by converting them into measurements will slowly get phased out. What has contributed to this? People are recognizing that "the conversion of perceptions into measurements is infeasible, unrealistic or counter productive." The exponential growth in computational power available through today's computing devices is making the move from measurements to perceptions more feasible. As a result, Zadeh [27] predicts an increase in the role of natural languages in scientific theories. If Zadeh's prediction is correct when he states that "in coming years, TFIG is likely to play an important role in the evolution of fuzzy logic and, in conjunction with computing with words, may eventually have a far-reaching impact on its applications," we should all actively participate in furthering our knowledge and understanding of human cognition by considering, if not fully subscribing, to this paradigm shift.

A concerted effort among the cognitive science community and those supporting the "computing with words movement" should bring about more concrete and interesting results that will take us closer to a unified theory of cognition. We should all recognize this. After all, all of us are cognitive scientists, to some degree or other, in our quest to understand more about our selves, our cognitive capabilities, and all our limitations.

REFERENCES

1. J. R. Anderson, A spreading activation theory of memory, *J. Verb. Learn. Verb. Behav.*, 22:261–295, 1983.
2. B. A. Juliano and W. Bandler, *Tracing Chains-of-Thought: Fuzzy Methods in Cognitive Diagnosis*, Physica-Verlag, Heidelberg, Germany, 1996.
3. B. A. Juliano and W. Bandler, Modeling the approximation of expert knowledge structures, in J. Liebowitz (ed.), *Proc. World Congress on Expert Systems*, Vol. 2, Pergamon Press, Elmsford, NY, 1991, pp. 820–827.
4. D. B. Lenat, *Building Large Knowledge-Based Systems: Representation and Inference in the CYC Project*, Addison-Wesley, Reading, MA, 1988.
5. D. B. Lenat and E. A. Feigenbaum, On the thresholds of knowledge, *Artif. Intell.*, 47: 185–250, 1991.
6. D. B. Lenat, *Hal's Legacy: 2001's Computer as Dream and Reality, http://www.cyc.com/halslegacy.html*, D. G. Stork, (ed.), current, Sept. 1999.
7. B. Markman, *Knowledge Representation*, Lawrence Erlbaum, Hillsdale, NJ, 1999.
8. N. J. Nilsson, Logic and artificial intelligence, *Artif. Intell.*, 47:31–56, 1991.
9. J. McCarthy, What is artificial intelligence? *http://www.formal.stanford.edu/jmc/whatisai.html*, current, Sept. 1999.
10. M. R. Quillian, Semantic memory, in M. Minsky (ed.), *Semantic Information Processing*, MIT Press, Cambridge, MA, 1968, pp. 216–260.
11. R. C. Schank and R. P. Abelson, *Scripts, Plans, Goals and Understanding*, Lawrence Erlbaum, Hillsdale, NJ, 1977.
12. C. Smith, The owl and the electric encyclopedia, *Artif. Intell.*, 47:251–288, 1991.
13. P. Thagard, Explanatory coherence, *Behav. Brain Sci.*, 12:435–502, 1989.
14. B. Von Eckardt, *What Is Cognitive Science*? MIT Press, Cambridge, MA, 1993.
15. M. Wagman, *Cognitive Science and the Symbolic Operations of Human and Artificial Intelligence: Theory and Research into the Intellective Processes*, Praeger, Westport, CT, 1997.
16. M. Wagman, *Cognitive Science and the Mind–Body Problem: From Philosophy to Psychology to Artificial Intelligence to Imaging of the Brain*, Praeger, Westport, CT, 1998.

17. M. Wagman, *Language and Thought in Humans and Computers: Theory and Research in Psychology, Artificial Intelligence, and Neural Science*, Praeger, Westport, CT, 1998.
18. R. R. Yager, Fuzzy logics and artificial intelligence, *Fuzzy Sets Syst.*, 90: 193–198, 1997.
19. L. A. Zadeh, Fuzzy sets, *Inf. Control*, 8:338–353, 1965.
20. L. A. Zadeh, Outline of a new approach to the analysis of complex systems and decision processes, *IEEE Trans. Syst. Man Cybern.*, 3:28–44, 1973.
21. L. A. Zadeh, The concept of a linguistic variable and its applications to approximate reasoning, Part I; *Inf. Sci.*, 8:199–249, 1975; Part II; *Inf. Sci.*, 8:301–357, 1975; Part III; *Inf. Sci.*, 9:43–80, 1975.
22. L. A. Zadeh, Fuzzy sets and information granularity, in M. Gupta, R. Ragade, and R. Yager (eds.), *Advances in Fuzzy Set Theory and Applications*, North-Holland, Amsterdam, 1979, pp. 3–18.
23. L. A. Zadeh, Fuzzy logic, neural networks, and soft computing, *Commun. ACM*, 37(3):77–84, 1994.
24. L. A. Zadeh, Soft computing and fuzzy logic, *IEEE Software*, November 1994, pp. 48–56.
25. L. A. Zadeh, Fuzzy logic = computing with words. *IEEE Trans. Fuzzy Syst.*, 4:103–111, 1996.
26. L. A. Zadeh, Toward a theory of fuzzy information granulation and its centrality in human reasoning and fuzzy logic, *Fuzzy Sets Syst.*, 90:111–127, 1997.
27. L. A. Zadeh, From computation with measurements to computation with perceptions: a paradigm shift, from the Abstract of a BISC seminar of the same title; seminar was held Sept. 16, 1999, Soda Hall, University of California–Berkeley, Berkeley, CA.

CHAPTER 8

COMBINING LINGUISTIC INFORMATION IN A DISTRIBUTED INTELLIGENT AGENT MODEL FOR INFORMATION GATHERING ON THE INTERNET

M. DELGADO, F. HERRERA, E. HERRERA-VIEDMA,
M. J. MARTIN-BAUTISTA, and M. A. VILA
University of Granada, Granada, Spain

8.1 INTRODUCTION

The fuzzy linguistic approach is an approximate technique that represents qualitative aspects as linguistic values by means of linguistic variables, that is, variables whose values are not numbers but words or sentences in a natural or artificial language [75]. The management of linguistic information implies the use of operators of comparison and aggregation. In Ref. 25 the *linguistic weighted averaging* (LWA) operator was presented as a tool to aggregate linguistic weighted information: namely, linguistic information which has associated different linguistic importance degrees. The fuzzy linguistic approach has produced very good results for solving different problems (decision, information retrieval, medicine, education, etc.). In the framework of information retrieval, one of the most current problems for which a linguistic approach is very useful is the retrieval, handling, and identification of relevant information through the Internet.

Intelligent software agents [21,23,24,44,52,62], a concept that appeared recently, deal with the information-gathering process assisting Internet users to locate the information that best fits their needs. Several proposals about intelligent software agents have been emerging in recent years, but the lack of connection, communica-

Computing with Words, Edited by Paul P. Wang.
ISBN 0-471-35374-4

tion, and consensus among them has led to a decrease in the quality and suitability of the information retrieved in addition to the efficiency of the system in the recovery and filtering task. This fact sustains the need for proposals in the field and emphasizes the importance of the design and development of intelligent software agent organizations as well as hierarchies and architectures that hold up such structures [8,12,37,41,55,62].

However, not only is some organization needed but also a protocol for communication among agents. The great variety of representations and evaluations of information on the Internet is the main obstacle to this communication, and the problem becomes more noticeable when a user takes part in the process. The complexity of this process reveals the need for more flexibility in communication among agents and between agents and the user. For this purpose, several approaches related to mechanisms to introduce and handle flexible information through linguistic labels have been proposed at both the agent [72,73] and user [6,35] levels.

In this chapter we present a distributed intelligent agent model for information gathering on the Internet, where communication of the evaluation of the information retrieved among agents is carried out by using the LWA operator as a way to endow the retrieval process with more flexibility and uniformity. To do so, the chapter is structured as follows: In Section 8.2 we present a short tutorial about the use of a linguistic approach to solving problems; in Section 8.3 we describe the LWA operator; and in Section 8.4 we show the structure of the distributed intelligent agent model, which uses the LWA operator for information gathering.

8.2 LINGUISTIC APPROACH TO SOLVING PROBLEMS

Many aspects of day-to-day activities cannot be assessed precisely in quantitative form but can in qualitative form. For example, when attempting to qualify phenomena related to human perception, we are often led to use words in natural language. As pointed out in Ref. 13, this may arise for different reasons. There are some situations in which the information may be unquantifiable due to its nature, and thus it may be stated only in linguistic terms (e.g., when evaluating the comfort or design of a car, terms such as *good*, *fair*, and *poor* can be used). In other cases, precise quantitative information may not be stated because either it is unavailable or the cost of its computation is too high, so an approximate value may be tolerated (e.g., when evaluating the speed of a car, linguistic terms such as *fast*, *very fast*, and *slow* may be used instead of numerical values).

Although a linguistic approach is less precise than a numerical approach, it has several advantages:

- In particular, a linguistic description is easily understood by human beings even if the concepts are abstract or the context is changing [3,56]. For example, everybody can figure out the concept of danger and can qualify it even if the context is unknown, and everybody is also able to classify colors without having explicit knowledge of their origin and the mechanisms of perception.

- On the other hand, a linguistic approach simplifies system–user interaction because the greater the required precision of assessments, the greater the difficulty in extracting them from users and the more likely it is that they will be inaccurate.
- Furthermore, a linguistic approach diminishes the effects of noise since, as is known, the more refined the assessment scale, the more sentitive it is to noise and, consequently, the more error-free it becomes.

In short, a linguistic approach is appropriate for a lot of problems, since it allows representation of the information in a more direct and adequate way when we are unable to express it with precision. In this way, the burden of quantifying a qualitative concept is eliminated.

The *fuzzy linguistic approach* has produced very good results in the modeling of qualitative information. It is an approximate technique, which represents qualitative aspects as linguistic values by means of *linguistic variables*, that is, variables whose values are not numbers but words or sentences in a natural or artificial language [75]. Each linguistic value is characterized by a *syntactic value* or *label* and a *semantic value* or *meaning*. The label is a word or sentence belonging to a linguistic term set, and the meaning is a fuzzy subset in a universe of discourse. Since words, in general, are less precise than numbers, the concept of a linguistic variable serves the purpose of providing a measure of an approximate characterization of the phenomena, which are too complex or too ill-defined to be amenable to their description by conventional quantitative terms.

From a formal point of view, a linguistic variable is defined by a quintuple, $\{L, H(L), U, G, M\}$. L is the name of the linguistic variable, and $H(L)$ (or simply H) is its term set (i.e., the collection of linguistic descriptors used to assess). For example, a term set for the linguistic variable *Importance*, denoted by H(*Importance*), can be defined as: H (*Importance*) = {*high, very high, medium, low, more or less low, not very low, ...*}.

A numerical variable u called the *base variable*, which takes values in the universe of discourse U (usually [0,1]), is associated with each linguistic variable L. G is a syntactic rule, which usually takes the form of a context-free grammar and generates the linguistic descriptors of H, and M is a semantic rule which associates the meaning $M(l)$ with a fuzzy subset of U to each linguistic value $l \in H$. Each l generated by G is the label for the fuzzy restriction $M(l)$ on the values of the base variable [75]. Furthermore, a fuzzy restriction is a fuzzy subset whose membership function is called a *compatibility function*, as it associates a number in [0,1] with each value of the base variable u and represents the degree of compatibility of u with the concept expressed by the linguistic value l [i.e., $M(l) = \{\langle u, \mu_l(u)\rangle, |u \in U\}$].

Computational models based on the linguistic approach can also be constructed to simulate approximate reasoning [4]. These linguistic models can accept a set of sentences as input, and based on the information contained in them, can derive conclusions or answer questions upon request. The implementation of these models presents several major problems:

- How to determine the linguistic descriptors of the term set (i.e., H)
- How to determine the semantic of these descriptors (i.e., M)
- How to perform arithmetic operations with linguistic terms

We deal with the first and second problems below the third problem is analyzed in Section 8.3.

8.2.1 On the Choice of Linguistic Term Set and Its Semantic

From a practical point of view, in any fuzzy linguistic approach, we have to choose the appropriate linguistic descriptors of the term set and their semantic. In the literature we can find two possibilities, which are detailed below. The first possibility is the classical linguistic approach, which is characterized by defining the linguistic term set by means of a context-free grammar. The semantics of the linguistic terms are represented by two elements: (1) fuzzy numbers described by parametric membership functions and (2), a semantic rule. The second possibility is characterized by defining the linguistic term set by means of an ordered structure of linguistic terms. The semantic of the linguistic terms is derived either from its own ordered structure or by means of subdomains of the [0,1] interval, which can be induced by negation functions defined over a linguistic term set.

Choice of Linguistic Term Set. The main aim of establishing the linguistic descriptors of a linguistic variable is to supply users with a few words by which they can naturally express their information needs. To accomplish this objective, an important aspect to analyze is the *granularity of uncertainty*, the level of discrimination among different countings of uncertainty, that is, the cardinality of the linguistic term set used to express the information. According to the uncertainty degree with which a user qualifies a phenomenon, the linguistic term set chosen to provide knowledge will contain more or fewer terms. The cardinality of this term set must be small enough so as not to impose useless precision to users, and it must be rich enough to allow discrimination of the assessments in a limited number of grades.

Typical values of cardinality used in the linguistic models are odd ones, such as 7 or 9, with an upper limit of granularity 11 or no more than 13, where the middle term represents an assessment of approximately 0.5 and with the rest of the terms being placed symmetrically around it [5]. These classical cardinality values seem to fall in line with Miller's observation that human beings can reasonably manage to keep in mind seven or so items [48,49].

A possibility of generating the linguistic term set consists in supplying a context-free grammar. However, this approach implies establishing previously the primary fuzzy sets associated with each term and the semantic rule that modifies them, and this task is not easy. An alternative possibility consists of supplying the term set directly by considering all terms distributed on a scale on which a total order is defined [70]. For example, a set of seven terms S could be given as follows:

$$S = \{s_0 = none,\ s_1 = very\ low,\ s_2 = low,\ s_3 = medium,$$
$$s_4 = high,\ s_5 = very\ high,\ s_6 = perfect\},$$

in which $s_a < s_b$ iff $a < b$. Usually, in these cases, it is often required that the linguistic term set satisfies the following additional characteristics:

1. There is a negation operator [e.g., $\text{neg}(s_i) = s_j$ such that $j = T - i$ ($T + 1$ is the cardinality)].
2. Maximization operator: $\max(s_i, s_j) = s_i$ if $s_i \geq s_j$.
3. Minimization operator: $\min(s_i, s_j) = s_i$ if $s_i \leq s_j$.

In most cases, as shown below, the semantics of the ordered terms are defined in a special way, by using as a basis some of these requested properties and the total order established in the linguistic term set.

Semantic of a Linguistic Term Set. Traditionally, the semantic of the primary terms in a linguistic term set is given by fuzzy numbers defined in the [0, 1] interval, which are usually described by membership functions or distributions [4–6,16,57,58]. A computationally efficient way to characterize a fuzzy number is to use a representation based on parameters of its membership function [4].

Because the linguistic assessments given by users are just approximate ones, some authors consider that linear trapezoidal membership functions are good enough to capture the vagueness of those linguistic assessments, since it may be impossible and unnecessary to obtain more accurate values [4,5,16,57,58]. This parametric representation is achieved by the 4-tuple $(a_i, b_i, \alpha_i, \beta_i)$. The first two parameters indicate the interval in which the membership value is 1; the third and fourth parameters indicate the left and right width [4]. For example, we may assign the following semantic to a set of seven terms:

$$P = Perfect = (1, 1, 0.25, 0)$$

$$VH = Very\text{-}High = (0.75, 0.75, 0.15, 0.25)$$

$$H = High = (0.6, 0.6, 0.1, 0.15)$$

$$M = Medium = (0.5, 0.5, 0.1, 0.1)$$

$$L = Low = (0.4, 0.4, 0.15, 0.1)$$

$$VL = Very\text{-}Low = (0.25, 0.25, 0.25, 0.15)$$

$$N = None = (0, 0, 0, 0.25).$$

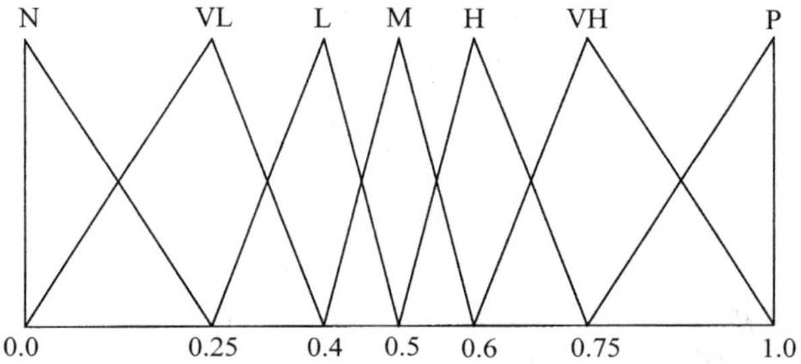

FIGURE 8.1 Set of seven terms with its semantic.

which is shown graphically in Figure 8.1. Others authors use a nontrapezoidal representation (e.g., Gaussian functions) [6,35].

In representations based on parameters, the problem is how to determine the parameters according to all users' attitudes. Formally speaking, it seems difficult to accept that all users should agree to the same membership functions associated with linguistic terms, and therefore there are no universal distribution of concepts. For example, two close perceptions of the same evaluation could be considered (Figure 8.2). Furthermore, it is not always possible that the user defines a fuzzy number for each primary linguistic term because it requires an excess of accuracy that the user cannot always supply. Hence many authors consider an environment where users can discriminate perfectly the same linguistic term set under a similar conception, taking into account that the concept of a linguistic variable serves the purpose of providing a measure of an approximated characterization of information of an imprecise preference [27].

An alternative possibility does not provide the semantic of the linguistic term set by means of fuzzy numbers, but it induces the semantic of the linguistic terms from the structure defined over the linguistic term set. In particular, this happens when users provide their assessments by using an ordered linguistic term set [68,70]. Usually, it is assumed that ordered linguistic term sets are uniformly distributed on a scale of [0,1], as aforementioned, with an odd cardinal and the middle term representing an assessment of approximately 0.5 and with the rest of the terms placed symmetrically around it. Then the semantic of the linguistic term set is established from the ordered structure of the term set, by considering that each linguistic

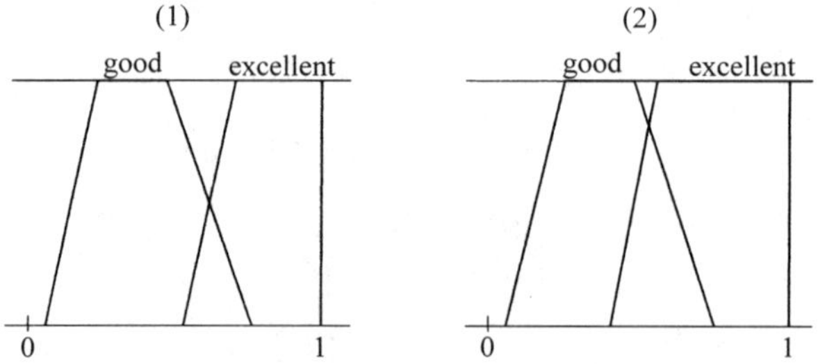

FIGURE 8.2 Different distribution concepts.

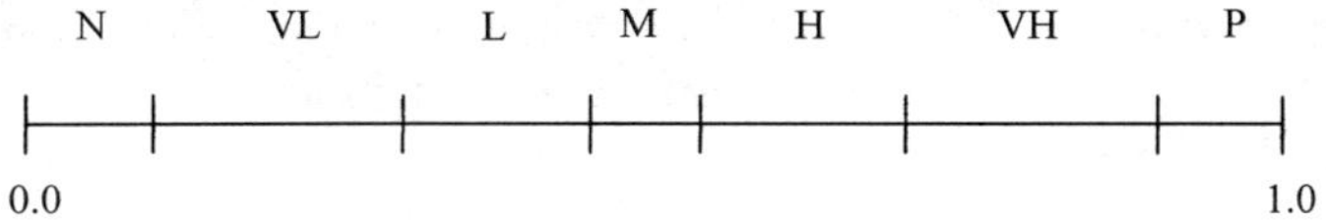

FIGURE 8.3 Uniformly distributed ordered set of seven linguistic terms.

term of pair (s_i, s_{T-i}) is equally informative [59]. This proposal may be defined explicitly by assigning a subdomain of the reference domain [0,1] to each linguistic term (Figure 8.3), or by assigning trapezoidal membership functions (Figure 8.1). In any case, as explained in Section 8.3, in this type of linguistic approach the semantic chosen has no effect on the final result.

However, sometimes it is possible that a subdomain of the reference domain may be more informative than the rest of the domain [59]. In this case, the density of linguistic labels in that subdomain would be greater than the density in the rest of the reference domain (i.e., the ordered linguistic term set would not be uniformly distributed). For these situations a method that induces the semantic (the subdomains) by using a negation function defined from the linguistic term set to parts of it was proposed in Ref. 59. In the following section we analyze briefly some more important applications of the linguistic approach.

8.2.2 Applications of the Linguistic Approach

In the literature we may find many applications of the fuzzy linguistic approach to solving problems in the real world (e.g., decision analysis, medicine, information retrieval, software development, education). A summary of these applications follows.

Decision Analysis. Decision theory is perhaps the field in which we find the greatest number of applications of the linguistic approach. In all of them, it is assumed that experts express their opinions of a set of options by means of linguistic assessments, and then an overall solution is obtained. Some of the more interesting linguistic models of decision making are the following:

- Linguistic models of multicriteria decision making [25,42,57,58,61,63,70]
- Linguistic models of group decision making [27,28,33,39]
- Linguistic models of consensus in group decision making [29–32]
- Linguistic models of multicriteria multiperson decision making [9,11,68]
- Linguistic models of consensus in multicriteria multiperson decision making [7,22,47]
- Linguistic models of decision making with linguistic evidence space states [16,18]

Information Retrieval. Several linguistic approaches in information retrieval have been proposed. In Refs. 6 and 35 authors use linguistic assessements to represent user queries, and in Ref. 72 a protocol for negotiations among multiple intelligent agents on the Internet is proposed by using a linguistic scale to represent the information used by the agents.

Medicine. In Ref. 15 a clinical diagnosis method whose results are linguistic labels is presented.

Marketing. The use of a variable to predict the value of another variable is an important tool in the field of market research. A methodology called FUZMAR (fuzzy market research system) to use information provided by market surveys to predict the values of related variables of interest to market research analysts is suggested in Ref. 74. An approach to validate models that contains linguistic variables is also introduced.

Education. In educational systems, a usual practice is evaluation of student performance to check who is good enough to pass a course. In Ref. 38 a fuzzy educational grading system is presented that assesses student performance by means of linguistic terms.

Software Development. Cost evaluation is a constant process in the life cycle of software system development. In Refs. 39 and 40 a linguistic structure model of risk in software development is presented. In such a model, evaluations of the rate of risk factors are given by means of linguistic terms.

8.3 AGGREGATION OF LINGUISTIC INFORMATION: THE LWA OPERATOR

In this section we analyze two ways to aggregate linguistic information and present the LWA operator to aggregate linguistic weighted information.

8.3.1 Aggregation of Linguistic Information

In line with the two main possibilities of defining the linguistic term sets given above, there exist also two principal approaches to the aggregation and comparison of linguistic terms. The first acts by direct computation on linguistic terms [17,25,26,66,67], whereas the second uses the associated membership functions [4,5,15,16,57,58,75]. In general, implementation of linguistic models based on techniques belonging to the second kind presents two major problems: how to perform arithmetic operations with fuzzy numbers [4] and how to associate a linguistic term with an unlabeled fuzzy set on the basis of the semantic similarity (linguistic approximation).

The fuzzy logic provides the logical operators (or, and, not $\rightarrow$), used to build the linguistic model, and the *extension principle* provides the mathematical tool to perform any arithmetic [4,75]. However, use of the extension principle with sampled membership distributions generates a considerable increase in the finite discrete support of the result. The classical solution to this problem consists of using a representation based on parameters for the fuzzy set, and then defining the arithmetic operations on the basis of these parameters without using the extension principle. For example, a table of basic arithmetic operations is given in Ref. 4.

On the other hand, it is well known that by using extended arithmetic operations to handle fuzzy numbers, the vagueness of the results increases step by step, and the shape of the membership functions does not keep when the linguistic variables are interactive. Thus the final results of those methods are fuzzy sets, which do not correspond to any label in the original linguistic term set. If we wish to have a label finally, a linguistic approximation is needed [4,15,16,57,75]. This linguistic approximation consists of finding a label, generally a sentence in a language, whose meaning is the same or closest (according to some metric) to the meaning of the unlabeled fuzzy set generated by the linguistic computational model. There is also no general method of associating a label with a fuzzy set, so that specific problems may require developed methods specifically. For example, the solution proposed for this problem in Ref. 4 is based on pattern recognition techniques. A review of some methods for linguistic approximation may be found in Ref. 15.

The symbolic approach acts by direct computations on labels, by taking into account the meaning and features of such linguistic assessments. These methods seem to be the most natural ones because the linguistic assessments are just approximations which are given and handled when obtaining more accurate values is impossible or unnecessary. Furthermore, they are computationally simple and quick because they are usually used in user-driven algorithms or decision-making processes [17]. Some of the main symbolic operators of linguistic aggregation may be found in Refs. 7,10,17,25,28,60, and 66–70. Therefore, we shall use the symbolic approach in the development of our model, and in particular, the operator of aggregation of linguistic information proposed in Ref. 25, which aggregates linguistic information weighted linguistically.

8.3.2 Aggregation of Linguistic Weighted Information

We may find situations where the information handled is not equally important. For example, when a group of medical experts express their opinions on a possible illness that a patient presents, on the one hand, their diagnostics must not be considered with equal relevance, given that there are medical experts with more experience than others, and on the other hand, a final and global diagnostic must be made using the initial and individual diagnostics. This heterogeneous framework has been considered by various authors in the aggregation of opinions [14,20,50,69], consensus models in group decision making [7,29–31], fuzzy pattern matching [19], and knowledge systems [54].

A way of modeling the first aspect is by assigning a weight to each medical expert. The weights can be quantitative or qualitative values and may be interpreted in at least two different ways [19,20]: (1) each medical expert is viewed as a subgroup and the weight reflects the relative size of this subgroup, or (2) the weight may reflect the relevance of the medical expert in the group. This level of relevance may act as a constraint on the opinions that a medical expert may express. A general way of dealing with the second aspect is to use adequate operators to combine information before reaching a final decision or action.

To aggregate weighted information, we have to combine linguistic information with the weights, which involves the transformation of the weighted information under the importance degrees. The transformation function depends on the type of aggregation of weighted information that is going to be performed [69]. In Refs. 63 and 64, Yager discussed the effect of the importance degrees on max and min aggregation and suggested a class of functions for importance transformation in both types of aggregation. For min aggregation he suggested a family of *t*-co-norms acting on the weighted information and the negation of the weights, which presents the nonincreasing monotonic property in these weights. For the max aggregation, he suggested a family of t-norms acting on weighted information and the weight, which presents the nondecreasing monotonic property in these weights.

A general specification of the requirements that any importance transformation function g must satisfy for any type of the aggregation operator is also proposed in Ref. 69. The function g must have the following properties:

1. If $a > b$, then $g(v, a) \geq g(v, b)$.
2. $g(v, a)$ is monotone in v.
3. $g(0, a) = \text{ID}$.
4. $g(1, a) = a$.

Here $a, b \in [0, 1]$ expresses satisfaction with regard to a criterion, $v \in [0, 1]$ the weight associated with the criterion, and ID an identity element, which is such that if we add it to our aggregations, it does not change the aggregated value. The first condition means that the function g is monotonically nondecreasing in the second argument, that is, if the satisfaction with regard to the criterion increases, the overall satisfaction should not decrease. The second condition may be viewed as a requirement of the effect of the importance of being consistent. It does not specify whether g is monotonically nonincreasing or nondecreasing in the first argument. It should be noted that conditions 3 and 4 actually determine the type of monotonicity obtained from condition 2. If $a > \text{ID}$, $g(v, a)$ is monotonically nondecreasing in v, whereas if $a < \text{ID}$, it is monotonically nonincreasing. The third condition is a manifestation of the imperative that zero-importance items do not affect the aggregation process. The final condition is essentially a boundary condition which states that the assumption of all importances equal to 1 is effectively like not including importances at all [69].

8.3.3 LWA Operator

According to the aforementioned ideas, the LWA operator to aggregate linguistic weighted information is provided in Ref. 25, which was defined using the linguistic ordered weighted averaging (LOWA) operator [26,28], the concept of *fuzzy majority* represented by a *fuzzy linguistic quantifier* [76], and two families of linguistic connectives [25]. Hence, before defining the LWA operator, we present its elements.

LOWA Operator. The LOWA operator [26] is an operator of aggregation of ordered linguistic information, which works by direct computation. It is based on the ordered weighted averaging (OWA) operator defined by Yager [65] and on the convex combination of linguistic labels defined by Delgado et al. [17].

Definition 8.1. *Let $A = \{a_k \in S, k = 1, \ldots, m\}$ be a collection of linguistic labels and assume that $a_m \leq a_{m-1} \leq \cdots \leq a_1$, without loss of generality. For any set of coefficients $\{\lambda_k \in [0,1], k = 1, 2, \ldots, m, \sum \lambda_k = 1\}$ the convex combination of these m labels is the one given by*

$$\mathcal{C}^m\{\lambda_k, a_k, k = 1, \ldots, m\} = \lambda_1 \odot a_1 \oplus (1 - \lambda_1) \odot \mathcal{C}^{m-1}\{\beta_h, a_h, h = 2, \ldots, m\}$$

$$\beta_h = \lambda_h \Big/ \sum_2^n \lambda_k \qquad h = 2, = \ldots, m,$$

$\mathcal{C}^2$ being defined as

$$\mathcal{C}^2\{\lambda_i, a_i, i = 1, 2\} = \lambda_1 \odot a_1 \oplus (1 - \lambda_1) \odot a_2 = s_k \in S,$$

such that assuming that $a_1 = s_j$, $a_2 = s_i (s_j, s_i \in S (j \geq i))$, then $k = min\{T, i + round(\lambda_1 \cdot (j - i))\}$, where "round" is the usual round operation. If $\lambda_j = 1$ and $\lambda_i = 0$ with $i \neq j \forall i$, the convex combination is defined as

$$\mathcal{C}^m\{\lambda_i, a_i, i = 1, \ldots, m\} = a_j.$$

An example follows.

Example 8.1. Assume the term set

$$S = \{s_8 = C,\ s_7 = EL,\ s_6 = ML,\ s_5 = MC,\ s_4 = IM,\ s_3 = SC,\ s_2 = VLC,\ s_1 = EU,\ s_0 = I\}$$

and $\lambda = 0.4$:

	$1 - \lambda = 0.6$			
$\lambda = 0.4$	**SC**	**VLC**	**C**	**EL**
ML	IM	IM	EL	EL
I	VLC	EU	MC	IM
IM	SC	SC	ML	ML
VLC	SC	VLC	ML	MC

where, for example,

$$k_{11} = \min\{8, 3 + \text{round}(0.4(6-3))\} = 4(IM)$$
$$k_{21} = \min\{8, 0 + \text{round}(0.6(3-0))\} = 2(VLC).$$

Definition 8.2. *Let $A = \{a_1, \ldots, a_m\}$ be a set of labels to aggregate; then the LOWA operator, ϕ, is defined as*

$$\phi(a_1, \ldots, a_m) = W \cdot B^T = \mathscr{C}^m\{w_k, b_k, k = 1, \ldots, m\}$$
$$= w_1 \odot b_1 \oplus (1 - w_1) \odot \mathscr{C}^{m-1}\{\beta_h, b_h, h = 2, \ldots, m\},$$

where $W = [w_1, \ldots, w_m\}$ is a weighting vector, such that $w_i \in [0, 1]$ and $\Sigma_i w_i = 1$. $\beta_h = w_h / \sum_2^m w_k, h = 2, \ldots, m$, and $B = \{b_1, \ldots, b_m\}$ is a vector associated with A such that

$$B = \sigma(A) = \{a_{\sigma(1)}, \ldots, a_{\sigma(n)}\},$$

where, $a_{\sigma(j)} \leq a_{\sigma(i)}\ \forall i \leq j$, with σ being a permutation over the set of labels A.

Example 8.2. Suppose that we want to aggregate by means of the LOWA operator the four labels $\{EU, VLC, EL, C\}$. Assuming that the weighting vector $W = [0.3, 0.2, 0.4, 0.1]$, the general expression of the aggregation of labels is

$$\phi(EU, VLC, EL, C) = [0.3, 0.2, 0.4, 0.1] \cdot (C, EL, VLC, EU)$$
$$= \mathscr{C}^4\{(0.3, C), (0.2, EL), (0.4, VLC), (0.1, EU)\}.$$

Then we obtain the final result applying the recursive definition of the convex combination, $\mathscr{C}^4$, as follows. First, we develop $\mathscr{C}^4$ until we obtain its simplest expression using the following steps:

1. For $m = 4$,

$$\mathscr{C}^4\{(0.3, C)(0.2, EL)(0.4, VLC), (0.1, EU)\}$$
$$= 0.3 \odot C \oplus \mathscr{C}^3\{(0.29, EL)(0.57, VLC)(0.14, EU)\}.$$

2. For $m = 3$,

$$\mathscr{C}^3\{(0.29, EL), (0.57, VLC), (0.14, EU)\}$$
$$= 0.29 \odot EL \oplus \mathscr{C}^2\{(0.57, VLC), (0.14, EU)\}.$$

Now we are going to go back solving the simplest cases until we obtain the final result:

1. For $m = 2$,

$$\mathscr{C}^2\{(0.57, VLC), (0.14, EU)\} = 0.57 \odot VLC \oplus (1 - 0.57) \odot EU = VLC(s_2),$$

since as $VLC = s_2$ and $EU = s_1$, then

$\min\{9, 1 + \text{round}(0.57.(2 - 1))\} = \min\{8, 1 + \text{round}(0.57)\} = \min\{8, 2\} = 2.$

2. For $m = 3$,

$$\mathscr{C}^3\{(0.29, EL), (0.57, VLC), (0.14, EU)\}$$
$$= 0.29 \odot EL \oplus \mathscr{C}^2\{(0.57, VLC)(0.14, EU)\} = SC(s_3),$$

since as $EL = s_7$ and $VLC = s_2$, then

$\min\{8, 2 + \text{round}(0.29 \cdot (7 - 2))\} = \min\{8, 2 + \text{round}(1.45)\} = \min\{8, 3\} = 3.$

3. Finally, we obtain the result for $m = 4$,

$$\mathscr{C}^4\{(0.3, C)(0.2, EL)(0.4, VLC)(0.1, EU)\}$$
$$= 0.3 \odot C \oplus \mathscr{C}^3\{(0.29, EL), (0.57, VLC\}(0.14, EU)\} = MC(s_5),$$

since as $C = s_8$ and $SC = s_3$, then

$\min\{8, 3 + \text{round}(0.3 \cdot (8-3))\} = \min\{8, 3 + \text{round}(1.5)\} = \min\{8, 5\} = 5.$

Next, we present an extension of the LOWA operator, an inverse LOWA operator, which will be used in the definition of the LWA operator.

Definition 8.3. *An inverse-linguistic ordered weighted averaging (I-LOWA) operator, ϕ^I, is a type of LOWA operator in which*

$$B = \sigma^I(A) = \{a_{\sigma(1)}, \ldots, a_{\sigma(n)}\},$$

where $a_{\sigma(i)} \leq a_{\sigma(j)} \forall\, i \leq j$.

The LOWA operator is a rational aggregation operator because it verifies the following properties and axioms of any acceptable aggregation operator [28]: increasingly monotonous, "orand" operator, unrestricted domain, unanimity or idempotence, positive association of social and individual values, independence of irrelevant alternatives, citizen sovereignty, neutrality with respect to alternatives, and neutrality with respect to voters.

A goal in the LOWA operator is that the final result reflects the information supplied by the majority of the aggregated elements of information. Traditionally, the majority is defined as a threshold number of people. Fuzzy majority is a soft majority concept, which is manipulated via a fuzzy logic–based calculus of linguistically quantified propositions. In Ref. 34, Kacprzyk specified fuzzy majority rule by means of a linguistic quantifier to derive various solution concepts for group decision-making problems. Here we work in a similar way, but in the field of quantifier-guided aggregations [71]. Before showing how to do so, we introduce the concept of fuzzy linguistic quantifier. As shown below, according to Yager's proposal [65], we represent explicitly the fuzzy majority via a fuzzy linguistic quantifier that is used to calculate the weights of LOWA operator. When a nondecreasing relative quantifier Q is used, the weights are obtained as [65]

$$w_i = Q(i/n) - Q((i-1)/n) \qquad i = 1, \ldots, n.$$

The membership function of a nondecreasing proportional quantifier is defined as follows:

$$Q(r) = \begin{cases} 0 & \text{if r<a} \\ \dfrac{r-a}{b-a} & \text{if a}\leq\text{r<b} \\ 1 & \text{if r}\geq\text{b,} \end{cases}$$

with $a, b, r \in [0, 1]$. Some examples of proportional quantifiers are "most," "at least half," and "as many as possible," where the parameters, (a, b) are $(0.3, 0.8)$, $(0, 0.5)$, and $(0.5, 1)$, respectively.

When a fuzzy linguistic quantifier Q is used to compute the weights of the LOWA operator ϕ, it is symbolized by ϕ_Q. Similarly, the I-LOWA operator is symbolized by ϕ_Q^I.

Example 8.3. Suppose that we want to aggregate by means of the LOWA operator the four labels $\{EU, VLC, EL, C\}$. If we use the fuzzy linguistic quantifier "as many as possible" to calculate the weighting vector [i.e., $W = \{0, 0, 0.5, 0.5\}$], the aggregation of the labels, working in the similar way, is the following:

$$\begin{aligned} \phi_Q(EU, VLC, EL, C) &= [0, 0, 0.5, 0.5](C, EL, VLC, EU) \\ &= \mathscr{C}^4\{(0, C), (0, EL), (0.5, VLC), (0.5, EU)\} = VLC. \end{aligned}$$

Two Families of Linguistic Connectives. The following two families of the linguistic connectives are used in the definition of the LWA operator to transform the weighted information under the importance degrees [25].

Linguistic Conjunction Functions $(LC^{\rightarrow})$. The linguistic conjunction functions used in our approach are the following t-norms, which are monotonically nondecreasing in the weights and satisfy the properties required for any transformation function g:

1. *Classical min operator*: $LC_1^{\rightarrow}(v, a) = \min(v, a)$, where a is the linguistic information $(a \in S = \{s_0, \ldots, s_T\})$ weighted by the linguistic importance degree $v (v \in S)$.
2. *Nilpotent min operator*:

$$LC_2^{\rightarrow}(v, a) = \begin{cases} \min(v, a) & \text{if } v > \text{neg}(a) \\ s_0 & \text{otherwise.} \end{cases}$$

3. *Weakest conjunction*:

$$LC_3^{\rightarrow}(v,a) = \begin{cases} \min(v,a) & \text{if } \max\ (v,a) = s_T \\ s_0 & \text{otherwise.} \end{cases}$$

Linguistic Implication Functions($LI^{\rightarrow}$). The linguistic implication functions that we use are monotonically nonincreasing in the weights and satisfy the properties required for any transformation function g:

1. *Kleene–Dienes implication function*:

$$LI_1^{\rightarrow}(v,a) = \max(\text{neg}(v), a).$$

2. *Gödel's implication function*:

$$LI_2^{\rightarrow}(v,a) = \begin{cases} s_T & \text{if } v \leq \text{a} \\ a & \text{otherwise.} \end{cases}$$

3. *Fodor's implication function*:

$$LI_3^{\rightarrow}(v,a) = \begin{cases} s_T & \text{if} v \leq a \\ \max(\text{neg}(v), a) & \text{otherwise.} \end{cases}$$

LWA Operator. By considering the aforementioned ideas, and assuming a linguistic framework, that is, an ordered linguistic term set S to express the information and the weights, the aggregation operators and transformation functions of the LWA operator [25] are the following:

1. *Aggregation operators*: LOWA or I-LOWA.
2. *Transformation functions*: $g_{(\text{LOWA})} = LC^{\rightarrow}(v,a)$ or $g_{(\text{I-LOWA})} = LI^{\rightarrow}(v,a)$.

Definition 8.4. *The aggregation of the set of weighted individual opinions,* $\{(p_1,a_1),\ldots,(p_m,a_m)\}$, *according to the LWA operator,* Ω, is defined as

$$\Omega[(p_1,a_1),\ldots,(p_m,a_m)] = f[g(p_1,a_1),\ldots,g(p_m,a_m)],$$

where $f \in \{\phi_Q, \phi_Q^I\}$ *is a linguistic aggregation operator of transformed information and* g *is an importance transformation function such that* $g \in \{LC_1^{\rightarrow}, LC_2^{\rightarrow}, LC_3^{\rightarrow}\}$ *if* $f = \phi_Q$, *and* $g \in \{LI_1^{\rightarrow}, LI_2^{\rightarrow}, LI_3^{\rightarrow}\}$ *if* $f = \phi_Q^I$.

The LWA operator is based on quantifier-guided aggregation operators (LOWA and I-LOWA operator guided by fuzzy majority), and therefore we may assert that it is a type of fuzzy majority-guided weighted aggregation operator. It should be observed that the LWA operator tries to reduce the effect of elements of low importance. To do so, when $f = \phi_Q$, the elements with low importance are transformed into small values, and when $f = \phi_Q^I$, into large values.

8.4 DISTRIBUTED INTELLIGENT AGENT MODEL FOR INFORMATION GATHERING

In this section we present an application of the LWA operator as a way to aggregate the evaluations of the information from intelligent agents on the Internet, in order to get the best and newest information for users. Other approaches of a similar type have been proposed. In Refs. 72 and 73, a combination of linguistic information is presented in order to negotiate and reach a consensus among agents. Linguistic information aggregation between relevant document and user importance is also detailed in Ref. 6 and 35. We shall board the problem of aggregation to match, once a user's weighted query has been given, the fulfilment of the agents to find relevant documents and the degrees of importance of the user. A possible use of this type of aggregation between documents and user weights over a certain query would be unsettled on a future work.

Next, the concept of intelligent software agents is presented, then an architecture for these agents is proposed, and finally, a way to aggregate this communication through the LWA operator is given.

8.4.1 Concept of Intelligent Software Agent

Intelligent software agents have been defined several times in the literature [21,23,24,44,52,62]. However, research work does not seem to agree regarding a profile of such agents, due to the large number of applications in which they are used, and to the evolution of the single term *agent* as opposed to such terms as *software agent* and *intelligent agent.* Hence we do not give a new definition of this concept, nor do we review those given previously, but present the primary ideas behind all these terms as they relate to our specific purpose.

The concept of *agent* or rather, *autonomous agent* must be explained first. This term is strongly associated with behavior-based AI as opposed to knowledge-based AI [44] and is led by expert systems. As defined by Maes in Ref. 44, an agent is a system that tries to achieve predefined goals in a complex and dynamic environment. Thus, depending on the environment, we can make the first clear distinction by splitting the concept of agent into those typically called *robots*, whose environment is basically physical, and those called *software agents*, which inhabit in an environment consisting of computers and networks. Both concepts share a primary characteristic: They are autonomous (i.e., they are able to operate by themselves and determine how to achieve their goals). However, as this feature is supposed to be inherent in an agent, an *autonomous agent* is usually simply called an *agent.* As for the term *intelligent*, there are several discussions in the literature [21,52] about how to determine whether or not an agent is intelligent by nature. We shall consider them as intelligent, since in some sense they present human behavior that lessens the work of Internet users. Hence the agents with which we are dealing are really *intelligent software agents*, even though we sometimes use the term *intelligent agent* without the term *software*, as they are supposed to be in an environment of computers and networks (i.e., the Internet).

8.4.2 Distributed Multiagent Architecture on the Internet

At present, designed intelligent agents are related closely to the Internet. These agents not only retrieve and filter information (in the sense of Web documents) [2,45,51], but also handle electronic mail, news lists, FAQ lists, and so on [36,43,62]. These are properly called *interface agents* [43], since they are closer to the user. However, all the information that these agents get comes from somewhere or something. There are servers throughout the Internet that proportionate these information, mail, news, and FAQ services. The agents closest to these data sources are called *information agents* [36,55]. But precisely because of this avalanche of agents, Internet users feel completely lost and overloaded with information, since they can access their interface or personal agents as well as general information agents. This problem reveals the need for an organization among the agents within the Internet that implies both agent hierarchy and architecture. Since the elements taking part in the retrieval information process are distributed, it seems sensible to consider the architecture as distributed. Several architectures for these multiagent distributed models have been proposed and reviewed [8,12,37,41,55,62]. However, the architecture that better fits our model is the one proposed by Sycara et al. [55]. In this architecture, in addition to the aforementioned *interface* and *information agents*, the authors consider a third type of agent, the *task agent*. These agents deal with the decision-making process and exchange of information with information agents, resolving conflicts and fusing information in order to release the interface agents from some of the tasks that make them ineffective. A hierarchical model with five levels is proposed:

1. *Internet users*, who look for Web documents on the Internet by means of a weighted query where a set of terms related to the documents desired is specified.
2. *Interface agents* (one for the user, generally), which communicate the user's weighted query to the task agents and filter the documents retrieved from task agents to give users those that best satisfy their needs.
3. *Task agents* (one for the interface agent, generally), which communicate the user's query to the information agents and get those documents from every information agent that best fulfills the query, fusing them and resolving the possible conflicts among information agents.
4. *Information agents*, which receive the weighted query from the task agents, look for the information in the data sources, and give the retrieved documents back to the preceding level.
5. *Information sources*, consisting of all data sources within the Internet, such as databases and information repositories.

This model is shown in Figure 8.4. In the next section, an application of the LWA operator used by the task agents is proposed as a way of carrying out the decision-making process and communication among these levels.

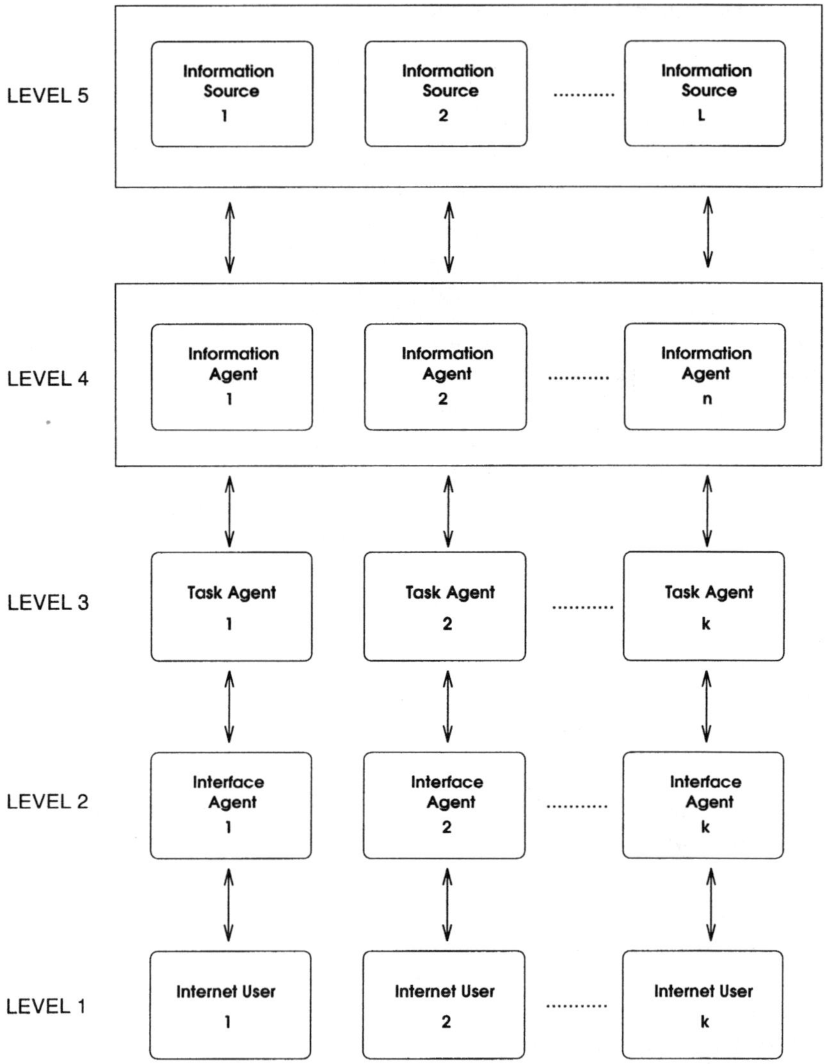

FIGURE 8.4 General overview of the distributed intelligent agent model.

8.4.3 Information Gathering Through the LWA Operator

In the process of information gathering, as a response to a user's query on the model presented, there are two parts:

1. On the one hand, there is communication between agents at levels 5–4 and 4–3, which is far from the user's participation and where the question that the task agent must answer concerns which information agents would better satisfy the user's needs.

2. On the other hand, there is communication between agents at levels 3–2 and the user, where the information element is specifically the set of retrieved documents that will be analyzed and filtered by the interface agents.

Several approaches based on multiagent models to carry out this process have been proposed in the literature [8, 12, 55], especially at levels 1 and 2 [2, 36, 43, 45, 46], where only the interface agent and the user act. We shall focus first on step 1 of the process, detailing the communication among agents at various levels and proposing the use of LWA as a possible aggregation operator between the importance of the criteria of the user query and satisfaction of these criteria on the part of each information agent.

In the levels considered (3–4 and 2–3), there are two main flows where the weighted information to be aggregated appears. Such flows are represented in Figure 8.5, where the elements related to a single-user have been considered. The process can be described as follows:

1. An *Internet user* makes a query to look for documents related to the terms $\{t_1, t_2, \ldots, t_m\}$, which are weighted by a linguistic degree of importance $\{p_1, p_2, \ldots, p_m\}$, $p_i \in S$ Both sets of values are given by the user to the *interface agent*.
2. The *interface agent* gives the terms and their importance weights to the *task agent*.
3. The *task agent* makes the query to all the information agents to which it is connected and gives them the terms $\{t_1, t_2, \ldots, t_m\}$.
4. All the *information agents* that have received the query look for the information that best satisfies it in the information sources, and retrieve from them the documents.
5 The *task agent* receives from every *information agent* h a set of documents and their relevances (D^h, R^h) ordered decreasingly by relevance [53], where every document d_j^h has an associated degree of relevance $r_j^h(j = 1, \ldots, \text{card}(D^h))$. It also receives a linguistic degree of satisfaction [6] $c_1^h, c_2^h, \ldots, c_m^h, c_i^h \in S$ of this set of documents with regard to every term of the query.
    5.1. The *task agent* aggregates through the LWA operator Ω linguistic information weights, the satisfactions of the terms of the query from every *information agent* c_i^h, and the importance weights that the user assigned to these terms p_i as follows. Let $((p_1, c_1^h), (p_2, c_2^h), \ldots, (p_m, c_m^h)), p_i, c_i^h \in S$ be the pairs of importance and satisfaction to be aggregated by every information agent h. According to the LWA operator definition given in Section 8.3, the aggregation of the pair associated with every term is obtained as

$$g(p_i, c_i^h) \qquad i = 1, \ldots, m,$$

where g is an importance transformation function $g \in \{LC_1^{\rightarrow}, LC_2^{\rightarrow}, LC_3^{\rightarrow}\}$. Hence the overall fulfilment of the information agent h, called

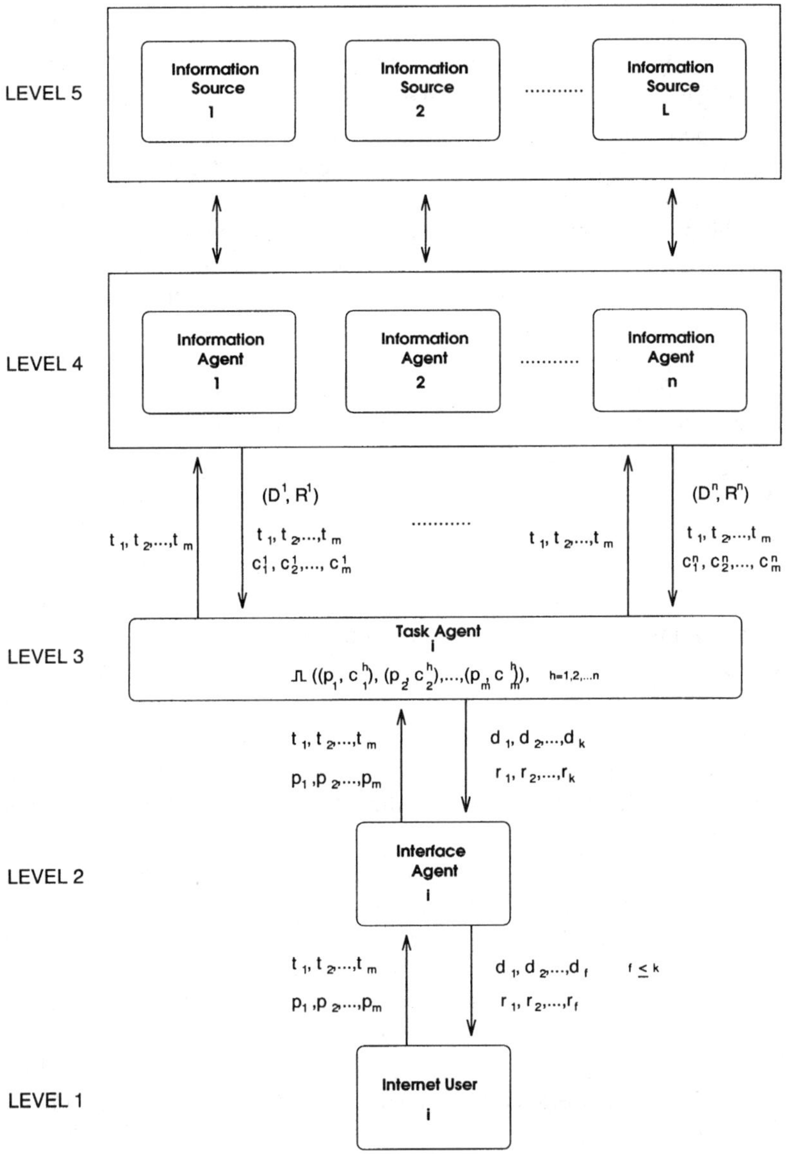

FIGURE 8.5 Overview of information flows in a single-user scheme.

λ^h, is defined by the following expression:

$$\lambda^h = \Omega((p_1, c_1^h), (p_2, c_2^h), \ldots, (p_m, c_m^h)) = f(g(p_1, c_1^h), \ldots, g(p_m, c_m^h)),$$

where $f = \phi_Q$ (i.e., a LOWA operator guided by a fuzzy majority represented by the quantifier Q, which could be fixed by an expert).

5.2. Once the *task agent* has calculated the overall performances $\{\lambda^1, \ldots, \lambda^n\}$, $\lambda^j \in S$ of the n *information agents* through the LWA operator, it must decide which agent best fulfills the user's query. For this purpose, the task agent orders the performances decreasingly and obtains the vector $\{\Theta_1, \ldots, \Theta_n\}$, $\Theta_j \in S$, as follows:

$$\{\Theta_1, \ldots, \Theta_n\} = \sigma(\{\lambda^1, \ldots, \lambda^n\}) = \{\lambda^{\sigma(1)}, \ldots, \lambda^{\sigma(n)}\},$$

where σ is a permutation over the set of labels $\{\lambda^1, \ldots, \lambda^n\}$

$$\lambda^{\sigma(j)} \leq \lambda^{\sigma(i)} \quad \forall i \leq j.$$

To better gather the documents, the task agent may decide on two alternatives:

(a) Selection of the information agent with the higher query satisfaction, Θ_1. This alternative has a significant disadvantage, as the set of documents of the agent selected contains some documents that probably will be less relevant to the query than some of the best documents of the other information agents. This problem leads us to the second alternative, based on selection of the best documents from every agent.

(b) For the purpose of selecting a number of documents from every agent being proportional to the degree of satisfaction of such an agent, we assign a probability of selection according to a scheme of selection probabilities called *linear ranking* [1], commonly used in the reproduction process of *evolutionary algorithms*, whose expression is as follows:

$$P_s(\Theta_h) = \frac{1}{n}\left(\eta_{\max} - (\eta_{\max} - \eta_{\min}) \cdot \frac{h-1}{n-1}\right),$$

$$\sum_{i=1}^{n} P_s(\Theta_i) = 1, \quad P_s(\Theta_i) \in [0, 1], \quad \textit{and} \quad P_s(\Theta_i) \geq P_s(\Theta_j), \quad i \leq j,$$

where $h = 1, \ldots, n$ and with $\eta_{\min}$ being a parameter that an expert can fix, such as $1 \leq \eta_{\max} \leq 2$ and $\eta_{\min} = 2 - \eta_{\max}$. This parameter should be approximately 1 when the difference in the satisfaction of the query by the information agents is small, and should be approximately 2 when this difference is notable, since the difference between the probabilities of the best and worse agents should be accentuated. Furthermore, as this scheme depends on the ranking, it assigns different probabilities to agents with the same label of satisfaction. To avoid this, we shall assign to these agents the average of the set of probabilities found using the scheme. Finally, the number of documents $k(\Theta_h)$ that the *task agent* would select from such an agent is expressed as

$$k(\Theta_h) = \frac{\sum_{i=1}^{n} \text{card}(D^i)}{n} \cdot P_s(\Theta_h).$$

6. The *interface agent* receives from the *task agent* an ordered list of documents and their relevances $\{(d_j^h, r_j^h)\}$, where $d_j^h \in D^h, r_j^h \in R^h, 1 \leq h \leq n$ and $j = 1, \ldots, k(\Theta_h)$.

7. The *interface agent* filters these documents to give to the user only those documents that best fulfill his or her needs.

8.5 SUMMARY

In this chapter we have satisfied two goals: (1) the study of fuzzy linguistic approach to solve problems, and (2) its application to a distributed intelligent agent system for information gathering on the Internet. We have analyzed various proposals of linguistic approach, showing how to choose the linguistic term set and its semantic and how to combine linguistic information. In particular, we have presented the LWA operator, which combines linguistic weighted information. This is a tool with a great potential to solve problems in which linguistic information with different degrees of importance appears.

We have presented a distributed intelligent agent system in which communication of the evaluation of the retrieved information among the agents is carried out by using the LWA operator. Using the LWA as an aggregation operator in the information-gathering process provides two outstanding advantages:

- The task agent can obtain an overall evaluation of the satisfaction of a query from any information agent, taking into account the degree of importance that the user assigns to the terms of the query.
- The LWA operator allows greater flexibility in the information-gathering process, reducing the effect of the low satisfaction rating of some terms within the overall performance of the information agent.

Finally, we must point out that an aggregation of linguistic information would be needed to filter the final set of documents by the interface agents. This aggregation would be unsettled on a future work.

REFERENCES

1. J. M. Baker, Adaptive selection methods for genetic algorithms, in *Proc. First International Conference on Genetic Algorithms and Their Applications*, Lawrence Erlbaum, Hillsdale, NJ, 1985, pp. 101–111.
2. M. Balabanovic, Y. Shoham, and Y. Yun, *An Adaptive Agent for Automated Web Browsing*, Stanford Univ. Tech. Rep. CS-TN-97-52, 1997.

3. F. Beyth-Marom, How probable is probable? A numerical taxonomy translation of verbal probability expressions, *J. Forecast.*, 1:257–269, 1982.
4. P. P. Bonissone, A fuzzy sets based linguistic approach: theory and applications, in M. M. Gupta and E. Sanchez (eds.), *Approximate Reasoning in Decision Analysis*, North-Holland, New York, 1982, pp. 329–339.
5. P. P. Bonissone and K. S. Decker, Selecting uncertainty calculi and granularity: an experiment in trading-off precision and complexity, in L. H. Kanal and J. F. Lemmer (eds.), *Uncertainty in Artificial Intelligence*, North-Holland, New York, 1986, pp. 217–247.
6. G. Bordogna and G. Passi, A fuzzy linguistic approach generalizing Boolean information retrieval: a model and its evaluation, *J. Am. Soc. Inf. Sci.* 44:70–82, 1993.
7. G. Bordogna, M. Fredizzi, and G. Passi, A linguistic modelling of consensus in group decision making based on OWA operators, *IEEE Trans. Syst. Man Cybern. A: Syst. Hum.*, 27:126–132, 1997.
8. C. Brown, L. Gasser, and D. E. O'Leary, AI on the WWW: supply and demand agents, *IEEE Expert*, 1995, pp. 50–55.
9. J. J. Buckley, The multiple judge, multiple criteria ranking problem: a fuzzy set approach, *Fuzzy Sets Syst.* 13:23–37, 1984.
10. C. Carlsson and R. Fullér, On fuzzy screening systems, in *Proc. 3rd European Congress on Intelligent Technologies and Soft Computing*, Aachen, Germany, 1995, pp. 1261–1264.
11. P. Chang and Y. Chen, A fuzzy multicriteria decision making method for technology transfer strategy selection in biotechnology, *Fuzzy Sets Syst.*, 63:131–139, 1994.
12. A. Chavez, A. Moukas, and P. Maes, Challenger: a multi-agent system for distributed resource allocation, in *Proc International Conference on Autonomous Agents*, CA, 1997.
13. S. J. Chen and C. L. Hwang, *Fuzzy Multiple Attribute Decision Making:Methods and Applications*, Springer-Verlag, New York, 1992.
14. W. Cholewa, Aggregation of fuzzy opinions: an axiomatic approach, *fuzzy Sets syst.* 17:249–259, 1985.
15. R. Degani and G. Bortolan, The problem of linguistic approximation in clinical decision making, *Int. J. Approx. Reason.*, 2:143–162, 1988.
16. M. Delgado, J. L. Verdegay, and M. A. Vila, Linguistic decision making models, *Int. J. Intell. Syst.*, 7:479–492, 1992.
17. M. Delgado, J. L. Verdegay, and M. A. Vila, On aggregation operations of linguistic labels, *Int. J. Intell. Syst.* 8:351–370, 1993.
18. M. Delgado, J. L. Verdegay, and M. A. Vila, A model for linguistic partial information in decision making problems, *Int. J. Intell. Syst.*, 9:365–378, 1994.
19. D. Dubois, H. Prade, and C. Testemale, Weighted fuzzy pattern matching, *Fuzzy Sets Syst.*, 28:313–331, 1988.
20. D. Dubois and J. L. Koning, Social choice axioms for fuzzy set aggregation, *Fuzzy Sets Syst.*, 43:257–274, 1991.
21. O. Etzioni and D. S. Weld, Intelligent agents on the Internet: fact, fiction and forecast, *IEEE Expert*, 1995, pp. 44–49.
22. M. Fedrizzi and L. Mich, Rule based model for consensus reaching group decisions support, in *Proc. 3rd Conference on Information Processing and Management of Uncertainty*, Palma de Mallorca, Spain, 1992, pp. 301–304.

23. S. Franklin and A. Graesser, Is it an agent, or just a program? A taxonomy for autonomous agents, in *Proc. 3rd International Workshop on Agent Theories, Architectures and Languages*, 1996.

24. J. A. Hendler, Intelligent agents: where AI meets information technology, *IEEE Expert*, 1996, pp. 20–23.

25. F. Herrera and E. Herrera-Viedma, Aggregation operators for linguistic weighted information, *IEEE Trans. Syst. Man Cybern.*, 27:646–656, 1997.

26. F. Herrera and J. L. Verdegay, Linguistic assessments in group decision, in *Proc. First European Congress on Fuzzy and Intelligent Technologies*, Aachen, Germany, 1993, pp. 941–948.

27. F. Herrera, E. Herrera-Viedma, and J. L. Verdegay, A sequential selection process in group decision making with linguistic assessment, *Inf. Sci.* 85:223–239, 1995.

28. F. Herrera, E. Herrera-Viedma, and J. L. Verdegay, Direct approach processes in group decision making using linguistic OWA operators, *Fuzzy Sets Syst.*, 79:175–190, 1996.

29. F. Herrera, E. Herrera-Viedma, and J. L. Verdegay, A model of consensus in group decision making under linguistic assessments, *Fuzzy Sets Syst.*, 79:73–87, 1996.

30. F. Herrera, E. Herrera-Viedma, and J. L. Verdegay, A rational consensus model in group decision making using linguistic assessments, *Fuzzy Sets Syst.*, 88:31–49, 1997.

31. F. Herrera, E. Herrera-Viedma, and J. L. Verdegay, Consensus based on fuzzy coincidence for group decision making in linguistic setting, in J. Kacprzyk, H. Nurmi, and M. Fedrizzi (eds.), *Consensus Under Fuzziness*, (Kluwer Academic, Dordrecht, The Netherlands, 1997, pp. 121–146.

32. F. Herrera, E. Herrera-Viedma, and J. L. Verdegay, Linguistic measures based on fuzzy coincidence for reaching consensus in group decision making, *Int. J. Approx. Reason.*, 16:309–334, 1997.

33. F. Herrera, E. Herrera-Viedma, and J. L. Verdegay, Choice processes for non-homogeneous group decision making in linguistic setting, *Fuzzy Sets Syst.*, 94:287–308, 1997.

34. J. Kacprzyk, Group decision making with a fuzzy linguistic majority, *Fuzzy Sets Syst.*, 18:105–118, 1986.

35. D. H. Kraft, G. Bordogna, and G. Pasi, An extended fuzzy linguistic approach to generalize Boolean information retrieval, *Inf. Sci.*, 2:119–134, 1994.

36. B. Krulwich, Learning user interests across heterogeneous document databases, in *Proc. AAAI Spring Symposium on Information Gathering from Heterogeneus, Distributed Environments*, 1995.

37. Y. Lashkari, M. Metral, and P. Maes, Collaborative interface agents, *Proc. 12th National Conference on Artificial Intelligence*, Vol. 1, Seattle, WA, 1994.

38. C. K. Law, Using fuzzy numbers in educational grading system, *Fuzzy Sets Syst.*, 83:311–323, 1996.

39. H. M. Lee, Group decision making using fuzzy sets theory for evaluating the rate of aggregative risk in software development, *Fuzzy Sets Syst.*, 80:261–271, 1996.

40. H. M. Lee, Applying fuzzy set theory to evaluate the rate of aggregative risk in software development, *Fuzzy Sets Syst.*, 80:323–336, 1996.

41. M. Lejter and T. Dean, A framework for the development of multiagent architectures, *IEEE Expert*, 1996, pp. 47–59.

42. C. Liu, M. Wang, and Y. Pang, A multiple criteria linguistic decision model (MCLDM) for human decision making, *Eur. J. Oper. Res.*, 76:466–485, 1994.
43. P. Maes, Agents that reduce work and information overload, *Commun. ACM*, 37:31–40, 1994.
44. P. Maes, Modeling adaptive autonomous agents, in C. G. Langton (ed.), *Artificial Life: An Overview*, MIT Press, Cambridge, MA, 1995, pp. 135–162.
45. M. J. Martin-Bautista, H. L. Larsen, J. Nicolaisen, and T. Svendsen, An approach to an adaptive information retrieval agent using genetic algorithms with fuzzy set genes, in *Proc. 6th IEEE International Conference on Fuzzy Systems*, Barcelona, Spain, 1997, pp. 1227–1232.
46. M. McElligot and H. Sorensen, An evolutionary connectionist approach to personal information filtering, in *Proc. Irish Neural Networks Conference*, Dublin, Ireland, 1994, pp. 141–146.
47. L. Mich, L. Gaio, and M. Fedrizzi, On fuzzy logic-based consensus in group decision, in *Proc. 5th International Fuzzy Systems Association World Congress*, Seoul, Korea, 1993, pp. 698–700.
48. G. A. Miller, The magical number seven or minus two: some limits on our capacity of processing information, *Psychol. Rev.*, 63:81–97, 1956.
49. G. A. Miller, The organization of lexical memory, in G. A. and N. C. Waugh (eds.), *The Pathology of Memory*, Talland, New York, 1969.
50. J. Montero, Aggregation of fuzzy opinions in a non-homogeneous group, *Fuzzy Sets Syst.*, 25:15–20, 1988.
51. M. Pazzani, L. Nguyen, and S. Mantik, Learning from hotlists and coldlists: towards a WWW information filtering and seeking agent, in *Proc. AI Tools Conference*, Washington, DC, 1995.
52. C. J. Petrie, Agent-based engineering, the Web and intelligence, *IEEE Expert*, 1996, pp. 24–29.
53. G. Salton and M. G. McGill, *Introduction to Modern Information Retrieval*, McGraw-Hill, New York, 1983.
54. E. Sanchez, Importance in knowledge systems, *Inf. Syst.*, 14:455–464, 1989.
55. K. Sycara, A. Pannu, M. Williamson, and D. Zeng, Distributed intelligent agents, *IEEE Expert*, 1996, pp. 36–46.
56. P. Szolovits and S. G. Pauker, Categorical and probabilistic reasoning in medical diagnosis, *Artifi. Intell. J.*, 11:115–144, 1978.
57. M. Tong and P. P. Bonissone, A linguistic approach to decision making with fuzzy sets, *IEEE Trans. Systems Man Cybern.*, 10:716–723, 1980.
58. M. Tong and P. P. Bonissone, Linguistic solutions to fuzzy decision problems, *Stud. Manag. Sci.*, 20:323–334, 1984.
59. V. Torra, Negation functions based semantics for ordered linguistic labels, *Int. J. Intell. Syst.*, 11:975–988, 1996.
60. V. Torra, The weighted OWA operator, *Int. J. Intell. Syst.*, 12:153–166, 1997.
61. T. Y. Tseng and C. M. Klein, A new algorithm for fuzzy multicriteria decision making, *Int. J. Approx. Reason.* 6:45–66, 1992.
62. M. Wooldridge and N. Jennings, Intelligent agents: theory and practice, *Knowledge Eng. Rev.*, 10:115–152, 1995.

63. R. R. Yager, A new methodology for ordinal multiobjective decisions based on fuzzy sets, *Decision Sci.*, 12:589–600, 1981.

64. R. R. Yager, A note on weighted queries in information retrieval systems, *J. Am. Soc. Inf. Sci.*, 38:23–24, 1987.

65. R. R. Yager, On ordered weighted averaging aggregation operators in multicriteria decision making, *IEEE Trans. Syst. Man Cybern.*, 18:183–190, 1988.

66. R. R. Yager, Applications and extension of OWA aggregation, *Int. J. Man–Mach. Stud.*, 37:103–132, 1992.

67. R. R. Yager, Fuzzy screening systems, in R. Lowen (ed.), *Fuzzy Logic: State of the Art*, Kluwer Academic, Dordrecht, The Netherlands, 1993, pp. 251–261.

68. R. R. Yager, Non-numeric multi-criteria multi-person decision making, *Group Decision Negot.*, 2:81–93, 1993.

69. R. R. Yager, On weighted median aggregation, *Int. J. Uncertainty Fuzziness Knowledge-Based Syst.*, 2:101–113, 1994.

70. R. R. Yager, An approach to ordinal decision making, *Int. J. Approx. Reason.*, 12:237–261, 1995.

71. R. R. Yager, Quantifier guided aggregation using OWA operators, *Int. J. Intell. Syst.*, 11:49–73, 1996.

72. R. R. Yager, Protocol for negotiations among multiple intelligent agents, in J. Kacprzyk, H. Nurmi, and M. Fedrizzi (eds.), *Consensus Under Fuzziness*, (Kluwer Academic, Dordrecht, The Netherlands, 1996, pp. 165–174.

73. R. R. Yager, Intelligent agents for World Wide Web, *Int. J. Intell. Syst.*, 12:379–390, 1997.

74. R. R. Yager, L. S. Goldstein, and E. Mendels, FUZMAR: an approach to aggregating market research data based on fuzzy reasoning, *Fuzzy Sets Syst.*, 68:1–11, 1994.

75. L. A. Zadeh, The concept of a linguistic variable and its applications to approximate reasoning, Part I, *Inf. Sci.* 8:199–249, 1975; Part II, *Inf. Sci.*, 8:301–357, 1975; Part III, *Inf. Sci.*, 9:43–80, 1975.

76. L. A. Zadeh, A computational approach to fuzzy quantifiers in natural languages, *comput. Math. Appl.*, 9:149–184, 1983.

Chapter 9

NUMERIC ROBUSTNESS AND LINGUISTIC PERSPICUITY: A HYBRID APPROACH TO KNOWLEDGE ACQUISITION

THOMAS WHALEN
Georgia State University, Atlanta, Georgia

GWANGYONG GIM
Soong Sil University, Seoul, Korea

9.1 INTRODUCTION

Acquiring knowledge from an expert is a major bottleneck in the development of expert systems. Automated knowledge acquisition methods, which generate expert systems based on sample data, circumvent this bottleneck partially. *Automated knowledge acquisition* (AKA) refers to a body of techniques that accept a database of examples and generate a formal system that displays expertlike behavior. Each example consists of a set of predictor variables and one or more criterion variables; the resulting formal system takes the predictor variables for new cases as inputs, and outputs the predicted value(s) of the criterion variable(s). The AKA concept is very similar to the concept of machine learning. Insofar as they differ, it is because machine learning has more of a flavor of fundamental research in cognitive science, whereas AKA connotes knowledge engineering aimed at developing knowledge-based tools to solve a practical problem. Three very important classes of AKA techniques are regressionlike techniques, supervised artificial neural networks, and rule induction.

In particular, the rule sets that simple example-based inductive mechanisms create can help knowledge engineers and domain experts during early stages of knowledge acquisition [21]. A computer-generated expert system, especially in

Computing with Words, Edited by Paul P. Wang.
ISBN 0-471-35374-4

the form of if–then rules, can do a better job of inspiring an expert to make improvements and corrections than a blank page and a request to "tell what you know" can. Therefore, what is important is not whether human judgment is better or worse than AKA but how different structures of computer-represented knowledge interact with an expert's ability to critique and modify computer-generated predictive models [9].

Although these systems are less robust than linear and neural models when dealing with noisy data, their perspicuity makes them useful for "breaking the ice" with a quick, inexpensive demonstration system. There is no guarantee the knowledge structures arising from AKA will represent meaningful ontological categories or causal relations [9]. However, they can stimulate a human expert to a better conceptualization and communication of his or her expertise. Experts should examine and validate the outputs of AKA to ensure that they are meaningful as well as predictive. For them to do so, it is important to present the structure and content of the knowledge system in a way that the experts can readily understand. Similarly, the end user is in a much better position to judge the appropriate degree of reliance to place on a decision support system if the knowledge it contains can be expressed clearly than if the system functions as a "black box."

9.2 DIMENSIONS OF KNOWLEDGE

Traditional epistemology has assumed that we acquire and represent knowledge symbolically by a collection of declarative sentences (or sentencelike expressions) that represent facts about the world. We observe ourselves conversing, writing, and lecturing by means of natural or technical language, and stating conclusions based on making inferences through transmitted sentences. In this chapter we refer to knowledge that is built up by joining together groups of sentencelike expressions as *articulate* knowledge, since the word *articulate* can mean either "composed of distinct, meaningful syllables or words" or "consisting of sections united by joints."

Epistemological analyses have focused primarily on this symbolically expressed declarative knowledge. However, Ryle [15], among others, objected to the preoccupation of philosophers with facts and argued that acquiring linguistically encoded knowledge is only a small part of human cognition. He emphasized a distinction between *knowing how* (procedural knowledge) and *knowing that* (declarative knowledge). In general, the expression *knowing that* requires completion by a declarative sentence, whereas the expression *knowing how* is completed by an infinitive specifying activity.

Some of what we know how to do, we can also explain using natural language, perhaps augmented with a technical vocabulary. However, there are also many things we know how to do without being able to state linguistically how we do them. The former case we refer to as *articulate procedural knowledge*, the latter as *inarticulate procedural knowledge*. Inarticulate knowledge is difficult to express in "meaningful syllables or words" in part because it is a relatively seamless unity of sensation, perception, and action—it does not consist of conceptual "sections united by joints." Even some of our declarative knowledge has an inarticulate element; for example, we may be able to name an image without being able to describe it or give rules for recognizing it. Much of the discipline of knowledge engineering has consisted of techniques for turning inarticulate knowledge into articulate knowledge prior to transcribing the knowledge into symbolic computer codes.

9.2.1 Articulate Versus Inarticulate

Strongly Articulate Approaches. Cognitive scientists involved in constructing models of knowledge representation have often used some version of articulate representation. Conventional database systems are an extreme case of the articulate approach for *knowing that*. While a database may consist largely of numbers, each number is clearly labeled with respect to what it is measuring and its units of measurement, and thus represents an articulate expression such as "The hourly wage of employee #436655 is $14.50." High-level programming languages use symbols to encode *knowing how*; an early example is COBOL, which mimics a restricted subset of natural language very closely. Almost all rule-based systems use symbols to represent or acquire expert knowledge. For example, the family of techniques derived from ID3 [13] treats the data as primarily nominal (articulate) to find a set of rules.

Mixed Articulate/Inarticulate Approaches. However, as cognitive science developed, psychologists and computer scientists found that simply listing all the applicable symbols was too impoverished an approach. Fuzzy logic systems are one highly developed way to combine the strengths of the qualitative and numeric approaches. Declarations about data and the rules for processing it are expressed in the language of symbolic logic, but with numerical grades of truth or applicability. Fuzzy inference retains much of the perspicuity of inferences made via linguistic expressions while acquiring the flexibility and power of inferences made via mathematical expressions. Three different orders of fuzzy approximate reasoning exist for finding (1) a nonfuzzy numeric output, (2) a discrete solution among a finite list of candidates, and (3) a linguistic assessment of interval or ordinal measures [17]. (The clearest example of a fuzzy system that combines the articulate and inarticulate is one that uses fuzzy truth values such as "not quite true." Such a truth value is represented by a vector of numbers collectively describing the appropriateness of various truth values in a many-valued nonfuzzy logic with the fuzzy concept "not quite true.")

Structural equation modeling [10] is an improved numerical approach for automated fitting and testing of models that incorporate latent variables. It lets analysts combine into a single model insights from a wide variety of experts or information sources with sample data. While the latent variables receive quantitative values, their purpose is to articulate deeper levels of knowledge, including concepts, abstractions, and problem-solving strategies that correspond explicitly to elements of a verbal theory. Such a model can describe complex interrelation among relevant facts of declarative knowledge. Specifically, structural equation modeling enables the investigator to move beyond correlation analysis to considerations of properly conceptualizing these related facts and estimating direct and indirect effects. A related automated knowledge acquisition tool, TETRAD [6], tries to discover latent structure automatically, unlike structural equation modeling, which takes structural elements as inputs derived from theory by the human user.

Strongly Inarticulate Approaches. Numerical tools to acquire or represent uncertain knowledge have played a large role in statistical analysis. Traditional statistical knowledge acquisition methods such as regression have been used for decades by many social scientists. This form of numerical representation of statistical knowledge is generally appropriate for the shallow or simple knowledge of descriptive and inferential statistics (*knowing that* the mean is 76.1) and forecasting (*knowing how* to forecast y for any given value of x).

Neural networks and other connectionist models [14] encode knowledge in a numeric format and access it by a process that is more like pattern recognition than like inference. The goal in connectionist models is a network type of system capable of carrying out cognitive types of operations through numerical methods. Since it is the weights of connections between units that are critical in determining the behavior of such a system, acquiring knowledge depends on procedures for changing these weights. A variety of such procedures exist that enable systems to learn complex structures on the basis of information locally available (at the units connected by the weight that is to be changed).

9.2.2 Declarative Versus Procedural

For many years, social science was dominated by the *behaviorist paradigm*, in which all behavior was to be explained in terms of learned and instinctive connections between stimulus and response. *Learning* meant changing the pattern of response to a given stimulus. Thus the fruit of learning was *knowing how* to respond to a stimulus in order to get a reward; there was no place in behaviorism for *knowing that* any proposition was or was not true. To the most extreme adherent of Skinner's behaviorist paradigm, learning to answer examination essay questions means reinforcing the stimulus–response connections that are rewarded by good grades.

The earliest modern researchers into cognitive representations were reacting against the behaviorist world view [4]. As a result, they tended to employ highly articulate declarative representations. Rule-based systems, such as Newell and Simon's general problem solver and Shortliffe's MYCIN, were written using "If A then B" rules. Such rules, on their face, are declarations that every instance of an A is also an instance of a B. However, rule-based systems give such rules a procedural interpretation. A forward-chaining system interprets "If A then B" as the procedural command "When you detect condition A, perform procedure B." A backward-chaining system interprets "If A then B" to mean "If you want to achieve goal B, try to achieve subgoal A." To the most extreme adherent of Simon's physical symbol system paradigm, learning to ride a bicycle means acquiring the right set of symbolic if–then production rules.

Conventional knowledge acquisition tools such as the ID3 family and statistical regression are used primarily for extracting declarative knowledge. As a result of difficulty with declarative formats in modeling language and cognition, a variety of new approaches to developing a modern, more direct cognitive representation of *knowing how* have been proposed. Semantic nets, frames, and scripts are examples of these alternatives [2]. Generative grammars represent linguistic knowledge in terms of a procedural "competence" rather than a descriptive list of grammatical facts. Anderson [1] suggests that initially, procedural knowledge is encoded declaratively and is converted into more procedural and often less articulate forms in the course of practice (see also Ref. 16). Newell [11] has emphasized the ongoing process of chunking rules into more complex productions that can be smoothly executed as integrated units.

Connectionist networks bear little resemblance to declarative formats. They consist of units that are interconnected rather than being ordered in strings, and typically, these units are not even symbols in the ordinary sense. When some of these units are activated, the network knows how to respond by propagating activation along weighted connections. Therefore, *knowing how* may consist in dynamic processing of inarticulate connectionist knowledge rather than sequential application of articulate declarative rules. On the other hand, some versions of genetic algorithms use automated knowledge acquisition to arrive at computer programs in a recognizable (articulate) symbolic language. Tunable fuzzy controllers acquire knowledge to modify the inarticulate definitions underlying a system of articulate fuzzy if–then rules.

9.3 ADVANTAGES OF HYBRID MODELS

Knowledge structures from AKA may be categorized as linguistic expressions, algebraic expressions, and inarticulate knowledge (see Table 9.1). In particular, the articulate linguistic expressions derived from a rule induction algorithm have higher perspicuity than logit's algebraic expressions or the inarticulate knowledge generated by neural networks. Therefore, it should be easier and more effective for a domain expert to understand, revise, and modify knowledge structured as articulate linguistic expressions rather than in a more inarticulate form.

Algebraic expressions from linear scoring approaches such as logit have low perspicuity compared to linguistic expressions. Under certain circumstances, the model parameters do tell the reader something about the role of the corresponding variables in making the prediction. But this knowledge is expressed in a fairly abstract, numerical form. It is very difficult or even impossible to explain cogently the logic behind any specific decision. And more seriously, the individual coefficients in a regression model lose much of their meaning under the very common case of multicollinearity in the data, a fact that unfortunately, does not prevent many authors from basing theoretical and practical decisions on them anyway. Finally, a very large body of research has shown that human experts' attempts to modify linear models are more apt to do harm than good [3].

TABLE 9.1. Summary of Three Approaches to Automated Knowledge Acquisition

Parameter	Rule Induction	Linear Scoring	Neural Network
Representative tool	Modified ID3	Logit	Neural network
Selection criteria	Entropy	Covariance	Delta rule
Selection process	Repetitive decomposition	Matrix operation	Feedforward, back-propagation
Assumption	No conflict in training	Normally distributed error term	None (?)
Knowledge representation	Rule set (decision tree)	Linear additive equation	Network with weight
Knowledge structure	Articulate knowledge	Pseudoarticulate knowledge	Inarticulate knowledge
Strength	Perspicuity	Robustness	Robustness, pattern recognition

Neural network models function essentially as a "black box." Neural networks' inarticulate nonpropositional knowledge structures have no perspicuity since knowledge resides holistically in the complicated connections among input, hidden, and output nodes. On the other hand, rule induction methods such as ID3 and its many derivatives are much less robust than linear models or neural nets. They are inconclusive if exposed to examples with identical predictors but different values of the criterion variable, and are easily led astray by outliers or errors in the data.

A hybrid approach has long been recognized as a potential way to overcome the two major limitations of the rule induction approach. First, a hybrid system makes it easy to solve the problem of contradictory examples (examples with identical values of all predictor variables but different criterion values) without deleting them. Since the dependent variable is computed as a function of the inputs from the continuous numerical system, the same set of input values is always associated with the same output value in the examples given to the rule induction algorithm. The criterion value that the rule induction engine sees for any set of predictor variable values depends on the criterion value(s) associated with those predictor values in the training data, but only in the context of the training data as a whole.

Second, the smoothing effect of using the output of numeric values from a neural net or logit should improve generalizability because the set of rules produced by rule induction will be less likely to be misled by anomalous cases in the raw data. Thus the input is not only consistent, it is also smoother and freer of the outliers that can unduly complicate the rule sets derived from the raw data by rule induction. In other words, through the hybrid approach, the robustness that is the major strength of linear scoring or neural net approach is integrated with high perspicuity, which is a major strength of the rule induction approach.

9.3.1 Computing with Words

Hybrid models for knowledge acquisition are an application of contemporary thinking about computing with words. The first stage of the knowledge acquisition process loads the computer with a body of inarticulate knowledge in the form of numerical coefficients or connection weights. At this point, a human expert can critique system behavior by producing pedagogical examples [21] even if the expert knowledge is inarticulate. Then the computer's inarticulate knowledge is converted into an articulate linguistic form using rule induction. The degree of correspondence between the vocabulary of the resulting rule set and the "real words" of human discourse about the subject matter is directly proportional to the skill and effort with which the inputs to the rule induction algorithm have been crafted. The text of this body of articulate knowledge can be critiqued and modified by human experts in a much more direct and sophisticated way than humans can modify inarticulate knowledge bases. Finally, the resulting system can compute with the articulate knowledge and explain the process and results to the user in words and phrases appropriate to the subject matter.

9.4 HYBRID APPROACH TO AUTOMATED KNOWLEDGE ACQUISITION

We have implemented a hybrid approach to knowledge acquisition which draws on the complementary strengths and weaknesses of robust numerical models, perspicuous linguistic models, and human expertise [5, 19]. The first step in generating a hybrid model is to fit a first-order model to a set of training examples containing predictor variables and a criterion variable. The second step is to convert the numerical outputs of the first-order model into a consistent set of ordinal categories based on the quantiles of the numeric model's output. The ordinal category assigned each training case, paired with the case's predictor variable values, make up the training data for the second-order model generated by the rule induction algorithm. The overall process, from raw data to working decision support system, is summarized in Figure 9.1.

If the resulting computer-generated rule-based functions as an expert system, it will give the user the ability to ask "why" about the system's requests for information and its conclusions. In addition, machine-generated rule sets, since they are expressed in words, can be modified by experts in the subject matter.

9.4.1 Experimental Results

In this section we report research into the usefulness of three approaches to AKA to provide stimuli to assist in acquiring knowledge from human experts. Hybrid approaches have been tested in a series of experiments involving a Korean surety insurance database, using logit and a neural net (Neuroshell) as first-order models, rule induction (1stClass) to generate second-order models, and human experts in surety insurance and bankruptcy risk assessment. Table 9.2 shows the 10 financial ratios that underlie the linguistic rules.

Experiment Hybrid Models. The purpose of the first experiment [19] is to verify the ability of articulate second-order models to capture the effective knowledge

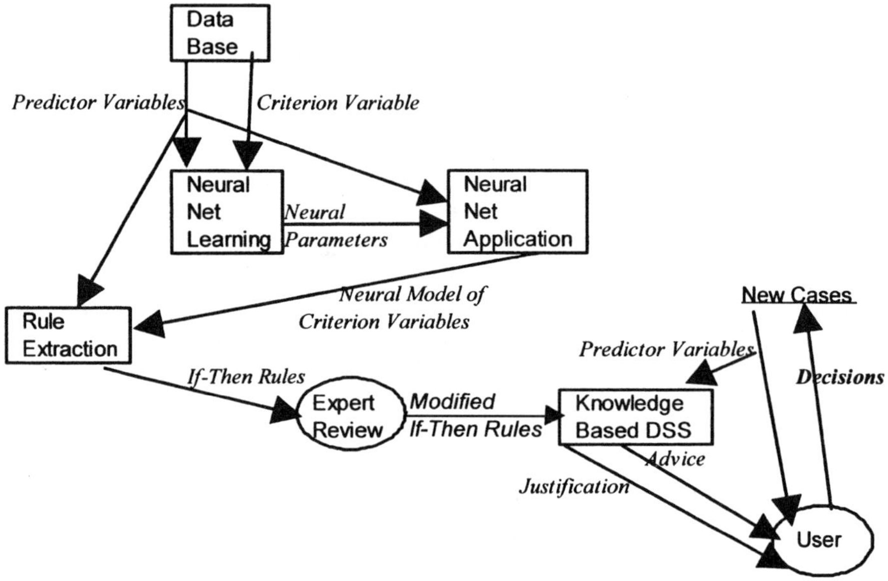

FIGURE 9.1. Data mining by second-order linguistic modeling.

TABLE 9.2. Financial Ratios

Name	Description
Fund expense ratio	Fund expense/sales revenue
Percent increase of receivables versus sales	Percent increase in receivables − percent increase in sales
Percent increase of inventories versus sales	Percent increase in inventories − percent increase in sales
Operating cash flow ratio	(Operating cash flow/sales) × 100
Percent increase in liabilities to total assets	(Percent increase in total liabilities − percent increase in long-term asset)/total asset
Working capital ratio	(*N* period accounts receivables − *N* period account payables)/ *N* monthly sales
Liability to sales	(*N* period total liabilities/*N* period monthly sales) × 100
Unfavorable change in liabilities	(Changes in liabilities − (monthly sales × changes of working capital ratio + changes of monthly sales))/ monthly sales
Operating cash flow	(Operating cash inflow/operating cash outflow) × 100
Disparity ratio	(| Change of receivables − (change of monthly sales) × liability ÷ sales | − | change of payables − (change of inventories) × payables ÷ sales|))/monthly sales

contained in inarticulate or quasiarticulate first-order models. The experiment compares the accuracy, evaluated on a test sample, of three nonhybrid approaches (logit, neural with two hidden nodes, and neural with five hidden nodes) and the corresponding hybrid approaches, all developed using a training sample.

The basis for comparison was θ, the area under the receiver operator characteristic curve. θ is equal to the probability that a randomly selected bankruptcy case will have a higher risk score than that of a randomly selected nonbankruptcy case (plus half the probability that they will have an equal risk score). For a dichotomous classifier, let α be the proportion of nonbankrupt firms classified as high risk, and β be the proportion of bankrupt firms classified as high risk. Then $\theta = (1-\alpha)\beta + 0.5(\alpha\beta + (1-\alpha)(1-\beta)$, which reduces to $\theta = 0.5(1-\alpha+\beta)$. θ takes type I and type II risk equally into account. $\theta = 0.5$ for a classifier that has no ability to discriminate bankrupts from nonbankrupts, and $\theta = 1$ for a perfect classifier. For classifiers with more than two categories (such as negligible, low, medium, high, and unacceptable risk), and for continuous-valued classifiers, θ provides a very natural generalization of these concepts.

Some authors have reported the "percentage classified correctly," but this is almost useless in assessing the power of a system to predict accurately rare events such as bankruptcy. Bias in favor of the more common event inflates the percentage classified correctly, but the resulting increase in false negatives is reflected in a smaller θ than that achieved by an unbiased system. If bankruptcies were only 1% in a population, then calling every case "low risk" regardless of any evidence would have a 99% proportion correctly classified but a θ value of only 0.5.

Each hybrid approach was generated by applying linguistic rule induction to a training sample (193 nonbankrupt firms and 56 bankrupt firms) but with a criterion variable based on the output of the logit or neural system. Logit output is an estimate of the probability that a firm will go bankrupt, while neural output is best viewed as the membership grade of a case in the fuzzy set of cases at risk for bankruptcy. Since ID3-type algorithms require a discrete criterion variable, we examined the effect of discretizing the numeric outputs at three, five, and seven levels of risk (see Table 9.3).

Overall, the performance of the hybrid models on a test sample (264 cases, including 58 bankruptcy cases) was roughly equal to that of the corresponding nonhybrid models; thus the gain in perspicuity was achieved at no significant cost in accuracy. Best performance on the test sample was found using logit (hybrid or

TABLE 9.3. Results of Experiment

Approach		For 3 Groups	For 5 Groups	For 7 Groups
Neural-2	Hybrid	0.67	0.68	0.73
	Nonhybrid	0.69	0.72	0.69
Neural-5	Hybrid	0.64	0.66	0.61
	Nonhybrid	0.66	0.67	0.68
Logit	Hybrid	0.69	0.74	0.78
	Nonhybrid	0.7	0.74	0.73

nonhybrid), followed by the neural net with two hidden nodes. Although the neural net with five hidden nodes fit the training sample well, its performance on the test sample was inferior to the neural model with two hidden nodes.

Experiment Expert Modification. The purpose of this experiment [5] was to compare the ability of three approaches to automated knowledge acquisition to provide a useful stimulus to elicit additional knowledge from human experts. The training sample for this experiment consisted of 121 nonbankrupt firms and 27 bankrupt firms selected at random from the full database. The predictor variables were the 10 financial ratios presented in Table 9.1. Three sets of if–then rules were generated from the database. The first set was generated using actual bankruptcy or nonbankruptcy from the raw data as the criterion variable for the linguistic rule induction algorithm. The criterion variable for the second set was based on dichotomized logit output. The cut point for the dichotomization was the one that generated the highest θ value on the training sample. The input to rule induction for the third set was developed in the same way, but using output from a neural net with two hidden nodes. (The logit and neural output were dichotomized in this experiment for compatibility with the raw data, which had only the two outcomes "bankrupt" and "nonbankrupt.")

Three experts, matched for their degree of expertise, independently modified each set of if–then rules (nine experts in all). Experts could (1) change the threshold levels at which ratios change from normal to risky, (2) simplify rules by removing unimportant variables, (3) refine rules by adding another variable (from the list of available data) that is important in classifying cases, or (4) leave rules the way the computer generated them.

At this point, we had 12 different sets of if–then rules: three machine-generated sets and three human modifications of each machine-generated set. Tables 9.4, 9.5, and 9.6 show the results of the various experts' modifications of the rules generated, respectively, by nonhybrid linguistic, hybrid logit-linguistic, and hybrid neural-linguistic. Since each set of rules generated only dichotomous outcomes (high or low risk of bankruptcy), theoretical calculations of the standard error of θ [7, 8] are suspect. To assess the reliability of differences between the accuracy of various models, we divided the database randomly into four samples: the training sample already mentioned, and three test samples. We ran each of the 12 sets of if–then rules against each of the three test samples, giving us 36 different values of θ.

Table 9.7 presents the results of a two-way analysis of variance that tests for main and interaction effects of two variables on the θ statistic. The "machine" variable has three values, depending on whether the rules are based on raw data, logit output, or neural network output. The "human" variable has two values, indicating whether or not the rules are modified by a human being. (The blocking factor indicates which of the three test samples was used.)

There is no significant evidence of a main effect of human modification, but there is a significant interaction effect between human modification and type of automated knowledge acquisition. This means that the effect of human modification is unpredictable without specifying the source of the rules the human is modifying. The

TABLE 9.4. Nonhybrid Linguistic[a]

Expert	Deleted Variables	Added Variables	Modified Threshold	Newly Added Variables	Newly Created Rule	Unchanged Rule	Deleted Rule	Total Modification	Result	Justification and Modification Procedure
Degree in accounting	—	1: R8	13	—	—	—	—	15	17 Rules and 76 clauses	1. Set up key variables, such as R3, R4, R10.
		7: R4								2. For each rules, tried to change threshold value.
Korean practitioner	14: R6	1: R4	22	R5	—	—	—	28	17 rules and 78 clauses (highest accuracy)	1. Did not try to set up key variables or threshold
	15: R6	7: R5		R7						2. For each rule, tried to change threshold value, delete variables, or add variables based on uses knowledge.
		8: R7 9: R9		R9						
Korean professor	1: R6, R2	2: R9	63	R9	—	—	Rule 9	78	14 rules and 49 clauses	1. Set up the key variable (R9) and unimportant variables (R2, R6, R8).
	2: R6, R2	3: R9					Rule 11			2. Deleted or added for that variable.
	4: R6, R10 5: R6, R2	16: R9 17: R9					Rule 15			3. Based on that variable, tried to change threshold values.
	6: R6, R2 14: R8 16: R8, R6 17: R8, R6							Avg. = 40		

[a]Seventeen rules, 74 clauses; ratios used: R1, R2, R3, R4, R6, R8, R10; modification result: 40/74 = 54%.

TABLE 9.5. Hybrid with Logit[a]

Expert	Deleted Variables	Added Variables	Modified Threshold	Newly Added Variables	Newly Created Rule	Unchanged Rule	Deleted Rule	Total Modification	Result	Justification and Modification Procedure
Degree in finance	1: R5, R6	—	0	R8	1 (Using R1, R5, R8, R10)	2	—	26	13 Rules and 32 clauses (highest accuracy)	1. Expert complained a lot because the rule did not make sense to him (only rule 2 makes sense).
	3: R10						(but almost deleted)			2. He is the only person who created his own rule.
	4: R6, R9									3. Almost deleted the computer-generated rules.
	5: R6, R9									
	6: R5									
	7: R5, R6, R9									
	8: R9									
	9: R5, R6, R9									
	10: R5									
	11: R4, R6									
	12: R4, R6									

Korean practitioner	1: R6	1: R1, R7	20	R7	—	—	—	45	13 rules and 42 clauses	1. Expert set up key variables but focused on the given rules and modified each rule.
	2: R6	2: R1								2. Expert is the only person who changed the direction of threshold value.
	3: R6	4: R7								
	4: R6, R2	6: R4, R7								
	5: R6, R2	7: R7								
	6–13: R6	9: R7								
		11: R7								
		13: R1								
Korean professor			22	—	—	Rule 8	—	22	13 rules and 51 clauses	1. Expert complained a lot because the rule didn't make sense to him.
								Avg. 31		2. Then he only tried to change the threshold value.

[a] Thirteen rules, 51 clauses; ratios used: R1, R2, R4, R5 R6, R9, R10; modification result: 31/51 = 61%.

TABLE 9.6. Hybrid with Neural Network[a]

Expert	Deleted Variables	Added Variables	Modified Threshold	Newly Added Variables	Newly Created Rule	Unchanged Rule	Deleted Rule	Total Modification	Result	Justification and Modification Procedure
Degree in finance	2:R5, R8, R7	3:R9, R10	5	R9	—	Rule 1	Rule 2	25	7 rules and 20 clauses	1. Set up key variable (R5), important variable (R9, 10), and deleted unimportant variables (R7,8).
		5: R9, R10		R10						2. For each rule, tried to change threshold value of key and important variables.
	3: R8, R7									
		6: R9, R10								
	4: R7									
		8: R10								
	5: R7, R8									
	6: R6, R4									
	7: R6									
	8: R6									
Korean practitioner	1: R8	1: R1	13	R1	—	Rule 3	Rule 8	18	8 rules and 25 clauses (highest accuracy)	1. Did not try to set up key variables or threshold.
		7: R1								2. For each rules, tried to change threshold value, delete variables, or add variables based on his knowledge.
										3. Only person to explain why he modified each rule based on accounting knowledge.

Korean professor	3: R7	—	9	—	—	—	—	9	8 rules and 23 clauses	1. Given rules, tried to change threshold value but the modification is very straightforward. That is, rather than considering each rule condition, he consistently changed threshold value for all rules (e.g., the threshold value of R4 is always 1.7 for all rules).
								Avg. = 17		

[a](Eight rules, 24 clauses, ratios used: R3, R4, R5, R6, R7, R8); modification result: 17/24 = 71%.

TABLE 9.7. ANOVA Results for Modification by Expert

Source of Variation	df	SS	*F*	Pr > F^a
Block	2	0.006	1.83	0.18
Human	1	0.0005	0.32	0.58
Machine	2	0.03	9.26	0.0008*
Human–machine	2	0.02	5.42	0.0102*
Error	28	0.04		
Total	35	0.1		

[a]Asterisk indicates significance at the 5% level.

interaction profile of these means, illustrating the nature of the human–machine interaction term, is shown in Figure 9.2. The profile shows that the prediction accuracy of a hybrid model based on neural net preprocessing is increased after experts' modification, whereas the prediction accuracy of a hybrid model based on logit is decreased after experts' modification. Nonhybrid linguistic shows almost no change after experts' modification.

9.5 DISCUSSION

The results of this investigation have some important implications about the relationships among four approaches to knowledge engineering that are often viewed in isolation or in competition with one another.

Linear models such as logit have long been known to be an extraordinarily powerful way to generate very accurate predictive models given a reasonable quantity and quality of historical data [3, 18]. However, these models are sometimes very counter-

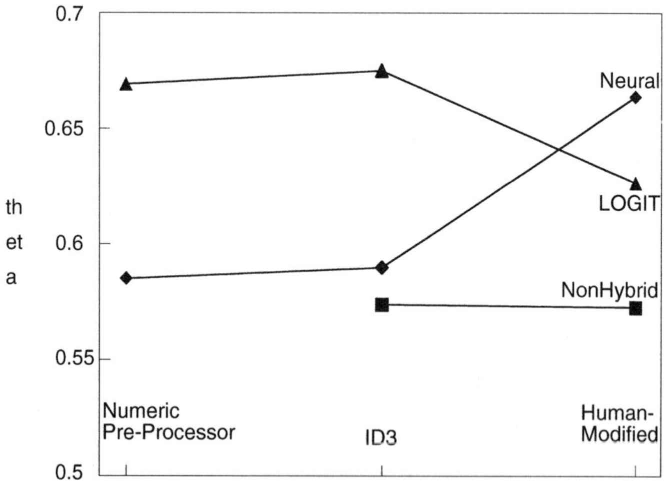

FIGURE 9.2. Interaction profile.

intuitive. It is common for an expert confronted with a linear model that closely matches the expert's own decisions, to object "But that's not the way I decide at all!" Other researchers have shown that an expert's attempt to improve a linear model directly by adjusting coefficients or introducing variables or interactions usually leads to degraded performance, even if the linear model is based on scanty information.

Neural networks are intentionally modeled on some of the functional characteristics of the living brain. Like regression, supervised neural nets take a database of classified cases and produce a model of the classification process. (Unsupervised neural nets are outside the scope of this chapter; they resemble cluster analysis in the same way that supervised neural nets resemble regression.) They are very robust and can perform well in applications that defeat conventional regression models. Despite their theoretical compatibility with human experts' own brains, neural networks are almost completely lacking in perspicuity; no explanation whatever is provided for why the system acts as it does. Thus it is impossible for a subject-matter expert to modify a neural network directly in an attempt to improve its performance. However, the present study demonstrated considerable success when experts modified if–then rules derived from a neural network by linguistic rule induction. Perhaps this is a reflection of the theoretical parallelism between artificial neural networks and human brains—this is an interesting question for future research.

Direct elicitation of knowledge from a human expert tends to produce encoded knowledge whose perspicuity is very high; what a human expert has written, presumably another expert can read. However, it is a very difficult and expensive process to get an expert system project of this sort off the ground.

Rule induction algorithms such as the modified ID3 algorithm embodied in 1st Class acquire knowledge automatically from data in much the same way that regression or neural nets do, but with an inherently higher level of perspicuity because rule induction algorithms produce if–then rules in a pseudo-natural language. These rule sets may be used for production just as they come out of the computer, using the improved perspicuity to support an articulate explanation facility in a decision support system. However, our focus is on the use of these rules as a stimulus to a subject matter expert. The expert can look at a set of computer-generated if–then rules and see where they need improvement; this process is often much more effective than giving the expert a blank page.

The most important finding of this research is that human experts can produce a substantial improvement in the accuracy of if–then rules based on neural net output, while they degrade the performance of rules produced from logit output. Expert modification has little effect on the (already lower) accuracy of rules generated directly from raw data. If these results generalize to other application areas, the implication is that data should be preprocessed before a rule induction engine is applied. If the rules are to be used as is, a linear preprocessor is appropriate, but if a human expert will be editing and modifying the rules, a neural preprocessor appears to be superior.

Further Research. Further research plans include taking advantage of the perspicuous second-order models of robust first-order models in a user-friendly expert system that responds to "why" queries. One important current research project is to investigate the compatibility between knowledge structures of inductive approaches and system users. For example, users get data for a case, a machine's assessment, and a machine's rationale (an equation for logit and a rule for linguistic). The user accepts or changes the machine's assessment, then the user's prediction accuracy using the two methods will be compared.

REFERENCES

1. J. R. Anderson, A theory of the origins of human knowledge, *Artif. Intell.*, 40:313–351, 1989.
2. W. Becthel, and A. A. Abrahamsen, *Connectionism and the Mind: An Introduction to Parallel Processing in Networks*, Basil Blackwell, Oxford, 1990.
3. R.M. Dawes, and B. Corrigan, Linear models, *Psychol. Bull.*, 81:2,95–106, 1974.
4. H. Gardner, *The Mind's New Science*, Basic Books, New York, 1985.
5. G. Gim, and T. Whalen, Hybrid approaches to automated knowledge acquisition and human knowledge elicitation, *Proc. 4th Annual Conference on Fuzzy Theory and Technology*, NC, 1995, pp. 526–529.
6. C. Glymour, R. Scheines, P. Spirtes, and K. Kelly, *Discovering Causal Structure: Artificial Intelligence, Philosophy of Science, and Statistical Modeling*, Acadmic Press, New York, 1987.
7. J. Hanley and B. McNeil, The meaning and use of the area under a receiver operating characteristic (ROC) curve. *Radiology*, 143:29–36, Apr. 1982.
8. J. Hanley and B. McNeil, A method of comparing the areas under ROC curves derived from the same cases. *Radiology*, 148:839–843, Sept. 1983.
9. A. Hart, *Knowledge Acquisition for Expert Systems*, 2nd ed., McGraw-Hill, New York, 1992.
10. J. G. Joreskog and D. Sorbom, Recent developments in structural equation modeling, *J. Market. Res.*, 19:404–416, 1982.
11. A. Newell, *Unified Theory of Cognition*, Harvard University Press, Cambridge, MA, 1989.
12. J. Quinlan, Discovering rules by induction from large collections of examples, in D. Michie, (ed.), *Expert Systems in the Microelectronic Age*, Edinburgh University Press, Edinbrugh, 1979, pp, 165–201.
13. R. Quinlan, Induction of decision trees. *Mach. Learn.*, 1(1):81, 1986.
14. D. E. Rumelhart, J. L. McClelland, and the PDP Research Group, *Parallel Distributed Processing: Explorations in the Microstructure of Cognition*, Vol. I, *Foundations*, MIT Press, Cambridge, MA, 1986.
15. G. Ryle, *The Concept of Mind*, Barnes & Noble, New York, 1949.
16. A. Sage, Behavioral and organizational considerations in the design of information systems and processes for planning and decision support, *IEEE Trans Syst. Man Cybern.*, 11(9):640–678, 1981.
17. T. Whalen, Three reasons for approximate reasoning, *Proc. IFSA*, 1987.

18. T. Whalen and G. Gim, Hybrid neural-statistical classification system for potential medical malpractice insurance claims, *Proc. 2nd International Decision Sciences Institute Conference*, 1993, pp. 216–218.
19. T. Whalen, G. Gim, and K. Son, Hybrid approach to automated knowledge acquisition: logical second order models making sense of neural nets and logistic regression, *Proc. 1996 World Congress on Expert Systems*, Seoul, Korea, 1996, pp. 839–846.
20. T. Whalen, and G. Gim, Second order logical system for risk classification in a newly developed country, *Int. J. Uncertainty Fuzziness Knowledge-Based Syst.* 4(5): 421–430, 1996.
21. T. Whalen, and B. Schott, Beginners' strategies in example based expert systems, *Proc. 1986 International Symposium on Methodologies for Intelligent Systems*.

CHAPTER 10

COMPUTING WITH DESCRIPTIVE AND VERISTIC WORDS: KNOWLEDGE REPRESENTATION AND REASONING

I. B. TÜRKŞEN
University of Toronto, Toronto, Ontario, Canada

10.1 INTRODUCTION

In computing with words, we need to implement several stages of development in building a rule base and reasoning with such a rule base for system modeling, analysis, prediction, decision, and control. First, a system's behavior knowledge must be stated linguistically, if such knowledge is available at the time. For example, for the laboratory-built-steam-engine model [8,9], a linguistic rule is stated as:

IF Speed Error is *Positive Big*
And Change in Speed Error is *Negative*
THEN Change in Throttle Opening must be *Negative Big*

In the second stage, the linguistic terms *Positive Big* (PB), *Negative* (N), and *Negative Big* (NB) of the linguistic variables Speed Error (SE), Change in Speed Error (CSE), and Change in Throttle Opening (CTO), respectively, are defined with fuzzy set membership functions. It is clear that linguistic terms that "describe" the fuzzy clusters of linguistic variables in the first stage are represented by numerical fuzzy membership functions in the second stage. Definitions of the membership functions are acquired generally in three different ways:

1. They are defined normatively as a function [e.g., $\mu_{\text{negative}}(x) = e^{-(x+\alpha)^2}$, $\alpha > 0$].

Computing with Words, Edited by Paul P. Wang.
ISBN 0-471-35374-4

2. They are extracted from a set of data via a fuzzy cluster algorithm (e.g., FMC algorithm) [3].
3. They are acquired through a membership measurement experiment via expert interviews [19].

Once the membership functions of the linguistic variables are defined, *descriptive words* (i.e., adjectives, or adjectives and adverbs) receive a meaning representation in the numerical domain. That is, we assign numerical functions to the fuzzy clusters of a base variable, where fuzzy clusters represent linguistic terms and base variables represent linguistic variables. In turn, we have a pattern-to-pattern representation of the linguistic rules in the numerical domain. This numerical representation is *many-to-many mapping*. It is in this manner that words are represented by numbers in computing with words.

On the other hand, there are cases where we have no linguistic information or knowledge of the system behavior but we have data that represent the behavior of the system. In such cases, the sequence of the first two stages is reversed. That is, in the first stage, we start out with a clustering algorithm to determine the clusters of the input and output variables. Second, we associate words, linguistic terms of the linguistic input–output variables, with the clusters determined at the first stage. In this alternative approach, we represent numbers with words.

In either case, we have methodologies to represent words with numbers and alternatively, numbers with words. Thus at the end of the second stage, the analyst has a representation of system behavior in numerical input patterns leading to output patterns. Furthermore, the analyst possibly knows that, for example, numerical input pattterns are AND aggregated to IMPLY the output patterns. But the analyst generally does not know, for example, how AND, IMPLY, and other operators are to be defined.

At this juncture, we move into the third stage, and restate the pattern-to-pattern numerical representation of the rules with symbolic fuzzy propositions. For example, numerical pattern-to-pattern representation of the linguistic rule of the steam-engine plant may be expressed as

$$\text{IF SE } isr \text{ PB AND CSE } isr \text{ N, THEN CTO } isr \text{ NB.}$$

More generally, we would express it as

$$\text{IF } x_1 \in X_1 \ isr \ A_{i1} \text{ AND } x_2 \in X_2 \ isr \ A_{i2}, \text{ THEN } y \in Y \ isr \ B_i$$

for the ith rule of the steam-engine plant as its symbolic rule base, which is in fact an implicit metalinguistic expression.

At this stage, we implicitly assume that the membership functions (e.g., PB, N and NB) are verified either by experts or by the algorithm in the case of clustering and that the analyst has confidence that they are a true representation of the descriptive words. In turn, the truth verification of the membership functions together attests to the truth of a given rule-pattern representation. The implicit truth verification means that we are implicitly stating the rule-based expressions in explicit form as follows:

$$\begin{aligned}&\text{IF } x_1 \in X_1 \textit{ isr } A_{i1} \text{ is verified to be true, T,}\\&\text{AND, } x_2 \in X_2 \textit{ isr } A_{i2} \text{ is verified to be true, T,}\\&\text{THEN } y \in Y \textit{ isr } B_i \text{ is verified to be true, T.}\end{aligned}$$

This explicitly detailed expression can be rewritten in a more compact and reduced form as

$$(A_{i1}, \mathrm{T}) \text{ AND } (A_{i2}, \mathrm{T}) \rightarrow (B_i, \mathrm{T}).$$

In this manner, we distinuguish A_{i1}, A_{i2}, and B_i as *descriptive words* that define the fuzzy sets and *true* (T) as the *veristic word* that establishes the veracity of the descriptive words and hence, the linguistic rule.

At the fourth stage of computing with words, we must determine the formulas that would represent the pattern-to-pattern representation of the original linguistic terms. At this stage, we face several alternatives: Let us first consider the alternatives of AND operation.

- *Alternative I.* We interpret AND as type I (myopic) representation. For example, we write

$$[\mathrm{FDNF_{AND}(PB, N) = PB \cap N}] \rightarrow \mathrm{NB}$$

for the steam-engine plant. More generally, we write

$$[\mathrm{FDNF_{AND}}(A_{i1}, A_{i2}) = A_{i1} \cap A_{i2}] \rightarrow B_i$$

- *Alternative II.* We interpret AND as type II representation with respect to fuzzy disjunctive normal form (FDNF) and fuzzy conjunctive normal form (FCNF), respectively [18,27]. For example, for the steam-engine plant, we write

(a) $[\mathrm{FDNF_{AND}(PB, N) = PB \cap N}] \rightarrow \mathrm{NB}$

(b) $[\mathrm{FCNF_{AND}(PB, N) = (PB \cup N) \cap (c(PB) \cup N) \cap (PB \cup c(N))}] \rightarrow \mathrm{NB},$

and more generally, we write

(a′) $[\mathrm{FDNF_{AND}}(A_{i1}, \mathrm{A}_{i2}) = A_{i1} \cap \mathrm{A}_{i2}] \rightarrow B_i$

(b′) $[\mathrm{FCNF_{AND}}(\mathrm{A}_{i1}, \mathrm{A}_{i2}) = (\mathrm{A}_{i1} \cup \mathrm{A}_{i2}) \cap (\mathrm{c}(\mathrm{A}_{i1}) \cup \mathrm{A}_{i2}) \cap (\mathrm{A}_{i1} \cup \mathrm{c}(\mathrm{A}_{i2})) \rightarrow B_i,$

where $\mathrm{c}(\cdot)$ is the standard complement.

Next let us consider the alternatives of the IMPLY operator.

- *Alternative I.1.* We interpret IMPLY as type I (myopic) with two different but extreme implication schemas. For example, for the steam-engine plant, we write:

$$\text{(a)}\ \ \mathrm{PB} \cap \mathrm{N} \cap \mathrm{NB} \quad \text{(interpolative) (Mamdani)}$$
$$\text{(b)}\ \ \mathrm{c}(\mathrm{PB} \cap \mathrm{N}) \cup \mathrm{NB} \quad \text{(CRI) (GMP)},$$

and more generally, we write

$$\text{(a}'\text{)}\ \ \mathrm{A}_{i1} \cap \mathrm{A}_{i2} \cap B_i \quad \text{(interpolative) (Mamdani)}$$
$$\text{(b}'\text{)}\ \ \mathrm{c}(\mathrm{A}_{i1} \cap \mathrm{A}_{i2}) \cup B_i \quad \text{(CRI) (GMP)}$$

- *Alternative II.1.* We interpret IMPLY as type II with two different implication schemas with respect to their fuzzy disjunctive and fuzzy conjunctive normal forms, respectively.
  - *Alternative II.1.1.* Thus for the interpolative schema, we have

$$\text{(a-1)}\ \ \mathrm{FDNF}_{\mathrm{AND}}(\mathrm{PD}, \mathrm{N}) \cap \mathrm{NB}$$
$$\text{(a-2)}\ \ \mathrm{FCNF}_{\mathrm{AND}}(\mathrm{PB}, \mathrm{N}) \cap \mathrm{NB} \text{ for the stream-engine plant.}$$

  More generally, we write first

$$\mathrm{FDNF}_{\mathrm{AND}}(\mathrm{FDNF}_{\mathrm{AND}}(A_{i1}, A_{i2}), B_i)$$
$$\mathrm{FDNF}_{\mathrm{AND}}(\mathrm{FCNF}_{\mathrm{AND}}(A_{i1}, A_{i2}), B_i)$$

  That is, we get

$$\text{(a}'\text{-1)}\ \ \mathrm{FDNF}_{\mathrm{AND}}(A_{i1}, A_{i2}) \cap B_i$$
$$\text{(a}'\text{-2)}\ \ \mathrm{FCNF}_{\mathrm{AND}}(A_{i1}, A_{i2}) \cap B_i.$$

  - Alternative II.1.2. Next, for the (CRI) (GMP) schema, we write

$$\mathrm{FCNF}_{\mathrm{IMP}}(\mathrm{FDNF}_{\mathrm{AND}}(\cdot), B_i)$$
$$\mathrm{FCNF}_{\mathrm{IMP}}(\mathrm{FCNF}_{\mathrm{AND}}(\cdot), B_i).$$

  That is,

$$\text{(b-1)}\ \ (\mathrm{FDNF}_{\mathrm{AND}}(\mathrm{PB}, \mathrm{N}) \cap \mathrm{NB}) \cup (\mathrm{c}(\mathrm{FDNF}_{\mathrm{AND}}(\mathrm{PB}, \mathrm{N})) \cap \mathrm{NB}) \cup (\mathrm{c}(\mathrm{FDNF}_{\mathrm{AND}}(\mathrm{PB}, \mathrm{N})) \cap \mathrm{c}(\mathrm{NB}))$$
$$\text{(b-2)}\ \ \mathrm{c}(\mathrm{FCNF}_{\mathrm{AND}}(\mathrm{PB}, \mathrm{N})) \cup \mathrm{NB} \text{ for the steam-engine plant.}$$

  More generally, we write

$$\text{(b}'\text{-1)}\ \ (\mathrm{FDNF}_{\mathrm{AND}}(A_{i1}, A_{i2}) \cap B_i) \cup (\mathrm{c}(\mathrm{FDNF}_{\mathrm{AND}}(A_{i1}, A_{i2})) \cap B_i) \cup (\mathrm{c}(\mathrm{FDNF}_{\mathrm{AND}}(A_{i1}, A_{i2}) \cap \mathrm{c}(B_i))$$
$$\text{(b}'\text{-2)}\ \ \mathrm{c}(\mathrm{FCNF}_{\mathrm{AND}}(A_{i1}, A_{i2})) \cup B_i.$$

There is a third alternative, known as the *compromise reasoning schema* [29], which we have identified formally and justified with the FCNF and FDNF structure analysis [27]. For example, for the steam-engine plant,

$$(1-\beta)[\mathrm{FDNF}_{\mathrm{AND}}(\mathrm{PB}(x_1),\mathrm{N}(x_2))\Delta\mathrm{NB}(y)] \\ +\beta[\mathrm{cFCNF}_{\mathrm{AND}}(\mathrm{PB}(x_1),\mathrm{N}(x_2)))\nabla\mathrm{NB}(y)]=\mathrm{NB}(y^*),$$

where Δ and ∇ are appropriate t-norm and t-co-norm operators, respectively, and $\mathrm{PB}(x_1),\mathrm{N}(x_2),\mathrm{NB}(y)$ are membership values of those linguistic terms (i.e., fuzzy sets). More generally, we write

$$(1-\beta)[\mathrm{FDNF}_{\mathrm{AND}}(A_{i1}(x_1),A_{i2}(x_2))\Delta B_i(y)] \\ +\beta[\mathrm{c}(\mathrm{FCNF}_{\mathrm{AND}}(A_{i1}(x_1),A_{i2}(x_2)))\nabla B_i(y)]=B_i(y^*).$$

Let us call this alternative *convex linear compromise reasoning* [27].

There is also a fourth alternative, which we call *exponential compromise reasoning*, which we propose to express as

$$[\mathrm{FDNF}_{\mathrm{AND}}(A_{i1}(x_1),A_{i2}(x_2))\Delta B_i(y)]^{1-\gamma}\cdot[\mathrm{c}(\mathrm{FCNF}_{\mathrm{AND}}(A_{i1}(x_1))) \\ \nabla B_i(y)^{\gamma}=B_i(y^*).$$

The reason for choosing FDNF and FCNF expressions and their combinations will be explained later after we develop the groundwork for the development of truth tables and the derivation of fuzzy normal forms. These derivations require an in-depth understanding of descriptive words and veristic words, as we alluded to earlier. These will also be explained later.

In the fifth stage, we either specify the t-norms and co-norms or introduce parametric t-norms and co-norms that can be determined with supervised learning.

The final stage is reasoning with the formulas that were presented in the preceding stage. For example, the convex linear compromized reasoning for a singleton observation of variables (x_1^0,x_2^0) would result in a consequent $\mathrm{NB}(y^*)$ for the steam-engine plant as follows:

$$(1-\beta)[\mathrm{FDNF}_{\mathrm{AND}}(\mathrm{PB}(x_1^0),\mathrm{N}(x_2^0))\Delta\mathrm{NB}(y)] \\ +\beta[\mathrm{c}(\mathrm{FCNF}_{\mathrm{AND}}(\mathrm{PB}(x_1^0),\mathrm{N}(x_2^0)))\nabla\mathrm{NB}(y)]=\mathrm{NB}(y^*).$$

For a singleton observation of variables (x_1^0,x_2^0), exponential compromise reasoning is expressed as

$$[\mathrm{FDNF}_{\mathrm{AND}}(\mathrm{PB}(x_1^0),\mathrm{N}(x_2^0))\Delta\mathrm{NB}(y)]^{1-\gamma} \\ \cdot[\mathrm{c}(\mathrm{FCNF}_{\mathrm{AND}}(\mathrm{PB}(x_1^0),\mathrm{N}(x_2^0)))\nabla\mathrm{NB}(y)]^{\gamma}=\mathrm{NB}(y^*).$$

In more general terms, we write

$$B_i(y^*) = (1-\beta)[\text{FDNF}_{\text{AND}}(A_{i1}(x_1^0), A_{i2}(x_2^0))\Delta B_i(y)$$
$$+ \beta[\text{c}(\text{FCNF}_{\text{AND}}(A_{i1}(x_1^0), A_{i2}(x_2^0)))\nabla B_i(y)]$$

for a single rule (i.e., the ith rule in convex linear compromise reasoning. For exponential compromise reasoning, we write

$$B_i(y^*) = [\text{FDNF}_{\text{AND}}(A_{i1}(x_1^0), A_{i2}(x_2^0))\Delta B_i(y)]^{1-\gamma}$$
$$\cdot [\text{c}(\text{FCNF}_{\text{AND}}(A_{i1}(x_1^0), A_{i2}(x_2^0)))\nabla B_i(y)]^{\gamma}.$$

Next, we should recall that the consequents of each rule should be aggregated. We should also recall that aggregation for interpolative reasoning requires maximum aggregation, whereas aggregation for GMP reasoning requires minimum aggregation. Thus the aggregation of two types of reasoning schemas are computed separately first, then are combined via the β operator for convex linear compromise reasoning. Thus we obtain

$$B(y^*) = (1-\beta)[\vee_i \text{FDNF}_{\text{AND}}(A_{i1}(x_1^0), A_{i2}(x_2^0))\Delta B_i(y)$$
$$+ \beta[\wedge_i \text{c}(\text{FCNF}_{\text{AND}}(A_{i1}(x_1^0), A_{i2}(x_2^0)))\nabla B_i(y)].$$

Similarly, for exponential compromise reasoning, we obtain

$$B(y^*) = [\vee_i \text{FDNF}_{\text{AND}}(A_{i1}(x_1^0), A_{i2}(x_2^0))\Delta B_i(y)]^{1-\gamma}$$
$$\cdot [\wedge_i \text{c}\,(\text{FCNF}_{\text{AND}}(A_{i1}(x_1^0), A_{i2}(x_2^0)))\nabla B_i(y)]^{\gamma}.$$

It should also be recalled that we have used a *first infer, then aggregate* (FITA) schema. It is known that FITA and *first aggregate, then infer* FATI give the same result for $A(x_i^0) = 1$, $x_i = x_i^0$ for all i [27], (i.e., FITA $\equiv$ FATI).

Finally, we need to execute a defuzzification algorithm, say, BADD of Yager and Filev [28]. This final stage takes us from pattern-to-pattern numerical representation of computing with words back to singleton numerical value. This is the consequence of our knowledge representation and reasoning schemas to enable us to implement analysis, prediction, decision, and control in systems modeling and its application.

At the beginning of this section it was stated that we start out either with (1) linguistic knowledge (if it is available from the experts) or (2) pattern-to-pattern representation extracted from input–output data (if such historical data are available), and then interpret the pattern-to-pattern representation linguistically to state the knowledge extracted from data in linguistic terms. A third alternative is to interpret classical mathematical expressions of systems via a systematic methodology to represent the knowledge of a system linguistically. This type of work was begun in the late 1980s by M. Sugeno [13]. But more recently, M. Margaliot proposed a systematic methodology that transforms our classical–mathematical knowledge to linguistic knowledge. For example, Margaliot shows how classical Lyapunov synthesis could be transformed into fuzzy Lyapunov synthesis [10]. Thus there are three approaches that provide us with a linguistic knowledge representation such that an analyst can start computing with words.

Within this framework of system modeling and reasoning structures, we now return to some of the critical assessment of computing with descriptive and veristic words for the derivation of FDNF and FCNF expressions.

10.2 BACKGROUND

Computing with words [31,32] is fundamental to our understanding of the foundations of fuzzy theory. Naturally, there are a large variety of words that we need to recognize and utilize in our computational paradigms. However, descriptive and veristic words are essential for the fundamental derivation of fuzzy set and logic formulas. Descriptive linguistic terms help us assign an element to a fuzzy set with a membership value, whereas veristic words determine the degree of truth associated with a descriptive membership value. Understanding this distinction between descriptive and veristic linguistic terms forms the basis of fuzzy truth tables. With the use of fuzzy truth tables we can derive the normal forms of fuzzy set and logic theory. Within this perspective, there are potentially a good number of possible fuzzy set and logic models. Each of these has its own unique formulas. Most of the current literature is based on a myopic theory which is a selection of one of the boundaries of the fuzzy set and two-valued logic-based formalism, which generates two boundaries. These issues are presented in our attempt to restructure the foundations of fuzzy theory.

In the IFSA '97–Prague, conference, Zadeh stated that there are four aspects to fuzziness: (1) sets, (2) logic, (3) relations, and (4) epistemology. Furthermore, Zadeh [31] points out that information granulation of elements results in a collection of granules, with a granule being a clump of elements (objects, persons) which are grouped or classified together by indistinguishability, similarity, proximity, or functionality. In this regard, Zadeh [31] identifies seven types of generalized constriants.

Naturally, information granulation may be crisp or fuzzy. It is well known and understood that the crisp case is the boundary of an infinite-valued (fuzzy) information granule. The essential conceptual issue from a fundamental perspective is to note that on the one hand, one type of information granulation, fuzzy or crisp, specifies the assignment of an element to a clump, a class, a group, and hence defines descriptive set membership, and on the other hand, another type of information granulation, fuzzy or crisp, specifies the assignment of the degree of truth or the membership specification for the abstract notion of truth which specifies the veristic constraint [31].

Thus there are in effect two distinct but related assignments. It appears that these two distinct assignments are implicitly assumed to be the same in most articles of the current fuzzy theory literature (e.g., Refs. 4 and 6). It appears further that this confusion arises because both of the assignments are values in {0,1} for two-valued theories. However, it is worthwhile to reemphasize that one specifies objects with their degree of belonging to a set identified by a *label*, a *word of a concept category*, and the other specifies the degree of belonging of the descriptive set assignment given in the first instance by our abstract concept of *verity*.

As a matter of fact, it is common knowledge that there are two distinct disciplines: (1) set theory and (2) logic theory. Furthermore, it is to be recalled that logicians usually start out discussions with an expression that states: "It is the case that (...), i.e., $\models$ (...), where (...) represents a proposition, a set definition, which is verified, asserted or denied, and where the symbol '$\models$' is a shorthand notation for 'it is the case that'. Many other examples of such expressions may be found in introductory logic books [2,5]: for example, "it is true that (...)," "It is affirmed that (...)," and so on. Introductory logic books make this point rather clear at the outset.

It is also worthwhile to note that Azzouni [1] states that "second-order logic with standard semantics is hardly set theory, if by that phrase is meant first-order set theory. They simply do not have the same models." In that statement Azzouni is responding to a statement of Quine [12]: "Second-order logic (with standard semantics) is set theory in sheep's clothing." Therefore, in fuzzy set and logic research, one needs to realize that the two concepts of descriptive sethood and veristic sethood must be given due recognition in the fundamental derivations of theoretical constructs such as truth tables, well-formed formulas, and normal forms.

In this context, the central concern of this chapter is directed to the formation of generalized truth tables and normal form expressions and their use in approximate reasoning. It is hoped that this will shed further light on future discussions while we are reassessing the foundations of fuzzy information granulation toward a well-founded fuzzy theory. To add further clarity to this issue of concern, we restate the categories of words and identify the nouns as linguistic variables and the adjectives and/or adjectives modified by adverbs as linguistic terms of the linguistic variables. It is to be recalled that the concern of fuzzy set theory is the clusters of linguistic variables fuzzily partitioned by adjectives and/or adjectives and adverbs.

10.2.1 Categories of Words

It is well known that there are four basic grammatical categories of words:

1. *Nouns*. Nouns are linguistic variables. They are labels that identify general classes of objects, entities, or activities. For example:
   (a) Age, height, inventory, profit, people, number, zero, chair, building
   (b) Truth, belief, probability, possibility, plausibility, necessity
2. *Adjectives*. Adjectives are linguistic terms. They are modifiers that describe subclasses of entities. For example:
   (a) Old people, tall building, low inventories, high profits, large numbers, negative zero, positive number, positive zero

   (b) High probability, low possibility, probable event, true sentence, false facts, high belief, or believable source, possible occurrences, necessary conditions, plausible events.

3. *Adverbs.* Adverbs are modifiers of linguistic terms. They qualify subclasses of adjectives. For example:
   (a) Very tall building, somewhat old people, very low inventories, very high profits
   (b) Very high probability, very high poissibility, highly probable event, very true sentence, very false facts, somewhat true statement, highly believable source, very necessary conditions, definitely possible occurrences, more or less plausible events
4. *Verbs.* Verbs are the grammatical center of predicates. They express an act, an event, an occurrence, a mode of being, and so on.

It is to be noted that such acts are also modified by adverbs, again generating fuzzy clusters that are treated by the fuzzy theory. It should also be noted that in the foregoing classification, we have identified two subclasses of linguistic variables: nouns as (a) and (b), and their corresponding linguistic terms (i.e., adjectives and/or adjectives modified by adverbs) as (a) and (b) categories. This separation helps us to clarify the confusion between the agenda of fuzzy theory and the agenda of other theories, such as probability, belief, and so on.

10.2.2 Structure of Sentences

For our purpose, we identify two distinct structures of sentences:

1. Descriptive sentences
2. Descriptive sentences that are verified with a truth-qualifying assertion

A descriptive sentence is a sentence that describes an entity, an object, an event, and so on, with the use of nouns, adjectives, adverbs, and verbs, whereas a verification sentence is a sentence that asserts the truth of a descriptive sentence which is taken as the subject. Let us give a few examples:

- *Description (crisp or fuzzy)*: "John is tall"; "inventory is high"; "belief is strong"; "probability is low."
- *Description (crisp or fuzzy) but verification (crisp)*: "John is tall" is true; or it is true that "John is tall"; "inventory is low" is false; or it is not the case that "inventory is low"; "belief is strong" is true; or it is the case that "belief is strong"; "probability is low" is false; or it is not the case that "probability is low," and so on.
- *Description (crisp or fuzzy) with first verification (crisp or fuzzy) and second verification (crisp)*: ' "John is tall" is true (or somewhat true)' is true; ' "inventory is low" is false (or very false)' is true; ' "belief is strong" is true

(or very true)' is false; '"probability is low" is false (or quite false)' is false; and so on.

In this last set of examples, we note a hierarchy of complex sentences with higher levels of verification. In classical logic, logicians discuss "truth of the truth, etc." in a similar hierarchy.

10.2.3 Nature of Truth

The nature of truth is one of the central philosophical concerns in studies of logic. It is expressed as a T-sentence.

Definition 10.1:. "$x \in X \; isr \, A, \mu_A(x) \in [0, 1]$ (or $\{0, 1\}$)" is true if and only if the sentence "$x \in X \; isr \, A, \mu_A(x) \in [0, 1]$ (or $\{0, 1\}$)" is itself true.

One needs to ask: How is this independent verification to be established? Generally, it is assumed that (1) there are experts who can verify that the sentence is itself true by their knowledge of a system, or (2) there are necessary and sufficient data vectors that are obtained from data files and/or sensor readings, and further, there is an algorithm that can identify clusters and construct membership functions, and hence our confidence in the data and the algorithm gives us the required verification.

Tarski [17] states that one cannot express the concept of truth (i.e., the concept of verification) in the same language that states the sentence of the concept of description. If there is $\mathrm{T}(s) \leftrightarrow s$, then alternatively, there is $\mathrm{T}(s) \leftrightarrow \rceil s$. Thus $s \leftrightarrow \rceil s$ is *crisp contradiction*.

Examples of contradicting T-sentences are: (1) "All Creatans are liars" as uttered by the Creatan Epimenides, and (2) "I am lying" as I utter in any discourse. Clearly, in these examples, if the truth were to be revealed by the sentence itself, we then get a crisp contradiction.

Recall that in a *court of law*, a witness is asked to affirm or deny a statement, event, or description in terms of two-valued logic as true or false separate from the statement that describes a situation and in addition to such a statement. Furthermore, the jury decides whether or not all the evidence given by all the witnesses can lead to truth beyond a reasonable doubt. This forms the second verification.

10.3 SET AND LOGIC COMBINATION

In light of the interpretation of membership functions given above, it is natural to propose a number of basic fuzzy set and logic models that combine the set and logic assignments that form the basis of our formal knowledge representation. We discuss next some of these models. For this discussion, we need the following concepts and their definitions.

Let us consider the linguistic variables that define the events or entities as $X = \{\text{events or entities}\}$, and linguistic terms that describe the fuzzy sets of the linguistic variables as $D = \{\text{qualifiers of events or entities}\}$. Let the membership in X be crisp:

$$\mu_X(x) \in \{0, 1\} \qquad \text{for all } x \in X.$$

Note that a base variable is associated with a *noun* (i.e., a linguistic variable). It identifies a general class, a label, such as "age," "height," "probability," "number," "possibility," "belief," "plausibility," or "truth." This is at times known as the *indicator function*. It should be recalled that classical theory deals ony with linguistic variables as the dimensions of any system analysis. Thus an n-dimensional system model is build over n variables.

Next, let the membership in D be either crisp or fuzzy:

$$\mu_D(X) \in \{0, 1\} \text{ or } [0, 1].$$

Recall that a descriptive membership associated with an adjective or an adjective and an adverb identifies a subclass of a general class, such as "high," "low," "small," "large," "positive small," or "negative large": for example, "old (age)," "tall (height) building," "low (probability)," "low (belief)," "high (plausibility)," "positive small (number)," "true sentence," "very false (sentence)."

Note again that "age," "height," "probability," "belief,' and so on, are nouns and that all nouns can be modified by adjectives and adverbs. Thus the agenda of fuzzy theory is clear. It takes probabilities or beliefs, from classical theory but fuzzifies them all. To the n-variable setting of classical theory, fuzzy theory introduces one additional dimension and hence deals with $(n + 1)$-dimensional space. Naturally, in classical theory, one could introduce $(n + 1)$-dimensional analysis when the qualification is taken to be dichotomous.

Beyond the descriptive sentence, there is either implicit or explicit verification. Next, we discuss the verification of a descriptive sentence. For this purpose, we consider the *external*, or last, *verfication* to be two-valued, whereas the *internal verification* could be two-valued or fuzzy-valued. We consider both of these options in our treatment. Let the external verification be $V' = \{\text{crisp truth qualifiers}\} = \{\text{true, false}\}$, with $\mu_{V'}(S) \in \{0, 1\}$, and the internal verification be $V = \{\text{fuzzy truth qualifiers}\}$ with $\mu_V(S) \in \{0, 1\}$ or [0,1], where s is a descriptive sentence. For fuzzy verification, the term set is $V = \{$very true, somewhat true, quite true, true, false, quite false, somewhat false, very false$\}$. Therefore, the truth qualification of a descriptive sentence generally can be written in two forms: (1) "s is true" and (2) "s is very true" is true. Based on these concepts and symbols, we now present several possible models of set and logic structures with descriptive and veristic words.

10.3.1 Models of Descriptive and Veristic Words

We consider four basic models with a number of subcases.

1. Consider over a two-valued classification of base-variable values in $x \in X$ a two-valued set description (qualification) D that is verified by the two-valued

logic assignment (assertion) V' as {T,F}, that is,

$$\{X_{\{0,1\}}, D_{\{0,1\}}, V'_{\{T,F\}}\}.$$

For example, the descriptive and veristic sentences would be written as

s =:: "John is heavy"; or
s =:: "John's weight is heavy"
s' =:: "John's is heavy" is true; or
s' =:: "John's weight is heavy" is true;

where $\mu_X(x) \in \{0, 1\}$ indicates "John's weight" to be in the class of people's weights in a dichotomous manner, $\mu_D(x) = \mu_H(x) \in \{0, 1\}$ qualifies the weight of John to be in the subclass of heavy people in a dichotomous-valued manner, and $\mu_{V'}(s) \in \{T, F\}$ verifies the sentence s to be true in a dichotomous manner. It should be noted that this is the classical two-valued set and logic theory that identifies fuzzy sets (i.e., vague linguistic terms such as "heavy" arbitrarily with a two-valued restriction).

2. (a) Next, consider over a two-valued classification (labeling) of base-variable values in $x \in X$ a fuzzy-valued set description (qualification) D that is verified by a two-valued logic assignment V' as {T,F}, that is,

$$\{X_{\{0,1\}}, D_{[0,1]}, V'_{\{T,F\}}\}.$$

For this case, the descriptive and veristic sentences would be written as

s =:: "John is heavy"; or
s =:: "John's weight is heavy"
s' =:: "John's is heavy" is true; or
s' =:: "John's weight is heavy" is true;

where again, $\mu_X(x) \in \{0, 1\}$ indicates 'John's weight" to be in the class of people's weights, but with $\mu_D(x) = \mu_H(x) \in [0, 1]$ qualifies John's weight to be in the subclass of heavy people to a certain degree in an infinite-valued fuzzy set, and $\mu_{V'}(s) \in \{T, F\}$ specifies a dichotomous verification of the sentence s to be true. This is the fuzzy set and two-valued logic model that is discussed in most of the current literature in a myopic manner. Why it is called myopic will be clarified later when FCNF and FDNF expressions are derived and discussed.

(b) Next consider over two-valued classification (labeling) of base-variable values $x \in X$ a probability measure P in the usual classical sense, where p is over an indicator function $\mu_{D'}$. But P is further qualified with a fuzzy-valued set description D whch is verified by a two-valued logic assignment V' as {T,F}, that is,

$$\{X_{\{0,1\}}, D'_{\{0,1\}}, \mathrm{Pr}_{[0,1]}, D_{[0,1]}, V'_{\{T,F\}}\}.$$

For this case, the descriptive and veristic sentences would be written as

$$s =:: \text{“Probability is large that John is heavy”; and}$$

$$s' =:: \text{“Probability is large that John is heavy” is true}$$

Note that "John is heavy" is interpreted dichotomously to provide an indicator function for the probability measure assignment. Again in this case, $\mu_X(x) \in \{0, 1\}$ indicates "John's weight" to be in the class of all possible people's weights; $\mu_D(x) = \mu_H(x) \in \{0, 1\}$ indicates whether or not the event "John's weight" is assigned to the class of "heavy" people; $\Pr(x \in X) = (p(x)|\mu_H(x) = 1) \in [0, 1]$ assigns a probability $\mu_H(x) = 1$ to the event $x \in X$ that "John's weight," which is classified as "heavy," has occurred; $\mu_D(p(x)) = \mu_L(p(x)) \in [0, 1]$ qualifies the event's probability to be in the subclass of "large probabilities" to a degree, (i.e., assigns it to be in the fuzzy set of "large probabilities"), and $\mu_{V'}(s) \in \{\mathrm{T}, \mathrm{F}\}$ specifies a dichotomous verification of the sentence s to be true. [*Note*: If we model it such that $\mu_D(p(x)) = \mu_L(p(x)) \in \{0, 1\}$, which qualifies the event Probabilities to be in the subclass of "large probabilities" in the two-valued manner crisply, we get the classical probability set up for an arbitrarily dichotomized concept of "large probabilities."]

(c) Next, consider over two-valued classification of base-variable values $x \in X$ a belief measure Bel in the usual classical sense, where Bel is over an indicator function $\mu_{D'}$. But Bel is further qualified with a fuzzy-valued set description D, whcih is verified by a two-valued logic assignmnt V' as {T,F}, that is,

$$\{X_{\{0,1\}}, D'_{\{0,1\}}, \mathrm{Bel}_{[0,1]}, D_{[0,1]}, V'_{\{\mathrm{T,F}\}}\}.$$

For this case, the descriptive and veristic sentences would be written as

s =:: "my belief that this sensor's information (reading) is good is low", or for short, we can write

s =:: "belief is low"

s' =:: "It is the case that (true that)" my belief is low for this sensor's information (reading) being good, or for short, we can write

s' =:: "belief is low" is true,

where $\mu_X(x) = \{0, 1\}$ indicates "the sensor's $x \in X$ reading" to be in the possible class of all readings, $\mu_D(x) = \mu_G(x) \in \{0, 1\}$ indicates whether or not the event "that sensor's reading" is good G has occurred in the sample space, $\mathrm{Bel}(x \in X) = (b(x)|\mu_G(x) = 1) \in [0, 1]$ assigns my belief to the information given by the sensor's reading being "good" G given that it has occurred for $X \in X$, $\mu_D(b(x)) = \mu_L(b(x)) \in [0, 1]$ qualifies my belief in the sensor reading that is dichotomously qualified as "good" to be in the subclass of "low beliefs" to a degree in a fuzzy manner, and

$\mu_{V'}(s) \in \{\text{T}, \text{F}\}$ specifies a dichotomous verification of the sentence s to be true. [*Note*: Again, if we model such that $\mu_D(b(x)) = \mu_L(b(x)) \in \{0, 1\}$, which qualifies my belief in the sensor reading to be in the subclass of "low beliefs" in the two-valued manner (i.e., crisply), we get the classical belief set up for an arbitrarily dichotomized concept of "low beliefs."]

3. (a) Next, consider over two-valued classification (labeling) of base-variable values $x \in X$ a two-valued set description (qualification) D that is first verified by a fuzzy-valued partial truth qualification which is next verified by a two-valued logic assignment as {T,F}, that is,

$$\{X_{\{0,1\}}, D_{\{0,1\}}, V_{[0,1]}, V'_{\{T,F\}}\}.$$

For example, for this case, the descriptive sentence s, the fuzzy-valued internal verification sentence s', and the two-valued external verification sentence s'' would be written as

s =:: "John is heavy";
s' =:: "John is heavy" is very true;
s'' =:: ' "John is heavy' is very true" is true,

where $\mu_X(x) \in \{0, 1\}$ indicates that John's weight is in the class of people's weights with a two-valued classification, $\mu_D(x) = \mu_H(x) \in \{0, 1\}$ quantifies John's weight to be in the subclass of "heavy people" with a two-valued clasification, $\mu_V(s) \in [0, 1]$ assigns a partial-truth qualification to the sentence s and $\mu'_V(s') \in \{T, F\}$ assigns a dichotomous verification to the sentence s'.

(b) Next, consider over two-valued classification of base-variable values $x \in X$ a probability measure P in the classical sense where P is over an indicator function $\mu_{D'}$. But P is further qualified in this case with a two-valued set description D which has an internal fuzzy-valued verfication V which is externally verified by a dichotomous verification V':

$$\{X_{\{0,1\}}, D'_{\{0,1\}}, \text{Pr}_{[0,1]}, D_{\{0,1}, V_{[0,1]}, V'_{\{\text{T,F}\}}\}.$$

For this case, the descriptive internal verification and external verification would be written as

s =:: "probability that John is heavy is large";
s' =:: " 'probability that John is heavy is large' is quite true";
s'' =:: " 'probability that John is heavy is large' is quite true" is true.

where $\mu_X(x) \in \{0, 1\}$ is the indicator function over X, $\mu_{D'}(x) = \mu_H(x) \in \{0, 1\}$ is the indicator function for "heavy" $(H), \text{Pr}(x \in X) = (p(x)|\mu_H(x) = 1) \in [0, 1]$ is the probability assignment, $\mu_D(p(x)) = \mu_L(p(x)) \in \{0, 1\}$ is a dichotomous subclass qualification for "large"

(L), $\mu_V(s) \in [0,1]$ is the partial-truth qualification of s, and $\mu_{V'}(s') \in \{T, F\}$ is a dichotomous verification of s'.

(c) Next, consider the same model for belief; without further detail we write it as

$$\{X_{\{0,1\}}, D'_{\{0,1\}}, \mathrm{Bel}_{[0,1]}, D_{\{0,1\}}, V_{[0,1]}, V'_{\{T,F\}}\}.$$

s =:: "belief is good is low";

s' =:: " 'belief is good is low' is quite false";

s'' =:: " 'belief is good is low' is quite false" is true,

where $\mu_X(x) \in \{0,1\}$ is an indicator function, $\mu_{D'}(x) = \mu_G(x) \in \{0,1\}$ is the indicator function for "good" (G), $\mathrm{Bel}(x \in X) = (b(x)|\mu_G(x) = 1) \in [0,1]$ is the belief assignment, $\mu_D(b(x)) = \mu_L(b(x)) \in \{0,1\}$ is a dichotomous subclass qualification for "low" (L), $\mu_V(s) \in [0,1]$ is a partial-truth qualification of s, and $\mu_{V'}(s') \in \{T, F\}$ is a dichotomous verification of s'.

4. (a) Next consider over two-valued classification of base-variable values $x \in X$ a fuzzy-valued set description (qualification) D that is first verified by a fuzzy-valued partial-truth qualification which is next verified by a two-valued logic assignment as {T,F}, that is,

$$\{X_{\{0,1\}}, D_{[0,1]}, V_{[0,1]}, V'_{\{T,F\}}\}.$$

The sentences for this case would be written as

s =:: "John is heavy";

s' =:: " 'John is heavy' is very true";

s'' =:: " 'John is heavy' is very true" is true,

where$\mu_X(x) \in 0, 1$ is an indicator function for the base-variable values, $\mu_D(x) = \mu_H(x) \in [0,1]$ is a fuzzy-valued subclassification, $\mu_V(s) \in [0,1]$ is a partial-truth qualification of the sentence s, and $\mu_{V'}(s')$ is a dichotomous verification of sentence s'.

(b) Next, consider, without detail, probability measure and fuzzy set classification as

$$\{X_{\{0,1\}}, D'_{\{0,1\}}, \mathrm{Pr}_{[0,1]}, D_{[0,1]}, V_{[0,1]}, V'_{\{T,F\}}\}.$$

s =:: "probability that John is heavy is large";

s' =:: " 'probability that John is heavy is large' is quite true";

s'' =:: " 'probability that John is heavy is large' is quite true" is false,

where $\mu_X(x) \in \{0,1\}$ is an indicator function, $\mu_{D'}(x) = \mu_H(x) \in \{0,1\}$ indicates that "John is classified as "Heavy" (H) has occurred,

$\Pr(x \in X) = (p(x)|\mu_H(x) = 1) \in [0, 1]$ is a probability assignment, $\mu_D(p(x)) = \mu_L(p(x)) \in [0, 1]$ is a fuzzy-valued subclasification of the probabilities, $\mu_V(s) \in [0, 1]$ is a partial-truth qualification of sentence s, and $\mu_{V'}(s') \in \{T, F\}$ is a dichotomous verification of sentence s'.

(c) It should be clear by now that all possible fuzzy models for probability, possibility, belief, plausibility, and necessity can be constructed in this framework as follows:

$$\{X_{\{0,1\}}, D'_{\{0,1\}}, \Pr_{[0,1]}, D_{[0,1]}, V_{[0,1]}, V'_{\{T,F\}}\}$$
$$\text{Poss}_{[0,1]}$$
$$\text{Bel}_{[0,1]}$$
$$\text{Pla}_{[0,1]}$$
$$\text{Nec}_{[0,1]}.$$

Detailed identification of each symbol could be made in agreement with the structure provided in previous models.

10.4 NORMAL FORM EXPRESSIONS

In Section 10.1 it was stated that fuzzy system modeling begins with linguistic expressions, next they are transformed into symbolic metalinguistic expressions, and then they are transformed into symbolic propositional expressions. In Section 10.2 a distinction is made between descriptive and veristic words that make up a metalinguistic expression. In Section 10.3, alternative models are proposed that combines descriptive and veristic words, depending on their representation in two-valued or infinite-valued set representations.

In this section, fuzzy truth table–based methodology is presented, which demonstrates how metalinguistic expressions are transformed into fuzzy propositional expressions. Fuzzy truth table methodology is applied to drive fuzzy disjunctive and fuzzy conjunctive normal forms (FDNF and FCNF) for all 16 combinations of concepts whose metalinguistic expressions are depicted in Table 10.1.

In classical theory, disjunctive and conjunctive normal forms (DNF and CNF) are derived from the classical truth table. Here it is shown that:

1. A classical truth table (Table 10.3) for two classical sets that contain four rows can be extended in a natural way to a fuzzy truth table (Table 10.5), which is a table of eight rows. The fuzzy truth table explicitly states that the membership values of fuzzy set A, a, and the membership values of fuzzy set B, b, are ordered (i.e., either $a \geq b$ or $a < bs$) [22, 24,26].
2. The classical DNF and CNF expressions, depicted in Table 10.2, turn out to be equivalent to FDNF and FCNF, *but in form only*, for the general class of computational predicate expressions, t-norms and t-co-norms, which correspond to the propositional operators $\cap$ and $\cup$ in the propositional

TABLE 10.1. Metalinguistic Expressions of Combined Concepts for Any *A* and *B*

No.	Metalinguistic Expression
1	Universe
2	Empty set
3	*A* or *B*
4	NOT *A* and not *B*
5	NOT *A* or not *B*
6	*A* and *B*
7	*A* implies *B*
8	*A* and not *B*
9	*A* or not *B*
10	Not *A* and *B*
11	*A* if and only if *B*
12	*A* exclusive or *B*
13	*A*
14	Not *A*
15	*B*
16	Not *B*

expressions shown in Table 10.2. It is well known that $\mathrm{DNF}(\cdot) = \mathrm{CNF}(\cdot)$, due to the axioms of classical set and logic theory shown in Table 10.4. It will be shown that $\mathrm{FDNF}(\cdot) \subseteq \mathrm{FCNF}(\cdot)$ in Section 10.4.3, due to monotonicity, and a subset of the axioms of classical set and logic theory, Table 10.4, which are involution, commutativity, associativity, identity (boundary), and De Morgan's laws.

3. FDNF and FCNF expressions provide a theoretical grounding [21] to the compensatory AND operators proposed on the basis of experimental results by Zimmermann and Zysno [33].
4. FDNF and FCNF expressions further provide a theoretical grounding [27,28] to he convex linear compromise reasoning proposed on the basis of heuristic considerations by Yager and Filev [29].
5. As an extension of items 3 and 4, it is proposed here that an alternative schema called *exponential compromise reasoning* should be investigated in some system modeling studies.

In summary, compensatory AND and compromise reasoning schemas are, in fact, further demonstrations of why we should not discard FDNF and FCNF formulas. In the rest of this section, we explain briefly the results stated above.

10.4.1 Fuzzy Truth Tables

For the formation of a fuzzy truth table, we start out with the metalinguistic expressions that explicitly state the descriptive and veristic words of our linguistic

TABLE 10.2. Classical and Fuzzy Disjunctive and Conjunctive Canonical Forms[a]

No.	Disjunctive Normal Forms				Conjunctive Normal Forms			
1	$(A \cap B) \cup$	$(A \cap c(B)) \cup$	$(c(A) \cap B) \cup$	$(c(A) \cap c(B))$		I		
2		ϕ			$(A \cup B) \cap$	$(A \cup c(B)) \cap$	$(c(A) \cup B) \cap$	$(c(A) \cup c(B))$
3	$(A \cap B) \cup$	$(A \cap c(B)) \cup$	$(c(A) \cap B)$		$(A \cup B)$			
4				$(c(A) \cap c(B))$		$(A \cup c(B)) \cap$	$(c(A) \cup B) \cap$	$(c(A) \cup c(B))$
5		$(A \cap c(B)) \cup$	$(c(A) \cap B) \cup$	$(c(A) \cap c(B))$				$(c(A) \cup c(B))$
6	$(A \cap B)$				$(A \cup B) \cap$	$(A \cup c(B)) \cap$	$(c(A) \cup B)$	
7	$(A \cap B) \cup$		$(c(A) \cap B) \cup$	$(c(A) \cap c(B))$			$(c(A) \cup B)$	
8		$(A \cap c(B))$			$(A \cup B) \cap$	$(A \cup c(B)) \cap$		$(c(A) \cup c(B))$
9	$(A \cap B) \cup$	$(A \cap c(B)) \cup$		$(c(A) \cap c(B))$		$(A \cup c(B))$		
10			$(c(A) \cap B)$		$(A \cup B) \cap$		$(c(A) \cup B) \cap$	$(c(A) \cup c(B))$
11	$(A \cap B) \cup$			$(c(A) \cap c(B))$		$(A \cup c(B)) \cap$	$(c(A) \cup B)$	
12		$(A \cap c(B)) \cup$	$(c(A) \cap B)$		$(A \cup B) \cap$			$(c(A) \cup c(B))$
13	$(A \cap B) \cup$	$(A \cap c(B))$			$(A \cup B) \cap$	$(A \cup c(B))$		
14			$(c(A) \cap B) \cup$	$(c(A) \cap c(B))$			$(c(A) \cup B) \cap$	$(c(A) \cup c(B))$
15	$(A \cap B) \cup$		$(c(A) \cap B)$		$(A \cup B) \cap$		$(c(A) \cup B)$	
16		$(A \cap c(B)) \cup$		$(c(A) \cap c(B))$		$(A \cup c(B)) \cap$		$(c(A) \cup c(B))$

[a] $\cap$ is a conjunction, $\cup$ is a disjunction, and c is a complementation operator.

TABLE 10.3. Classical Truth Table Interpretations of "*A* AND *B*"

Truth Assignments to Classical Metalinguistic Variables *A*	*B*	Truth Assignments to the Metalinguistic Expression "*A* AND *B*"	Primary Conjunctions
$T(A)$	T(*B*)	T(*A* AND *B*)	$A \cap B$
T(*A*)	F(*B*)	F(*A* AND *B*)	$A \cap c(B)$
F(*A*)	T(*B*)	F(*A* AND *B*)	$c(A) \cap B$
F(*A*)	F(*B*)	F(*A* AND *B*)	$c(A) \cap c(B)$

TABLE 10.4. Axioms of Classical and Set Operations

Involution	$c(c(A)) = A$
Commutativity	$A \cup B = B \cup A$
	$A \cap B = B \cap A$
Associativity	$(A \cup B) \cup C = A \cup (B \cup C)$
	$(A \cap B) \cap C = A \cap (B \cap C)$
Distributivity	$(A \cup (B \cap C) = (A \cup B) \cap (A \cup C)$
	$A \cap (B \cup C) = (A \cap B) \cup (A \cap C)$
Idempotence	$A \cup A = A$
	$A \cap A = A$
Absorption	$A \cup (A \cap B) = A$
	$A \cap (A \cup B) = A$
Absorption by X and $\varnothing$	$A \cup X = X$
	$A \cap \varnothing = \varnothing$
Identity	$A \cup \varnothing = A$
	$A \cap X = A$
Law of contradiction	$A \cap c(A) = \varnothing$
Law of excluded middle	$A \cup c(A) = X$
De Morgan's laws	$c(A \cap B) = c(A) \cup c(B)$
	$c(A \cup B) = c(A) \cap c(B)$

TABLE 10.5. Newly Constructed Fuzzy Truth Table of "*A* AND *B*" where $a, b \in [0,1]$

A			*B*			*A* AND *B*
(1.1.1)	$a \geq b$	T	(2.1.1)	$a \geq b$	T	T
(1.1.1)	$a \geq b$	T	(2.2.1)	$a < b$	F	F
(1.2.1)	$a < b$	F	(2.1.1)	$a \geq b$	T	F
(1.2.1)	$a < b$	F	(2.2.1)	$a < b$	F	F
(1.1.2)	$a < b$	T	(2.1.2)	$a < b$	T	T
(1.1.2)	$a < b$	T	(2.2.2)	$a \geq b$	F	F
(1.2.2)	$a \geq b$	F	(2.1.2)	$a < b$	T	F
(1.2.2)	$a \geq b$	F	(2.2.2)	$a \geq b$	F	F

knowledge as shown expressions (1.1.1), (1.2.1), (2.1.1), (2.2.1) for any element $x \in X_1$ and (1.1.2), (1.2.2), (2.1.2), (2.2.2) for $x \in X_2$, where $X_1 \cup X_2 = X$ and $X_1 \cap X_2 = \phi$, $\mu_X(x) \in \{0, 1\}$. Thus any x that belongs to X_1, does not belong to X_2 on the base axis domain of X. Thus there is an "exclusive or" concept that applies to $x \in X$. Furthermore, A and B are two fuzzy sets with membership values $\mu_A(x) = \text{a}, \mu_B(x) = b, a, b \in [0, 1]$ for all possible combinations of $a \geq b$ or $a < b$ for the external verification V', such that $\mu_{V'}(s) = \tau \in [\text{T}, \text{F}]$, where

$$s \in S = \{(1.1.1), (1.2.1), (2.1.1), (2.2.1) \text{ and } (1.1.2), (1.2.2), (2.1.2), (2.2.2)\}$$

as shown below.

Basic Metalinguistic Expressions. For all $x \in X_1$:

(1.1.1) $x \in X_1$ is in the infinite-valued (fuzzy) set A with membership degree $a \geq b$ is V' = "true, "$\tau = \text{T}$; that is,

$$x \in X_1 \ isr \ A, a \geq b, \ isv \ V', \tau = \text{T}$$

(1.2.1) $x \in X_1$ is in the infinite-valued (fuzzy) set A with membership degree $a < b$ is V' = "false," $\tau = \text{F}$; that is,

$$x \in X_1 \ isr \ A, a < b, \ isv \ V', \tau = \text{F}.$$

(2.1.1) $x \in X_1$ is in the infinite-valued (fuzzy) set B with membership degree $a < b$ is V' = "true," $\tau = \text{T}$; that is,

$$x \in X_1 \ isr \ B, a \geq b, \ isv \ V', \tau = \text{T}.$$

(2.2.1) $x \in X_1$ is in the infinite-valued (fuzzy) set B with membership degree $a < b$ is V' = "false," $\tau = \text{F}$; that is,

$$x \in X_1 \ isr \ B, a < b, \ isv \ V', \tau = \text{F}.$$

For all $x \in X_2$, analogous expressions can be written, but we will write the shorthand notation only. That is, we have for all $x \in X_2$:

(1.1.2) $x \in X_2 \ isr \ A, a < b, \ isv \ V', \tau = \text{T}$.
(1.2.2) $x \in X_2 \ isr$ is $A, a \geq b, \ isv \ V', \tau = \text{F}$.
(2.1.2) $x \in X_2 \ isr \ B, a < b, \ isv \ V', \tau = \text{T}$.
(2.2.2) $x \in X_2 \ isr \ B, a \geq b, \ isv \ V', \tau = \text{F}$.

These two sets of linguistic expressions form the bases on which one can construct the fuzzy truth table for the definition of the combined fuzzy set A AND B in the model $\{X_{\{0,1\}}, D_{[0,1]}, V_{\{0,1\}}\}$ discussed in Section 10.3. With these metalinguistic expressions, we are able to construct the combination of predicate expressions to form the fuzzy truth table as depicted in Table 10.5 for any of the 16 concept combinations.

Construction of Fuzzy Truth Table. The combination of the metalinguistic predicate expressions (1.1.1), (1.2.1), (2.1.1), (2.2.1) and (1.1.2), (1.2.2), (2.1.2), (2.2.2) together form the basis of rows of a fuzzy truth table as follows, row by row from top to bottom, for example, for a A AND B combination as follows:

(1.1.1) AND (2.1.1)	"$x \in X_1$ *isr* $A, a \geq b$, *isv* $V', \tau = \text{T}$" AND "$x \in X_1$ *isr* $B, a \geq b$, *isv* $V', \tau = \text{T}$" is T;
(1.1.1) AND (2.2.1)	"$x \in X_1$ *isr* $A, a \geq b$, *isv* $V', \tau = \text{T}$" AND "$x \in X_1$ *isr* $B, a < b$, *isv* $V', \tau = \text{F}$" is F;
(1.2.1) AND (2.1.1)	"$x \in X_1$ *isr* $A, a < b$, *isv* $V', \tau = \text{F}$" AND "$x \in X_1$ *isr* $B, a \geq b$, *isv* $V', \tau = \text{T}$" is F;
(1.2.1) AND (2.2.1)	"$x \in X_1$ *isr* $A, a < b$, *isv* $V', \tau = \text{F}$" AND "$x \in X_1$ *isr* $B, a < b$, *isv* $V', \tau = \text{F}$" is F.
(1.1.2) AND (2.1.2)	"$x \in X_2$ *isr* $A, a < b$, *isv* $V', \tau = \text{T}$" AND "$x \in X_2$ *isr* $B, a < b$, *isv* $V', \tau = \text{T}$" is T;
(1.1.2) AND (2.2.2)	"$x \in X_2$ *isr* $A, a < b$, *isv* $V', \tau = \text{T}$" AND "$x \in X_2$ *isr* $B, a \geq b$, *isv* $V', \tau = \text{F}$" is F;
(1.2.2) AND (2.1.2)	"$x \in X_2$ *isr* $A, a \geq b$, *isv* $V', \tau = \text{F}$" AND "$x \in X_2$ *isr* $B, a < b$, *isv* $V', \tau = \text{T}$" is F;
(1.2.2) AND (2.2.2)	"$x \in X_2$ *isr* $A, a \geq b$, *isv* $V', \tau = \text{F}$" AND "$x \in X_2$ *isr* $B, a \geq b$, *isv* $V', \tau = \text{F}$" is F.

A similar set of eight expressions can be written for any of the 16 linguistic concept combinations, where, for example, for "IMPLIES" ($\rightarrow$), all we need to change is "AND" with "IMPLIES" in the template shown above with additional changes for the consequents to be {T,F,T,T,T,F,T,T}, as shown in the last colums of Table 10.5.

As a result of these metalinguistic expressions, which explicitly identify the components of the descriptive and veristic statements, we can form the fuzzy truth table in Table 10.5. In this table, descriptive components are shown in the columns which indicate $a \geq b$ or $a < b$ alongside the veristic component column, where it is shown whether a description is verified to be true (T) or false (F). It should be recalled that in two-valued classical truth tables, this distinction is never made explicitly, even though it is there implicitly. That is, classical truth tables do not say anything about the definition of the sets A and B, but implicitly it is assumed that elements of A and B belong or do not belong to the sets A and B absolutely (i.e., $a, b \in \{0, 1\}$). In fuzzy truth tables, fuzzy membership values $a, b \in [0, 1]$ are shown with respect to their order relation. This is a bit of knowledge that is stated in Kaufmann [7] in assessments of fuzzy functions.

It is this simple bit of knowledge that helps us respond positively to the negative position stated by Marinos [11], where it is stated that "it is impossible to form fuzzy truth tables since $a, b \in [0, 1]$" (i.e., fuzzy truth tables must have infinitely many rows). A more detailed discussion of this and other related issues can be found in Türkşen et al. [24,26].

Remark: Readers are warned that in our previous publications [22–24, 26] there is a minor but important error. The "exclusive or" nature of $x \in X_1$ and $x \in X_2$, $X_1 \cup X_2 = X$, and $X_1 \cap X_2 = \phi$, was overlooked in those writtings. Thus FDNF and FCNF expressions are stated with duplicate terms. For example, FCNF(*A* OR *B*) is written as $(A \cup B) \cap (B \cup A)$ and FDNF(*A* AND *B*) is written as $(A \cap B) \cup (B \cap A)$. But in the light of more recent results, it is shown that we just have FCNF(*A* OR *B*)$= A \cup B$ and FDNF(*A* AND *B*)$= A \cap B$. Readers should make these corrections in reviewing the previous papers. The main essence of all the discussions, however, is still valid in those papers.

10.4.2 FDNF and FCNF Expressions

Application of the normal form derivation algorithm (see the Appendix) gives us the derivation of FDNF and FCNF expressions for "*A* AND *B*" from the fuzzy truth table (Table 10.5) as

$$\text{FDNF}(A \text{ AND } B) = (A \cap B), A \supseteq B \text{ or } A \subset B \text{ is T}$$
$$\text{FCNF}(A \text{ AND } B) = (A \cup B) \cap (B \cup \text{c}(A) \cap (\text{c}(B) \cup A), A \supseteq B \text{ or } A \subset B \text{ is T},$$

for all *t*-norm *t*-co-norm, and standard complements that correspond to $\cap, \cup$, and c, respectively, in the computational domain.

We can also drive FDNF and FCNF expressions for all 16 metalinguistic combinations shown in Table 14.1. For example, for "*A* OR *B*" we get

$$\text{FDNF}(A \text{ OR } B) = (A \cap B) \cup (A \cap \text{c}(B)) \cup (\text{c}(A) \cap B)$$
$$\text{FCNF}(A \text{ OR } B) = A \cup B.$$

For another example, for "*A* IMPLIES *B* ($A \rightarrow B$), we get

$$\text{FDNF}(A \rightarrow B) = (A \cap B) \cup (\text{c}(A) \cap B) \cup (\text{c}(A) \cap \text{c}(B))$$
$$\text{FCNF}(A \rightarrow B) = (\text{c}(A) \cup (B),$$

where $A \supseteq B$ or $A \subset B$ is T, again for all *t*-norm, *t*-co-norm, and standard complementation that correspond to $\cap, \cup$, and *c*, respectively, in the numerical domain.

10.4.3 Containment Versus Equivalence

In classical theory we have $\text{DNF}(\cdot) \equiv \text{CNF}(\cdot)$ for all 16 cases. It is shown that $\text{FDNF}(\cdot) \subseteq \text{FCNF}(\cdot)$ for all 16 cases in fuzzy theory [18,28]. This is now demonstrated very briefly. We will first show the equivalence of $\text{DNF}(\cdot) \equiv \text{CNF}(\cdot)$, and then that $\text{FDNF}(\cdot) \subseteq \text{FCNF}(\cdot)$.

Equivalence of DNF and CNF. In classical theory, we have, for example,

$$\text{CNF}(A \text{ AND } B) \equiv \text{DNF}(A \text{ AND } B).$$

To show this, we start out with the expressions

$$\text{DNF}(A \text{ AND } B) = A \cap B$$
$$\text{CNF}(A \text{ AND } B) = (A \cup B) \cap (A \cup \text{c}(B)) \cap (\text{c}(A) \cup (B).$$

Next, we apply certain axioms to CNF($\cdot$), as follows:

$$\begin{aligned}(\text{idempotency and distributivity}) &= [A \cup (B \cap \text{c}(B))] \cap [B \cup (A \cap \text{c}(A))] \\ (\text{law of contradiction}) &= [A \cup \varnothing] \cap [B \cup \phi] \\ (\text{identity, boundary}) &= A \cap B.\end{aligned}$$

Containment of FDNF and FCNF. In fuzzy theory we have

$$\text{FDNF}(A \text{ AND } B) \subseteq \text{FCNF}(A \text{ AND } B).$$

To show this, we start out again with the expressions

$$\text{FDNF}(A \text{ AND } B) = A \cap B$$
$$\text{FCNF}(A \text{ AND } B) = (A \cup B) \cap (A \cup \text{c}(B)) \cap (\text{c}(A) \cup B).$$

As indicated, the expressions are the same but *in form only*. In general, for the class of t-norms, t-co-norms, and standard complement De Morgan triples that correspond to the propositional operators $\cap$, $\cup$, and c, respectively, the axioms of idempotency, distributivity, and the law of contradiction are not applicable. It is because these axioms are relaxed in general in fuzzy theory that we get the containment of FDNF in FCNF.

Next, let us demonstrate this containment relationship as an example of the case of "A OR B" combination, this time in the numerical domain where t-norm (Δ) and t-co-norm (∇) operators are applicable. That is, we need to show that

$$\text{FDNF}(A \text{ OR B}) \subseteq \text{FCNF (A OR B)};$$

that is,

$$(A \cap B) \cup (\text{c}(A) \cap B) \cup (A \cap \text{c}(B)) \subseteq A \cup B.$$

In the numerical membership domain, we need to show that

$$\nabla[\triangle(a,b), \triangle(\bar{a},b)] \leq b \tag{10.1}$$

and

$$\triangle(a, \bar{b}) \leq a \tag{10.2}$$

hold in general, where $\bar{a} = 1 - a, \bar{b} = 1 - b$, and $a, b \in [0, 1]$. While (10.2) is true in general, (10.1) requires a bit of work but can be shown to hold in general, as well be done below. If (10.1) and (10.2) hold, it is true that the following inequality holds:

$$\nabla[\nabla[\triangle(a, b), \triangle(\bar{a}, b)], \triangle(a, \bar{b})] \leq \nabla(a, b). \tag{10.3}$$

Next, we show that (10.1) holds in general. The following statements are true in general for the class of t-norms. First it is clear that

$$a i_{\min} b \leq a \beta_{\min} b \leq a \odot b \leq a \wedge b. \tag{10.4}$$

Next, it is well known that

$$\bar{a} i_{\min} b \leq \bar{a}\, \beta_{\min} b \leq \bar{a} \odot b \leq a \wedge b, \tag{10.5}$$

with the monotonicity of t-norms.

Consider next the following inequalities, which are all true:

$$\nabla[\triangle(a, b), \triangle(\bar{a}, b)] \leq b \qquad (\text{for } \nabla = V, \triangle = \Lambda, \text{ and -}) \tag{10.6}$$

$$\nabla[\triangle(a, b), \triangle(\bar{a}, b)] \leq b \qquad (\text{for } \nabla = \oplus, \triangle = \odot, \text{ and -}) \tag{10.7}$$

$$\nabla[\triangle(a, b), \triangle(\bar{a}, b)] \leq b \qquad (\text{for } \nabla = \beta_{\max}, \triangle = \beta_{\min}, \text{ and -}) \tag{10.8}$$

$$\nabla[\triangle(a, b), \triangle(\bar{a}, b)] \leq b \qquad (\text{for } \nabla = u_{\max}, \triangle = i_{\min}, \text{and -}). \tag{10.9}$$

In expressions (10.3), (10.4), (10.6), (10.7), (10.8), and (10.9), $u_{\min}$, $\beta_{\min}$, $\odot$, and $\wedge$ are "drastic," "bold," "algebraic," and "minimum" intersection operators, respectively; and $u_{\max}$, $\beta_{\max}$, $\oplus$, and V are "drastic," "bold," "algebraic," and "maximum" union operators, respectively.

Because (10.4), and (10.5) hold, it is natural that (10.6) to (10.9) must hold with the monotonicity of t-norms (Δ) and t-co-norms (∇). Thus it can be shown that (10.3) holds for the four well-known cases of t-norm and t-co-norms discussed above for all 16 combinations shown in Table 10.1.

10.4.4 Compensatory AND

Zimmermann and Zysno [33] proposed *compensatory AND*, based on their experiments to be either

$$\mu_{A \ominus B} = \mu_{A \cap B}^{1-\gamma} \mu_{A \cup B}^{\gamma} \qquad \text{exponential compensation} \tag{10.10}$$

or

$$\mu_{A \ominus B} = (1 - \gamma)\mu_{A \cap B} + \gamma\mu_{A \cup B} \qquad \text{convex linear compensation} \tag{10.11}$$

A generalization of the compensatory AND defined by (10.10) and (10.11) can be written as

$$\mu_{A \ominus B} = [\triangle(a,b)]^{1-\gamma}[\nabla(a,b)]^{\gamma} \tag{10.12}$$

or

$$\mu_{A \ominus B} = (1-\gamma)\triangle(a,b) + \gamma\nabla(a,b) \tag{10.13}$$

Türkşen [21] showed that

$$\mu_{\text{FDNF}(A \text{ AND } B)} \leq \mu_{A \ominus B} \leq \mu_{\text{FCNF}(A \text{ OR } B)}$$

for both cases of (10.10) and (10.11) for $\gamma \in [0, 1]$. This results in a theoretical grounding of the Zimmermann and Zysno [33] result, with the realization that

$$\mu_{\text{FDNF}(A \text{ AND } B)} = \triangle(a,b) \quad \text{and} \quad \mu_{\text{FCNF}(A \text{ OR } B)} = \nabla(a,b)$$

are boundary values in human communications. In natural language use, humans mean an infinite gradation of "AND"ness between (1) either FDNF(*A* AND *B*) and FCNF (*A* AND *B*), or (2) a mixture of graded "AND"ness and "OR"ness between FCNF(*A* AND *B*) and FDNF (*A* OR *B*) expression, as in natural expressions where we write "and/or," or (3) a gradation of "OR"ness between FDNF(*A* OR *B*) and FCNF(*A* OR *B*). The γ operator thus specifies this gradation of "AND"ness, or a mixture or "AND"ness, and "OR"ness or the gradation of "OR"ness.

Zimmermann [34] indicated that γ values were determined by interviews of experts in decision-support systems. We have found that γ values can be determined with the application of parametric *t*-norms and *t*-co-norms that are determined by supervised learning in industrial applications [25] where γ operators are used as compensation between two extreme reasoning schemas proposed by Yager and Filev, [29] as compromized reasoning. Let us look next into this issue.

10.1.5 Compromised Reasoning

Yagar and Filev [29] proposed *compromised reasoning* as a convex linear combination of the two extreme reasoning methods that are used in the current literature as $F(y) = (1-\beta)\ F_{\text{M}}(y) + \beta F_{\text{GMP}}(y)$, where $F_{\text{M}}(y)$ is the consequent of Mamdani-type reasoning and $F_{\text{GMP}}(y)$ is the consequent of GMP-type reasoning. It should be recalled that in Mamdani reasoning, the implication $A \to B = A \times B$ is used, and in GMP reasoning, the implication $A \to B = \text{c}(A) \cup B$ is used. Naturally, for a singleton observation $A'(x) = 1$ for $x = x^0$, we get

$$A'(x^0) \bigcirc (A(x) \to B(y)) = A(x^0) \triangle B(y)$$

in Mamdani reasoning, and

$$A'(x^0) \bigcirc (A(x) \rightarrow B(y)) = \mathrm{c}(A(x^0)\nabla B(y)$$

in GMP reasoning.

We observe that

$$\begin{aligned} \text{FDNF}(A \text{ AND } B) &= A \cap B \\ \text{FCNF } (A \rightarrow B) &= (A) \cup B. \end{aligned}$$

Therefore, we can write

$$\begin{aligned} A(x^0)\triangle B(y) &\leq (1-\beta)[A(x^0)\triangle B(y)] + \beta[\mathrm{c}(A(x^0))\nabla\beta(y)] \\ &\leq \mathrm{c}\,(A(x^0))\nabla\beta(y) \text{ for } \beta \in [0,1]. \end{aligned}$$

But we need to show that $A \cap B \subseteq \mathrm{c}(A) \cup B$ in general in order to prove that β values can be found either experimentally or computationally via supervised learning.

FDNF(AND) ⊆ FCNF(→). Let us show that FDNF(A AND B) is included in FCNF($A \rightarrow B$) in a manner similar to FDNF(A AND B) ⊆ FCNF(A OR B), which is shown in Türkşen [21]. However, we show the alternative proof here. Recall that

$$\begin{aligned} \text{FDNF}(A \text{ AND } B) &= A \cap B \\ \text{FCNF}(A \text{ AND } B) &= (A \cup B) \cap (\mathrm{c}(A) \cup B) \cap (A \cup \mathrm{c}(B)) \\ \text{FDNF}(A \rightarrow B) &= (A \cap B) \cup (\mathrm{c}(A) \cap B) \cup (\mathrm{c}(A) \cap \mathrm{c}(B)) \\ \text{FCNF}(A \rightarrow B) &= \mathrm{c}(A) \cup B. \end{aligned}$$

With the general result of Section 10.4.3, it can be shown that

$$\begin{aligned} \text{FDNF}(A \text{ AND } B) &\subseteq \text{FCNF}(A \text{ AND } B) \\ \text{FDNF}(A \rightarrow B) &\subseteq \text{FCNF}(A \rightarrow B). \end{aligned}$$

Also, it is clear that

$$\text{FDNF}(A \text{ AND } B) \subseteq \text{FCNF}(A \rightarrow B).$$

Next, let us examine

$$\text{FCNF}(A \text{ AND } B) \subseteq \text{FDNF}(A \rightarrow B)$$

which cannot be shown to hold for all t-norms and t-co-norms. However, it can be shown that

$$\text{FDNF}(A \text{ AND } B) \subseteq \text{FDNF}(A \rightarrow B).$$

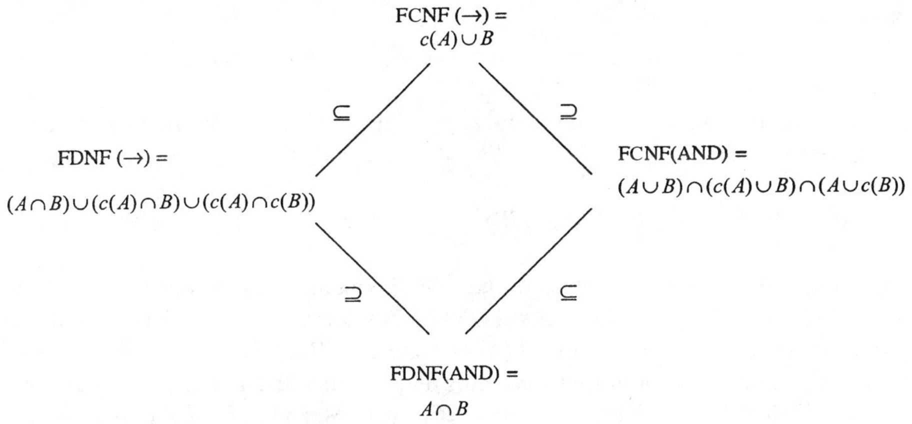

FIGURE 10.1. The lattice diagram showing the containment relationship between FDNF (AND), FCNF(AND) and FDNF(→) and FCNF(→).

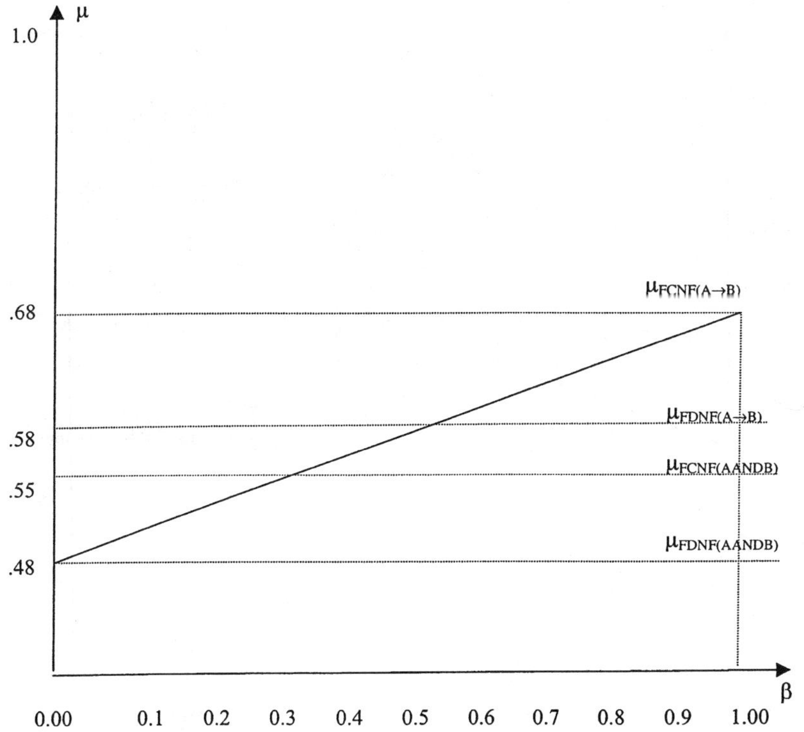

FIGURE 10.2. Graph of convex linear compromise reasoning $\mu = (1\text{-}\beta)\ (A(x^*)\Delta B(y)) + \beta\ (c(A(x^*))\nabla B(y))$ for $A(x^*) = (.8)$ and $B(y) = (.6)$, for algebraic operators.

because

$$A \cap B \subseteq (A \cap B) \cup (c(A) \cap B) \cup (c(A) \cup c(B)).$$

These arguments are shown graphically in Figure 10.1. Therefore, convex linear compromised reasoning

$$A(x^0) \triangle B(y) \leq (1 - \beta)[A(x^0) \triangle B(y)] + \beta[c(A(x^0))\nabla B(y)] \leq c(A(x^0))\nabla B(y)$$

represents all gradations between the two boundaries of Mamdani reasoning identified by FDNF(A AND B) and FCNF(A AND B), and the two boundaries of GMP reasoning identified by FDNF($A \rightarrow B$) and FCNF($A \rightarrow B$).

Convex linear compromised reasoning is demonstrated graphically in Figures 10.2 and 10.3 for particular $A(x)$ and $B(y)$ values and for algebraic and bold operators.

Exponential Compromised Reasoning. In analogy with exponential compensation, we next proposed exponential compromised reasoning. That is,

$$F(y) = [F_M(y)]^{1-\gamma}[F_{GMP}(y)]^{\gamma}.$$

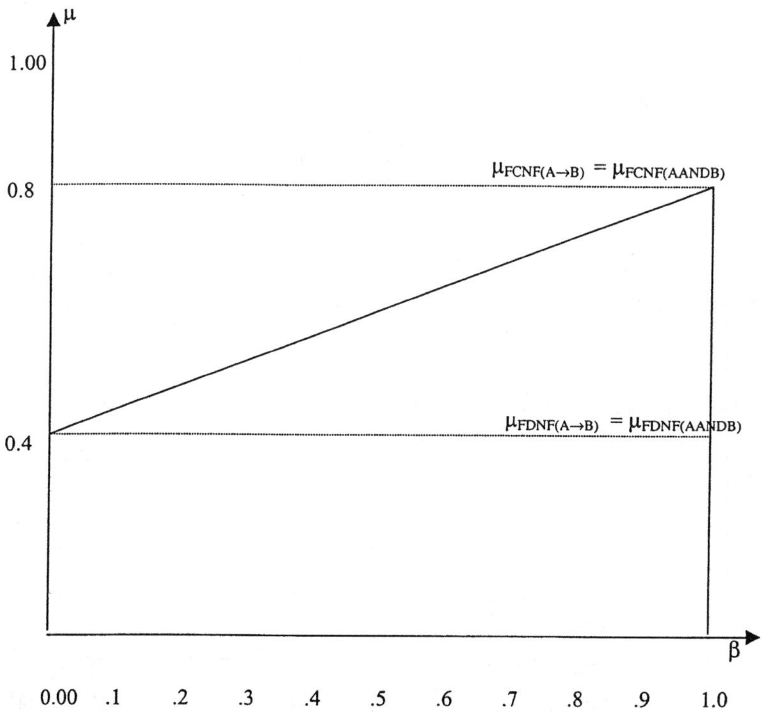

FIGURE 10.3. Graph of convex linear compromise reasoning μ = (1-β) (A(x*)ΔB(y)) + β(c(A(x*))∇B(y)) for A(x*) = (.8) and B(y) = (.6), for bold operators.

It can be shown that

$$A(x^0) \triangle B(y) \leq [A(x^0) \triangle B(y)]^{1-\gamma}[\mathrm{c}(A(x^0))\nabla B(y)]^{\gamma} \leq \mathrm{c}(A(x^0))\nabla B(y)$$

since $A \cap B \subseteq \mathrm{c}(A) \cup B$, as shown above.

Currently, we are experimenting with exponential compromised reasoning to determine if it may provide a better reasoning schema for certain system models. Exponential compromised reasoning is demonstrated graphically in Figures 10.4 and 10.5 for particular values of $A(x)$ and $B(y)$ and for algebraic and bold operators. The curvature of the compromise is to be observed in Figures 10.4 and 10.5.

10.5 CONCLUSIONS

Within a framework of fuzzy system modeling, we have shown how we start out with our linguistic knowledge acquired either from an expert via an interview and/or from algorithmic data processing of historical information. This linguistic knowl-

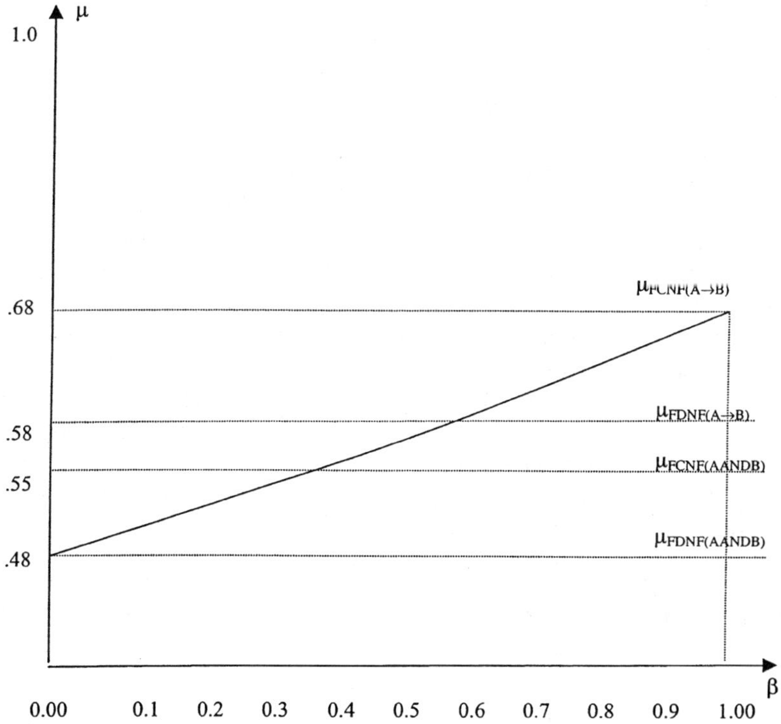

FIGURE 10.4. Graph of exponential compromise reasoning $\mu = [A(x^*)\Delta B(y)]^{(1-\beta)} + [c(A(x^*))\nabla B(y)]^{\beta}$ for $A(x^*) = (.8)$ and $B(y) = (.6)$, for algebraic operators.

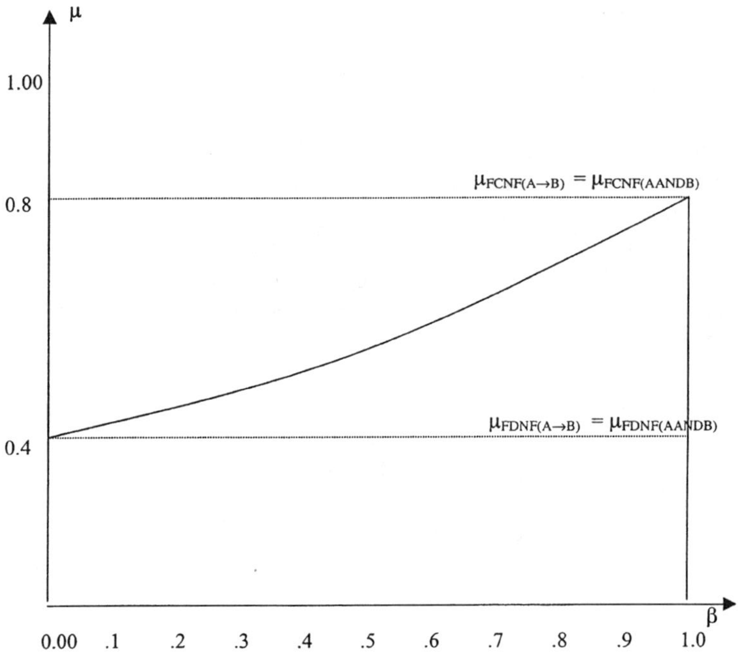

FIGURE 10.5. Graph of exponential compromise reasoning $\mu = [A(x^*)\Delta B(y)]^{(1-\beta)} + [c(A(x^*))\nabla B(y)]^{\beta}$ for $A(x^*) = (.8)$ and $B(y) = (.6)$, for bold operators.

edge is usually expressed in terms of descriptive words. The veristic word that asserts the truth of the descriptive knowledge is expressed either implicitly or explicitly. When the veristic assessment is expressed explicitly, we can form fuzzy truth tables and derive the FDNF and FCNF expressions. FDNF and FCNF expressions generate type II knowledge representation because FDNF$(\cdot) \subseteq$ FCNF$(\cdot)$ for all 16 combinations of any two fuzzy sets A and B and for the four well-known t-norms and t-co-norms.

Furthermore, FCNF and FDNF expressions show that there is theoretical verification of the experimentally discovered heuristics of compensatory AND and compromised reasoning proposed by Zimmermann and Zysno [33] and Yager and Filve [29], respectively. Finally, we propose yet a newer compromised reasoning called exponential compromised reasoning.

APPENDIX: NORMAL FORM DERIVATION ALGORITHM

1. Assign truth values T and F to the metalinguistic values (labels, variables) A and B and then assign truth values T and F to the metalinguistic expression of concern, say A AND B, in order to define its meaning.

2. Construct primary conjunctions of the set symbols *A* and *B* corresponding to linguistic values such that in a given row:
   (a) If a T appears, take the set affirmation symbol of that metalinguistic variable.
   (b) If an F appears, take the set of complementation symbols of that metalinguistic variable.
   (c) Conjunct the two symbols.
3. Construct the disjunctive normal form of the metalinguistic expression of concern.
   (a) Take the conjunctions corresponding to the T's of the truth assignment made under the column of the metalinguistic expression, such as "*A* AND *B*."
   (b) Combine these conjunctions with disjunctions.
4. Construct the conjunctive normal form of the metalinguistic expression of concern.
   (a) Take the conjunctions corresponding to F's of the truth assignment made under the column of the metalinguuistic expression, such as "*A* AND *B*."
   (b) Combine these conjunctions with disjunctions.
   (c) Take the complement of these disjunctions of conjunctions.

REFERENCES

1. J. Azzouni, *Metaphysical Myths, Mathematical Practice: The Ontology and Epistemology of the Exact Science*, Cambridge University Press, Cambridge, 1994.
2. M. Bergmann, J. Moor, and J. A. Nelson, *The Logic Book*, McGraw-Hill, New York, 1988.
3. J. C. Bezdek, *Pattern Recognition with Fuzzy Objective Function Algorithms*, Plenum Press, New York, 1981.
4. R. R. Christensen, *Belief and Behaviour*, Entropy Ltd., Lincoln, MA, 1982.
5. I. M. Copi, *Introduction to Logic*, Macmillan, New York, 1982.
6. D. Dumitrescu and D. Tatar, Normal forms of fuzzy formulas and their minimization, *Fuzzy Sets Syst.*, 64:113–117, 1994.
7. A. Kaufmann, *Introduction to the Theory of Fuzzy Subsets, Vol 1, Fundamental Theoretical Elements*, Academic Press, New York, 1975.
8. E. H. Mamdani, Applications of fuzzy algorithms for simple dynamic plant, *Proc. IEE*, 121, 12:1585–1588, 1974.
9. E. H. Mamdani and S. Assilian, An experiment in linguistic synthesis with a fuzzy logic controller, *Int. J. Man-Mach. Stud.*, 7(1):1–13, 1975.
10. M. Margaliot, New methods for design and analysis of fuzzy controllers, Ph.D. dissertation, Tel-Aviv University, Tel Aviv, Israel, 1999.
11. P. N. Marinos, Fuzzy logic and its applications to switching systems, *IEEE trans. Comput.*, 18(4):343–348, 1969.

12. W. V. O. Quine, *Philosophy of Logic*, Prentice Hall, Englewood Cliffs, NJ, 1970.
13. M. Sugeno, and G. T. Kang, Structure identification of fuzzy model, *Fuzzy Sets Syst.*, 28(1):15–33, 1998.
14. M. Sugeno, and T. Yasukawa, A fuzzy-logic-based approach to qualitative modeling, *IEEE Trans. Fuzzy Syst.*, 1:7–31, 1993.
15. T. Tagaki and M. Sugeno, Fuzzy identification of systems and its applications to modeling and control, *IEEE-Trans. Syst. Man Cybern.*, 15:116–132, 1985.
16. K. Tanaka and M. Sugeno, Stability analysis and design of fuzzy control systems, 45(1):135–156, 1992.
17. A. Tarski, The concept of truth in formalized languages, in J. H. Woodger (ed.), *Logic, Semantics, Mathematics*, Oxford University Press, Oxford, 1956.
18. I. B. Türkşen, Interval-valued fuzzy sets based on normal forms, *Fuzzy Sets Syst.*, 20:191–210, 1986.
19. I. B. Türkşen, Measurement of membership functions and their acquisition, *Fuzzy Sets Syst.*, 40:5–38, 1991.
20. I. B. Türkşen, fuzzy normal forms, *Fuzzy Sets Syst.*, 20:253–266, 1994.
21. I. B. Türkşen, Interval-valued fuzzy sets and "compensatory AND," *Fuzy Sets Syst.*, 51:295–307, 1992.
22. I. B. Türkşen, Type I and "interval valued" type II fuzzy sets and logics, in P. P. Wang (ed.), *Fuzzy Theory Technol.*, III:31–82, 1995.
23. I. B. Türkşen, Non-specificity and internal valued fuzzy sets, *Fuzzy Sets Syst.*, :87–100, 1996.
24. I. B. Türkşen, A. Kandel, and Y.-Q. Zhang, Universal truth tables and normal forms, *IEEE Fuzzy Syst.* 6(2):295–303, 1998.
25. I. B. Türkşen and M. H. F. Zarandi, Fuzzy System models for aggregate scheduling analysis, *IJAR*, 19:119–143, 1998.
26. I. B. Türkşen, A. Kandel, and Y.-Q. Zhang, Normal forms of fuzzy middle and fuzzy contradiction, *IEEE Trans. Syst. Man Cybern., B: Cybern.*, 29(2)237–253, 1999.
27. I. B. Türkşen, Type I and type II fuzzy system modeling, *Fuzzy Sets Syst.*, 106:11–34, 1999.
28. I. B. Türkşen, Computing with descriptive and veristic words, *Proc. NAFIPS '99*, New York, June 10–12, 1999, pp. 13–17.
29. R. Yager and D. Filev, *Essentials of fuzzy reasoning*, Wiley, New York, 1994.
30. L. A. Zadeh, Outline of a new approach to the analysis of complex systems and decisions processes, *IEEE Trans. Syst. Man. Cybern.*, 3:28–44, 1973.
31. L. A. Zadeh, Toward a theory of fuzzy information granulation and its centrality in human reasoning and fuzzy logic, *Fuzzy Sets Syst.* 90:111–127, 1997.
32. L. A. Zadeh, From computing with numbers to computing with words—from manipulation of measurements to manipulation of perceptions, *IEEE Trans. Circuits Syst.*, 45(1): 105–119, 1999.
33. H.-J. Zimmermann and P. Zysno, Latent connectives in human decision making, *Fuzzy Sets Syst.*, 4:37–51, 1980.
34. H. J. Zimmermann, *Fuzzy Sets, Decision Making and Expert Systems*, Kluwer Academic Publishers, Boston, 1986.

CHAPTER 11

PRINCIPLES OF WORD-BASED KNOWLEDGE REPRESENTATION AND KNOWLEDGE PROCESSING FOR CW

ALEXANDER M. MEYSTEL
Drexel University, Philadelphia, Pennsylvania

11.1 INTRODUCTION

Computing with words (CW) was invoked by the concept of *linguistic variable* [1], which relied on the *meaning* of words and statements composed in words. Zadeh admitted that fuzzy logic (FL) is theoretically equivalent to computing with words if FL is considered in a broader paradigm as a set of tools for analysis of intelligent systems [2]. In his recent paper [3], Zadeh explored other consequences of the emerging of CW: its expansion into analysis of perception, its merger with the theory of language interpretation, and the need in analysis of multigranular (multiresolutional) systems of words—systems of word-based knowledge (WBK) representation.

We will be especially interested in the process of obtaining words for computing out of corpora related to the particular area of design. Thus the high-resolution details might be contained in a text in a form inappropriate for use in computing. A process of prior compression via generalization is presumed. Methods of context-dependent generalization for compression purposes are discussed in a separate paper.

Computing with words presumes relying on having problems of knowledge representation resolved prior to the start of CW. Theories of *knowledge representation and organization* for CW are related to the notion of *fuzzy syntax, knowledge organization, and interpretation*; to the formation of *fuzzy semantic fields* and *knowledge generation and utilization;* and to *fuzzy pragmatics*. These three areas belong to the body of semiotics and are applicable to knowledge transmitted by any type of

Computing with Words, Edited by Paul P. Wang.
ISBN 0-471-35374-4

sign system. We focus on a subset of it denoted by a term we have not yet defined: *word-based knowledge* (WBK). We can no longer postpone focusing on this term since interest in *meaning extraction* is pervasive, yet without understanding what WBK is, we would not be able to define all other concepts related to it: WBK *representation, organization, generation*, and *utilization*. These definitions can be deduced from what we already know about these ideas from our experience of dealing with WBK in our professional domains. We have already tacitly assumed some definitions for both WBK and its different incarnation as well as different stages of its processing. These assumptions seemed to be plausible since a lot of our considerations were acceptable in our professional activities.

But what do we know about these issues from our previous activities? Theoretical approaches relevant to CW are extremely diversified, and they are dispersed within sources related to application domains. Their consideration would first require a discussion of general principles of WBK representation for CW. In this section we formulate a number of principles that encompass and reflect the essence of what we know about WBK and the laws governing its representation and processing.

11.2 PRINCIPLES OF WORD-BASED KNOWLEDGE

The following principles of dealing with WBK should be discussed as a prerequisite for developing the theory of computing with words:

1. Principle of thesaural interpretation of words assignment (labeling)
2. Principle of entity-relational WBK representation
3. Principle of multiresolutional representation (coarsening/refinement) or principle of nested hierarchical representation
4. Principle of heterogeneity, or principle of multiple WBK representation systems
5. Principle of causality
6. Principle of efficiency
7. Principle of incompleteness
8. Feedforward principle
9. Principle of feedback
10. Principle of limited resource, or principle of focusing attention
11. Principle of continuity
12. Principle of creativity

These principles are discussed in sequence, organized in a manner that allows for consecutive buildup of the conceptual background, with a gradual increase in complexity of the issues involved. Since this chapter is part of a discussion of a new, nascent scientific area, each principle is supported by formulating its premises (if they are not obvious) and includes selected questions that cannot necessarily be answered immediately but rather, serve the purpose of stimulating further discussion.

11.2.1 Principle of Thesaural Interpretation of Word Assignment (Labeling)

Assertion. Any WBK representation is a system of interrelated statements in natural language with words and strings of words lumped to be interpreted with the help of a *thesaurus*. These statements pursue a goal (or a set of goals) that are typically not presented explicitly and should be explicated from the larger set of related statements, the overall text, or a group of texts. This missing part of the discourse that can be restored or assumed is called the *context*. It is assumed that the context is provided as necessary.

Definition 1.1. *WBK representation* consists of (is a list of) meaningful natural language statements. The latter include definitions (together with the related explanations) of the concepts related to the world to be represented, or encoding of these concepts and the relationships among them, as well as encoding any other messages. All encoding is done with the help of single words or strings of words, or the signs and symbols introduced for brevity.

Premise 1.1.1. It is presumed that the word-based statements of interest are *meaningful*, or otherwise *goal oriented*. Thus the very existence of the *meaning* is assumed to reflect a knowledge representation with all elements oriented toward and interpreted via a system of goals.

- *Question 1.1.1.1.* What is the *meaning* of a word-based statement (WBS), how is it related to the *sense* of WBS, and how is it related to a *goal* of WBS and to the *context*?
- *Question 1.1.1.2.* Is it possible to contemplate that the meaning conveys the essence of relations between perceptions, representations, and behavior generations in their *closure* through the actuators, world, and sensors? This closure is outlined in Ref. 11. The conjecture of this closure being a meaning carrier could be introduced after analysis of cases within the particular domain of interest.

We have to remind the reader that the literature on meaning is scarce and belongs primarily to the field of pure linguistics [12–14].

Premise 1.1.2. The phenomena of reality are represented in the form of statements of *existence* (for both entities and the relationships among them), statements of *interpretation* containing linkages between the statements of existence and the context, and statements of *implication* that invoke related statements of existence from prior experience and/or logical transformations. It generates a problem: How can knowledge be extracted from the account of experiences, and how trustworthy can it be?

From Ref. 13 we would expect that the tool of knowledge extraction is the joint mechanism of generalization/instantiation.

- *Question 1.1.2.1.* How should we categorize the statements of generalization or of instantiation?
- *Question 1.1.2.2.* How should we categorize questions formulated for helping in the process of knowledge extraction?

Premise 1.1.3. (*A corollary*) Any meaningful statement can be encoded in words.

- *Question 1.1.3.1.* Are the terms *representation* and *coding* just synonyms (e.g., for recommended use in such constructions as: "representation with words," "encoding with symbols or signs")?
- *Question 1.1.3.2.* (This question is simply another version of the preceding question.) Is there any difference between "coding in words" and "coding in symbols"? "representing in words" and "representing in symbols"?
- *Question 1.1.3.3.* Should we admit the mandatory loss of (or distortion of) meaning during the processes of representation and encoding? Why does it happen? Can it be avoided?

Premise 1.1.4. Communication messages circulate between the adjacent subsystems of any intelligent system. The latter is often described as an elementary functioning loop (ELF) consisting of the following components: sensors, sensory processing, world model, behavior generation, and actuators (see Question 1.1.1.2). This loop is closed through the world [4,17]. Each subsystem is presumed to carry a representation required for its functioning. These representations are generally presumed to be symbolic. However, all of them can and are being explained in words of natural language (i.e., can be represented by using WBK). A conjecture is looming about the homomorphism between two mappings: the mapping from WBK to symbolic representation, and vice versa.

- *Question 1.1.4.1.* What is the resemblance and distinction (more generally, what is the relation) between the terms *statements* and *concepts*, and *concepts* and *messages*?
- *Question 1.1.4.2.* Should we expect any difference in using WBK representation as opposed to any symbolic representation? Thus, should we determine any difference between symbol-based representation and word-based representation?

Definition 1.2. A *word* (label or symbol) is understood as a sign consistent with and interpretable within natural languages, convenient to use and efficient when applied within a real computer system that can be assigned to perform the operation of *interpretation.*

Premise 1.2.1. A multiplicity of available natural languages is presumed to exist; it does not matter which of the existing natural languages is used in the system.

- *Question 1.2.1.1.* Is it possible to expect that WBK represented in different natural languages will entail different algorithms and strategies of behavior generation? A hypothesis similar to the Sapir–Whorf hypothesis seems to be plausible for the CW domain (see Ref. 15).
- *Question 1.2.1.2.* How do the conditions, forms, and number of loops of closure affect Premise 1.2.1 (the premise of independence from the kind of NL applied)?

Premise 1.2.2. The difference between a word and a symbol is in the fact that words belong associatively to the general body of language and that the context plays the decisive role in their interpretation. Symbols are either a part of a rigid protocol, as in scientific papers, or are tightly linked to a particular application subdomain. This implies that systems of symbols have a context, too, as do natural language texts.

- *Question 1.2.2.1.* Even in the cases of rigid protocol and ultimate attachment to the domain of application, symbols can be translated into WBK form, and no difference would exist between symbols and words. Should we make this distinction between words and symbols?
- *Question 1.2.2.2.* Do we ever interpret symbols without explicating their context and the domain of application (e.g., given in the form of protocols)?

Definition 1.3. *Interpretation* is the explanation of a word, or of a particular statement consisting of words, which carries meaning that exceeds the usual (thesaural) meaning of the components of the statement; interpretation is usually done within an external subsystem. *Note:* Interpretation is not equivalent to *symbol grounding*; it presumes a discovery that exceeds routine symbol grounding procedures (for a discussion of symbol grounding, see Refs. 16 and 17).

Premise 1.3.1. A human operator (or human operator–like subsystem) is presumed to be a part of the overall CW system which performs the role of ultimate symbol grounder for statements, or ultimate interpreter of commands, experiences, images, and situations.

- *Question 1.2.1.1.* Can the operation of symbol grounding be performed without human participation, automatically?
- *Question 1.2.1.1.* How is it possible that from an interaction of units of WBK new knowledge emerges that is not accounted for in the thesauri statements?

Premise 1.3.2. A domain dictionary (a subset of the thesaurus) is presumed that contains interpretations for a particular WBK domain.

- *Question 1.3.2.1.* Is the role of interpretation just to narrow down the domain of application for a particular WBK representation?
- *Question 1.3.2.2.* Is it possible to expect that anything consistent and symbol grounded but not having its explanation in the thesaurus should be included in the thesaurus as its own interpretation?

Premise 1.3.3. The interpretation dictionary should allow for a learning procedure: As new concepts arrive at the system, they should appear within the dictionary with the interpretations that pertain to them that have been agreed to by the human operator. This alludes to the accepted approach to the process of verifying acquired knowledge.

- *Question 1.3.3.1.* Who develops interpretations for emerging concepts?
- *Question 1.3.3.2.* Is it possible to have more than one valid interpretation? How should such cases be handled?

Definition 1.4. A *thesaurus* is a global dictionary that contains interpretations for all words (labels) and combination of words that can be expected in a CW system based on its prior experiences.

Conjecture. All messages built on words are considered information carriers; after assigning the interpretation, they become WKB.

11.2.2 Principle of Entity-Relational WKB Representation

Assertion. Words represent *objects, relations* among objects, and *actions* imposed by one object upon another.

Assertion. Any word (W) and/or word-based statement (WBS) is a part of the coalition of multiple word–object sets ({WO}) and word–relationship sets ({WR}). Thus any WBK representation is built on the concept of objects represented by words and the concept of relationships represented by words.

Assertion. Any change in a word (ΔW) and/or any change in a word-based statement (ΔWBS) can only emerge due to multiple word–action sets ({A}), which pursue a particular set of goals ({G}) and are entailed by an evaluation of "goodness" ("cost") under this set of goals ({J[G]}). Thus any evolution of WBK representation can be obtained by applying the concepts of changes, concepts of actions that produce the concepts of changes, concepts of goals that are being pursued in producing the concepts of changes, and concepts of costs that are incurred during these processes. All of these concepts are represented by words and together form the representation of world.

Definition 2.1. The *world* (of interest, or under consideration) is a subset of reality that should be observed and/or controlled, or it should serve as a medium for the ELF activities (which is the same). The goals (tasks) are being formulated to determine what directs the ELF activities. Goals are considered to be the final states for the temporal process called *task* and denoted by a *command.* WBK representation is being developed (created) ultimately to allow for this process to develop in systems. States are the units on the list of descriptive and/or numerical characterization of objects existing in the world.

Premise 2.1.1. The world (W) and the system of word-based knowledge representation (WBKR) are ideally presumed to allow for isomorphic mapping in principle; CW should employ this mapping; WBKR is the ideal concept that underlies CW efforts.

Premise 2.1.2. The correspondence between the world (W) and WBK representation is our main object of interest; the mapping W $\rightarrow$ WBKR is presumed to exist. Mapping that constructs a realistic WBKR system is a *homomorphism.*

Premise 2.1.3. Existence of semiotic closure through the world is presumed as a part of ELF, with its ability to sense, perceive (organize the results of sensing), collect, and organize *knowledge;* make decisions under a goal (or task); and actuate in the world as a result of the decision. The existence of information channels among the subsystems is also assumed.

Premise 2.1.4. The same world can be represented at various degrees of granularity (levels of resolution). If the resolution is reducing, many objects represented at initial resolution become indistinguishable at a new resolution. They merge and form a smaller number of lower-resolution objects out of the multiplicity of higher-resolution objects (aggregation). If the resolution increases, many objects that were indistinguishable at initial resolution become distinguishable and appear as parts of the previously represented lower-resolution objects (decomposition, or partitioning). The same can be stated about relationships. All representations at all resolutions of interest can exist simultaneously as a multiresolutional knowledge representation.

Conjecture. Premise 2.1.4 contains a conjecture that can be formulated as follows: *Representation at every adjacent level of resolution is obtained by a recursively applied algorithm of nesting: for decomposition, top down, and for aggregation, bottom up.* This conjecture entails ideas of *granularity, multiscale* representation, and *nesting.*

- *Question 2.1.4.1.* The concept of granularity ascends to the concept of distinguishability, which is implicitly a perception-oriented concept. Does it mean that all these interrelated concepts are totally perception dependent?

Definition 2.2. A *word–object* is an elementary conceptual formation of discourse (related to the world, it is distinguishable under resolution of consideration and attributed to the possible existence of an elementary formation of the world). This formation is characterized by a conceptual unity and is frequently called an *entity.* It is also characterized by such values as (a) adjacency to one or more other objects, (b) resemblance to one or more other objects, (c) belonging to one or more other objects as a part, (d) having one or more other objects as its parts, (e) ability to generate actions affecting other objects, and (f) ability to be subjected to other objects' actions applied to the object under consideration.

Premise 2.2.1. More than one elementary object is always under consideration.

- *Question 2.2.1.1.* Which concept should be called elementary? As opposed to what?
- *Question 2.2.1.2.* An elementary formation is distinguishable from what?
- *Question 2.2.1.3.* What is *resolution under consideration*?
- *Question 2.2.1.4.* Is there any resolution other than that under consideration?
- *Question 2.2.1.5.* Does resolution under consideration (or of interest) imply necessity of an external person who has this interest and makes these considerations?

Premise 2.2.2. Any consideration has limited accuracy (resolution, scale, granularity).

- *Question 2.2.2.1.* How should the word *can* be understood if knowledge is complete but the computations required for prediction are so cumbersome and time consuming that exact prediction is inefficient and thus our statement cannot be verified?

Clearly, entity-relational WKB representation is very closely related to the object-oriented approach [10].

Definition 2.3. *Resolution* is a measure of distinguishability of the objects; this measure is determined by the number of bits of information that are carried within the system of representation of a particular object; the minimum-resolution representation carries one bit of information.

Premise 2.3.1. A digital system of information representation is presumed.

- *Question 2.3.1.1.* Is it possible to represent information continuously?
- *Question 2.3.1.2.* Are we talking about resolution of knowledge or resolution of information?
- *Question 2.3.1.3.* Is it possible to expect continuous change of resolution in a discrete system of information representation?

Premise 2.3.2. The existence of the procedure of *distinguishing* is presumed; this in turn appeals to the possible procedure of *identification*; intuitively, these procedures refer to the ideas of *recognition* and *matching.*

- *Question 2.3.2.1.* Distinguishing presumes dealing with two items that are to be distinguished from one another; what are these two items?
- *Question 2.3.2.2.* Identification and recognition require some prior knowledge for comparison; what if this knowledge does not exist?
- *Question 2.3.2.3.* Under our conditions, how can you contemplate the expected procedure for matching?

Definition 2.4. *Relationship* is a name for the phenomenon of present or memorized interaction between objects, and it can be assigned to any pair of objects. Relations depend on the values of features (a) through (d) in Definition 2.2.

Premise 2.4.1. The phenomena of interaction exist for each pair of objects.

- *Question 2.4.1.1.* Do the relationships exist for n-tuples that cannot be represented by a set of relationships between each existing couple of the n-tuple?
- *Question 2.4.1.2.* Does the idea of *resolution* apply to the relationships as well as to the objects?
- *Question 2.4.1.3.* What is the value of the discrete time between two consecutive states? Is it related to resolution of the state representation? Is it related to resolution of object description?
- *Question 2.4.1.4.* What is the link between time resolution and resolution of change at a particular level of the entity-relational network?

Premise 2.4.2. Relation presumes the existence of memory in the related objects.

11.2.3 PRINCIPLE OF MULTIRESOLUTIONAL REPRESENTATION (COARSENING/REFINEMENT) OR PRINCIPLE OF NESTED HIERARCHICAL REPRESENTATION

Assertion. It is impossible to organize a system of WBK representation that would use the same resolution for all objects, objects that are parts of them, objects to which they are parts, and so on. Indeed, if some particular resolution is chosen *for everything*, then all phenomena of higher resolution will not be represented. In this particular case it is impossible to construct WBKR at a higher resolution since (a) it is expected that an object can be found that requires higher resolution for the representation and (b) the complexity of representation grows rapidly with growth of resolution (see Section 11.2.6). Thus all efforts related to WBKR construction were related to coarsening and refinement, fuzzification and defuzzification, aggregation and decomposition, abstraction and specialization, and generalization and instantiation.

Definition 3.1. Coarsening and refinement are two opposing procedures of forming multiresolutional WBKR system. *Coarsening* presumes lowering resolution of representation via increase of elementary granules. *Refinement* transforms representation by using smaller granules.

Premise 3.1.1. It is presumed that any representation has its elementary basis: minimal elementary granules.

- *Question 3.1.1.1.* Are all minimal granules the same?
- *Question 3.1.1.2.* Is the change of granulation equivalent to the change of scale?

Definition 3.2. *Fuzzification* and *defuzzification* are methods of coarsening/refinement via algorithms of the fuzzy sets and fuzzy logic theory.

Definition 3.3. Aggregation is a merging together of objects of a higher-resolution level within one object of the lower-resolution level. Aggregation leads to refinement or defuzzification.

Premise 3.3.1. It is presumed that objects are meaningfully *composable* (aggregable) out of parts; in other words, that objects are assemblies of parts; this consideration seems to be recursively applicable to parts.

- *Question 3.3.1.1.* Is there any limit for continuing this recursive process?

Premise 3.3.2. It is presumed that a technique or algorithm exists that allows us to average the properties and characteristics of the higher-resolution parts within the expected low-resolution object; a technique and algorithm should also exist for recognition of candidates having the value of *uniformity* at the lower-resolution level.

- *Question 3.3.2.1.* How would you suggest choosing the property of expected uniformity (at a level of resolution)?

Definition 3.4. *Decomposition* is partitioning of an object at a lower-resolution level into two or more objects at a higher-resolution level. Decomposition leads to refinements, or defuzzification.

Premise 3.4.1. Objects are meaningfully decomposable in parts.

Premise 3.4.2. A technique or algorithm exists that allows for recognition of higher-resolution parts within the prior low-resolution uniformity of a lower-resolution object.

- *Question 3.4.1.1.* Is there any limit for continuing this recursive process?
- *Question 3.4.2.1.* How would you suggest choosing the property of expected uniformity?

Definition 3.5. *Abstraction* and *specialization* are methods of coarsening and refinement via classification and categorization algorithms (and their inverses).

Definition 3.6. *Generalization* and *instantiation* are methods of coarsening and refinement via combinatorial synthesis, focusing attention, and search within the domain of possible instantiations.

Definition 3.7. *Multiscale hierarchy* is a structure that emerges as a result of multiple repetition of processes of refinement (top down) or coarsening (bottom up); hierarchy is formed from the objects and their parts, or from the classes and their members, or from generalities and their instantiations, and so on. The relations of inclusion are recorded for objects and their parts.

Definition 3.8. *Multiscale heterarchy* is a structure in which in addition to the top-down and bottom-up relationships of multiresolutional (multiscale) inclusion (nestedness), relations among objects at a particular level of resolution are also demonstrated [5].

Definition 3.9. *Change in a system* is defined as a difference between two consecutive (in time) hierarchical or heterarchical representations of a system. This difference is also expected to be representable by a hierarchy or heterarchy. One can therefore expect that changes also allow for decomposition and/or aggregation.

Conjecture. Multiresolutional or multigranular representations (representations based on the hierarchy of levels of coarsening and refinements) are a constructive result of the law reflected in the Godel theorem of incompleteness. Indeed, each level evokes a metalevel which would serve for interpreting the statements that otherwise could not be interpreted within the level itself.

11.2.4 Principle of Heterogeneity, or Principle of Multiple WBK Representation Systems

Assertion. Any WBK representation is to be heterogeneous based on multiplicity of WBK representation systems complementary in their ability to describe entity-relational structures with desirable completeness and consistency.

Definition 4.1. A *homogeneous system of representation* represents the object using only one language of representation; a heterogeneous system uses more than one language; the exact relationships between languages in the heterogeneous system are never known.

Premise 4.1.1. WBK representation is intuitively expected to be homogeneous.

Premise 4.1.2. A homogeneous system of representation deals with *objects* of a similar nature (belonging to the same class or functioning within the same domain) and/or a context: A need for other languages appears because objects of another nature are part of the system, or because the original set of objects is not described exhaustively and does not satisfy the criteria of completeness and consistency required in the system.

Premise 4.1.3. A representation system uses various dialects of a natural language possibly as a tool of representation; different general classes of objects and application domains generate different dialects.

Definition 4.2. *Heterogeneity* is the property of using more than one WBK system for representation.

Definition 4.3. A *WBK system* of describing entity-relational structures is a language with a vocabulary and grammar and axioms and rules which was accepted for building the models of a particular knowledge domain; selection of a particular language is explained by a variety of causes, one being the convenience of application for a particular purpose.

Premise 4.3.1. WBK representation of the world is possible to obtain in various verbal forms.

Premise 4.3.2. The same WBK constructed for different application domains can be presented in different dialects.

Premise 4.3.3. A single method of exhaustive WBK representation does not exist.

Premise 4.3.4. We do not know the world well enough to imagine that a single language could be selected that would represent the world.

11.2.5 Principle of Causality

Assertion. WBK representation is based on records of cause–effect (C-E) relationships in all cases. Causal relationships can be contained in explicit statements or groups of categorized data. It is important that CW can be organized so that causal relationships are explicated.

Definition 5.1. Two items of knowledge are said to be in *C-E relationships* if one of them (C) happens before the other (E), and within a particular interpretation frame of WKB representation, a model can be built in which C can be considered as an input which after being activated entails the output E.

Premise 5.1.1. C-E relationships depend on the interpretation frame, and in one frame they can exist, whereas in another they are not considered to be a C-E pair.

Premise 5.1.2. C-E relationships presume existence of the *model*, which is constructed for a subset of the world; this model can be understood as a control model: All models are control models, they have inputs, states, and outputs.

Premise 5.1.3. C-E couples never exist without a reference to time.

Premise 5.1.4. WBK frequently presumes existence of verbal records.

Premise 5.1.5. WBK representation should be ordered in both space and time (see examples in Ref. 6).

Definition 5.2. A *model* is a representation system which often indicates for the user what is (are) the *cause(s)* and what is (are) the *effect(s)* as well as what the relationships among them are.

Definition 5.3. A *representation* is a phenomenon of functioning in the metasystem with more than one agent: The essence of this phenomenon can be described as delegation of the duties of one agent to another. The latter requires forming a categorized list of C-E couples.

Definition 5.4. A *metasystem* is a system in which the system under consideration is enclosed; the external observer who builds the model is always presumed to be situated within the metasystem.

Conjecture. The *structure* is always secondary and the linguistic (word-based) *discourse* primary in representation systems.

11.2.6 Principle of Efficiency

Assertion. Different systems of WBK representation using homogeneous as well as heterogeneous principles of representation are judged on by their efficiency, which includes the following components: expressive power, computability, and complexity. The decisions are preferable if they demonstrate higher values of these criteria.

Definition 6.1. *Expressive power* (EP) is the ability of the representation to convey interpretations using interpretable logical statements; EP can be evaluated quantitatively by the rate of generating interpretations per memory and/or time required, or per cost.

Premise 6.1.1. A human operator is presumed to whom these interpretations are being addressed.

Definition 6.2. *Computability* is the ability of a system with mathematical or linguistic representation to arrive with a complete and consistent solution in a reasonable time.

Premise 6.2.1. The existence of a solution in principle does not make a problem solvable.

Definition 6.3. *Complexity* is a characterization of logical and mathematical systems which allows for approximate evaluation of the number of computations required for solving the problem, or the order of the number of computations.

Conjecture. The higher the completeness, the less the efficiency of a knowledge representation system.

11.2.7 Principle of Incompleteness

Assertion. Any knowledge representation is incomplete.

Definition 7.1. Knowledge is called *complete* if it provides an opportunity to *predict* the outcomes of the situation (of interest) exactly.

Premise 7.1.1. The goal of dealing with knowledge is to *predict* the situation (of interest).

- *Question 7.1.1.1.* What should be predicted?
- *Question 7.1.1.2.* What for?
- *Question 7.1.1.3.* What horizon of prediction is required?
- *Question 7.1.1.4.* What is a situation of interest?
- *Question 7.1.1.5.* How many outcomes are to be considered?

Premise 7.1.2. The situation can be predicted exactly (with no error) if the knowledge is complete.

- *Question 7.1.2.1* How should the word *can* be understood if the knowledge is complete but the computations required for prediction are very cumbersome and time consuming, so that exact prediction is inefficient and thus our statement cannot be verified?

Premise 7.1.3. The system of interest is always expressed (represented) by a set of states varying in time.

- *Question 7.1.3.1.* What is the content of the states available—their dimensions? What is the set of variables that compose a single state?
- *Question 7.1.3.2.* What is the size (in time) of an available set of time-varying states?
- *Question 7.1.3.3.* What is the value of the discrete time between two consecutive states?

Definition 7.2. *Uncertainty* is a form of incompleteness: The statements that would help to distinguish right from wrong (e.g., noise from a useful signal) are absent, the higher-resolution information is not available, the sources of disturbances are unknown, some of the statements demand disambiguation, and so on.

Premise 7.2.1. It is presumed that all methods of uncertainty evaluation are explored and put into correspondence logically (some examples can be found in Ref. 7).

Premise 7.2.2. It is possible to demonstrate that all methods of uncertainty evaluation are based on similar axiomatic premises (compare Refs. 8 and 9).

The principle of incompleteness can actually be rephrased as the *principle of uncertainty*, which states that inaccurate information regarding state variables is an intrinsic property of the system under consideration and can be evaluated quantitatively. The uncertainty principle also deals with knowledge representation.

11.2.8 Feedforward Principle

Assertion. At any moment in time, a level of resolution can be determined for which the time interval exceeds the operational time of interest, and thus a single directional operational flow can be considered from knowledge representation to desirable activities, with no changes in the world to be taken into account.

Definition 8.1. A *single-directional operational flow* is a subset of the six-box diagram which can be considered with no changes in the world taken in account. (Principle 8 deals with the subset from knowledge representation to the desirable activities in the world.)

Premise 8.1.1. In the ELF diagram [4,17], knowledge representation is utilized in order to imply a chain of decisions extended in time which are required for receiving a time-extended chain of desirable activities, which in turn create changes in the world which are being recorded, organized, and utilized to enrich the knowledge representation.

Premise 8.1.2. A time interval can be assigned that makes it possible to think about this subset in an open-loop sense; this determines the level of resolution (generalization).

11.2.9 Principle of Feedback

Assertion. Knowledge about the results of activities (decision and actuation) are acquired and utilized to compensate for the incompleteness of knowledge stored in a system of WBK representation. This process of knowledge updating triggers subsequent processes of decision making and is called *feedback*. This process is related to closurc (as in ELF) but is not equivalent to closure.

Definition 9.1. *Acquisition of WBK statements* concerning the results of activities is a process required to maintain the level of completeness of knowledge accepted in the system under consideration.

Premise 9.1.1. It is presumed that feedback is required only to compensate for the growing incompleteness of knowledge, that in the beginning the level of incompleteness was minimal, and that the feedforward operation was properly determined.

- *Question 9.1.1.1.* Does the growing incompleteness of WBK representation occur during the process of operation?

- *Question 9.1.1.2.* What does "to determine the feedforward operation properly" mean?

11.2.10 Principle of Limited Resource, or Principle of Focusing Attention

Assertion. Only a subset of WBK representation can be considered.

Definition 10.1. Any system of WBK representation and processing for CW is built on the need to provide its operation under *system constraints* (constraints in acceptable time of operation, available computer power, accessible information, and available sum of money).

Premise 10.1.1. Constraints in acceptable time of operation, available computer power, accessible information, and available sum of money are the components of the cost-functional which should be extremized as a result of ELF operation.

Premise 10.1.2. Acceptable time of operation, available computer power, accessible information, and available sum of money are limited.

Definition 10.2. The subset of consideration is called the *focus of attention.*

11.2.11 Principle of Continuity

Assertion. WBK representation should reflect the fact that all changes in the world with no external control applied are dominated by a tendency to maintain the least deviation from earlier states.

Definition 11.1. The *continuity of the world* is an intrinsic property of all systems under consideration.

Premise 11.1.1. Any changes in WBK representation should reflect the continuity of the world, including the evolutionary character of development of the objects and relationships among them.

Premise 11.1.2. Every next snapshot of the world is a result of the next iteration of the control operation applied to a limited subset of the world.

Definition 11.2. A *snapshot of the world* is defined as a WBK representation with no changes recorded during the process of recording. This phenomenon of "instance" pertains to a particular level of resolution.

Definition 11.3. The *evolutionary character of development* of objects and relationships among them are the changes in state variables that can be computed, taking into account knowledge of prior developments.

11.2.12 Principle of Creativity

Assertion. The system of WBK representation allows for and is usually equipped by the mechanisms of creativity, which combine units of knowledge not taken from the reality. (This principle is also formulated as follows: *The system of knowledge representation is capable of generating possible worlds.)*

Definition 12.1. The *mechanism of new WBK generation* is a combinatorial algorithm of forming strings of the labels according to the laws of a particular domain of interest.

Premise 12.1.1. Processes of new knowledge generation are driven by a particular interest linked with the goal of functioning of the system.

Premise 12.1.2. It is presumed that all possible mechanisms of forming strings of labels are included into a *combinatorial* set of mechanisms.

11.3 CONCLUSIONS

Any system for CW is equipped with a WBK representation that presumes the need for collection and organization of knowledge in the form of specifically constructed and synthesized units consisting of *words* and *word-based statements.* Knowledge of what? To answer this question, let us recall the ELF structure. Two groups of entities can be noted: the hardware and the software. The hardware includes the material world, external events, and objects of our interest: the *domain for future decision making.* Usually, these are all things that we can sense, measure, and experiment within the real world, everything that is material, exists, and is given for us to perceive and formulate our problems upon. Everything else in ELF is the software. But there is some kind of entity that can be understood as a common entity for these two worlds. This entity is *knowledge about the external world.* This means that knowledge is the invariance of the two worlds mentioned above: the hardware and software worlds.

The central part of ELF is a subsystem in which *perceptions* and *decision-making activities* are being mutually interpreted, translated into each other, and brought to matching. We call it a knowledge base. Perception implies a knowledge base, which in turn implies decision making (or planning/control). In this dual process of consecutive knowledge transformation, the bulk of information comes from the external world and the task comes from the upper level. (Through all these stages each subsystem deals with a *multiresolutional world representation*, so the task that is coming from the upper level is apparently a decision which is a result of upper-level activities.)

This process is different within each subsystem; it uses different vocabularies but has the same *essence*: knowledge of the state of the world represented in a way that is commensurate with the tools and techniques applicable within each subsystem being considered. This common essence is determined by the fundamentally uniform assignment typical for the intelligent systems: *extraction of meaning.*

In systems for natural language processing this is the most challenging central problem. As CW systems were introduced, most computational problems have evolved into the domain of meaning extraction. In this overview we have addressed the typical common traits and all-encompassing fundamental principles of CW.

REFERENCES

1. L. A. Zadeh, Fuzzy sets, *Inf. Control*, 8:417–435, 1965.
2. L. A. Zadeh, Fuzzy logic = computing with words, *IEEE Trans. Fuzzy Syst.*, 4(2):103–111, 1996.
3. L. A. Zadeh, From computing with numbers to computing with words—from manipulation of measurements to manipulation of perception, *IEEE Trans. Circuits Syst. I: Fundam. Theory Appl.*, 45(1):105–119, 1999.
4. J. Albus and A. Meystel, *Behavior Generation in Intelligent Systems*, National Institute of Science and Technology, Gaithersburg, MD, 1998.
5. P. McCauley-Bell and A. Badiru, Fuzzy modeling and analytic hierarchy processing to quantify risk levels associated with occupational injuries, part I: The development of fuzzy-linguistic risk levels, *IEEE Trans. Fuzzy Syst.*, 4(2):124–131, 1996.
6. D. Dubois and H. Prade, Processing fuzzy temporal knowledge, *IEEE Trans. Syst. Man Cybern.*, 19(4):729–744, 1989.
7. A. Basu and A. Dutta, Reasoning with imprecise knowledge to enhance intelligent decision support, *IEEE Trans. Syst. Man Cybern.*, 19(4):756–770, 1989.
8. A. Kolmogorov, Über die Analytishen Methoden in der Wahrscheinlichkeitsrechnung, *Math. Ann.*, 104:415–458, 1931.
9. V. Sridhar and M. N. Murty, Belief revision: an axiomatic approach, *J. Intell. Robot. Syst.*, 8:127–153, 1993.
10. G. Booch, *Object-Oriented Analysis and Design*, Benjamin-Cummings, Redwood City, CA, 1994.
11. A. Meystel, *Intelligent Systems as an Object of Semiotic Research: Proc. 1996 Biennial Conference of the North American Fuzzy Information Processing Society*, Berkeley, CA, 1996.
12. J. F. Sowa (ed.), *Principles of Semantic Networks: Explorations in the Representation of Knowledge*, Morgan Kaufmann, San Mateo, CA, 1991.
13. A. Meystel, Learning algorithms generating multigranular hierarchies, in B. Mirkin, R. R. McMorris, F. S. Roberts, and A. Rzhetsky (eds.), *Mathematical Hierarchies and Biology*, DIMACS, Vol. 37, American Mathematical Society, Providence, RI, 1997, pp. 357–384.
14. G. Brown and G. Yule, *Discourse Analysis*, Cambridge University Press, Cambridge, 1993.
15. J. A. Lucy, *Language Diversity and Thought*, Cambridge University Press, Cambridge, 1992.
16. S. Harnad, Symbol grounding problem, in S. Forrest (ed.), *Emergent Computation*, MIT Press, Cambridge, MA, 1991, pp. 335–346.
17. A. Meystel, *Semiotic Modeling and Situation Analysis: An Introduction*, AdRem, Bala Cyncoyd, PA, 1995.

CHAPTER 12

FUZZY QUALITATIVE REASONING WITH WORDS

DIDIER DUBOIS
Université Paul Sabatier, Toulouse, France

ALLEL HADJ-ALI
Institut d'Informatique, Université Mouloud Mammeri, Tizi-Ouzou, Algeria

HENRI PRADE
Université Paul Sabatier, Toulouse, France

12.1 INTRODUCTION

Computing in its traditional sense involves manipulation of numbers for the most part. Symbolic computation has been developed in the meantime, especially in artificial intelligence, but often without preserving the ability to interface the symbolic processing of information with numerical data. By contrast, humans employ mostly words and qualitative descriptions when providing assessments of situations, or reasoning about complex physical or human systems, even if some of the data refer to numerical scales. For a long time, fuzzy sets have been advocated by Zadeh [24] as a methodology for interfacing numerical data about the world (which are often imprecisely perceived), with linguistic categories or classes used in reasoning. In particular, it is the case for fuzzy rules or fuzzy algorithms where words are interpreted as the labels of fuzzy sets. There are different types of situations where the underlying reasoning process can be handled within the framework of a limited vocabulary. When developing his approach to approximate reasoning, Zadeh [25] was already separating the combination/projection machinery acting at the levels of fuzzy set membership functions from the knowledge representation and linguistic approximation steps which, respectively, turn the linguistic input information into possibility distributions and restate the conclusions obtained into a prescribed vocabulary

Computing with Words, Edited by Paul P. Wang.
ISBN 0-471-35374-4

understandable by the user. The fuzzy set framework should supply the proper tools for mixing a symbolic treatment to be performed at the level of linguistic labels, with facilities for interfacing them permanently with their fuzzy set semantics along the reasoning process. Indeed, fuzzy sets restore gradual transitions between categories on continuous universes, which would be lost if the interface between labels and data were provided by crisp sets only. In this chapter we investigate the feasibility of such a view on a particular type of reasoning: the order-of-magnitude reasoning in terms of closeness and negligibility relations. The same line of research has been explored on more general patterns of approximate reasoning by Dubois et al. [6].

Qualitative reasoning, handled at the level of comparative relations, may be viewed as a simple illustration of the idea of computing with words recently emphasized by Zadeh [26,27]. As the expression suggests, *computing with words* is a methodology in which words are used in place of numbers for computing and reasoning. As pointed out by Zadeh [26], there are two major imperatives for computing with words. "First, computing with words is a necessity when the available information is too imprecise to justify the use of numbers, and second, when there is a tolerance for imprecision which can be exploited to achieve tractability, robustness, low solution cost, and better report with reality. Exploitation of the tolerance for imprecision is an issue of central importance in computing with words." A key idea underlying computing with words is that it involves a fusion of symbolic processing and computation with fuzzy variables. The following summarizes Zadeh's main points. Computing with words is based on a granulation process, which generally serves as a way of achieving data compression. A granule g is a fuzzy set of points drawn together by similarity. A word w (e.g., young) is a label of granule g. In computing with words, a granule g which is a denotation of a word w is viewed as a fuzzy constraint on a variable. The rules of inference in fuzzy logic are employed to propagate fuzzy constraints from premises to conclusions. Thus the techniques of computing with words underlie, in one way or another, almost all the apparatus of fuzzy logic.

This chapter focuses on a particular type of reasoning where computation can be handled at the word level, as will be shown: qualitative reasoning about relative orders of magnitude, where fuzzy constraints expressing closeness or negligibility relations have to be propagated. Building inference systems endowed with the ability to reason about physical systems in the same way as humans—or at least engineers—do has led to the development of qualitative reasoning [16,19,23]. The main aim of qualitative reasoning is both to address the need to deal with physical systems where some magnitudes are not easy to quantify (numerical data are not available) and to be able to reason at a qualitative or symbolic level (e.g., reasoning directly in terms of orders of magnitude). The last decade has seen significant progress toward the development of formal methods for qualitative reasoning about the behavior of physical systems. The simplest formalism used in qualitative reasoning is based on the sign algebra $(-, 0, +)$; see, for instance, [4,16]. Such models are enough to represent the sign of quantities and the direction in which each quantity affects another quantity. Information about magnitudes or relative orders of magnitude is not represented. As a consequence, the sign-based approach has too limited an expressive power in some practical cases to be widely applicable. A major limitation lies in the fact that the sign of the result of an operation can often be determined only if the order of magnitude of the parameters involved is considered. The only knowledge of the sign of quantities involved in mathematical expressions often leaves completely indeterminate the sign of the result. Reasoning with relative orders of magnitude is an attempt to overcome these limitations. See Ref. 22 for a general discussion.

This type of qualitative reasoning corresponds to a particular form of common-sense reasoning in which ideas of closeness, comparability, and negligibility are involved. The first attempt to formalize such reasoning appeared with the formal system FOG, proposed by Raiman [20,21]. FOG is based on three basic relations, expressing the relations "negligible in relation to" (Ne), "close to" (Cl), and "has the same sign and order of magnitude as" [i.e., "is comparable to" (Co)]. FOG includes one axiom and 31 inference rules, which allow for deduction from pieces of knowledge expressed in terms of relative orders of magnitude. This set of rules was proved to be consistent by interpreting the three relations in the framework of non-standard analysis. Note that FOG handles relative orders of magnitude through a purely symbolic computation process. Nevertheless, no numerical interpretation is provided for the symbolic computation of orders of magnitude in the FOG approach, which thus does not allow for the incorporation of numerical values. This drawback is remedied in the system O(M) proposed by Mavrovouniotis and Stephanopoulos [17,18], where the primitive relations ("much smaller than", "moderately smaller than," "slightly smaller than," "exactly equal," "slightly larger than," "moderately larger than," "much larger than") are interpreted in terms of the location of the quotient of the two quantities compared in some interval. All these intervals are disjoint and defined via a unique parameter that is fixed according to the application context. The fact that this parameter is fixed creates a problem since the result of (repeated) composition of the primitive relations cannot always be expressed by a primitive relation if we want to adhere perfectly to the interval semantics. For instance, if $x/y \in [a,b]$ and $y/z \in [a,b]$, with $a>0$, then $x/z \in [a^2,b^2]$ and $[a^2,b^2]$, or more generally, $[a^n,b^n]$, are not necessarily included in an interval corresponding to the semantics of a primitive relation. Dague [2] also provides a numerical interpretation of FOG-like relations manipulated in a formal way. However, FOG and O(M) do not take into account the fact that the satisfaction of relations such as Ne, Cl, or "much larger than" by two numerical values is often a matter of degree. Moreover, FOG does not cope with the fact that it is also context-dependent. FOG does not acknowledge either that a relation of closeness (respectively, negligibility) is usually transitive in a weak (respectively, strong) sense (which will be made precise in the following) rather than just transitive [10]. The same type of limitation applies to O(M) as well. The modeling of relations Ne, Cl, and Co by means of fuzzy relations constitutes an appropriate framework for solving these problems.

The chapter is organized as follows. In Section 12.2 we provide the background necessary to understand the formal system FOG. In Section 12.3 we introduce fuzzy equality and inequality relations (such as "approximately equal," "much larger than") modeled in terms of difference and present a set of inference rules based on these relations. We show that the composition of such relations reduces to simple fuzzy arithmetic operations. However, a simple example suggests that the modeling in terms of difference may be more appropriate for temporal relations. In Section 12.4 we discuss modeling of the basic relations of FOG using fuzzy relations in terms of ratios of values. New inference rules, based on the relations Ne and Cl, are established. The composition of fuzzy relations representing relations Ne and Cl also reduces to simple arithmetic operations on fuzzy numbers which play the role of parameters underlying the semantics of Ne and Cl. The results of inferences are always expressed in terms of the relations Ne and Cl but based on fuzzy parameters, which are computed symbolically from the fuzzy parameters underlying the relations appearing in the premises. This machinery contributes to providing standard numerical semantics for the symbolic computation performed by the FOG's rules, as well as by the new inference rules that are proposed. Illustrative examples for solving equations in an approximate way are presented in Section 12.5, and the concluding remarks point out some problems that are faced for the development and efficient implementation of the approach.

12.2 FORMAL SYSTEM FOG

The FOG system is based on three relations, which capture closeness, negligibility, and comparability, and which are denoted by Cl, Ne, and Co, respectively. These three operators are:

x Ne y	Stands for x is negligible in relation to y
x Cl y	Stands for x is close to y, understood as $(x–y)$ is negligible in relation to y
x Co y	Stands for x has the same sign and order of magnitude as y

The underlying idea is that if x Ne z then y Ne z (when x Co y). FOG has one axiom (A1: x Cl x) and 31 inference rules. Hereafter we give some of these rules ($[x]$ denotes the sign $(+, -, 0)$ of the quantity x):

1. $x \text{ Cl } y \Rightarrow y \text{ Cl } x$
2. $x \text{ Cl } y \Rightarrow x \text{ Co } y$
3. $x \text{ Cl } y,\ y \text{ Cl } z \Rightarrow x \text{ Cl } z$
4. $x \text{ Cl } y,\ y \text{ Ne } z \Rightarrow x \text{ Ne } z$
5. $x \text{ Co } y,\ y \text{ Co } z \Rightarrow x \text{ Co } z$
6. $x \text{ Ne } y,\ y \text{ Ne } z \Rightarrow x \text{ Ne } z$
7. $x \text{ Co } y,\ y \text{ Cl } z \Rightarrow x \text{ Co } z$
8. $x \text{ Ne } y \Rightarrow (x + y) \text{ Cl } y$
9. $(x + y) \text{ Cl } z, y \text{ Ne } x \Rightarrow x \text{ Cl } z$
10. $x \text{ Ne } y, z \text{ Cl } t \Rightarrow x \cdot z \text{ Ne } y \cdot t$
11. $x \text{ Ne } y, z \text{ Ne } x \Rightarrow x \cdot z \text{ Ne } y \cdot t$

12. $x \cdot y$ Cl $z \cdot t, x$ Cl $z, [x] \neq 0 \Rightarrow y$ Clt
13. $x \cdot y$ Cl $z \cdot t, x$ Ne $z, [z] \neq 0 \Rightarrow t$ Ne y
14. $x \cdot y$ Ne $z \cdot t, z$ Ne $x, [x] \neq 0 \Rightarrow y$ Ne t

Note that both Cl and Co are equivalence relations (i.e., reflexive, symmetric, and transitive), with Co coarser than Cl. The FOG rules, which can be justified from the point of view of non-standard analysis, describe how the three relations work together and allow for the propagation of initial qualitative information. Most of the rules have an explicit intuitive interpretation and need no explanation. Note that they are not independent (e.g., rules 2 and 5 $\Rightarrow$ rule 7). Note that FOG has been used successfully in the DEDALE system of analog circuit diagnosis [3], and in macroeconomics [1]. Nevertheless, FOG has several limitations, as announced in the introduction:

- No standard numerical interpretation of the three relations Ne, Cl, and Co is provided in this approach. It may create interface problems with genuine numerical values. It does not allow for the incorporation of quantitative information such as the assessment of numerical values. However, such information is often available and useful when solving engineering problems. FOG cannot use this type of information because it does not relate numbers to order-of-magnitude relations. Moreover, FOG is unable to express a gradual change from one order of magnitude to another in the computation process, due to the absence of gradual transitions between the orders of magnitude [2].
- FOG does not take into account the fact that the extent to which two numerical values satisfy the relations Ne, Cl, and Co is often a matter of degree and is also context-dependent (e.g., the relation "negligible" does not mean the same thing in to the preliminary and detailed-design contexts).
- FOG cannot express that the relations are "weakly" or "strongly" transitive rather than just transitive in the usual sense. For instance, if "a is close to b" and "b close to c," it is not so true that we should conclude that "a is close to c" in any case (at least with a too restrictive acceptance of "close"). This exemplifies the weakening of transitivity. To avoid undesirable transitivity effects and obtain results at least approximately valid with respect to a numerical semantics, Raiman is obliged to introduce arbitrary limitations on the chaining of rules (by means of control techniques).

The use of fuzzy relations for modeling the relations Ne, Cl, and Co can solve the foregoing problems and provide numerical semantics to the symbolic calculus of orders of magnitude performed by the FOG system.

12.3 FUZZY EQUALITIES AND INEQUALITIES

In this section we consider particular fuzzy relations which are of interest in practice in some forms of qualitative reasoning. Approximate equalities and strong inequalities (e.g., "much greater than") are examples of binary fuzzy relations which can easily be handled using fuzzy arithmetic techniques. An approximate equality can be modeled by a fuzzy relation E of the form $\mu_E(x,y) = \mu_L(|x-y|)$. For instance,

$$\mu_E(x,y) = \begin{cases} 1 & \text{if} |x-y| \leq \delta \\ 0 & \text{if} |x-y| \geq \delta + \varepsilon \\ \dfrac{\delta + \varepsilon - |x-y|}{\varepsilon} & \text{otherwise,} \end{cases} \tag{12.1}$$

where δ and ε are, respectively, positive and strictly positive parameters which modulate the approximate equality. Then the approximate equality of quantities a and b (in the sense of E) will be denoted by

$$a - b \in L \tag{12.2}$$

with the following intended meaning: The possible values of the difference $a - b$ are restricted by the fuzzy set L. Here L is a fuzzy set centered in 0 [i.e., $\mu_L(d) = \mu_L(-d)$], or if we prefer, $\mu_E(x,y) = \mu_E(y,x)$ (see Figure 12.1). It ensures the symmetry of the approximate equality relation. Classical equality is recovered for $\delta = 0$ and $\epsilon \to 0$. We shall write equivalently $(a,b) \in E(\delta,\epsilon)[\Leftrightarrow (b,a) \in E(\delta,\epsilon)]$. Moreover, $(a,b) \in E(\delta,\epsilon) \Leftrightarrow (a-b,0) \in E(\delta,\epsilon)$.

Similarly, a more or less strong inequality can be modeled, for instance, by a relation I of the form

$$\mu_I(x,y) = \begin{cases} 1 & \text{if} x \geq y + \lambda + \rho \\ 0 & \text{if} x \leq y + \lambda \\ \dfrac{x - y - \lambda}{\rho} & \text{otherwise,} \end{cases} \tag{12.3}$$

with $\lambda \geq 0$ and $\rho > 0$. A constraint of the form "a is slightly/moderately/$\cdots$/much larger than b" (in the sense of I) can then be written, with $\mu_I(x,y) = \mu_K(x-y)$,

$$a - b \in K, \tag{12.4}$$

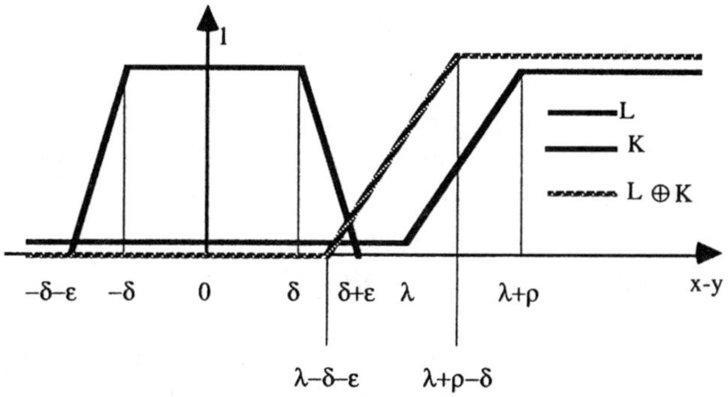

FIGURE 12.1.

where K is a fuzzy interval such that $K = [K, +\infty)$, where $\mu_{[K,+\infty]}(t) = \sup_{s \le t} \mu_K(s)$. It means that K identifies itself with the set of values equal or greater than a value restricted by K (see Figure 12.1). According to the values of parameters λ and ρ, the modality which specifies how much a is larger than b may be linguistically expressed by "slightly," "moderately," "much,"..., in a given context. When $\lambda = 0$ and $\rho \to 0$, the usual inequality relations $>$ or $\geq$ are recovered. We shall write $(a, b) \in I(\lambda, \rho)$ equivalently to $a - b \in K$.

The composition of two fuzzy relations E and I, with $\mu_I(x, y) = \mu_K(x - y)$ and $\mu_E(y, z) = \mu_L(y - z)$, is defined by

$$\begin{aligned}\forall x, \forall z, \mu_{E \circ I}(x, z) &= \sup_{y \in Y} \min(\mu_K(x - y), \mu_L(y - z)) \\ &= \sup_{\substack{s,t \\ x-z=s+t}} \min(\mu_K(s), \mu_L(t)) \\ &= \mu_{K \oplus L}(x - z),\end{aligned} \tag{12.5}$$

where $\oplus$ denotes the addition extended to fuzzy intervals (e.g., Ref. 9). Indeed, arithmetic operations are extended to fuzzy quantities in the following way:

$$\mu_{K \circledcirc L}(u) = \sup_{s,t:\mu=s*t} \min(\mu_K(s), \mu_L(t)),$$

where $\circledcirc$ denotes the extension of the arithmetic operation $*$ to fuzzy sets of the real line.

Note that if K and L have trapezoidal membership functions, that is, $K = (k1, k2, k3, k4)$ where $[k1, k4]$ is the support of μ_K and $[k2, k3]$ is the core of μ_K, and $L = (l1, l2, l3, l4)$, with a similar understanding of the components of the 4-tuple, then $K \oplus L = (k1 + l1, k2 + l2, k3 + l3, k4 + l4)$ and $K \ominus L = (k1 - l4, k2 - l3, k3 - l2, k4 - l1)$. In Figure 12.1, $L = (-\delta - \epsilon, -\delta, \delta, \delta + \epsilon), K = (\lambda, \lambda + \rho, +\infty, +\infty)$, and $L \oplus K = (\lambda - \delta - \epsilon, \lambda + \rho - \delta, +\infty, +\infty)$. For more details about fuzzy arithmetic, see Ref. 9.

Let us look at an example. If we know, for instance, that "a is approximately equal to b" (i.e., $a - b \in L$) and that "b is much greater than c" (i.e., $b - c \in K$), using (12.5) we can deduce that $a - c \in L \oplus K$. This result is represented in Figure 12.1. Symbolically, this inference can be written

$$(a, b) \in E(\delta, \epsilon) \text{ and } (b, c) \in I(\lambda, \rho) \Rightarrow (a, c) \in I(\lambda - \delta - \epsilon, \rho + \epsilon), \tag{12.6}$$

which means that if a and b are approximately equal (in the sense of the approximate equality relation E defined with parameters δ and ϵ) and b is (more or less) larger than c (in the sense of the fuzzy inequality relation I defined with parameters λ and ρ), we infer that a is (more or less) larger than c (in the sense of the fuzzy relation I defined with parameters, $\lambda - \delta - \epsilon$ and $\rho + \epsilon$). Note that $I(\lambda - \delta - \epsilon, \rho + \epsilon)$ means "larger than" only if $\lambda - \delta - \epsilon > 0$, strictly speaking. Otherwise, if $\lambda - \delta - \epsilon \leq 0$, it is at least somewhat possible that a is not greater than c when $(a, c) \in I(\lambda - \delta - \epsilon,$

$\rho + \epsilon$); and it is fully possible that a is not greater than c if $\lambda + \rho - \delta \leq 0$. Note also that $(a, b) \in I(\lambda, \rho) \Leftrightarrow (a - b, 0) \in I(\lambda, \rho)$.

In the same way, we can justify the following inference rules:

$$(a, b) \in E(\delta, \epsilon) \text{ and } (b, c) \in E(\delta', \epsilon') \Rightarrow (a, c) \in E(\delta + \delta', \epsilon + \epsilon') \quad (12.7)$$

$$(a, b) \in I(\lambda, \rho) \text{ and } (b, c) \in I(\lambda', \rho') \Rightarrow (a, c) \in I(\lambda + \lambda', \rho + \rho'). \quad (12.8)$$

Other rules expressing the behavior of fuzzy relations E and I with respect to arithmetic operations can easily be derived. For instance, we have

$$(a, b) \in E(\delta, \epsilon) \Rightarrow (a + c, b + c) \in E(\delta, \epsilon) \quad (12.9)$$

$$(a, b) \in I(\lambda, \rho) \Rightarrow (a + c, b + c) \in I(\lambda, \rho) \quad (12.10)$$

$$(a, b) \in E(\delta, \epsilon) \text{ and } (c, d) \in E(\delta', \epsilon') \Rightarrow (a + c, b + d) \in E(\delta + \delta', \epsilon + \epsilon') \quad (12.11)$$

$$(a, b) \in I(\lambda, \rho) \text{ and } (c, d) \in I(\lambda', \rho') \Rightarrow (a + c, b + d) \in I(\lambda + \lambda', \rho + \rho') \quad (12.12)$$

$$(a, b) \in E(\delta, \epsilon) \text{ and } (c, d) \in I(\lambda, \rho) \Rightarrow (a + c, b + d) \in I(\lambda - \delta - \epsilon, \rho + \epsilon) \quad (12.13)$$

$$(a + b, c) \in E(\delta, \epsilon) \text{ and } (a, b) \in I(\lambda, \rho) \Rightarrow (a, c - a) \in I(\lambda - \delta - \epsilon, \rho + \epsilon) \quad (12.14a)$$

$$(a + b, c) \in E(\delta, \epsilon) \text{ and } (a, b) \in I(\lambda, \rho) \Rightarrow (c - b, b) \in I(\lambda - \delta - \epsilon, \rho + \epsilon) \quad (12.14b)$$

$$(a + b, c) \in I(\lambda, \rho) \text{ and } (c, a) \in I(\lambda', \rho') \Rightarrow (b, 0) \in I(\lambda_+\lambda', \rho_+\rho') \quad (12.15)$$

$$(a + b, c) \in E(\delta, \epsilon) \text{ and } (a, c) \in E(\delta', \epsilon') \Rightarrow (0, b) \in E(\delta + \delta', \epsilon + \epsilon') \quad (12.16)$$

$$(a + b, c) \in E(\delta, \epsilon) \text{ and } (c, a) \in I(\lambda, \rho) \Rightarrow (b, 0) \in I(\lambda - \delta - \epsilon, \rho + \epsilon) \quad (12.17)$$

$$(a - c, b) \in E(\delta, \epsilon) \text{ and } (c, a) \in E(\delta', \epsilon') \Rightarrow (0, b) \in E(\delta + \delta', \epsilon + \epsilon') \quad (12.18)$$

$$(a + b, c + d) \in E(\delta, \epsilon) \text{ and } (c, a) E(\delta', \epsilon') \Rightarrow (b, d) \in E(\delta + \delta', \epsilon + \epsilon') \quad (12.19)$$

$$(a + b, c + d) \in I(\lambda, \rho) \text{ and } (c, a) \in E(\delta, \epsilon) \Rightarrow (b, d) \in I(\lambda - \delta - \epsilon, \rho + \epsilon) \quad (12.20)$$

$$(a + b, c + d) \in I(\lambda, \rho) \text{ and } (c, a) \in I(\lambda', \rho') \Rightarrow (b, d) \in I(\lambda + \lambda', \rho + \rho'). \quad (12.21)$$

Proof: Let us look at the proof of some of these inference rules. The left side of (12.11) can be written in the form

$$\sup_{\substack{x,y,z,t \\ u=x+z;\ v=y+t}} \min(\mu_{E(\delta,\epsilon)}(x, y), \mu_{E(\delta',\epsilon')}(z, t))$$

$$= \sup_{\substack{x,y,z,t \\ u-v=(x-y)+(z-t)}} \min(\mu_L(x - y), \mu_{L'}(z - t)) = \mu_{L \oplus L'}(u - v)$$

with $L' = (-\delta' - \epsilon', -\delta', +\delta', \delta' + \epsilon')$. This result implies that $(a+c, b+d) \in E(\delta+\delta', \epsilon+\epsilon')$.

Rule (12.17) can be established noting that

$$\begin{aligned} &\sup_{x,z} \min(\mu_E(x+y,z), \mu_I(z,x)) \\ &= \sup_{x,z} \min(\mu_L(x+y-z), \mu_K(z-x)) \\ &= \mu_{L\oplus K}(y) \end{aligned}$$

observing that $y = (x+y-z)+(z-x)$. Thus we conclude that $(b,0) \in I(\lambda-\delta-\epsilon, \rho+\epsilon)$ when $(a+b,c) \in E(\delta,\epsilon)$ and $(c,a) \in I(\lambda,\rho)$. Note that it is certain that $b>0$ only if $\lambda-\delta-\epsilon>0$.

Now, considering rule (12.20), the composition of relations $(a+b, c+d) \in I(\lambda,\rho)$ and $(c,a) \in E(\delta,\epsilon)$ is given by

$$\begin{aligned} &\sup_{x,z} \min(\mu_I(x+y,z+t), \mu_E(z,x)) \\ &= \sup_{x,z} \min(\mu_K((x+y)-(z+t)), \mu_L(z-x)) \\ &= \mu_{K\oplus L}(y-t), \end{aligned}$$

observing that $y-t = [(x+y)-(z+t)]+(z-x)$. This means that $(b,d) \in I(\lambda-\delta-\epsilon, \rho+\epsilon)$.

Rules (12.9) to (12.21) are not independent. Rules (12.9) to (12.10) are particular cases of (12.11) and (12.12) replacing (c,d) by (c,c), noting that $(c,c) \in E(0,0)$ and $(c,c) \in I(0,0)$. Similarly, (12.16) and (12.15) are particular cases of (12.19) and (12.21), respectively, for $d = 0$. Rule (12.18) can be obtained from (12.16) by noting that $(a-c,b) \in E(\delta,\epsilon) \Leftrightarrow (a, b+c) \in E(\delta,\epsilon)$ and $(a,c) \in E(\delta',\epsilon') \Leftrightarrow (c,a) \in E(\delta',\epsilon')$. Besides, rule (12.17) can be generalized into the rule

$$(a+b, c+d) \in E(\delta,\epsilon) \text{ and } (c,a) \in I(\lambda,\rho) \Rightarrow (b,d) \in I(\lambda-\delta-\epsilon, \rho+\epsilon).$$

Then, letting $a+b = C, c+d = A, c = A+B, a = C+D$, we obtain

$$\begin{aligned} &(C,A) \in E(\delta,\epsilon) \text{ and } (A+B, C+D) \in I(\lambda,\rho) \Rightarrow \\ &\quad (-D,-B) \in I(\lambda-\delta-\epsilon, \rho+\epsilon), \end{aligned}$$

which is nothing but (12.20), noting that $(-d,-b) \in I(\lambda',\rho') \Leftrightarrow (b,d) \in I(\lambda',\rho')$ always holds.

As can be seen, arithmetic computations on fuzzy numbers are mirrored at a symbolic level by inference rules that exhibit formal manipulations of the parameters underlying the approximate equality and inequality relations. The fuzzy number–based interpretation of these relations provides a natural semantics and interfaces the symbolic level with the numerical level. From these inference rules, new conclusions can be drawn symbolically, still keeping the ability to interpret the obtained result numerically. For instance, from (12.7) and the equivalence $(a+b,c) \in E(\delta,\epsilon) \Leftrightarrow (a,c-b) \in E(\delta,\epsilon)$, we can conclude, for instance, that

$$\text{if } (a-c,b) \in E(\delta,\epsilon) \text{ and } (d+b,c) \in E(\delta',\epsilon'),$$
$$\text{then} (a-c,c-d) \in E(\delta+\delta',\epsilon+\epsilon').$$

Finally, let us recall that this kind of fuzzy relation (i.e., relations E and I) can offer a useful setting for representing and processing temporal knowledge [11]. For example:

- Knowing that the date b takes place "much after" the date a is represented by $\pi_{(a,b)}(x,y) = \mu_I(y,x)$, where I is defined by (12.3) and where the meaning of "much" is modeled by means of the parameters λ and $\rho.\pi_{(a,b)}$ is a joint possibility distribution expressing the precedence relations between dates a and b.
- Knowing that dates a and b are "approximately equal" is represented by $\pi_{(a,b)}(x,y) = \mu_E(x,y)$, where E is defined by (12.1) and where the meaning of "approximately" is modeled by means of the parameters δ and ϵ.

Let us consider an example of reasoning involving temporal knowledge, where we have the following information about dates a, b, c, and d:

(i) Dates a and b almost coincide [in the sense of $E(\delta,\epsilon)$].
(ii) Dates b and c are "approximately equal" [in the sense of $E(\delta',\epsilon')$].
(iii) Date $a+b$ takes place "much after" date $c+d$ [in the sense of $I(\lambda,\rho)$].

Let us consider the question: What can be said about date b with respect to d? Information in points (i) to (iii) can be represented, respectively, by the following relations:

(i) $(a,b) \in E(\delta,\epsilon)$ or $(b,a) \in E(\delta,\epsilon)$
(ii) $(b,c) \in E(\delta',\epsilon')$
(iii) $(a+b,c+d) \in I(\lambda,\rho)$

By the transitivity rule (12.7), we obtain $(a,c) \in E(\delta+\delta',\epsilon+\epsilon')$. Since E is symmetric, the last result implies that $(c,a) \in E(\delta+\delta',\epsilon+\epsilon')$. Rule (12.20), applied to this last relation and to the relation in (iii), enables us to conclude that

$$(b,d) \in I[\lambda-(\delta+\delta')-(\epsilon+\epsilon'), \rho+(\epsilon+\epsilon')].$$

This means that date b is "much after" date d, where the meaning of "much" is modeled by means of parameters $\lambda' = \lambda-(\delta+\delta')-(\epsilon+\epsilon')$ and $\rho' = \rho+ (\epsilon+\epsilon')$, provided that $\lambda' > 0$.

12.4 SYMBOLIC REASONING WITH FUZZY NEGLIGIBILITY AND CLOSENESS RELATIONS

12.4.1 Modeling Closeness and Negligibility

In Section 12.3 we have seen that some relational order-of-magnitude information can be expressed in practice by fuzzy relations whose membership functions depend on difference of values. If we prefer, we can also work in terms of the ratio x/y rather than in terms of the difference $x - y$, especially when both x and y are positive. Then an approximate equality is modeled by a fuzzy relation $\mu_E(x, y) = \mu_M(x/y)$, where M is a fuzzy interval such as $\mu_M(1) = 1$ (i.e., M represents a "fuzzy 1"). More or less strong inequality relations can be obtained by sustituting x/y for $x - y$ in definition (12.3) of μ_K [i.e., $\mu_I(x, y) = \mu_K(x/y)$]. The use of ratios looks natural for the modeling of negligibility relations. When μ_K and μ_L are functions of x/y (instead of $x - y$), we obtain $\mu_{I \circ E}(x, z) = \mu_{K \otimes L}(x/z)$ instead of (12.5), where $\otimes$ denotes the product extended to fuzzy numbers. In the following, we omit "$\otimes$" when writing products.

As pointed out by Dubois and Prade [10], the idea of relative closeness (Cl) can be captured by the following approximate equality relation between numbers x and y:

$$\mu_{\mathrm{Cl}}(x, y) = \mu_M(x/y), \tag{12.22}$$

where the characteristic function μ_M is such that $\mu_M(1) = 1$ (since x is close to x), $\mu_M(t) = 0$ if $t \leq 0$ (since two numbers which are close should have the same sign), and $\mu_M(t) = \mu_M(1/t)$ in order to ensure that $\mu_{\mathrm{Cl}}(x, y) = \mu_{\mathrm{Cl}}(y, x)$. In other words, M is a fuzzy interval which restricts values around 1 and is equal to its inverse, M^{-1}, which is defined by $\mu_{M^{-1}}(t) = \sup_{t=1/s} \mu_M(s) = \mu_M(1/t)$. Thus we have the semantic equivalence

$$(a, b) \in \mathrm{Cl} \Leftrightarrow (b, a) \in \mathrm{Cl}. \tag{12.23}$$

Strict equality is recovered for $M = \mathbf{1}$ [i.e., $\mu_{\mathbf{1}}(x/y) = 1$ if $x = y$ and $\mu_{\mathbf{1}}(x/y) = 0$ otherwise].

Raiman, in his inference system FOG, relates the ideas of closeness and of negligibility in the following way: "a is close to b" is equivalent to "a–b is negligible in comparison with b". In other words, "a is negligible in comparison with b" if and only if "$a + b$ is close to b" (see rule 8 of FOG). It leads us to define the extent to which x is negligible in comparison with y by

$$\mu_{Ne}(x, y) = \mu_M((x + y)/y) = \mu_M(1 + x/y). \tag{12.24}$$

By definition, the following equivalences hold $\forall C \neq 0$:

$$(a, b) \in \mathrm{Cl} \Leftrightarrow (ac, bc) \in \mathrm{Cl}$$
$$(a, b) \in \mathrm{Ne} \Leftrightarrow (ac, bc) \in \mathrm{Ne}.$$

The third relation, Co, is such that (see rule 2 of FOG) a Cl $b \Rightarrow a$ Co b, which means that comparability is a less restrictive notion than closeness. Note that it is desirable to have not only the fuzzy relation inclusion Cl $\subseteq$ Co but also to express that a and b are no longer comparable (in the sense of Co) when a becomes negligible in comparison with b, or b becomes negligible in comparison with a. This leads to the definition

$$((a,b) \in \text{Co} \Leftrightarrow \neg[(a,b) \in \text{Ne or } (b,a) \in \text{Ne}])$$

That is,

$$\begin{aligned}\mu_{\text{Co}}(x,y) &= 1 - \max(\mu_{\text{Ne}}(x,y), \mu_{\text{Ne}}(y,x)) \\ &= \min(1 - \mu_M(1 + x/y), 1 - \mu_M(1 + y/x)). \qquad (12.25)\end{aligned}$$

However, in the rest of the paper, we only consider rules involving the more basic relations Cl and Ne.

12.4.2 Inference Rules with Cl and Ne Relations

In the following we show that it is possible to develop inference rules where the fuzzy sets that parametrize the closeness and negligibility relations are manipulated at a symbolic level. As we shall see, the use of fuzzy relations can provide appropriate numerical semantics to the order-of-magnitude symbolic calculus performed by the formal system FOG. From now on we use the notations Cl[M] and Ne[M] to express that Cl (respectively, Ne) is defined from a membership function μ_M by (12.22) [respectively, (12.24)]. Using fuzzy arithmetic, the following inference rules can be established [10, 13]:

$$(a,b) \in \text{Ne}[M] \Leftrightarrow (a+b,b) \in \text{Cl}[M] \qquad (12.26)$$

$$(a,b) \in \text{Cl}[M] \Leftrightarrow (a-b,b) \in \text{Ne}[M] \qquad (12.27)$$

$$(a,b) \in \text{Ne}[M] \Leftrightarrow (-a,b) \in \text{Ne}[2 \ominus M] \qquad (12.28)$$

$$(a,a+b) \in \text{Ne}[M] \Leftrightarrow (b,a+b) \in \text{Cl}[2 \ominus M] \qquad (12.29)$$

$$(a,b) \in \text{Cl}[M] \text{ and } (b,c) \in \text{Cl}[N] \Rightarrow (a,c) \in \text{Cl}[MN] \qquad (12.30)$$

$$(a,b) \in \text{Ne}[M] \text{ and } (b,c) \in \text{Ne}[N] \Rightarrow (a,c) \in \text{Ne}[(M \ominus 1)(N \ominus 1) \oplus 1] \qquad (12.31)$$

$$(a,b) \in \text{Cl}[M] \text{ and } (b,c) \in \text{Ne}[N] \Rightarrow (a,c) \in \text{Ne}[M(N \ominus 1) \oplus 1] \qquad (12.32)$$

$$(a,c) \in \text{Cl}[M] \text{ and } (b,a) \in \text{Ne}[N] \Rightarrow (a+b,c) \in \text{Cl}[MN] \qquad (12.33)$$

$$(a,c) \in \text{Cl}[M] \text{ and } (b,c) \in \text{Ne}[N] \Rightarrow (a+b,c) \in \text{Cl}[M \oplus N \ominus 1] \qquad (12.34)$$

$$(a,c) \in \text{Ne}[M] \text{ and } (b,c) \in \text{Ne}[N] \Rightarrow (a+b,c) \in \text{Ne}[M \oplus N \ominus 1] \qquad (12.35)$$

$$(a,b) \in \text{Cl}[M] \text{ and } (c,d) \in \text{Ne}[N] \Rightarrow (a \cdot c, b \cdot d) \in \text{Ne}[M(N \ominus 1) \oplus 1] \qquad (12.36)$$

$$(a,b) \in \text{Ne}[M] \text{ and } (c,d) \in \text{Ne}[N] \Rightarrow (a \cdot c, b \cdot d) \in \text{Ne}[(M \ominus 1)(N \ominus 1) \oplus 1] \qquad (12.37)$$

$$(a,b) \in \text{Cl}[M] \text{ and } (c,d) \in \text{Cl}[N] \Rightarrow (a \cdot c, b \cdot d) \in \text{Cl}[MN] \qquad (12.38)$$

$$(a+b,c) \in \text{Cl}[M] \text{ and} (b,a) \in \text{Ne}[N] \Rightarrow (a,c) \in \text{Cl}[MN]. \qquad (12.39)$$

Most of these rules have counterparts in the FOG system. For instance, rules (12.30) to (12.32) and (12.39) are the counterparts of the following FOG rules:

$$(a, b) \in \mathrm{Cl} \text{ and } (b, c) \in \mathrm{Cl} \Rightarrow (a, c) \in \mathrm{Cl}$$

$$(a, b) \in \mathrm{Ne} \text{ and } (b, c) \in \mathrm{Ne} \Rightarrow (a, c) \in \mathrm{Ne}$$

$$(a, b) \in \mathrm{Cl} \text{ and } (b, c) \in Ne \Rightarrow (a, c) \in \mathrm{Ne}$$

$$(a + b, c) \in \mathrm{Cl} \text{ and } (b, a) \in \mathrm{Ne} \Rightarrow (a, c) \in \mathrm{Cl}.$$

The fuzzy relations approach shows that these rules are only "qualitatively valid." Repeated use of some of these rules without control can lead to dubious conclusions. Fuzzy relations enable us to acknowledge that the relation Cl is "weakly transitive" [since for $M = N, \mathrm{Cl}[M] \subseteq \mathrm{Cl}[M^2]$ [i.e., "a may be less close to c" than "a is close to b"] and that the relation Ne is "strongly transitive" (since for $M = N, \mathrm{Ne}[M] \supseteq \mathrm{Ne}[(M \ominus 1)(M \ominus 1) \oplus 1]$ (i.e., "a is more negligible in comparison with c" than "a in comparison with b," and "b with c")].

To equip all the FOG rules with numerical semantics, we propose new inference rules (not studied in Ref. 10) involving the product of the quantities considered:

$$(a \cdot b, c \cdot d) \in \mathrm{Ne}[M] \text{ and } (c, a) \in \mathrm{Ne}[N] \Rightarrow \\ (b, d) \in \mathrm{Ne}[(M \ominus 1)(N \ominus 1) \oplus 1] \tag{12.40}$$

$$(a \cdot b, c \cdot d) \in \mathrm{Cl}[M] \text{ and } (c, a) \in \mathrm{Cl}[N] \Rightarrow (b, d) \in \mathrm{Cl}[MN] \tag{12.41}$$

$$(a \cdot b, c \cdot d) \in \mathrm{Cl}[M] \text{ and } (a, c) \in \mathrm{Ne}[N] \Rightarrow \\ (d, b) \in \mathrm{Ne}[M(N \ominus 1) \oplus 1]. \tag{12.42}$$

Proof: The composition of relations $(a \cdot b, c \cdot d) \in \mathrm{Ne}[M]$ and $(c, a) \in \mathrm{Ne}[N]$ can be written in the form

$$\begin{aligned}
&\sup_{x,z} \min(\mu_{\mathrm{Ne}[M]}(x \cdot y, z \cdot t), \mu_{\mathrm{Ne}[N]}(z, x)) \\
&= \sup_{x,z} \min(\mu_M(1 + [x \cdot y/z \cdot t]), \mu_N(1 + z/x)) \\
&= \sup_{\substack{u,v \\ (u-1)(v-1)+1=1+y/t}} \min(\mu_M(u), \mu_N(v)), \text{ letting } u = 1 + [x \cdot y/z \cdot t] \text{ and } v = \\
&\quad 1 + z/x \\
&= \mu_{[(M\ominus 1)(N\ominus 1)\oplus 1]}(1 + y/t).
\end{aligned}$$

This implies that $(b, d) \in \mathrm{Ne}[(M \ominus 1)(N \ominus 1) \oplus 1]$.

In the same way, we can establish rules (12.41) and (12.42). Considering rule (12.42), the composition of relations $(a \cdot b, c \cdot d) \in \mathrm{Cl}[M]$ and $(a, c) \in \mathrm{Ne}[N]$ can be written in the form

$$\begin{aligned}
&\sup_{x,z}\min\left(\mu_{\mathrm{Cl}[M]}(x\cdot y, z\cdot t), \mu_{\mathrm{Ne}[N]}(x,z)\right)\\
&\quad = \sup_{x,z}\min(\mu_M(x\cdot y/z\cdot t), \mu_N(1+x/z))\\
&\quad = \sup_{x,z}\min(\mu_M(z\cdot t/x\cdot y), \mu_N(1+x/z))\\
&\quad = \sup_{\substack{u,v\\ u(v-1)+1=1+t/y}} \min(\mu_M(u), \mu_N(v)), \text{letting } u = z\cdot t/x\cdot y \text{ and } v = 1+x/z\\
&\quad = \mu_{[M(N\ominus 1)\oplus 1]}(1+t/y).
\end{aligned}$$

The latter result implies that $(d,b)\in \mathrm{Ne}[M(N\ominus 1)\oplus 1]$.

The syntactic approximations of rules (12.40), (12.41), and (12.42) are given by the following FOG rules:

$$\begin{aligned}
(a\cdot b, c\cdot d)\in \mathrm{Ne} \text{ and } (c,a)\in \mathrm{Ne} \Rightarrow (b,d)\in \mathrm{Ne}\\
(a\cdot b, c\cdot d)\in \mathrm{Cl} \text{ and } (a,c)\in \mathrm{Cl} \Rightarrow (b,d)\in \mathrm{Cl}\\
(a\cdot b, c\cdot d)\in \mathrm{Cl} \text{ and } (a,c)\in \mathrm{Ne} \Rightarrow (d,b)\in \mathrm{Ne}.
\end{aligned}$$

In the following we show that it is possible to derive other symbolic inference rules which are not explicit in the formal FOG system. First, we start with simple rules whose premises are not compound, namely,

$$(a, a\cdot b)\in \mathrm{Ne}[M] \Rightarrow (1+b, b)\in \mathrm{Cl}[M] \quad \text{if } a\neq 0 \tag{12.43}$$

$$(a, a\cdot b)\in \mathrm{Cl}[M] \Rightarrow (1, b)\in \mathrm{Cl}[M] \quad \text{if } a\neq 0 \tag{12.44}$$

$$(a-b, a)\in \mathrm{Ne}[M] \Rightarrow (b,a)\in \mathrm{Cl}[2\ominus M] \tag{12.45}$$

$$(a-b, a)\in \mathrm{Cl}[M] \Rightarrow (b,a)\in \mathrm{Ne}[2\ominus M]. \tag{12.46}$$

These rules can be proved easily by using the definitions of relations Cl and Ne given in (12.22) and (12.24), respectively.

More complex rules expressing the behavior of the relations Cl[M] and Ne[N] with respect to arithmetic operations (addition, subtraction, and product) in either the premise or the conclusion can be derived as well:

$$(a,c)\in \mathrm{Ne}[M] \text{ and } (b,a)\in \mathrm{Ne}[N] \Rightarrow (a+b, c)\in \mathrm{Ne}[(M\ominus 1)N\oplus 1] \tag{12.47}$$

$$(a,b)\in \mathrm{Ne}[M] \text{ and } (c,b)\in \mathrm{Ne}[N] \Rightarrow (a, b+c)\in \mathrm{Ne}[(M\ominus 1)N\oplus 1] \tag{12.48}$$

$$(a\cdot b, c\cdot d)\in \mathrm{Ne}[M] \text{ and } (a,c)\in \mathrm{Cl}[N] \Rightarrow (b,d)\in \mathrm{Ne}[(M\ominus 1)N\oplus 1] \tag{12.49}$$

$$(a+b, c)\in \mathrm{Cl}[M] \text{ and } (b,c)\in \mathrm{Cl}[N] \Rightarrow (a,c)\in \mathrm{Ne}[M\ominus N\oplus 1] \tag{12.50}$$

$$(a+b, c)\in \mathrm{Cl}[M] \text{ and } (b,c)\in \mathrm{Ne}[N] \Rightarrow (a,c)\in \mathrm{Cl}[M\ominus N\oplus 1] \tag{12.51}$$

$$(a+b, c)\in \mathrm{Ne}[M] \text{ and } (b,c)\in \mathrm{Ne}[N] \Rightarrow (a,c)\in \mathrm{Ne}[M\ominus N\oplus 1] \tag{12.52}$$

$$(a-b, c)\in \mathrm{Cl}[M] \text{ and } (b,a)\in \mathrm{Ne}[N] \Rightarrow (c,a)\in \mathrm{Cl}[M(2\ominus N)] \tag{12.53}$$

$$(a-b, c)\in \mathrm{Cl}[M] \text{ and } (a,c)\in \mathrm{Cl}[N] \Rightarrow (b,c)\in \mathrm{Ne}[N\ominus M\oplus 1] \tag{12.54}$$

$$(a-b, c)\in \mathrm{Ne}[M] \text{ and } (a,c)\in \mathrm{Cl}[N] \Rightarrow (b,c)\in \mathrm{Cl}[N\ominus M\oplus 1] \tag{12.55}$$

$$(a-b, c)\in \mathrm{Cl}[M] \text{ and } (b,c)\in \mathrm{Ne}[N] \Rightarrow (a,c)\in \mathrm{Cl}[M\oplus N\ominus 1]. \tag{12.56}$$

Proof: Let us look at the proof of some of these rules. Rule (12.47) can be established noting that

$$\begin{aligned}
&\sup_{\substack{x,y\\ x+y=w}} \min(\mu_{\mathrm{Ne}[M]}(x,z), \mu_{\mathrm{Ne}[N]}(y,x)) \\
&\quad = \sup_{\substack{x,y\\ x+y=w}} \min(\mu_M(1+x/z), \mu_N(1+y/x)) \\
&\quad = \sup_{\substack{u,v\\ (u-1)v+1=1+w/z}} \min(\mu_M(u), \mu_N(v)), \quad \text{letting } u = 1+x/z \text{ and } v = 1+y/x \\
&\quad = \mu_{[(M\ominus 1)N\oplus 1]}(1+w/z).
\end{aligned}$$

This means that $(a+b,c) \in \mathrm{Ne}[(M\ominus 1)N \oplus 1]$. Rule (12.48) can be obtained similarly by noting that

$$\left[\left(1+\frac{x}{y}\right)-1\right]\frac{y}{y+z}+1 = 1+\frac{x}{y+z} \quad \text{and} \quad \text{using } \mu_N\left(1+\frac{z}{y}\right) = \mu_N\left(\frac{y}{y+z}\right).$$

The result of rule (12.50) can be obtained easily noting also that

$$\begin{aligned}
&\sup_y \min(\mu_{\mathrm{Cl}[M]}(x+y,z), \mu_{\mathrm{Cl}[N]}(y,z)) \\
&\quad = \sup_y \min(\mu_M((x+y)/z), \mu_N(y/x)) \\
&\quad = \mu_{[M\ominus N\oplus 1]}(1+x/z), \quad \text{observing that } 1+(x/z) = [(x+y)/z] - (y/z) + 1.
\end{aligned}$$

Then we conclude that $(a,c) \in \mathrm{Ne}[M \ominus N \oplus 1]$.

In rule (12.53), the composition of relations $(a-b,c) \in \mathrm{Cl}[M]$ and $(b,a) \in \mathrm{Ne}[N]$ leads to

$$\begin{aligned}
&\sup_y \min(\mu_{\mathrm{Cl}[M]}(x-y,z), \mu_{\mathrm{Ne}[N]}(y,x)) \\
&\quad = \sup_y \min(\mu_M((x-y)/z), \mu_N(1+y/x)) \\
&\quad = \sup_y \min(\mu_M(z/(x-y)), \mu_N(1+y/x)) \\
&\quad = \sup_{\substack{u,v\\ u(2-v)=z/x}} \min(\mu_M(u), \mu_N(v)), \quad \text{letting } u = z/(x-y) \text{ and } v = 1+y/x \\
&\quad = \mu_{[M(2\ominus N)]}(z/x).
\end{aligned}$$

This expresses the fact that $(c,a) \in \mathrm{Cl}[M(2\ominus N)]$.

12.5 PROPAGATION OF RELATIVE ORDERS OF MAGNITUDE: SOME EXAMPLES

In this section we show that the previous inference rules can be useful for solving equations in an approximate way. Such equations involve arithmetic expressions and order-of-magnitude relations (expressed in terms of parametrized relations Cl and Ne).

Example 12.1. The following relations are supposed to be known to hold:

$$(c \cdot d, a \cdot b) \in \mathrm{Cl}[M]; (a + c, c) \in \mathrm{Cl}[N]; (d/b, f/e) \in \mathrm{Cl}[P].$$

The problem is to compare the orders of magnitude of quantities e and f. The following relations can easily be obtained:

$$(a \cdot b, c \cdot d) \in \mathrm{Cl}[M] \quad \text{(since the relation Cl is symmetrical)}$$
$$(a, c) \in \mathrm{Ne}[N] \quad \text{[using the definition of Ne in terms of Cl, i.e., rule (12.27)].}$$

By applying rule (12.42), we can deduce that $(d, b) \in \mathrm{Ne}[M(N \ominus 1) \oplus \in 1]$. The relation $(d/b, f/e) \in \mathrm{Cl}[P]$ implies that $(d \cdot e, b \cdot f) \in \mathrm{Cl}[P]$. Rule (12.42), based on the latter relation and $(d, b) \in \mathrm{Ne}[Q]$ with $Q = M(N \ominus 1) \oplus 1$, enables us to conclude that $(f, e) \in \mathrm{Ne}[PM(N \ominus 1) \oplus 1]$. If we start with classical equalities, (i.e., $a \cdot b = c \cdot d$ and $d/b = f/e$), then letting $M \doteq 1$ and $P = 1$, it leads to $(f, e) \in \mathrm{Ne}[N]$. Now, if the parameter $e = 100$, we can come up with an estimate of the parameter f under the form of a fuzzy number F, namely:

$$\mu_F(x) = \mu_{\mathrm{Ne}[N]}(x, 100) = \mu_N(1 + x/100) = \mu_{[100(N \ominus 1)]}(x)$$

[i.e., $F = 100(N \ominus 1)$], which can easily be computed. This illustrates that fuzzy relations can provide a natural framework for interfacing symbolic information and numerical data.

Example 12.2 [18]

$$(d, b) \in \mathrm{Ne}[M]; (b, c) \in \mathrm{Ne}[N]; (e, g) \in \mathrm{Ne}[P];$$
$$a - b - c - d = 0; a \cdot e \cdot f - c \cdot g \cdot h = 0.$$

The question now is to compare the values of f and h. By applying rule (12.26), we get $(d + b, b) \in \mathrm{Cl}[M]$. Substituting $a - c$ to $d + b$ (because $a - b - c - d = 0$), we obtain $(a - c, b) \in \mathrm{Cl}[M]$. Rule (12.32), based on the latter relation and $(b, c) \in \mathrm{Ne}[N]$, enables us to deduce that $(a - c, c) \in \mathrm{Ne}[M(N \ominus 1) \oplus 1]$. This relation implies that $(a, c) \in \mathrm{Cl}[M(N \ominus 1) \oplus 1]$. Using rule (12.36), we get $(a \cdot e, c \cdot g) \in \mathrm{Ne}[Q(P \ominus 1) \oplus 1]$, with $Q = M(N \ominus 1) \oplus 1$. Since $(a \cdot e/c \cdot g) = h/f$, the pair (h,f) should satisfy the same fuzzy relation (i.e., $(h,f) \in \mathrm{Ne}[Q(P \ominus 1) \oplus 1]$). This example can be solved using other inference rules. For example, the chaining of rules (12.31), (12.35), and (12.27) enables us to obtain $(a, c) \in \mathrm{Cl}[R \oplus N]$, with $R = (M \ominus 1)(N \ominus 1)$; then using rule (12.36), we get $(a \cdot e, c \cdot g) \in \mathrm{Ne}[(R \oplus N)\ (P \ominus 1) \oplus 1]$ and finally, $(h,f) \in \mathrm{Ne}\ [(R \oplus N)\ (P \ominus 1) \oplus 1]$.

Generally, different results (some less restrictive than others) can be obtained from different chainings of inference rules, as suggested by Example 12.2. The conjunctive combination of these partial results restricting the possible values of a ratio of interest enables us to refine the conclusion. Note that the most restrictive result would be obtained by applying the combination/projection method [25], because in this approach all the existing constraints are exploited. Nevertheless, this approach can be computationally untractable in practice, and no explanation can be provided for the results obtained using such a global handling of the constraints.

Example 12.3. Let us now consider a practical example of a countercurrent heat exchanger as described in Ref. 18. The important parameters in the analysis of the device are the molarheat (KH) and the molarflow rate (FH) of the hot stream, and the molarheat (KC) and molar flowrate (FC) of the cold stream. Four temperature differences are defined: DTH the temperature drop of the hot stream, DTC the temperature rise of the cold stream, DT1 the driving force at the left end of the device, and DT2 the driving force at the right end of the device. The following two equations hold:

$$\text{(e1)}\quad \mathrm{DTH} - \mathrm{DT1} - \mathrm{DTC} + \mathrm{DT2} = 0$$
$$\text{(e2)}\quad \mathrm{DTH}\cdot\mathrm{KH}\cdot\mathrm{FH} = \mathrm{DTC}\cdot\mathrm{KC}\cdot\mathrm{FC}.$$

The first is a consequence of the definition of the temperature differences, and the second is the energy balance of the device. Let us take the following assumptions expressed as order-of-magnitude relations:

(i) (DT2,DT1] $\in$ Cl[M]
(ii) (DT1,DTH) $\in$ Ne[N]
(iii) (KC,KH) $\in$ Cl[P].

The problem now is to deduce the relation between the parameters FC and FH. Rule (12.32), based on the relations (i) and (ii), enables us to obtain

$$(\mathrm{DT2}, \mathrm{DTH}) \in \mathrm{Ne}[M(N \ominus 1) \oplus 1].$$

The following inferences are easily obtained as well:

$$(\mathrm{DT1},\mathrm{DTH}) \in \mathrm{Ne}[N] \Rightarrow (-\mathrm{DT1}, \mathrm{DTH}) \in \mathrm{Ne}[2 \ominus N] \qquad \text{[by rule (12.28)]}$$
$$(\mathrm{DT2},\mathrm{DTH}) \in \mathrm{Ne}[M(N \ominus 1) \oplus 1] \text{ and } (-\mathrm{DT1}, \mathrm{DTH}) \in \mathrm{Ne}[2 \ominus \mathrm{N}]$$
$$\Rightarrow (\mathrm{DT2} - \mathrm{DT1}, \mathrm{DTH}) \in \mathrm{Ne}[M(N \ominus 1) \oplus 2 \ominus N] \qquad \text{[by rule(12.35)]}.$$

In the latter result, we can substitute DTC − DTH for DT2 − DT1 using equation (e1), and we get

$$(\mathrm{DTC} - \mathrm{DTH}, \mathrm{DTH}) \in \mathrm{Ne}[M(N \ominus 1) \oplus 2 \ominus N].$$

Then applying rule (12.27), we get

$$(\mathrm{DTC}, \mathrm{DTH}) \in \mathrm{Cl}[M(N \ominus 1) \oplus 2 \ominus N].$$

Rule (12.38), based on this relation and relation (iii), enables us to conclude that

$$(\mathrm{DTC} \cdot \mathrm{KC}, \mathrm{DTH} \cdot \mathrm{KH}) \in \mathrm{Cl}[(M(N \ominus 1) \oplus 2 \ominus N)P],$$

and finally, since DTC · KC/DTH · KH = FH/FC [see equation (e2)], the pair (FH,FC) should satisfy the same fuzzy relation, that is,

$$(\mathrm{FH}, \mathrm{FC}) \in \mathrm{Cl}[(M(N \ominus 1) \oplus 2 \ominus M)P].$$

12.6 CONCLUSIONS

Fuzzy relations can provide an appropriate semantics for inference rules about relative orders of magnitude. Each rule has a precise interpretation in terms of fuzzy sets. The composition of relations Ne[M] and Cl[N] reduces to simple arithmetic operations on the fuzzy numbers M and N. Moreover, fuzzy relations calculus enables us to reason about closeness and negligibility in a rigorous way without being obliged to introduce arbitrary limitations on the chaining of rules (by means of control techniques)—to avoid undesirable transitivity effects, for instance. The approach is faithful to the gradual nature of comparators. Another clear advantage of the use of fuzzy relations is that it enables us to interface numbers with symbolic information in a convenient way, as hinted in Example 12.1. Thus it provides an example of computing with the words *negligible* and *close to* in a symbolic manner, in full agreement with the numerical semantics underlying these words. As suggested briefly in Section 12.3, a similar approach based on other fuzzy relations could also be developed in temporal reasoning (where approximate equalities or fuzzy ordering relations can apply to dates), or even in spatial resoning.

A notable feature of the approach is the separation of the symbolic processing of the labels of inferred relations from expression of their semantics in terms of their membership functions. It is why it is important to always check that the conclusions produced are semantically meaningful (e.g., that the relation of closeness obtained is not too permissive). If a relation Ne[P] of negligibility is obtained, we should make sure that it is in agreement with the intuitive semantics underlying this notion [e.g., $\mu_P(2) = 0$; otherwise, x would be negligible with respect to itself, since $\mu_P(1 + x/x) = \mu_P(2)$]. Indeed, even if we start with relations having semantically meaningful parameters, it may happen that after several chainings of the rules, the result is no longer a closeness or negligibility relation semantically speaking, despite its appearance at the syntactic level.

Future work should deal especially with (1) the conception of a complete system of inference rules (for particular types of equation systems: for example, linear equations involving only addition and subtraction operations, and product by a constant);

(2) the choice of a set of formal computation rules which enables us to write equations in a suitable way when necessary (since the form of equations can interfere with the possibility of applying inference rules); (3) implementing this system and the set of computation rules in order to obtain automated strategies for simplifying equations involving relative order-of-magnitude relations and arithmetic expressions. This should be useful for solving numerical equations, in an approximate way, for physicochemical systems or for the qualitative calculus of probabilities [7,13].

Finally, it should also be emphasized that reasoning with relative orders of magnitude can be seen as a particular type of fuzzy constraint satisfaction problems [5] which may provide a source of inspiration for implementation. Thus there is a balance to be located between a minimal complete set of rules and a larger set of rules exhibiting some redundancy but offering more possibilities of being applicable to a given set of constraints. See Refs. 8 and 14 for the study of a reduced set of rules from which all the rules provided in Section 12.4 can be derived. Moreover, it is possible to approximate all these rules using symmetrical fuzzy numbers as parameters (e.g., in terms of MN, if both M and N are symmetrical); a method for establishing the inconsistency of a set of hypotheses with respect to a set of equations is also hinted at [15].

REFERENCES

1. P. Bourgine and O. Raiman, Economics as reasoning on a qualitative model, *Proc. International Conference on Economics and Artificial Intelligence*, Aix-en-Provence, France, 1986, pp. 185–189.
2. P. Dague, Symbolic reasoning with relative orders of magnitude, *Proc. 13th International Joint Conference on Artificial Intelligence (IJCAI'93)*, Chambéry, France, 1993, pp. 1509–1514.
3. P. Dague, O. Devès, and O. Raiman Troubleshooting when modeling is the trouble, *Proc. National Conference on Artificial Intelligence (AAAI'87)*, Seattle, WA, July, 1987, pp. 600–605.
4. J. L. Dormoy, Nouvelles méthodes de calcul qualitatif, *Rev. Intell. Artif.*, 3(4): 39–53, 1989.
5. D. Dubois, H. Fargier, and H. Prade, Possibility theory in constraint satisfaction problems: handling priority, preference and uncertainty, *Appl. Intell.*, 6:287–309, 1996.
6. D. Dubois, L. Foulloy, S. Galichet, H. Prade, Two views of approximate reasoning. *Proc. 7th International Fuzzy Systems Association World Congress (IFSA'97)*, Prague, Czech Republic, June 25–29, 1997, Academia, Prague, pp. 238–242. A revised version entitled "Performing approximate reasoning with words" (Tech. Rep. IRIT/98-29 R) in *Computing with Words* (J. Kacpryk, ed.) Physica-Verlag, Heidelberg, Germany, 1999, pp. 24–49.
7. D. Dubois, L. Godo, R. Lòpez de Màntaras and H. Prade, Qualitative reasoning with imprecise probabilities. *J. Intell. Inf. Syst.*, 2:319–363, 1993.
8. D. Dubois, A. Hadj-Ali, and H. Prade, Granular computing with fuzzy closeness and negligibility relations, to appear in *Granular Computing* (T. Y. Lin, Y. Y. Yao, and L. A. Zadeh, eds.), Physica-Verlag, Heidelberg, Germany, in the series "Studies in Fuzziness and Soft Computing."

9. D. Dubois and H. Prade, Fuzzy numbers: an overview, in J. C. Bezdek (ed.), *Analysis of Fuzzy Information*, Vol. 1, and *Mathematics and Logic* CRC Press, Boca Raton, FL, 1987, pp. 3–39.
10. D. Dubois and H. Prade, Order of magnitude reasoning with fuzzy relations, *Rev. Intell. Artif.*, 3(4):69–94, 1989.
11. D. Dubois and H. Prade, Processing fuzzy temporal knowledge, *IEEE Trans. Syst. Man Cybern.*, 19:729–744, 1989.
12. D. Dubois and H. Prade, Traitements numérico-symboliques d'informations symbolico-numériques. *Actes des 3èmes Journées Nationales du PRC-GDR Intelligence Artificielle*, Hermès, Paris, 1990, pp. 113–126.
13. D. Dubois and H. Prade, Semantic considerations on order of magnitude reasoning, in M. G. Singh and L. Travé-Massuyès, (eds.), *Decision Support and Qualitative Reasoning*, North-Holland, Amsterdam, 1991, pp. 223–228.
14. A. Hadj-Ali, D. Dubois, and H. Prade, Raisonnement sur les ordres de grandeurs relatifs avec des relations floues: Appliqué aux probabilits qualitatives, in *Actes de la 8ème Conférence sur la Logique Floue et ses Applications (LFA '98)*, Rennes, France, 1998, pp. 229–234.
15. A. Hadj-Ali, D. Dubois, and H. Prade, Résolution approchée d'équations par le raisonnement qualitatif flou, in *Actes de la 9 ème Conférence sur la Logique Floue et ses Applications (LFA'99)*, Valenciennes, France, Oct. 21–22, 1999, pp. 293–300.
16. B. Kuipers, *Qualitative Reasoning: Modeling and Simulation with Incomplete Knowledge*, MIT Press, Cambridge, MA, 1994.
17. M. L. Mavrovouniotis and G. Stephanopoulos, Reasoning with orders of magnitude and approximate relations, *Proc. 6th National Conference on Artificial Intelligence (AAAI '87)*, Seattle, WA, 1987, pp. 626–630.
18. M. L. Mavrovouniotis and G. Stephanopoulos, Formal order of magnitude reasoning in process engineering, *Comput. Chem. Eng.*, 12(9/10):867–880, 1988.
19. MQ&D Project (coordinator, P. Dague) Qualitative reasoning: a survey of techniques and applications. *AICOM, Eur. J. Artif. Intell.*, 8(3/4):119–192, 1995.
20. O. Raiman, Order of magnitude reasoning, *Proc. National Conference on Artificial Intelligence (AAAI '86)*, Philadelphia, PA, 1986, pp. 100–104.
21. O. Raiman, Le raisonnement sur les ordres de grandeur, *Rev. Intell. Artif.*, 3(4):55–67, 1989.
22. O. Raiman, Order of magnitude reasoning, *Artif. Intell.*, 51:11–38, 1991.
23. L. Travé-Massuyès, P. Dague, and F. Guerrin, *Le Raisonnement Qualitatif pour les Sciences de l'Ingénieur*, Hermès, Paris, 1997.
24. L. A. Zadeh, Outline of a new approach to the analysis of complex systems and decision processes, *IEEE Trans. Syst. Man Cybern.*, 3:28–44, 1973.
25. L. A. Zadeh, A theory of approximate reasoning, in J. E. Hayes, D. Michie, and L. I. Mikulich (eds.), *Machine Intelligence*, Vol. 9, Elsevier, New York, 1979, pp. 149–194.
26. L. A. Zadeh, Fuzzy logic = computing with words, *IEEE Trans. Fuzzy Syst.*, 4(2):103–111, 1996.
27. L. A. Zadeh From computing with numbers to computing with words—from manipulation of measurements to manipulation of perceptions, *IEEE Trans. Circuits Syst. I: Fundam. Theory Appl.*, 45(1):105–119, Jan. 1999.

Chapter 13

BEYOND PROCESS AND ACTION SYMBOLS

TAO YANG
University of California, Berkeley, California

13.1 PROLOGUE

In *Timaeus*, Plato set a very clear boundary between two concepts, being and becoming. For him, *being* is "apprehensible by intelligence with the aid of reasoning, being eternally the same," and *becoming* "is the object of opinion and irrational sensation, coming to be and ceasing to be, but never fully real." However, the boundary between being and becoming is not crisp. This leads to a big unsolved problem in physics, as shown in a conversation reported by Carnap. "Einstein said that the problem of the *now* worried him seriously. He explained that the experience of the now means something special for humans, something essentially different from the past and the future, but that this important difference does not and cannot occur within physics. That this experience cannot be grasped by science seemed to him a matter of painful but inevitable resignation: There is something essential about the now which is just outside the realm of science." For the greatest physicists, this is the problem of the *arrow of time* [21,32], the origin of the universe, and the reason for the existence of human species. Since *reality*, which means the existence of a universe, is a perception of human beings, this essential problem which has puzzled generations of philosophers and physicists will soon become an engineering problem, because the next step in information science will embed human perceptions into machines.

In the preceding chapters of this book, the authors deal primarily with the world of being, where a truth value can be assigned to each object or event. This chapter deals with the world of becoming and provide a technical boundary between being and becoming—namely, now. What is happening now in a human brain? In fact,

Computing with Words, Edited by Paul P. Wang.
ISBN 0-471-35374-4

now is a "moment of awareness" and is a "moment when *becoming* is becoming being *being*." Now is a bridge connecting the past and the future along the arrow of time. Now is a mechanism to assign something a truth value and make it being.

Based on the discussion above, computational verb systems consist of two different phases. In the first phase the now does not function. This means that verbs are used to model actions (dynamics) that do not concern the truth of the perceptions or do not lead to any perceptions at all. From a biological and psychological point of view, these kinds of dynamics correspond to many emotion-driven dynamics [32]. These dynamics were called "irrational" by Plato and are shared by human beings and many animals. The first phase is addressed primarily in this chapter. The second phase involves the now. The now is treated as a collapsing process of becomings, which are modeled by verbs. In a word, a collapsing process assigns a truth value to the result of a verb. This corresponds to the death of a dynamic process. The logic under this framework, called verb logic, as addressed in Ref. 62, is impossible unless a proper collapse of verb is defined. It is then understood explicitly that the now is the moment when a collapsing action is happening.

Remark: The term *computational verb system* [57–64] has been used in a very broad sense and cannot simply be interpreted as *computational verb system* = *assign dynamics to symbolized verbs*. This is because computational verb systems can be used to model nonsymbolized communications[1] between *machinselves* (from "machines themselves") or human selves. It is my belief that human beings are connected by an intuitive level of communications whereby nonsymbolized communications play a very important role either between two brains or within the same brain. Without the help of nonsymbolized dynamics, a symbolized system will lose many features of a living brain, such as emotions, intuitions, and very high level creativity. Since application of computational verb systems to nonsymbolized dynamics and communications is outside the scope of this book, I use *computational process symbol* or *computational action symbol* to denote the narrow meanings of *computational verb*. The reader will find the difference between a computational process (action) symbol and a computational verb from Definitions 13.1 and 13.2, in section 13.5.3; namely, a computational process (action) symbol is a *brainless* computational verb. To avoid clutter, in this and the next chapter, *computational process (action) symbol systems* will be written simply as *computational verb systems*.

13.2 MOTIVATIONS

At the beginning of twentieth century the relativity theory and quantum mechanics introduced an entirely new point of view of the reality as a dramatic revolution. At the end of twentieth century, a silent revolution happened over the entire scale of our reality and all scientific principles because of the challenge of complexity [16].

[1] Some nonverbal communications are still symbolized communications to some degree.

Complexity is not a new phenomenon, although it fell into the scope of modern science only in the twentieth century. Human beings had survived for a long time without knowing it (or precisely, without knowing how to model it using formulas). Complexity imposes an enormous challenge to scientific and engineering methods based on precise models. In the history of science, precise modeling methods were so excellent that when fuzzy sets [71] embedded imprecision and vagueness into a scientific framework, fuzzy theory encountered many misunderstandings. Today, fuzzy theory has been established and used widely because it meets the natural tendency of human beings to use linguistic models [72,24] to cope with complexities.

From a physical point of view, an electronic digital computer is a simulation running in an analog computer based on electromagnetic dynamics of silicon. Similarly, a human linguistic system is a symbolic simulation running in the analog structure called the *human brain*. Encountering complexities in all scales of the universe, how real should our linguistic simulations be for solving the most critical problem—the survival of human species and individuals? We may ask this question in an other way: Why can humans survive complexities painlessly, whereas digital computers (no matter how powerful they may be) cannot? The answer is that our brains simulate complexities in correct ways, whereas digital computers simulate them incorrectly.

If we view our languages as systems of symbols, how do human beings use these symbolic processes to simulate complexities? It seems to me that all human species use the same structure to simulate complexities. Although in China analog methods are used to encode simulations in the Western world, symbolic methods and in Japan, both analog and symbolic methods, we understand each other very well. This is because we confront the same complexities in our lives, independent of coding methods. We encounter two types of complexities in our circumstances: One is static, such as fractal structures and randomness and the second is dynamic, such as chaotic and random processes. The relationship between static and dynamic complexity cannot simply be stated as the former being only a snapshot of the latter. The boundaries between these two complexities are fuzzy. It appears that no one can unify complexities into a single framework. In our linguistic system, we have developed different types of words to cope with these two types of complexities.

We use verbs to describe dynamic complexities. Computational verb systems [57–64] are a new framework of artificial intelligence. They embed into machine intelligence the knowledge and experiences that human experts express or imply with verbs. Computing with words is a systematic consideration of coping with complexities. Fuzzy logic provides a computing framework of adjectives and nouns, but it does not cope with verbs (process symbols). It turns out that process symbols are very important in describing the dynamics of complexities for the survival of human beings. Process symbols are very important building blocks for transferring and representing human experiences. They are very important tools for the next generation of expert system.

As with many other things, computational verb systems have many facets. In this chapter I address the nonsymbolic facet of computational verb systems. This means that there are some perceptions that correspond to nonsymbolized verbs.[2] The are two reasons why nonsymbolized verbs are necessary. The first one is that the corresponding process symbol of a perception has not been invented. For example, if 25 years ago I said: "I will *e-mail* you my files," nobody would understand me, but today we know exactly what that means. The second reason is that it is not necessary or even possible to generate a process symbol for each perception of a dynamical process. Different dynamics have entirely different priorities in the lives of different human beings. Although there is a definite set of process symbols in each human language, each human being has his or her own set of process symbols. Since computational verb systems view each process symbol as a granular representation of dynamical process, approaches similar to those described in the preceding chapters can also be used to extract process symbols from dynamical processes. The principle presented in this chapter can help linguists to gain more insight into the birth of new process symbols and the death of old process symbols. Roughly speaking, each process symbol is a communication network. The number of users of a process symbol determines the value of that symbol. In a certain historical period, if many people experience the same (but new) dynamics, a new process symbol might be invented. Typical examples are such process symbols as xerox, fax, and e-mail. Many other process symbols are forgotten because the associated dynamics are no longer used. In the future I will describe a way to make "irrational" process symbols "rational" and to define their computations.

13.3 MODELING WITH COMPUTATIONAL PROCESS SYMBOLS

Process symbols represent the dynamics of linguistic expressions. They provide systematic granular approaches for representing continuous dynamics ("becomings") using discrete symbols. This is a process similar to that described in Parts III and IV, where the continuous uncertainties in "beings" are represented as discrete symbols. In this section, nonlinear and linear dynamic systems are used to model and classify computational process symbols. Based on these models of computational process symbols, the dynamical aspects of linguistic expressions, which are associated with qualitative descriptions of human experiences, can be described quantitatively. In particular, verb models of both simple and complex dynamical systems are provided to show how to use computational process symbols to model dynamics. In this section, verb models are also used to solve real-life problems in chaotic cryptanalysis.

13.3.1 What Are Verbs (Process Symbols)?

In this section the terms *verb* and *process symbol* are generally used exchangeably. Can we write down in words all that we think, feel, and want? Can we train our off-

[2] However, to avoid clutter, I will use process symbols to represent both symbolic and non symbolic verbs.

spring only by letting them read books? The answer is no[3] because there exist some interconnections between humans and definitely between animals because they do not have advanced languages and words) that are far beyond what we can express (speak and write). Two typical examples are cited from Ref. 23:

Example 1

A: These two wines taste different.

B: But *how* do they taste different?

A: It's hard to say: Try them yourself.

Example 2

A: What does it feel like when you do a double back flip on the trampoline?

B: It's hard to say, but when you can do one, you'll know when it feels right and when it doesn't.

It is clear that between the teacher and the learner something behind the "meaningless dialogues" is communicated implicitly. Many factors contribute to this kind of communication between humans, such as equivalent knowledge and experience, similar reactions to some things and even the same evolutionary process encoded in human genes [5]. What the teacher tries to do is to show the learner how his or her own experience should be formed after following these instructions. This kind of experience is full of dynamic complexities, implied by verbs such as *taste*, *try*, and *feel*. Since a teacher cannot relate this experience explicitly, the learner has to learn by tasting, trying, and feeling personally. If this kind of experience is not a dynamic process (in memory),[4] it should easily be written as explicit expressions such that the classical expert system can easily record and retrieve it. However, the classical expert system cannot record this kind of experience. It is almost impossible to model all these implicit factors in a single model or paradigm because any complex system must have many different aspects, and each aspect may need a framework to model.

It is verbs that introduce dynamics into our language and transfer dynamics of brain states between human beings. Since brain dynamics are closely connected with our intuitions and emotions [25], there may exist many information exchanges via verbs using implicit (intuitive) ways among humans. Unfortunately, whenever a verb is recorded as a representation (its symbol),[5] the details of dynamics defined by the person who spoke it is generally lost and could be recovered only by those humans who read it later using their own dynamics associated with this verb (some-

[3]The human consciousness is closely tied to the capacity for natural language [28]. Human language is an infinitely flexible system of thought and communication. However, the capacity for language does not exclude humans' prelinguistic, evolutionary, ancient ways of knowing themselves and the world. Although nonlinguistic processing is often overshadowed in consciousness by linguistic coding, its underlying role in human mental life is crucial.

[4]The experience is constructed by the conscious self in conscious–nonconscious dynamics [28].

[5]This process may be viewed as the extraction of knowledge from experiences [37, p. 16].

times we call the dynamics associated with a set of verbs, *experiences*). When a machine reads this verb, it cannot recover the dynamics even if it has a huge pool of knowledge [36].

Since a verb contains so many different dynamics in different contexts, the implications behind verbs are very complex. This is the reason why we can express our feelings efficiently if we talk to someone in person instead of communicating only via mails. This is also believed to be one of the motivations that will drive the computer industry in the next 50 years [14].

To maintain the dynamics of a verb, we need to set up a model for describing it. Although dynamics of verbs should be very complex, we can lump them qualitatively into the following classes.[6]

1. *Static verbs.* This type of verb does not have any dynamics; they are just fixed at a static point such as *be*. Since this class has been studied very carefully in fuzzy logic and other chapters in this book, I do not discuss it here.

2. *Smooth dynamic verbs.* This type of verb can be described by smooth dynamic systems whose ω sets [20,22] may be fixed points (asymptotic processes), limit cycles (oscillated processed), toruses (quasiperiodic processes), and strange attractors (chaotic processes). Some verbs converge to fixed points such as "become" in the following sentence:

Gina becomes a pretty girl.

While "pretty girl" is a fuzzy item that can be modeled by a membership function $x(t) = \mu_{\text{pretty girl}}(\text{Gina,Time})$, "becomes" is a dynamic process that can be modeled only in different contexts. For example, if Gina was an ugly girl before, and I meet her only once a year, "become" is a converge process that approaches its fixed point asymptotically with the initial value $x(0) = \mu_{\text{pretty girl}}(\text{Gina}, 0)$, which is give by

$$\begin{aligned} \dot{x} &= -x + \mu_{\text{pretty girl}}(\text{Gina}, \infty) \\ x(0) &= \mu_{\text{pretty girl}}(\text{Gina}, 0). \end{aligned} \tag{13.1}$$

If I meet Gina more often, say once a month, then in some months Gina may seem to be a little worse than in some other months. In this case, the dynamics of "become" can be modeled by an asymptotic oscillating dynamics as

$$\begin{aligned} \frac{d^2x}{dt^2} &= -x + \mu_{\text{pretty girl}}(\text{Gina}, \infty) \\ x(0) &= \mu_{\text{pretty girl}}(\text{Gina}, 0). \end{aligned} \tag{13.2}$$

If a person can observe Gina in a very fine time resolution, say Gina's mother, then the "become" can be described by a chaotic process whose mean value converges

[6]Observe that in grammar books [48], verbs are classified as *transitive verbs* and *intransitive verbs*. This classification is useless for our purposes.

to a high value of "pretty." Such a system could be

$$\begin{aligned} \dot{x} &= -x + ky + \mu_{\text{pretty girl}}(\text{Gina}, \infty) \\ x(0) &= \mu_{\text{pretty girl}}(\text{Gina}, 0), \end{aligned} \tag{13.3}$$

where k is a constant and y is a chaotic process given by a chaotic system, say, the Lorenz system [31]

$$\begin{aligned} \dot{x} &= -\sigma x + \sigma y \\ \dot{y} &= rx - y - xz \\ \dot{z} &= xy - bz, \end{aligned} \tag{13.4}$$

where σ, r, and b are three real positive parameters.

3. *Impulsive dynamic verbs.* In this case the verbs are modeled by impulsive differential equations [4,27] whose states are subject to sudden changes (jumps) whenever some conditions are satisfied. This kind of verb can also have different types of ω sets, such as fixed points, limit cycles, toruses, and strange attractors. One example is given by the description of a rule from psychotherapy:

If whenever you feel at the edge of crazy, you tell yourself "calm down, please!", "calm down, please!", you can regain control of yourself.

To trivialize this statement, let us suppose that "feel crazy" is a chaotic status of emotional trajectory in a (mental) phase space [40]. When one can control oneself, the emotional trajectory is supposed to be a kind of limit cycle. "Calm down, please!" can be modeled by an impulsive control effect which acts only when some conditions are satisfied. We then use the following Rössler chaotic system [41] to represent "feel crazy" as

$$\begin{aligned} \dot{x} &= -y - z \\ \dot{y} &= x + ay \\ \dot{z} &= zx + b - cz, \end{aligned} \tag{13.5}$$

where a, b, and c are three parameters, chosen as $a = 0.398$, $b = 2$, and $c = 4.0$. A fourth-order Runge–Kutta algorithm with a step size of 0.005 is used. The initial condition is given by $(x(0), y(0), z(0)) = (-2.277838, -2.696438, 0.304911)$. Figure 13.1$a$ shows the corresponding chaotic attractor. The "calm down, please!" is modeled by a set of impulsive control laws:

$$\begin{aligned} x(\tau_k^+) &= x(\tau_k) \\ y(\tau_k^+) &= \psi_2(\mathbf{x}(\tau_k)) = [1 - \lambda \operatorname{sgn}(y(\tau_k))]y(\tau_k), \quad |\lambda| < 1 \\ z(\tau_k^+) &= z(\tau_k) \end{aligned} \tag{13.6}$$

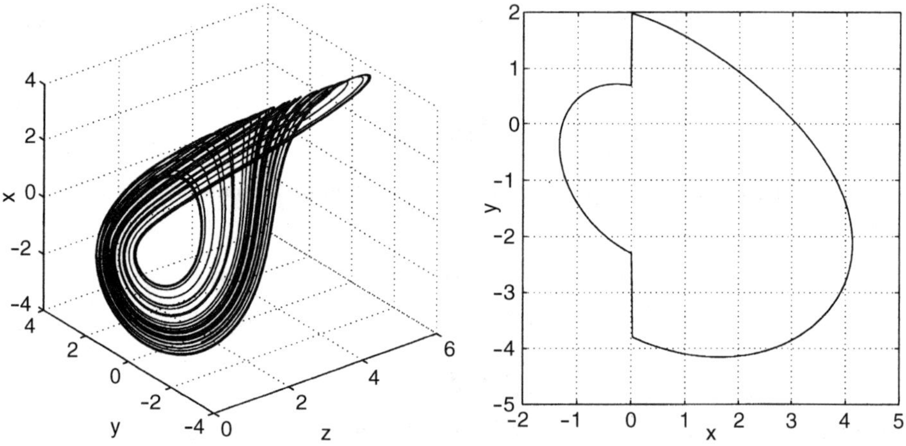

(a) (b)

FIGURE 13.1. Demonstration of impulsive dynamic verbs: (*a*) representation of "feel crazy" in mental phase space; (b) result of repeating "calm down, please!".

where $\mathbf{x}^{\mathrm{T}} = (x, y, z)$. The impulsive control law above works only when the condition $x = 0$ is satisfied. The impulsively controlled Rössler system is then given by

$$\begin{aligned} \dot{x} &= -y - z \\ \dot{y} &= x + ay \qquad\qquad x(t) \neq 0 \\ \dot{z} &= zx + b - cz \end{aligned} \tag{13.7}$$

and

$$\mathbf{x}(\tau_k^+) = \Psi_k(\mathbf{x}(\tau_k)), \quad x(\tau_k) = 0, \tag{13.8}$$

where $\Psi_k(\mathbf{x})$ is given by (13.6). We choose $\lambda = 0.65$; the simulation result is shown in Figure 13.1*b*, which represents a controlled emotional state. The detail of impulsive control of chaotic systems can be found in Ref. 70.

4. *Terminal dynamic verbs.* This kind of verb can have an effect only in a finite time period, such as

Gina *arrive*s on campus.

Although Gina could use different dynamics of "arrive," such as walk, take a bus, or whatever, "arrive" is terminated whenever she is on campus. This kind of verb can be modeled by dynamic systems with non-Lipschitz singular solutions. One example is given by

$$\dot{x} = -(x - x^*)^{\frac{1}{3}}. \tag{13.9}$$

Since at $x = x^*$ the Lipschitz condition is violated, $x(t)$ will arrive x^* within finite time. The simulation results are given in Figure 13.2*a*. The initial condition is

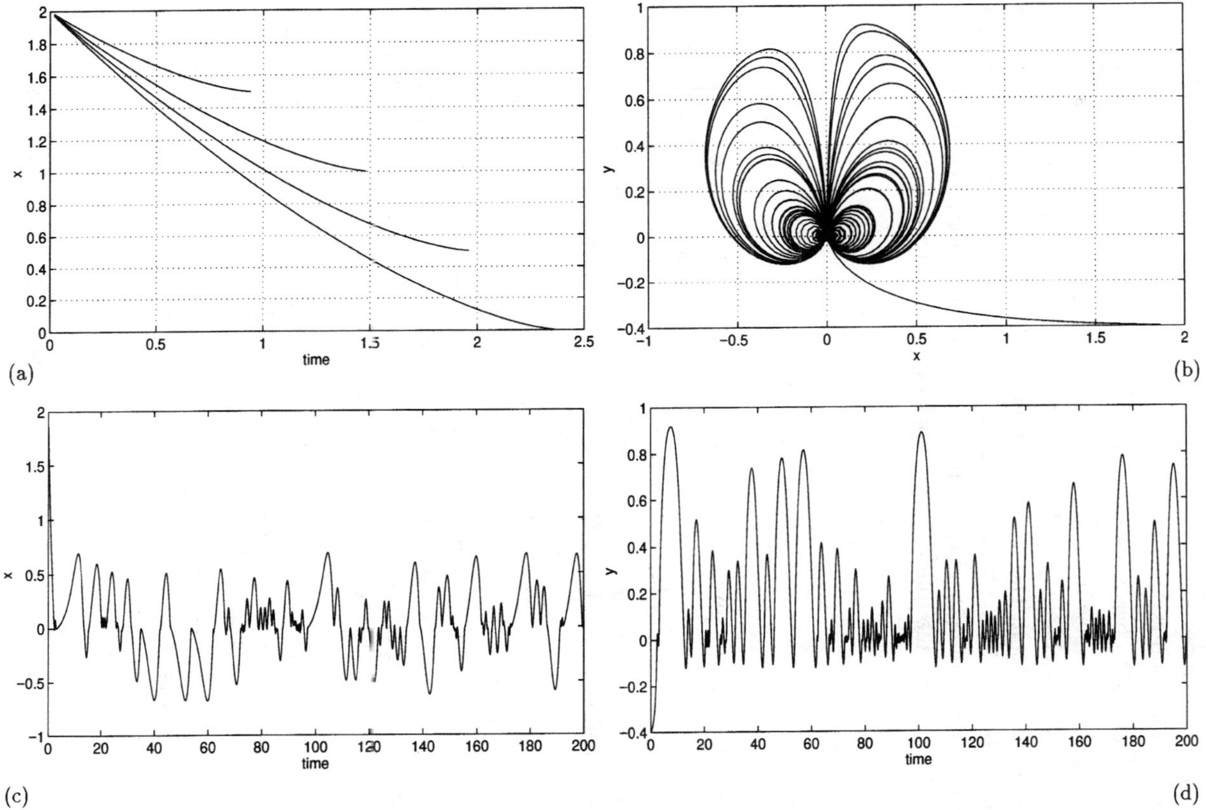

FIGURE 13.2. Terminal dynamic verbs and their complexities: (*a*) trajectories of "arrive" with different initial conditions; (*b*) stochastic attractors for modeling "keep changing widely"; (*c*) wave form of $x(t)$ of the attractor in part (*b*); (*d*) waveform of $y(t)$ of the attractor in part (*b*).

$x(0) = 2$. In Figure 13.2*a* the four curves correspond to four different x^*'s of $0, 0.5, 1$, and 1.5, respectively. In each case the system arrives at x^* within a finite time.

Terminal verbs are not always so simple; they may have stochastic attractors [74]. One example follows:

Gina keeps changing her ideas widely.

If we define the universe of Gina's ideas as a two-dimensional space, and if we want to show "keeps changing widely" is an irrational process, we cannot use a chaotic system to model it. The reversible property of chaotic process (at least for a short period) seems to be too "rational" because whenever we know the result, we can reverse it and find the "cause." A promising candidate for modeling this kind of irrational process is the following terminal dynamic system [15]:

$$\begin{aligned} \dot{x} &= \frac{\lambda xy}{x^2 + y^2} - \epsilon x \\ \dot{y} &= \frac{\lambda y^2}{x^2 + y^2} - \gamma y - (\lambda - \gamma). \end{aligned} \tag{13.10}$$

The simulation results are given in Figure 13.2*b* with $\lambda = 1.0$, $\epsilon = 0.6$, and $\gamma = 0.7$. The Lipschitz condition is violated at the origin. The initial condition is $(x(0), y(0)) = (2, -0.4)$. In this simulation, a fourth-order Runge–Kutta method with fixed step size 0.1 is used. The waveforms of $x(t)$ and $y(t)$ are also shown in Figure 13.2*c* and *d*, respectively. Observe that the waveforms of this system are somehow more complex than those of some low-dimensional chaotic systems.

5. *Discrete-time verbs.* This kind of verb can be modeled by difference equations or discrete mathematics. They may be used to describe the experiences associated with discrete events. The dynamics of this kind of verbs are similar to that of other kinds of verbs and may be very complex, such as cellular automata [45], and many chaotic systems are discrete in time. A hybrid discrete-time/continuous system can also be used to model verbs that involve discrete-time events and continuous dynamics.

While examples of possible verb models in this section are demonstrated using low-dimensional models, very high dimensional models can also be used in actual applications. Although final applications of the dynamic models of verbs may be in areas where complexities cannot easily be decomposed by using bottom-up methods, for the purpose of demonstrating the use of verb models, two classical examples are presented in the next two sections.

13.3.2 Computational Process-Symbol Model of a Simple System

To avoid clutter, we call a *computational process-symbol model* simply a *verb model*. In this section we build a verb model for a simple nonlinear dynamic system. We investigate the following second-order piecewise linear oscillator. In the outer region, this system is governed by

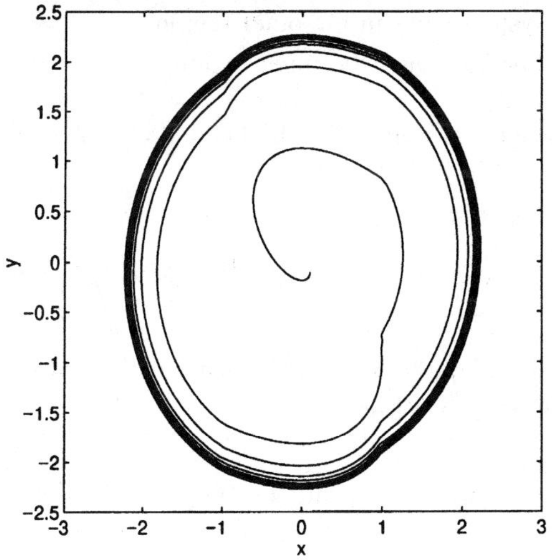

FIGURE 13.3. Attractor of the second-order piecewise linear dynamic system.

$$\begin{aligned} \dot{x} &= 2y - 0.1x \\ \dot{y} &= -2x, \end{aligned} \qquad |x| > 1 \tag{13.11}$$

whereas in the inner region it is governed by

$$\begin{aligned} \dot{x} &= y + x \\ \dot{y} &= -x \end{aligned} \qquad |x| \leq 1. \tag{13.12}$$

The attractor of this system is shown in Figure 13.3. The initial condition for this trajectory is $(x(0), y(0)) = (0.1, 0.1)$. Observe that the trajectory converges to a limit cycle.

By inspecting the trajectory of the limit cycle, we can qualitatively describe the evolution of this system using a linguistic statement such as

> The trajectory *leaves* the inner region and *stays* in the outer region for a while; then it *enters* the inner region again, such that it forms a limit cycle.

This qualitative statement describes a way of forming a limit cycle. This type of general description is a powerful tool for human beings to express, remember, and classify different experiences. Humans can also change and share their experiences by using this kind of qualitative model because it can easily be understood by others (including their offspring). However, if we want to share this kind of experience with a machine, we have to introduce quantitative descriptions of the verbs in the linguistic statement above. For the system in (13.11) and (13.12), a verb model is given by:

- If $|x - 1| \leq \xi$ and $\dot{x} < 0$ or $|x + 1| \leq \xi$ and $\dot{x} > 0$, the system *enter*s the inner region; **else**

- If $|x|>1$, the system *stays* in the outer region.
- If $|x|<1$, the system *leaves* the inner region.

The verbs *stay* and *leave* are given by (13.11) and (13.12), respectively. The verb "enter" is given by the following system:

$$\begin{aligned}\dot{x} &= w_1 y + w_2 x \\ \dot{y} &= -2x\end{aligned} \qquad |x-1| \leq \xi \text{ and } \dot{x}<0 \text{ or } |x+1| \leq \xi \text{ and } \dot{x}>0. \quad (13.13)$$

We choose $\xi = 0.01$. Adaptive learning laws are then used to find w_1 and w_2 by minimizing the following cost function:

$$E = \frac{1}{2}(\dot{x}_o - \dot{x})^2 \qquad |x-1| \leq \xi \text{ and } \dot{x}<0 \text{ or } |x+1| \leq \xi \text{ and } \dot{x}>0, \quad (13.14)$$

where $\dot{x}_o$ and $\dot{x}$ are, respectively, obtained from the trajectories of the original system as shown in Figure 13.3 and the verb model system at "enter" status.

The updating law for w_1 is given by

$$\begin{aligned}\dot{w}_1 &= -\delta \frac{\partial E}{\partial w_1} \\ &= \delta(\dot{x}_o - \dot{x}) \frac{\partial \dot{x}}{\partial w_1} \\ &= \delta(\dot{x}_o - \dot{x}) y,\end{aligned} \quad (13.15)$$

where $\delta > 0$ is the learning rate. Similarly, we have

$$\dot{w}_2 = -\delta \frac{\partial E}{\partial w_2} = \delta(\dot{x}_o - \dot{x}) x. \quad (13.16)$$

We choose the learning rate $\delta = 0.1$. The learning processes of parameters for "enter" are shown in Figure 13.4. The solid line shows $w_1(t)$ and the dashed line shows $w_2(t)$. The initial conditions are $w_1(0) = 0$ and $w_2(0) = 0$. The trained parameters are $w_1 = 0.977687$ and $w_2 = -0.533483$.

Figure 13.5 shows the performance of a verb model. The dotted line shows the original trajectory, and the solid line shows the output of the verb model. Observe that the verb model gives almost an error-free result for this problem.

Here I do not want to claim that the verb model has an advantage over the other identification schemes for this simple problem. One should always bear in mind that verb models are most possibly used as high-level machine languages for the next generation of expert systems. Verb models can be viewed as experiences of machines that are supposed to share with human experts an experience *qualitatively related* to the same complex processes.

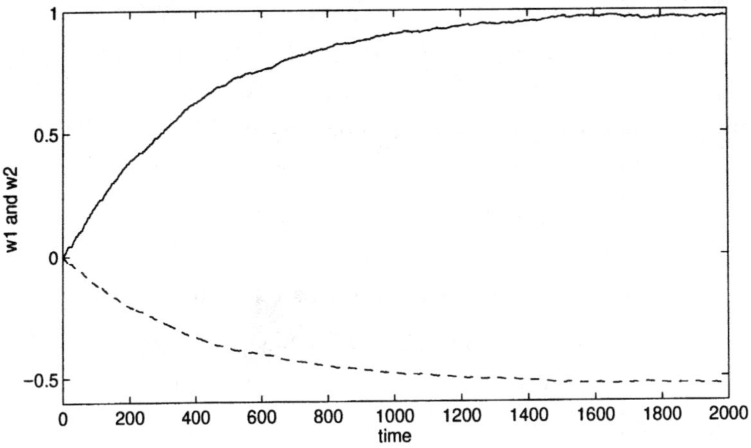

FIGURE 13.4. Learning processes of the parameters of *enter* for the verb model of a second-order system.

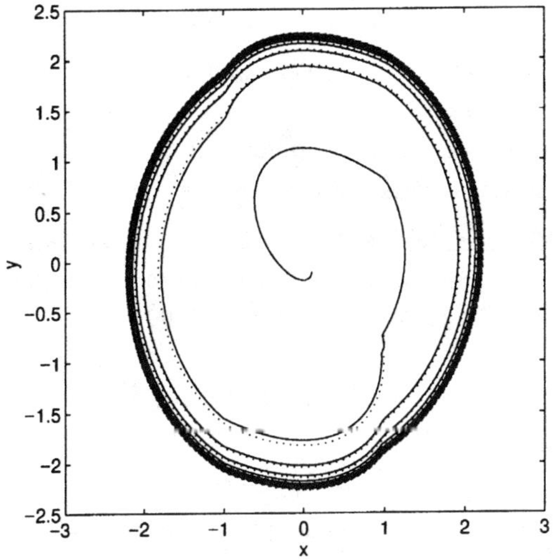

FIGURE 13.5. Performance of the verb model of a second-order system.

13.3.3 Computational Process-Symbol Model of a Complex System

In this section a verb model is used to describe a complex dynamic system—a chaotic system. We consider the following piecewise linear chaotic system, called a *Chua oscillator* [8]:

$$\begin{aligned}\dot{x} &= \alpha[y - x - f(x)] \\ \dot{y} &= x - y + z \\ \dot{z} &= -\beta y - \gamma z,\end{aligned} \tag{13.17}$$

where

$$f(x) = bx + \tfrac{1}{2}(a - b)(|x + 1| - |x - 1|). \tag{13.18}$$

Observe that this system is divided into an inner region that is governed by the following linear ordinary differential equation (ODE):

$$\begin{aligned} \dot{x} &= \alpha(y - x - ax) \\ \dot{y} &= x - y + z \qquad |x| < 1 \\ \dot{z} &= -\beta y - \gamma z \end{aligned} \tag{13.19}$$

and two outer regions which are governed by the following linear ODE:

$$\begin{aligned} \dot{x} &= \alpha[y - x - bx + (a - b)\ \mathrm{sgn}(x)] \\ \dot{y} &= x - y + z \qquad |x| > 1, \\ \dot{z} &= -\beta y - \gamma z \end{aligned} \tag{13.20}$$

where sgn(·) is the signum function. One of the chaotic attractors of this system is shown in Figure 13.6*a*.

We also use verbs "stay," "leave," and "enter" to model this chaotic system. The verb model of this system is given by

- If $|x - 1| < \xi$ and $\dot{x} < 0$ or $|x + 1| < \xi$ and $\dot{x} > 0$, the system *enter*s the inner region; **else**
- If $|x| > 1$, the system *stay*s in the outer region.
- If $|x| < 1$, the system *leave*s the inner region.

The verb *stay* and *leave* are given by (13.19) and (13.20) respectively. The verb *enter* represents a kind of transient process from outer regions to the inner region. We need to learn parameters for this process. Suppose that the verb *enter* is given by the following system:

$$\begin{aligned} \dot{x} &= \alpha y + w_1 x \\ \dot{y} &= y + x + z \\ \dot{z} &= -\beta y - w_2 z. \end{aligned} \tag{13.21}$$

We learn parameter w_1 by using an adaptive learning law that minimizes the following cost function:

$$E(t) = \tfrac{1}{2}(\dot{x}_o - \dot{x})^2 \qquad |x_o - 1| < \xi \text{ or } |x_o + 1| < \xi, \tag{13.22}$$

where x_o is obtained from the objective trajectory of the original chaotic system within the transient regions. We have

$$\begin{aligned} \dot{w}_1 &= -\delta \frac{\partial E}{\partial w_1} \\ &= \delta(\dot{x}_o - \dot{x}) \frac{\partial \dot{x}}{\partial w_1} \\ &= \delta(\dot{x}_o - \dot{x}) x. \end{aligned} \tag{13.23}$$

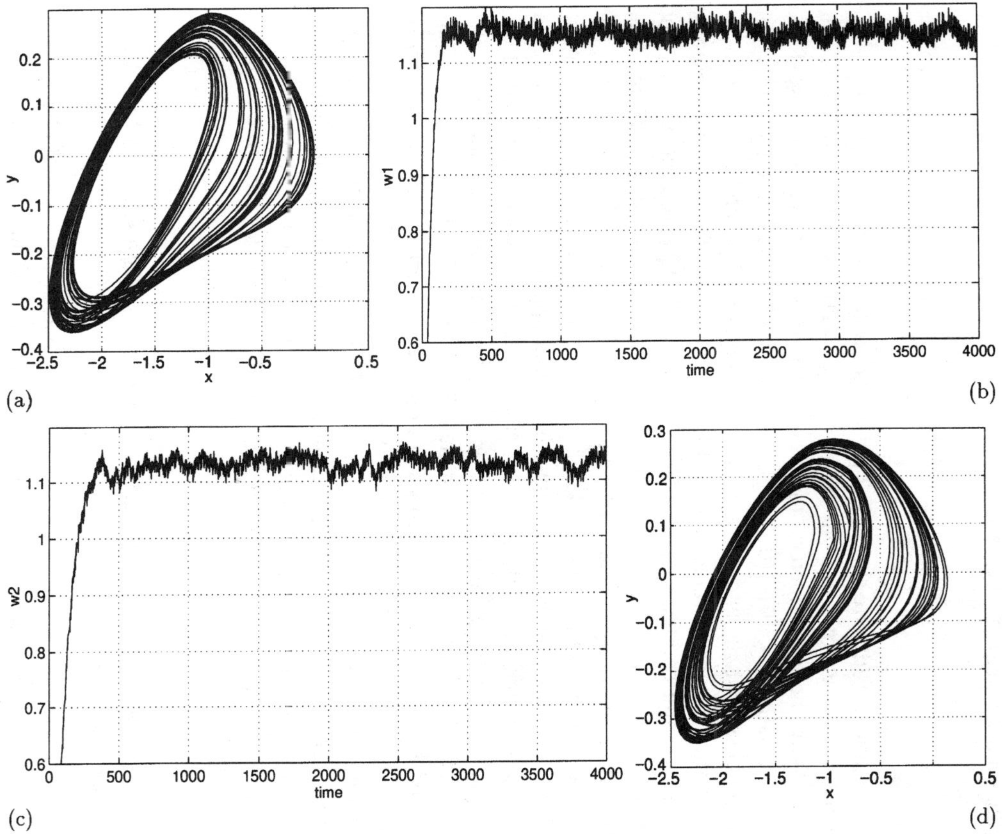

FIGURE 13.6. Learning processes of the parameters of the verb *enter* for modeling the chaotic system: (*a*) original strange attractor; (*b*) learning process of w_1 for the verb *enter*; (*c*) learning process of w_2 for the verb *enter*; (*d*) output of the trained verb model of the chaotic system.

Similarly, we learn parameter w_2 by using an adaptive learning law that minimizes the following cost function:

$$E(t) = \frac{1}{2}(\dot{z}_o - \dot{z})^2 \qquad |x_o - 1| < \xi \text{ or } |x_o + 1| < \xi, \tag{13.24}$$

where z_o is the third variable of the objective trajectory of the original chaotic system within the transient region. We have

$$\dot{w}_2 = -\delta(\dot{z}_o - \dot{z})z. \tag{13.25}$$

The simulation results are shown in Figure 20.6. In this simulation we choose the parameters of the chaotic system as $\alpha = 15, \beta = 20, \gamma = 0.56, a = -8/7$, and $b = -5/7$. With these parameters, the strange attractor is shown in Figure 13.6*a* with initial condition $(x(0), y(0), z(0)) = (-1.087613, 0.012802, 0.312794)$. The learning processes of w_1 and w_2 are shown in Figure 13.6*b* and *c*, respectively. We choose the learning parameter $\delta = 0.1$. The parameter for *enter* is chosen as $\xi = 0.2$. The initial conditions are $w_1(0) = w_2(0) = 0$. Observe that both w_1 and w_2 fluctuate around their average values with small fluctuation if the training time is big enough. The average values of w_1 and w_2 are 1.15 and 1.13, respectively. The output of the verb model is shown in Figure 13.6*d*. Although there exist some modeling errors, we find that the verb model is a good approximation of the original chaotic system. Since the verb system is also a chaotic system, in Figure 13.6*d* we show only the stable strange attractor with the same initial condition as that used in Figure 13.6*a*. Since chaotic systems are very sensitive to initial conditions, mismatch of parameters, and differences in structure, the verb model can only repeat the qualitative property of the original system.

Comparing the results in Sections 13.3.2 and 13.3.3, we can see that the same verb model can be used to model different processes qualitatively given different definitions of verbs. This makes our language vivid and rich in the sense that humans can transfer different experiences by using a small number of verbs in a relatively huge number of contexts.

13.3.4 Application of Computational Process–Symbol Models to Chaotic Cryptanalysis

In this section, verb modeling is used to break a cipher system called *chaotic shift keying* [13]. In chaotic shift keying, a binary information signal $m(t)$ is hidden in a chaotic time series generated by two different chaotic attractors in the following way. When bit 1 of $m(t)$ is sent, the transmitted signal $s(t)$ is generated by chaotic attractor 1, and when bit 0 of $m(t)$ is sent, $s(t)$ is generated by chaotic attractor 0. To make these two attractors indistinguishable from the signal transmitted is the basis for achieving chaotic shift keying security. Given that two chaotic attractors are generated by the same chaotic system with slightly shifted parameter sets, we can hopefully find two attractors with similar statistic properties in the time domain. Two

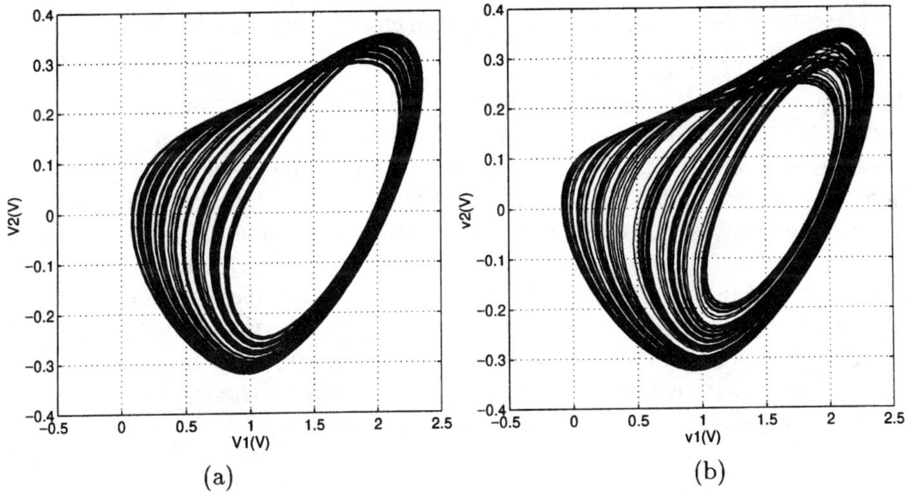

FIGURE 13.7. Two chaotic attractors used in chaotic shift keying: (*a*) chaotic attractor of a Chua circuit for encoding "1"; (*b*) chaotic attractor of a Chua circuit for encoding "0."

similar chaotic attractors generated by a Chua circuit is shown in Figure 13.7. These two chaotic attractors are statistically similar in the time domain and have already been used in chaotic shift keying.

I have been working in chaotic cryptography and chaotic cryptanalysis for many years [50–52,67] and qualify as a human expert in this area. My experiences in chaotic cryptanalysis are extensive [53–56,69]. To share with machines the experience of breaking a chaotic shift keying system, the machines should be told that the dynamics of a spectrogram of the transmitted signal should be used. I prefer to share my experiences with my computer, named *fred.eecs.berkeley.edu* by telling it: "Hi, Fred, to break a chaotic shift keying system you should first get a spectrogram of the signal intercepted.[7] By inspecting the spectrogram and the message signal (suppose that we have been lucky enough to have a few bits of the message signal) you can find the differences between bit 1, bit 0, and the switching process from bit 0 to bit 1. It's difficult to describe the differences, but you can absolutely find them by yourself."[8] Since a human being is very well equipped to perform pattern recognition tasks [14], if Fred is a human being, he will follow the instruction above and before long will have his own experiences and be familiar with decoding the spectrogram. Unfortunately, since my Fred is a computer, I had to write down my experiences in the form of the following computational verb model:

- If transmitted signal $s(t)$ $stay_1$'s in chaotic attractor 1, then 1 is output.
- If transmitted signal $s(t)$ $stay_0$'s in chaotic attractor 0, then 0 is output.

[7] I can imagine a big smile on its face because this task seems too easy at the beginning.

[8] Although all of my human students would find this task incredibly easy, my poor computer student Fred feels that it is very difficult to program "inspect" and "find the differences" because I really do not tell it what the differences are.

- If transmitted signal $s(t)$ *switch*$_{01}$'s from chaotic attractor 0 to chaotic attractor 1, then 1 is output.

In the computational verb model above the switching process from bit 1 to bit 0 is not needed because detection of bit 0 is much more robust than that of bit 1. This observation is based totally on my experience; I have no reason for why this happens. So I do not want to bother my computer with something that I have no idea about. To embed the rule above into a machine, a set of examples should be used to give the machine its own *experience* of the verbs *stay*$_1$, *stay*$_0$, and *switch*$_{01}$. The experiences of these verbs constitute verb models. To get these models, machines are trained by examples. Suppose that we get a pair of transmitted signals $s(t)$ and the corresponding message signal $m(t)$, as shown in Figure 13.8*a*. Since spectral–temporal characteristics are more robust than temporal characteristics for cryptanalysis purposes, the spectrogram of $s(t)$ given in Figure 13.8*b* is used to build the verb models. We denote the spectrogram by $\mathscr{S}(t,n)$, where $t = 1, 2, \ldots$ is the discrete sampling time instant with a constant sampling interval of 5 μs, and $n = 1, 2, \ldots, 20$ are the discrete frequency slots, whose physical meaning is not important in cryptanalysis. The window for FFT is 128 sampling points. The energy density of the spectrogram shown in decibels is represented by 256 gray levels.

In this case, the verb models are two-dimensional spectral–temporal patterns which are determined by clustering the examples in the corresponding spectrogram segments. For making *stay*$_1$ and *stay*$_0$, spectrograms of the central region of bit 1's and bit 0's, respectively, are used. For training *switch*$_{01}$, spectrograms at the corresponding switching edges are used. Since $m(t)$ has a 1000-point bit duration, the center region is chosen as the central 800 points. The other two 100-point regions are chosen as switching regions. The time length for each verb model is chosen as 50 points. We simply move a 50-point window along the corresponding regions and average all samples to get the verb models, as shown in Figure 13.8*c*.

Then the verb models are used to process the original spectrogram by finding distances between each 50-point windows and verb models. The results for *stay*$_1$, *stay*$_0$, and *switch*$_{01}$ are given, respectively, by

$$r_1(t) = \frac{1}{50} \sum_{i=t-24}^{25} \sum_{j=1}^{20} [\mathscr{S}(i,j) - stay_1(t-i+25,j)]^2 \tag{13.26}$$

$$r_0(t) = \frac{1}{50} \sum_{i=t-24}^{25} \sum_{j=1}^{20} [\mathscr{S}(i,j) - stay_0(t-i+25,j)]^2 \tag{13.27}$$

$$r_{01}(t) = \frac{1}{50} \sum_{i=t-24}^{25} \sum_{j=1}^{20} [\mathscr{S}(i,j) - switch_{01}(t-i+25,j)]^2 \tag{13.28}$$

The results are shown in Figure 13.8*d*, *e*, and *f*, respectively. Combining the information from $r_1(t)$, $r_0(t)$, and $r_{01}(t)$, an intermediate decision $d_1(t)$ shown in Figure 13.8*g* is made by the following rule:

- If $stay_1(t) < 5000$ or $stay_0(t) < 6000$ or $switch_{01}(t) > 5000$ or $switch_{01}(t) < 1500$, then $d_1(t) = 1$; else, $d_1(t) = 0$.

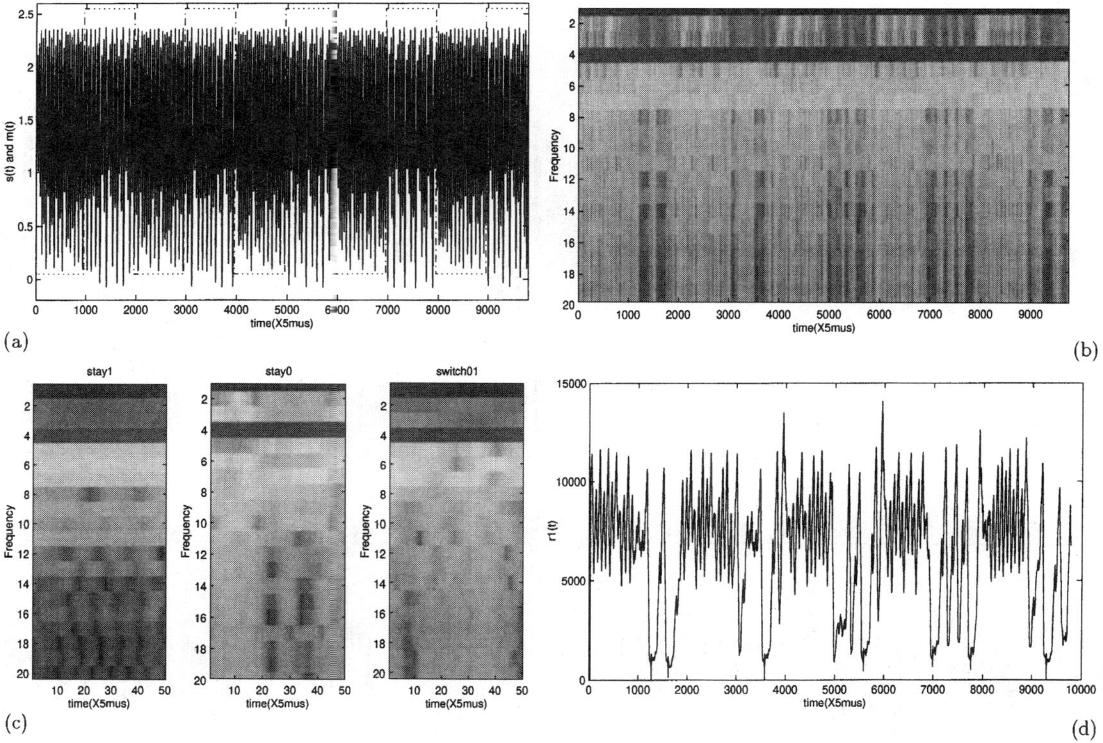

FIGURE 13.8. Breaking chaotic shift keying using computational verb models—learning experiences: (*a*) transmitted signal $s(t)$ of the chaotic shift keying and the massage signal $m(t)$(dashed-dotted); (*b*) spectrogram of $s(t)$, $\mathscr{S}(t,n)$; (*c*) computational verb models of verbs $stay_1$, $stay_0$, and $switch_{01}$; (*d*) output of the distance $r_1(t)$ between $\mathscr{S}(t,n)$ and $stay_1$; (*e*) output of the distance $r_0(t)$ between $\mathscr{S}(t,n)$ and $stay_0$; (*f*) output of the distance $r_{01}(t)$ between $\mathscr{S}(t,n)$ and $switch_{01}$; (*g*) intermediate decision result $d_1(t)$; (*h*) averaging and thresholding result from $d_1(t)$, $d_2(t)$ (solid) and $m(t)$ (dashed-dotted).

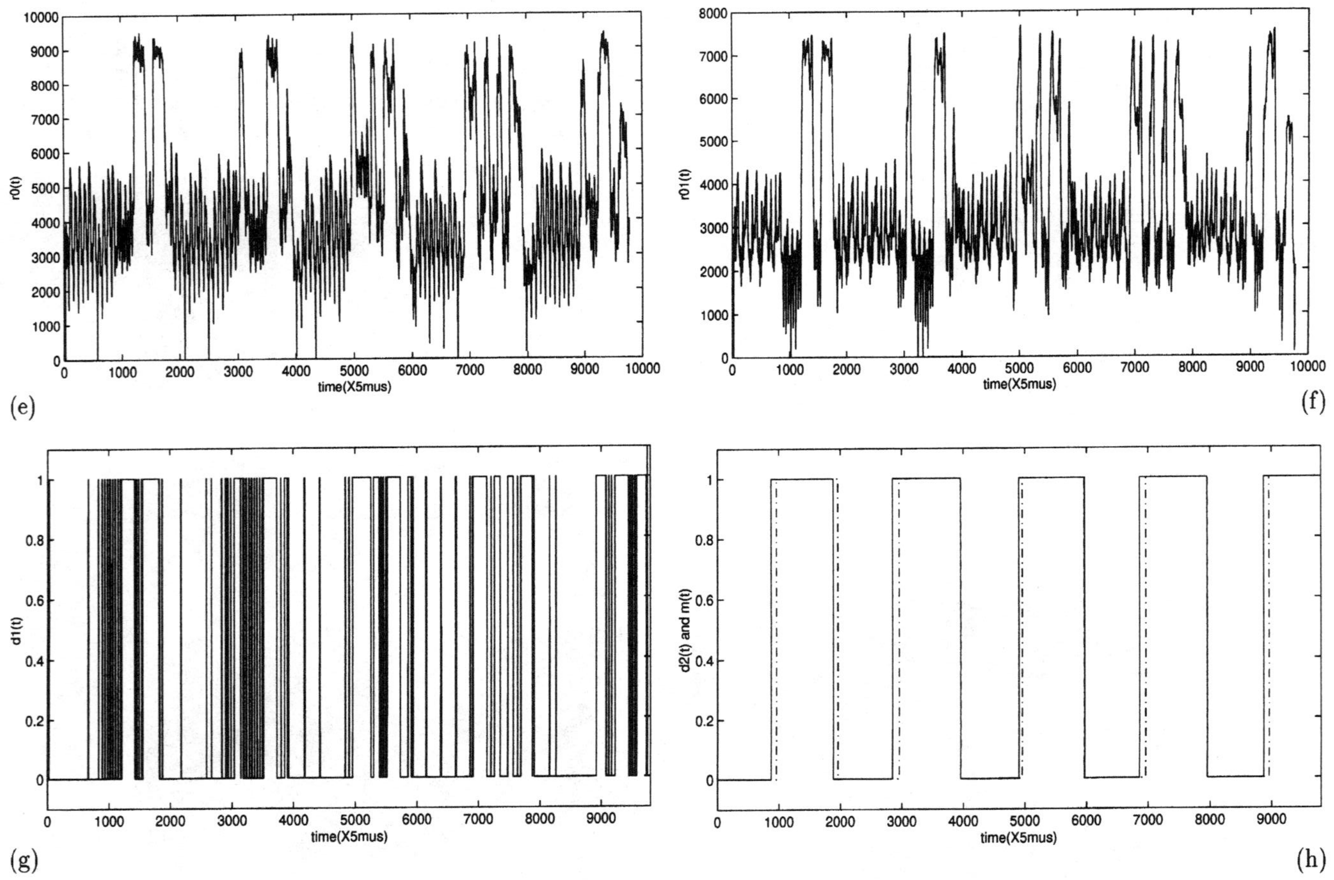

FIGURE 13.8. (*Continued*)

The final decision $d_2(t)$, shown in Figure 13.8*h* is then given by averaging $d_1(t)$ with a 100-point window and then thresholding with a 0.35 threshold. For comparison, $m(t)$ is also shown in Figure 13.8*h*, dashed-dotted lines. Observe that $m(t)$ is recovered perfectly, with little shifts on some edges.

To test the machine's experiences, the method described above is used to break a new sample with totally different initial conditions and bit duration 800 points. The results are shown in Figure 13.9. Figure 13.9*a* shows the transmitted signal and the message signal. Figure 13.9*b* shows the spectrogram of $s(t)$. Figure 13.9*c*,*d*, and *e* show the distances between the verb models and the spectrogram. Figure 13.9*f* shows the intermediate decision result. Figure 13.9*g* shows the final decision and the message signal. Observe that the chaotic shift keying is broken by the machine itself, with only small shifts at the bit edges. From $d_2(t)$ we can recover the clock signal and then each bit can be recovered perfectly.

13.4 COMPUTING WITH COMPUTATIONAL PROCESS SYMBOLS

In this section, relationships and computations between computational process symbols are modeled by relations between different dynamics. To avoid clutter, we call *computation of computational process symbols* and *computing with computational process symbols* simply *verb computation*. Another important concept, *verb equality*, also addressed in this section, has a very unique meaning and thus cannot be translated into something related to computational process symbols without serious confusion arising. This is because verb equality uses the broad sense of computational verbs. The classical "equality" is generalized to verb equality, which is synchronization or generalized synchronization between dynamic systems. Verb computation deals with vagueness in dynamical processes and relations. To illustrate the application of verb computation, an example of "understand music" is presented to show how emotions and intuitions can be transmitted through music by verb computation. There are different methods of setting up intuitive connections between human beings. Music is one of these methods. Music is said to be a form of communication between humans beyond words (where the words end, the music begins). What is music from a physical point of view? It is a *dynamic process* characterized by a $1/f$ spectrum [46]. The dynamics behind a piece of music may be periodic, quasiperiodic, or even chaotic [38,39]. Musicians can code their feelings and emotions into this kind of "noise," and audiences with trained ears can decode the feelings and emotions in their own ways. This kind of communication via music between people is very similar to a dynamic process called *adaptive synchronization* [49]. In this case, the synchronization happens in high neural levels (high brain functions). In this section, I show what happens when a chaotic signal (a kind of music) is transmitted between two human beings.

Since chaotic phenomena are very complex, the possibilities for exploring chaos to secure communication have drawn lots of attention from both the scientific and engineering communities [9,10,50–52,66]. In this section, verb computation is used

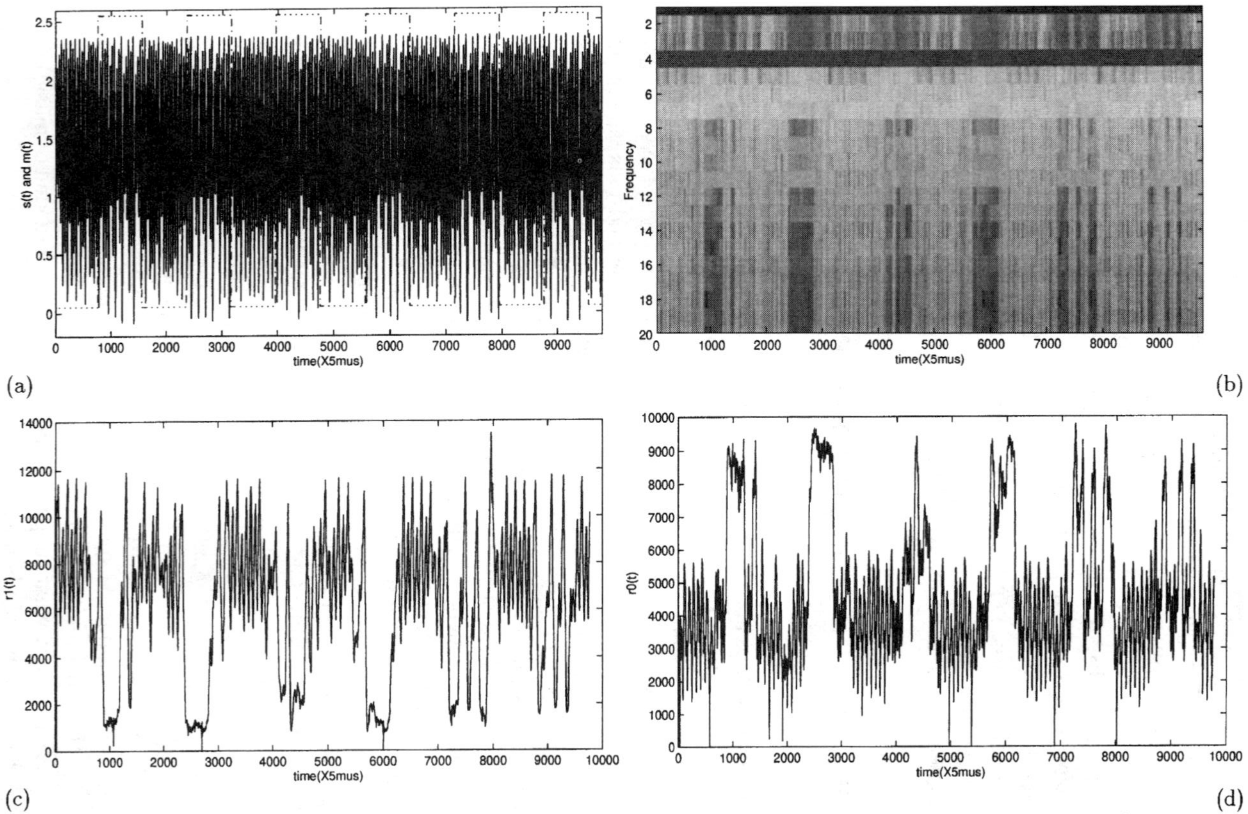

FIGURE 13.9. Breaking chaotic shift keying using computational verb models—testing the experiences: (*a*) transmitted signal $s(t)$ of the chaotic shift keying and the massage signal $m(t)$ (dashed-dotted); (*b*) spectrogram of $s(t)$, $\mathscr{S}(t,n)$; (*c*) output of the distance $r_1(t)$ between $\mathscr{S}(t,n)$ and $stay_1$; (*d*) output of the distance $r_0(t)$ between $\mathscr{S}(t,n)$ and $stay_0$; (*e*) output of the distance $r_{01}(t)$ between $\mathscr{S}(t,n)$ and $switch_{01}$; (*f*) intermediate decision result $d_1(t)$; (*g*) averaging and thresholding result from $d_1(t)$, $d_2(t)$ (solid), and $m(t)$ (dashed-dotted).

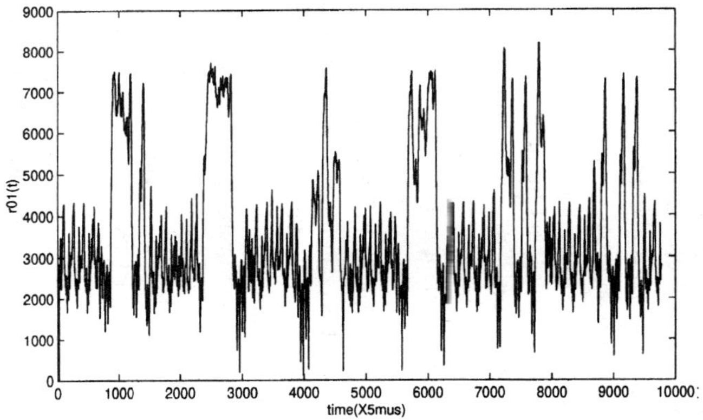

(e)

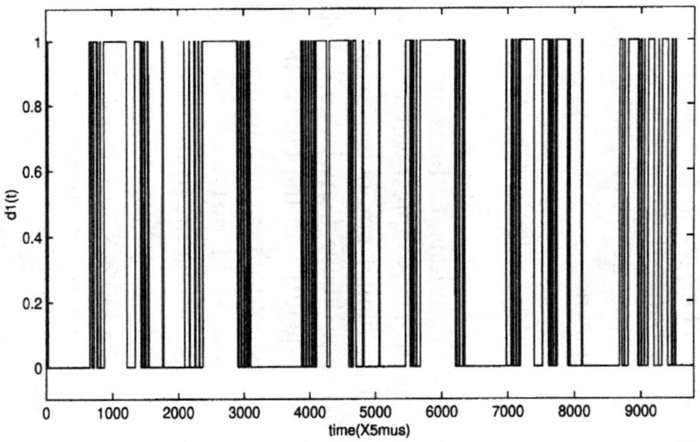

(f)

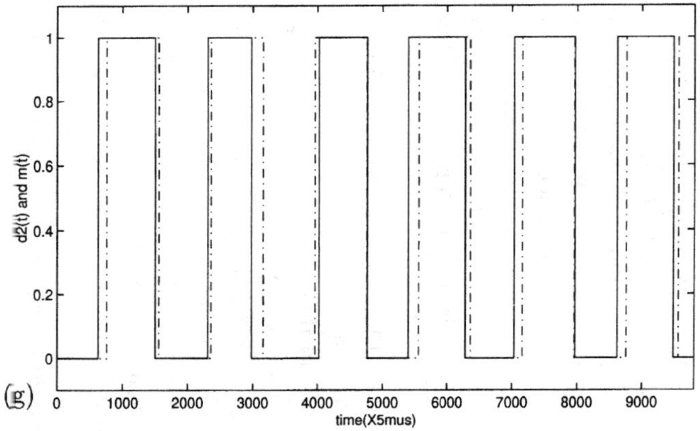

(g)

FIGURE 13.9. *(Continued)*

to unmask the chaotic secure communication scheme called chaotic shift keying [13]. First a reference system is chosen as the "machinself." Then the reference system "hears" the transmitted signal and "feels" different styles in the transmitted signal when different bits of the message signal are scrambled. Different feelings of the reference system reveal the scrambled message signal even though the structure and parameters of the chaotic transmitter are unknown.

13.4.1 Motivations

How can we *understand* process symbols which imply emotions, feelings, or intuitions? There exist many methods to model this problem. The simplest way is to use "equality." This kind of equality is used by modern digital computers where a "copying" operation is supposed to make the machine "have knowledge." This kind of machine intelligence is a static map. Since "equality" in the conventional sense is only a static map between two processes, it is not rich enough to describe different interactions between verbs (dynamic processes) in different contexts. When a human being "understands" other people, it seems that the resulting understandings are different in different contexts. In one word, the verb "understand" is much richer than a static equality although it connects closely to the concept of "equality."[9] In fact, there exist many verbs that have the characteristics of equalities [29]. Some of them are "know," "feel," "recognize," "perceive," "be aware of," "learn," and "comprehend." Although these computational process symbols have different functions in our natural languages, they share a characteristic: namely, they are used to describe dynamic processes by which humans acquire experiences, intuitions, or knowledge [34]. By using these computational process symbols, a person is aware of a kind of "copying" process happening in his or her brain from nonconscious self to conscious self [34]. It had been reported that humans can construct experiences from the nonconscious self via behaviors [28] (i.e., a conscious–nonconscious dynamics is needed to gain and retrieve experiences). In this "copying" process, people assumes that they are getting equivalent copies of something from their counterparts.

We need a systematic method called *verb computation* to build a relationship between different computational process symbols or between computational process symbols and circumstances. The verb computation is a framework for organizing and processing the implied information behind the dynamics of computational process symbols. Since verbs are dynamic processes, the verb computation should also be a dynamic process in some prescribed contexts. The verb computation is based on the dynamic models of verbs [57], in which verbs are viewed as linear or nonlinear dynamic models of human experiences. Computational process symbols are also viewed as a means of sharing experiences between humans.

Before verb computation can be defined in a mathematical framework, a quantitative description of each computational process symbol should be used. We use an *evolving function* (or *evolving system*) to describe a computational process symbol.

[9] "Understand" is also very different from equivalent relation although some aspects of "understand" are equivalent relations.

Since *time* is so deeply rooted in our brain and reality, it is convenient to define an evolving function as an explicit function of time. In different contexts, evolving functions (systems) may be defined by simple functions or complex behaviors of nonlinear dynamic systems. For example, let us study the following sentence:

Mei usually *goes* to the office by bus.

Here the evolving function of "go" can be found by tracing the route and time schedule of a bus. In this case, "go" is a simple process that can be observed explicitly. However, in most cases, verb computation involves processes that cannot easily be observed. This may impose a big problem in finding evolving functions of computational process symbols.

13.4.2 Equality and Similarity Between Computational Process Symbols

Before we can provide verb computation, the most important thing is to define verb *equality*. Equality is an elementary axiom in any computation framework, although in most cases it is embedded implicitly. However, classical equality is an idealized concept which cannot be found in the nature. In a word, equality can only exist in our mental experiments. When we consider the static aspects of nature, this kind of mental idealization may be useful to handle computations of static objects. But verb computation is used to handle dynamic aspects of nature, and idealized equality is no longer valid. If idealized equality is used in verb computation, the rich dynamics and resulting complexities of our natural language will be destroyed.

Verb Equalities. In our natural language, *equality* and *similarity* are represented by a verb such as "understand" and "feel." We model this kind of verb by using dynamic processes called *(generalized) synchronization*. For example, examining the following sentence:

Mary *feels* what Tom *feels*

We can define a synchronizing process between the feelings of Mary and Tom. If Mary can "feel" what Tom "feels" exactly, both of them are intuitively connected. In this case we cannot distinguish the feelings of both. We call this process an *identical synchronization*, which is a generalization of classical equality by combining it with dynamics. If what Mary "feels" is not an exact copy of what Tom "feels" but the two feelings are correlated, a *generalized synchronization* (GS) is needed. We use the following two examples to show the difference between these two kinds of synchronizations.

Example 13.1: Identical Synchronization. Given the evolving function of "feel" from Mary as

$$feel_{\text{Mary}}(t) = \sin(t + \pi) \tag{13.29}$$

and that from Tom as

$$feel_{\text{Tom}}(t) = \sin(t + \pi) \tag{13.30}$$

we have

$$feel_{\text{Mary}}(t) = feel_{\text{Tom}}(t). \tag{13.31}$$

This is identical synchronization and classical equality, which means that Mary and Tom "feel" the same thing. In this case, identical synchronization degrades to classical equality. However, identical synchronization may be a dynamic process whose ω set [22] is the classical equality as shown below the section "Examples of Verb Equalities."

Example 13.2: Generalized Synchronization. Given the evolving function of "feel" from Mary as

$$feel_{\text{Mary}}(t) = 2\sin(t + \pi) \tag{13.32}$$

and that from Tom as

$$feel_{\text{Tom}}(t) = sin(t), \tag{13.33}$$

we have

$$feel_{\text{Mary}}(t) = g(feel_{\text{Tom}}(t)), \tag{13.34}$$

where

$$g(x(t)) = 2x(t + \pi) \tag{13.35}$$

is called *GS transformation*. This is a GS that is connected by a GS transformation. The GS transformation itself can be a chaotic system if verbs are modeled by chaotic systems, such as "I *think* what you *think*" or "I *am thinking* what you *dreamed* last night."

Verb equalities, which include different types of synchronizations, are dynamic processes. A verb equality is a system characterized either by synchronization errors in the case of identical synchronizations or some kinds of correlations in the case of generalized synchronizations.

Examples of Verb Equalities. We then study how can two computational process symbols be synchronized. Without loss of generality, we use a chaotic system, the Lorenz system [31], to demonstrate synchronization between two computational process symbols. The state equation of a Lorenz system is given by

$$\begin{aligned} \dot{x} &= -\sigma x + \sigma y \\ \dot{y} &= rx - y - xz \\ \dot{z} &= xy - bz, \end{aligned} \tag{13.36}$$

where $\sigma = 10$, $r = 28$, and $b = 8/3$ are three real positive parameters.

Identical Synchronizations

Example 13.3. We first consider the identical synchronization of two computational process symbols, which are modeled by two Lorenz systems. The first thing that we should specify is the manner of interconnections between these two verbs. If the two computational process symbols occur during an active conversation between two people such that each is affected by its counterpart in this conversation, we can use mutual coupling between two Lorenz systems to model interconnections of these two computational process symbols during the conversation.

1. The evolving system of computational process symbol 1 is given by

$$\begin{aligned} \dot{x} &= -\sigma x + \sigma y + k(\tilde{x} - x) \\ \dot{y} &= rx - y - xz + k(\tilde{y} - y) \\ \dot{z} &= xy - bz + k(\tilde{z} - z). \end{aligned} \tag{13.37}$$

2. The evolving system of computational process symbol 2 is given by

$$\begin{aligned} \dot{\tilde{x}} &= -\sigma\tilde{x} + \sigma\tilde{y} + k(x - \tilde{x}) \\ \dot{\tilde{y}} &= r\tilde{x} - \tilde{y} - \tilde{x}\tilde{z} + k(y - \tilde{y}) \\ \dot{\tilde{z}} &= \tilde{x}\tilde{y} - b\tilde{z} + k(z - \tilde{z}), \end{aligned} \tag{13.38}$$

where k is used to model the mutual influence between two computational process symbols. These two computational process symbols are coupled by sharing states with each other. This kind of mutual coupling can be a model of sensation verbs [29], such as "touch," "hear," "listen to," and "look."

The simulation results are shown in Figure 13.10 with $k = 1$. In Figure 13.10*a* the evolving processes of $x(t)$ and $\tilde{x}(t)$ are shown. The solid and dashed waveforms show $x(t)$ and $\tilde{x}(t)$, respectively. In Figure 13.10*b* the evolving processes of $y(t)$ and $\tilde{y}(t)$ are shown. The solid and dashed waveforms show $y(t)$ and $\tilde{y}(t)$, respectively. In Figure 10*c* the evolving processes of $z(t)$ and $\tilde{z}(t)$ are shown. The solid and dashed waveforms show $z(t)$ and $\tilde{z}(t)$, respectively. Observe that these two verbs influence each other such that they go to the same process after about 2 time units. This simulation is an implementation of the verb equality in the following sentence:

Mary and Tom *understand* what each other *says* (in their conversation).

Here *understand* is the verb equality and two *say*'s are omputational process symbol 1 and computational process symbol 2 respectively. The mutual coupling between Mary and Tom is set up by both linguistic and nonlinguistic links in their conversations [34].

Example 13.4. In some contexts, the influence between two computational process symbols is unidirectional. For example, one reads a book and tries to understand the computational process symbols in the book. Since these computational process sym-

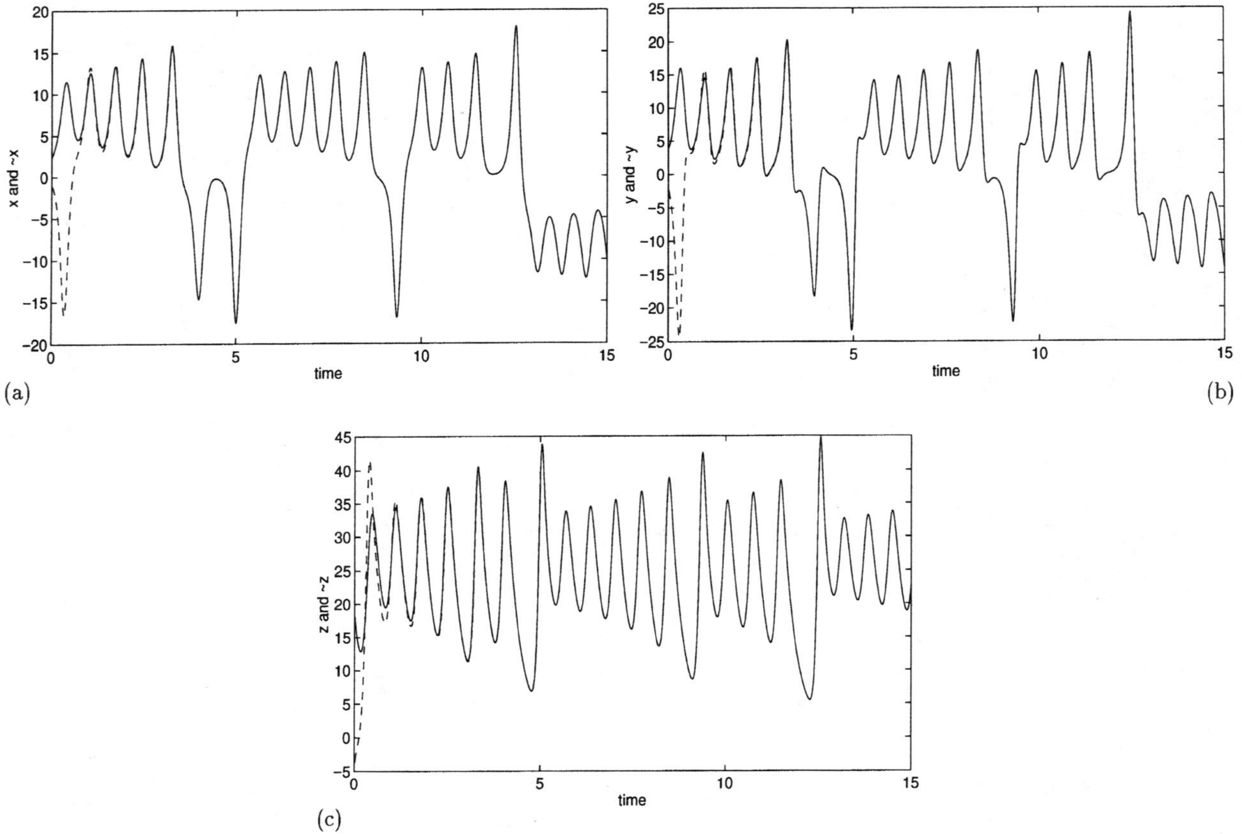

FIGURE 13.10. Identical synchronization of two Lorenz systems as the model of verb equality using mutual coupling: (*a*) evolving processes of $x(t)$ and $\tilde{x}(t)$; (*b*) evolving processes of $y(t)$ and $\tilde{y}(t)$; (*c*) evolving processes of $z(t)$ and $\tilde{z}(t)$.

bols cannot be affected by the reader, understanding of the computational process symbols by the reader is a unidirectional synchronizing process. One example of verb equality using unidirectional coupling is as follows.

1. The evolving system of computational process symbol 1, which is printed in a book and fixed, is given by

$$\begin{aligned} \dot{x} &= -\sigma x + \sigma y \\ \dot{y} &= rx - y - xz \\ \dot{z} &= xy - bz. \end{aligned} \tag{13.39}$$

2. The evolving system of computational process symbol 2, which is the understanding of computational process symbol 1 by the reader, is given by

$$\begin{aligned} \dot{\tilde{x}} &= -\sigma\tilde{x} + \sigma\tilde{y} + k(x - \tilde{x}) \\ \dot{\tilde{y}} &= r\tilde{x} - \tilde{y} - \tilde{x}\tilde{z} + k(y - \tilde{y}) \\ \dot{\tilde{z}} &= \tilde{x}\tilde{y} - b\tilde{z} + k(z - \tilde{z}). \end{aligned} \tag{13.40}$$

The simulation results are shown in Figure 13.11 with $k = 2$. In Figure 13.11*a* the evolving processes of $x(t)$ and $\tilde{x}(t)$ are shown. The solid and dashed waveforms show $x(t)$ and $\tilde{x}(t)$, respectively. In Figure 13.11*b* the evolving processes of $y(t)$ and $\tilde{y}(t)$ are shown. The solid and dashed waveforms show $y(t)$ and $\tilde{y}(t)$, respectively. In Figure 13.11*c* the evolving processes of $z(t)$ and $\tilde{z}(t)$ are shown. The solid and dashed waveforms show $z(t)$ and $\tilde{z}(t)$, respectively. Although the simulations in both Figures 13.10 and 13.11 have the same synchronization error system and with the same initial condition, the simulation results are totally different. This simulation is an implementation of the verb equality in the following sentence:

Mary *understands* what Tom wrote.

Here the verb equality is *understand*, computational process symbol 1 is Tom's *write* and computational process symbol 2 is Mary's *read*, which is implicit in this sentence.

From the examples in Figure 13.10 and 13.11 we can see that identical synchronization is not a classical equality, although the former approaches the latter asymptotically.

Generalized Synchronizations. Although full understanding is a goal we always try to achieve, misunderstanding is the most common case in human conversation. Misunderstanding is also a kind of understanding, although it may not be "correct" (or identical to the original one). In this sense, there should be a kind of verb equality for modeling this type of nonperfect understanding. On the other hand, because of the richness of personalities, different understandings of the same object are inner factors that contribute to the variety of human society. The variety of behaviors,

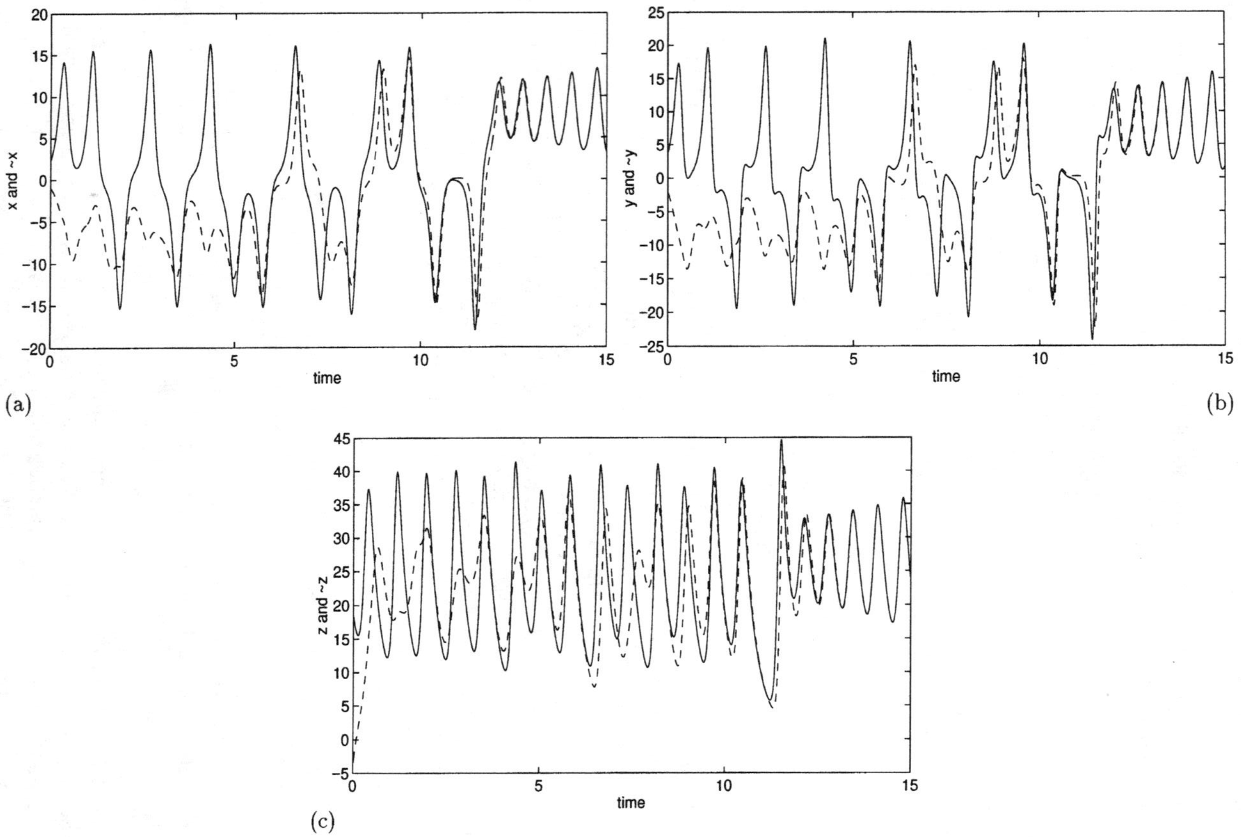

FIGURE 13.11. Identical synchronization of two Lorenz systems as the model of verb equality using unidirectional coupling: (*a*) evolving processes of $x(t)$ and $\tilde{x}(t)$; (*b*) evolving processes of $y(t)$ and $\tilde{y}(t)$; (*c*) evolving processes of $z(t)$ and $\tilde{z}(t)$.

which cannot happen in classical equalities, is another aspect of verb equality. The model for this kind of variety is generalized synchronization. Coupling between two verbs in generalized synchronization can also be mutual or unidirectional. To save space, only cases of unidirectional coupling are presented in this section.

Example 13.5. In this example [50], verb equality distorts the original dynamics with a scalar factor. This can be used to model the verb equality in the following sentence:

> When she reads these sentences, (the reader) Mary *feels* what (the author) Tom *felt* when he was seriously hurt in that accident.

Although Mary can use her mental experiment to reconstruct some virtual pain, she will not be hurt as seriously as Tom was by reading these sentences. The two "feel's" may be qualitatively similar but not necessarily the same. The quantitative difference and qualitative similarity are another aspects of verb equality, which can be modeled by the following GS.

1. The evolving system of computational process symbol 1, which is fixed, is given by

$$\begin{aligned}\dot{x} &= -\sigma x + \sigma y \\ \dot{y} &= rx - y - xz \\ \dot{z} &= xy - bz.\end{aligned} \tag{13.41}$$

2. The evolving system of computational process symbol 2, which is the understanding of computational process symbol 1 by the reader, is given by

$$\begin{aligned}\dot{\tilde{x}} &= -\sigma\tilde{x} + \sigma\tilde{y} \\ \dot{\tilde{y}} &= \lambda(r - \mu)x + \mu\tilde{x} - \tilde{y} - \lambda xz \\ \dot{\tilde{z}} &= \lambda xy - b\tilde{z}.\end{aligned} \tag{13.42}$$

The simulation results with $\lambda = 0.5$ are shown in Figure 13.12. Figure 13.12*a* shows the attractor of computational process symbol 1 and Figure 13.12*b* shows the attractor of computational process symbol 2. Observe that the attractor of computational process symbol 2 is a scaled version of that of computational process symbol 1 by a scaling factor $\lambda = 0.5$. Figure 13.12*c*, *d*, and *e* show the relations of x versus $\tilde{x}$, y versus $\tilde{y}$, and z versus $\tilde{z}$, respectively.

Example 13.6. In this example [68], the verb equality distorts the original dynamics with a linear transformation. This can be used to model the verb equality in the following sentence:

> When she reads these sentences, although (the reader) Mary *does not understand* why, she *knows* that (the author) Tom was right in some way.

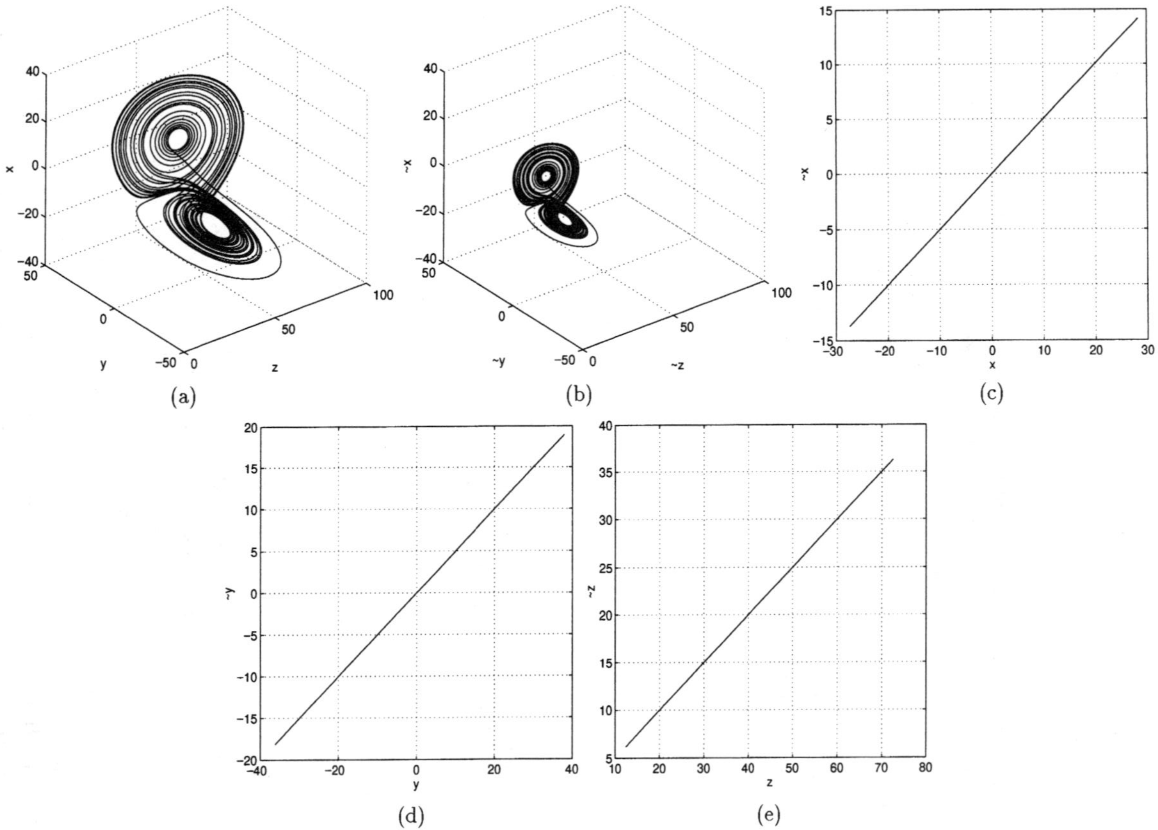

FIGURE 13.12. Scaled GS of two Lorenz systems for modeling verb equality with qualitative similarity: (*a*) attractor of computational process symbol 1; (*b*) attractor of computational process symbol 2; (*c*) x versus $\tilde{x}$ plot; (*d*) y versus $\tilde{y}$ plot; (*e*) z versus $\tilde{z}$ plot.

Although Mary does not fully understand what she is reading, she feels something, which may be a transformation of the original feeling. This "know" may be a very complex system (e.g., a chaotic system) which functions as a GS transformation. To avoid clutter, only the case with linear GS transformation is presented in this example. In this case, "know" is a kind of verb equality.

In this example, the computational process symbol 1 is the same as that used in Example 13.5, and the evolving system of computational process symbol 2 is given by

$$\begin{aligned}\dot{\tilde{x}} &= -\sigma\tilde{x} + \sigma\tilde{y} + \sigma x(r - \mu - z)\\ \dot{\tilde{y}} &= \mu\tilde{x} - \tilde{y} - x(r - \mu - z)\\ \dot{\tilde{z}} &= -b\tilde{z} - bxy.\end{aligned} \tag{13.43}$$

If GS between computational process symbol 1 and computational process symbol 2 is achieved, the following relations should be satisfied:

$$\begin{aligned}\tilde{x} &= -\sigma x + \sigma y \triangleq f_1(x, y)\\ \tilde{y} &= \mu x - y \triangleq f_2(x, y)\\ \tilde{z} &= -bz.\end{aligned} \tag{13.44}$$

The simulation results are shown in Figure 13.13. Figure 13.13*a* shows the attractor of computational process symbol 2. Observe that this attractor is totally different to the famous "butterfly" attractor as shown in Figure 13.12*a* although the former is only a linearly transformed version of the latter. Figure 13.13*b* and *c* show plots of $\tilde{x}$ versus $f_1(x, y)$ and $\tilde{y}$ versus $f_2(x, y)$, respectively. Observe that the linear GS transformation is true. Figure 13.13*d* shows a plot of $\tilde{z}$ versus z. To show the difference between GS and identical synchronization, we also show the $\tilde{x}$ versus x plot and $\tilde{y}$ versus y plot in Figure 13.13*e* and *f*, respectively. Verb equality based on GS is more flexible than the identical synchronization-based verb equality because some kinds of personalities are allowed in verb computation.

13.4.3 Using Music to Transfer Feelings and Emotions

In this section we use verb computation to model intuitive connections between human beings via music. Although music is usually simpler than a chaotic signal [12], for the purpose of demonstrating, I suppose that there exists a kind of chaotic "music" [38], which is generated by the following chaotic system [8]:

$$\begin{aligned}\dot{x} &= \frac{1}{\alpha}[G(y - x) - f(x)]\\ \dot{y} &= \frac{1}{\beta}[G(x - y) + z]\\ \dot{z} &= -\frac{1}{\gamma}(y + Kz),\end{aligned} \tag{13.45}$$

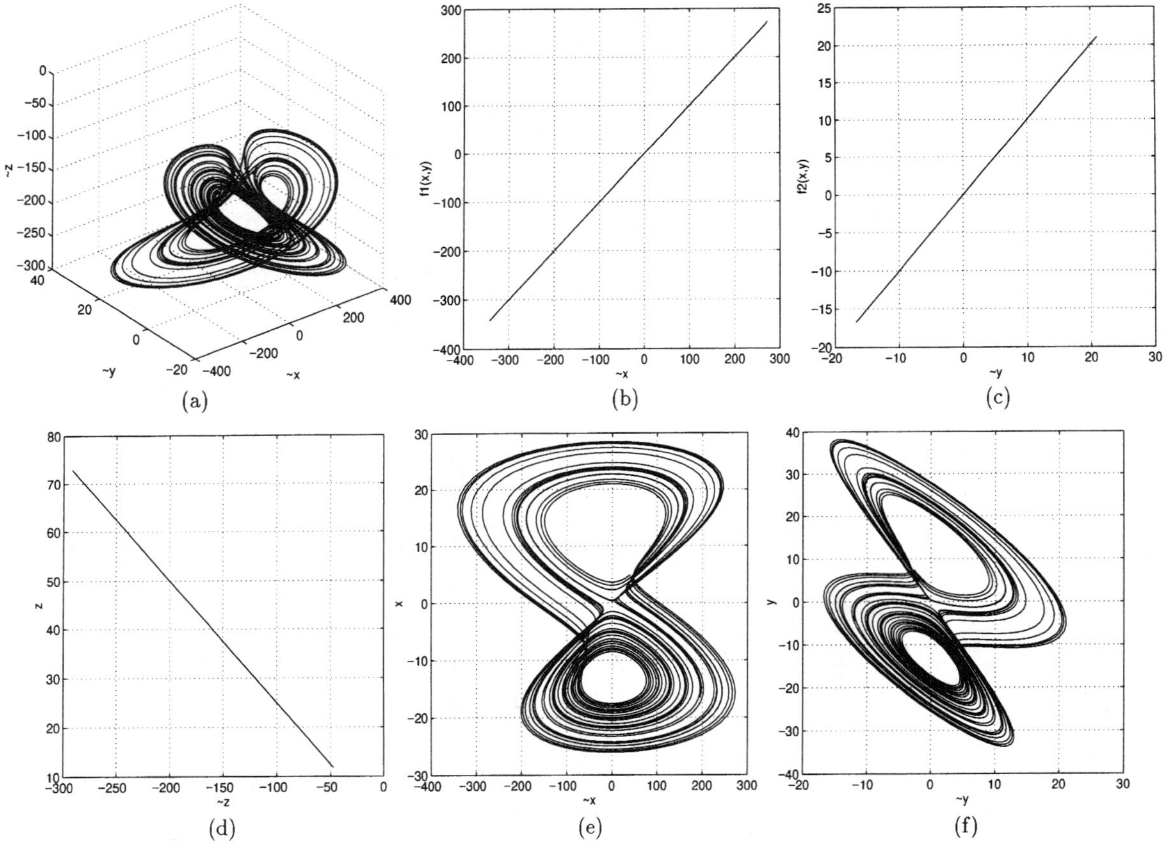

FIGURE 13.13. Linear GS of two Lorenz systems for modeling verb equality with linear transformation: (*a*) attractor of computational process symbol 2; (*b*) $\tilde{x}$ versus $f_1(x, y)$ plot; (*c*) $\tilde{y}$ versus $f_2(x, y)$ plot; (*d*) $\tilde{z}$ versus z plot; (*e*) $\tilde{x}$ versus x plot; (*f*)$\tilde{y}$ versus y plot.

where $\alpha = 5.56 \times 10^{-9}$, $\beta = 50 \times 10^{-9}$, $\gamma = 7.14 \times 10^{-3}$, $G = 7.20461 \times 10^{-4}$, and $K = 2$ are constant parameters. $f(\cdot)$ is given by

$$f(x) = b(t)x + \tfrac{1}{2}(a(t) - b(t))(|x+1| - |x-1|) + c(t), \tag{13.46}$$

where $a(t), b(t)$, and $c(t)$ are time-varying parameters.

We suppose that the emotions or feelings of a musician are used to tune some parameters of his brain such that different tones are generated. For example, "play happily" is encoded by the following parameter dynamics:

$$a_{\text{play happily}}(t) = -0.9 \times 10^{-3}[1 - 0.01\sin(300t)], \tag{13.47}$$

"play anxiously" is encoded by

$$b_{\text{play anxiously}}(t) = -0.5 \times 10^{-3}[1 - 0.01\sin(100t)], \tag{13.48}$$

and "play calmly" is encoded by

$$c_{\text{play calmly}}(t) = 5 \times 10^{-6}\sin(75t). \tag{13.49}$$

Then we assume that music is given by the state variable $x(t)$ because sound is a one-dimensional signal. Since all humans have the same genetic brain structure, we suppose that an audience has the following chaotic system, which functions as the biological basis for understanding music, in their brains:

$$\begin{aligned} \dot{x}_1 &= \frac{1}{\alpha}[G(y_1 - x_1) - f_1(x_1) + d(x - x_1)] \\ \dot{y}_1 &= \frac{1}{\beta}[G(x_1 - y_1) + z_1] \\ \dot{z}_1 &= -\frac{1}{\gamma}(y_1 + Kz_1), \end{aligned} \tag{13.50}$$

where

$$f_1(x) = b_1(t)x + \tfrac{1}{2}[a_1(t) - b_1(t)](|x+1| - |x-1|) + c_1(t). \tag{13.51}$$

Observe that the chaotic system of the audience has almost the same structure as that of the musician except that an additional term $d_1(x - x_1)$ is embedded in the first equation. The additional term in (13.50) is reasonable for modeling the "driven" effect of the music in the audience. Since the model of the musician in (13.45) is used to model the fact that the "music is coming from the heart of the musician," outer "driven" music to drive the musician toward new music does not exist. In this sense, the musician is an autonomous system, whereas the audience is a forced system.

We suppose that initially, there exist some differences between parameters of the two brains of the musician and the audience. When the music is heard by the audience, we suppose that the audience has dynamic processes corresponding to "play happily," "play anxiously," and "play calmly." Since the audience cannot "play" the music, we choose the verb "listen" to describe the passive position of the audience when they try to "understand" ("enjoy," or whatever) the music.

Then the problem is how the audience "listens." From our experiences we know that different ears have different understandings of the same piece of music. For example, for a traditional Chinese, some American jazz and rock music involves very strong noises, whereas American folksongs may be acceptable. I only study the case in which the audience can totally "understand" what the musician is attempting to transmit. Here, "understand" is a verb equality. To do this, "listen" can be modeled as the following dynamic systems:

$$\dot{a}_{1\text{listen happily}} = -\tfrac{1}{2}\alpha\phi_1(x - x_1)(|x_1 + 1| - |x_1 - 1|) \tag{13.52}$$

$$\dot{b}_{1\text{listen anxiously}} = \alpha\phi_2(x - x_1)[x_1 - \tfrac{1}{2}(|x_1 + 1| - |x_1 - 1|] \tag{13.53}$$

$$\dot{c}_{1\text{listen calmly}} = -\alpha\phi_3(x - x_1), \tag{13.54}$$

where $\phi_1 = 5 \times 10^9$, $\phi_2 = 5 \times 10^9$, and $\phi_3 = 5 \times 10^9$ are three constants.

"Pay attention" is used to model the process that the audience uses to try to catch the important details in the music by using time-varying attention weight, given by

$$\dot{d}_{\text{pay attention}} = \alpha\phi_4(x - x_1)^2, \tag{13.55}$$

where $\phi_4 = 10^9$ is a constant. The initial conditions in the simulation are given by $a_1(0) = -0.01 \times 10^{-3}$, $b_1(0) = -10 \times 10^{-3}$, $c_1(0) = 0.1 \times 10^{-3}$, and $d(0) = 0.08 \times 10^{-3}$. A fourth-order Runge–Kutta method with a 10^{-6} fixed step is used.

To summarize, we model the entire process, called "understand music," as the following verb computation:

understand music $\underline{\underline{\Delta}}$

emotions and feelings of musician modeled by verbs "play happily," "play anxiously," and "play calmly"

$\Longrightarrow$ "play" music

$\Longrightarrow$ the audience "pays" attention to details of the music

$\Longrightarrow$ the audience "listens" happily, anxiously, and calmly, corresponding to the music as it comes from the heart of the musician

$\Longrightarrow$ the audience gets the same emotions and feelings as those of the musician.

In the simulation, we present the result when the musician has time-varying emotions during the playing of the music. The simulation is shown in Figure 13.14.

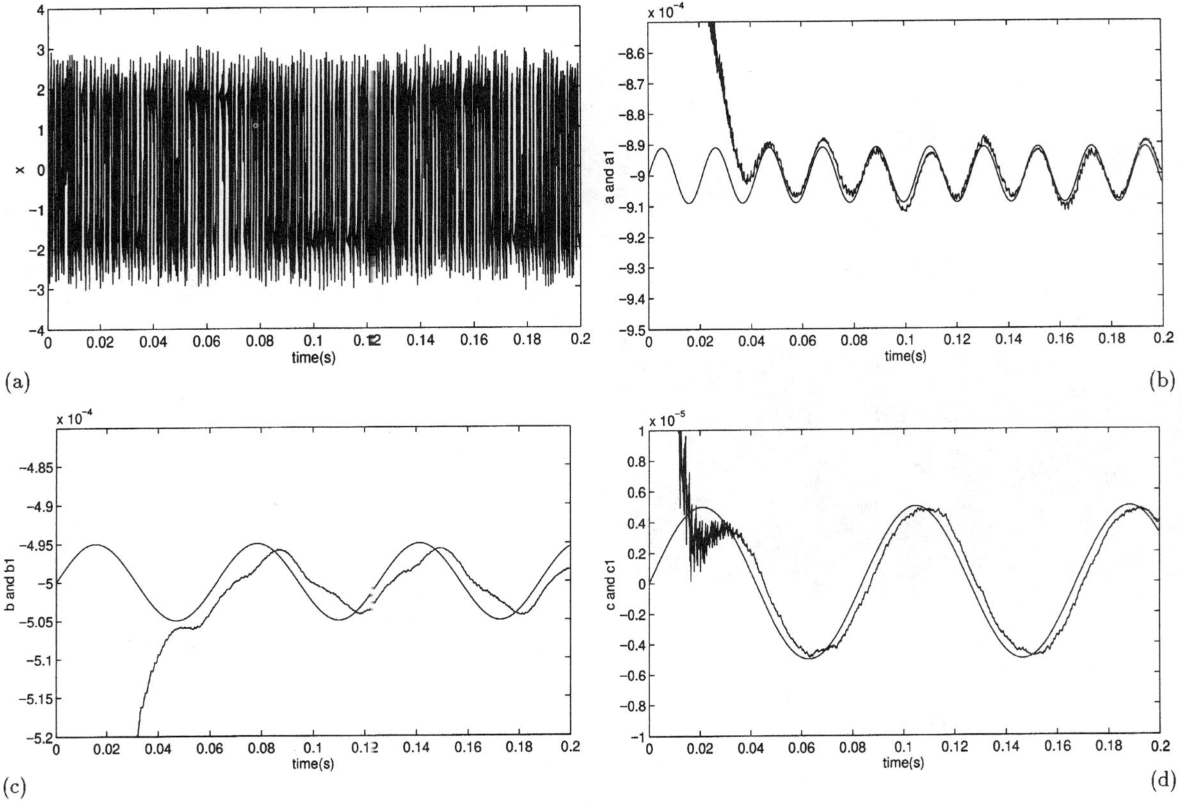

FIGURE 13.14. "Understand music" process: (*a*) the music waveform embedded different emotions and feelings of the musician; (*b*) time-varying property of *a(t)* and the emotional resonance of $a_1(t)$; (*c*) time varying property of *b(t)* and the emotional resoance of $b_1(t)$; (*d*) time-varying property of *c(t)* and the emotional resoance of $c_1(t)$; (*e*) "pay attention" process; (*f*) evolution process of what the audience "understands."

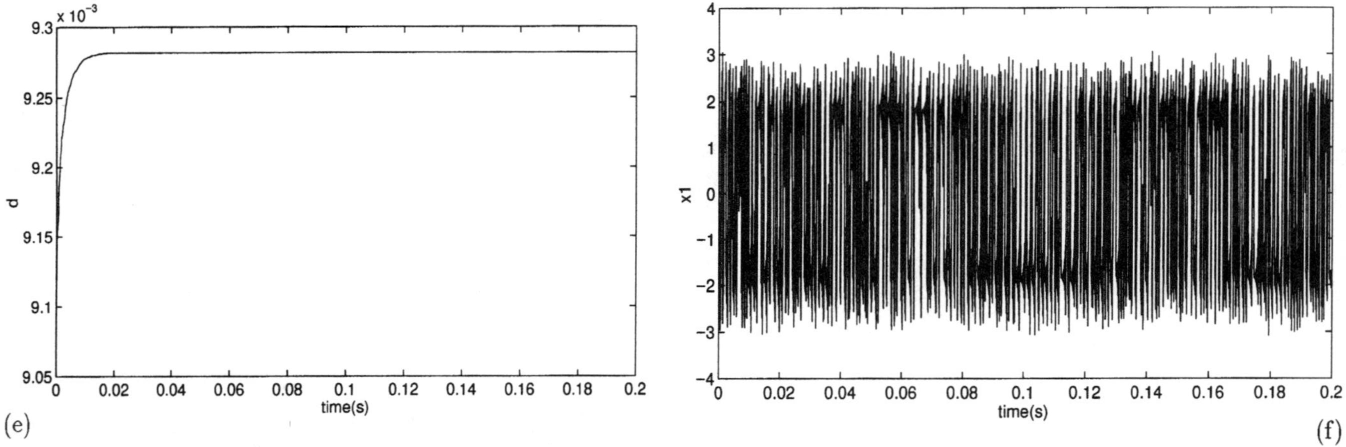

FIGURE 13.14. (*Continued*)

Figure 13.14*a* shows the waveform of the music, $x(t)$, which is really complex. Figure 13.14*b,c*, and *d* show the emotional processes of the musician and the emotional resonances of the audience, respectively. In Figure 13.14*b,c*, and *d*, the smooth waveforms model the emotions of the musician and the other waveforms model the emotions of the audience. Observe that the emotions of the audience follow those of the musician with strong correlations, although some significant delays and errors exist. Figure 13.14*e* shows the process "pay attention." Observe that at first the audience does not focus on the important characteristics of the music (such as classic or not, noise or music). However, after awhile they can focus on some characteristics and interpret the music in their own manner. Figure 13.14*f* shows the music that the audience "understands", which is reproduced by their own brains. Comparing Figure 13.14*a* and *f*, we can see that an almost identical synchronization is achieved. It is a verb equality of "understand."

13.4.4 Application of Verb Computation to Breaking Chaotic Secure Communication

The verb equality can also be used to solve real-life engineering problems. In this section human expert's experiences of breaking chaotic shift keying [53,56] are embedded into verb computations and give a method of breaking the chaotic shift keying without knowing the structure and parameters of the chaotic transmitter.

The human experience in breaking the chaotic shift keying is based on hearing the signal transmitted, which changes its tune patterns constantly. The tunes of a chaotic transmitted signal $s(t)$ are very complex and irregular; however, after hearing it for a long time, a human expert can feel some tune patterns in $s(t)$ and changes of tune patterns can be distinguished when bits of the message signal are changed. This kind of human experience is really very sensitive, yet cannot be described efficiently by words. If you want to learn from me how to distinguish tune patterns, I can tell you this: "Try it yourself; after an hour you will know when the tune pattern is changed and when it remains unchanged." I cannot imagine how I can tell a machine to do this for me. Should I program whatever I cannot express using words? Or shall I just tell my cumbersome machine the truth—that I can only *feel* the changes in tune patterns? Instead of programming my machine, I prefer to tell it directly the following computational verb rule:

> The message signal can be found if you *feel* different tune styles by *hear*ing the transmitted signal $s(t)$.

So far, a machine does not have self-reflection [34,36]; it does not know the definition of "you.". Thus the computational verb rule above is not operational. To make an operational computational verb rule, we should define a *reference system* to represent the machine itself; then the rule is given as:

> The message signal can be found if the reference system *feel*s different tune styles by *hear*ing the transmitted signal $s(t)$.

We then set up the entire computational verb system for unmasking chaotic shift keying. The two chaotic attractors used to scramble the message signal are shown in

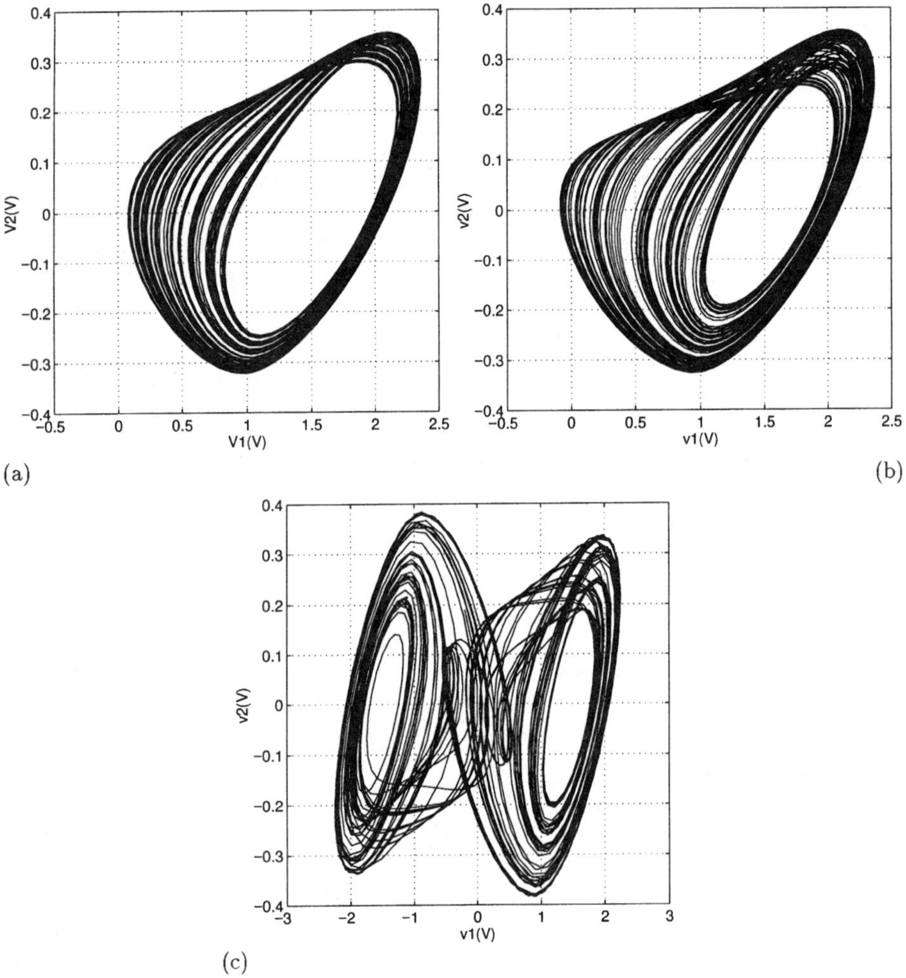

FIGURE 13.15. (*a*) Chaotic attractor for encoding "1"; (*b*) chaotic attractor for encoding "0"; (*c*) chaotic attractor of the reference system.

Figure 13.15*a* and *b*, respectively. This two chaotic attractors are statistically similar and yet distinguishable by the authorized receiver. The reference system is then given by

$$\begin{aligned} \dot{x} &= \frac{1}{\alpha}[G(y-x)-f(x)] \\ \dot{y} &= \frac{1}{\beta}[G(x-y)+z] \\ \dot{z} &= -\frac{1}{\gamma}(y+Kz), \end{aligned} \tag{13.56}$$

whose chaotic attractor is shown in Figure 13.15*c*. Observe that the reference system is much different from both chaotic systems, shown in Figure 13.15*a* and *b*.

The verb *hear* in the computational verb rule is implemented by inserting $s(t)$ into the second equation of the state equation of the reference system as follows:

$$\begin{aligned}\dot{x} &= \frac{1}{\alpha}[G(y-x) - f(x)]\\ \dot{y} &= \frac{1}{\beta}[G(s(t)-y) + z]\\ \dot{z} &= -\frac{1}{\gamma}(y + Kz).\end{aligned} \tag{13.57}$$

Observe that *hear* is modeled by a force driven from the transmitted signal. This is exactly the case when our ears are driven by mechanical air waves called *sound*.

To quantitize the "*feel*" of the reference system when it *hear*s *s(t)*, a moving average of the error $w_1(t)$ between $s(t)$ and $x(t)$ is used:

$$w_1(t) = \frac{1}{T}\int_{t-T}^{t} [s(t) - x(t)]^2 dt, \tag{13.58}$$

where $T = 100$ sampling points is the window length for averaging.

The results are shown in Figure 13.16. Figure 13.16*a* shows the transmitted signal, from which we can not distinguish the scrambled binary message signal $m(t)$. Figure 13.16*b* shows the dynamics of the *feel*ing process, when the reference system *hear*s *s(t)*. This is a verb equality. The quantitative description of this dynamic process is shown as $w_1(t)$, in Figure 13.16*c*, from which we can distinguish that the reference system has felt something quantitatively different in different time intervals. To make the scrambled binary signal more visible, we threshold $w_1(t)$ by

$$w_2(t) = \begin{cases} 0 & \text{if } w_1(t) > 1.2 \\ 1 & \text{else} \end{cases} \tag{13.59}$$

$w_2(t)$ is shown in Figure 13.16*d*. Then $w_2(t)$ is low-pass filtered by a moving average with a window of 101 points. The result is $w_3(t)$, shown in Figure 13.16*e*. The final result, $w_4(t)$, is given by low-pass filtering and thresholding $w_3(t)$. Figure 13.16*f* shows $w_4(t)$ in solid lines and the message signal $m(t)$ in dashed lines. Observe that the message signal is recovered by the reference system through *hear*ing and *feel*ing the transmitted signal.

13.5 ADVERBS AND ADVERBIALS AS MODIFIERS OF COMPUTATIONAL PROCESS SYMBOLS

In this section, the relations between computational process symbols and adverbs (adverbials) are modeled from a systematic point of view. Adverbs (adverbials)

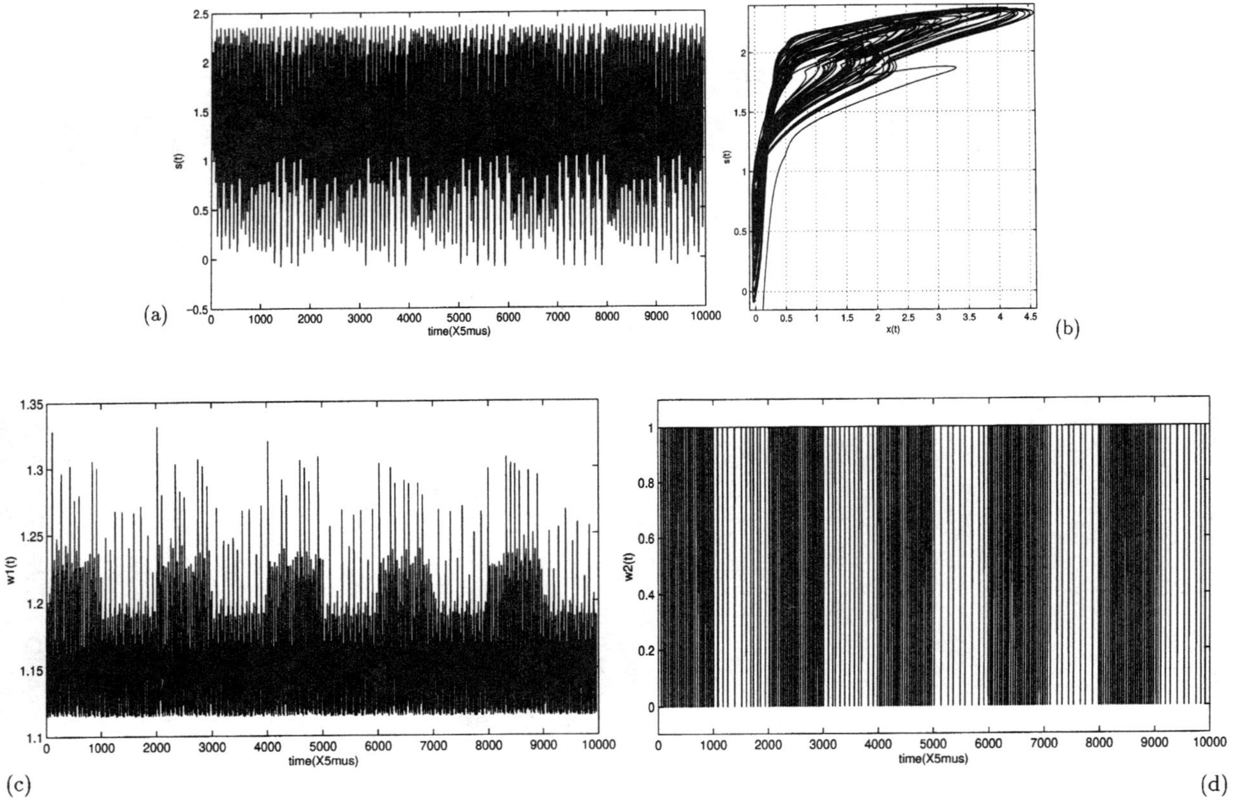

FIGURE 13.16. Unmasking the chaotic shift keying by verb computation: (*a*) transmitted signal *s(t)*; (*b*) dynamics of *feel*ing *s(t)* by the reference system; (*c*) quantitative description of the *feel*ing dynamics of the reference system; (*d*) thresholding results of (*c*); (*e*) moving average of (*d*); (*f*) final low-pass filtering and thresholding result of (*e*) (solid line) and the message signal *m(t)* (dashed line).

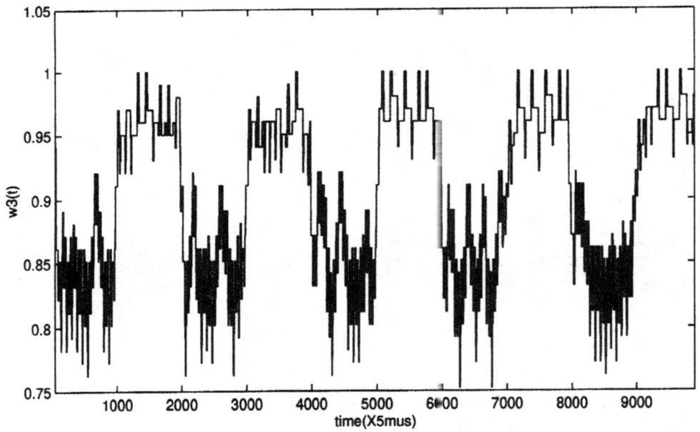

(e)

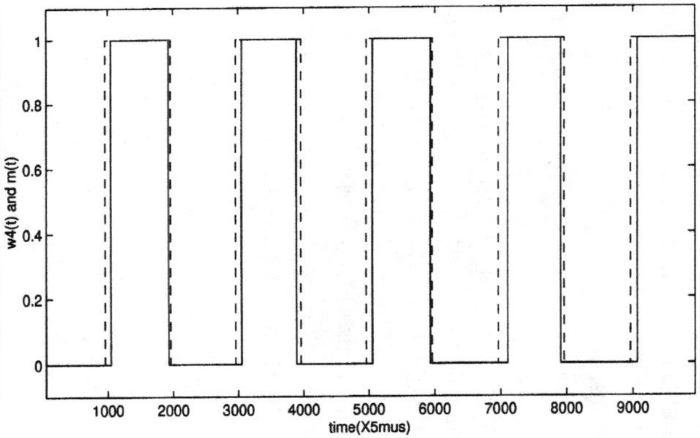

(f)

FIGURE 13.16. (*Continued*)

are viewed as modifiers of verbs by linguistic definitions. Adverbs (adverbials) are characterized by *modifying systems (functions)*. Different types of relationships between computational process symbols and adverbs (adverbials) are presented and modeled. Unlike the relations between adverbs and adjectives, which are only static maps, the relations between verbs and adverbs (adverbials) have very rich interpretations in different contexts.

As an application, computational verb systems with adverbs are used to preprocess speech signals for speech recognition. Speech signals are modeled by a computational process symbol "speak," with different adverbs, such as "fast," "slowly," and "normally." A computational verb system is built as the *machinself*, which uses a computational process symbol "hear" to preprocess the input speech signal and find the corresponding adverbs of "speak" for each speech signal. Then a corresponding adverb (or adverbial) is used to modify "hear" to improve the preprocessing of speech signals. A comparison of the results of computational verb systems with and without adverbs (adverbials) is provided.

13.5.1 Background

In classical artificial intelligence (AI), the *syntax entry* can be any kind of word, such as noun, verb, adverb, or adjective. In today's object-oriented computer programming languages such as C^{++} and Java, *objects* can be viewed as nouns and *actions (functions)* can be viewed as computational process symbols. Then one may question the necessity of inventing computational verb systems. To clear this doubt, let us check the universe of English words as shown in Figure 13.17. English consists of two grammatical centers: noun and verb. A noun is the passive center that answers "what," a verb is an active center that answers "how." In fact, syntactic categories such as *noun*, *noun phase*, and *verb* exist universally in the grammars of all natural human languages [17, p. 81]. Since verbs and nouns form two centers of human languages [48], which are used efficiently to describe and communicate human intelligence, AI should use artificial nouns and verbs. With the enormons achievements in the computer industry in the second half of the twentieth century, AI successfully established the artificial noun as a center in digital computers. Here I do not want

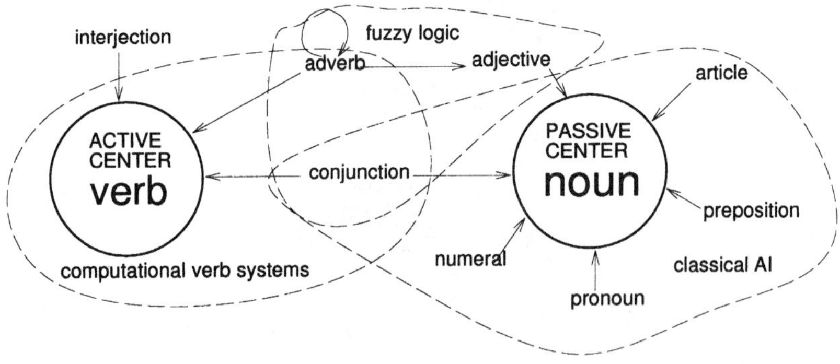

FIGURE 13.17. Different types of words in English and their relations.

to give the reader the impression that no computational process symbol exists in modern computer programming languages. In fact, computer programming languages are full of verbs such as "go to," "do ... loop," "continue," "while ... do," and "call function...." The problem is that these verbs represent *actions* without dynamics. The accuracy of Boolean logic cannot allow different computers to assign different dynamics to these verbs. The entire computer community would not exist if we allow a computer to go wherever it (not the programmer) wants when it meets a "go-to" instruction. The verbs used in today's computer programming languages are *dead* verbs and are very different from those used by humans.

On the other hand, fuzzy logic [71] deals primarily with adjectives and their adverbs. Since in fuzzy logic adjectives are modeled by membership functions, which are static entries, the corresponding adverbs are also modeled by static maps. Although fuzzy logic is a kind of platform of "computing with words" [72,73], only adjectives and the corresponding adverbs are involved. The core of fuzzy logic for computing with words is the adjective; this makes it, in fact, a platform for "computing with adjectives + nouns." Although some adverbs are studied in fuzzy logic, adverbs cannot be the core of fuzzy logic because only a few adverbs can be used to modify adjectives. The adverbs studied in fuzzy logic are *adverbs of degree* [3]. For example, consider the following fuzzy rule:

If the pressure is *high*, the control is *small*.

To modify the adjectives *high* and *small*, we can use adverbs such as *very*, *almost*, *a little*, *mildly*, and so on. But most adverbs cannot modify adjectives [48]. For example, we cannot use *yesterday, here, bravely, firstly, therefore*, and so on, to modify adjectives. On the other hand, all these adverbs can be used to modify verbs [48]. In a word, fuzzy logic is only an extension of the implementation of the passive center of English into computers, because the final users of adjectives are nouns.

The computational verb system [57–62] is the first step to building the active center of English into computers. Unlike in classical AI, where syntax entries are only static symbols, computational verbs are *dynamic systems* (even chaotic systems). Since dynamic systems can also be modeled by fuzzy variables [6,7,30,35,47], one may wonder why we need to invent computational verbs. To clear this doubt, let us examine how dynamic systems are modeled by fuzzy variables. To model a dynamic system by fuzzy variables, one needs to fuzzify the parameter space [6,35] and/or phase space [47], and then a set of fuzzy expressions (e.g., a set of fuzzy if...then rules) or structures (e.g., fuzzy neural network structures [30]) are used to set up models of dynamic systems. A dynamic system modeled by fuzzy variables is the combining result of structures of models (either fuzzy rule set or fuzzy neural networks) and fuzzy variables. Fuzzy variables themselves are not dynamic systems. This is the essential difference between fuzzy variables and computational verbs because computational verbs are *dynamic systems*, which by definition should evolve along physical time or any general event sequence (reversible or irreversible).

Human actions are emotion-driven [25]. Without emotions all human existence will be pointless [43]. The basic emotions are branches of two fundamental streams:

fear and *pleasure* [2]. Fear and pleasure are closely related to *retracting* and *forward-going* attitudes. Emotions are associated with actions: namely, the dynamics of verbs. Moreover, Sloman [44] found that emotions and moods were involved with various kinds of disturbances of the central processes. In this sense, emotions function not only as the driving forces of the dynamics of verbs but also as modifiers of the dynamics of verbs: namely, adverbs.

Since adverbs can be modifiers of adverbs and verbs, they fall within the scope of computational verb systems. Adverbials are equivalent to adverbs in respect to modifying verbs. To avoid further clutter, in this section when we say adverbs, we also imply their equivalences. As already mentioned, fuzzy logic uses adverbs as static maps to modify adjectives. This makes the relation between adverb and adjective very simple in fuzzy logic. However, in many cases since each computational process symbol in computational verb systems is a dynamic system, adverbs cannot be modeled as static maps. This makes computational verb systems very flexible but also makes them very difficult to study. In this section we give a general framework for the relation between adverbs and verbs in computational verb systems.

13.5.2 Revisiting English Grammar

Since in this section we provide only the relevant parts of the elements of English grammar for the purpose of computational verb systems, it is neither a rigorous nor a complete linguistic statement. Details and exceptions to English grammar rules would disturb the central idea; thus the statements in this section are, in the main, correct. As mentioned before, there are two grammar centers in English: noun and verb.

A noun*[10] *is the name of anything [48]. Anything can be an object of thought, whether this object has life or is without it, is material or immaterial, is real or imaginary. In a word, every object that we can think about, whether or not it has an existence, is a thing whose name is a noun.

A verb*[11] *is a word with which we can make an assertion [48]. What is asserted is either an *action* or a *state*. However, English grammar books do not tell the reader how the "action" happens or where the "state" comes from, because all these *dynamics* are defaulted as the shared experiences of all human beings who use the same language [34]. Unfortunately, since today's computers are totally different from people, they cannot truly appreciate the essence of language. Yes, we can use a database to built an entire dictionary into a computer. We can use mathematical linguistics [19] to build a grammar into a computer. But where are the defaulted experiences that are shared by human beings? The evolution of language is closely connected to the biological evolution of the human species [5], so how should we evolve computer language while the hardware evolution of computers is subject to Moore's law [42]? What should our computers share when they are globally connected and form a virtual "society" [14]? We need to build verbs into computers.

[10]Noun stems from the Latin *nomen*, which means a *name*

[11]Verb stems from the Latin *verbum*, which means a *word*.

We use *transitive verbs* to indicate actions directed toward objects, and we use *intransitive verbs* to indicate either actions not directed toward objects, or states. In fact, since a state is a static entry, it can be well defined by classical AI and fuzzy logic. In computational verb systems, only verbs dealing with actions are studied because "actions" embed "dynamics."

No sentence can be constructed without involving a noun, or something equivalent to a noun, expressed or implied, and a verb, also expressed or implied. In a sentence, nouns indicate things about which the statement is made, and verbs indicate the ways that the statement is made.

An adjective is a word that is used with a noun to limit its applications. Adjectives are classified into three groups as follows: (1) *adjective of quality*, (2) *adjective of quantity*, and (3) *demonstrative adjectives*.

An adverb is a word that modifies the meanings of a verb, adjective, or other adverb [48]. Adverbs are used to express variations in the manners and conditions under which verbs indicate actions.

Since adjectives denote attributes some of which vary in degree, adverbs can be applied to adjectives to indicate this variation. Adverbs can only apply to some (not all) adjectives. On the other hand, only some adverbs can be applied to adjectives. For example, adverbs of time, place, and manner cannot be used to qualify adjectives, although they qualify verbs. The same happens when adverbs are used to qualify other adverbs.

Although adverbs can be classified on three different principles [48], in computational verb systems, they are classified according to their meanings.

1. Time
   (a) *When?* today, tonight, yesterday, soon, then, ...
   (b) *How long?* always, forever, ...
   (c) *How often?* monthly, yearly, rarely, usually, ...
2. Place
   (a) *Where?* there, above, below, here, ...
   (b) *Whence?* hence, thence, ...
   (c) *Whither?* hither, thither, ...
   (d) *In what order?* first, finally, last, ...
3. Degree, or quantity: *How much?* little, exactly, ...
4. Manner, or quality: *How?* well, ill, bravely, ...
5. Certainty: not, perhaps, ...
6. Reason and consequence: why, therefore, thus, ...

13.5.3 Formal Definitions of Computational Verb and Computational Process Symbol

In Sections 13.3 and 13.4 we have a qualitative description of computational verbs and their computations. To set up a good framework for computational verb systems, we need to define computational verbs quantitatively because computational verbs are basic building blocks of computational verb systems. As the primary concept of computational verb systems, a computational verb is generally defined as a dynamical process associated with brain dynamics—even connected to the unconscious dynamics of human brains.

The formal definition of computational verbs is based on human cognitive structures because nature languages are only simulations of these structures. Since evolution of human cognitive structures are shaped by the environment, evolution of human language is also shaped by the environment [5]. A human being experiences a space spanned by time, physical space, and perception. Time is one-dimensional and physical space is three-dimensional for normal human beings. None of us know the dimension of our perception [43].

Definition 13.1: Computational Verb [57–64]. A computational verb α is defined by an evolving system, an inner system and an outer system as follows:

1. The *evolving system*, $\mathscr{E}_\alpha$, summarizes α as a whole:

$$\mathscr{E}_\alpha = [T, X_s, X_p, \mathscr{I}_\alpha, \mathscr{F}_\alpha], \tag{13.60}$$

   where $T \subset \mathbb{R}$, $X_s \subset \mathbb{R}^3$, and $X_p \subset \mathbb{R}^k$ are the time, three-dimensional physical space, and perception, respectively. The evolving system is an inner representation of a verb in a human brain.
2. The *inner system*

$$\mathscr{I}_\alpha : T \times X_s \times X_p \mapsto T \times X_s \times X_p \tag{13.61}$$

   models the self-reflection of a human being. If a brain wants to know the inner representation of a verb in another brain, communication between the two brains should be set up. To make communication possible, each evolving system must have outputs, which are described by
3. The *outer system*

$$\mathscr{F}_\alpha : T \times X_s \times X_p \mapsto T' \times X_s' \times X_p', \tag{13.62}$$

   where $T' \subset \mathbb{R}$, $X_s' \subset \mathbb{R}^3$, and $X_p' \subset \mathbb{R}^l$ are the "observed" or "expressed" time, three-dimensional physical space, and perception obtained by the observing brain, which is usually (not necessarily) different from the observed brain. The observing brain can find the outputs of $\mathscr{E}_\alpha$ from a visual medium (facial expression, gesture, etc.), sounds (speech, music, etc.), chemical agencies (smell, taste, etc.), and mechanical sensations (touch, tap, etc.).

Remark: The time, three-dimensional physical space, and perception may be any kind of set because all mathematical abstractions are reflections of human perceptions. They may be discrete, continuous, crisp, fuzzy, or hybrid.

Definition 13.2: *Computational Process (Action) Symbol.* A computational process (action) symbol α is defined by the following outer system:

$$\mathscr{F}_{\alpha} : T \times X_s \times X_p \mapsto T' \times X'_s \times X'_p, \tag{13.63}$$

where $T \subset \mathbb{R}, X_s \subset \mathbb{R}^3$, and $X_p \subset \mathbb{R}^k$ are the time, three-dimensional physical space, and perception, respectively. $T' \subset \mathbb{R}$, $X'_s \subset \mathbb{R}^3$, and $X'_p \subset \mathbb{R}^l$ are the "observed" or "expressed" time, three-dimensional physical space, and perception obtained by the observing brain, which is usually (not necessarily) different from the observed brain.

Remark: Observe from Definitions 13.1 and 13.2 that a computational verb degrades to a computational process (action) symbol when the inner system is dead. This is a very straightforward way to denote that a *symbol* does not have a "brain" or "machinself." We usually assume that a computational verb does have a brain or machinself behind it. However, in this chapter I use a computational process symbol to represent both concepts.

Since computational process symbols in computational verb systems are dynamic systems, the computation in computational verb systems must be handled as the relationship between dynamical systems. There are two ways to tame a dynamic system; the first one is to control it [58], the second is to modify it. To modify a computational process symbol, we need adverbs just like those used in the English language.

13.5.4 Adverbs and Their Models

Since adverbs modify computational process symbols, we can define an adverb as a general operator in the evolving systems of computational process symbols within the same brain or over the outer system when observed from outside. Give an adverb β, which is used to modify a computational process symbol α, the modified computational process symbol $\beta \circ \alpha$ is given as follows:

1. Evolving system

$$\Psi_{\beta} \circ \mathscr{E}_{\alpha} = [T, X_s, X_p, \mathscr{I}_{\alpha}, \mathscr{F}_{\alpha}, \Psi_{\beta}], \tag{13.64}$$

where the *modifying system* of the adverb β is given by

$$\Psi_{\beta} : T \times X_s \times X_p \mapsto T^{\Psi} \times X_s^{\Psi} \times X_p^{\Psi}, \tag{13.65}$$

which is the model of the modifying effect of the adverb β within the same brain. $T^{\Psi} \subset \mathbb{R}$, $X_s^{\Psi} \subset \mathbb{R}^3$, and $X_p^{\Psi} \subset \mathbb{R}^m$ are the *modified* time, three-dimensional physical space, and perception, respectively.

2. Outer system

$$\Phi_{\beta} \circ \mathscr{F}_{\alpha} : T \times X_s \times X_p \mapsto T^{\Phi} \times X_s^{\Phi} \times X_p^{\Phi} \tag{13.66}$$

where the *modifying function* of the adverb β is given by

$$\Phi_{\beta} : T' \times X'_s \times X'_p \mapsto T^{\Phi} \times X_s^{\Phi} \times X_p^{\Phi}, \tag{13.67}$$

which is the model of the modifying effect of the adverb β outside the brain, which generates verb α. $T^{\Phi} \subset \mathbb{R}$, $X_s^{\Phi} \subset \mathbb{R}^3$, and $X_p^{\Phi} \subset \mathbb{R}^n$ are the *modified* observed time, three-dimensional physical space, and perception, respectively.

There are two kinds of adverbs that can be explicitly represented by modifying functions with clear physical meanings: time adverbs and place adverbs. A *time adverb* is defined as an adverb concerned with time, and a *place adverb* is defined as an adverb concerned with three-dimensional physical space. For many other adverbs, the situation may be very complex if they are concerned with perceptions. We call adverbs concerned with perceptions *perception adverbs*.

Remark: Observe that the classification of adverbs according to their meanings as presented in Section 13.5.2 is different from that according to different spaces. In actual applications, the contexts may impose important criteria on the classification of a certain adverb because many adverbs can be perception adverbs in some contexts but time adverbs or place adverbs in other contexts.

Adverbs Concerning Time. For time adverbs, the modifying effect in (13.64) and (13.66) is degraded into the following form:

1. Evolving system

$$\Psi_\beta \circ \mathscr{E}_\alpha = [T, X_s, X_p, \mathscr{I}_\alpha, \mathscr{F}_\alpha, \psi_\beta], \tag{13.68}$$

where

$$\psi_\beta : T \mapsto T^{\psi} \tag{13.69}$$

is the modifying system.

2. Outer system

$$\phi_\beta \circ \mathscr{F}_\alpha : T \times X_s \times X_p \mapsto T^{\phi} \times X_s' \times X_p', \tag{13.70}$$

where

$$\phi_\beta : T' \mapsto T^{\phi} \tag{13.71}$$

is the modifying function.

Examples. Let the time period of a day be $\Delta = 24$ hours and the origin of time be chosen at 0 hours today; then if at time t one says:

I met Tom **yesterday**.

the corresponding modifying function can be written as

$$\phi_{\text{yesterday}}(t) : [0, t) \mapsto [-\Delta, 0) \tag{13.72}$$

where $\phi_{\text{yesterday}}(t)$ is a time-varying map. This kind of time adverb just transfers the time period from one to the other. Since the time in daily life can also be characterized as a fuzzy variable, this kind of time adverb can also be used to transfer crisp time to fuzzy time, fuzzy time to crisp time, or fuzzy time to fuzzy time.

The second kind of time adverb provides a different modification. For example, consider the following sentence:

I **often** meet Tom.

The corresponding modifying function can be written as

$$\phi_{\text{often}} : t \mapsto a \times t, \tag{13.73}$$

where $0 \leq a \leq 1$ is a scaling factor. This modifier rescales the time axis such that every time interval is shrunken. The resulting effect is that events along the time axis became denser—thus "often." If one wants to say

I meet Tom **very often**.

the corresponding modifying function can be written as

$$\phi_{\text{very often}} : t \mapsto b \times t, \tag{13.74}$$

where $0 < b \ll a < 1$ is a scaling factor. Although we use two constant scaling factors to denote "**often**" and "**very often**," in many cases, the scaling factors may be functions of time or even three-dimensional physical space and perception.

Adverbs Concerning Place. For place adverbs, the modifying effect in (13.64) and (13.66) is degraded into the following form:

1. Evolving system

$$\Psi_\beta \circ \mathscr{E}_\alpha = [T, X_s, X_p, \mathscr{I}_\alpha, \mathscr{F}_\alpha, \Psi_\beta] \tag{13.75}$$

   where

$$\Psi_\beta : X_s \mapsto X_s^\Psi \tag{13.76}$$

   is the modifying system.

2. Outer system

$$\Phi_\beta \circ \mathscr{F}_\alpha : T \times X_s \times X_p \mapsto T' \times X_s^\Phi \times X_p' \tag{13.77}$$

   where

$$\Phi_\beta : T' \times X_s' \times X_p' \mapsto T' \times X_s^\Phi \times X_p' \tag{13.78}$$

   is the modifying function.

This kind of adverb transfers the occurring position of verbs from one place to another. This can be expressed explicitly by either crisp mathematics or fuzzy mathematics. To save space, no example is given.

Adverbs Concerning Perception. Since the perception is so complex, the evolving systems and the outer systems of perception adverbs are kept the same in (13.64) and (13.66). Let us consider the following examples.

Mary and Tom *understand* each other.

In this case, we model *understand* as a generalized synchronization [58] process between two Lorenz systems [31], The state equation of a Lorenz system is given by

$$\begin{aligned}\dot{x} &= -\sigma x + \sigma y \\ \dot{y} &= rx - y - xz \\ \dot{z} &= xy - bz,\end{aligned} \tag{13.79}$$

where $\sigma = 10$, $r = 28$, and $b = 8/3$ are three parameters; x, y, and z are state variables.

To make the verb computation well defined, let us first assume the context of the verb. Suppose that Mary and Tom is in a progress of conversation, they both share and contribute to this conversation, and their evolving systems are mutually coupled. This is modeled by the following two mutually coupled Lorenz systems.

1. The inner system of the evolving system of Mary's *understand* is given by

$$\mathscr{I}^{\text{Mary}}_{\text{understand}} = \begin{cases} \dot{x} = & -\sigma x + \sigma y + k(\tilde{x} - x) \\ \dot{y} = & rx - y - xz + k(\tilde{y} - y) \\ \dot{z} = & xy - bz + k(\tilde{z} - z)\,, \end{cases}$$

   where k is used to model the mutual influence between two verbs (Mary's *understand* and Tom's *understand*). x, y, and z are three state variables of Mary's evolving system: $\tilde{x}$, $\tilde{y}$ and $\tilde{z}$ are state variables of Tom's evolving system. This implies that Tom's outer system, which is communicated to Mary, is

$$\mathscr{F}^{\text{Tom}}_{\text{understand}} = k\tilde{\mathbf{x}} = k\begin{pmatrix}\tilde{x} \\ \tilde{y} \\ \tilde{z}\end{pmatrix}. \tag{13.81}$$

2. The inner system of the evolving system of Tom's *understand* is given by

$$\mathscr{I}^{\text{Tom}}_{\text{understand}} = \begin{cases} \dot{\tilde{x}} = & -\sigma\tilde{x} + \sigma\tilde{y} + k(x - \tilde{x}) \\ \dot{\tilde{y}} = & r\tilde{x} - \tilde{y} - \tilde{x}\tilde{z} + k(y - \tilde{y}) \\ \dot{\tilde{z}} = & \tilde{x}\tilde{y} - b\tilde{z} + k(z - \tilde{z})\,. \end{cases} \tag{13.82}$$

Similarly, Tom's evolving system implies that Mary's outer system, which is communicated to Tom, is

$$\mathscr{F}^{\text{Mary}}_{\text{understand}} = k\mathbf{x} = k\begin{pmatrix} x \\ y \\ z \end{pmatrix}. \tag{13.83}$$

Since there is no adverbs/adverbials to modify *understand*, this kind of *understand* can be very general and loose. For example, in Figure 13.18*a* the relationship between these two evolving systems is shown. They are in a generalized synchronization status [50], which is very loose. Note that when both Mary and Tom go to topics that both evolving systems change smoothly, they can achieve good understanding [an almost identical time period [20,25] (time units)]. But if they go to topics that their evolving systems change rapidly, local misunderstandings may occur, such as those involving the time period [27,33] (time units). The time period [0,5] (time units) is the process of building understanding between Tom and Mary. In this case, the coupling $k = 0.35$ is used.

If we want to modify the *understand* by adverbs concerned with the degree of understanding, we may use the following sentence:

Mary and Tom *understand* each other **well**.

In this example, the modifying function of **well**, Ψ_{well}, can be explicitly assumed to be a function

$$\Psi_{\text{well}} \circ \mathscr{F} = \psi_{\text{well}}(t) \times \mathscr{F}, \tag{13.84}$$

where $\psi_{\text{well}}(t) \in \mathbb{R}$ is a scalar. In (13.84) we assume that the *understand* in this conversation is affected only by time. Figure 13.18*b* shows the example when $\psi_{\text{well}}(t) = 0.5/0.35$. Although this is also a kind of generalized synchronization, the time period of misunderstanding is much shorter than that shown in Figure 13.18*a*. Misunderstandings probably happen at moments when both brains were subjected to sudden changes. This implies that either the vagueness of our perception (e.g., fuzziness in language expressions, facial expressions, voice tones, and postures) or the uncertainty of conversation topics (e.g., explanation of a complex phenomenon using different descriptions) can create more misunderstanding. The time period for building understanding between Tom and Mary is shorter than that in Figure 13.18*a*.

Moreover, if we want to modify *understand* further, we can use the following sentence:

Mary and Tom *understand* each other **very well**.

Similarly, we choose the modifying function as follows:

$$\Psi_{\text{very well}} \circ \mathscr{F} = \psi_{\text{very well}}(t) \times \mathscr{F} \tag{13.85}$$

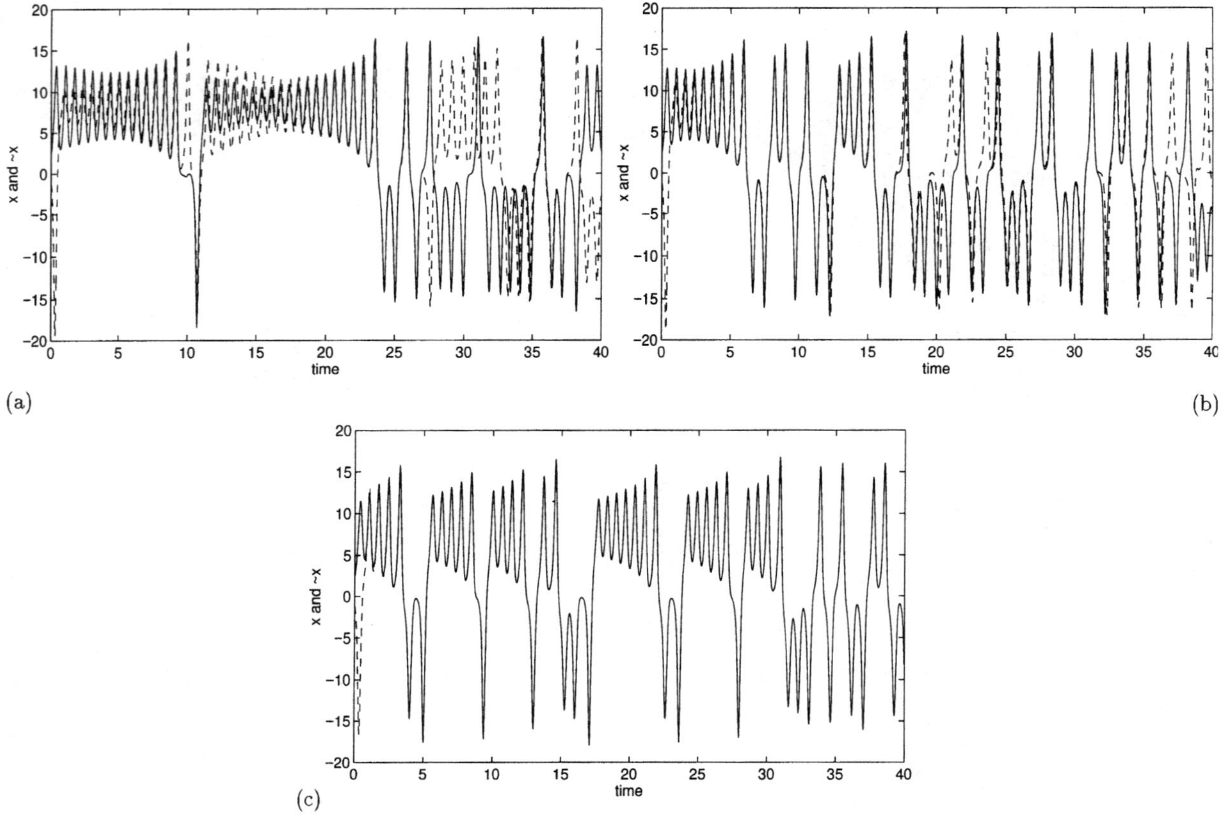

FIGURE 13.18. Examples of adverbs concerned with perception: (*a*) *understand*; (*b*) *understand* well; (*c*) *understand* very well. In this figure, only the first state variables of both evolving systems are shown. The solid lines denote $x(t)$ and the dashed lines denote $\tilde{x}(t)$.

where $\psi_{\text{very well}}(t) = 1.0/0.35$. The simulation result is shown in Figure 13.18*c*. In this case an identical synchronization is achieved.[12] This is perfect understanding. Also, the time period for building understanding between Tom and Mary is shorter than that in Figure 13.18*b*.

13.5.5 Applications to Speech Recognition

Communication between human beings is dominated by speech and hearing [1,18]. Sight and the other modalities are also used, but the immediate transfer of complex information relies heavily on speech. The human speech system is a very complex mechanical system driven by airflow. This complexity provides us with various manners of expressing our emotions and linguistic flows. On the other hand, this complexity imposes a very big difficulty in machine speech recognition. Psychological and physiological evidence shows that the dynamic features of the speech spectrum and the speech waveform over time intervals of 2 to 3 ms and 20 to 50 ms play crucially important roles in speech recognition [18]. However, almost all speech analysis methods assume the stationarity of the speech signal. To invent new speech analysis methods, transitional or dynamic features should be used.

As we have seen in Refs. 57, 58, and 60, the computational verb systems stemmed from the complexities and dynamics, and it is then reasonable to find applications of verb computation to speech recognition. In this section, examples are presented to show the application to Chinese speech recognition of verb computation with adverbs.

Without loss of generality, a speech signal is denoted by $s(t)$. For processing purposes, $s(t)$ is sampled by a 12-bit analog-to-digital (A/D) converter at a sampling rate of 8 kHz. In this section, computational verb rules for preprocessing speech signal are provided to demonstrate how to design verb rules with adverbs. The computational verb rule of speech recognition is very simple for a human being and can be given as follows:

You *hear* what that person *speak*s.

To make an operational computational verb rule, we should define a *reference system* to represent the machine itself; then the rule is rewritten for a computer as follows:

The reference system *hear*s what that person *speak*s.

In this sense, the reference system is a simplified version of a human brain. The beauty of verb computation is that the brain model can be anything, regardless of the biological evidence because to solve the engineering problem is the first priority of this model. In the verb rule above, there are two verbs, *speak* and *hear*. The reference system does not know the evolving system of *speak*, $\mathscr{E}_{\text{speak}}$. However, the outer system of *speak* is measured as the speech signal: namely, $\mathscr{F}_{\text{speak}} = s(t)$. The

[12]This can be proved rigorously.

inner system of *hear* is modeled by the following three coupled Chua circuits [8]:

$$\mathscr{I}_{\text{hear}} = \left\{ \begin{array}{l} \left\{ \begin{array}{l} \dfrac{dv_{11}}{dt} = \dfrac{1}{C_1}[G(v_{12} - v_{11}) - f(v_{11}) + Ks(t)] \\ \dfrac{dv_{12}}{dt} = \dfrac{1}{C_2}[G(v_{11} - v_{12}) + i_{13}] \\ \dfrac{di_{13}}{dt} = \dfrac{1}{L}(-v_{12} - R_0 i_{13}) \end{array} \right. \\ \left\{ \begin{array}{l} \dfrac{dv_{21}}{dt} = \dfrac{1}{C_1}[G(v_{22} - v_{21}) - f(v_{21}) + v_{11}] \\ \dfrac{dv_{22}}{dt} = \dfrac{1}{C_2}[G(v_{21} - v_{22}) + i_{23}] \\ \dfrac{di_{23}}{dt} = \dfrac{1}{L}(-v_{22} - R_0 i_{23}) \end{array} \right. \\ \left\{ \begin{array}{l} \dfrac{dv_{31}}{dt} = \dfrac{1}{C_1}[G(v_{32} - v_{31}) - f(v_{31}) + v_{21}] \\ \dfrac{dv_{32}}{dt} = \dfrac{1}{C_2}[G(v_{31} - v_{32}) + i_{33}] \\ \dfrac{di_{33}}{dt} = \dfrac{1}{L}(-v_{32} - R_0 i_{33}), \end{array} \right. \end{array} \right. \tag{13.86}$$

where

$$f(v_1) = G_b v_1 + \tfrac{1}{2}(G_a - G_b)(|v_1 + E| - |v_1 - E|). \tag{13.87}$$

The parameters are $C_1 = 5.56 \times 10^{-9}$, $C_2 = 50 \times 10^{-9}$, $G = 7 \times 10^{-4}$, $L = 7.14 \times 10^{-3}$, $R_0 = 0$, $G_a = -8 \times 10^{-4}$, $G_b = -5 \times 10^{-4}$, and $E = 1$. $K = 10^{-12}$ is the sensation scaling factor. A fourth-order Runge–Kutta method, with a fixed step size of 10^{-6}, is used in the simulations. The initial conditions are

$$\begin{pmatrix} v_{11}(0) \\ v_{12}(0) \\ i_{13}(0) \end{pmatrix} = \begin{pmatrix} v_{21}(0) \\ v_{22}(0) \\ i_{23}(0) \end{pmatrix} = \begin{pmatrix} v_{31}(0) \\ v_{32}(0) \\ i_{33}(0) \end{pmatrix} = \begin{pmatrix} -0.2 \\ -0.2 \\ -0.001 \end{pmatrix}. \tag{13.88}$$

In this case, the time, (physical space), perception space $[t, X_s, X_p]$ of *hear* is spanned by

$$t, \begin{pmatrix} v_{11}(t) \\ v_{12}(t) \\ i_{13}(t) \end{pmatrix}, \begin{pmatrix} v_{21}(t) \\ v_{22}(t) \\ i_{23}(t) \end{pmatrix}, \begin{pmatrix} v_{31}(t) \\ v_{32}(t) \\ i_{33}(t) \end{pmatrix}, s(t),\ K, \begin{pmatrix} C_1 \\ C_2 \\ G \\ L \\ R_0 \\ G_a \\ G_b \\ E \end{pmatrix}. \tag{13.89}$$

Observe that the time appears explicitly while the three-dimensional physical space and perception are mixed. This means that the three-dimensional physical space information is either defaulted or ignored when we say *hear.* Since *hear* is a sensation verb [29], the speech signal is plugged directly into the inner function in (13.86) scaled by a sensation scaling factor K.

The outer system of *hear* is given by

$$\mathscr{F}_{\text{hear}} = i_{13} - i_{33}, \tag{13.90}$$

which will be used by other computational verbs or other conventional digital signal processing blocks. We can then conclude that the evolving system of *hear* of the reference system, $\mathscr{E}_{\text{hear}}$, is defined by the space defined in (13.89), the inner system in (13.86), and the outer system in (13.90). The forgoing statements are used to give the reader an impression of what an *actual* evolving system looks like.

The simulation results of this verb rule are shown in Figure 13.19. For demonstration purposes, speech samples of two female Chinese are used. Observe from Figure 13.19 that the outer system of the verb *hear* is similar to a (nonlinear) low-pass-filtered version of the speech signal. The main goal of this preprocess is to make the similarity of $\mathscr{F}_{\text{hear}}$'s of the same sound from different persons as large as possible, while the difference in $\mathscr{F}_{\text{hear}}$'s of different sounds stays significantly large. However, the output results (the outer systems of *hear*) in Figure 13.19 are not good because there exist significant differences between $\mathscr{F}_{\text{hear}}$'s of the same sound from different persons. Different speaking speeds are attributed to this kind of difference. Observe from Figure 13.19 that person A speaks each sound much slower than person B does, which causes the outputs of the corresponding outer systems to have different time scales. To overcome this problem, we would like to make the time scales of different speech signals as similar as possible. To do this, we need to add time adverbs and perception adverbs to modify verbs in the computational verb rule, as follows:

The reference system *hear*s what that person *speak*s.$\Longrightarrow$
When the person *speak*s **fast**, the reference system *hear*s **carefully**.
When the person *speak*s **slowly**, the reference system *hear*s **casually**.
When the person *speak*s **normally**, the reference system *hear*s **normally**$_h$.

Here we need to combine two verbs, *speak* and *hear*, with five adverbs, **fast**, **slowly**, **carefully**, **normally**, and **casually**. Since the evolving system of *speak* is inaccessible, what the computer can sense is the (modified) outer system of *speak*: namely, the sampled speech signal $s(t)$. In this sense, $s(t)$ is given by

$$s(t) = \Phi_\beta \circ \mathscr{F}_{\text{speak}}, \tag{13.91}$$

where β is any of **slowly, normally**, and **fast**. Then we face an inverse problem: how to find the adverb β from the modified outer system $s(t)$. Since all three adverbs are time adverbs, we can use a very simple criterion to solve this inverse problem by

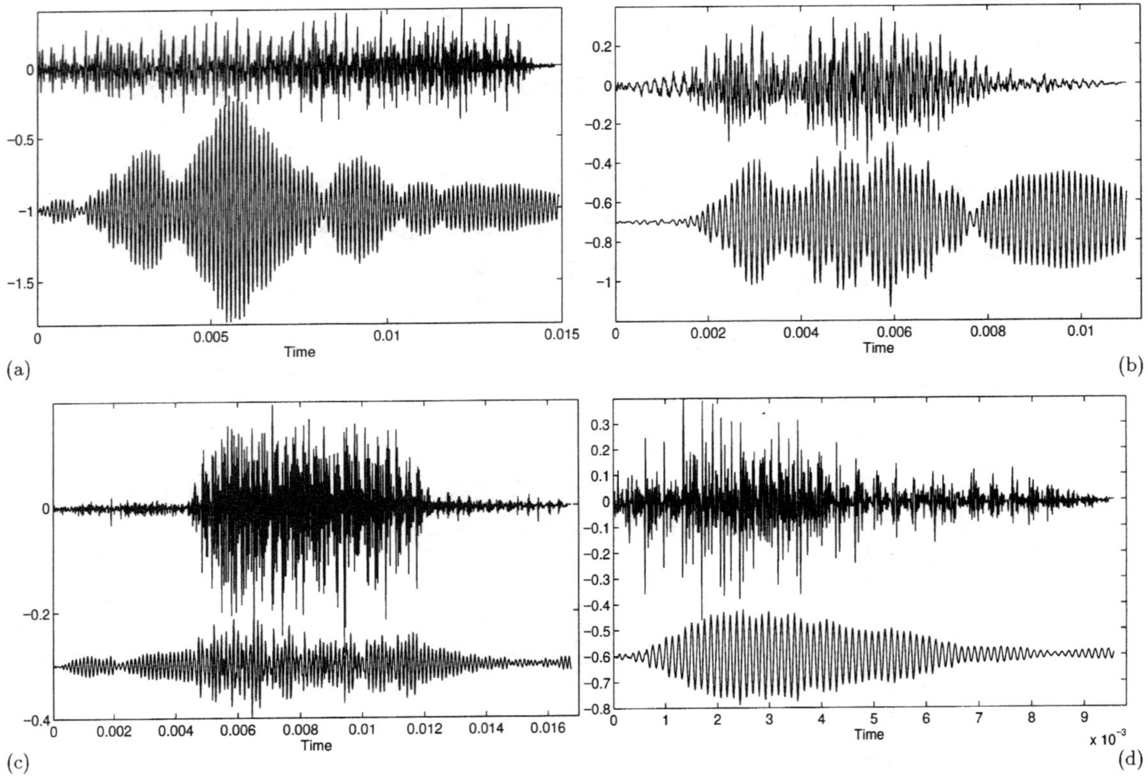

FIGURE 13.19. Outer systems of the verb *hear* for different speech signals: (*a*) speech sample of Chinese *yi* (Chinese 1) from person A; (*b*) speech sample of Chinese *yi* (Chinese 1) from person B; (*c*) speech sample of Chinese *san* (Chinese 3) from person A; (*d*) speech sample of Chinese *san* (Chinese 3) from person B. The simple verb rule without adverbs is used. In each figure the upper trace shows the speech signal $s(t)$ and the lower trace shows the outer system of verb *hear*.

measuring the time duration of the speech signal $s(t)$. The corresponding results are provided in Table 13.1.

Unfortunately, since $s(t)$ is a recorded sampled time sequence with a fixed sampling rate, we have to interpolate some points between two samples if the person speaks fast. To do this, we make the *time constant* of the *hear* bigger such that more sampling points can be obtained by using a fixed number of samples of $s(t)$ and a fixed sampling rate of $\mathscr{F}_{\text{hear}}$. The method of changing the time constant of Chua's circuit can be found in Ref. [26]. Only three sets of parameters are used to model the modifying systems of the adverbs **carefully**, **normally**, and **casually**. In this case, the modifying system of an adverb β is given by

$$\Psi_\beta \circ \mathscr{E}_{\text{hear}} : C_1 = \lambda \times 5.56 \times 10^{-9}, C_2 = \lambda \times 50 \times 10^{-9}, L = \lambda \times 7.14 \times 10^{-3}, \tag{13.92}$$

where $\lambda > 0$ is the factor of time scale. Observe that the modifying system of the adverb β provides parameters adapting laws to the evolving system of *hear*. This is also an example to show that the relation between verbs and adverbs can be very general. The corresponding parameters for different adverbs of *hear* are listed in Table 13.2.

The simulation results of computational verb rule with adverbs are shown in Figure 13.20. By inspecting Figure 13.19 and Table 13.1, we find that person A speaks *yi* **normally**, person B speaks *yi* **fast**, person A speaks *san* **slowly**, person B speaks *san* **fast**. Then by checking the computational verb rule and Table 13.2, the reference system should *hear* the *yi* from person A **normally** (the result is the same as that in Figure 13.19*a* and copied in Figure 13.20*a*), the *yi* from person B **carefully** (the result is shown in Figure 13.20*b*), the *san* from person A **casually** (the result is shown in Figure 13.20*c*), and the *san* from person B **carefully** (the result is shown in Figure 13.20*d*). Comparing the results in Figure 13.19 and 13.20 we find that the preprocessing results become much better when adverbs are used in computational verb rules.

Of course, the computational verb systems presented in this section are only preprocessing blocks of an actual speech recognition system. They can be viewed intuitively as a kind of "chaotic filter." However, to understand this kind of chaotic filter

TABLE 13.1. Look-up Table for the Inverse Problem of the Verb *speak*

Time duration of $s(t)$	<0.013	$[0.013, 0.015]$	>0.015
Adverb β for *speak*	**fast**	**normally**	**slowly**

TABLE 13.2. Look-up Table for the Adverbs Used to Modify the Verb *hear*

Adverb β for *hear*	**carefully**	**normally$_{\mathbf{h}}$**	**casually**
Time scaling factor λ	18/13	1	10/13

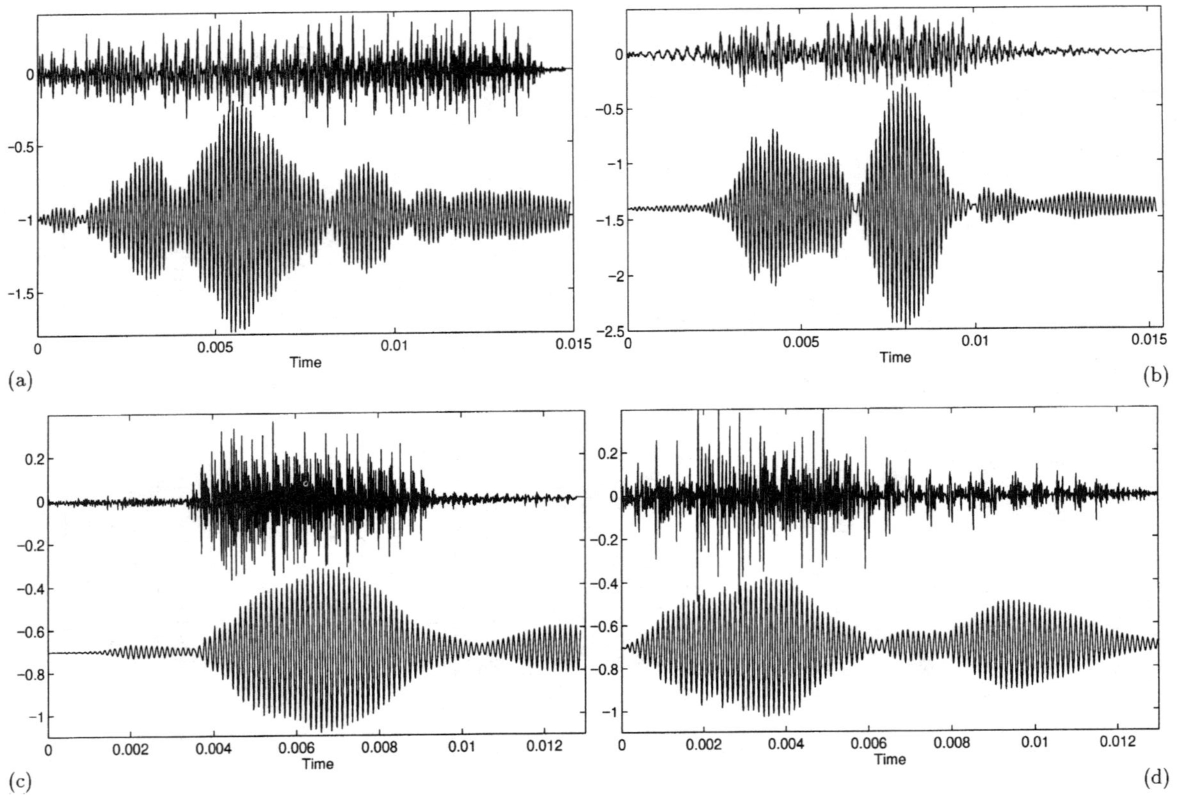

FIGURE 13.20. Outer systems of verb *hear* for different speech signals. (*a*) speech sample of Chinese *yi* (Chinese 1) from person A modified by adverb **normally**; (*b*) speech sample of Chinese *yi* (Chinese 1) from person B modified by adverb **carefully**; (*c*) speech sample of Chinese *san* (Chinese 3) from person B modified by adverb **casually**; (*d*) speech sample of Chinese *san* (Chinese 3) from person B modified by adverb **carefully**. The verb is modified by different adverbs. In each figure the upper trace shows the original speech signal and the lower trace shows the outer system of the verb *hear*.

is a very advanced topic in today's science of complexity because it is hyperchaos. The outputs of these computational verb systems are then fed into some characteristic-extraction blocks, such as a linear predictive coding (LPC) block, and some pattern processing blocks, such as hidden Markov models (HMMs). The main function of this kind of computational verb system is to exploit chaotic information processing technology, which is a sort of "stochastic resonance" [65], to find new features in speech signals. Thus the method presented here is a compensation for conventional methods.

13.6 CONCLUSIONS

The linguistic description of complexity is a well-developed strategy for human beings to survive circumstantial complexities. Besides fuzzy theory, which can characterize beings in our linguistic statements, we still need a theoretic framework for characterizing becomings. This is systematic consideration of the invention of computational verb systems. Humans have survived different kinds of complexities in nature for a long time and have developed linguistic systems for handling these complexities which are far beyond the capability of modern science. It would be very useful to characterize linguistic systems and use *artificial linguistic systems* to help cope with the complexities. A combination of fuzzy theory and computational verb systems can result in such artificial linguistic systems.

In English grammar there are two grammar centers: nouns and verbs [48]. In fact, in all human natural languages found on earth, nouns and verbs are two kinds of elementary elements [17]. Nouns are *things*, which are *found* or *perceived* by humans, and verbs are *words*, which are *generated* by or *acted* on by humans. Nouns provide the context of the existence of our inner (mental) and outer worlds while verbs provide the relations and dynamics of nouns. Verbs represent the dynamical experiences of humans. To embed into machines dynamical experiences coded by verbs, verbs are modeled explicitly and quantitatively by dynamical systems called *computational verbs*. In ordinary artificial intelligence, any word is treated as a static entry. A computational process symbol used in symbolic logic loses its dynamics and thus degrades into a *symbolic verb* [33].

By using computational verb systems, we can embed our dynamical knowledge and experiences into machine intelligence. This strategy benefits sciences in two ways: (1) we can build a machine that can produce artificial complexities, and (2) it will ease communication between human experts and machines by sharing experiences. Although we cannot hope that a machine has the same "feeling" regarding a certain experience as that of a human expert [36], the qualitatively related nature of these two experiences should be helpful in developing a new generation of expert systems. The backbone behind computational verb systems is pattern thinking [11], which is used very efficiently by human brains. So far, the purpose of computational verb systems has been to set an interface between the dynamic aspect of computational verb systems and the static technical reality of digital computers, which are based on Boolean logic.

As a substantial axiom of many computation frameworks, equality is the most important building block. In classical computations, equality is used as a mental construct, an idealized operation. However, since verb computation itself copes with the mental world of human beings idealized equality loses its validity. Instead, dynamic verb equalities can reflect the real aspects of processes, encoded by verbs such as *feel, know, be like*, and *understand.* Verb equalities are dynamic relations which allow for variety and richness in the context of different (machine) personalities for modeling the same objects (experiences). I believe that these kinds of varieties can introduce machine personality [14] (*machinality*) into machine intelligence. Although in this chapter I use the well-established synchronizing theory of dynamic (chaotic) systems to model verb equality, I am afraid that synchronization is not the only way that nature copes with this kind of phenomenon.

Based on an understanding of verb equality, we can develop a framework of verb computation. Direct application of this kind of verb computation is the next generation of machine intelligence, which should have a core called *machinself* ("machine itself"). At first hearing, giving a machine a *self* sounds uncomfortable to humans. But it is the price we have to pay if we want our machines to have *creativity.* This kind of creativity is neither something that can be programmed, as in classical AI, nor something that can be learned, as current artificial neural networks do, but something *generated* by *machinself.*

The computation of verbs is not only the relation between beings and becomings, but also that among becomings. The invention of adverbs is a very smart way to compress the total number of verbs needed in a language system. From this point of view, all adverb + verb structures can be treated as composite verbs. We can define computation between adverbs and verbs by treating adverbs as modifiers. Adverbs are much more advanced than simple static functions. They can modify the evolving systems of verbs at different levels. For example, they can modify not only the outputs of evolving systems, but also the parameters or structures of evolving systems. Although the principles presented in this chapter are based on uncollapsed verbs, the relation between adverbs and verbs can also be used in collapsed verbs.

REFERENCES

1. W. A. Ainsworth, *Speech Recognition by Machine*, Vol. 12 of IEE Computing series, Peregrinus on behalf of the Institution of Electrical Engineers, London, 1988.
2. I. Aleksander, *The Human Machine: A View of Intelligent Mechanisms*, Georgi, St. Saphorin, Switzerland; distributed by Renouf, New York; 1978.
3. U. Backlund, *The Collocation of Adverbs of Degree in English*, Uppsala, Sweden, 1973.
4. D. D. Bainov and P. S. Simeonov. *Systems with Impulsive Effect: Stability, Theory and Applications*, Ellis Horwood, Chichester, West Sussex, 1989.
5. B. H. Bichakjian, *Evolution in Language*, Vol. 18 of Linguistica Extranea Studia, Karoma, Ann Arbor, MI, 1988.

6. S. G. Cao and N. W. Rees, Identification of dynamic fuzzy models, *Fuzzy Sets Syst.*, 74(3):307–320, Sept. 29, 1995.
7. M. Chen and D. A. Linkens, Neuro-expert approach to characteristics recognition for process monitoring and performance evaluation, *Int. J. Intell. Syst.*, 12(5):359–377, May 1997.
8. L. O. Chua, Chua's circuit: an overview ten years later, *J. Circuit, Syst. Comput.*, 4(2): 117–159, Jan. 1994.
9. L. O. Chua, T. Yang, G. Q. Zhong, and C. W. Wu, Adaptive synchronization of Chua's oscillators, *Int. J. Bifurcat. Chaos*, 6(1):189–201, Jan. 1996.
10. L. O. Chua, T. Yang, G. Q. Zhong, and C. W. Wu, Synchronization of Chua's circuits with time-varying channels and parameters, *IEEE Trans. Circuits Syst. I: Fundam. Theory Appl.*, 43(10):862–868, Oct. 1996.
11. L. A. Coward, *Pattern Thinking*, Praeger, New York, 1990.
12. D. S. Dabby, Musical variations from a chaotic mapping, *Chaos*, 6(2):95–107, June 1996.
13. H. Dedieu, M. P. Kennedy, and M. Hasler, Chaotic shift keying: modulation and demodulation of chaotic carrier using self-synchronization Chua's circuits, *IEEE Trans. Circuits Syst.* II, 40(10):634–642, Oct. 1993.
14. P. J. Denning, *Beyond Calculation: The Next Fifty Years of Computing*, Copernicus, New York, 1997.
15. D. D. Dixon, F. W. Cummings, and P. E. Kaus, Continuous chaotic dynamics in 2-dimensions, *Physica D*, 65(1/2):109–116, 1993.
16. L. Lam (ed.), *Introduction to Nonlinear Physics*, Springer-Verlag, New York, 1997.
17. V. Fromkin and R. Rodman, *An Introduction to Language*, 5th ed., Harcourt Brace Jovanovich, Forth Worth, TX, 1993.
18. S. Furui, *Digital Speech Processing, Synthesis, and Recognition*, Vol. 55 of Electrical Engineering and Electronics Series, Marcel Dekker, New York, 1989.
19. A. V. Gladkij and I. A. Mel'cuk, *Elements of Mathematical Linguistics*, Vol. 110 of Janua Linguarum Series Maior, Mouton, New York, 1983.
20. J. Guckenheimer and P. Holmes, *Nonlinear Oscillations, Dynamical Systems, and Bifurcations of Vector Fields*, Springer-Verlag, New York, 1983.
21. S. W. Hawking, *A Brief History of Time*, Bantam Books, New York, 1998 (updated and expanded tenth anniversary ed.).
22. M. W. Hirsch and S. Smale, *Differential Equations, Dynamical Systems, and Linear Algebra*, Academic Press, New York, 1974.
23. R. S. Jackendoff, *Consciousness and the Computational Mind*, Vol. 3 of *Explorations in Cognitive Science*, MIT Press, Cambridge, MA, 1987.
24. S. L. Jaki, Words: blocks, amoebas, or patches of fog? Artificial intelligence and the conceptual foundations of fuzzy logic, in *Proc. International Society for Optical Engineering*, Orlando, FL, 1996, Vol. 2761, pp. 138–144.
25. J. A. Jauregui, *The Emotional Computer*, Blackwell, Cambridge, MA, 1995.
26. M. P. Kennedy, Robust OP AMP realization of Chua's circuit, *Frequenz*, 46(3/4):66–80, 1992.
27. V. Lakshmikantham, D. D. Bainov, and P. S. Simeonov, *Theory of Impulsive Differential Equations*, Series in Modern Applied Mathematics, World Scientific, Teaneck, NJ, 1989.

28. J. E. LeDoux, Brain, mind and language, in David A. Oakley (ed.), *Brain and Mind: Psychology in Progress*, Methuen, New York, 1985, pp. 197–216.

29. B. Levin, *English Verb Classes and Alternations: A Preliminary Investigation*, University of Chicago Press, Chicago, 1993.

30. C. T. Lin and C. S. G. Lee, *Neural Fuzzy Systems: A Neuro-Fuzzy Synergism to Intelligent Systems*, Prentice Hall, Upper Saddle River, NJ, 1996.

31. E. N. Lorenz, Deterministic nonperiodic flow, *J. Atmos. Sci.*, 20:130–141, 1963.

32. A. Magnon, *Arrow of Time and Reality: In Search of a Conciliation*, World Scientific, River Edge, NJ 1997.

33. T. J. McKay, *Modern Formal Logic*, Collier Macmillan, New York; Macmillan, London, 1989.

34. D. A. Oakley (ed.), *Brain and Mind: Psychology in Progress*, Methuen, New York, 1985.

35. R. Palm, D. Driankov, and H. Hellendoorn, *Model Based Fuzzy Control: Fuzzy Gain Schedulers and Sliding Mode Fuzzy Controllers*, Springer-Verlag, New York, 1997.

36. R. Penrose, *The Emperor's New Mind: Concerning Computers, Minds, and the Laws*, Oxford University Press, New York, 1989.

37. R. Riedl, *Biology of Knowledge: The Evolutionary Basis of Reason*, Wiley, New York, 1984; Robert Kaspar's translation of *Biologie der Erkenntnis*.

38. X. Rodet, Models of musical instruments from Chua's circuit with time delay, *IEEE Trans. Circuits Syst. II: Analog Digital Signal Process.*, 40(10):696–701, Oct. 1993.

39. X. Rodet, Sound and music from Chua's circuit, *J. Circuits Syst. Comput.*, 3(1):49–61, Mar. 1993.

40. E. T. Rolls, *The Brain and Emotion*, Oxford University Press, New York, 1999.

41. O. E. Rössler, An equation for continuous chaos, *Phys. Lett. A*, 57(5):397–398, 1976.

42. R. R. Schaller, Moore's law: past, present and future, *IEEE Spectrum*, 34(6):52–59, June 1997.

43. G. Simons, *Is Man a Robot?* Wiley, New York, 1986.

44. A. Sloman, *The Computer Revolution in Philosophy: Philosophy, Sicence, and Models of Mind*, Harvester Studies in Cognitive Science, Harvester Press, Hassocks Engineering, Brighton, Essex, England, 1978.

45. T. Toffoli, *Cellular Automata Machines: A New Environment for Modeling*, Series in Scientific Computation, MIT Press, Cambridge, MA, 1987.

46. R. F. Voss and J. Clarke, 1/f noise in music: music from 1/f noise, *J. Acoust. Soc. Am.*, 63:256–263, 1978.

47. H. O. Wang, K. Tanaka, and M. F. Griffin, An approach to fuzzy control of nonlinear systems: stability and design issues, *IEEE Trans. Fuzzy Syst.*, 4(1):14–23, Feb. 1996.

48. A. S. West, *The Elements of English Grammar*, Pitt Press Series, Cambridge University Press, Cambridge, 1901.

49. C. W. Wu, T. Yang, and L. O. Chua, On adaptive synchronization and control of nonlinear dynamical systems, *Int. J. Bifurcat. Chaos*, 6(3):455–471, Mar. 1996.

50. T. Yang and L. O. Chua, Channel-independent chaotic secure communication, *Int. J. Bifurcat. Chaos*, 6(12B):2653–2660, Dec. 1996.

51. T. Yang and L. O. Chua, Secure communication via chaotic parameter modulation, *IEEE Trans. Circuits Syst. I: Fundam. Theory Appl.*, 43(9):817–819, Sept. 1996.

52. T. Yang, C. W. Wu, and L. O. Chua, Cryptography based on chaotic systems, *IEEE Trans. Circuits Syst. I: Fundam. Theory Appl.*, 44(5):469–472, May 1997.
53. T. Yang, C. M. Yang, and L. B. Yang, Break chaotic switching using generalized synchronization: examples, *IEEE Trans. Circuits Syst. I: Fundam. Theory Appl.*, 45(10):1062–1067, Oct. 1998.
54. T. Yang, L. B. Yang, and C. M. Yang, Cryptanalyzing chaotic secure communication using return maps, *Phys. Lett. A*, 245(6):495–510, Aug. 31, 1998.
55. T. Yang, L. B. Yang, and C. M. Yang, Breaking chaotic secure communication using a spectrogram, *Phys. Lett. A*, 247(1/2):105–111, Oct. 5 1998.
56. T. Yang, Recovery of digital signals from chaotic switching, *Int. J. Circuit Theory Appl.*, 23(6):611–615, Nov.–Dec. 1995.
57. T. Yang, *Verbal Paradigms*, Part I; *Modeling with Verbs*, Tech. Rep. Memo. UCB/ERL M97/64, Electronics Research Laboratory, College of Engineering, University of California, Berkeley, CA, Sept. 9, 1997, pp. 1–15.
58. T. Yang, *Verbal Paradigms*, Part II, *Computing with Verbs*, Tech. Rep. Memo. UCB/ERL M97/66, Electronics Research Laboratory, College of Engineering, University of California, Berkeley, CA, Sept. 18, 1997, pp. 1–27.
59. T. Yang, Computational verb systems: adverbs and adverbials as modifiers of verbs, *Inf. Sci.*, 121(1/2):127–148, Dec. 1999.
60. T. Yang, Computational verb systems: modeling with verbs and applications, *Inf. Sci.*, 117(3/4): 147–175, Aug. 1999.
61. T. Yang, Computational verb systems: computing with verbs and applications, *Int. J. Gen. Syst.*, 28(1):1–36, 1999.
62. T. Yang, Computational verb systems: verb logic, *Int. J. Intell. Syst.*, 14(11):1071–1087, Nov. 1999.
63. T. Yang, Computational verb systems: a new paradigm for artificial intelligence, *Inf. Sci.*, 124(1/4): 103–123, May 2000.
64. T. Yang, Computational verb systems: towards a unified paradigm for artificial languages, *Proc. 7th International Conference on Fuzzy Theory and Technology*, Atlantic City, N.J, Feb. 27–Mar. 3, 2000, Vol. 1, pp. 137–140.
65. T. Yang, Optimizing stochastic resonance in visual system, *Phys. Lett. A*, 245(1/2):79–86, Aug. 10, 1998.
66. T. Yang and L. O. Chua, Impulsive control and synchronization of nonlinear dynamical systems and application to secure communication, *Int. J. Bifurcat. Chaos*, 7(3):645–664, Mar. 1997.
67. T. Yang and L. O.Chua, Impulsive stabilization for control and synchronization of chaotic systems: theory and application to secure communication, *IEEE Trans. Circuits Syst. I: Fundam. Theory Appl.*, 44(10):976–988, Oct. 1997.
68. T. Yang, Channel-independent chaotic secure communication system using general chaotic synchronization, *Telecommun. Rev.*, 7(2):240–254, Mar.–Apr. 1997.
69. T. Yang, L. B. Yang, and C. M. Yang, Application of neural networks to unmasking chaotic secure communication, *Physica D*, 124(1/3):248–257, Dec. 1, 1998.
70. T. Yang, L. B. Yang, and C. M. Yang, Control of Rössler system to periodic motions using impulsive control methods, *Phys. Lett. A*, 232(5):356–361, Aug.4, 1997.
71. L. A. Zadeh, Fuzzy sets, *Inf. Control*, 8:338–353, 1965.

72. L. A. Zadeh, Fuzzy logic = computing with words, *IEEE Trans. Fuzzy Syst.*, 4(2):103–111, May 1996.
73. L. A. Zadeh, From computing with numbers to computing with words—from manipulation of measurements to manipulation of perceptions, *IEEE Trans. Circuits Syst. I: Fundam. Theory Appli.*, 45(1):105–119, Jan. 1999.
74. M. Zak, J. P. Zbilut, and R. E. Meyers, *From Instability to Intelligence: Complexity and Predictability in Nonlinear Dynamics*, Vol. m49 of Lecture Notes in Physics, New Series m Monographs, Springer-Verlag, New York, 1997.

SUBJECT INDEX

Page references followed by italic *t* indicate material in tables. Page references followed by italic *n* indicate material in footnotes.

abstraction, 338
acoustics
  sensory input ambiguity, 3–4
  and speech recognition, 23
actions, 80, 334, 410
ACT (semantic network model), 244
actuators, 1
adaptive synchronization, 387
adjectives, 304–305
  defined, 413
  and fuzzy logic, 411
  handling in speech recognition, 26
adult's normal, typical cognition (ANTCOG), 236–238, 247
adverbs, 305, 407, 410–412
  computational process symbol models of, 415–421
  concerning perception, 418–421
  concerning place, 417–418
  concerning time, 416–417
  defined, 413
  and fuzzy logic, 411
  handling in speech recognition, 26
  models of, 415–421
afterset, 99, 105–106
agents, 20, 104–105
  intelligent software, 266–267
age of syntactics, 15–16
aggregation, 81
  defined, 335, 338
  linguistic information, 258–259
  linguistic weighted information, 259–260
aggregation operators, 265
α-cuts, 60
ambiguity
  handling in speech recognition, 26–27
  sensory input, 3–4
amorphic concepts, 40
analog-to-digital conversion, crisp granulation in, 37
analyzing with words, 8
AND connective, 100
AND operation, 298
  alternatives to, 299–301
  compensatory, 320–321
animals, 4
  decision analysis, 2
ANTCOG (adult's normal, typical cognition), 236–238, 247
antecedent constraints, 47–48
antecedent phrases (a-phrase), queries, 129
anthropology, 17
application-specific semiotic knowledge, 136
a-relation, 133
arrive (verb), 374–375
articulate procedural knowledge, 82, 278–280
artificial intelligence, 153
  and cognitive sciences, 17, 241–243
  and computing with words, 20–21
  languages issues as key to success, 15
  qualitative reasoning in, 84
  syntax entry, 410
artificial linguistic systems, 427
artificial neural networks, 155
  supervised, 155
associative dependencies, 193
atomic words, 42
attention focusing, 78, 330, 334
attractors
  Chua oscillator, 383–384
  general synchronization, 398, 400
  second-order piecewise linear oscillator, 377

attributes, 2, 104
attribution, in fuzzy information granulation, 245–246
automated knowledge acquisition, 81–82, 277
  hybrid approaches, 283–294
  summary of three approaches to, 282*t*
automated rule learning, 224
automatic speech recognition, 21, 22
autonomous agents, 266
AutoSlog, 224
axioms, 315*t*

Backus-Naur form, 124–125
BADD defuzzification algorithm, 302
base variable, 253
basic interpolative rule, 56–57
B-CUBED scoring algorithm, 229–232
becoming, problem of, 367–368
behavior generation and control, 85–86
behaviorist paradigm, 280
being, problem of, 367–368
belief, partial, 37
bigrams, 173
binary fuzzy relations, 351–352
BK-products. *See* fuzzy relational BK-products
bold connectives, 100
Boolean logic, 427
bottom-up processing, 4
branching quantifiers, 138

calculus
  fuzzy, 70
  predicate, 28–29, 242
  relational, 99–101
CAMP system, 226–228
canonical forms
  of generalized constraint language, 76, 91
  normal form expressions, 314*t*
  of proposition, 47
cartesian granules, 45
causality (causation), 18, 147, 236, 245
  as amorphic concept, 40
  partial, 37
  word-based knowledge, 330, 340–341
cause-effect relationship, 340–341
CELEX database, with TIMES system, 212
cellular automata, 376
certainty
  granularity of (uncertainty), 254
  partial, 37
change in a system, 339
chaotic shift keying, computational verbs for breaking, 383–388, 405–407
chaotic systems
  for Chinese speech recognition application, 425, 427
  dynamic verbs, 373–376
  piecewise linear chaotic system, 379–383
  for secure communications, 387–388
characteristic-extraction blocks, 427
Chinese speech recognition, computational verb application, 421–427
Chomsky linguistics, 154, 157–159
Chua oscillator, 379–383
  for chaotic shift keying, 384
  for Chinese speech recognition application, 422, 425
chunking, 37
circuit theory, 35
classical min operator, 264
Clinaid, 108, 109
  generic architecture, 110–113
  medical diagnosis process dynamics, 109–110
  multicontext fuzzy relational inference, 114–118
  semiotics of modes and strategies of inference, 113–114
closeness (Cl) relation, 349, 350–351, 364
  inference rules, 358–361
  modeling, 357–358
Cl relation. *See* closeness (Cl) relation
cluster analysis, 37
clustering, fuzzy aspects of, 72, 304
coarsening, 337–338
cognitive sciences
  adult's normal, typical cognition (ANTCOG), 236–238, 247
  and artificial intelligence, 241–243
  and computing with words, 17–19, 79–80, 235–244
  defined, 236
  domain-specifying assumptions, 237–238
  knowledge representation, 243–245
  methodological assumptions, 239–241
  substantive assumptions, 238–239
  uncertain questions in, 236–237
combination function, TIMES system, 217
combination rules, TIMES system, 217
combinatorial search, 78
commonsense knowledge, 28, 243
communication and information theory, 23
comparability (Co) relation, 349, 350–351
comparators, 364
comparison, 81
compatibility function, 253
compensatory AND operation, 320–321

complete knowledge, 342
complexity, 70, 341
  human brain's handling of, 368–370
  of inference in clinical practice, 110
composable objects, 338
composite constraints, 76
composite words, 42
compositionality, 139
compositional rule, 55–56
compromised reasoning schema, 301, 321–325
computability, 341
computational action symbols, 368
computational linguistics, 14, 149, 153
computational process symbols, 370–376
  adverbs and adverbials as modifiers of, 407–427
  chaotic shift keying applications, 383–387, 405–407
  complex system model, 379–383
  computing with, 387–407
  equality and similarity between, 391–399
  formal definition, 413–415
  music to transfer feelings and emotions, 399–405
  simple system model, 376–379
  speech recognition application, 421–427
computational semiotics, 149–150, 152, 162–171
computational systems, 154
computational theory of perceptions (CTP), 76, 241, 246–247
  computing with words framework for, 15, 39–42
computational verbs, 86, 368, 427
  as dynamic systems, 411
  formal definition, 413–415
computational verb systems, 26, 85–86. *See also* computational process symbols
  defined, 368
  motivations for, 368–370
computer science, 23
computing, 347
computing with numbers, 78
computing with thoughts, 10–11, 78
computing with words. *See also* artificial intelligence; cognitive science; fuzzy logic and numerous other terms beginning with "fuzzy"; granularity; language; linguistic variables; natural language
  and artificial intelligence, 20–21
  basic concepts, 42–48
  behavior generation implied from words, 85–86
  brief introduction, 1–5
  and cognitive science, 17–19, 79–80, 235–244
  connection to mind and perception, 8–10
  connection to natural language, 7–8
  defined, 14–16, 91, 245–247
  descriptive and veristic words, 303–324
  evolution of, 27
  and fuzzy expert systems, 30–31
  fuzzy relational BK-product architectures for, 107–108
  fuzzy relational front end system for, 118–136
  history of early papers concerning, 42
  how senses talk to our actuators, 1–11
  knowledge acquisition application, 282–283
  knowledge representation, 80–81
  and language and intelligence, 31
  new gestalt for, 69–75
  new reality of intelligent systems engineering, 74–75
  problems and issues, 24–25, 75–77
  rationales for using, 27, 39–42
  semiotic, 193–202
  theoretical fundamentals, 77–80
  von Neumann computer architecture contrasted, 75
  word-based knowledge reasoning, 83–85
  word-based knowledge representation, 82–83, 329–345
computing with words and images, 11
conjunction, 54
conjunctive normal form (CNF), 84. *See also* fuzzy conjunctive normal form
conjunctive rules, 54–55
connectionist models, 280, 281
connotative dependencies, 193
co-norms, 301, 318–321
consequent constraints, 48
constraint-centered semantics of natural languages (CSNL), 76, 246–247
constraint modification rules, 57
constraint programming, 37
constraints, 76, 246
containment, 71, 319–320
contents words, 159
context, 4
  and activity of clinicians, 109
  defined, 331
  and fuzziness of words, 7
  and partial information, 37
  semiotic descriptor, 105
  and speech recognition, 25
continuity principle, of word-based knowledge, 330, 344
converse relation, 102
convex linear compromise reasoning, 301, 302, 321–324

Co relation, 349, 350–351
corpora, 157
cosine normal factor, 228
countercurrent heat exchanger, 363
creativity, 428
word-based knowledge principle, 330, 334
crisp contradiction, 306
crisp information granulation (crisp IG), 37, 303
disadvantage of, 38
criterion variable, 277
cross-document coreferences, 225–232
cryptanalysis, computational process symbols application, 383–387, 405–407

databases, 90
articulate knowledge, 279
information extraction system, 209
data dictionary, 125
data mining, 284
decision analysis
animals, 2
and computational theory of perceptions, 76
and computing with words, 61
and fuzzy logic, 91–92, 257
group decision making, 259, 263
decision trees, 37
declarative knowledge, 278, 280–281
decomposition, 335, 338
DEDALE system, 351
defuzzification, 338
defuzzification algorithm, 302
degree, of relation, 99
de Morgan's laws, 313, 315*t*
de Morgan triples, 319
Dempster-Shafer theory, 37, 53
depth information, 139
derived rules, for fuzzy logic inference, 55–64
descriptive statistics, 280
descriptive words, 298, 299–303
computing with, 83–84
models of, 307–312
Dextron, 108
diakoptics, 37
dictation machines, 22
direct elicitation, of knowledge from experts, 293
disambiguation, 70, 73
word sense, 79, 211, 213
discourse knowledge, in natural language processing, 22
discrete-time verbs, 376
disjunction, 54
disjunctive (possibilistic) constraints, 51, 76, 247
disjunctive normal form (DNF), 84. *See also* fuzzy disjunctive normal form
disjunctive rules, 54–55
dispositional dependencies, 193, 194–195
dispositional dependency structure, 195
distinguishing, 336
distributed intelligent agents, information gathering on Internet, 81, 252, 266–272
divide and conquer, 37
domain dictionary, 333–334
domain set class, 129
dynamic complexity, 368
dynamic descriptor structures, 113
dynamic systems, 29–30
dynamic verbs, 371–376
dyslexia, 123*n*

ECHO (semantic network model), 244
ecological information processing, 162–163
educational applications, 258
efficiency principle, of word-based knowledge, 330, 341
E-language (externalized language), 149, 154
elementary functioning loop (ELF), 332, 334, 343
emotions, 411–412
endo-exo dichotomy, 158
English, 173*n*
grammar, 412–413, 427
modifying systems (adverbs), 410–412
English query language (EQL), 119, 120, 127–128
English query language interpreter, 131–135
enter (verb), 377–381
entity, 80, 335
entity-relational WBK representation principle, of word-based knowledge, 330, 334–337
epistemology, 17, 82, 278
equality constraints, 51, 246–247
equivalence, 100
erkenntnisinteresse, 154
Euclidian metric, 178
events, 80
temporal extent, 244
evolutionary algorithms, 271
evolutionary-computing-based methods, 59, 64
exclusive afterset, 106
exclusive foreset, 106
existence statements, 331
experts
direct elicitation of knowledge from, 293
and truth, 306
expert systems, 20

knowledge acquisition, 277–278
explanatory database, 49–50
explication, and fuzzy constraint propagation, 60
exponential compromise reasoning, 301, 302, 313, 324–325
expressive power, 341
extension principle, 56, 258–259
externalized language (E-language), 149, 154
external linguistic correspondence, 107
external logical correspondence, 107
external verification, 307

FCNF. *See* fuzzy conjunctive normal form
FDNF. *See* fuzzy disjunctive normal form
fear, 412
feedback principle, of word-based knowledge, 330, 343–344
feedforward principle, of word-based knowledge, 330, 343
feel crazy (verb), Rössler chaotic system representation, 373–374
feel (verb), 371
fernordnung (linear long-distance orderings), 154*n*
f.g. generalization, 246
f-granulation, 246
financial ratios, 284*t*
financial systems, hybrid automated knowledge acquisition, 284–294
first aggregate, then infer (FATI), 302
first infer, then aggregate (FITA), 302
first-order predicate calculus, 28–29
FMC algorithms, 298
F-measure, 213
focusing attention principle, 78
word-based knowledge, 330, 344
Fodor's implication function, 265
FOG system, 349, 350–351
foreset, 99, 105–106
formal languages, 148
formal language theory, 14
forschungsgegenstände, 154
frames, 281
French, 173*n*
front end system, for computing with words, 107–108, 118–136
functionality, 37, 94
functional words, 159
FUZMAR method, 258
fuzzification, 338
fuzzy calculus, 70
fuzzy cluster algorithm, 298, 306
fuzzy clusters, 305
fuzzy cognitive maps, 248
fuzzy computational semiotics, 78, 149–150. *See also* semiotic cognitive information processing systems (SCIPs)
fuzzy conjunctive normal form (FCNF), 84
canonical forms, 314*t*
in compromised reasoning, 322–324
containment, 319–320
and descriptive/veristic words, 299, 301, 318
fuzzy truth tables, 312–313
fuzzy constraint modification rules, 57
fuzzy constraint networks, 28–29
fuzzy constraint propagation, 42, 43, 47–48, 93. *See also* generalized constraint language
and explication, 60
and fuzzy logic inference, 54–64
fuzzy constraints, 42, 43, 47–48
representation of, 48–54, 93
fuzzy controllers, 8–9
fuzzy disjunctive normal form (FDNF), 84
canonical forms, 314*t*
containment, 319–320
and descriptive/veristic words, 299, 301, 318
fuzzy truth tables, 312–313
fuzzy equalities, 351–356
fuzzy equivalence relation, 94
fuzzy expert systems, and computing with words, 30–31
fuzzy granularity
knowledge acquisition, 81–83
and knowledge representation, 80–81
learning, 81–83
fuzzy granules, 148
fuzzy graph constraints, 76, 247
fuzzy graphs, 19
basic interpolative rule, 56–57
as disjunction of cartesian granules, 45
and fuzzy information granulation, 245
fuzzy if-then rules, 44–48
and cognitive science, 19
and fuzzy information granulation, 245
fuzzy inequalities, 351–356
fuzzy information granulation (fuzzy IG), 38, 303
and cognitive science, 19
role in computing with words, 92–94
theory of, 241, 245–247
fuzzy linguistic quantifier, 261
fuzzy linguistics, semiotic cognitive information processing systems (SCIPs), 166, 171–179
fuzzy logic, 1, 15. *See also* linguistic variables
and adverbs and adjectives, 411
and cognitive science, 19
defined, 8, 91–92

fuzzy logic (*Continued*)
further research, 27–29
history of theory, 36, 42
inability to cope with verbs, 368
inference rules, 54–64, 348
and linguistic variables, 71, 72
mixed articulate/inarticulate knowledge approaches, 279–280
and soft computing, 21
fuzzy Lyapunov synthesis, 303
fuzzy majority, 260–261
fuzzy pattern matching, 159
fuzzy pragmatics, 82, 329
fuzzy qualitative reasoning, 84–85
fuzzy relational BK-products, 85, 89, 98
architectures for computing with words, 107–108
and calculus of relations, 99–101
communicating with other computing systems, 136–137
front end system for computing with words, 107–108, 118–136
future developments, 137–140
information-intelligent systems, 108–118
in logic notation, 99–100, 101
role in computing with words, 97–98
semiotics and mathematics of granularity, 94–98
semiotics of relational computations, 101–107
in set notation, 100–101
fuzzy relational computations, 90
semiotics of, 101–107
fuzzy relational knowledge, 136
fuzzy relational representation, 85, 89
fuzzy relations, 71
binary, 351–352
characteristics of, 92
fuzzy representation, 70–74
fuzzy rules generation, 72
fuzzy semantic fields, 82, 329
fuzzy semiotic models, 96
fuzzy semiotic representation structures, 98
described, 102–104
internal SD correspondence, 107–108
fuzzy sets
aspects of, 303
characteristics of, 92
defined, 1, 7, 15
and fuzzy qualitative reasoning, 347
history of theory, 36
importance of, 71–72
fuzzy syntax, 82, 329
fuzzy systems, 7–8, 72. *See also* linguistic variables
fuzzy truth tables, 84, 304, 315*t*
constructing, 313–318
fuzzy variables, 8, 9

gedankenexperimente, 162
generalization, 71–72, 80*n*
defined, 338
TIMES system, 216–219
generalized constraint language (GCL), 76
described, 60–64
generalized constraints, 50–54
semiotically generalized, 195–197
generalized extension principle, 56, 58–64
generalized modus pens, 56
generalized morphisms, 138
generalized synchronization (verb equalities), 391, 392, 395–399, 400
general problem solver (Newell and Simon), 280
generative grammars, 281
generic knowledge, 136
German
SCIP applications (*See* semiotic cognitive information processing systems)
soft categories in, 173–175, 176
gestalt processes, 71
global property, 96–97
GMP reasoning, 302, 321
goals
of speech act, 25
of tasks, 334
Gödel's implication function, 265
Gödel's incompleteness theorem, 339
grammars, 157
English, 412–413, 427
generative, 281
Montague, 42
queries, 124–127
granularity, 6–7, 92. *See also* fuzzy relational BK-products
levels of, 103
locality of granular structures, 96–97
multiple resolution dynamic systems, 29–30
nonmonotonicity of reasoning, 74
relational characterization of types, 94–95
and relevance, 96–97
semiotics and mathematics of, 94–98
of uncertainty, 254
granular word meaning, 197
granulation, 147, 236
crisp IG and fuzzy IG contrasted, 37–39, 303
defined, 245–246, 348

history of theory, 37
human cognition, 47
and image processing, 18
granules, 92, 245–247
cartesian, 45
defined, 18, 42, 45–47, 95, 348
ground, of a mental representation, 239
grounding, 2, 30, 333
group decision making, 259, 263
grouping, 4, 78
GSM diagram, 343

harsh products, 100
Hasse diagrams, 122
header phrase (h-phrase), queries, 128
heat exchanger, 363
Heisenberg uncertainty principle, 70
heterogeneity, 330, 339–340
hidden Markov models, 427
higher-order relational structures, 244
homogeneous system of representation, 339
homomorphism, 335
human brain, 369
pattern thinking by, 427
human cognition, 147, 151
adult's normal, typical cognition (ANTCOG), 236–238, 247
cognitive science assumptions about, 239–241
granulation in, 47
linguistic mechanisms, 156–159
modeling, 151–153, 281
human consciousness, 371*n*
human intelligence, 4–5, 72. *See also* language; natural language
exceptional aspects of, 235–236
importance of language and speech in, 13
and language, 31

iconic representations, 4, 6, 11
ID-3, 282, 293
identical synchronization (verb equalities), 391–395, 400
identification, 336
I-language (internalized language), 149, 154
I-LOWA operator (inverse-linguistic ordered weighted averaging), 263, 265
image interpretation, 10
image processing, and granulation, 18
image segmentation, 37
implication operators, 100
implications, 100
implication statements, 331
IMPLY operation, 298, 300
impulsive dynamic verbs, 373–374
inarticulate procedural knowledge, 82, 278–280
inclusive afterset, 106
inclusive foreset, 106
incompleteness principle, 330, 342–343
indicator function, 307
indistinguishability, 37
inference rules
Cl and Ne relations, 358–361
for fuzzy logic, 54–64, 348
inferential statistics, 280
information, depth and surface, 139
information agents, 267–272
information extraction systems, 209–211. *See also* trainable information extraction system (TIMES)
CAMP system, 226–228
cross-document coreferences, 225–232
information granulation. *See* granulation
information-intelligent systems, 90
fuzzy relational BK-products for, 107, 108–118
information retrieval, 257–258
information systems view, 162–164
inheritance systems, 214
initial data set, 27, 44–48, 137
instantiated explanatory database, 49
instantiation, 338
intelligence. *See* human intelligence; machine intelligence
intelligent control, 1, 13, 80
multiple resolution mathematical modeling, 29
intelligent information systems, 13
intelligent machines, 65, 72, 242, 247
intelligent software agents, information gathering on Internet, 81, 251–252, 266–267
intelligent systems, 72, 74–75, 80
fuzzy relational BK-products for, 89
interactions, 104
interface agents, 267–272
internalized language (I-language), 149, 154
internal SD correspondence, 107–108
internal verification, 307
Internet, distributed intelligent agent model for information gathering on, 81, 252, 266–272
interpretant, 239
interpretation, 102–103
defined, 332, 333
interpretation statements, 331
interval analysis, 37
intransitive verbs, 372*n,* 413
invariance, 139
inverse-linguistic ordered weighted averaging (I-LOWA) operator, 263, 265

inverse mapping rule, 56
inverse relation, 102
isoreferentials, 189
isr (*X* isr *R*), 51, 76, 246–247

Kleene-Dienes implication, 100, 265
knowledge, 80
  commonsense, 243
  dimensions of, 278–281
  partial, 37
knowledge acquisition. *See also* automated knowledge acquisition
  computing with words, 282–283
  in fuzzy granular systems, 81–83
  hybrid model advantages, 281–283
knowledge engineering, 90
knowledge generation, 82
knowledge interpretation, 82, 329
knowledge organization, 82, 329
knowledge representation, 1, 20, 75, 329. *See also* word-based knowledge representation
  and cognitive sciences, 243–245
  and fuzzy granularity, 80–81
knowledge systems, 159
knowledge utilization, 82
Korean surety insurance database, 283

label, 304
  linguistic variables, 253
labeling, 330, 331
laboratory-built-steam-engine model, 297–303
language, 13–14. *See also* natural language
  as action, 25–26
  formal languages, 148
  and intelligence, 31
  and linguistics, 153–156
  modeling, 281
  universals, 157
  word-based, 83
language competence, 154, 281
language games, 169–170
language performance, 154, 155–156
large, in fuzzy if-then rule, 44–48
learnability, 139
learning, 280
  automated rule learning, 224
  knowledge acquisition in fuzzy granular systems, 81–83
  machine learning, 20, 37, 277
leave (verb), 377–378, 380
levels of granularity, 103
levels of resolution, 103
lexemes, 133
lexical analyzer phase, 133
  TIMES system, 212
lexicon, 154
limited resource principle, 330, 344
linear long-distance orderings, 154*n*
linear models, 292
linear predictive coding (LPC) blocks, 427
linear ranking, 271
linear scoring, 281, 282
linear short-distance orderings, 154*n*
linguistic approximation, 48
linguistic coding, 371*n*
linguistic connectives, 264–265
linguistic descriptors, 104
linguistic elements, 135
linguistic implication functions, 265
linguistic information management, 251
linguistic ordered weighted averaging (LOWA) operator, 260, 261–263, 265
linguistic perspicuity, 278, 282
linguistic qualifiers, 121
linguistic quantifiers, 134, 261
linguistics, 14, 17, 23
  internal and external languages, 149
  and language, 153–156
  problem solving approach, 252–258
linguistic term sets, 254–255
  semantics, 255–257
linguistic universals, 157
linguistic variables, 6, 7, 71–72, 75
  and fuzzy information granulation, 245, 253
  history of theory, 36–37
  and word-based knowledge representation, 329
linguistic weighted averaging (LWA) operator, 81, 251
  described, 260–265
  information gathering on Internet using, 268–272
  summarized, 272
local composed properties, 96
locality
  of granular structures, 96–97
  of inference in clinical practice, 110
local reflexivity, 96
logic, 41, 71, 304
  of questions and relational queries, 105–107
  with set theory, 306–307
logical parallelism, 93–94
logic notation, 99–100, 101
logic theory of models, 103
logit, 281, 282
  Korean surety insurance database, 283, 292, 294
Lorenz systems, 372

general synchronization, 395, 397–399, 400
identical synchronization, 392–395, 396, 400
LOWA operator (linguistic ordered weighted averaging), 260, 261–263, 265
Lukasiewicz connectives, 100
Lukasiewicz implication, 100
lumping, 6, 83
LWA operator. *See* linguistic weighted averaging (LWA) operator
Lyapunov synthesis, fuzzy set theory application, 303

machine intelligence, 65, 72, 242, 247
machine learning, 20, 37
and automated knowledge acquisition, 277
Mamdani reasoning, 321
many-to-many mapping, 298
mapping rule, 56
market research applications, 258
matching, 336
mathematical modeling, 16–17
mathematics, fuzzy, 16–17
maximization of a function, 59
meaning
approximation in fuzzy semiotic models, 96
and knowledge representation, 75
linguistic variables, 253
and semiotic triangle, 103
syntactics age view of, 16
and thesauri, 331
meaning extraction, 72, 78–79
and word-based knowledge, 330, 346
mean products, 100
measurement, perception contrasted, 37
medical diagnosis applications, 108–110, 258, 259–260. *See also* Clinaid
medium, in fuzzy if-then rule, 44–48
membership, 71
grades of, 91–92
membership functions, 247
truth verification, 297–299, 306
memory, 163*n*
mental grammar, 158
mental representation, 238–239
Message Understanding Conferences, 209
metalinguistic expressions, 84
metasystem, 341
mind
and computing with words, 8–10
mind/brain processes, 148
min operator, 264
modal logic, 41
model, 341
modeling, 16–17
model-theoretic semantics, 14
Modified ID-3, 282
modifying systems, adverbs, 410–412
Montague grammar, 42
morphemes, 21
morphological knowledge, in natural language processing, 21
most, 62–64
MUC-4 system, 224, 225
multicontext fuzzy relational inference, in Clinaid, 114–118
multigranular representation, 339
multiple resolution dynamic systems, 29–30
multiple resolution mathematical modeling, 29
multiple WBK representation systems principle, of word-based knowledge, 330, 339–340
multiresolutional representation, 339, 345
multiscale heterarchy, 339
multiscale hierarchy, 338–339
multiscale representation, 335
music, 387
to transfer feelings and emotions, 399–405
mutisymbol fusion, 10
MYCIN, 280

nahordnung (linear short-distance orderings), 154*n*
names, 2
in semiotic triangle, 103
natural language, 1, 2. *See also* computing with words; language
and computing with words, 7–8, 41–42
mathematical modeling using fuzzy mathematics, 16–17
multigranular nature of, 74
precisiated, 76–77
as recent development, 4
restricted fragment of, 107, 135
and thinking, 77–78
types of, 13–14
natural language processing, 20, 21–22, 153–154
negligibility (Ne) relation, 349, 350–351, 364
inference rules, 358–361
modeling, 357–358
Ne relation. *See* negligibility (Ne) relation
nested hierarchical representation, 330, 337–339
nesting, 335
NetOwl, 225
neural networks, 20, 21
artificial, 155, 277
automated knowledge acquisition, 280, 282
modeling, 293

neurocomputing, 59, 64
neuroscience, 17
Neuroshell, 283
n-grams, 173
nilpotent min operator, 264
nonlinear dynamic systems, second-order piecewise linear oscillator, 376–379
nonlinguistic processing, 371*n*
nonmonotonicity of reasoning, 74
normal form expressions, 304, 312–315. *See also* fuzzy conjunctive normal form; fuzzy disjunctive normal form
  derivation algorithms, 304, 312–315
noun phrase coreference, 211
noun phrases, 410
  identification by TIMES, 212
nouns, 304, 307, 410
  defined, 412
  handling in speech recognition, 26
  universality in all languages, 427
now, problem of, 367–368
numbers, 80
numerical analysis, 90

objects, 80, 104, 334, 410
  in semiotic triangle, 103
  spatial extent, 244
O(M) system, 349
ontologies, 104
OpenMath standard, 108, 136–137
OR connective, 100
orders of magnitude. *See* relative orders of magnitude
organization, 18, 92, 147, 236, 245

PALKA, 224
parallel distributed processing, 18
parallelism, 93–94, 139
parser subsystem, front end of relational system, 123–131
parse tree, 133
partial information, 37
partial parser, 212
partial relational structures, 138
pattern processing blocks, 427
pattern recognition, and speech recognition, 23
pattern thinking, 427
PDP, 18
perception. *See also* computational theory of perceptions (CTP)
  and computing with thoughts, 10–11
  and computing with words, 8–10
  dimension of, 414
  measurement contrasted, 37
  validity as matter of degree, 37
perception adverbs, 416, 418–421
perceptual images, 4, 80
permutation function, TIMES system, 217–218
permutation rules, TIMES system, 218
perspectives, 105
perspicuity, 278, 282
philosophy, 14, 17
phonetic knowledge, in natural language processing, 21
phonological knowledge, in natural language processing, 21
physics, and speech recognition, 23
physiology, 23
piecewise linear chaotic system, 379–383
piecewise linear oscillator, second-order, 376–379
pixel size, 18
place adverbs, 416, 417–418
plan recognition problem, 26
pleasure, 412
possibilistic constraints, 51, 53, 76, 247
pragmatically homogeneous texts (PHTs), 149–150, 162
pragmatic knowledge, in natural language processing, 21–22
pragmatics, 25–27
  fuzzy, 82, 329
  syntax-semantics-pragmatics distinction, 23, 103
Prague Linguistic Circle, 137, 139
precisiated natural language, 76–77
precision, 213
predical logic, 41
predicate calculus, 28–29, 242
predicate form, of relations, 92
predicates, 305
prediction, goal of complete knowledge, 342
predictor variable, 277
prelinguistic brain, 4
prepositions, identification by TIMES, 212
probabilistic constraints, 51, 52, 76, 247
probabilistic reasoning, 21
probability qualification rule, 57–58
probability value constraints, 51
procedural knowledge, 82, 278, 280–281
product phrases, queries, 129–131
product relation, 99
projective rule, 55
pronouns, handling in speech recognition, 26
propositional logic, 41
propositions, 47–48, 304
  fuzzy constraint representation, 48–54

fuzzy inference rules, 54–64
proximity, 37
psycholinguistics, 14
psychology, 17, 23
qualitative process theory, 37
qualitative reasoning, fuzzy, 84–85, 347–365
quantization, 37
queries
antecedent and subsequent phrases, 129
grammar, 124–127
header phrases, 128
logic of, 105–107
metaformula translation, 120
product phrases, 129–131
semantic analyzer, 134–135
semantic interpreter, 135
syntax analysis, 131–134
query parser, 133
questions, logic of, 105–107

random fuzzy set constraints, 51, 247
random graph constraints, 51, 247
random set constraints, 51, 53, 247
RAPIER, 224
reasoning
fuzzy qualitative, 84–85, 347–365
nonmonotonicity of, 74
with word-based knowledge, 83–85
recall, 213
recognition, 336
refinement, 337–338
reflexivity, 95, 96
relational calculus, 99–101
relational queries. *See* queries
relational semiotic structures, 96
relations, 334
relationships, 2
defined, 336
relative orders of magnitude, 348–350
propagation, 361–364
relevance, of granularity, 96–97
relevancy rate, 219
representation. *See also* word-based knowledge representation
defined, 341
modes of, 163–164
problems with, 5–7
symbolic and iconic, 4, 6, 11
representational content, 239
representational objects, 238
representation bearer, 238, 239
representation relations, 238
representation system, 5
resolution, 6–7, 18. *See also* granularity
defined, 336
levels of, 103
restricted fragment of natural language (RFNL), 107, 135
robotic systems, fuzzy relational BK-products for, 89
robots, 20
Rössler chaotic systems, 373–374
rough set constraints, 51
rough set theory, 37
rule based formats, 153
automated knowledge acquisition, 282, 293
automated rule learning, 224
development stages, 297
rule generalization, TIMES system, 216–219
rule learning, automated, 224
rules, for fuzzy logic inference, 54–64, 348

sampling frequency, 18
satisfaction set, 99
SCIPs. *See* semiotic cognitive information processing systems
scripts, 281
event representation, 244
search, 20
second-order logic, 304
second-order piecewise linear oscillator, 376–379
semantic analyzer, 134–135
semantic dispositional dependencies, 194–195
semantic generalization, TIMES system, 218–219, 221–223
semantic hyperspace, 175–179
semantic interpreter, 135
semantic knowledge, in natural language processing, 21
semantic networks, 244, 281
crisp granulation in, 37
semantics, 148
defined, 2, 16–17
linguistic term sets, 255–257
model-theoretic, 14
syntax-semantics-pragmatics distinction, 23, 103
semantic space, 7
semantic value, linguistic variables, 253
semiosis, 102–103, 152, 165, 168
semiotically generalized constraints, 195–197
semiotic attunement, 170–171
semiotic cognitive information processing systems (SCIPs), 78, 202–204
cognitive background, 150–161

semiotic cognitive information processing systems (SCIPs) (*Continued*)
  computational semiotics, 162–171
  formal properties, 185*t*
  fuzzy linguistics, 166, 171–179
  language games, 169–170
  reconstructing reference, 179–193
  reconstructive procedures, 166–171
  semantic hyperspace, 175–179
  semiotic attunement, 170–171
  semiotic computing with words, 193–202
  semiotic enactment, 164–166
  word space, 172–175
semiotic computing with words, 193–202
semiotic descriptors, 91, 101. *See also* fuzzy relational BK-products
  Clinaid, 113, 115–116
  conceptual categories, 104–105
  defined, 103
  external linguistic correspondence, 107–108
semiotic enactment, 164–166
semiotic parallelism, 93, 94
semiotic relational models, constructing, 95–96
semiotics, 26, 148
  Clinaid modes and strategies of inference, 113–114
  computational, 149–150, 152, 162–171
  defined, 29–30
  fuzzy relational computations, 101–107
  granularity, 94–98
  and word-based knowledge representation, 330
semiotic triangle, 103
sense disambiguation (word sense), 79, 211, 213
senses, 1–11, 37
sensory input, 2–5, 37
  ambiguous nature of, 3–4
SentenceExtractor module, CAMP system, 226–228
sentences, 305–306
serial-symbolic model, 18
set-theoretical notation, 100–101
set theory, 304
  axioms of, 315*t*
  with logic theory, 306–307
shared knowledge and experiences, 243
signal processing, 23
similarity, 37, 94
similarity relation, 71
single-directed operational flow, 343
60% barrier, on MUC-like data sets, 225
small, in fuzzy if-then rule, 44–48
smooth dynamic verbs, 372
snapshot, 344
s-norms, 54
soft computing, 21, 42
soft linguistic categories, 148
  German language, 173–175, 176
software agents, 266
software development applications, 258
sound, 407
spatial extent, 244
specialization, 338
specific concepts, 216
speech, 13, 14
speech acts, 25
speech recognition
  automatic, 21, 22
  computational process symbols application, 421–427
speech segmentation, 24
square product, 98, 99
  semiotic aspects, 101–102
s-relation, 133
states, 2
static complexity, 368
static verbs, 372
statistical analysis, 280
stay (verb), 377–378, 380, 382, 385
steam-engine model, laboratory-built-, 297–303
strata, 156–159
strongly inarticulate knowledge approaches, 280
structural equation modeling, 279–280
structural linguistics, 159
structure, 341
subsequent phrase (s-phrase), queries, 129
subsumption functions, TIMES system, 215–216
summarization, 71–72, 80*n*
surface information, 139
surjective rule, 55
switch (verb), 382, 385
syllogistic rule, 57
symbol grounding, 2, 333
symbolic computation, 347
symbolic processing, 29
symbolic reasoning, 1
symbolic representations, 4, 6, 11
symbolic verbs, 427
symbols, 6–7
  mutisymbol fusion, 10
symmetry, 95
syndrome, 115–116
syntactic generalization, TIMES system, 216–218, 220–224
syntactic knowledge, in natural language processing, 21
syntactics age, 15–16

syntactic value, linguistic variables, 253
syntax, 148
  age of syntactics, 15–16
  defined, 2
  generic abbreviations, 134*t*
  syntax-semantics pragmatics distinction, 23, 103
syntax analysis, of queries, 131–134
syntax entry, 410
syntax tree, 133
system constraints, 344
system theory, 35–36
  change, 339

target phrase, TIMES system, 215
task agents, 267–272
taste (verb), 371
t-co-norms, 301, 318–321
telephone applications, of speech recognition systems, 25
temporal extent, 244
terminal data set, 27, 44–48
terminal dynamic verbs, 374–376
test-score semantics, 28, 48, 54
TETRAD, 280
text, 7. *See also* trainable information extraction system (TIMES)
  extracting information from, 78–79
  extracting meaning from, 72
text interpreters, 139
Textract, 225
theory of fuzzy information granulation (TFIG). *See* fuzzy information granulation
thesaural interpretation, 330, 331–334
thinking, and natural language, 77–78
tiling, 159–161
time, arrow of, 367
time adverbs, 416–417
t-norms, 54, 301, 318–321
tokens, 133, 148, 216–217
top-down processing, 4
trainable information extraction system (TIMES), 212–213, 224
  experiments, 219–223
  rule generalization, 216–219
  rules, 215–216
  training phase, 214–215
  and WordNet, 212, 213–214, 218
transformation functions, 265
transitive verbs, 372*n*, 413
transitivity, 95
transposed relation, 102
triangle products, 98, 99
  semiotic aspects, 101–102
triangle subproduct, 98
triangle superproduct, 98, 99
Trier dpa-Corpus, 156*n*
Trisys, 108
  local properties, 96
truth. *See also* veristic words
  degrees of, 92
  membership function verification, 297–299, 306
  nature of, 299, 306
  partial, 37
  syntactics age view of, 16
truth tables, 315*t*. *See also* fuzzy truth tables
try (verb), 371
T-sentence, 306
tunable fuzzy controllers, 281
two-dimensional generalization, TIMES system, 219, 221–223

uncertainty, 342–343
  granularity of, 254
understanding
  lack of human, in dictation machines, 22
  partial, 37
untersuchungsmethoden, 154
usuality constraints, 51, 52, 247
utterances, 157

valuation, in fuzzy information granulation, 245–246
values, 104
vector space model, CAMP system, 228–232
verb equalities, 387, 391–399, 428
verb logic, 368
verb phrases, identification by TIMES, 212
verbs, 305, 410–411. *See also* computational process symbols; computational verb systems
  defined, 412–413
  to describe dynamic complexities, 368
  handling in speech recognition, 26
  universality in all languages, 427
verification, 297–299, 306. *See also* truth
  external and internal, 307
veristic constraints, 51–52, 76, 247
veristic words, 299–303
  computing with, 83–84
  models of, 307–312
verity, 304
very large language corpora (VLCC), 155, 156
views, 105
vision systems, 20
visual sensory input, ambiguous nature of, 3

Viterbi decoding, 23
von Neumann computer architecture, 18
  computing with words contrasted, 75
VSM-Disambiguate module, CAMP system, 226–228

WBK system, 340
wetware, 8
WHISK, 224
word-based computers, 8
word-based knowledge, 330
  principle of causality, 330, 340–341
  principle of continuity, 330, 344
  principle of creativity, 330, 334
  principle of efficiency, 330, 341
  principle of entity-relational WBK representation, 330, 334–337
  principle of feedback, 330, 343–344
  principle of feedforward, 330, 343
  principle of focusing attention, 330, 344
  principle of heterogeneity, 330, 339–340
  principle of incompleteness, 330, 342–343
  principle of limited resource, 330, 344
  principle of multiple WBK representation systems, 330, 339–340
  principle of multiresolutional representation (coarsening/refinement), 330, 337–339
  principle of nested hierarchical representation, 330, 337–339
  principle of thesaural interpretation (labeling), 330, 331–334
word-based knowledge representation, 82–83, 329–330
  principles of, 330–345
  reasoning with, 83–85
word-based statements, 331, 345
WordNet
  other rule learning tools, 224
  with TIMES system, 212, 213–214, 218
word-object, 335
words, 2, 83, 345. *See also* computing with words; descriptive words; veristic words
  atomic and composite, 42
  behavior generation implied from, 85–86
  categories, 304–305
  connection to natural language, 7–8
  defined, 332
  difficulties with meaning of, 17
  fuzzy denotations, 42–43
  fuzzy qualitative reasoning, 84–85, 347–365
word sense disambiguation, 79
  information extraction system, 211, 213
word space, 172–175
world, 5, 334
  snapshot, 344
world knowledge, in natural language processing, 22, 153

NAME INDEX

Page numbers in regular type refer to citations in the text. Page numbers in **bold type** refer to material in the reference section of a chapter.

Abbot, J., 108, 136, **140**
Abelson, R. P., 243, 244, **249**
Abrahamsen, A. A., 281, **294**
Ainsworth, W. A., 421, **428**
Albus, J. S., 29–30, **33**, 74, **88**, 332, **346**
Aleksander, I., 412, **428**
Allen, J., 14, 21, **32**
Anderson, J., 90, 95, 108–111, 114, 119, **140**, **141**, **142**, **145**
Anderson, J. R., 181, 244, **249**, **294**
Armstrong-Warwick, S., 155, **204**
Assilian, S., 297, **327**
Azzouni, J., 304, **327**

Backlund, U., 411, **428**
Bagga, A., 212, 225, 229, **232–233**, 235
Bahler, D., 28, **33**
Bainov, D. D., 373, 419, **428**, **429**
Baker, J. M., 271, **272**
Balabanovic, M., 267, 269, **272**
Baldwin, B., 225, 226, 229, **232–233**, 235
Bandler, W., 89–90, 95–102, 104–105, 108–111, 119, 121, 136–137, **140–141**, **143–144**, 248, **249**
Barwise, J., 168, 171, **204**
Bechtel, W., 281, **294**
Behrooz, A., 90, 109–110, **140**, **141**, **143**
Bellman, R. E., 71, **86**
Ben-Ahmeida, B., 108, **141**
Bergmann, M., 304, **327**
Bever, T. G., 31, **33**
Beyth-Marom, F., 252, **273**
Bezdek, J. C., 298, **327**
Bichakjian, B. H., 371, 412, 414, **428**
Biermann, A., 212–218, 224, **232**, **233**
Bierwisch, M., 156, 157, **204**
Blum, J., xiv
Bonissone, P. P., 253–255, 257–259, **273**, **275**
Booch, G., 336, **346**
Bordogna, G., 252, 255–257, 259, 266, **273**
Bortolan, G., 258, 259, **273**
Bourgine, P., 351, **365**
Bowen, J., 28, **33**
Briscoe, T., 156, **204**
Brown, C., 252, 267, **273**
Brown, G., 331, **346**
Brown, P., 156, **204**
Bruce, R., 73, **87**
Buckley, J. J., 257, **273**
Bunke, H., 155, **204**

Califf, M., 209, 224, **233**
Calvin, W. H., 15, **32**
Cao, S. G., 411, **429**
Carlsson, C., 259, **273**
Carpenter, G. A., 155, **204**
Carroll, J., 156, **204**
Carroll, J. M., 31, **33**
Casti, J. L., 31, **33**, 152, **205**
Cawsey, A., 20, 22, 24, **32**
Chai, J., 211, 212, 214, 215, 216, 218, 224, **232**, **233**
Chalmers, D., 164, **205**
Chang, P., 257, **273**
Charniak, E., 209, **234**
Chavez, A., 252, 267, **273**
Chen, M., 411, **429**
Chen, S. J., 252, **273**
Chen, Y., 257, **273**
Cholewa, W., 259, **273**
Chomsky, N., 147, 154, **205**
Christensen, R. R., 303, **327**

Chua, L. O., 379, 384, 387, 397, 399, 419, 422, **429**, **430**, **431**
Church, K., 73, **87**, 154, 156, **205**
Clarke, J., 387, **430**
Cooper, L., 155, **205**
Copi, I. M., 304, **327**
Corrigan, B., 281, 292, **294**
Coward, L. A., 427, **429**
Cowie, J., 209, **233**
Creswell, M. J., 49, **66**
Culicover, P., 155, **205**

Dabby, D. S., 399, **429**
Dague, P., 351, **365**, **366**
DARPA:TIPSTER text program, 209, **233**
Dawes, R. M., 281, 292, **294**
Dean, T., 252, 267, **274**
DeBaets, B., 98, **141**
Decker, K. S., 254–255, 258, **273**
Dedieu, H., 383, 390, **429**
Degani, R., 258, 259, **273**
Delgado, M., 255, 257–259, 261, **273**
DellaPietra, S., 156, **204**
DellaPietra, V., 156, **204**
Denning, P. J., 372, 384, 412, 428, **429**
Devès, O., 351, **365**
DiPasquo, D., 209, **233**
Dixon, D. D., 376, **429**
Doignon, J. P., 98, **141**
Dormoy, J. L., 348, **365**
Dowlatshahi, F., 139, **141**
Dowty, D., 72, **87**
Driankov, D., 411, **430**
Dubois, D., 259, **273**, 349, 356–358, 365, **365**, **366**
Dubrosky, B., 96, 104, 119, **141**, **142**
Dumitrescu, D., 303, **327**
Dusková, 139, **146**

Einstein, A., 17, **32**
Erickson, R., 16
Etzioni, O., 251, 266, **273**

Fargier, H., 365, **365**
Fedrizzi, M., 257, **273**, **275**
Feigenbaum, E., 15, 241, **249**
Filev, D. P., 72, **86**, 301, 313, 321, **328**
Fodor, J., 98, **141**, 155, **205**
Fogelman-Soulié, F., 155, **206**
Foulloy, L., 348, **365**
Franklin, S., 251, 266, **274**
Freitag, D., 209, **233**
Freuder, E. C., 48, **66**
Fromkin, V., 410, 427, **429**
Fucks, W., 154, **205**
Fullér, R., 259, **273**
Furui, S., 421, **429**

Gaines, B. R., 139, **141**
Gaio, L., 257, **275**
Gale, W., 73, **87**
Galichet, S., 348, **365**
Gao, S., 90, 108–110, 113, **143**, **144**
Gardner, H., 17, **32**, 280, **294**
Gasser, L., 252, 267, **273**
Ghalia, M. B., 20, 24, 28, 30, **32**, **33**
Gibson, J., 162, **205**
Gim, G., 283, 286, 292, **294**, **295**
Gindikin, S. G., 28, 29, **33**
Gladkij, A. V., 412, **429**
Glymour, C., 279, **294**
Godo, L., 365, **365**
Goldstein, L. S., 258, **276**
Gomide, F., 54, **67**
Gould, S. J., 16, **32**
Granville, B., 119, 121, **142**
Graven, M., 209, **233**
Griffin, M. F., 411, **430**
Grishman, R., 224, 225, **233**
Grossberg, S., 155, **204**
Guckenheimer, J., 372, 419, **429**
Guerrin, F., 348, **366**
Guinn, C., 216, **233**
Gupta, M. M., 47, **66**

Hadj-Ali, A., 365, **365**
Hájek, P., 98, **142**
Halliday, T., 27, **32**
Hanks, P., 154, **205**
Hanley, J., 286, **294**
Harnad, S., 333, **346**
Harnish, R., 155, **205**
Harris, M., 136, 138, **144**
Hart, A., 278, **294**
Hasler, M., 383, 390, **429**
Hawking, S. W., 367, **429**
Hellendoorn, H., 411, **430**
Hendler, J. A., 251, 257, 258, **274**
Herrera, F., 256–261, 263, 264, 271, **274**
Herrera-Viedma, E., 256–261, 263, 264, **274**
Hindle, D., 154, **205**
Hintikka, J., 138, 139, **142**
Hinton, G., 155, **205**
Hirsch, M. W., 372, 392, **429**
Hoare, C. A. R., 98
Hobbs, J. R., 42, **66**
Holland, J., 19, **33**

Holmes, P., 372, 419, **429**
Huffman, S., 209, **233**
Hwang, C. L., 252, **273**

Infeld, L., 17, **32**

Jackendoff, R. S., 371, **429**
Jaki, S. L., 369, **429**
James, W., 17, **32**
Jauregui, J. A., 371, 411, 419, **429**
Jennings, N., 251, 266, 267, **275**
Johnson, A. P., 74, **88**
Jones, R., 209, **234**
Joreskog, J. G., 279, **294**
Juang, B.-H., 22–23, **32**
Jubak, J., 16, **32**
Juliano, B. A., 98, **142**, 248, **249**

Kacprzyk, J., 263, **274**
Kahan, W., 37
Kalantar, H., 90, 110, 113, 114, **144**, **145**
Kaliappan, V., 90, 108, **142**
Kallala, M., 108, **144**
Kalman, R., 36, 37
Kandel, A., 312, 317–318, **328**
Kang, G. T., 302, **328**
Karlqvist, A., 31, **33**
Kaufmann, A., 47, **66**, 317, **327**
Kelly, K., 279, **294**
Kelvin, William Thomson (Lord Kelvin), 36, 37
Kennedy, M. P., 383, 390, 425, **429**
Keravnou, E., 90, 108, **142**, **144**
Kerre, E., 98, **141**
Khalfa, J., 13, 32, **32**
Kim, E., 96, 104, 108, 119, **141**, **142**, **144–145**
Kim, J., 224, **233**
Kim, Y.-G., 119, **145**
Kimble, G., 17
Klein, C. M., 257, **275**
Klir, G. J., 54, **66**, 91, **142**
Knuth, D. E., 175, **205**
Köhler, R., 155, **205**
Kohler, W., 71, **86**
Kohonen, T., 188, **205**
Kohout, L. J., 72, **86**, 89–91, 95–105, 108–111, 113–114, 119, 121, 136–140, **140–144**
Koning, J. L., 259, **273**
Kraft, D. H., 252, 256, 257, 266, **274**
Krulwich, B., 267, 269, **274**
Kuipers, B., 348, **366**
Kulas, J., 139, **142**

Lai, R., 28, **33**
Lakshmikantham, V., 373, 419, **429**
Lam, L., 368, **429**
Larsen, H. L., 267, 269, **275**
Lashkari, Y., 252, 267, **274**
Law, C. K., 258, **274**
LeDoux, J. E., 371, 390, **430**
Lee, C. S. G., 411, **430**
Lee, H. B., 73, **87**
Lee, H. M., 257, 258, **274**
Lehnert, W., 209, **233**
Lejter, M., 252, 267, **274**
Lenat, D. B., 241–243, **249**
Lettvin, J. Y., 1
Levin, B., 390, 393, 423, **430**
Lin, C. T., 411, **430**
Linkens, D. A., 411, **429**
Liu, C., 257, **275**
Lòpez de Màntaras, R., 365, **365**
Lorch, R., 180, 194, **205**
Lorenz, E. N., 373, 392, **430**
Lucy, J. A., 333, **346**

Macleod, C., 224, **233**
Maes, P., 251, 252, 267, 269, **273**, **274**, **275**
Magnon, A., 367, 368, **430**
Mamdani, E. H., 48, **66**, 297, 324, **327**
Mancini, V., 96, 98, **141**, **145**
Mantik, S., 267, **275**
Marek, M., 41, **67**
Margaliot, M., 303, **327**
Marinos, P. N., 317, **327**
Markman, B., 243, 244, **249**
Marr, D., 171, **205**
Martin-Bautista, M. J., 267, 269, **275**
Matejka, L., 139, **145**
Maturana, H., 1
Mavrovouniotis, M. L., 349, 362, 363, **366**
McCallum, A., 209, **233**
McCarthy, J., 74, **87**, 241, **249**
McClelland, J. L., 18, **32**, 280, **294**
McCulloch, W. S., 1
McElligot, M., 269, **275**
McGill, M. G., 269, **275**
McKay, T. J., 419, 427, **430**
McNeil, B., 286, **294**
Mel'cuk, I. A., 412, **429**
Mendels, E., 258, **276**
Mercer, R. L., 156, **204**, **205**
Metral, M., 252, 267, **274**
Meyers, R. E., 376, **432**
Meystel, A., 29, **33**, 74, **88**, 152, **205**, 331–333, 343, **346**
Mich, L., 257, **273**, **275**
Miller, G., 212, 213, 214, **233**, 254, **275**

Miller, L. A., 31, **33**
Minsky, M., 18, **32**
Mitchell, T., 209, **233**
Moldovan, D., 224, **233**
Monjardet, M., 98, **141**
Montague, R., 72, **87**
Montero, J., 259, **275**
Mooney, R., 209, 224, **233**
Moor, J., 304, **327**
Moukas, A., 252, 267, **273**
MQ&D Project, 348, **366**

Nadel, L., 155, **205**
Nagarajan, S., 138, **145**
Nelson, J. A., 304, **327**
Newell, A., 281, **294**
Ng, H. T., 73, **87**
Nguyen, L., 267, **275**
Nicolaisen, J., 267, 269, **275**
Nigam, K., 209, **233**
Nilsson, N. J., 241, 242, **249**
Niskanen, V., 10

Oakley, D. A., 390, 393, 405, 411, **430**
O'Hara, K., 164, **205**
O'Leary, D. E., 252, 267, **273**

Palm, R., 411, **430**
Pang, Y., 257, **275**
Pannu, A., 267, 269, **275**
Partee, B., 42, **67**
Passi, G., 252, 255–257, 259, 266, **273**, **274**
Pattee, H., 148, 152, 166, 181, **205–206**
Pauker, S. G., 252, **275**
Pazzani, M., 267, **275**
PDP Research Group, 18, **32**, 280, **294**
Pedersen, T., 73, **87**
Pedrycz, W., 54, **67**
Peirce, C., 165, 168, 170, **206**
Penrose, R., 372, 405, **430**
Perry, J., 168, 171, **204**
Petrie, C. J., 251, 266, **275**
Pfeiffer, R., 155, **206**
Piaget, J., 14–15
Pitts, W. H., 1
Plato, 367
Prade, H., 259, **273**, 348–349, 356–358, 365, **365**, **366**
Pret, J.-C., 74, **88**
Prim, R. C., 195, 197, **206**
Pylyshyn, Z., 155, **205**

Quillian, M. R., 244, **249**
Quine, W. V. O., 304, **327**
Quinlan, R., 279, **294**

Rabiner, L., 22–23, **32**
Raiman, O., 349, 351, **365**, **366**
Rangaswamy, S., 28, **33**
Rasiowa, H., 41, **67**
Ratsch, V., 21, **32**
Rees, N. W., 411, **429**
Richter, M. M., 21, **32**
Riedl, R., 371, **430**
Rieger, B., 150, 152, 155, 156, 160–162, 165, 169, 171–173, 180, 188, 193, **205**, **206–207**
Riguet, J., 98, **145**
Riloff, E., 209, 224, **233–234**
Ritter, H., 188, **207**
Roark, B., 209, **234**
Rodet, X., 387, 399, **430**
Rodman, R., 410, 427, **429**
Rolls, E. T., 373, **430**
Rooth, M., 154, **205**
Rosch, E., 151, 162, **208**
Rosen, R., 15
Rössler, O. E., 373, **430**
Roubens, B., 98, **141**
Rumelhart, D. E., 18, **32**, 280, **294**
Ryle, G., 278, **294**

Sagan, C., 24, **32**
Sage, A., 281, **294**
Salton, G., 228, **234**, 269, **275**
San-Andres, M., 90, 114, **145**
Sanchez, E., 259, **275**
Sandu, G., 139, **142**
Schaller, R. R., 412, **430**
Schank, R. C., 243, 244, **249**
Scheines, R., 279, **294**
Schnelle, H., 154, 155, **207–208**
Schott, B., 277, 283, **294**
Schreter, Z., 155, **206**
Scott, T., 164, **205**
Shafer, G., 53, **67**
Shoham, Y., 267, 269, **272**
Simeonov, P. S., 373, 419, **428**, **429**
Simon, A., 74, **88**
Simon, H. A., 163, 165, **208**
Simons, G., 411, 414, **430**
Slattery, S., 209, **233**
Sloman, A., 412, **430**
Smale, S., 372, 392, **429**
Smith, C., 244, **249**
Smolensky, P., 155, **208**
Snow, P., 48, **66**

Soderland, S., 209, 224, **234**
Son, K., 283, **294**
Sorbom, D., 279, **294**
Sorenson, H., 269, **275**
Sowa, J. F., 331, **346**
Spirtes, P., 279, **294**
Stabile, I., 90, 95, 108–110, 114, 119, **142**, **145**
Stamatescu, I. O., 21, **32**
Steels, L., 155, **206**
Steiner, P., 139, **145–146**
Stephanopoulos, G., 349, 362, 363, **366**
Sterling, J., 224, **233**
Strotmann, A., 108, 136, **140**
Sugeno, M., 21, 302, **328**
Sundheim, B., 213, **234**
Svendsen, T., 267, 269, **275**
Sycara, K., 267, 269, **275**
Szolovits, P., 252, **275**

Tanaka, K., 411, **430**
Tarski, A., 306, **328**
Tatar, D., 303, **327**
Testemale, C., 259, **273**
Thagard, P., 244, **249**
Thiopoulos, C., 169, 171, 179, **207**, **208**
Thompson, C., 209, **234**
Thompson, E., 151, 162, **208**
Toffoli, T., 376, **430**
Tong, M., 255, 257–259, **275**
Torra, V., 257, 259, **275**
Travé-Massuyès, L., 348, **366**
Traynor, C., 90, 108–110, **143**
Trnka, B., 139, **146**
Tseng, T. Y., 257, **275**
Tsonis, D., 136, **146**
Türksen, I. B., 298–302, 312, 317–318, 321, **328**
Tyan, C. Y., 28, **33**

Vachek, J., 139, **145–146**
Valee, R., 41, **67**
van Leuwen, A., 108, 136, **140**
Varela, F., 151, 162, **208**
Verdegay, J. L., 255–261, 263, 271, **273**, **274**
Vila, M. A., 255, 257–259, 261, **273**
Vincke, P., 98, **141**
von Eckardt, B., 236–244, 247, **249**
Voss, R. F., 387, **430**

Wagman, M., 242, **249**
Walker, R. M., 96, 104, **141**
Wang, H. O., 411, **430**
Wang, H. P., 96, 104, **141**
Wang, M., 257, **275**
Wang, P. P., 20, 24, 28, **32**, **33**, 74, **88**
Wang, S. W. T., xiv
Watson, J. B., 70, **86**
Weizsäcker, E., 162, **208**
Weld, D. S., 251, 266, **273**
West, A. S., 372, 410, 411, **430**
Whalen, T., 279, 283, 286, 292, **294**
Wiebe, J., 73, **87**
Williamson, M., 267, 269, **275**
Wittgenstein, L., 169, 171, **208**
Woolridge, M., 251, 266, 267, **275**
Wu, C. W., 387, **429**, **430**, **431**

Yager, R. R., 72, **86**, 248, 251–253, 255–261, 263–264, 266, **276**, 301, 313, 321, **328**
Yang, C. M, 384, 387, 405, **431**
Yang, L. B., 384, 387, 405, **431**
Yang, T., 368–370, 374, 384, 387, 397, 405, 411, 414–415, 418–419, 421, 427, **429**, **430**, **431**
Yarowsky, D., 73, **87**
Yoh-Han, P., 30, **33**
Yuan, B., 54, **66**
Yule, G., 331, **346**
Yun, Y., 267, 269, **272**

Zadeh, L. A., 6, 7, 13, 15, 18–21, 25–31, **32**, **33**, 35–36, 42, 45, 47–51, 54, 56–64, **67–68**, 71–72, 74–75, 79, 84, **86**, **87**, 91–97, 137–138, **146**, 147, 195, 196, **208**, 235–236, 241, 245–248, **250**, 251, **276**, 303, **328**, 329, **346**, 347–348, 363, **366**, 369, 411, **431–432**
Zak, M., 376, **432**
Zarandi, M. H. F., 321, **328**
Zbilut, J. P., 376, **432**
Zeng, D., 267, 269, **275**
Zenz, G., 108, **145**
Zhang, H. J., 312, 317–318, **328**
Zimmermann, H.J., 313, 320, 321, **328**